COLONIAL GEOGRAPHIES, TOURIST IMAGINARIES, AND MYSTICAL LANDSCAPES

Sophia Rose Arjana

Routledge
Taylor & Francis Group

NEW YORK AND LONDON

Designed cover image: Tourists at the Pyramids of Giza, Egypt, 1920s.
Wikimedia Commons, George Rinhart, 1920s

First published 2026
by Routledge
605 Third Avenue, New York, NY 10158

and by Routledge
4 Park Square, Milton Park, Abingdon, Oxon, OX14 4RN

Routledge is an imprint of the Taylor & Francis Group, an informa business

ISBN: 978-1-032-42213-8 (hbk)
ISBN: 978-1-032-42211-4 (pbk)
ISBN: 978-1-003-36172-5 (ebk)

DOI: 10.4324/9781003361725

Typeset in Sabon
by Apex CoVantage, LLC

COLONIAL GEOGRAPHIES, TOURIST IMAGINARIES, AND MYSTICAL LANDSCAPES

The first study to examine the intersection between imaginative geographies and mystical tourism, this book presents a detailed discussion of how tourism is linked to mystical experiences, consumer products, and wellness resorts.

The many forms of colonialism have enabled governments, colonial agents, settlers, writers, and artists to reorder the world as a new space that mystifies invasion, occupation, and reterritorialization as it reestablishes a new binary of what is natural and what is unnatural. *Colonial Geographies, Tourist Imaginaries, and Mystical Landscapes* provides an account of this colonial practice and its influence on the creation of mystical landscapes in modern tourism. Including case studies on more familiar cases of colonialism, such as Kenya and Algeria, which are known as Europe's "classic colonies," as well as settler colonies, including the United States of America, its Pacific colony in the Hawaiian Islands, and Israel, this book examines how colonial culture inserted itself into these spaces and looks to anti-colonial and indigenous voices to help us understand and counter this mystification.

This engaging and accessible work bridges cultural theory, sociology of religion, and human geography and tourism studies through an examination of film, television, theme parks, travel, and leisure activities focused on the wellness industry to illustrate how imaginative geographies function in European and American colonial and imperial projects.

Sophia Rose Arjana is Associate Professor of Religious Studies at Western Kentucky University and is the author of *Buying Buddha, Selling Rumi: Orientalism and the Mystical Marketplace* (2020); *Veiled Superheroes: Islam, Feminism, and Pop Culture* (2018); *Pilgrimage in Islam: Traditional and Modern Practices* (2017); and *Muslims in the Western Imagination* (2015).

To my children, S, M, M, and N,
the loves of my life and joy of my heart.

CONTENTS

List of Images   *x*
Acknowledgments   *xi*

Introduction: Colonial Dreams and Mystical Landscapes   1

1   Colonial Geographies   24

2   Tourism's Mystical Landscapes   52

3   Imagining Africa   83

4   Shangri-La   119

5   Bali Ha'i   158

6   Dreams of the South Pacific   191

7   Holy Landscapes   228

8   The Mystic West   266

    Postscript   301

    Bibliography   *305*
    Glossary of Indigenous and Local Places   *331*
    Index   332

IMAGES

0.1 Bakery, Bandung, Indonesia.   2
1.1 Old Batavia Restaurant, Jakarta, Indonesia.   34
2.1 Ebstorf Map, Thirteenth Century.   68
3.1 Fatima Cigarette.   95
4.1 Photo of Prambanan, Yogyakarta Region, Indonesia.   130
4.2 Photo of Prambanan, Yogyakarta Regency, Indonesia.   131
5.1 Photo of Bali Rice Field, Bali, Indonesia.   163
6.1 Photo of Hula Girls.   207
7.1 Photo of Group of Explorers, Judea District, Palestine, 1867.   244
8.1 Across the Continent: "Westward the Course of Empire
     Takes Its Way," Frances Flora Bond Palmer, 1868.   269

ACKNOWLEDGMENTS

Over the past decade, my writing community has gone through many changes, brought upon by a move from Colorado to Kentucky, new projects (this is my fifth book), new colleagues, and steadfast friends. To these fellow writers and friends, I am so grateful—Andrew Rosa, Nassima Neggaz, Eric Reed, Julie Todd, Sarah Eltantawi, and Blayne Harcey (who has been my writing buddy through three books)—thank you for reading chapters and offering your expertise, critiques, and notes. My dear family friend and personal editor Jean, I am forever grateful for your wisdom and sharp wit, for catching details I would miss.

This book would not have been possible without the support of the staff at the Western Kentucky University library, and most of all, I am thankful to Kathy Foushee, for the countless interlibrary loans and academic articles she obtained for me. The broad focus of this book included an almost insurmountable number of books and articles that our university library did not have in their collections. Scholars cannot survive without libraries and the wonderful people who manage them and support our work.

I am above all thankful to my children, who endured many long hours of me in my home and campus offices—so many hours that by the end stages of this book, my two youngest had made a game of pretend espresso maker, which included them making me imaginary lattes.

Lastly, I would like to acknowledge that during the writing of this book, universities in Gaza were destroyed and their libraries turned to dust. May this book be a reminder that what stood before, even when destroyed, can be remembered and rebuilt. May the people of Palestine rise from the ashes and be free.

INTRODUCTION

Colonial Dreams and Mystical Landscapes

Bandung, a city located in the mountains of West Java, was home to some of the most brutal fighting in WW2. I have often visited an old bakery in one of the old Dutch areas of the city. The bakery maintains the colonial style, with the same pastry cases, signs, and furniture. An old cash register sits in its original location and signs on the walls date from before the war—relics of a past that now exists as a tourist site reflecting colonial nostalgia. The chairs are the same ones that colonial settlers used to eat pastries and drink *kopi* (coffee), perhaps after church or an outing to a nearby volcano. Bandung is a place that serves as a reminder of a failed colonial project, its Dutch spaces now identified with an independent and free Indonesia.

Colonial memories are like the recipes original to the bakery, still remembered but consumed. Today, the bakery's pastries are eaten by Indonesians and foreign tourists, including Dutch visitors, who might imagine what they once controlled when they tour their former colony, longing for a past that is gone. My husband's grandfather had his eye poked with a bayonet for teaching Arabic, and even though it happened two generations ago, it is not forgotten. Indonesia, like many former colonial territories, is a landscape haunted by its colonial past.

During the colonial occupation of Java and other islands in the Dutch East Indies, the local population intermarried with colonial settlers, but more often, they worked as employees for the regime or as servants in colonial households. The policies designed to separate Europeans and locals included everything from dress to food: "Housing, dress codes, transport, food, clubs, conversation, recreation, and leaves marked a distinct social space in which

DOI: 10.4324/9781003361725-1

IMAGE 0.1   Bakery, Bandung, Indonesia.

Source: photo courtesy of author

Europeans were internally stratified but from which Asians were barred."[1] Derek Gregory describes this as *dispossession through spatializing*.[2]

The Dutch gave Indonesian spaces names like *Batavia* and *Europeesche Buurt*, which was part of a complex effort to remap the islands as the Dutch East Indies. These policies created a new map onto which the Dutch imposed their European vision of space. Maps are a critical part of the story of Indonesia under colonial rule. In his study of colonial Orientalism in maritime Southeast Asia, Farish Noor deconstructs the map of Java found in Raffles's 1817 *The History of Java*. As he explains,

> Java was never simply another island to be explored, but also a market to be dominated and controlled, a territory to be defended, a data-bank to be analysed and ordered, and a collection of antiquities to be categorised, inventoried and vaulted in a colonial museum.[3]

This study illustrates how colonialism, mapping, and landscapes are linked. Newly enacted colonial spaces became tableaus where escape, solitude, and transformation were attached to the land. The modern landscapes of tourism examined in the following chapters were created out of this colonial (and imperial) violence, erasing the lives and cultures that once occupied the mountains, islands, deserts, and forests of a precolonial world, and in their place, new imaginative spaces were created. For the tourist, mystical experience is often focused on transcendent experiences that reflect the construction of "meaning and purpose in their lives."[4] This quest for transcendence is predicated on a history of colonialism that has often been mitigated, forgotten, or ignored, and mystical landscapes have often been created out of this violence.

The old Dutch neighborhoods of Bandung, Jakarta, and Semarang inspired this book. Bandung is famous today for its many fashion designers and boutiques, its active volcanic attractions, and as the site of the Asian African Congress. Here, in 1955, the leaders of newly independent states who had escaped from the claws of colonialism converged to establish a path forward in a new postwar world. Indonesia has long been free from the Dutch, the British, and the Japanese, but the ghosts of colonialism linger. As a scholar of religion who has focused much of my scholarship on religious and secular pilgrimage, space and place, and the Orient, I am interested in how colonized spaces become tourist spaces, and how *landscapes* are constructed as part of cartography and other descriptive narratives about place. In the words of Claudio Minca, "Tourism is, above all, a spatial phenomenon."[5]

Maps are only one way we create the geographical knowledge that results in tourist spaces. As Denis Cosgrove has argued, the visual of the map and the "written narrative and description" are different but complementary forms of geographical description.[6] For this reason, this book sees maps as one type of geographical mapping, existing as part of a wider field of representations that include novels, painting, and cinema.

Colonial powers surveyed and reimagined their territories, transforming them into new landscapes, many of which became identified with spiritual and mystical experience. The relationship between these things—maps as "precise" ways of knowing (colonial geography), landscapes as the "idealization" of the spectator's view (tourism), and experiences of a sublime and mystical natural world (mystical landscapes)—is the subject of this book. The late scholar of tourism John Urry wrote that landscapes involve "the language of views" that create "places of visual desire, as the inhospitable was turned into a place of emotion, of landscape, especially for rich (male) European visitors."[7]

Colonial geography, tourism, and mystical landscapes are linked. Colonial maps provided a reliable way of knowing the world, landscapes represented the ideal views of the tourist, and mystical spaces were necessary in a world in which enchantment had been largely extinguished through the Protestant discomfort with pilgrimage, sainthood, and Gnosticism. Many different modes of visual representation (maps, paintings, literature) helped to connect the individual to both the past and the present.[8] They also created opportunities for new, colonized spaces to be reimagined as places of spiritual transformation—mystical landscapes.

Religious Map-Making

Jonathon Z. "JZ" Smith was one of the most important American religious scholars of the twentieth century. He spent his career at the University of Chicago, writing books that would forever challenge the ways students think about religion. When he passed away, I had a memorial to him on my office door, and to this day, I play old, grainy clips of him saying something clever or provocative for my students. I was lucky enough to see him lecture once, and when he walked in the room, he was like Gandalf, the great wizard from the Hobbit stories—wise, brilliant, and majestic. He even had a cane that resembled Gandalf's magical staff.

In *Map Is Not Territory* (1978), JZ asks scholars to reflect on space and movement, the scholarly construction of sacred space, and the position of religious people within it. JZ reminds us that the West is the mapmaker, "The West is active, it makes history, it is visible, it is human. The non-Western world is static, it undergoes history, it is invisible, it is non-human."[9] Smith demonstrates this point by tabulating the population numbers of people in the world's religions; as he points out, only some religions are studied as the *great world religions*, leaving the rest invisible.[10] As he explains, "Let me emphasize that I do not mean this word 'invisible' in any merely hyperbolic fashion. I mean, quite literally, that they may as well not exist."[11] This is the power of maps.

Map-making is a project that relies on the colonial cartographer to make some people visible and others a distant memory. As one study notes, "there is no doubt that the appropriation of space through the production of geographical knowledge did play a key role in the military conquest and political domination of the colonized territories."[12] John Brian Harley, the great scholar of cartography who died prematurely but left us with a corpus of scholarship on maps as a *discourse of power*, argued that every small space on a map represented power, lack of power, or the imposition of power. As he explained,

> The white places which abound on the maps of early modern Europe, for example, cannot be explained simply by positing "fact" against "no fact." Silence and utterance are not alternatives but constituent parts of map language, each necessary for the understanding of the other.[13]

Harley helps us understand what maps are—constructions of national and colonial vision that pushed some people to the margins or erased them completely.

Cartographic language may be a "classic case of Foucault's 'power-knowledge,'" but also has a strongly religious voice.[14] Postcolonial scholar Anne McClintock has described map-making as "the servant of colonial plunder" and the map as "a technology of possession."[15] Renaming is one way that maps are created. In some cases, indigenous or local names were erased and completely new names were attached to places.[16] In 1691, Fray Damián Massanet came upon a place called Yanaguana, which he named San Antonio de Pádua, because this was a day that marked the celebration of San Antonio de Pádu in the Roman Catholic calendar.[17] This is now the city of San Antonio, Texas. In other cases, an English, French, Spanish, or Dutch translation of an indigenous or local place was adopted. Yellowstone was taken from the Minnetaree Indian expression *Mi tse a-da-zi*, which likely referred to the yellow color of the sandstone bluffs that surround much of the river.[18]

Christianity played a powerful role in the mapping and renaming of many landscapes, but it took different forms. For many Britons living in the nineteenth century, the Holy Land had been identified with Palestine for many centuries. At a meeting of the Palestine Exploration Fund in 1875, the Archbishop of York stated, "Our reason for turning to Palestine is that Palestine is our country."[19] In U.S. national parks, Biblical language was used to describe impressions of nature, which included describing Yellowstone's bubbling mud pits as a hellish landscape and its mountains as heavenly outdoor churches.[20]

Maps are constructed through colonial bodies and the power they exert. In 1898, U.S. ships carrying soldiers to the Philippines to fight in the Spanish-American War stopped in Waikiki harbor. As the Honolulu *Commercial Advertiser* reported, "the best thing possible for the corps would be a march to Waikiki and a swim in the surf."[21] The identification of the military with Hawai'i as a tropical playground began at this moment. As Carolyn O' Dwyer explains, "The excerpt from the Commercial Advertiser expresses a confluence of contemporaneous ideas about Hawaii, mapping it simultaneously as an idyllic recreational site and as an available space for the inscription of United States military power."[22] Hawai'i's transition from a territory (1893) to a state (1959) relied on these inscriptions of power, identified with the U.S. military and the missionaries who helped secure the islands as part of the American nation.

In British India, Darjeeling was represented as a landscape with little or no human presence, for locals were "treated as passive components of the landscape" and in some cases, as interruptions to the "picturesque" scenes that were a critical part of the "visual consumption of the tourist gaze."[23] For Europeans, place was identified with territory, the establishment of settlements, and the creation of borders and empire.[24] Locative structures helped to form the colonial map through the building of settlements, military outposts, and churches, working to shape the environment into a new space.[25]

Space also was transformed into landscape, which required the sight, meaning, and emotions linked to sublime and spiritual experience. Colonists in Kenya figuratively erased the indigenous population, an act that allowed for the mapping of East Africa as an empty landscape full of wildlife and led to the modern safari. In North America, the national parks were enacted as oases of wilderness with no human presence, making them perfect as a site for American leisure and contemplation.

Mapping colonized territories often included these examples of "place production," where the idea of a place involved the tourist gaze and what John Urry has described as a specific "way of seeing."[26] Colonial ways of seeing, perceiving, and recording the world often erased the local population, who were thought of as interruptions to the colonial gaze. The erasure of indigenous and local populations became a critical part of modern tourism, an industry that often promises respite from the disenchantment brought about by labor and other forces, resulting in the glorification of nature and attempts to escape the "mechanized, regulating, and alienating" lifestyle of the urban and industrial life.[27] The landscapes of tourism are preferably pristine and empty—tableaus for fantasies about magical valleys, mountains, and islands. Tourists are often involved in efforts to create intimacy in a world of consumerism.[28] This intimacy often requires an empty space perfect for contemplation, enlightenment, and mystical experience.

Imaginative Geographies and Mystical Landscapes

Colonialism and imperialism have an intimate relationship with geography, cartography, and imaginary spaces, "The fact that a densely populated and culturally remolded land was seen as 'virgin' reflects a kind of mental 'ethnic cleansing,' a discourse of imaginary removal."[29] The creation of landscapes involves these cleansings and removals. As Peter Bishop proposes, "In a sense, natural landscapes do not exist. We inescapably shape the world, even if only with our minds and not our hands. When we shape the world, we create *places*."[30]

At one time, the lands of North America were filled with Indians, buffalo, and other wildlife, along with civilizations that included great cities. In his book *Facing East from Indian Country*, Daniel Richter asks us to imagine looking out upon the lands that now contain St. Louis and seeing Cahokia, the largest city in what is now the United States.[31] His description provides an image of a world that was erased through the mapping of Indian territory as new white lands,

> In its heyday it was home to more than twenty thousand people. Towering a hundred feet above a fifty-acre artificial plaza, its main temple mound covered sixteen acres at its base and contained twenty-two million cubic

feet of hand-deposited earth. Surrounding the temple and plaza, at least a hundred smaller mounds supported ceremonial structures or covered the accumulated burials of generations of the city's elite residents.[32]

Through European explorers, then early American settlers, this world was erased from memory and replaced with a new one—the world of a new America. Indians were transformed from real people to specters that haunt the Euro-American. As Renée Bergland puts it,

> First and foremost, the ghosting of Indians is a technique of removal. By writing about Indians as ghosts, white writers effectively remove them from American lands, and place them, instead, within the American imagination.[33]

The removal of Indians from their ancestral lands included massacres, executions, rape, and death from disease—what John P. Bowes describes as "relentless in its tales of death, dispossession, and dislocation."[34]

In John B. Harley's essay "New England Cartography and the Native Americans," he discusses the 1676 *Map of New England*, which portrays English settlements but no Indians, a "territorial void" over which the large letters New England are transposed, like the watermark one can put on a document today with a click of a computer.[35] Native Americans were also erased in other ways, such as in the massacre of the Pequot in May 1637, when the Pequot disappeared from maps.[36] The story of Indian removal is one of the many cases of colonial violence and remapping documented in this book. Where the lands that became the United States were once Indian land that was filled with wildlife, today these lands are largely occupied by non-Indian populations, and only an astounding 2.5 percent of land remains "untrammeled by man" (mostly in Alaska).[37] We don't have the mystical tourist destinations of the American West like Sedona, Arizona, without the settler colonialism and imperial struggles between the English, French, Spanish, and Americans that "drew, erased, and imposed political borders in territories that were more naturally delineated by rivers, portages, and lakes."[38] This is the work of *imaginative geographies*.

The creation of the national park system is linked to a new concept of American wilderness. Views of nature changed in modernity, from dangerous places to sites of beauty and contemplation. As Evan Berry explains,

> Although it is true that certain strands of American religiosity, fundamentalism in particular, preserved the tradition's intense otherworldliness and Augustinian fixation on the return of the immortal soul to God, the prevalence and power of theological repudiations of the natural world were greatly diminished in twentieth-century American culture.[39]

The American imagination about natural spaces required that American Indians be erased, for they did not fit into the new theology of the environment and its mystical potential.

Imaginative geographies are an important part of American history. The remapping of the American West was dependent upon Indian removal and the mapping of place through religion, new cosmologies, and bodies. In her study of Sedona, Susannah Crockford explains how the city and its environment are described by its white inhabitants as a vortex with different access points within a cosmology and belief system that "implicitly" reflects American Christianity.[40] The codewords used in Sedona's own brand of spirituality, like "manifestation" and "ascension," replace "Jesus-talk" with "energy-talk."[41] Energy, which is at the center of the "cosmologies of spirituality" popular in Sedona, also includes the remapping of bodies through claims of Native American heritage or other links to indigenous roots in the land.[42] One individual discussed in Crockford's study is Sierra Neblina, who was reincarnated as a woman of "Cherokee and Irish descent," although she was born as Shannon Marie Hare, a woman with no Native American ancestry.[43]

The colonial imagination about Asia also created mystical landscapes. Tourists visiting the Himalayas have a particular idea about the landscape and its potential for mystical experience. In Nepal, this includes Buddhist sites like Lumbini (the Buddha's birthplace) and the great stupas of Boudhanath and Swayambhunath, where Western Buddhists regularly seek to be transformed by the mystical power of the Buddha's homeland. Western tourists in Tibet complain that the goal of authentic experience is being disrupted by China and often fail to consider whether modernity or the agency of Tibetans might play a role in modern Tibet. As anthropologist Vincanne Adams's explains,

> For many Westerners visiting Tibet, but particularly for those involved in the movement to free Tibet who have come to Lhasa to validate their time-consuming intentions and efforts, karaoke is usually discussed as a sign of the "decline" of Lhasa and the "loss" of an authentic Tibet at the hands of the Chinese.[44]

Mapping often includes renaming. The Solu-Khumbu region of Nepal is famous to its European, American, and other foreign climbers, a history that began with Sir Edmund Hillary's ascent in 1953. The landscape of Nepal has been mapped by its European, and particularly its British, history. Its tallest mountain, which is known as Chomolungma in Sherpa and Tibetan and as Sagarmatha in Nepali, is better known as Everest, named after Sir George Everest, the head of the Great Trigonometrical Survey of 1852 that first measured it.[45] The Sherpas, who are a critical part of the climbing industry, are an integral part of the history of Nepal. As Sherry Ortner points out, they are not as dominant as the foreigners who created the business of trekking and climbing, "But Himalayan mountaineering was originally, and is still, for the most part, defined by the international mountaineers. It is their sport, their game, the enactment of their desires."[46]

Nepal has older maps constructed by Hindu and Buddhist traditions. Nepal includes the area known as Mustang, an ancient trade route between Nepal and Tibet that is over a 1,000 years old.[47] The area around Muktinath (sacred to Hindus and Buddhists) is referenced in *the Ramayana*, a text that is 2,500–3,000 years old, and as Holly Walters notes, it "was likely highly revered as a landscape possibly as far back as the Vedic landscape."[48] While this landscape remains sacred, the colonial mapping of Nepal has affected the ways in which the region is understood—instead of a sacred Hindu and Buddhist landscape, Nepal is better known as the site of the highest mountain in the world and a destination for thousands of adventure travelers per year who seek special kinds of experiences in an environment they have mapped as mystical. This study is concerned with both the processes through which these geographies are formed and their creation of mystical landscapes. As Stephen Britton explains, tourism persuades the consumer that they will "receive more than the product is capable of delivering."[49]

Colonialism exists in different forms—the classic colonies of Europe and settler colonialism are two of these. The former are focused on "controlling the 'natives,'" while the latter requires "the prior extermination or expulsion of a majority of indigenous populations, followed by the demographic 'swamping' of these territories by settlers from the metropole and/or a variety of other locales."[50] America and Israel, with its white settlers from Europe, are two such examples of this swamping, which use renaming to claim territory. For example, the Israeli news media uses Yershalaim for Jerusalem and its shortened version, Urshalim, instead of Al Quds or Jerusalem, as a way to remap the city as a solely Jewish space.[51] There are also landscapes that fall under "colonialism without colonies."[52] The "blank spaces" in the study of colonialism signal how Western hegemony is a force seen not only in locations, but also in the machinations of modernity like tourism, a business that relies on colonialism as its foundation. As we shall see, tourism is a form of cognitive mapping that requires the exploitation or erasure of people whose ancestral lands are now mystical landscapes.

Chapter Outline and Theoretical Voices

Each chapter in this book focuses on a region—Africa, the Himalayas, Southeast Asia, the South Pacific, the Muslim Orient, the American West, and on specific sites within these places. These landscapes were chosen for specific reasons. For example, how could I not include Kenya and its role in the British and American imaginations about Africa? How could I not include Nepal and Tibet as places indispensable to fantasies about the East? The American West could not be ignored, for it is a landscape so foundational to American imperialism around the world that even our weapons are named after its people (e.g., the Apache helicopter). India, Persia, and China are also important places that illustrate the power of mystical landscapes, but perhaps a book on these places is a project for another volume.

The places examined in this book are diverse, ranging from the savannahs of Kenya to the jungles and beaches of Bali. Landscape is often created through an "empty-land imaginary" where indigenous people are removed, followed by the destruction of "the 'deficient' indigenous flora and fauna" and an establishment of a neo-Europe.[53] This often followed the pattern of settler expansion that prioritized the "control of Indigenous land and its environmental transformation" from Australia and New Zealand to the Americas.[54] In other cases like Nepal, the tourist gaze was a colonizing force that did not involve the taking of territory, but transformed it from being a Hindu and Buddhist sacred landscape to one dominated by the mountaineering industry and the adventurer's search for sublime and mystical experiences.

In these chapters, I try to be attentive to the role of history, colonial ideology, and cultural discourse in the mapping of mystical landscapes. Each chapter provides a colonial history of each site, discusses the ways it was remapped, and includes at least one case study of the ways that cultural discourse contributed to this remapping of space. Examples of this discourse include travel writing, literary fiction, paintings, and films, all of which helped to map a territory as a site of the European (and at times, American) imagination. These include the paintings of native people like Mai (called Omai by Europeans), artists like Gauguin, writings of French romantics like Pierre Loti, travelogues about the Holy Land, and the many films about the Orient that portray the East as a mystical, magical land.

These pieces of cultural discourse about mystical places are critical because they are linked to tourist imaginaries. Some of my analyses are highbrow, such as the writings of educated Orientalist scholars, colonial agents, and famous explorers. Tibet's Mount Kailash (Kailās) is an important pilgrimage site for Hindus, Buddhists, and Bonpo today. However, it long functioned in the Western imagination about Shangri-La. In 1715, the Jesuit Ippolito Desideri came upon the magnificent mountain and wrote about it, as did Yeats, over 200 years later, in his poem about Meru.[55] In other cases, my analyses focus on writings that are "middlebrow," such Loti's romance novels and Hilton's "lost worlds romance" of Tibet, rejected by some literati but popular with the masses.[56]

This book is a history of mystical landscapes, which includes forms of colonial violence used against indigenous/native/local populations and their lands, oceans, and deserts. These forms of violence range from the establishment of the national parks and Indian reservation systems in the United States to the expulsion of Palestinians from their homes with the founding and expansion of Israel. It is my hope that through this book, we will come to understand more about the relationship of colonialism, mapping, and mystical landscapes but also that we will think more intentionally about the spaces we occupy and ask what our responsibilities are moving forward to honor the peoples whose lands now are the sites of hotels, resorts, hiking trails, campsites, and other forms of tourism. The following outline of chapters provides an overview of each chapter and its contents.

Chapters 1 and 2 contain the discussions that lay the groundwork for the remainder of the book, which is focused on geographical regions. In these first two chapters, I present several intersecting topics critical to this study. Chapter 1 focuses on colonialism and technologies of mapping, including paper maps and other forms of mapping like renaming of sites. Chapter 2 focuses on landscapes, mystical landscapes, and tourism.

The remainder of the book is organized around geographical case studies: Chapter 3 on the continent of Africa (Kenya, Morocco, and Tunisia); Chapter 4 on the Himalayas (Nepal and Tibet); Chapter 5 on the island of Bali (with a short digression on Thailand); Chapter 6 on the South Pacific; Chapter 7 on the Holy Land (and Egypt); and Chapter 8 on the American Southwest. These chapters do not tell a chronological story of mystical landscapes, although certainly the reader should understand that the West's "global imagination," as Peter Bishop calls it, can be understood through a series of shifts—in the eighteenth-century China and Tahiti, in the nineteenth-century Egypt and Palestine, and in the twentieth-century Tibet and Nepal.[57] However, in organizing this book's chapters, I propose an understanding of this imagination that begins with Africa and ends with the United States—telling a long story that begins with the early colonies of Europe and ends in the settler colonialism of white American colonists. The Postscript includes some of the ways that indigenous, local, and anti-colonial movements use counter-mapping to disrupt the maps of colonialism.

This book employs Soja's theory of space as a force of political power, which provides the conceptual infrastructure to frame my analysis of mystical landscapes. Conceptions of space (both material space and "ideational space") are "socially produced and reproduced."[58] Edward Soja argued that power was intimately connected to our understanding of space through capitalism, patriarchy, and racism.[59] Space is political:

A knowable and unknowable, real and imagined lifeworld of experiences, emotions, events, and political choices that is existentially shaped by the generative and problematic interplay between centers and peripheries, the abstract and concrete, the impassioned spaces of the conceptual and the lives marked out materially and metaphorically in spatial praxis, the transformation of (spatial) knowledge into (spatial) action in a field of unevenly developed (spatial) power.[60]

Space is not just there, it is constructed, and as Soja's later work argues, space has different meanings. Soja's theory of Thirdspace understands these as Firstspace (physical), Secondspace (social), and Thirdspace (the meaning created by the body acting upon a space). Barbara Bender gives an example of Thirdspace in Leskernick Hill on Bodmin Moor in England, where geologists and anthropologists viewed the placement of stones as significant, but in different ways. As Bender states, "A person may, more or less in the same breath, understand a landscape in a dozen different ways."[61] Landscapes, including mystical landscapes, offer individual experiences that are shaped by the production and deployment of political power.

Tourism is an embodied activity defined by the bodies that engage with these spaces. According to Soja's formulation of Thirdspace, we can see space as "constructed and signified by the tourist," and thus, "space is a medium through which the tourist negotiates her or his world, tourism signs and contexts, and may construct her or his own distinctive meanings."[62] Soja's linking of space and power is influenced by Lefebvre's "production of space" and its identification with power and its scopic regimes.[63] The creation of these meanings is predicated on a past that is situated in colonial violence. This results in mystical landscapes.

Embodiment is a key part of the tourist experience, "Tourist sites, destinations, cultures and places are (at least in part) made significant through the way we encounter them, and the encounter happens in an embodied way. Cultures, places, memories, actions, and time are embodied."[64] As I will show, bodies create meaning in spaces that have been colonized and mapped. The bodies that are creating meaning in these spaces are predominantly white. Colonialism is dominated by Europeans and Americans. Here, Sara Ahmed's work is very useful in understanding how white bodies assume positions of power and take up space. As she puts it, "In other words, whiteness may function as a form of public comfort *by allowing bodies to extend into spaces that have already taken their shape.*"[65]

As an interdisciplinary scholar, I also draw on theorists from numerous fields, reflecting the diverse voices in Religious Studies as well as the need to be attentive to the historical, postcolonial, and minority voices that inform good scholarship. In the past, my scholarship has been keenly interested in the questions of how religion and tourism overlap in pilgrimage, the religious marketplace, and in the identities that mystical tourists form for themselves. Religion has a prominent role in this study in numerous ways. Tourism is embedded in religious matters. In his 1973 study, Dean McCannell argues that "sightseeing is a form of ritual respect" and points out how "tourism absorbs some of the social functions of religion in the modern world."[66]

The spaces of mystical tourism also reflect a preoccupation with authenticity and experience. Zygmunt Bauman has suggested that tourism may be a modern form of the human impulse to travel and find meaning, which was once done through pilgrimage.[67] Pilgrimage scholars, who have often focused their studies on *communitas*, the transformational experience that is identified with religious journeys, have also suggested that tourism has the potential to provide salvific experiences.[68] By visiting these places, tourists believe that they can benefit from their sacredness and find "restoration and salvation to the progressive, rational, but dispirited West."[69] Tourists believe that the disenchantment in modernity can be remedied by visiting places invested with mystical power. These places are mystical landscapes.

The *imaginaire* is linked to the search for enchantment, as discussed by Canadian philosopher Charles Taylor in his great book *A Secular Age* (2007). My last book explored the question of how consumers in North America and Europe seek enchantment through products identified with the East.[70] Taylor asks us to consider "the dissolution of the 'enchanted' world, the world of spirits and meaningful causal forces" and its links to the search for mystical experience at tourist sites.[71] Lefebvre has written about how leisure activities like tourism provide a space in which to find meaning in a world where individuals are cogs in the capitalist machine.[72] Tourism includes marketing designed for consumers' "individual spiritual needs."[73]

This study also has a strong historical voice. In Carl Becker's famous *Everyman* address in 1984, he said, "[Everyman has his own history] which he imaginatively recreates as an artificial extension of his personal experience . . . an engaging blend of fact and fancy."[74] Some historians have suggested that this intervention is a call to consider historiography as a craft that involves one's own perspectives and feelings.[75] I am not a trained historian, but I am attentive to the work of historiography and have attempted to be balanced, thorough, and fair in the rewriting of colonial history and its links to tourist landscapes that are at the center of much of this book.

The role of maps in imaginary landscapes is a key theme in this study and reflects historian John Harley's attentiveness to maps and power, "the particular role of maps, as images with historically specific codes."[76] Without Harley and his brilliant work, I would not have undertaken this book, at least in the way I did. For Harley, maps have a cartographic language, an iconology, and they represent an immense form of power.[77] Beyond this, maps are not only the creations of cartography—maps exist in the renaming of places, in their silences (those "empty spaces"), and in the imposition of European and American ideas on lands they conquered, settled, and then identified as home.

Anthropology plays an important role in the history of tourism that is linked to this study in several ways. One of these is through the museumification of cultures. This includes the classification of foreign lands into types, the map-making that this book documents, and the representation of tropes and stereotypes in the form of exhibitions. The world expositions, the small and large museums, and the ethnographic scenes within these spaces that presented exotic places as "evolutionary messages" helped to affect the construction of place and space for tourism.[78] We see this in films about Africa, Oceania, and the Middle East, which feature portrayals of colonized peoples in forms that are either "zoological" or "theatrical" or both, suggesting that Europe existed in a different time than its colonial subjects.[79] This view casts the anthropological subject as a colonial object that exists somewhere else.[80]

In recent years, anthropologists and cultural theorists have been interested in determining what the *imaginary* is with models including the imaginary as a *social ethos, cultural model*, or *fantasy*.[81] Without digressing into a complex and lengthy discussion on psychology and the human penchant for imaginary lands, monsters, and dreams, it is worth stating that the imagination has a powerful role in Western thought. Several philosophers have suggested ways to think about the imagination. Lacan's imaginary is "a fantasy, an illusion in response to a psychological need."[82] The *Real*, an idea also at the center of Slavoj Zizek's work, is obscured by both symbols and the imaginary.[83] In the spaces examined in this study, the symbols identified with mysticism are part of the *imaginaire* about a place, whereas the Real has been lost to the ravages of colonial power.

The work of Michel Foucault has become controversial in recent years due to his exploitation of young men in his international travels. I have reservations about bringing him into discussion here, but Foucault has important things to say about the imagination, which he located in colonial power—specifically, the writings that emerged from it. He claimed that "the imaginary now resides between the book and the lamp," a reference to the role of colonial agents and scholars in the creation of fantasy about the Other.[84] Foucault's theories of power/knowledge (*pouvoir savoir*) and his concept of an episteme are especially important in the context of maps. As Harley reminds us, the map has been "an instrument of power" since the early modern period.[85] Furthermore, the silences (or "blank spaces") on maps are "active performances" that form an *episteme*.[86]

Foucault's ideas of utopia and heterotopia are important parts of the tourist imagination. To begin with, we have the utopias of tourism, which serve as projections of our fantasies and in some cases fulfill these fantasies in different ways. Utopias, in the words of Michel Foucault and Jay Miskowiec, are "society itself in a perfected form," and as such, they are "fundamentally unreal places."[87] One example of a utopia is Bali, whose resorts present a world that it is idyllic, peaceful, tranquil, and beautiful—an island paradise. Once we scratch the surface, however, we see the problems that plague the island, ranging from political violence and terrorism to environmental devastation. As one study notes, Balinese culture is the thing that defines them and sustains the tourist industry as "both an identity marker (*ciri khas*) and a trademark."[88]

The heterotopia is a bit more complex, a place that is simultaneously a utopia and its flipside. These are spaces that are the "upside down" of *Stranger Things* without the monsters. They are true counter-sites through their representation, contestation, and inversion.[89] Heterotopias are also places of crisis and we see how they are an apt way to understand the spaces identified with mystical tourism—the desert, the mountain summit, the tropical island. These are privileged and often sacred, making them perfect destinations for individuals seeking an escape, a solution, or a mystical transformation.

The study of tourism is also a study of the imagination. One scholar describes it as: "Tourism fantasies are always situated within wider sociocultural frameworks."[90] One of the ways these fantasies are played out is in the search for mystical experience in landscapes viewed as sacred, powerful, or transformative. In these spaces, tourists often practice transitory identities that are exotic, different, or foreign. Laura Donaldson describes this as *postmodern neocolonialism*, "*postmodern* because they deterritorialize and consume original spiritual traditions in particular ways and *neocolonial* because they reproduce historical spiritual traditions in particular ways and because they reproduce historical imperialism."[91]

Mystical tourism involves the movement of bodies that are engaging in a form of pilgrimage that takes them from their ordinary lives to special places. Victor and Edith Turner's model of pilgrimage provides a way to understand why mystical landscapes are so appealing. The pilgrim, including the tourist, seeks an experience removed from ordinary life. The island, desert, and high mountain spaces offer the promise of mystical experience. As Victor Turner explains, "I wish to briefly indicate, too, that as the pilgrim moves away from his structural involvements at home his route becomes increasingly sacralized at one level and increasingly secularized at another."[92] Both pilgrimage and tourism entail a search for authenticity. In mystical tourism, these intersections are amplified, because disenchantment pushes individuals to seek meaning outside of the mundaneness of their lives.

This is a project about the legacy of colonialism, imaginative geographies, and their role in modern tourism, out of which mystical tourism emerges. Originally envisioned as a book that brought the reader on a world tour of mystical tourism, it became a book more about colonialist systems of mapping and their force in the world today. As a white scholar, I have tried to be inclusive of indigenous and postcolonial voices. I also have adopted the practice of renaming sites that were given European or American names. Anna Carr, in her work on the natural spaces of Aotearoa (New Zealand), utilizes an approach where the Māori and English names are both given. Carr's usage includes examples like Aoraki/Mount Cook and the inclusion of Māori names such as *tangata whenua* to denote the original inhabitants of the land.[93] I began by including a footnote with the English, French, or Spanish language name and then used the indigenous name throughout the main text. I decided to revert to the indigenous or original name for places out of respect for the people whose ancestral lands are now known by other names.

Biographical Note

The South Pacific, on which Chapter 5 focuses, is a part of my past and present. I went to college in Hawai'i, to a wonderful little college (now gone; a casualty of the overdevelopment of Oahu's land) called Hawai'i Loa, named after the Polynesian explorer. The college is now being razed for another housing development, but when I was there my classmates included many Native Hawaiians as well as Pacific Islanders from Tonga and Samoa, who performed a war dance at our basketball games at halftime and whose kindness marked me forever, so much so that my life today is still centered on the Pacific region. My college travels included the Cook Islands (named after Captain James Cook); Western Samoa (the Samoa that is *not* a U.S. military base and where Robert Louis Stevenson's house still stands); Fiji (famous in colonial literature for its cannibals and today the home of many Indians, brought by the British); the Kingdom of Tonga (home of one of my best college friends); and Aotearoa, better known as New Zealand, where I spent a year abroad and learned history from the perspective of formerly colonized people.

It was perhaps no accident, but providence, that placed me as a student in the Māori Studies program at the University of Waikato for a year. I struggled through my lessons, helped at one point by a sweet Māori classmate named Maui. I was the only white person in the language classes and during the time I was in Aotearoa, there was a high level of racial tension between the Māori and white New Zealanders (kiwis). The bar we went to was segregated along racial lines and my Tongan friend was the focus of more than one racial incident, including one I was witness to, where a guest of a friend made offensive comments about her hair, its length, and its texture. It was an eye-opening year, coming from a family whose politics were leftist. My year abroad was paid for by a scholarship from a foundation established by two of the oldest white families in Hawai'i and linked to the Dole pineapple fortune. I plan to send them a copy of this book, for without that year my life would not have taken the path it did.

By the time my year was over, I wondered if I was going to leave the Pacific permanently: today, I return to Indonesia almost yearly to visit my husband's extended family, although I have only been back to Polynesia twice since college. I look back on my undergraduate days with such fondness and have always felt that the people I met in the islands, including the Hawaiian Islands (a colony that should be free), many of whose names I have forgotten, were somehow preparing me for this book, for without the stories they told me about the past and the present, I would never have gone on to graduate school and entered an academic life. To them, I owe a huge debt of gratitude. *Tēnā koutou.*

Notes

1 Ann Laura Stoler, *Carnal Knowledge and Imperial Power: Race and the Intimate in Colonial Rule* (Berkeley: University of California Press, 2010), 32.
2 Derek Gregory, *Geographical Imaginations* (Cambridge: Blackwell, 1994), 173.
3 Farish A. Noor, *The Long Shadow of the 19th Century: Critical Essays on Colonial Orientalism in Southeast Asia* (Petaling Jaya: Matahari, 2021), 125.
4 Gregory B. Willson, Alison J. McIntosh, and Anne L. Zahra, "Tourism and Spirituality: A Phenomenological Analysis," *Annals of Tourism Research* 42 (2013): 153.
5 Claudio Minca, "'The Bali Syndrome': The Explosion and Implosion of 'Exotic' Tourist Spaces," *Tourism Geographies* 2, no. 4 (2000): 389.
6 Denis Cosgrove, *Geography and Vision: Seeing, Imagining and Representing the World* (New York: I. B. Tauris, 2008), 6.
7 John Urry, "The Place of Emotions within Place," in *Emotional Geographies*, ed. Liz Bondi, Joyce Davidson, and Mick Smith (London: Routledge, 2016), 77, 78.
8 Simon Coleman, "From the Sublime to the Meticulous: Art, Anthropology and Victorian Pilgrimage to Palestine," *History and Anthropology* 13, no. 4 (2002): 277.
9 Jonathon Z. Smith, *Map Is Not Territory* (Chicago: University of Chicago, 1993), 295.
10 Smith 1993, 295–296.
11 Smith 1993, 295.
12 Hélène Blais, Florence Deprest, and Pierre Singaravelou, "French Geography, Cartography, and Colonialism: Introduction," *Journal of Historical Geography* 37 (2011): 146.
13 John Brian Harley, "Silences and Secrecy: The Hidden Agenda of Cartography in Early Modern Europe," *Imago Mundi* 40 (1988): 58.
14 Harley 1988, 59.
15 Anne McClintock, *Imperial Leather: Race, Gender and Sexuality in the Colonial Contest* (New York: Routledge, 1995), 25–26.
16 Aubrey L. Haines, *The Yellowstone Story: A History of Our First National Park*, Volume 1 (Niwot: University Press of Colorado, 1996), 4.
17 Thomas S. Bremer, *Blessed with Tourists: The Borderlands of Religion and Tourism in San Antonio* (Chapel Hill: University of North Carolina Press, 2004), 11.
18 Haines, 4.
19 Barbara W. Tuchman, *Bible and Sword: England and Palestine from the Bronze Age to Balfour* (New York: Ballantine Books, 1984), 1. In her book, Tuchman documents the long history of England and Palestine, which begins with the claim that Noah was the ancestor of the British. See Tuchman, 2–21.
20 Thomas S. Bremer, "The Religious and Spiritual Appeal of National Parks," in *The Routledge Handbook of Religious and Spiritual Tourism*, ed. Daniel H. Olsen and Dallen J. Timothy (New York: Routledge, 2022), 170.
21 Carolyn O' Dwyer, "Tropic Knights and Hula Belles: War and Tourism in the South Pacific," *Journal for Cultural Research* 8, no. 1 (2004): 33.
22 O' Dwyer, 34.
23 Rune Bennike, "'A Summer Place': Darjeeling in the Tourist Gaze," in *Darjeeling Reconsidered: Histories, Politics, Environments*, ed. Townsend Middleston and Sara Schneidermann (New York: Oxford University Press, 2018), 61.

24 Bremer 2004, 16.
25 Bremer 2004, 20.
26 Bennike, 57.
27 Joe Bandy, "Managing the Other of Nature: Sustainability, Spectacle, and the Global Regimes of Capital in Ecotourism," *Public Culture* 8 (1996): 556.
28 Dina Glouberman and Josée-Ann Cloutier, "Community as Holistic Healer on Health Holiday Retreats: The Case of Skyros," in *The Routledge Handbook of Health Tourism*, ed. Melanie Kay Smith and László Puczkó (New York: Routledge, 2017), 153.
29 Robert Stam and Ella Shohat, *Race in Translation: Culture Wars around the Postcolonial Atlantic* (New York: New York University Press, 2012), 6.
30 Peter Bishop, *The Myth of Shangri-La: Tibet, Travel Writing and the Western Creation of Sacred Landscape* (Berkeley: University of California Press, 1989), 1. (emphasis original)
31 Daniel K. Richter, *Facing East from Indian Country: A Native History of Early America* (Cambridge: Harvard University Press, 2001), 3.
32 Richter, 3.
33 Renée Bergland, *The National Uncanny: Indian Ghosts and American Subjects* (Hanover: University Press of New England, 2000), 4.
34 John P. Bowes, *Land Too Good for Indians: Northern Indian Removal* (Norman: University of Oklahoma Press, 2016), 4.
35 John B. Harley, "New England Cartography and the Native Americans," in *The New Nature of Maps: Essays in the History of Cartography*, ed. Paul Laxton (Baltimore: John Hopkins University Press, 2001), 188–189.
36 Harley 2001, 181.
37 Michael McCloskey, "The Wilderness Act of 1964: Its Background and Meaning," *The Oregon Law Review* 45, no. 4 (1966): 288.
38 Bowes, 20.
39 Evan Berry, *Devoted to Nature: The Religious Roots of American Environmentalism* (Berkeley: University of California Press, 2015), 102.
40 Susannah Crockford, *Ripples of the Universe: Spirituality in Sedona, Arizona* (Chicago: University of Chicago Press, 2021), 5, 11.
41 Crockford, 3, 11.
42 Crockford, 12.
43 Crockford, 101, 102.
44 Vincanne Adams, "Karaoke as Modern Lhasa, Tibet: Western Encounters with Cultural Polities," *Cultural Anthropology* 11, no. 4 (1996): 514.
45 Sherry Ortner, *Life and Death on Mt. Everest: Sherpas and Himalayan Mountaineering* (Princeton: Princeton University Press, 1999), 26.
46 Ortner 1999, 4.
47 Holly Walters, *Shaligram Pilgrimage in the Nepal Himalayas* (Amsterdam: Amsterdam University Press, 2020), 112.
48 Walters 2020, 113.
49 Stephen Britton, "Tourism, Capital, and Place: Towards a Critical Geography of Tourism," *Society and Space* 9, no. 14 (1991): 464.
50 Lorenzo Veracini, "The Other Shift: Settler Colonialism, Israel and the Occupation," *Journal of Palestine Studies* 42, no. 2 (2013): 27.
51 Rashid Khalidi, *Palestinian Identity: The Construction of Modern National Consciousness* (New York: Columbia University Press, 1999), 14. Rashidi has a more extensive history of the word Urshalim in his book; see pages 15–16 for the usage of Urshalim in the nineteenth century.
52 Barabara Lüthy, Francesca Falk, and Patricia Purtschert, "Colonialism without Colonies: Examining Blank Spaces in Colonial Studies," *National Identities* 18, no. 1 (2016): 4.

53 Tom Lynch, *Outback & Out West: The Settler-Colonial Environmental Imaginary* (Lincoln: University of Nebraska Press, 2022), 183–184.

54 Jarrod Hore, *Visions of Nature: How Landscape Photography Shaped Settler Colonialism* (Berkeley: University of California Press, 2022), 43.

55 Simon Piasecki, "A Mountain as Multiverse: Circumnavigating the Realities and the Meta-Realities of a Kailas Pilgrim," *Performance Research* 24, no. 2 (2019): 16. Meru is the mythical mountain identified as the center of the universe in many Asian religions, but for some Buddhists, this place is Kailash.

56 Jeffrey Mather, "Captivating Readers: Middlebrow Aesthetics and James Hilton's *Lost Horizon*," *College English Association Critic* 79, no. 2 (2017): 231.

57 Bishop, 143.

58 Edward Soja, *Postmodern Geographies: The Reassertion of Space in Critical Social Theory* (New York: Verso, 1989), 120.

59 Margarida Queirós, "Edward Soja: Geographical Imaginations from the Margins to the Core," *Planning Theory & Practice* 17, no. 1 (2016): 155.

60 Edward Soja, *Thirdspace: Journeys to Los Angeles and Other Real and Imagined Places* (Oxford: Blackwell, 1996), 31.

61 Barbara Bender, "Time and Landscape," *Current Anthropology* 43, no. S4 (2002): S106.

62 David Crouch, Lars Aronsson, and Lage Wahlström, "Tourist Encounters," *Tourist Studies* 1, no. 3 (2001): 254.

63 Derek Gregory, "Colonial Nostalgia and Cultures of Travel: Spaces of Constructed Visibility in Egypt," in *Consuming Tradition, Manufacturing Heritage: Global Norms and Urban Forms in the Age of Tourism*, ed. Nezar Al Sayyad (New York: Routledge, 2001), 114.

64 Crouch, David, Aronsson, and Wahlström, "Tourist Encounters," 259.

65 Sara Ahmed, "A Phenomenology of Whiteness," *Feminist Theory* 8, no. 2 (2017): 158. (emphasis in original)

66 Dean MacCannell, "Staged Authenticity: Arrangements of Social Space in Tourist Settings," *American Journal of Sociology* 79, no. 3 (1973): 589.

67 Zygmunt Bauman, "From Pilgrim to Tourist: Or a Short History of Identity," in *Questions of Cultural Identity*, ed. Stuart Hall and Paul Du Gay (London: Sage, 1996), 26.

68 Michael Stausberg, *Religion and Tourism: Crossroads, Destinations and Encounters* (New York: Routledge, 2011), 21.

69 Adrian J. Ivakhiv, *Claiming Sacred Ground: Pilgrims and Politics at Glastonbury and Sedona* (Bloomington: Indian University Press, 2001), 51.

70 See Sophia Arjana, *Buying Buddha, Selling Rumi: Orientalism and the Mystical Marketplace* (London: Oneworld, 2020).

71 Charles Taylor, *A Secular Age* (Cambridge: Harvard University Press, 2007), 553.

72 Boris Vukoníc, *Tourism and Religion* (New York: Pergamon, 1996), 13.

73 Vukoníc, 18.

74 Milton M. Klein, "Everyman His Own Historian: Carl Becker as Historiographer," *The History Teacher* 19, no. 1 (1985): 105.

75 Klein 1985, 107.

76 John B. Harley, "Maps, Knowledge and Power," in *The Iconography of Landscape: Essays on the Symbolic Representation, Design and Use of Past Environments*, ed. Denis Cosgrove and Stephen Daniels (Cambridge: Cambridge University Press, 1988), 277.

77 Harley, 278–279.

78 Emma Sandon, "Projecting Africa: Two 1920s British Travel Films," in *Cultural Encounters: Representing 'Otherness'*, ed. Elizabeth Hallam and Brian V. Street (New York: Routledge, 2000), 136.

79 Sandon, 138.
80 See Johannes Fabian, *Time and the Other: How Anthropology Makes Its Object* (New York: Columbia University Press, 2014).
81 Claudia Strauss, "The Imaginary," *Anthropological Theory* 6, no. 3 (2006): 323–332.
82 Strauss, 326.
83 Strauss, 328.
84 Michel Foucault, "Fantasia of the Library," in *Language, Counter-Memory, Practice: Selected Essays and Interviews*, ed. Donald Bouchard (Ithaca: Cornell University Press, 1977), 90.
85 Harley 1988, 58.
86 Harley 1988, 59.
87 Michel Foucault and Jay Miskowiec, "Of Other Spaces," *Diacritics* 16, no. 1 (1986): 24.
88 Michel Picard, "'Cultural Tourism' in Bali: Cultural Performances as Tourist Attraction," *Indonesia* 49 (1990): 74.
89 Foucault and Miskowiec, 24.
90 Noel B. Salazar, "Tourism Imaginaries: A Conceptual Approach," *Annals of Tourism Research* 39, no. 2 (2012): 871.
91 Laura E. Donaldson, "On Medicine Women and White Shame-Ans: New Age Native Americanism and Commodity Fetishism as Pop Culture Fetishism," *Signs* 24, no. 3 (1999): 680. (emphasis in original)
92 Victor Turner, "The Center Out There," *History of Religions* 12, no. 3 (1973): 204.
93 Anna Carr, "Mountain Places, Cultural Spaces: The Interpretation of Culturally Significant Landscapes," *Journal of Sustainable Tourism* 12, no. 5 (2004): 437, 433.

Bibliography

Adams, Vincanne. "Karaoke as Modern Lhasa, Tibet: Western Encounters with Cultural Polities." *Cultural Anthropology* 11, no. 4 (1996): 510–546.
Ahmed, Sara. "A Phenomenology of Whiteness." *Feminist Theory* 8, no. 2 (2007): 149–168.
Arjana, Sophia. *Buying Buddha, Selling Rumi: Orientalism and the Mystical Marketplace*. London: Oneworld, 2020.
Bandy, Joe. "Managing the Other of Nature: Sustainability, Spectacle, and Global Regimes of Capital in Ecotourism." *Public Culture* 8 (1996): 539–566.
Bauman, Zygmunt. "From Pilgrim to Tourist: Or a Short History of Identity." In *Questions of Cultural Identity*, edited by Stuart Hall and Paul Du Gay, 18–36. London: Sage, 1996.
Bender, Barbara. "Time and Landscape." *Current Anthropology* 43, no. 4 (2002): S103–S112.
Bennike, Rune. "'A Summer Place': Darjeeling in the Tourist Gaze." In *Darjeeling Reconsidered: Histories, Politics, Environments*, edited by Townsend Middleton and Sara Shneidermann, 54–73. New York: Oxford University Press, 2018.
Bergland, Renée L. *The National Uncanny: Indian Ghosts and American Subjects*. Hanover: University Press of New England, 2000.
Berry, Evan. *Devoted to Nature: The Religious Roots of American Environmentalism*. Berkeley: University of California Press, 2015.
Bishop, Peter. *The Myth of Shangri-La: Tibet, Travel Writing and the Western Creation of Sacred Landscape*. Berkeley: University of California Press, 1989.

Blais, Hélène, Florence Deprest, and Pierre Singaravelou. "French Geography, Cartography and Colonialism: Introduction." *Journal of Historical Geography* 37 (2011): 146–148.

Bowes, John P. *Land Too Good for Indians: Northern Indian Removal.* Norman: University of Oklahoma Press, 2016.

Bremer, Thomas S. *Blessed with Tourists: The Borderlands of Religion and Tourism in San Antonio.* Chapel Hill: University of North Carolina Press, 2004.

Bremer, Thomas S. "The Religious and Spiritual Appeal of National Parks." In *The Routledge Handbook of Religious and Spiritual Tourism*, edited by Daniel H. Olsen and Dallen J. Timothy, 166–178. New York: Routledge, 2022.

Britton, Stephen. "Tourism, Capital, and Place: Towards a Critical Geography of Tourism." *Society and Space* 9, no. 4 (1991): 451–478.

Carr, Anna. "Mountain Places, Cultural Spaces: The Interpretation of Culturally Significant Landscapes." *Journal of Sustainable Tourism* 12, no. 5 (2004): 432–459.

Coleman, Simon. "From the Sublime to the Meticulous: Art, Anthropology and Victorian Pilgrimage to Palestine." *History and Anthropology* 13, no. 4 (2002): 275–290.

Cosgrove, Denis. *Geography and Vision: Seeing, Imagining and Representing the World.* New York: I.B. Tauris, 2008.

Crockford, Susannah. *Ripples of the Universe: Spirituality in Sedona, Arizona.* Chicago: University of Chicago Press, 2021.

Crouch, David, Lars Aronsson, and Lage Wahlström. "Tourist Encounters." *Tourist Studies* 1, no. 3 (2001): 253–270.

Donaldson, Laura E. "On Medicine Women and White Shame-ans: New Age Native Americanism and Commodity Fetishism as Pop Culture Feminism." *Signs* 24, no. 3 (1999): 677–696.

Fabian, Johannes. *Time and the Other: How Anthropology Makes Its Object.* New York: Columbia University Press, 2014.

Foucault, Michel. "Fantasia of the Library." In *Language, Counter-Memory, Practice: Selected Essays and Interviews*, edited by Donald Bouchard, 87–109. Ithaca: Cornell University Press, 1977.

Foucault, Michel and Jay Miskowiec. "Of Other Spaces." *Diacritics* 16, no. 1 (1986): 22–27.

Glouberman, Dina and Josée-Ann Cloutier. "Community as Holistic Healer on Health Holiday Retreats: The Case of Skyros." In *The Routledge Handbook of Health Tourism*, edited by Melanie Kay Smith and László Puczkó, 152–167. New York: Routledge, 2017.

Gregory, Derek. *Geographical Imaginations.* Cambridge: Blackwell, 1994.

Gregory, Derek. "Colonial Nostalgia and Cultures of Travel: Spaces of Constructed Visibility in Egypt." In *Consuming Tradition, Manufacturing Heritage: Global Norms and Urban Forms in the Age of Tourism*, edited by Nezar Al Sayyad, 111–151. New York: Routledge, 2001.

Haines, Aubrey L. *The Yellowstone Story: A History of Our First National Park, Volume One.* Niwot: University Press of Colorado, 1996.

Harley, John Brian. "Maps, Knowledge, and Power." In *The Iconography of Landscape: Essays on the Symbolic Representation, Design and Use of Past Environments*, edited by Denis Cosgrove and Stephen Daniels, 277–312. Cambridge: Cambridge University Press, 1988.

Harley, John Brian. "Silences and Secrecy: The Hidden Agenda of Cartography in Early Modern Europe." *Imago Mundi* 40 (1988): 57–76.

Harley, John Brian. "New England Cartography and the Native Americans." In *The New Nature of Maps: Essays in the History of Cartography*, edited by Paul Laxton, 169–196. Baltimore: John Hopkins University Press, 2001.

Hore, Jarrod. *Visions of Nature: How Landscape Photography Shaped Settler Colonialism*. Berkeley: University of California Press, 2022.

Ivakhiv, Adrian J. *Claiming Sacred Ground: Pilgrims and Politics at Glastonbury and Sedona*. Bloomington: Indiana University Press, 2001.

Khalidi, Rashid. *Palestinian Identity: The Construction of Modern National Consciousness*. New York: Columbia University Press, 1997.

Klein, Milton M. "Everyman His Own Historian: Carl Becker as Historiographer." *The History Teacher* 19, no. 1 (1985): 101–109.

Lüthy, Barbara, Francesca Falk, and Patricia Purtschert. "Colonialism without Colonies: Examining Blank Spaces in Colonial Studies." *National Identities* 18, no. 1 (2016): 1–9.

Lynch, Tom. *Outback & Out West: The Settler-Colonial Environmental Imaginary*. Lincoln: University of Nebraska Press, 2022.

MacCannell, Dean. "Staged Authenticity: Arrangements of Social Space in Tourist Settings." *American Journal of Sociology* 79, no. 3 (1973): 589–603.

Mather, Jeffrey. "Captivating Readers: Middlebrow Aesthetics and James Hilton's *Lost Horizon*." *CEA Critic* 79, no. 2 (2017): 231–243.

McClintock, Anne. *Imperial Leather: Race, Gender and Sexuality in the Colonial Contest*. New York: Routledge, 1995.

McCloskey, Michael. "The Wilderness Act of 1964: Its Background and Meaning." *The Oregon Law Review* 45, no. 4 (1966): 288–321.

Minca, Claudio. "'The Bali Syndrome': The Explosion and Implosion of 'Exotic' Tourist Spaces." *Tourism Geographies* 2, no. 4 (2000): 389–403.

Noor, Farish A. *The Long Shadow of the 19th Century: Critical Essays on Colonial Orientalism in Southeast Asia*. Petaling Jaya: Matahari Books, 2021.

O'Dwyer, Carolyn. "Tropic Knights and Hula Belles: War and Tourism in the South Pacific." *Journal for Cultural Research* 8, no. 1 (2004): 33–50.

Ortner, Sherry. *Life and Death on Mt. Everest: Sherpas and Himalayan Mountaineering*. Princeton: Princeton University Press, 1999.

Piasecki, Simon. "A Mountain as Multiverse: Circumnavigating the Realities and Meta-Realities of a Kailas Pilgrim." *Performance Research* 24, no. 2 (2019): 16–23.

Picard, Michel. "'Cultural Tourism' in Bali: Cultural Performances as Tourist Attraction." *Indonesia* 49 (1990): 37–74.

Queirós, Margarida. "Edward Soja: Geographical Imaginations from the Margins to the Core." *Planning Theory and Practice* 17, no. 1 (2016): 154–160.

Richter, Daniel. *Facing East from Indian Country: A Native History of Early America*. Cambridge, MA: Harvard University Press, 2001.

Salazar, Noel B. "Tourism Imaginaries: A Conceptual Approach." *Annals of Tourism Research* 39, no. 2 (2012): 863–882.

Sandon, Emma. "Projecting Africa: Two British Travel Films of the 1920s." In *Cultural Encounters: Representing 'Otherness'*, edited by Elizabeth Hallam and Brian V. Street, 109–147. New York: Routledge, 2000.

Smith, Jonathon Z. *Map Is Not Territory*. Chicago: University of Chicago Press, 1993.

Soja, Edward. *Postmodern Geographies: The Reassertion of Space in Critical Social Theory*. New York: Verso, 1989.

Soja, Edward. *Thirdspace: Journeys to Los Angeles and Other Real and Imagined Places*. Oxford: Blackwell, 1996.

Stam, Robert and Ella Shohat. *Race in Translation: Culture Wars Around the Postcolonial Atlantic*. New York: New York University Press, 2012.

Stausberg, Michael. *Religion and Tourism: Crossroads, Destinations and Encounters*. New York: Routledge, 2011.

Stoler, Ann Laura. *Carnal Knowledge and Imperial Power: Race and the Intimate in Colonial Rule*. Berkeley: University of California Press, 2010.

Strauss, Claudia. "The Imaginary." *Anthropological Theory* 6, no. 3 (2006): 322–344.

Taylor, Charles. *A Secular Age*. Cambridge, MA: Harvard University Press, 2007.

Tuchman, Barbara W. *Bible and Sword: England and Palestine from the Bronze Age to Balfour*. New York: Ballantine Books, 1984.

Turner, Victor. "The Center Out There: Pilgrim's Goal." *History of Religions* 12, no. 3 (1973): 191–230.

Urry, John. "The Place of Emotions within Place." In *Emotional Geographies*, edited by Liz Bondi, Joyce Davidson, and Mick Smith, 77–83. London: Routledge, 2016.

Veracini, Lorenzo. "The Other Shift: Settler Colonialism, Israel and the Occupation." *Journal of Palestine Studies* 42, no. 2 (2013): 26–42.

Vuconíc, Boris. *Tourism and Religion*. New York: Pergamon, 1996.

Walters, Holly. *Shaligram Pilgrimage in the Nepal Himalayas*. Amsterdam: Amsterdam University Press, 2020.

Willson, Gregory B., Alison J. McIntosh, and Anne L. Zahra. "Tourism and Spirituality: A Phenomenological Analysis." *Annals of Tourism Research* 42 (2013): 150–168.

1

COLONIAL GEOGRAPHIES

> Imperialism after all is an act of geographical violence through which vir-
> tually every space in the world is explored, charted, and finally brought
> under control.[1]
>
> Edward Said

Colonialism

This book is a *counter-map* of the modern world that explores the ways
colonial power, including settler colonialism, is involved in creating mystical
landscapes around the world. As Camilla Fojas explains, "The strict definition of empire" is "direct political and administrative control over a sovereign territory."[2] While the Hawaiian Islands may be part of the American
empire, they are not sovereign; nor are the Indian lands of the American
West.

Anti-colonial and indigenous voices help us understand how colonialism
and imperialism take numerous forms. For example, when the Samoan
writer Albert Wendt castigates the modern hotel in Western Samoa as a
soulless monstrosity, he reveals how colonialism and tourism are inextri-
cably linked.[3] French colonies in the Maghrib (Algeria, Tunisia, Morocco,
and Tripolitania) included major building projects—a theater and the
Chemin de Télemely (a promenade)—designed to serve colonial settlers
and the tourists who would come.[4] The farms of French settlers were
viewed as revivals of North Africa's ancient role as a producer of grain,
and including the farms on tours was a part of the promotion of the territories (visiting the colonies was an important part of being a good French
citizen) of the "Second France."[5]

DOI: 10.4324/9781003361725-2

Maps are common features of tourist materials. Benedict Anderson describes how the colonial map becomes "pure sign, no longer compass to the world," found in everything from posters to hotel walls.[6] In colonial Africa, we find several examples linked in an imaginative geography and told in symbols and products:

> The map of Africa, with its gouache of imperial red and its spinal serpent of Rhodes's projected railway, a seeming extension of the uraeus-like Nile, entered into the realm of the iconic. It was adopted by the Africana bibliographer Sidney Mendelssohn as his bookplate, and it became a Cook poster and a design for dust jackets.[7]

Colonialism allowed governments, colonial agents, settlers, writers, and artists to reorder the world as a new space, often resulting in mystical landscapes. The way in which colonial culture inserted itself into these spaces was viewed as *natural*. However, colonialism is *unnatural*. Isak Dinesen, the colonial farmer in Kenya whose book is examined in Chapter 3, is one example. As Simon Lewis explains,

> Having the farm, according to Blixen's formulation, a formulation faithfully repeated in the movie with Meryl Streep's beautifully nuanced voice-over, at once proud and regretful, naturalizes Blixen's presence in Africa; she had a farm the same way as one might have brown hair or a bad temper, a particular experience or disease. Her having the farm is no more a political act than Old MacDonald's having of his farm in the nursery song.[8]

The places examined in this book include territories distant from their colonial overlords as well as places invaded and occupied by settlers. The United States is one case where neither colonialism nor imperialism is a sufficient framing device:

> On the one hand, America is and always has been a colony of Europe; on the other, America is an imperial power. But both of these facts are somehow shameful in an American context, since American nationhood is built on the denial of colonialism.[9]

I use "colonialism" in a broad sense to describe the occupation, militarily, socially, and culturally, of land that one is not tied to through indigeneity. In some cases, imperialism is a more appropriate term, as Said reminds us when he defines imperialism as "an act of geographical violence through which virtually every space in the world is explored, charted and finally brought under control."[10]

Stories of colonialism told in this book are different, but they have commonalities—invasion, occupation, and reterritorialization. Colonialism takes different forms. The more familiar cases, such as India and Algeria, are known as Europe's "classic colonies," but there are also settler colonies, including the United States of America, its Pacific colony in the Hawaiian Islands, and Israel, all of which are examined in this book.[11] Today, settler colonialism is upheld through national narratives about a promised land and manifest destiny. Systems of representation, including the museum, are also key parts of the settler colonial project. In Karen Kosasa's study of museum and art gallery exhibitions in Hawai'i, she analyses an exhibit about the Pacific Islands in the eighteenth century at the Honolulu Academy of Arts—no histories of colonialism were included.[12]

The British in the Victorian era had a fondness for classification, maps, and other kinds of enumeration.[13] These practices help to explain British colonies, the large geographical surveys in the Himalayas and other parts of Asia, the mapping of Palestine, and the collections at British museums, but the French, Germans, Americans, and others were also interested in controlling and classifying the world as part of a larger colonial project. Neocolonialism is evident in Nepal's economic reliance on the mountaineering business, and for some tourists, Bali exists as an "imaginary periphery of the Australian nation."[14]

The focus of this book is on European and American colonialism, which includes places shaped by settler colonialism such as Kenya and the Hawaiian Islands. Other empires are not included for many reasons (two of them being the large size of this project and its focus on tourism). However, spurious techniques of map-making have been a part of action of non-European empires as well, such as the Ottomans, who used the map (*harita*) to satisfy its leaders and for the purposes of propaganda.[15]

Explorers' maps provided the outlines for colonies in Kenya, North America, and Palestine, but cartography is more than a scientific endeavor, "Explorers were not merely the agents of geography, but landscape artists, whose views of the unknown were filtered, embellished, and sometimes imagined."[16] Colonial mapping included not only soldiers and cartographers, but also poets and painters, "missionaries, tradesmen, explorers, settlers, mercenaries."[17] Bali became famous because of its colonial encounter with the Dutch and popularity with artists and writers. Later, it became a place whose mystique was present in numerous spaces. As Michael Hitchcock writes, "Over time Bali became one of the most romantic stops on the tourist itinerary, underpinned by a host of new books, articles, photographic studies and films."[18] Today, Indonesia has had to develop new resorts to re-create what tourists have already destroyed on the rest of island.

The kidnapping of indigenous people who were displayed as part of Europe's human zoos is another legacy of colonial cartography. At the

World's Columbian Expedition of 1893, 400 natives from the French colonies were put on display; and in the Moskauer Panoptikum of 1899 held in Frankfurt, Amazons were presented as barbaric and Samoans as cheerful and sexually available natives.[19] A few of these captives became celebrities. Mai (called Omai in the press) toured around Europe, while others were released after a few days of being held on a British ship. Early studies in human ethnography were part of these colonial projects, something that remains a stain on the field of anthropology today. The discipline of anthropology is also linked to tourism. In the early twentieth century, a group of anthropologists helped to cast Bali as an island of friendly rice farmers. This was the same era in which Bali was seen as "the last paradise" and other places in the Pacific became popular mystical landscapes.[20]

In colonially occupied territories, the local population was dealt with in different ways. Sometimes, the indigenous population was replaced with white settlers through a coup, such as in Hawai'i's "Bayonet Constitution." The creation of the American West was dependent on the idea of the "vanishing Indian," which made way for a new vision of the landscape that resulted in the erasure of indigenous space and memory. As Kenneth Olwig explains,

> [T]he wilderness ideal helped to naturalize a colonial imperialism that simultaneously required the removal, even extermination, of the previous native population, often deemed to be radically inferior, and the obliteration of the memory of this population.[21]

This erasure involved the *ghosting* of Indians, "one specific discursive technique of Indian removal—describing them as insubstantial, disembodied, and finally spectral beings."[22] The "vanishing Indian" is an example of the ways that the colonial mapping project succeeded in erasing Indians from their lands. Dependent on mythologies of Indians as savage and primitive, early Americans justified the seizure of natives' land. As one scholar points out, "Although native agricultural practice had sustained indigenous people for millennia, it was not recognized by Europeans as authentic agriculture but only as a kind of animal-like foraging."[23]

New forms of colonization seem to constantly emerge, something seen in theme parks that capitalize on the appeal of other cultures. Cinema is also a space where the colonial imagination is richly expressed, seen in films about Africa, Oceania, or Asia where the inhabitants are part of the setting, existing as a kind of decorative element for the viewer. Predating these films are the drawings and paintings of exoticized spaces that present people in romantic and idealized ways. As one example, the artist William Hodges portrayed the famous Tahitian Tu, also known as Otoo, in a style fitting the words of George Forster who described his "majestic and intelligent air" and the "great expression in his black eyes."[24] Part of Romanticism was a quest for experience that was often visited upon women in foreign lands: "Henceforth, vitality and sensuous enjoyment were considered highly informative."[25] As we shall learn, the romanticism attached to Otoo is only one side of the history of colonial imagination and its map-making project. The story told in this book includes the massacres of Native Americans, Africans, and most recently, of Arabs in Gaza. The geographical imagination is indeed a violent and terrible thing.

Orientalism(s) and Other Discourses of Difference

Orientalism is strongly identified with many of the places examined in this study, including Morocco, Algeria, Egypt, Palestine, Nepal, and Tibet. The British *imaginaire* about the East often referred to Orientalist ideas about India. Richard King has shown how instrumental India is in propagating ideas about the East, and I direct readers to his book for a full account of this history.[26] As one example, Romantic ideas about the mountains, which lie at the center of attitudes toward Nepal and Tibet and their mystical landscapes, have their cultural references in India. As Mark Liechty explains,

> From mountain tourism and mountaineering to mountain resorts, sanatoria, and "hill stations" in colonial India, mountains became exhilarating and grand places to escape the evils of modern civilization. As the world's highest mountains, the Himalayas were second to none in inspiring romantic attraction, serving as a magnet of the disaffected of all sorts.[27]

In Edward Said's words, "The Arab world compelled fascination and interest yet withheld affection or enthusiastic and particular knowledge."[28] Colonial regimes often offered fallacious theories of why a region was in decline. In Egypt, colonial administrators claimed that the Arabic absence of a vowel was indicative of the debilitated "Oriental mind," which was incapable of governing itself.[29] Because Arabic words don't always have the vowels marked with diacritics, this was used to assert a racialized topography on the region, which would be remedied by white Europeans controlling Arab territory. A similar myth was constructed around the Lakota, who used sign language. This fact was used to argue that they were "savages," as opposed to Europeans, who communicated with "an advanced written and verbal language."[30] This is the colonial logic that constructed new maps of the world. As Mark Liechty has pointed out, the Western mind has constructed many Orients, reflecting the territorial and colonial programs of the day. In his words,

> For centuries Jerusalem was the source of the "light of the East"—*ex lux oriente*—but certainly by the 19th century more and more people critical

of Western modernity were looking further east for their spiritual *axis mundi*. Colonial knowledge systems that spawned a host of Orientalisms, and eventually Anthropology itself, inevitably made "the East" not just the focus of scholarly and administrative scrutiny, but a resource for the Western popular imagination.[31]

Another example of the imagination running wild is Tibet. In part due to its isolation, Tibet has functioned as a site of fantasy for Europeans and more recently, for Americans, for several centuries. As Tom Neuhaus explains, the interest in a "privately experienced spirituality" and the fact that it was so isolated led to the creation of Tibet as a magical and mystical landscape.[32] As he puts it, the stories about Tibet "could hardly ever be verified."

Orientalism is often focused on conquest and penetration, both territorial and bodily, and this is seen in "the function of the East as the desired imaginary of the West."[33] The hypersexualization of foreign lands is, of course, not limited to the East, and we see Orientalism in other spaces outside the "East." French fantasies of Black women reflected ideas about Africa and other French colonial territories; here, the Orient often made itself known in paintings that referred "the viewer to a type of Orientalist fantasy about Africa."[34] Suren Lalvani calls this the "colonial fetish," explaining, "It arrives only within the specular zone of desire as a 'consumable difference' and is subsequently generative of power within the domain of consumption."[35]

Orientalism's fetishism of the Other is often located in desires about Africans and other colonized people. Orientalism is also racist in ways that are less obvious. Sherry Ortner, whose scholarship studies the experiences of Sherpa in the mountaineering business, has suggested that we recognize Orientalism as a racist system. As she explains, "By Orientalism here I mean not only a kind of racist 'othering,' but also at the same time a yearning for solidarity and even identity with the other that (perhaps) makes Orientalism different than classic racism."[36] But of course, and Ortner points this out, the *sahib* (foreign climber) and Sherpa are not the same; for one thing, the climber attempts Everest for glory and the Sherpa for money.[37] This racial dynamic is part of the global mountaineering industry, which includes sports climbing, trekking, mountain biking, and canyoning.[38]

Ortner's point—that Orientalism can include a kind of role-playing of the Other—is seen in numerous places throughout this book—the cross-dressing of Europeans as Arabs, the fetishizing of Africans, and the fantasies about "going native" in Polynesia. The social imaginary about the Other also includes a kind of paternalism over the colonized subject. The "dusty maiden" (the Polynesian woman) is part of the "knowledge" about the Pacific, which is "refracted through a distorted lens—a lens that has been systematically shaped by Westerners."[39] Said describes this as the process of "dominating, restructuring, and having authority over" colonized peoples through which a social imaginary about them is created.[40]

Perhaps the better theoretical frame is *Orientalizing*, where the difference of the colonized subject reflects the geographical imagination also found in mapping. In Edward Said's words, "The orient was almost a European invention, and had been since antiquity a place of romance, exotic beings, haunting memories and landscapes, remarkable experiences."[41] As he suggests, although the East is often viewed as the "land of spiritual origins," there are many mystical lands of the imagination.[42] Said calls us to think about the "orientalizing" of the world, where all places outside of our own are exotified and categorized as Other.

Orientalizing can be understood as a technique used both within and outside the border of the East. As Christopher Howard explains, "This modern, geographical imaginary reflects a long-standing set of oppositions found in the discourse of the 'West and the rest,' orient and occident (Said, 1978) and an imagined 'Great Divide' separating moderns and non-moderns (Latour, 1993)."[43] This allows the mystical tourist to legitimize their conquests through a sense of cultural superiority and often, a financial privilege only available to their social class. The process of *orientalizing* determines the ways that mystical landscapes are constructed, visited, and deployed in the global business of tourism. The formation of these spaces is directly linked to colonialism and spatial relations in the modern period, "the ongoing effects that colonial encounter, dispossession and power have in shaping the familiar social, spatial and political structures, as well as the uneven global interdependencies of the world as we know it."[44]

Orientalism is both an academic methodology and a style—two things that are seemingly contradictory. Orientalist scholars like Lane and de Sacy are known for their classification of language, cultures, and collections of artifacts. The documentation of Egypt, for example, included both photography and drawing. William John Bankes (1786–1855) made more than 1,500 drawings, which include works on archaeology that became critical in Egyptology due to the damage to ancient sites caused by Lake Nasser.[45] An example is found in nineteenth-century writings about the Holy Land, which often focused on its Biblical importance. As Mohammad Sakhnini explains, for many Europeans, "traveling to a land many exclusively associated with the birth and rise of Christianity should be seen as a practice of immense importance for all regardless of education, class, religion, and political creed."[46] Biblical Geography is popular in this period, but it is a practice that originates in the *Onomastikon*, compiled by Eusebius in the early fourth century.[47]

Orientalist style is irreconcilable with the exact and detailed work seen in the work of Lane, de Sacy, and Bankes. It is an aesthetic that reflects a patchwork of styles and motifs arranged to elicit a feeling of wonder and nostalgia. Hossam Mahdy explains Orientalist methodology and style here:

> On the one hand, travellers were obsessed with the accurate recording of medieval life in Egypt, but, on the other hand, what really mattered was to see and portray a lively exotic image, even if it needed to be patched up wither from imagination or from images of other exotic places, such as Turkey, Persia or India.[48]

As I argued in my most recent book, Orientalism is an indiscrete concept that is perhaps best understood by the phrase *muddled Orientalism*, which is the anachronistic and nonsensical assortment of Oriental motifs, symbols, and designs often used to sell mystical products.[49] Orientalism did not stick to the territories within the Orient's borders and often included places in Africa or the Americas, all of which were viewed as exotic and strange enough to include in the fictive place associated with the East. Museum collections often classified artifacts as "Oriental," no matter where they were from. In Frederick Horniman's collection, we have one example:

> Oriental artefacts included Chinese furniture, paintings (showing different occupations), Japanese embroideries, dresses, porcelain and wooden carvings and panels, Indian figures, metalwork, paintings on talc, bidri ware, Japanese, Chinese, Indian, Inuit, Swiss and African ivory carvings.[50]

In many cases, "the Orient" was shorthand for the world outside of Europe.

Colonialism's Geographical Imagination

Euro-Americans generally see the rest of the world through a colonial gaze. Under such a system, Muslims are viewed as "childlike but nevertheless progressing toward full untutored maturity," while Europeans and Americans are fully realized modern subjects.[51] This is the social imaginary, what Charles Taylor describes as "the way ordinary people 'imagine' their social surroundings" that is "carried in images, stories, and legends."[52] Colonial geographies often reflected the impressions people had of a particular place. As Shalini Singh explains, "Cultural geographers have for some time sought to explain the impact of places and spaces (environmental information) on human imagination and subsequent interpretation of landscapes."[53] Photography was a critical part of the colonial project that included boosting the government seizure of land, promoting its potential for mining and other ventures, illustrating the role of technology including railroads, and representing the absence of indigenous people in these new landscapes.[54] Jarrod Hore describes photography as a kind of "settler careering" in which individual photographers were interested in the natural world and in spreading the colonial message worldwide through their pictures.[55]

In the Holy Land, photography was used by American, British, and French explorers, writers, and other visitors to Palestine, and included scholars like James Turner Barclay (an American) and missionaries like James Graham, who was interested in converting Jews as part of his work for the London Jew's Society.[56] The Palestine Exploration Fund included early photos of the area now known as Gaza and the first-ever photos of Masada.[57] Photography was also used to put down colonial rebellions, illustrating the link between documentation and surveillance. The British shifted aerial photography in Palestine from intelligence used in the First World War (WWI) to the crushing of anti-colonial insurgencies after the war.[58]

The geographical imagination is rooted in these systems of power, for "our close-at-hand geographical imaginations, as well as many of the material geopolitical realities of the modern world have their formative roots in colonial encounters, mappings and representations."[59] Imaginative geographies also involved the gendering of landscapes. Colonized spaces were often feminized, along with the people who originally inhabited them, rendering them conquerable and, in the language of some European writers, subject to penetration. The language of sexual conquest was frequently placed upon these spaces, which often became sites of sexual conquest, including rape. Lord Curzon famously remarked about the British having "destroyed the virginity of the bride to whom [we] aspired."[60] This allusion to the conquest of India illustrates the gendering of territory that lies at the center of colonial narratives.

Gendered landscapes also include fantasies of conquering local girls and women. Loti's affair with a harem girl in the Orientalist novel *Aziyadé* (1876) is one example; he describes his paramour's teeth as "two even rows of tiny white pearls" and her lips like "the pulp of a ripe cherry."[61] In *Marriage of Loti* (1880), his novel of Otaheite (Tahiti), the island is a "feminized and eroticized" island.[62] In the novel, this gendering of space includes the author having an affair with an island maiden (Rarahu) and as discussed in a later chapter, her status as a sexual object and a product for European consumption. As is often the case in colonial fantasies about the Other, in her death Rarahu becomes an object of terror, transformed into the Polynesian *tupapa'u*, the monstrous undead.[63] In his majestic study of the construction of the South Seas, which relied strongly on the imagination of fiction writers, more so than the reality of encounters by explorers, Neil Rennie writes,

> So travel from civilization tended to be regressive, the traveller discovering not a new land so much as a new location for the old, nostalgic fictions about places lost in the distant past, now found in the distant present, found and confirmed, it seems, in the form of exotic facts.[64]

Imaginative geographies are written on pages, drawn in sketchbooks, painted on canvases, and portrayed by actors on film. Cinema is linked to these imaginaries through the mediation of experience. As one study notes, "Film plays a powerful role in framing popular understandings of events and experiences in a changing political-economic world order by mapping out geopolitical assemblages that mediate touristic imaginaries of place."[65] The Hollywood Western is one example of the power of these geographies, so powerful that it formed an idea about the American West still in force today. As Susan Courtney notes,

> Film scholars have long recognized the key role of open space in the Western, where (along with other generic elements) such space is routinely used to articulate, expand, and glorify the nation and its most idealized subjects. And such identity projects in that genre, we know, are routinely structured in distinct, antagonistic, binary terms that routinely shape and exploit empty western screen space to mark (and sometimes trouble) differentiations of us versus them, civilization versus savagery, and so on.[66]

The empty space of the West has been transposed onto other places like the Arabian desert and outer space to illustrate the dangers of uncivilized spaces and the need to colonize them.

Imaginative geographies exist in relation to colonial power, what Said described as "a poetics of space" being "a politics of space."[67] At times, the efforts of Europeans (and later Americans) to map new territories as their own borders on the comical. The genre of stories of the colonial tropics is perhaps the best example of "the jungle planter sweating through a five-course dinner in formal attire."[68] Ann Laura Stoler describes the items that settlers brought with them to hot climates: "heavy clothing that mildewed, rich food and liquor that was hard to digest, furniture that retained the heat and sometimes rotted onboard ship before it arrived."[69]

At times, the lines between colonizer and colonized became blurred, such as through adoption or marriage.[70] However, the mapping of territories always remained a colonial project, only to be undone through revolution, expulsion of the occupier, and the remapping of lands taken. In Jakarta, the old Dutch neighborhood is called Old Batavia. Now it is a tourist site where Indonesians and foreign tourists take photos in front of the old Dutch buildings and eat at a restaurant whose walls are lined with black and white photos of old celebrities who once sat at the same tables.

In other cases, the geographical imagination creates a new national history. The claim that Palestine (*Filastin*) is a reaction to Zionism and came into existence after 1948 has been dispelled by scholars. In his study of Orientalism as a tactic deployed against Palestinians, Israeli historian Haim Gerber demonstrates how *Filastin* was in use from the medieval period, found in

IMAGE 1.1   Old Batavia Restaurant, Jakarta, Indonesia.

Source: photo courtesy of author

texts like the one written by Mujir al-Din al-'Ulaymi, referred to in the *fatwa* collection of Khayr al-Din al-Ramli, in the newspapers of the Young Turks, and only went slightly out of fashion with Turkification of the region, to have a resurgence with the Great Palestinian Revolt of 1936–1939.[71] Thus, the notion of Palestine as a solely modern concept is a fallacy, one that helps to legitimize the mapping of Israel on a territory long referred to as "Palestine," or *Filastin*. This is an example of colonial mapping and the "modes of spatial control" that are both enforced and resisted.[72]

The geographical imagination was also at play closer to home. The American West is a space often identified with scarcity and asceticism, seen in novels, films, and other images of landscape available for the individual to experiment with asceticism. This is an example of Denis Cosgrove's understanding of landscape as ideological:

It represents a way in which certain classes of people have signified themselves and their world through their imagined relationship with nature, and through which they have underlined and communicated their own social role and that of others with respect to external nature.[73]

Maps often reflect these ideologies.

The geographical imagination has a powerful voice in creating the tourist spaces that people visit today. As Edwin James Aiken eloquently puts it, "the world's geography itself can be thought of as a textual surface."[74] As mentioned earlier, settler colonialism also played a role in these maps, something we see in many of the cases included in this study—Kenya, the American West, Tahiti, Hawai'i, Palestine. In these places, settlers created new spaces out of old ones once the local population had been subdued, moved out, or exterminated.

Vision and visualization are key parts of the stories told in this book, which scholars have described as *scopic regimes*. As Derek Gregory explains, "In general, scopic regimes are constituted through grids of power, desire and knowledge, and their visual structures and practices enter intimately into the production of imaginative geographies."[75] The mapping of landscapes often perpetrated great cultural harm due to the replacement of an indigenous, communal system with a capitalist, land-owner system disconnected from nature. In American Indian societies, humans were intimately linked with the creatures they shared the land with. The Muscogee Creek, for example, believed that their ancestors emerged from the earth and because of this, nature was respected, "All things were related and belonged to nature's order or system, leading the Muscogee Creek to develop kinship relations with the earth's plants and animals as expressed in clans and animism."[76] The consumption of places included not only physical travel, but also imaginary tourism. As Rune Bennike reminds us, the imagination plays such a strong role in tourism that when people experienced a place in person, the idea of the place remained the "established sense of that place mediated by the tourist industry."[77] This the power of *tourism imaginaries*.

Technologies of Mapping

The history of mapping illuminates its arbitrary character. The academic field of "colonial geography" was founded at the height of colonialism. In France, it was a popular field that included centers in Paris, Bordeaux, and Algiers. The first chair in "colonial geography" was established in 1893 at the Sorbonne.[78] Mapping was one of the practices in which, along with the census and the museum, Europeans and later, Americans, deployed their colonial grammar.[79] Colonial geography was intimately connected to other aspects of governance, something seen in its inclusion in the education of colonial agents: "From the end of the nineteenth century, 'colonial geography' was also taught in the context of new colonial courses within the École supérieures de commerce."[80]

In colonial French Africa, numerous approaches were used in mapmaking. As one study notes, "But this program of constructing homogeneous territorial nations through the production of rational ethnic boundaries based on linguistic criteria quickly became impractical."[81] The same was true of the Orient. In Rana Kabbani's study of the West's fantasies about the Orient, she describes the beginnings of Orientalism as an academic field that was linked directly to the colonial project, "Orientalist studies were officially inaugurated by Sir William Jones, a servant of the East India Company, in order to deepen Europe's acquaintance with the peoples over whom it would ultimately come to have control."[82]

Farish Noor describes map-making as an invention process. He writes, "a map of Asia therefore does not really 'discover' Asia, but it really *invents* Asia as it goes along."[83] The distortion found on maps reflects the role the imagination played in the visualization of the world. George R. Parkin's *British Empire Map* (1893) includes large versions of Britain, Canada, South Africa, and Australia, with Canada's distortion (twice its real size) influenced by Parkin's New Imperialist sympathies and Canadian origins.[84] The British Empire was shown as enormous, spanning the world not through land, but through its control of the oceans, which in Parkin's view was the key to the New Imperialist vision of a "rejuvenation of Anglo-Saxon civilization."[85] Some maps were just fantasies built upon Classical, Biblical, and other mythologies. One example is the map of Asia by Jean Baptiste Calude de Sales in *Histoire du Monde Primitif* (1780), which showed India and the Malay Peninsula "cut off from the Asian continent."[86]

Outside of mapping, the colonial project had other practices including the collections that wound up in museums. As discussed earlier, this included captive indigenous people who were held in cages and exhibited at local fairs, where observers often had "hostile or fearful responses."[87] Later, these became *Völkerschauen*, the ethnographic exhibits that are found today in natural history museums around the world.[88] The links between colonialism, anthropology, museums, and tourism include the collection of cultural artifacts that encouraged travel to exotic places. It also included the creation of entire tourist markets in these places. As Anthony Allen Shelton explains,

> The close complicity between colonialism and ethnographic museum collecting, interpretation and display, has not only helped determine the categories of objects which have entered Western collections, but also established an indigenous manufacturing market that produced objects that reflected native perception of the focus of intrusive European demands.[89]

As noted earlier, the European, and later, American, practice of collecting and cataloguing was not restricted to collecting artifacts from the world's cultures. Alongside the exhibitions, museums, and other forms of display, human beings were placed in public venues. At times, these individuals were forcibly taken from their homeland; in other instances, they were encouraged to travel to Europe, often with disastrous consequences that included illness and death, usually due to exposure to European diseases. The arts also contained characters that expressed sentiments about foreign peoples as if they were objects in a vitrine case. In *The Marriage of Loti*, the author describes Rarahu, his Tahitian love interest, as "a little creature" and "a perfect specimen."[90] The museumification of cultures included all these things and provided a cultural experience close to home for those unwilling or unable to travel abroad. The beginnings of the tourism industry relied upon such experiences, for they promised the exotic and mystical experiences found in faraway places from Egypt to Nepal.

The topographies of colonized territories represent another form of mapping that was often linked to gender. Gendered Orientalism is one place we see this, in representations of Egypt as a woman waiting consummation with a European lover, who would conquer her "territory." Perhaps the most famous example of this is Lane's famous statement about feeling like a bridegroom meeting his beloved. The Orient was not the only place in which mapping was gendered. Eighteenth-century European travelers feminized Italy, describing it as "the home of emotion and superstition," and as a result, "the Italian nation was more easily moulded to a stereotypical womanhood."[91]

In the South Pacific, topography was represented in "erotic terms."[92] Writers like Edwin Pallander and Robert Louis Stevenson described their encounters with islands in the South Seas with phrases like "her bridal veil of cloud" and a "first love," and others described features of the landscape as "volcanic breasts."[93] The mapping of the South Pacific as an erotic landscape was influenced by European sexual politics of the time, which included the Enlightenment's sexual hedonism and the popularity of pornography and "licentious literature."[94]

Writings about new lands often included the theme of strangeness, used to cast new landscapes as special places that could offer transformation and other forms of mystical experience. In Charles Fletcher Lummis's 1892 book, *Some Strange Corners of Our Country*, he writes about an environment marked by environmental oddities. Lynch explains these characterizations as "freaks of nature" that could not be placed in England or New England, simply because they didn't fit into the Euro-American imagination about what a proper plant should look like.[95]

Language is an important mapping technology. In 1896, Robert T. Hill, writing for the *National Geographic* magazine, lamented the inadequacies of English as a language to describe landscape.[96] In other words, English was not always the ideal colonial language. In some cases, Spanish was preferred, for it had words like "*rincon* (sloping meadow high on a mountain), *bolson* (flat desert valley), *ceja* (jutting edge of a mesa), and *cuesta* (a hill with a gentle slope on one side and a steep slope on the other)."[97] Renaming is another way that places were remapped. Mountains were often renamed after the first Europeans who mapped or explored them, even though they had been the homes of indigenous people for hundreds or thousands of years. Mount Denali became Mount McKinley, Sagarmatha (or Chomolongma) became Everest, and Aoraki became Mt. Cook (although in this case, Aoraki has returned as one of its names due to long fought efforts to recognize Māori ancestral lands).[98] In other cases, mountains in far off lands just became the more exotic or larger versions of European peaks, seen in the use of Matterhorn to describe Shivling (the Matterhorn of Asia) and Ama Dablam (the Matterhorn of the Himalayas).[99]

Artists also created maps through their portraits and landscapes of places they viewed as European or Christian spaces. William Holman Hunt "portrayed himself as equipped with a paintbrush in one hand, and a gun in the other" and even had a photo taken of himself at his home in London holding a gun and a brush.[100] Hunt was an "artist-pilgrim" whose paintings included Biblical figures looking at the viewer, becoming a part of stories located in the landscape of Palestine.[101] Literature, painting, and film are included in this book because they are powerful examples of the ways that colonialism involves numerous actors and forms of cultural production.

The popularity of mysticism also helped to map landscapes in literature, both nonfiction and fiction. In the nineteenth and twentieth centuries, books like *With Mystics and Magicians in Tibet* (1929) and *Foundations of Tibetan Mysticism* (1969) popularized Tibet.[102] As this book shows, fictional literature often helped to map mystical landscapes, whether they were mountains, islands, or deserts. Landscapes are "structures of feeling" that can be constructed and deconstructed, created and erased, part of the process of "both remembering past events and reordering them, a technology for forgetting."[103]

Spaces construed as isolated, ranging from the American West to the islands of Polynesia, offer an ideological framework for the reimagining of physical environments necessary for the occupation and control of territory. Occupants of these territories have been variously erased, vilified, romanticized, and reimagined in ways that uphold the goals of colonial and imperial administrations. As John Connell explains,

> Linked processes of exploring, mapping, settling, administering and converting are implicated in a wider imperial politics of place, that, in talking back to the home lands, tended to glamourize the various enterprises that were linked to the colonial endeavour, at this great distance from the hearts and hearths of empire.[104]

The ways in which people from these imagined spaces have been represented is a lynchpin in the colonial system. Obviously, portrayals of these societies differ—the savage Indian, the lascivious Tahitian, the mystical Tibetan—but they all function in similar ways, as characters that enable the supremacy of Western power. As Dibyesh puts it,

> Cultural representation of the non-Western Other lies at the core of Western colonial and neocolonial discourses. A critical political analysis of the Western imagination of the Other involves a recognition at two levels—the practices of essentializing and stereotyping that provide the backbone as well as various strategies (such as infantilization, eroticization, debasement, idealization, and self-affirmation) that put flesh on the imagined Other.[105]

Erasure was often used to remap territory as mystical landscape. One example is Tibet, which has been framed as Shangri-La—an idyllic, mystical Buddhist land. Scholars erased its Muslim population, effectively wiping them from the history of Tibet because they did not fit the vision of Tibet as a mystical Buddhist kingdom. As David G. Atwill writes in his groundbreaking study on the Muslims of Tibet, "It is often assumed that to be Tibetan is to be Buddhist and, axiomatically, that to be Muslim precludes one from being Tibetan."[106] Not only were the Khache [Tibetan Muslims] considered to be Tibetan, they were also "among the most literate and multilingual lay element of the society."[107]

Blank Spaces and Mystical Landscapes

The colonial fantasies explored in the following chapters are neither disparate nor congruous. As Stoler remarks, "in such a model, some country's legacy was always more benevolent, another's violences were truly atrocious, and yet another's integrative efforts were more effective or more benign."[108] The theme of emptiness is often present, seen in claims about a blank space ideal for colonial occupation, and later, for mystical tourist experiences. The British experience in Kenya (occupation) is unlike the American experience in the Hawaiian Islands (annexation), although both involved white settlers. The imagination about territory also repeats itself in different places, such as the idea of *terra nullius*, an empty land with no human populations, which is seen in both European colonialism in Africa (the extinct African) and American internal colonialism in North America (the vanishing Indian). The "empty land theory" promoted in the eighteenth century included the map by John Barrows of South Africa that specified areas of empty land "ideal for the cultivation of fruits" or "deserted because of the bushman," making the future garden, orchard, or farm an imaginative possibility for the white settler.[109]

Empty spaces on maps also denoted populations that were said to have no culture or civilization. Zionist visions of Palestine viewed the land as empty before the 1880s, when the first Jewish immigrants arrived.[110] These visions of the landscape were eventually replaced with the Zionist project, with its modernist architecture, health programs promoting sanitization of the people (including the local Oriental Jew), and agricultural projects that sought to replace smaller-scale Palestinian farming.

The deserts of the American Southwest, described as empty, were populated with Native peoples—lives that are often erased. In the recent film *Oppenheimer* (2023), New Mexico was portrayed as a dry wasteland, ignoring the presence of Native Americans and Latino communities who were expelled from the Los Alamos area. The use of "empty spaces" in colonized landscapes is not limited to the American West; as we learn in this book, it is common in colonial regimes in Africa and other sites of occupation and European and American settlement. The sparsity and asceticism associated with the desert are expansive, connected to many capitalist ventures that reflect these themes in different ways at different places. The meditation retreats located in places like Sedona are one example. Burning Man capitalizes on the remoteness of the desert and an expression of the exotic, seen in the Indian costumes worn by its mostly white, affluent participants and the activities at the festival, which reflect noninhibition, nonrestraint, and the primitive.[111]

In addition to these kinds of experiences, the colonized American West also inspires New Age and wellness products built upon the idea of sparsity and the ascetic life. In her analysis of Gwyneth Paltrow's *Goop*, Dana Logan points to the ways in which the brand focuses on fasting, detoxification regimens, and vacations focused on a pseudo-religious practice. As she writes, "Detox in *goop* is a form of consumption that requires purchase at every turn, including juices for cleansing diets, sauna treatments for sweating, and most expensively, retreats where Gwyneth pays thousands of dollars to live like a monk."[112]

Images of mystical, vast spaces recall the early Christian Church fathers who retreated into the wilderness to find God, the sparse landscapes of the American West, and the isolated mountains of Tibet. The desert also plays a role in the Oriental landscape, especially in places like Egypt and Morocco, both examined in this book. Often the desert exists as a location of primitive introspection or discovery, which is juxtaposed to the modern and spiritually vacant West. In Tarek Shamma's study of the film *The Sheltering Sky* (examined in the following chapter), he writes, "In this regard, the desert and its inhabitants serve as a means of exteriorising the existential predicament of the characters and their search for a way out of the spiritual void which has presumably afflicted the West."[113]

It is important to understand that maps, which help us understand how landscapes were constructed and then promoted as sites of tourism, are a European project that was focused on the creation of knowledge as a system of power. The blank spaces on maps signify how maps could include visions of places, either that were highly inaccurate due to ignorance, or that represented the wishes of the colonial power. In the map of Java created by Petrus Bertius (1565–1629), the entire southern coast was blank:

> Interestingly, the small map also features a charming vignette of a sailing ship coasting along the southern shore of Java; though presumably the crew on board were not very attentive and did not knock on any doors as they sailed past the island.[114]

Foucault's model of discourse suggests that maps are literally a way to construct space and non-space, those empty spaces on maps. In Alex McKay's discussion of the European construction of Mount Kailash in Tibet, he writes,

> Geographical information was at the centre of the early phase of the European knowledge-building process. With the rise of scientific mapping it became possible to precisely locate every geographical feature and site of human habitation on a map—something of obvious military value—and the blank spaces on maps were rapidly filled in as a result of two interweaving and often inter-related imperatives, the political and the intellectual.[115]

Maps were also recomposed with empty spaces for financial reasons. In the British maps of the region between the Savannah and Altamaha rivers (Georgia), we find a long list of inscriptions that were deleted, including "Apalachy Indians 200 Men" and "Chaktas 700 Men."[116] These edits made the land being promoted more favorable to colonists, who did not know that they would have to contend with American Indians and others in their land grab.

As described earlier, emptiness is often attached to mystical landscapes. In one study of tourists in the Tunisian Sahara, the study notes a congruity in the comments by their subjects visiting the desert. These include remarks like, "No one is around me," "It is emptiness," and "The desert represents an empty space," all of which signal the belief that this space, a desert occupied by local people, is empty.[117] The sites of mystical tourism are one result of these mythologies of space, in what one study calls the "Aha-experience" identified with natural spaces, where the "mountains, quietness, remoteness and limitless facilitate and/or provoke a spiritual feeling."[118]

Alongside these empty spaces are places like the tropical islands of the South Pacific and Southeast Asia, where the human communities who live there are part of another kind of construction of mystical landscape— the isolated paradise. Tahiti, Hawaii, Bali, and Thailand are all places where the local population was an important part of the colonial construction of space, not as absent or missing, but as exotic, seductive, and idealized humans who were often the focus of sexual conquest. Paradise is a fluid term, as Vernadette Vicuña Gonzalez explains: "Paradise in not a generic or static term—it specifically refers to an idea of passivity and penetrability engendered by imperialism as an alibi for domination."[119] In this study, paradise takes on a multiplicity of images. In mystical tourism, paradise is often expressed in the form of an exotic environment and its locals, if they have survived.

In Otaheite (Tahiti), this was expressed in the writings of explorers and the fantasies penned by writers. In one famous example, *The Marriage of Loti* (1878), a Frenchman lives out his fantasies of the flesh on a local island maiden, Rarahu. The opening page of the novel establishes the difference between Europe and the islands, "In Europe it was a cold and dismal winter's day. On the other side, in the queen's gardens, it was a calm, languorous, enervating summer's night" of "mimosas and orange trees, in a fervid and fragrant air, under a sky starry with southern constellations."[120] The difference and exoticism of the environment was also seen in its people, for Rarahu is introduced a few pages later as "a very strange little person, whose startling and savage charm was a thing quite part from all the conventional rules of beauty recognized by the nations of Europe."[121]

Colonialism was a global competition for territory, something seen in the race to explore and map the world. While this book is less interested in this aspect of the mapping of the world, it is important to note that, for all the energy and resources spent in competition, to colonize one part of the world or another, there were also moments of colonial allyship, seen in the passing of the colonial torch from Europe to the Americas. One such moment is found in *Buffalo Bill's Rough Riders of the World*, an entertainment show that played to audiences in the United States and Europe. As one author describes the spectacle,

> Now audiences witnessed cowboys and Indians riding alongside well-disciplined cavalrymen representing Germany, France, and Great Britain, giving the impression that frontier experience made Americans equal to European soldiers.[122]

In addition to providing entertainment, this colonial spectacle suggested that the world's non-white peoples were subject to occupation, violence, and extermination, as if these were normal human activities. *Spectacle* is an apropos term for these colonial activities, but it also lies at the center of modern tourism, which includes the "spectacle of a postmodern commodity culture of deferred aesthetic pleasure."[123] This book attempts to provide an account of this colonial spectacle and its influence on the creation of mystical landscapes in modern tourism. It is these mystical landscapes we now shift our attention to.

Notes

1 Edward Said, "Yeats and Decolonization," in *Nationalism, Colonialism, and Literature: Terry Eagleton, Fredric Jameson, and Edward Said* (Minneapolis: University of Minnesota Press, 1990), 77.
2 Camilla Fojas, *Islands of Empire: Pop Culture & U.S. Power* (Austin: University of Texas Press, 2014), 20.
3 Robert Chi, "Toward a New Tourism: Albert Wendt and Becoming Attractions," *Cultural Critique* 37 (1997): 74.
4 Kenneth J. Perkins, "The Compagnie Générale Transatlitique and the Development and the Development of Saharan Tourism in North Africa," in *The Business of Tourism: Place, Faith, and History* (Philadelphia: University of Pennsylvania Press, 2009), 34.
5 Perkins, 36, 50, 54.
6 Benedict Anderson, *Imagined Communities: Reflections on the Origin and Spread of Nationalism* (New York: Verso, 1991), 175.
7 Peter Merrington, "A Staggered Orientalism: The Cape-to-Cairo Imaginary," *Poetics Today* 22, no. 2 (2001): 356.
8 Simon Lewis, "Culture, Cultivation, and Colonialism in 'Out of Africa' and Beyond," *Research in African Literatures* 31, no. 1 (2000): 63–64.
9 Bergland, 13.
10 Edward Said, *Culture and Imperialism* (New York: Vintage, 1993), 271.
11 Said, 3.
12 Karen Kosasa, "Searching for the 'C' Word: Museums, Art Galleries, and Settler Colonialism in Hawai'i," in *Studies in Settler Colonialism: Politics, Identity and Culture* (New York: Palgrave MacMillan, 2011), 157.
13 Alan McNee, *The New Mountaineer in Late Victorian Britain: Materiality, Modernity, and the Haptic Sublime* (New York: Palgrave Macmillan, 2016), 3.
14 Fiona Allon, "Bali as Icon: Tourism, Death, and the Pleasure Periphery," *Humanities Research* 11, no. 1 (2004): 27.
15 Yuval Ben-Bassat and Yossi Ben-Artzi, "Ottoman Maps of the Empire's Arab Provinces, 1850s to the First World War," *Imago Mundi* 70, no. 2 (2018): 199, 201.
16 Michael F. Robinson, *The Lost White Tribe: Explorers, Scientists, and the Theory That Changed a Continent* (New York: Oxford University Press, 2016), 17.
17 Lüthiy, Falk, and Purtschert, 2.
18 Michael Hitchcock, *Tourism, Development, and Terrorism in Bali* (New York: Routledge, 2007), 30.
19 Raymond Corbey, "Ethnographic Showcases: Account and Vision," in *Human Zoos: Science and Spectacle in the Age of Colonial Empires*, ed. Pascal Blanchard, Nicolas Bancel, Gilles Boëtsch, Eric Deroo, Sandrine Lemaire, and Charles Forsdick (Liverpool: Liverpool University Press, 2008), 96–97.
20 Shinji Yamashita, *Bali and Beyond: Explorations in the Anthropology of Tourism* (New York: Bergahn Books, 2003), 7.
21 Kenneth Olwig, *Landscape, Nature, and Body Politic* (Madison: University of Wisconsin Press, 2002), 12.
22 Bergland, 3.
23 Shohat and Stam 2012, 6.
24 George Forster, *A Voyage around the World*, Volume 1 (London, 1777), 327. Quoted in Bernard Smith, *Imagining the Pacific: In the Wake of the Cook Voyages* (New Haven: Yale University Press, 1992), 104.
25 Suren Lalvani, "Consuming the Exotic Other," *Critical Studies in Mass Communication* 12 (1995): 267.

26 See Richard King, *Orientalism and Religion: Postcolonial Theory, India, and 'the Mystic East'* (New York: Routledge, 1999).
27 Mark Liechty, *Far Out: Countercultural Seekers and the Tourist Encounter in Nepal* (Chicago: The University of Chicago Press, 2017), 4.
28 Said 1993, 294.
29 Timothy Mitchell, *Colonising Egypt* (Berkeley: University of California Press, 1988), 140.
30 Sam Maddra, "American Indians in Buffalo Bill's Wild West," in *Human Zoos: Science and Spectacle in the Age of Colonial Empires*, ed. Pascal Blanchard, Nicolas Bancel, Gilles Boëtsch, Eric Deroo, Sandrine Lemaire, and Charles Forsdick (Liverpool: Liverpool University Press, 2008), 135.
31 Mark Liechty, "Building the Road to Kathmandu: Notes on the History of Tourism in Nepal," *Himalaya* 25, nos. 1/2 (2005): 20.
32 Tom Neuhaus, *Tibet in the Western Imagination* (New York: Palgrave Macmillan, 2012), 142.
33 Yosefa Loshitzky, "Orientalist Representations: Palestinians and Arabs in Some Postcolonial Film and Literature," in *Cultural Encounters: Representing 'Otherness'*, ed. Elizabeth Hallam and Brian V. Street (New York: Routledge, 2000), 53.
34 Robin Mitchell, *Vénus Noire: Black Women and Colonial Fantasies in Nineteenth-Century France* (Athens: University of Georgia Press, 2020), 24.
35 Lalvani, 265.
36 Sherry Ortner, "Thick Resistance: Death and the Cultural Construction of Agency in Himalayan Mountaineering," *Representations* 59 (1997): 139.
37 Ortner, 139.
38 Paul Beedie and Simon Hudson, "Emergence of Mountain-Based Adventure Tourism," *Annals of Tourism Research* 30, no. 3 (2003): 626.
39 A. Marata Tamaira, "From Full Dusk to Full Tusk: Reimagining the 'Dusky Maiden' through the Visual Arts," *The Contemporary Pacific* 22, no. 1 (2010): 14.
40 Edward Said, *Orientalism* (New York: Vintage, 1978), 3.
41 Said 1978, 1.
42 Liechty 2005, 20.
43 Christopher A. Howard, "Touring the Consumption of the Other: Imaginaries of Authenticity in the Himalayas and Beyond," *Journal of Consumer Culture* 16, no. 2 (2016): 357.
44 Tariq Jazeel, "Postcolonialism: Orientalism and the Geographical Imagination," *Geography* 97, no. 1 (2012): 5.
45 Patricia Usick, "William John Bankes' Collection of Drawings of Egypt and Nubia," *Travellers in Egypt*, ed. Paul and Janet Starkey (London: Tauris Parke Paperbacks, 2001), 52–53.
46 Mohammad Sakhnini, "James Silk Buckingham (1786–1855) and the Politics of Travel in the Holy Land," *Studies in Romanticism* 62, no. 2 (2023): 249.
47 Robin A. Butlin, "Ideological Contexts and the Reconstruction of Biblical Landscapes in the Seventeenth and Early Eighteenth Centuries: Dr. Edward Wells and the Historical Geography of the Holy Land," in *Ideology and Landscape in Historical Landscape: Essays on the Meanings of Some Places in the Past*, ed. Alan R. H. Baker and Gideon Biger (Cambridge: Cambridge University Press, 1992), 45.
48 Hossam Mahdy, "Travellers, Colonisers and Conservationists," in *Travellers in Egypt*, ed. Paul and Janet Starkey (London: Tauris Parke Paperbacks, 2001), 162.
49 Sophia Arjana, *Buying Buddha, Selling Rumi: Orientalism and the Mystical Marketplace* (London: Oneworld, 2020), 96.
50 Alan Anthony Shelton, "Museum Ethnography: An Imperial Science," in *Cultural Encounters: Representing 'Otherness'*, ed. Elizabeth Hallam and Brian V. Street (New York: Routledge, 2000), 165.

51 William Rasch, "Enlightenment as Religion," *New German Critique* 108 (2009): 122.
52 Charles Taylor, "Modern Social Imaginaries," *Public Culture* 14, no. 1 (2002): 106.
53 Shalini Singh, "Secular Pilgrimages and Sacred Tourism in the Indian Himalayas," *GeoJournal* 64, no. 3 (2005): 217.
54 Hore, 17, 23, 29, 135.
55 Hore, 18–19.
56 Yeshayahu Nir, *The Bible and the Image: The History of Photography in the Holy Land 1839–1899* (Philadelphia: University of Pennsylvania Press, 1985), 12. Nir's study includes a collection of photos from Palestine and analyses of the technology used. His discussion of the differences between Protestant and Catholic photographers in terms of their interests (what he calls "nuances") is very interesting, found in pages 103–106.
57 Nir, 95–97. For a fuller discussion of the Palestine Exploration Fund's activities, see Chapter 7.
58 Nadi Abusaada, "Combined Action: Aerial Imagery and the Urban Landscape in Interwar Palestine, 1918–40," *Jerusalem Quarterly* 81 (2020): 34. See also Nadi Abusaada, "Urban Encounters: Imaging the City in Mandate Palestine," in *Imaging and Imagining Palestine: Photography, Modernity and the Biblical Lens, 1918–1948*, ed. Karène Sanchez Summerer and Sary Zananiri (Boston: Brill, 2021), 367.
59 Jazeel, 10.
60 Liechty 2017, 10.
61 Pierre Loti, *Aziyadé* (1876; repr., Paris: North Star, 1996), 201.
62 Rod Edmond, *Representing the South Pacific: From Cook to Gaugin* (Cambridge: Cambridge University Press, 2009), 242.
63 Roslyn Jolly, "South Sea Gothic: Pierre Loti and Robert Louis Stevenson," *English Literature in Translation, 1880–1920* 47, no. 1 (2004): 34.
64 Neil Rennie, *Far-Fetched Facts: The Literature of Travel and the Idea of the South Seas* (Oxford: Clarendon Press, 1995), 1.
65 Mary Mostafanezhad and Tanya Promburom, "'Lost in Thailand': The Popular Geopolitics of Film-Induced Tourism in Northern Thailand," *Social & Cultural Geography* 19, no. 1 (2018): 96.
66 Susan Courtney, *Split Screen Nation: Moving Images of the American West and South* (New York: Oxford University Press, 2017), 195.
67 Derek Gregory, "Between the Book and the Lamp: Imaginative Geographies of Egypt, 1849–50," *Transactions of the Institute of British Geographers* 20, no. 4 (1995): 29.
68 Stoler, 35.
69 Stoler, 35.
70 Stoler, 39.
71 Haim Gerber, "Zionism, Orientalism, and the Palestinians," *Journal of Palestine Studies* 33, no. 1 (2003): 26–29.
72 Annabel Jane Wharton, *Selling Jerusalem: Relics, Replicas, Theme Parks* (Chicago: University of Chicago Press, 2006), 1.
73 Denis E. Cosgrove, *Social Formation and Symbolic Landscape* (Madison: University of Wisconsin Press, 1984), 15.
74 Edwin James Aiken, *Scriptural Geography: Portraying the Holy Land* (New York: Bloomsbury Academic, 2010), 188.
75 Derek Gregory, "Emperors of the Gaze: Photographic Practices and Productions of Space in Egypt, 1839–1914," in *Picturing Place: Photography and the Geographical Imagination*, ed. Joan M. Schwartz and James R. Ryan (New York: I.B. Tauris, 2003), 224.

76 Donald L. Fixico, *The Invasion of Indian Country in the Twentieth Century: American Capitalism and Tribal Natural Resources* (Niwot: University Press of Colorado, 1998), 5.
77 Bennike, 58.
78 Pierre Singaravelou, "The Institutionalisation of 'Colonial Geography' in France, 1880–1940," *Journal of Historical Geography* 37 (2011): 149.
79 Anderson, 163.
80 Singaravelou, 150.
81 Camille Lefebvre, "We Have Tailored Africa: French Colonialism and the 'Artificiality' of Africa's Borders in the Interwar Period," *Journal of Historical Geography* 37 (2011): 193.
82 Rana Kabbani, *Europe's Myths of Orient* (Bloomington: Indiana University Press, 1986), 138.
83 Noor, 126.
84 Terry Cook, "A Reconstruction of the World: George R. Parkin's British Empire Map of 1893," *Cartographica* 21, no. 4 (1984): 59, 57.
85 Cook 1984, 56.
86 Noor, 131.
87 Julia S. Setler, " 'Painting the Town Red': Buffalo Bill's Indians in the German Media," in *The Popular Frontier: Buffalo Bill's Wild West and Transnational Mass Culture*, ed. Frank Christianson (Norman: University of Oklahoma Press, 2017), 157.
88 Setler, 157.
89 Shelton, 185.
90 Loti, *The Marriage of Loti (Rarahu)*, 15.
91 James Buzard, *The Beaten Track: European Tourism, Literature, and the Way to 'Culture,' 1800–1918* (New York: Oxford University Press, 1993), 133.
92 Michael Sturma, *South Sea Maidens: Western Fantasy and Sexual Politics in the South Pacific* (Westport: Greenwood Press, 2002), 6.
93 Edwin Pallander, *The Log of an Island Wanderer: Notes of Travel in the Eastern Pacific* (London: C. Arthur Pearson, 1901), 58, Robert Louis Stevenson, *In the South Seas* (London: Chatto and Windus, 1912), 6, Mel Kernahan, *White Savages in the South Seas* (London: Verso, 1995), 135. Quoted in Sturma, 6.
94 Sturma, 27.
95 Lynch, 102.
96 Lynch, 106.
97 Lynch, 107.
98 James Higham, Anna Thompson-Carr, and Ghazali Musa, "Mountaineering Tourism: Activity, People, and Place," in *Mountaineering Tourism*, ed. Ghazali Musa, James Higham, and Anna Thompson-Carr (New York: Routledge, 2015), 2.
99 Zac Robinson, "Early Alpine Club Culture and Mountaineering Literature," in *Mountaineering Tourism*, ed. Ghazali Musa, James Higham, and Anna Thompson-Carr (New York: Routledge, 2015), 114.
100 Simon Coleman, "A Tale of Two Centres? Representing Palestine to the British in the Nineteenth Century," *Mobilities* 2, no. 3 (2007): 331.
101 Kristine Kelly, "Aesthetic Desire and Imperialist Disappointment in Trollope's *The Bertrams* and the Murray *Handbook for Travellers in Syria and Palestine*," *Victorian Literature and Culture* 43 (2015): 625.
102 Liechty 2017, 11–12.
103 Christopher Tilley, "Introduction: Identity, Place, Landscape and Heritage," *Journal of Material Culture* 11, nos. 1/2 (2006): 25.
104 John Connell, "Island Dreaming: The Contemplation of Polynesian Paradise," *Journal of Historical Geography* 29, no. 4 (2003): 545–555.

105 Dibyesh Anand, "Western Colonial Representations of the Other: The Case of Exotica Tibet," *New Political Science* 29, no. 1 (2007): 23.
106 David G. Atwill, *Islamic Shangri-La: Inter-Asian Relations and Lhasa's Muslim Communities, 1600–1960* (Oakland: University of California Press, 2018), 7.
107 Atwill, 7.
108 Stoler, 141.
109 Margaret Hanzimanolis, "Eight Hens per Man per Day: Shipwreck Survivors and Pastoral Abundance in Southern Africa," in *Navigating African Maritime History*, ed. Carina E. Ray and Jeremy Rich (Liverpool: Liverpool University Press, 2009), 44.
110 Beshara B. Doumani, "Rediscovering Ottoman Palestine: Writing Palestinians into History," *Journal of Palestine Studies* 21, no. 2 (1992): 8. The Zionist slogan "a land without a people for a people without a land" is another example.
111 Robert Kozinets, "The Moment of Infinite Fire," in *Time, Space and the Market: Restroscapes Rising*, ed. Stephen Brown and John F. Sherry, Jr. (New York: Routledge, 2015), 201.
112 Dana W. Logan, "The Lean Closet: Asceticism in Postindustrial Consumer Culture," *Journal of the American Academy of Religion* 85, no. 3 (2017): 602.
113 Tarek Shamma, "Horror and Likeness: The Quest for Self and the Imagining of the Other in *The Sheltering Sky*," *Critical Arts* 25, no. 2 (2011): 131.
114 Noor, 128.
115 Alex McKay, *Kailas Histories: Renunciate Traditions and the Construction of Himalayan Sacred Geography* (Leiden: Brill, 2016), 376.
116 Louis de Vorsey, "Maps in Colonial Promotion: James Edward Oglethorpe's Use of Maps in 'Selling' the Georgia Scheme," *Imago Mundi* 38 (1986): 37.
117 Omar Moufakkir and Noureddine Selmi, "Examining the Spirituality of Spiritual Tourists: A Sahara Desert Experience," *Annals of Tourism Research* 70 (2018): 116, 114.
118 Moufakkir and Selmi, 111.
119 Vernadette Vicuña Gonzalez, *Securing Paradise: Tourism and Militarism in Hawai'i and the Philippines* (Durham: Duke University Press, 2013), 7.
120 Loti 1878, 11.
121 Loti 1878, 13.
122 Jeremy M. Johnston, " 'The Wild West Side of American Existence': Theodore Roosevelt, Buffalo Bill Cody, and American Military Exceptionalism," in *The Popular Frontier: Buffalo Bill's Wild West and Transnational Mass Culture*, ed. Frank Christianson (Norman: University of Oklahoma Press, 2017), 76.
123 Bandy, 541.

Bibliography

Abusaada, Nadi. "Combined Action: Aerial Imagery and the Urban Landscape in Interwar Palestine, 1918–40." *Jerusalem Quarterly* 81 (2020): 20–36.
Abusaada, Nadi. "Urban Encounters: Imaging the City in Mandate Palestine." In *Imaging and Imagining Palestine: Photography, Modernity and the Biblical Lens, 1918–1948*, edited by Karène Sanchez Summerer and Sary Zananiri, 360–389. Boston: Brill, 2021.
Aiken, Edwin James. *Scriptural Geography: Portraying the Holy Land*. New York: Bloomsbury Publishing, 2010.
Allon, Fiona. "Bali as Icon: Tourism, Death, and the Pleasure Periphery." *Humanities Research* 11, no. 1 (2004): 24–41.
Anand, Dibyesh. "Western Colonial Representations of the Other: The Case of Exotica Tibet." *New Political Science* 29, no. 1 (2007): 23–42.

Anderson, Benedict. *Imagined Communities: Reflections on the Origin and Spread of Nationalism*. New York: Verso, 2006.

Arjana, Sophia. *Buying Buddha, Selling Rumi: Orientalism and the Mystical Marketplace*. London: Oneworld, 2020.

Atwill, David G. *Islamic Shangri-La: Inter-Asian Relations and Lhasa's Muslim Communities, 1600 to 1960*. Oakland: University of California Press, 2018.

Bandy, Joe. "Managing the Other of Nature: Sustainability, Spectacle, and Global Regimes of Capital in Ecotourism." *Public Culture* 8 (1996): 539–566.

Beedie, Paul and Simon Hudson. "Emergence of Mountain-Based Tourism." *Annals of Tourism Research* 30, no. 3 (2003): 625–643.

Ben-Bassat, Yuval and Yossi Ben-Artzi. "Ottoman Maps of the Empire's Arab Provinces, 1850s to the First World War." *Imago Mundi* 70, no. 2 (2018): 199–211.

Bennike, Rune. "'A Summer Place': Darjeeling in the Tourist Gaze." In *Darjeeling Reconsidered: Histories, Politics, Environments*, edited by Townsend Middleton and Sara Shneidermann, 54–73. New York: Oxford University Press, 2018.

Bergland, Renée L. *The National Uncanny: Indian Ghosts and American Subjects*. Hanover: University Press of New England, 2000.

Bertolucci, Bernardo, dir. *The Sheltering Sky*. Warner Brothers, 1990.

Butlin, Robin A. "Ideological Contexts and the Reconstruction of Biblical Landscapes in the Seventeenth and Early Eighteenth Centuries: Dr. Edward Wells and the Historical Geography of the Holy Land." In *Ideology and Landscape in Historical Perspective: Essays on the Meanings of Some Places in the Past*, edited by Alan R. H. Baker and Gideon Biger, 31–62. Cambridge: Cambridge University Press, 1992.

Buzard, James. *The Beaten Track: European Tourism, Literature, and the Way to 'Culture,' 1800–1918*. New York: Oxford University Press, 1993.

Chi, Robert. "Toward a New Tourism: Albert Wendt and Becoming Attractions." *Cultural Critique* 37 (1997): 61–105.

Coleman, Simon. "A Tale of Two Centres? Representing Palestine to the British in the Nineteenth Century." *Mobilities* 2, no. 3 (2007): 331–345.

Connell, John. "Island Dreaming: The Contemplation of Polynesian Paradise." *Journal of Historical Geography* 29, no. 4 (2003): 554–581.

Cook, Terry. "A Reconstruction of the World: George R. Parkin's British Empire Map of 1893." *Cartographica* 21, no. 4 (1984): 53–65.

Corbey, Raymond. "Ethnographic Showcases: Account and Vision." In *Human Zoos: Science and Spectacle in the Age of Colonial Empires*, edited by Pascal Blanchard, Nicolas Bancel, Gilles Boëtsch, Sandrine Lemaire, and Charles Forsdick, 95–113. Liverpool: Liverpool University Press, 2008.

Cosgrove, Denis. *Social Formation and Symbolic Landscape*. Madison: University of Wisconsin Press, 1984.

Courtney, Susan. *Split Screen Nation: Moving Images of the American West and South*. New York: Oxford University Press, 2017.

De Vorsey, Louis. "Maps in Colonial Promotion: James Edward Oglethorpe's Use of Maps in 'Selling' the Georgia Scheme." *Imago Mundi* 38 (1986): 35–45.

Doumani, Beshara B. "Rediscovering Ottoman Palestine: Writing Palestinians into History." *Journal of Palestine Studies* 21, no. 2 (1992): 5–28.

Edmond, Rod. *Representing the South Pacific: From Cook to Gaugin*. Cambridge: Cambridge University Press, 2009.

Fixico, Donald L. *The Invasion of Indian Country in the Twentieth Century: American Capitalism and Tribal Natural Resources*. Niwot: University Press of Colorado, 1998.

Fojas, Camilla. *Islands of Empire: Pop Culture & U.S. Power*. Austin: University of Texas Press, 2014.

Forster, George. *A Voyage Around the World: Volume 1*. London, 1777.

Gerber, Haim. "Zionism, Orientalism, and the Palestinians." *Journal of Palestine Studies* 33, no. 1 (2003): 23–41.

Gonzalez, Vernadette Vicuña. *Securing Paradise: Tourism and Militarism in Hawai'i and the Philippines*. Durham: Duke University Press, 2013.

Gregory, Derek. "Between the Book and the Lamp: Imaginative Geographies of Egypt, 1849–50." *Transactions of the Institute of British Geographers* 20, no. 1 (1995): 29–57.

Gregory, Derek. "Emperors of the Gaze: Photographic Practices and Productions of Space in Egypt, 1839–1914." In *Picturing Place: Photography and the Geographical Imagination*, edited by Joan M. Schwartz and James R. Ryan, 196–225. New York: I.B. Tauris, 2003.

Hanzimanolis, Margaret. "Eight Hen Per Man Per Day: Shipwreck Survivors and Pastoral Abundance in Southern Africa." In *Navigating African Maritime History*, edited by Carina E. Ray and Jeremy Rich, 33–55. Liverpool: Liverpool University Press, 2009.

Higham, James, Anna Thomason-Carr, and Ghazali Musa. "Mountaineering Tourism: Activity, People and Place." In *Mountaineering Tourism*, edited by Ghazali Musa, James Higham, and Anna Thompson-Carr, 1–15. New York: Routledge, 2015.

Hitchcock, Michael. *Tourism, Development, and Terrorism in Bali*. New York: Routledge, 2007.

Hore, Jarrod. *Visions of Nature: How Landscape Photography Shaped Settler Colonialism*. Berkeley: University of California Press, 2022.

Howard, Christopher A. "Touring the Consumption of the Other: Imaginaries of Authenticity in the Himalayas and Beyond." *Journal of Consumer Culture* 16, no. 2 (2016): 354–373.

Jazeel, Tariq. "Orientalism and the Geographical Imagination." *Geography* 97, no. 1 (2012): 4–11.

Johnston, Jeremy M. "'The Wild West Side of American Existence': Theodore Roosevelt, Buffalo Bill Cody, and American Military Exceptionalism." In *The Popular Frontier: Buffalo Bill's Wild West and Transnational Mass Culture*, edited by Frank Christianson, 73–95. Norman: University of Oklahoma Press, 2017.

Jolly, Roslyn. "South Sea Gothic: Pierre Loti and Robert Louis Stevenson." *English Literature in Translation, 1880–1920* 47, no. 1 (2004): 28–49.

Kabbani, Rana. *Europe's Myths of Orient*. Bloomington: Indiana University Press, 1986.

Kelly, Kristine. "Aesthetic Desire and Imperialist Disappointment in Trollope's *The Bertrams* and the Murray *Handbook for Travellers in Syria and Palestine*." *Victorian Literature and Culture* 43 (2015): 621–639.

Kernahan, Mel. *White Savages in the South Seas*. London: Verso, 1995.

King, Richard. *Orientalism and Religion: Postcolonial Theory, India and 'The Mystic East'*. New York: Routledge, 1999.

Kosasa, Karen. "Searching for the 'C' Word: Museums, Art Galleries, and Settler Colonialism in Hawai'i." In *Studies in Settler Colonialism: Politics, Identity and Culture*, edited by Fiona Bateman and Lionel Pilkington, 153–168. New York: Palgrave MacMillan, 2011.

Kozinets, Robert V. "The Moment of Infinite Fire." In *Time, Space and the Market: Retroscapes Rising*, edited by Stephen Brown and John F. Sherry, Jr., 199–216. New York: Routledge, 2015.

Lalvani, Suren. "Consuming the Exotic Other." *Critical Studies in Mass Communication* 12 (1995): 263–286.

Lefebvre, Camille. "We Have Tailored Africa: French Colonialism and the 'Artificiality' of Africa's Borders in the Interwar Period." *Journal of Historical Geography* 37 (2011): 191–202.

Lewis, Simon. "Culture, Cultivation, and Colonialism in 'Out of Africa' and Beyond." *Research in African Literatures* 31, no. 1 (2000): 63–79.

Liechty, Mark. "Building the Road to Kathmandu: Notes on the History of Tourism in Nepal." *Himalaya* 25, nos. 1/2 (2005): 19–28.

Liechty, Mark. *Far Out: Countercultural Seekers and the Tourist Encounter in Nepal.* Chicago: The University of Chicago Press, 2017.

Logan, Dana W. "The Lean Closet: Asceticism in Postindustrial Consumer Culture." *Journal of the American Academy of Religion* 85, no. 3 (2017): 600–628.

Loshitzky, Yosefa. "Orientalist Representations: Palestinians and Arabs in Some Postcolonial Film and Literature." In *Cultural Encounters: Representing 'Otherness'*, edited by Elizabeth Hallam and Brian V. Street, 51–71. New York: Routledge, 2000.

Loti, Pierre. *Aziyadé*, 1867. Reprint. Paris: North Star, 2016.

Loti, Pierre. *The Marriage of Loti (Rarahu)*, 1878. Reprint. London: Forgotten Books, 2012.

Lüthy, Barbara, Francesca Falk, and Patricia Purtschert. "Colonialism without Colonies: Examining Blank Spaces in Colonial Studies." *National Identities* 18, no. 1 (2016): 1–9.

Lynch, Tom. *Outback & Out West: The Settler-Colonial Environmental Imaginary.* Lincoln: University of Nebraska Press, 2022.

Maddra, Sam. "American Indians in Buffalo Bill's Wild West." In *Human Zoos: Science and Spectacle in the Age of Colonial Empires*, edited by Pascal Blanchard, Nicolas Bancel, Gilles Boëtsch, Sandrine Lemaire, and Charles Forsdick, 134–141. Liverpool: Liverpool University Press, 2008.

Mahdy, Hossam. "Travellers, Colonisers, and Conservationists." In *Travellers in Egypt*, edited by Paul and Janet Starkey, 157–167. London: Tauris Parke Paperbacks, 2001.

McKay, Alex. *Kailas Histories: Renunciate Traditions and the Construction of Himalayan Sacred Geography.* Leiden: Brill, 2016.

McNee, Alan. *The New Mountaineer in Late Victorian Britain.* London: Palgrave Macmillan, 2016.

Merrington, Peter. "A Staggered Orientalism: The Cape-to-Cairo Imaginary." *Poetics Today* 22, no. 2 (2001): 323–364.

Mitchell, Timothy. *Colonising Egypt.* Berkeley: University of California Press, 1988.

Mostafanezhad, Mary and Tanya Promburom. "'Lost in Thailand': The Popular Geopolitics of Film-Induced Tourism in Northern Thailand." *Social & Cultural Geography* 19, no. 1 (2018): 81–101.

Moufakkir, Omar and Noureddine Selmi. "Examining the Spirituality of Spiritual Tourists: A Sahara Desert Experience." *Annals of Tourism Research* 70 (2018): 108–119.

Neuhaus, Tom. *Tibet in the Western Imagination.* New York: Palgrave Macmillan, 2012.

Nir, Yeshayahu. *The Bible and the Image: The History of Photography in the Holy Land 1839–1899.* Philadelphia: University of Pennsylvania Press, 1985.

Nolan, Christopher, dir. *Oppenheimer.* Universal Pictures, 2023.

Noor, Farish A. *The Long Shadow of the 19th Century: Critical Essays on Colonial Orientalism in Southeast Asia.* Petaling Jaya: Matahari Books, 2021.

Olwig, Kenneth. *Landscape, Nature, and Body Politic.* Madison: University of Wisconsin Press, 2002.

Ortner, Sherry. "Thick Resistance: Death and the Cultural Construction of Agency in Himalayan Mountaineering." *Representations* 59 (1997): 135–162.

Pallander, Edwin. *The Log of an Island Wanderer: Notes of Travel in the Eastern Pacific.* London: C. Arthur Pearson, 1901.

Perkins, Kenneth J. "The Compagnie Générale Transatlantique and the Development of Saharan Tourism in North Africa." In *The Business of Tourism: Place, Faith, and History*, edited by Philip Scranton and Janet F. Davidson, 34–55. Philadelphia: University of Pennsylvania Press, 2009.

Rasch, William. "Enlightenment as Religion." *New German Critique* 108 (2009): 109–131.

Rennie, Neil. *Far-Fetched Facts: The Literature of Travel and the Idea of the South Seas*. Oxford: Clarendon Press, 1995.

Robinson, Michael F. *The Lost White Tribe: Explorers, Scientists, and the Theory that Changed a Continent*. New York: Oxford University Press, 2016.

Robinson, Zac. "Early Alpine Club Culture and Mountaineering Literature." In *Mountaineering Tourism*, edited by Ghazali Musa, James Higham, and Anna Thompson-Carr, 105–117. New York: Routledge, 2015.

Said, Edward. *Orientalism*. New York: Vintage, 1978.

Said, Edward. "Yeats and Decolonization." In *Nationalism, Colonialism, and Literature: Terry Eagleton, Fredric Jameson, and Edward Said*, 69–95. Minneapolis: University of Minnesota Press, 1990.

Said, Edward. *Culture and Imperialism*. New York: Vintage, 1993.

Sakhnini, Mohammad. "James Silk Buckingham (1786–1855) and the Politics of Travel in the Holy Land." *Studies in Romanticism* 62, no. 2 (2023): 249–267.

Shamma, Tarek. "Horror and Likeness: The Quest for the Self and the Imagining of the Other in *The Sheltering Sky*." *Critical Arts* 25, no. 2 (2011): 242–258.

Shelton, Anthony Alan. "Museum Ethnography: An Imperial Science." In *Cultural Encounters: Representing 'Otherness'*, edited by Elizabeth Hallam and Brian V. Street, 157–193. New York: Routledge, 2000.

Singaravelou, Pierre. "The Institutionalisation of 'Colonial Geography' in France, 1880–1940." *Journal of Historical Geography* 37 (2011): 149–157.

Singh, Shalini. "Secular Pilgrimages and Sacred Tourism in the Indian Himalayas." *GeoJournal* 64, no. 3 (2005): 215–223.

Smith, Bernard. *Imagining the Pacific: In the Wake of the Cook Voyages*. New Haven: Yale University Press, 1992.

Stam, Robert and Ella Shohat. *Race in Translation: Culture Wars Around the Postcolonial Atlantic*. New York: New York University Press, 2012.

Stetler, Julia S. "'Painting the Town Red': Buffalo Bill's Indians in German Media." In *The Popular Frontier: Buffalo Bill's Wild West and Transnational Mass Culture*, edited by Frank Christianson, 155–174. Norman: University of Oklahoma Press, 2017.

Stevenson, Robert Louis. *In the South Seas*. London: Chatto and Windus, 1912.

Stoler, Ann Laura. *Carnal Knowledge and Imperial Power: Race and the Intimate in Colonial Rule*. Berkeley: University of California Press, 2010.

Sturma, Michael. *South Sea Maidens: Western Fantasy and Sexual Politics in the South Pacific*. Westport: Greenwood Press, 2002.

Tamaira, A. Marata. "From Full Dusk to Full Tusk: Reimagining the 'Dusky Maiden' through the Visual Arts." *The Contemporary Pacific* 22, no. 1 (2010): 1–35.

Tilley, Christopher. "Introduction: Identity, Place, Landscape and Heritage." *Journal of Material Culture* 11, no. 1/2 (2006): 7–32.

Usick, Patricia. "William John Bankes' Collection of Drawings of Egypt and Nubia." In *Travellers in Egypt*, edited by Paul and Janet Starkey, 51–60. London: Tauris Parke Paperbacks, 2001.

Wharton, Annabel Jane. *Selling Jerusalem: Relics, Replicas, Theme Parks*. Chicago: University of Chicago Press, 2006.

Yamashita, Shinji. *Bali and Beyond: Explorations in the Anthropology of Tourism*. New York: Berghahn Books, 2003.

2

TOURISM'S MYSTICAL LANDSCAPES

Modernity's great social and environmental upheavals were accompanied by romantic longings for nature as a source of inspiration, escape, and belonging, whether it was in transcendentalist philosophy, in the literary glorification of the American frontier, or in orientalist fascination with subaltern people.[1]

Joe Bandy

Tourism and Authenticity

Tourism was created out of the "discipline of detail" at the center of colonial regimes. The *Description de l'Egypte*, created by 165 scholars from Napoleon's *Commission des Sciences et des Arts de l'Armée de l'Orient*, included 897 illustrated plates, 3,000 drawings, and 9 folios of text.[2] It resulted in a map of Egypt that satisfied colonial claims, inspired the photography and painting that followed the expedition, produced volumes of academic studies, and inspired tourists to visit the pyramids and other sites.

Tourism is a political and colonial project. Tourist attractions often reflect national narratives and mythologies and symbols of nationhood, even at places that once belonged to someone else. As Kobi Cohen-Hattab argues, tourism was used during the British Mandate in Palestine to project a cognitive map on Palestine, "The Jews consciously sought to exploit the tourist market in order to market a Zionist view of Palestine while, at the same time, preventing the Arabs from peddling their Arab-oriented image of the country."[3] Cohen-Hattab explains how tourism often creates " 'mythic' cultures" that redefine a place's "realities."[4] As discussed in the previous chapter, Orientalism is often at the center of these mapping projects, even in places

DOI: 10.4324/9781003361725-3

outside "the East," signifying the ways that Orientalism pervades all kinds of spaces in its quest to define the Other as different, odd, and exotic. As Suren Lalvani notes, Orientalism is "a heterogeneous and contradictory discourse" that both fixates upon and derides its colonial subject.[5]

Scholars have pointed to the introduction of leisure time and workers' rights movements as key factors in the development of tourism. As Boris Vukonić explains, in the late nineteenth century the average worker in Europe worked 3,900 hours per year; by the mid-twentieth century, this had dropped to 2,000 hours; by 1950, this had dropped again, and is even lower today.[6] The state of tourism in Europe in the early nineteenth century was quite undeveloped, with a London-to-Paris trip requiring a train, a ship, and a lot of time (often taking up to 39 hours), resulting in "disorienting effects."[7] This quickly changed, and by the 1840s, travelers could get to Egypt from London by steamship in as little as two-and-a-half weeks, experiencing Orientalism firsthand, visiting the port of Alexandria and experiencing the Nile.[8] The year 1840 was a watershed year for tourism, with several important developments including "the invention of the camera, the organization of the first packaged holiday, and the introduction of the first national railway timetable."[9] The entire enterprise of early European tourism was focused on the exotic. After his European tours were established, Thomas Cook famously remarked that the next step was travels "even amongst strange people, and in strange countries."[10] Cook's background as a minister helped to motivate his evangelical interest in the Holy Land and Egypt.

Scholars have suggested different theories about tourism: that it is a search for authenticity, an event centered on images and their meanings, or an escape from the "real world." Typologies of tourism are based on the experiences of the tourist. Erik Cohen has proposed five modes: recreational, diversionary, experiential, experimental, and existential.[11] Scholars of tourism have also introduced typologies of different kinds of tourism experiences. This book includes examples like adventure tourism (in Kenya) and spa and wellness tourism (in Bali and numerous other places), but there are other forms of tourism this book does not address, such as collector tourism, "dark" or "disaster" tourism, and gambling tourism.[12]

Mystical landscapes are part of many modern tourist experiences. These include the "green" (land-based natural environments) and "blue" (ocean-related environments such as islands) spaces that Sharpley discusses in his work.[13] Safaris and extreme sports in the Himalayas are two examples of "green places" and the islands of Bali, Tahiti, and Hawai'i are "blue spaces," all of which may be understood as landscapes that "elicit some sort of spiritual response."[14] While this book is less interested in typologies and more interested in mystical landscapes, Cohen's modes are helpful ways to think about the great variety of experiences offered to modern tourists.[15]

Modern tourism is framed around concerns like design, accessibility, and attractions, all of which are focused on maximizing profit. In Clare Gunn's study of vacation tourist locations, he explains how design is a central factor in the development of a tourist place, with the goal of attracting large numbers of tourists and, thus, dollars. In the case of natural environments, design includes things like parking spaces and hiking trails.[16] For example, in national parks zones are created based on "objectives."[17] These objectives are focused on the promotion of the park as a space that is designed, constructed, and presented as a particular space. Today, American national parks, which are on Indian ancestral lands, are constructed spaces used for the enjoyment of tourists, unconcerned with resources like water and food or traditions like religious ceremonies. The focus of design is on consumers—an example of the mapping of indigenous space for tourism.

The search for a special, spiritually charged experience is often at the center of tourist experiences; an effort to escape the disenchantment of modernity.[18] The wide expanses of the West are presented as mystical spaces in which bodily and spiritual healing can take place, effectively erasing the history of people who once occupied lands that are now empty of the buffalo and people who once lived there in large numbers. Enchantment is believed to be readily available in the environment at places like Sedona, Arizona. However, in other cases, enchantment is produced, and it is important to remember that "the tourist industry is under pressure to generate novel fantasy magical loci."[19] One quality that tourist spaces often have in common is their perceived *difference*, which is often a reflection of fetishism for the exotic and reflects geographical distance. As Noel Salazar has written, this is a foundational theme in the tourism industry: "After all, tourists and tourism service providers alike rely on a shared frame of reference in relation to ethnic and cultural difference: globally circulating tourism imaginaries infused with outdated scientific knowledge."[20]

Tourism also represents struggles over identity in which, due to colonial mapping, entire continents often are perceived to have a distinct personality. As Noel Salazar explains,

> Imaginaries often become the symbolic objects of a significant contest over economic supremacy, territorial ownership, and identity. In the eyes of Western tourists, for example, Africa is often seen as dangerous and to be avoided, while Asia is construed as simultaneously risky but also exotic and worth experiencing.[21]

Today, these spaces are often sites of colonial nostalgia, ranging from the Karen Blixen Safari Camp in Kenya to the renovated colonial hotels of Southeast Asia. As Maurizio Peleggi notes, there is an entire "nostalgia-oriented tourism industry" that allows visitors to Singapore, Vietnam, and other countries to experience the "authentication" of the wealthy, elite colonial past.[22]

Authenticity is a key part of the tourist industry. As Bruner points out,

> The tourist pursuit of the exotic and the Other has been conceptualized as a quest for authenticity by MacCannell (1976), who accepts the myth of European decadence, arguing that alienated Western persons, unable to find satisfaction and authenticity in their own society look for it elsewhere, in places thought to be more original and authentic.[23]

The Western quest for authenticity is often built into tourism promotion materials that combine exotic locals with the promise of sensual, even sexual, experiences with locals. As one study on Thailand notes, in a video titled *Fields of Jade*, "The new age ambience of the production plays on this purportedly 'authentic' spirituality, supplementing it with crude sexual imagery."[24] The "dusky maiden," the "bare-breasted, nubile Polynesian *wāhine* (women)," is another motif that helps to represent the exoticism and eroticism identified with island cultures in the South Pacific.[25]

Tourism offers authentic experience in numerous forms, including wellness resorts and religious (or spiritual) retreats. As Brooke Schedneck has noted, the retreat is distinct from the vacation because it offers the possibility of transformation using a therapeutic model such as mindfulness.[26] Offering retreats in mystical landscapes imbues the experience with an added layer of authenticity due to the different and exotic nature of places like India and Bali. In Bali, marketing includes an exploitation of the Hindu and Buddhist cultures and taglines like "the island of the gods" and "Shangri-La."

Scholars of marketing have noted how authenticity, through the interest in retro products, has been an important trend over the past century: "Under modern conditions, the place of the individual in society is preserved, in part, by newly institutionalized concerns for the authenticity of his social experiences."[27] The "staging" of time and space is part of this trend, much like tourism that relies on colonial nostalgia.[28] The production of mystical tourist spaces is the result of the disconnection from wonder and transcendence that is part of the modern project. As Joe Bandy reminds us, "For the wealthy, adventure tours—safaris, hunting trips, journeys through the great American wilderness, excursions to remote locations in the Far East, or sea voyages to 'exotic' regions—become more frequent during the late nineteenth and early twentieth centuries."[29]

Authenticity has often been tied to class. In Nepal, money could enable entry to the nation (which was closed to tourists until the 1950s). As Liechty notes, "In the early years Nepal was a trophy-destination reserved for members of the 'jet-set' who were basically the only ones who could afford to stay there."[30] Authenticity also reflects the interest in alterity (the exotic) in which tourists, predominantly of European descent, visit places that are conceptualized as special based on their geographic difference and cultural/social/racial exoticism. Historically, these tourist experiences "operated as an ideal existential state that was activated by coming into contact with places and people perceived to be 'authentic.'"[31]

Eat, Pray, Love, Elizabeth Gilbert's wildly successful account of her own search for meaning following a painful divorce, provides an example of how *poverty is a form of authentic experience* for affluent tourists visiting exotic locations. For Gilbert, poverty is an experience, one that she can leave whenever she wishes. One indigenous scholar from Indonesia describes her own encounter with this part of Gilbert's book:

> I open to the part about India, where she expresses longing for an imaginary Ashram life. She even allows herself to scrub the floor. She wants to transform *herself* into a "mystical" girl who "performs menial tasks as a way to achieve a constant meditative state."[32]

For Larasati, a Balinese scholar, Gilbert is overly romantic about the lives of indigenous people. As a child, the scholar was made to clean an ashram as a part of her religious duty, something she was excused from while menstruating and which she and her girlfriends escaped by claiming to "have three menstrual cycles a month."[33]

For the European or American tourist, the authentic is often found in spaces identified with traditional, premodern, or exotic cultures. For moderns seeking a different experience, the forests of the Indian/Native American, the desert of the Arab, and the island of the Polynesian all offer the authenticity they desire. As Philip Deloria puts it,

> Because those seeking authenticity have already defined their own state as inauthentic, they easily locate authenticity in the figure of an Other. This Other can be coded in terms of time (nostalgia or archaism), place (the small town), or culture (Indianness).[34]

The search for authentic experience is a large part of the modern condition. As Deloria writes in *Playing Indian* (1998), "The authentic serves as a way to imagine and idealize the real, the traditional, and the organic in opposition to the less satisfying qualities of everyday life."[35] Tourism, and especially mystical tourism, suggests that certain spaces are optimal, regardless of the histories and peoples attached to them. In one study of Nepal, the author explains it in this way: "After all, the tourist imagination does not merely *represent* what tourists come in search of; it *produces* it. It is this agency in constructing places that is enabled by the tourist imagination: *making* spaces rather than moving through them."[36]

Charles Taylor proposes that the world of enchantment passed away with the Enlightenment. During the Middle Ages, enchantment was believed to be attached to the wonder and delight found in religion, but a goal of the Enlightenment was to free people from this and situate them in the world of science and reality.[37] For those who believe that enchantment has disappeared in their lives, authentic, often mystical, experience must replace it. Zygmunt Bauman argues that this is one of the goals of the consumer—to purchase authenticity. Authenticity is not only one of tourism's aims, but it is also something we find more discretely in mystical tourism, in its creation of communities and experiences that offer *both* authenticity and spiritual transformation. As Bauman argues, "Perceiving the world, complete with its inhabitants, as a pool of consumer items, makes the negotiation of human bonds exceedingly hard."[38] Perhaps this is why mystical landscapes are so important.

The imagination, the remapping of territory, and the search for authentic and meaningful experience are what led to *tourism imaginaries*. This questions whether there is *any* authentic tourist experience. The tourist thinks they are seeking something different, located in ideas of the magical landscapes discussed in this book, but perhaps what they are really doing is looking at a projection of their own desires. As one author puts it, "the Other reflected back to them is their own imaginary projection."[39] The primary "source" in the construction of tourist space is the imagination. Nepal is a place few had visited but had fixated in their mind. Gustave Flaubert wrote that he was born to live there, despite never having left France.[40] Another writer simply loved the name Kathmandu, describing it as "one of the best sounding place names in the world" that belonged with "Xanadu and the fictional Shangri-La."[41] Visitors to Tahiti also had a vision of the islands constructed upon colonial fantasies about the noble savage, premodern societies, and sensuality being located in non-white bodies.

Tourism imaginaries did not magically appear with the emergence of international tourism. They were embedded in the colonial past and then monetized for profit as tourism emerged as a global business. As anthropologists Nelson Graham and Naomi M. Leite explain, "Formed of images, discourses, fantasies, stereotypes, advertising, folklore, and more, these imaginaries prompt tourist expectations, provide fodder for tour guide presentations, and lend meaning to the traveler's experience."[42] The creation of tourist sites is dependent upon forgetting, silencing, and erasure. At times, these processes are centered upon places that are internally colonized or are sites of settler colonialism. George Hughes writes about Scotland,

> To the current tourist Scotland is clearly a picturesque Scotland, based on a landscape which embodies a history of much human suffering. That this goes largely unremarked in the tourism brochures is but one aspect of depiction, for not only is the landscape of Scotland partially a product of economic parvenus, but the issue of "landscape" itself has been problematized and shown to be a more modern "way of seeing."[43]

The European and American construction of place is embedded in the history of colonialism, resulting in travel destinations like Kenya, Tahiti, and Nepal. Colonial nostalgia promotes "reminiscences and evocations of a past lifestyle."[44] These moments are found in the African safari, resorts like the Karen Blix Camp, and the reconstruction of Paul Gauguin's home for tourists. Called *Maison du Jouir*, it literally means the "house of pleasure." For Gauguin and other artists, the islands of the South Pacific represented the "ends-of-the-earth, cultural-limit cases unencumbered by notions of sin," and for colonial powers, they were the stepping-stones to Asia's riches.[45] This is the history of mystical landscapes—imaginary lands that provide both spiritual transformation and monetary wealth.

Pilgrims and Mystical Tourists

In my last book, I likened mystical tourism to a form of spiritual tourism, but here I would like to point out a key difference.[46] Mystical tourism involves the perceived religious power of a landscape such as an island, desert, or mountain range, while spiritual tourism is typically focused upon the wellness and growth offerings of a place, which are commonly visited to "address a problem in their lives" and focus on their health.[47] Thus, mystical tourism is a form of pilgrimage that often relies on the power within a landscape, which may include therapies that emerge from it. The landscape as a kind of spiritual center is one of the things that makes mystical tourism a form of pilgrimage, for the true pilgrim is "committed to the centre" and is on a "search" for meaning.[48]

Alex Norman's definition of spiritual tourism argues that it is a kind of tourism focused on "a desire to seek answers to problems in life."[49] As scholars have pointed out, spiritual tourism is very focused on a goal—weight loss, a reduction in stress, or a new yoga technique.[50] Spiritual tourism is focused on "spiritual betterment," but this is not necessarily tied to a landscape; as one example, spiritual tourists travel to retreat centers in major cities.[51] Mystical tourism is focused on the sacred and powerful qualities of a place. As one study of Chiang Mai reminds us, mystical tourists visit a city due to its "spiritual atmosphere" that is linked to its many temples and monks, but the land is not believed to be intrinsically powerful.[52] Looking at a definition of spiritual tourism helps us understand this difference. "Spiritual tourism can be defined as a reflexive well-being intervention driven by the sense that some aspects of everyday life need improving, and oriented toward the space of nonwork from home where such problems can be given full attention."[53] Mystical tourism, on the other hand, is focused on gaining mystical power from a place. While this may involve wellness and "spiritual activities are beneficial for their health and well-being," mystical tourists are focused on the landscape as the source of radical transformation.[54]

This is not a book that is primarily *about* pilgrimage. However, mystical landscapes often involve acts of pilgrimage.[55] When a tourist travels to Nepal or Tibet to experience the mystical power of its land, they are seeking a religious experience, which is often expressed in the language of authenticity. "I am seeking something different" is one way the search for authentic experience is phrased, and, as scholars know, these quests are a feature of modern life. In the sites discussed in this book, the "natural features" that are often a part of the religious pilgrimage are also present—in the Himalayan mountains, the deserts of North Africa, the savannahs of Kenya, and the lagoons and waterfalls of the Hawaiian Islands.[56]

Pilgrimage is a phenomenon linked to "movement, place, belief, and transformation."[57] In my book on Islamic pilgrimage, one of my concerns was how pilgrimage is a malleable and extremely diverse phenomenon that, among Muslims, includes literally hundreds of traditions. Pilgrimage is about experiencing something special, and as such, it is identified with certain places different from our usual, normal, familiar spaces. As one study notes, "The pilgrim attains solidarity with place of person through the journey."[58]

How religion is involved in these quests is a tricky question, because "religion" is a category of meaning created by European and American academics. Its referent, Protestant Christianity, remains powerful even for those who are not self-described Christians. J.Z. Smith has described how the concept of religion is a way to subsume other people's traditions and refer them back to European ideas about theology, divinity, and meaning.[59] As one study notes,

> By the colonial era, "religions" became used by Western colonial powers to describe a category of belief systems that appeared to be parallel (yet subordinate to) the Christian tradition, despite the fact that such categories are not always indigenous.[60]

Religion, spirituality, and mysticism are discrete concepts that are often conflated as one phenomenon. *Religion*, as scholars know, is an invention of Protestant Christian scholars who created the field. Definitions of religion often include things like a belief in a higher power, rituals, a shared set of traditions, and a set of religious authorities who determine doctrine and practice. However, not all religions have these elements, and as indigenous scholars have pointed out, the concept of a divine being is often incongruous. In the Osage tradition, the "sacred Other" is bigender, experienced as "Above and Below, as grandfather and grandmother."[61] Spirituality and mysticism are equally problematic because they do not have discrete definitions that are helpful to understanding the parameters of spiritual or mystical states, practices, or traditions. Like *religion*, both spirituality and mysticism embrace obscurity and vagueness.[62]

Tourism often involves religion through places that are sacred or part of a religious history. As Nelson Graburn reminds us, a main reason for travel was the search for religious meaning:

> In medieval Europe, travel was usually for avowedly religious purposes, as were pilgrimages and crusades; for ordinary people travel was difficult and dangerous, and even for the ruling classes, who also traveled for reasons of state, travel required large protective entourages. Those who could afford it often retired to retreats or endowed religious institutions in their spiritual quest for the ultimate "truth."[63]

Religious tourism still exists, but other forms of modern tourism have emerged, including adventure, wellness, and environmental tourism. Pilgrimage is a critical part of the intersections between the colonial gaze, tourism, and landscapes, seen in the ways that tourist activities constitute modern ritual forms. Dean MacCannell contends that pilgrimage is not the same as tourism, yet he suggests that its resemblance is striking and sees tourism as a collection of ritualized acts of sightseeing.[64] For many early tourists, their travels were a collection of sights or views—of a great mountain, a beautiful island, or an ancient city. For Christians in the Holy Land, the Bible became "a book of views" identified with Palestine.[65] Other scholars have shown how tourism and pilgrimage have numerous commonalities—the journey, souvenirs, the seeking of a new experience. Zygmunt Bauman has argued that the tourist is *on the move*, but this movement has a purpose, also found in the pilgrim.[66]

Religious pilgrimages were likely the precursors to modern tourism; as scholars have shown, the two may be part of a continuum that persists today.[67] Dean MacCannell has argued that tourism is a religious act—a way of escaping the mundane existence of modernity: "sightseeing is a kind of collective striving for a transcendence of the modern totality, a way of attempting to overcome the discontinuity of modernity."[68] The two categories are messy; as Sean Gammon has remarked, one can be both a tourist and a pilgrim—something that is true of both *religious* and *secular* voyages.[69]

Pilgrimage and tourism have many similarities, including a journey to a special place, the search for authentic experience, and the importance of souvenirs. They also share "the requirements of free time, social sanction and income, as well as the process of transfer from ordinary/profane to non-ordinary/sacred time and place."[70] Pilgrimages are not always religious and may involve popular tourist sites including sporting events, graves of famous people, and "sites of civil religion" like the Lincoln Memorial.[71] The landscapes examined in this book include places that blur the lines between religious and secular pilgrimage such as Sagarmatha/Chomolungma (Everest), which is both a site of spiritual experience for many climbers and the site of the tallest mountain in the world. While this book is less concerned with how people define such places, I am interested in the ways that these spaces are created as tourist sites linked to mystical and spiritual experience.

As noted earlier, modern domestic tourism in Europe began in the eighteenth century when roads and later railways became major modes of transportation in places like England.[72] However, it was much earlier, during Shakespeare's time, that we see the advent of modern souvenirs that surrounded stories about the bard.[73] Scholars of tourism understand these connections to religion and see tourism as a kind of modern replacement for religion. It is not merely a matter of "organizational similarities," but rather a matter of having an *authentic experience*.[74] As Dean MacCannell explains, "Pilgrims attempted to visit a place where an event of religious importance actually occurred. Tourists present themselves at places of social, historical, and cultural importance."[75]

Religious scholars have argued that pilgrims often *are* tourists. Pilgrims buy souvenirs, they desire proof of their journey, and they travel to distant places in search of a different experience—all things tourists do. Scholars also have pointed to the difference between religious pilgrims, who go to a religious center, and tourists, who seek an Other.[76] In modernity, "landscapes are transformed into 'attractions,' not because they symbolize one's culture, but precisely because they are different—allegedly harboring an 'authenticity' which modernity has lost."[77] The religious tourist is doing both of these things—seeking a spiritual center that is also a site of difference.

It can also be argued that the culture of consumption that characterizes modern pilgrimage is linked to capitalism and moreover, to the commodification of religious goods. A consumer can buy a prayer carpet on Amazon made in China, and then use it in a mosque in Iowa. The ways in which the Buddha appears on T-shirts, bumper stickers, and coffee cups are another example of how the sacred is part of the larger marketplace. This is also true for tourist places, whose commodification is "invoked when marketing precepts are applied," resulting in a shift in "the focus from simply 'selling places' to the production of what will sell."[78]

Do religious acts make a secular pilgrimage or tourist journey religious? I am not sure, but it is difficult to completely exclude religious elements at places like Graceland, which hosts altars to Elvis at its gates.[79] One study included an axis that contains secularism, pilgrimage, sacredness, and tourism, showing some of the ways they intersect.[80] In the work of Victor Turner, we see how the pilgrim wishes to travel to a place "out there," away from the normal life they are living. Distance is a large part of the pilgrim's experience, and mystical tourists are also mystical pilgrims, what Turner describes where he writes that these journeys are also viewed as life-changing rituals. In his words, "The peripherality of pilgrimage shrines and the temporal structure of the pilgrimage process, beginning in a Familiar Place, going to a Far Place, and returning, ideally 'changed,' to a Familiar Place" is a rite of passage.[81]

Most spaces examined in this book are located at far distances from Europe and North America, but other sites examined here are not "out there" in the Turnerian sense. In particular, the American West functions as a kind of *internal exterior*—it is located within the United States but is viewed as being different, a center of mysticism. The Outback in Australia is viewed as an example of a "frontier destination" and one of the "places imagined to be standing outside of modernity."[82] A result of this social imaginary is that the places created, which include the Orient, the American West, Africa, and Oceania, all once occupied by colonial powers, become mystic territory. As Noel Salazar has argued, "tourist imaginaries do not float spontaneously and independently; rather, they 'travel' in space and time through well-established conduits."[83]

Tourist imaginaries can be powerful, for they replace the authenticity once attached to religion that has been lost in modernity. Colonial regimes imposed an entire system on the places they occupied, creating the maps, names, texts, and traditions that replaced the indigenous, local, or other precolonial culture. Anthony Alan Shelton explains how this took place in British colonialism:

> Empire became an image, represented by the pink shadings on the map, titular claims (Victoria as Empress of India, imperial viceroys and governors), a hagiography of secular heroes (David Livingstone, Richard Burton, Charles George Gordon, Herbert Kitchener, Clive of India, Cecil Rhodes), archives, compiled, collated and attemptedly synthesized from cartographic, geographical, archaeological and ethnographic surveys, natural history expeditions, population censuses, economic statistics, all tenuously connected by repositories of information and networks of telegraph wire threading together lonely and far-flung outposts.[84]

As we will learn, mystical landscapes are often sacred spaces and include sacred lands taken from indigenous people, "produced through the spatial, material, and discursive practices of social groups."[85] However, many places are subjected to colonial imaginings. As Dibyesh Anand explains, "The Other is both a prisoner of time (frozen in a stage of history) and an escapee (outside the time grid, timeless, outside history). The West is the present, the now."[86] At times, these fantasies transform economies into tourism sites that sell culture as an exotic product. For example, Bali has been "turned into a tourist commodity via policy intervention by the state."[87] These policies began with the Dutch colonial vision of Bali as the last paradise.

Colonial Tourism

At its core, tourism is a very colonial and very white activity. White bodies, for the most part, do this work. As Sara Ahmed writes, "Not all those at the borders, such as tourists, migrants, or foreign nationals, are recognized as strangers; some will seem more 'at home' than others, some will pass through, with their passports extending physical motility into social mobility."[88] Thus, mystical tourism is a form of white power that constructs, defines, and experiences those places where spiritual or cultural growth is believed to be located, at the cost of what existed before. In Isak Dinesen's books *Out of Africa* and *Shadows on the Grass*, she reflects the sensibilities of Europe at the time, which included a distaste for modernity and a search for transcendent, mystical experience. Europe was identified with "the urban, the industrial, the plutocratic, the tame, and the tacky" against Dinesen's "pristine Africa marked by adventure, freedom, and power."[89]

The branding of cultures for profit is a large part of tourism. Colonialism has touched every corner of the world, and the places examined in this book have suffered its effects. These include the impact on local traditions that includes the marketing of entire cultures as part of a national tourism strategy. Bali is one example of this process—the culture is both significant to Balinese character and a necessary part of the island's tourism industry. As Picard notes,

> In other words, their culture has become for the Balinese, on the one hand what characterizes them as a specific society, and on the other hand what provides their tourist product with its distinguishing features—both an identity marker (*ciri khas*) and a trademark.[90]

The acquisition of objects, or in some cases, of territory, through the purchase of real estate is another way in which tourism functions as a colonial act. It is this "white body's extension into space" that is under examination in this book—the way it erases the past, adopts it as white culture, or commercializes it as a mystical activity.[91] Sara Ahmed describes this as a natural function of whiteness. For the mystical tourist, it is natural "to be so at ease with one's environment that it is hard to distinguish where one's body ends and the world begins."[92] An example of this is when tourists make statements about how they are citizens of the world. In one study of Nepal, one tourist talked about how the world was her "global abode."[93] But of course, she does not realize that her quest to be a world traveler and experience authenticity through exotic, underdeveloped places is a paradox, for the very act of traveling, visiting, and consuming destroys her object of desire.[94] The extension of white colonialism is also seen in the commodification of Buddhist sites, where the focus is on satisfying the desire of tourists. As Brooke Schedneck and other scholars have shown us, "ancient Buddhist temples, Buddhism, and even monks have become overly commoditized to attract and satisfy tourist imaginaries, and deliver only economic benefits."[95]

Islands are another environment subjected to the wishes of colonizers. As John O'Carroll explains, islands are "tiny, away from it all, peripheral and carnivalesque."[96] This has allowed foreigners, including European explorers and colonists, to create their own ideas about the new environments they were encountering. Tahiti is one of the best examples of this as a place that was constructed as a paradise, a vision inspired by the philosophical ideals focused on nature that had overtaken much of Europe and further substantiated by the natural beauty of the islands. As one scholar described Tahiti, "This was a region of groves, glades, intersecting paths and gentle rivulets familiar to any reader of Renaissance pastoral, and moreover in keeping with pre-Romantic ideals of gentle disorder as a desirable outdoor setting."[97]

Mystical tourism is often focused on the power of place, which the tourist narrates through their experience. Scholars have argued that melancholy is one emotional state attached to these spaces, where affluent tourists (especially white women) are able to stage a "fantasized escape" from the unhappiness in their lives.[98] The sites of mystical tourism created out of colonial occupation are visited by tourists who tell stories that have power. As one study argues, "The tourist is an agent, considered from a dynamic point of view, an acting person, involved in a *narrative process*, from which the successive positions, translations, and semantic value of his topological transformations can be decoded."[99]

Tourism is place-driven; however, when a spiritual tourist "undertakes a spiritual practice or seeks spiritual progression in the course of their travels," this may include the belief that the place they visit is a mystical landscape.[100] Alex Norman contends that a sacred site not essential to spiritual tourism, and I think this is a valuable and correct distinction.[101] Thus, mystical tourism can reflect spiritual tourism, but only when it involves a tourist believing in or placing value upon a mystical landscape.

Ideas about place lie at the center of mystical landscapes. In this way, mystical tourism is more about an *idea* than about the reality of a location. For the mystical pilgrim, this is not merely an idea, or ideas, but a fantasy about far-off places and what one's experience will be. As one scholar puts it, it is the representation of a place that is important, more than what is "offered."[102] Mystical tourism involves mystical places and often "the bodies attached to these places," which are viewed as having mystic power.[103] The attraction to exotic bodies can be coupled with a repulsion, seen in the narratives of the passion and danger attached to miscegenation. As Tarek Shamma has written, there is a "dynamic of attraction and repulsion" that is "characteristic of Orientalist and colonialist narratives in general."[104] In the occupation of the East Indies (Indonesia) by the Dutch, the repulsion was represented in the separation between Europeans and local population.

Mystical experience is not simply tourism, or even pilgrimage, for what constitutes the mystical experience depends on the imaginings of spaces that are imbued with religious power. As Said reminds us, the imagination plays a central role in the construction of geographic spaces. True of colonialism, this is also true of tourism and the spaces this book explores—the American West, Oceania, Nepal, Bali, the continent of Africa, and Palestine. As Noel Salazar explains,

> For Said (1994), geographic imaginaries refer, literally, to how spaces are imagines, how meanings are ascribed to physical spaces (such that they are perceived, represented and interpreted in particular ways), how knowledge about these places are produced, and how these representations make various courses of action possible.[105]

As I have discussed, tourism often entails the search for meaning in a disenchanted world. Perhaps no one has written as eloquently about this disenchantment as Charles Taylor. He argues that this world has things missing—the belief in enchantment is gone as is the lack of choice, for modernity is a marketplace of consumable products and secular experiences. As he writes,

> The number one problem of modern social science is modernity itself. By *modernity* I mean that historically unprecedented amalgam of new practices and institutional forms (science, technology, industrial production, urbanization), of new ways of living (individualism, secularization, instrumental rationality), and of new forms of. Malaise (alienation, meaninglessness, a sense of impending social dissolution) (Italics are in original source).[106]

In some cases, such as Bali, a culture is commercialized to the extent that outsiders can experience the spiritual benefits of the island's Hinduism without being Hindu. For example, tour agencies advertise not only the beautiful landscape, but also "the experience of Balinese culture, especially spiritual culture."[107] Whether one can truly possess a tourist destination is under debate.

Dean MacCannell argues that such places can be created but not possessed. As he puts it, "Tourist destinations may be treated as classic commodities up to a point; that is, they can be manufactured, as at Disneyland, and they can be marketed."[108] According to MacCannell, they cannot be owned.[109]

The mystical or spiritual quest is at the center of many tourist sites. It is important to understand that these quests are, by their very nature, colonial. The quests are also situated in neoliberal values about womanhood, capitalism, wellness, and success. The successes women have in their wellness goals are linked to their productivity as workers, seen in the self-help books by writers like Elizabeth Gilbert and in the many ways that mystical tourism is identified as both a reward and remedy for hard work, weekends lost to employers, deadlines, children, and elder care. As Ethel Mickey writes, when individuals fail at their wellness goals, they are also seen as failures in the capitalist superstructure due to their unproductive bodies.[110]

Elizabeth Gilbert's *Eat, Pray, Love* has garnered much attention from scholars (including myself) who have critiqued its tone-deaf observations about other cultures, the way white womanhood is viewed as a path to saving women trapped in poverty, and its fantasies about self-discovery and spiritual growth. Spiritual growth is viewed as being centered in other places, which is a way of saying that American (and European) society is focused on the more rational, economical, and liberative aspects of the modern human experience. As Anca-Luminata Iancu writes, the "processes of self-discovery the protagonists experience in order to discover an individual identity" are focused on formerly colonized territories whose status as sites of mystical growth is largely intact.[111] In *Eat, Pray, Love*, Gilbert finds her salvation in her travels to India and Indonesia (and to a lesser degree, Italy). As Kendra Marston explains,

> The appeal of these films, however, lies not merely in the postcard-perfect images of carefully selected international locations and artfully constructed sets designed to evoke romance and excitement, mystery and glamour, but rather in the transformative potential they offer their white, middle-class tourists who frequently initiate their journeys while suffering from a form of urban bourgeois malaise.[112]

Tourism is a business focused on escape, at times through a quest or special experience.[113] These experiences are created through colonial histories and the strategies of mapping enforced at these sites. Mystical landscapes are "places of power" believed to have a particular religious or mystical gravitas, what scholars have called "spiritually stimulating places."[114] As stated in the previous chapter, mystical landscapes are often, but not always, part of mystical tourism. Like other forms of modern capitalism, mystical landscapes may include the erasure of histories and communities or their exploitation.

As Miriam Kahn explains, "Capitalist markets, while economically needing other peoples and environments, may politically seek to eliminate them through consciously crafted representations."[115] These representations include mystical landscapes.

Mystical Landscapes

Landscapes are a form of imaginative geography that involve the imposition of a particular ideology on a space. The idea of "landscape" originates in an Anglo-Saxon word, related to the German word *Landscaft*, "a small patch of cultivated ground" and perhaps the "peasant's view of the world."[116] When the word *landskip* emerged in the seventeenth century, it meant something different—a "masculine and class-conscious way of 'seeing.'"[117] John Urry's "tourist gaze" is a very useful frame for understanding the ways landscapes function as part of the set of tourists' expectations. As Urry writes, "the gaze in any historical period is constructed in relationship to its opposite, to non-tourist forms of social experience and consciousness."[118] Urry also explains how landscape is a site of difference and is "out of the ordinary."[119]

Tourism has an intimate relationship with the history of transportation, which influenced ideas about sight and landscape. Scholars have documented how the railway changed the way people viewed the world, and specifically, how they perceived the landscape, which became "a 'panorama' unfolding outside the carriage window."[120] The landscape reflects the paintings that became an instrumental part of the tourist imaginary and create a loss of depth. As Wolf Sternberger explains, "The views . . . have entirely lost their dimension of depth and have become mere particles of one and the same panoramic world that stretches all around and is, at each and every point, a painted surface."[121]

As one scholar puts it, "Landscapes are not something uncontested and objective that are simply 'out there.'"[122] Scholars sometimes call this process cognitive mapping. This book explores some of the ways that Europeans and North Americans replaced indigenous and local ways of understanding the natural environment with their own visions of meaning. For example, when Egeria visited Palestine in the fourth century, her experience imitated "the actual experience of someone viewing a landscape," in which she matched her "scriptural" knowledge with the "geographical testimony" that she observed.[123] While not all the places examined in this book are as overtly religious as the Holy Land, they often contained Biblical or other religious references, suggesting that colonial landscapes were often shaped by Christian thought. As Blake Leyerle explains, "Her [Egeria] willingness to connect biblical markers to relatively unmarked geographical spots, moreover, illustrates Pred's contention that place always represents a human product."[124]

The mapping of the world as a Christian space followed in the centuries after Egeria's pilgrimage and included a vision of the world modeled upon the Biblical story of Noah's three sons, each of whom was associated with a different continent. As Michael Robinson explains in his monumental book on the fantasies of white Africans, Asians, and Native Americans, medieval mapmakers created T-O maps (called this due to their shape) with "each son taking dominion over a different, pie-wedged continent" and even superimposed Christ over the world, "a way to show the Messiah's dominion over the earth" in a grand "cosmic tapestry."[125] In the *Ebstorf* map (thirteenth century), the T shows the dividing lines of the three continents linked to Noah's sons and the O the outer ring of the ocean.[126]

These beginnings predate the mapping of landscapes that took place in the age of exploration and the colonial period. The landscapes that emerge

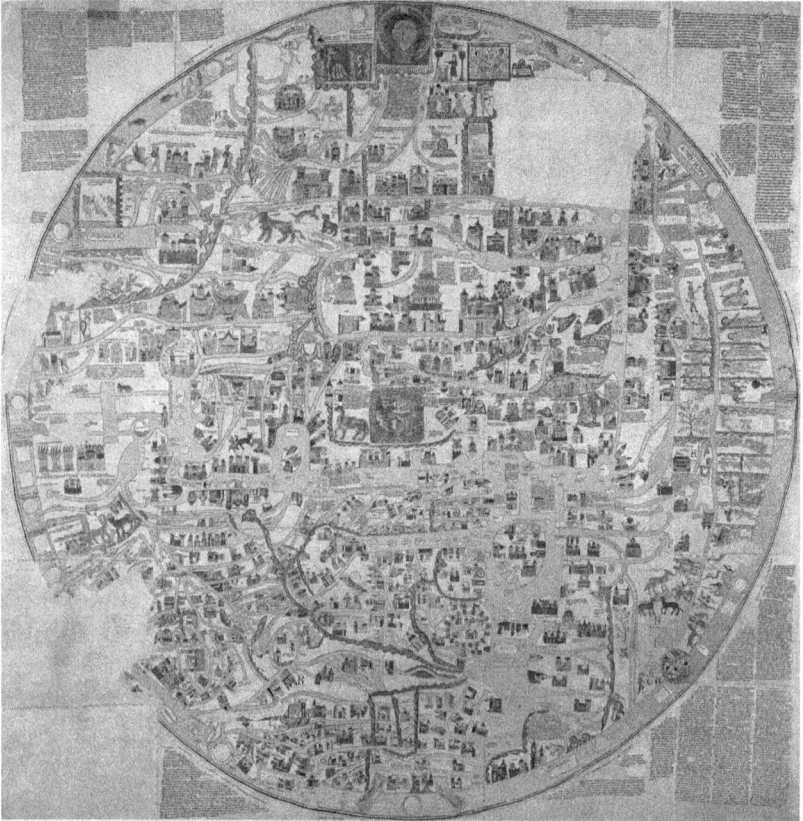

IMAGE 2.1 Ebstorf Map, Thirteenth Century.

Source: photo courtesy of Wikimedia

from these mappings are often attached to ideas of Christian religious experiences embedded in tourism. Landscapes became tourist sites through these imaginative processes, which involve the viewer's formation of spatial knowledge.[127] Places deemed important are included on maps, and places that are not are the "silences" and "empty spaces" that represent a form of encoding.[128] Landscapes are encoded through sight. Derek Gregory describes this as "the ways in which vision and visuality were imbricated in its colonizing gestures."[129]

So, what are mystical landscapes?

In his study of Nepal, Mark Liechty proposes that tourists traveled to the Himalayas "less to find the people who resided there than to find the selves they wished to be—or imagined to have lost."[130] Mystical landscapes are places that hold a powerful place in the Western imagination, but they are not simply wellness resorts that could be built anywhere. Mystical landscapes are tied to the land. This makes them different than wellness tourism, spiritual tourism, or spirituality tourism. Kenya, Nepal, Tahiti, Sedona, and other places in this book are viewed as having mystical qualities. Said's concept of the geographical imaginary is a critical piece of mystical landscapes, for it "rests on the logic that the more remote, non-Westernised or perhaps not-yet-globalised places are the more 'authentic.'"[131]

Zygmunt Bauman suggests that the modern subject is tempted by the desert and other vacant places, whose "trails are blazed by the destination of the pilgrim."[132] These places are often mystical landscapes. In *Orientalism*, Edward Said asks us to understand space as an entity that "acquires emotional and even rational sense by a kind of poetic process" and to see imaginative geography as something that creates both a sense of history and geography—a product of the colonial mind.[133] The mapping of the world from indigenous and foreign lands into mystical landscapes is a project about this *politics of vision*, what Derek Gregory explains where he writes, " 'sightseeing' has shaped and scripted the routines of tourism."[134]

As discussed earlier, religion has a prominent voice in the formation of landscapes. The desert as a place of contemplation is rooted in the experiences of early Christian monks in the Thebaid, and early maps of Jerusalem were drawn from the Mount of Olives, the place where it was believed that Christ stood and prophesied, which was also the site of his ascension.[135] Because maps are more of a language than a precise science, they form ideas about landscapes that may be religiously charged. These visions of space are so powerful that they can be transposed onto other distant spaces with a similar appearance. One example is the Australian desert, viewed as a site of spiritual and mystical power due to the desert's "divine status" in the Christian imagination and more broadly, its sacred status across other religions popular in the West (including "nature religion").[136]

Research on the links between nature and spiritual experiences that qualify as mystical—transformation, union with the Divine, and enlightenment— often includes the fact that "spirituality" is an idea embedded in Christian consciousness.[137] Judith Adler has written about the long history of the intersection of Christianity and nature. In early Christian monastic literature, the Thebaid was idealized for its mystical qualities and became the "paradise of monks."[138] Adler calls us to be attentive to the "enduring motifs of wilderness romance" that show themselves all over the world.[139] The idea that life's answers are found in nature, whether that be a tropical beach, a mountaintop, or a desert, is at the core of the places examined in this book.

Mystical landscapes and people may indeed exist—a question this book does not fully explore. Europeans and Americans, whether explorers, writers, artists, or tourists, are also not alone in believing that certain spaces and bodies were imbued with something magical, unexplained, or mystical. In one account from Qing China, the Panchen Lama was believed to have a mirror that illuminated different colors, dependent on one's state of mind, and other accounts attributed medical healing and miraculous bodily changes to the religious figure from Tibet.[140]

As noted earlier, the spaces examined in this book range from tropical islands like Tahiti to the mountain region of the Himalayas and the deserts of the American West and North Africa, all of which offer different experiences based on a particular vision of exoticized and mystic environments. Kenya, Morocco, and Algeria have all been framed as having empty places, an expression of *Terra Nullius* (Nobody's Land) that offered a way to legitimize colonial occupation.[141] Nepal began with a mythology that has been monetized for the tourist industry, "Nepal has long existed as a mythical destination for travellers, with many parts of the country now frequently marketed by adventure tour operators as accessible, consumable Orients."[142]

In the mountainous regions of Nepal and Tibet, the imagination prefabricated a space long before tourists traveled there. Tibet was described as Shangri-La, a magical land of "pious noble savages and god-kings" that was both mysterious and somewhat mythical.[143] As Christiaan Klieger notes, "The mystical Western attitude toward Tibet and the conceit of its oracles of occult knowledge is Orientalism at its finest."[144] In Liechty's historical work on Nepal's development as a popular tourism destination, he writes about Michael Hollingshead's impression of Nepal,

> As for so many other tourists, Kathmandu was an "Other" place already largely prefabricated: one had only to reminisce in order to find what they had come "halfway across the world" looking for. It's this prefiguring, or prefabrication of worlds, and the global spatial imaginaries that people

carry with them that intrigue me and, I think, have to be part of our theoretical understandings of the cultural history of tourism.[145]

Islands were identified as examples of paradise on earth. Hawai'i, Bali, and Tahiti are all examples of the "animated foreign imaginings of 'exotic landscapes' that have existed for hundreds of years."[146] When people visit these places, they have a particular set of expectations shaped by colonial history and the business of tourism. As Miriam Kahn has written about Tahiti, "Before setting out, they imagine what they will find: tropical sunshine, warm fragrant air, snow-capped peaks, plunging cliffs, shimmering sand dunes, historical sites, exotic people, or simply a lounge chair by a pool."[147]

Islands were mapped based on Western mythologies about difference and then transformed into tourist capitals that promised mystical experience. As John Connell has written about islands, "Such places demand imaginations, where Bachelard's poetics of space, the systematic study of the sites of our intimate lives, can be realized, both there and afar."[148] Bali's identification as a "dream island" for American military, tourists, and other foreigners is one example of how fantasies can slowly replace the reality of a place.[149]

The desire for a *sublime* experience is often at the center of mystical landscapes. The focus on the human imagination, the paintings of artists like Turner, "whose powerful prospects liberated the observer from his finite limits," and the influence of nineteenth-century Continental and British philosophers all pointed toward the importance of the sublime for the European tourist.[150] Mountains, most notably the Alps, became a popular region where sublime experiences were sought out, but as the numbers of tourists grew, climbers began seeking more isolated places, influencing the interest in travel farther away.[151] Kant's concept of the sublime includes two parts—the mathematical (related to size) and the dynamical (related to awe)—which are seen in the experiences of climbers at Everest who remark on an experience that includes both of these.[152] Researchers have determined that these sublime experiences are, at least in part, due to the effects of physical experiences like sensory deprivation, isolation, and in the case of mountaineering at extreme altitudes, a lack of oxygen.[153]

Mystical landscapes rely on the imaginary created out of colonial violence and the erasure of the past. "Prospective tourists are invited to imagine themselves in a paradisiacal environment, a vanished Eden, where local landscape and population are to be consumed through observation, embodied sensation, and imagination."[154] In the colonial past, indigenous inhabitants were erased from their land in numerous ways. In photos from the Dutch East Indies, the Javanese and servants were included in photographs, but their names were never recorded.[155]

Mystical places are viewed as stuck in the past before the world became disenchanted. The view that the West has moved beyond this condition is a key theme in tourism, seen in the ways the exotic is linked to the past. As one study puts it, this is a business that places "the Other in a timeless present."[156] This denial of common time is central in Johannes Fabian's indictment of anthropologists' tendency to place the subject in the past—a critique that goes far beyond this one discipline.[157] The mystic quest is central to the story of the tourist.

Mystical landscapes not only rely on modes of cultural production like literature and film, but they also are mediated by tourists who have their own visions of the places they visit. As Brooke Schedneck notes, "These imaginaries are transmitted in promotional materials and through any visual or textual medium about a place, including novels, art, movies, postcards, memoirs, and blogs."[158] The chapters in this book include at least one of these visual or textual mediums, which are included to show how colonized spaces are transformed into landscapes that are identified with mystical experience. In the next chapter, Paul Bowles's *The Sheltering Sky* helps us to understand how American tourists Port and Kit experienced the region of North Africa as an imaginary mystical landscape. As one study notes,

> Port's desire to find a desert-space uncorrupted by mechanized modernity might be interpreted as a quest for pure essence or authenticity, which is what some theorists, such as Dean MacCannell in his book *The tourist*, argue is the drive behind travel.[159]

Mystical landscapes are at the center of these tourist quests.

Notes

1 Bandy, 542.
2 Gregory 2003, 197.
3 Kobi Cohen-Hattab, "Zionism, Tourism, and the Battle for Palestine: Tourism as a Political-Propaganda Tool," *Israel Studies* 9, no. 1 (2004): 62.
4 Cohen-Hattab, 64.
5 Lalvani, 263.
6 Vukonić, 7–8.
7 Buzard, 42.
8 Buzard, 41.
9 Bennike, 56.
10 Buzard, 46.
11 See Erik Cohen, "A Phenomenology of Tourist Experiences," *Sociology* 13 (1979): 179–201.
12 Stausberg, 27–28.
13 Richard Sharpley, "Tourism and Spirituality: Green Places, Blue Spaces, and Beyond," in *The Routledge Handbook of Religious and Spiritual Tourism*, ed. Daniel H. Olsen and Dallen J. Timothy (New York: Routledge, 2022), 156, 157.
14 Sharpley 2022, 152.
15 Cohen's "Existential Mode" fits the tourists going to mystical landscapes due to its focus on an "elective" or different, spiritual center outside one's own society.

However, it does not fit all cases of mystical landscapes and mystical tourism. See Cohen 1979, 189–190.

16 Clare A. Gunn, *Vacationscape: Designing Tourist Regions* (New York: Van Nostrand Reinhold, 1988), 86.

17 Gunn, 86.

18 Jane Lovell and Howard Griffin, "Unfamiliar Light: The Production of Enchantment," *Annals of Tourism Research* 92 (2022): 1.

19 Lovell and Griffin, 2.

20 Noel B. Salazar, "Imagineering Otherness: Anthropological Legacies in Contemporary Tourism," *Anthropological Quarterly* 86, no. 3 (2013): 691.

21 Salazar, 869.

22 Maurizio Peleggi, "Consuming Colonial Nostalgia: The Monumentalisation of Historic Hotels in Urban South-East Asia," *Asia Pacific Viewpoints* 46, no. 3 (2005): 261, 263.

23 Edward M. Bruner, "Transformation of Self in Tourism," *Annals of Tourism Research* 18, no. 2 (1991): 240.

24 Jaeyeon Choe and Luh Putu Mahyuni, "Sustainable and Inclusive Spiritual Tourism Development in Bali as a Long-Term Post-Pandemic Strategy," *International Journal of Religious Tourism and Pilgrimage* 11, no. 2 (2023): 180.

25 Tamaira, 1.

26 Brooke Schedneck, "Religious and Spiritual Retreats," in *The Routledge Handbook of Religious and Spiritual Tourism*, ed. Daniel H. Olsen and Dallen J. Timothy (New York: Routledge, 2022), 192.

27 MacCannell 1973, 590.

28 Stephen Brown, "No Then There: Of Time, Space, and the Market," in *Time, Space, and the Market: Retroscapes Rising*, ed. Stephen Brown and John F. Sherry (New York: Routledge, 2015), 3.

29 Bandy, 542.

30 Mark Liechty, "The Key to an Oriental World: Boris Lissanevitch, Kathmandu's Royal Hotel, and the 'Golden Age' of Tourism in Nepal," *Studies in Nepali History and Society* 15, no. 2 (2010): 260.

31 Howard, 355.

32 R. Diyah Larasati, "Eat, Pray, Love Mimic: Female Citizenship and Otherness," *South Asian Popular Culture* 8, no. 1 (2010): 92; (emphasis in original; Gilbert 190).

33 Larasati, 92.

34 Philip J. Deloria, *Playing Indian* (New Haven: Yale University Press, 1998), 101. Dr. Deloria is a member of the Standing Rock Sioux Tribe.

35 Deloria, 101.

36 Roger Edward Norum, "The Unbearable Likeness of Being a Tourist: Expats, Travel and Imaginaries in the Neo-Colonial Orient," *International Review of Social Research* 3, no. 1 (2013): 43. (emphasis in original)

37 Lovell and Griffin, 1.

38 Zygmunt Bauman, *Liquid Modernity* (New York: Polity, 2000), 165.

39 Bruner, 244.

40 Norum, 33.

41 Colin Simpson, *Katmandu* (Sydney: Angus and Robertson, 1967), 1. Quoted in Norum, 33.

42 Nelson Graburn and Naomi M. Leite, "Always in Process: Edward Bruner, American Anthropology, and the Study of Tourism," in *The Ethnography of Tourism: Edward Bruner and Beyond*, ed. Naomi M. Leite, Quetzil E. Castañeda, and Kathleen M. Adams (Lanham: Lexington Books, 2019), 61.

43 George Hughes, "Tourism and the Geographical Imagination," *Leisure Studies* 11, no. 1 (1992): 37.

44 Patricia M. E. Lorkin, "Imperial Nostalgia; Colonial Nostalgia: Differences of Theory, Similarities or Practice?," *Historical Reflections* 39, no. 3 (2013): 103.

45 Paul Lyons, *American Pacificism: Oceania in the U.S. Imagination* (New York: Routledge, 2006), 24.

46 Arjana 2020, 154.

47 Choe and O'Regan, 178–179.

48 Singh, 217.

49 Alex Norman and Jennifer J. Pokorny, "Meditation Retreats: Spiritual Tourism Well-Being Interventions," *Tourism Management Perspectives* 24 (2017): 202.

50 Choe and O'Regan, 179.

51 Alex Norman, *Spiritual Tourism and Religious Practice in Western Society* (London: Continuum, 2011), 20.

52 Choe and O'Regan, 187.

53 Choe and O'Regan, 179.

54 Choe and O'Regan, 179.

55 See Sophia Arjana, *Pilgrimage in Islam: Traditional and Modern Practices* (London: Oneworld Academic, 2017).

56 Richard Scriven, "Geographies of Pilgrimage: Meaningful Movements and Embodied Mobilities," *Geography Compass* 8, no. 4 (2014): 252.

57 Scriven, 251.

58 David L. R. Houston, "Five Miles Out: Communion and Commodification among the Mountaineers," in *Tarzan Was an Eco-Tourist . . . and Other Tales in the Anthropology of Adventure*, ed. Luis Vivanco and Robert Gordon (New York: Berghahn Books, 2006), 151.

59 Jonathon Z. Smith, "Religion, Religions, Religious," in *Critical Terms for Religious Studies*, ed. Mark C. Taylor (Chicago: University of Chicago, 1998), 275–281.

60 Michael Di Giovine and Jaeyeon Choe, "Geographies of Religion and Spirituality: Pilgrimage beyond the 'Officially' Sacred," *Tourism Geographies: An International Journal of Tourism Space, Place, and Environment* 21, no. 3 (2019): 363.

61 George E. Tinker, "Native/First Nation Theology: Response," *Journal of Feminist Studies in Religion* 22, no. 2 (2006): 121.

62 Nick J. Watson, "Nature and Transcendence: The Mystical and Sublime in Extreme Sports," in *Sport and Spirituality: An Introduction*, ed. Jim Parry, Simon Robinson, Nick Watson, and Mark Nesti (New York: Routledge, 2007), 99.

63 Nelson H. Graburn, "Tourism: The Sacred Journey," in *Hosts and Guests: The Anthropology of Tourism*, ed. Valene L. Smith (Philadelphia: University of Pennsylvania Press, 1989), 28–29.

64 Dean MacCannell, *The Tourist: A New Theory of the Leisure Class* (New York: Schocken, 1989), 42.

65 Coleman 2007, 337.

66 Bauman 1996, 29.

67 Singh, 215.

68 MacCannell 1989, 13.

69 Sean Gammon, "Chapter 2: Secular Pilgrimage and Sport Tourism," in *Sport Tourism: Interrelationships, Impacts and Issues*, ed. Brent W. Richie and Daryl Adair (Clevedon: Channel View Publications, 2004), 32.

70 Richard Sharpley and Priya Sundaram, "Tourism: A Sacred Journey? The Case of Ashram Tourism, India," *International Journal of Tourism Research* 7 (2005): 164.

71 Daniel H. Olsen, "Religious Tourism: A Spiritual or Touristic Experience?," in *Routledge Handbook of Tourist Experience*, ed. Richard Sharpley (New York: Routledge, 2022), 394.

72 Hughes, 32.

73 Hughes, 32.

74 MacCannell 1973, 593.

75 MacCannell 1973, 593.

76 Erik Cohen, "Pilgrimage and Tourism: Convergence or Divergence," in *Sacred Journeys: The Anthropology of Tourism*, ed. Alan Morinis (Westport: Greenwood Press, 1992), 50–51.

77 Cohen 1992, 68.

78 Hughes, 39.

79 Singh, 216.

80 Singh, 216.

81 Turner, 213.

82 Howard, 358.

83 Salazar 2012, 868.

84 Shelton, 156.

85 Ivakhiv, 45.

86 Anand, 36.

87 Ruth Williams, "*Eat, Pray, Love*: Producing the Female Neoliberal Spiritual Subject," *The Journal of Popular Culture* 47, no. 3 (2014): 617. See Chapter 5 for a discussion of how Indonesia has been forced to re-create an authentic Bali.

88 Ahmed, 162.

89 Thomas R. Knipp, "Kenya's Literary Ladies and the Mythologizing of the White Highlands," *South Atlantic Review* 55, no. 1 (1990): 3. Quoted in Lewis, 65.

90 Picard 1990, 74.

91 Kendra Marston, "The World Is Her Oyster: Negotiating Contemporary White Womanhood in Hollywood's Tourist Spaces," *Cinema Journal* 55, no. 4 (2016): 21.

92 Ahmed, 158.

93 Howard, 362.

94 Howard, 368.

95 Jaeyeon Choe and Michael O'Regan, "Faith Manifest: Spiritual and Mindfulness Tourism in Chiang Mai, Thailand," *Religions* 11, no. 4 (2020): 185.

96 John O'Carroll, "The Island after Plato: A 'Western' Amnesia," *Southern Review* 31, no. 3 (1998): 165.

97 W. H. Pearson, "Intimidation and the Myth of Tahiti," *Journal of Pacific History* 4 (1969): 200.

98 Marston, 10.

99 Jean-Didier Urbain, "The Tourist Adventure and His Images," *Annals of Tourism Research* 16 (1989): 110. (emphasis in original)

100 Norman 2011, 17.

101 Norman 2011, 188.

102 Norum, 43.

103 Arjana 2020, 50.

104 Shamma, 125.

105 Salazar 2012, 872.

106 Taylor 2002, 91.

107 Williams, 627.

108 Dean MacCannell, "The Ego Factor in Tourism," *Journal of Consumer Research* 29, no. 1 (2002): 147.

109 MacCannell, 147.

110 Ethel L. Mickey, "'Eat, Pray, Love Bullshit': Women's Empowerment through Wellness at an Elite Professional Conference," *Journal of Contemporary Ethnography* 48, no. 1 (2018): 18.

111 Anca-Luminata Iancu, "Spaces of Their Own: Emotional and Spiritual Quests in *Under the Tuscan Sun* and *Eat, Pray, Love*," *Journal of Research in Gender Studies* 4, no.1 (2014): 440.
112 Marston, 3.
113 Urbain, 112.
114 Harald Friedl, " 'Places of Power': Can Individual 'Sacred Space' Help Regain Orientation in a Confusing World?: A Discussion of Mental Health Tourism to Extraordinary Natural Sites in the Context of Antonovsky's 'Sense of Coherence' and Maslow's 'Hierarchy of Needs,' " in *The Routledge Handbook of Health Tourism*, ed. Melanie Kay Smith and László Puckzó (New York: Routledge, 2017), 358.
115 Miriam Kahn, "Tahiti Intertwined: Ancestral Land, Tourist Postcard, and Nuclear Test Site," *American Anthropologist* 102, no. 1 (2000): 8.
116 Barbara Bender, "Place and Landscape," in *Handbook of Material Culture*, ed. Christopher Tilley, Webb Keane, Susanne Küchler, Michael Rowlands, and Patricia Spyer (SAGE Publications, 2006), 307.
117 Bender, 307.
118 John Urry, *The Tourist Gaze* (London: SAGE Publications, 2002), 1.
119 Urry 2002, 3.
120 Yamashita, 15.
121 Wolf Sternberger, *Panorama, Oder Ansichten Vom 19. Jahrhundert* (Hamburg, 1955) (English version published as *Panorama of the Nineteenth Century* [New York: Urizen Books, 1977]), 53. Quoted in Yamashita, 15.
122 Alexa Weik von Mossner, "Encountering the Sahara: Embodiment, Emotion, and Material Agency in Paul Bowles's *The Sheltering Sky*," in *Environmental Awareness and the Design of Literature*, ed. Francois Specq (Leiden: Brill, 2016), 119.
123 Blake Leyerle, "Landscape as Cartography in Early Christian Pilgrimage Narratives," *Journal of the American Academy of Religion* 64, no. 1 (1996): 129.
124 Leyerle, 129.
125 Robinson 2016, 59.
126 Tamara Bellone, Salvatore Engel-Di Mauro, Francesco Fiermonte, Emiliana Armano, and Linda Quiquivix, "Mapping as Tacit Representations of the Colonial Gaze," in *Mapping Crisis: Participation, Datafication and Humanitarianism in the Age of Digital Mapping*, ed. Doug Specht (London: University of London Press, 2020), 19.
127 Leyerle, 120.
128 Leyerle, 125.
129 Gregory, 195.
130 Liechty 2017, 4.
131 Howard, 360.
132 Bauman 1996, 21.
133 Said 1978, 55.
134 Gregory 2003, 195.
135 Rehav Rubin, "Ideology and Landscape in Early Printed Maps of Jerusalem," in *Ideology and Landscape in Historic Perspective: Essays on the Meanings of Some Places in the Past*, ed. Alan R. H. Baker and Gideon Biger (Cambridge: Cambridge University Press, 1992), 19.
136 Yamini Narayanan and Jim Macbeth, "Deep in the Desert: Merging the Desert and the Spiritual through 4WD Tourism," *Tourism Geographies* 11, no. 3 (2009): 373.
137 Paul Heintzman, "Nature-Based Recreation and Spirituality: A Complex Relationship," *Leisure Sciences* 32, no. 1 (2009): 73.

138 Judith Adler, "Cultivating Wilderness: Environmentalism and Legacies of Early Christian Asceticism," *Comparative Studies in Society and History* 48, no. 1 (2006): 7–8. The Thebaid is the region of the Egyptian desert where Christian monks went to contemplate God.
139 Adler, 10.
140 Hanung Kim, "Another Tibet at the Heart of Qing China: Location of Tibetan Buddhism in the Mentality of the Qing Chinese Mind at Jehol," in *Greater Tibet: An Examination of Borders, Ethnic Boundaries, and Cultural Areas*, ed. P. Christiaan Klieger (Lanham: Rowman & Littlefield, 2015), 50.
141 Mohammed Saissi, "The Symptoms of Orientalism in Pre-Contemporary Western Travel Writings on Morocco," *International Uni-Scientific Research Journal* (2021): n.p.
142 Norum, 30.
143 P. Christiaan Klieger, "Research Notes: Shangri-La and the Politicization of Tourism in Tibet," *Annals of Tourism Research* 19 (1992): 122.
144 Klieger, 123.
145 Liechty 2005, 27. See also Michael Hollingshead, *The Man Who Turned on the World* (London: Blond and Briggs, 1973).
146 Siobhan McDonnell, "Selling 'Sites of Desire': Paradise in Reality Television, Tourism, and Real Estate Promotion in Vanuatu," *The Contemporary Pacific* 30, no. 2 (2018): 413.
147 Miriam Kahn, "Tahiti: The Ripples of a Myth on the Shores of the Imagination," *History and Anthropology* 14, no. 4 (2003): 307.
148 Connell, 555.
149 Hitchcock, 25.
150 Ann C. Colley, *Victorians in the Mountains: Sinking the Sublime* (Burlington, VT: Ashgate, 2010), 14.
151 Colley, 37, 39.
152 Watson, 107–108.
153 Watson, 110.
154 Salazar 2012, 866.
155 Stoler, 190.
156 Mary Louise Pratt, "Scratches on the Face of the Country: Or, What Mr. Barrow Saw in the Land of the Bushmen," *Critical Inquiry* 12, no. 1 (1985): 120.
157 See Fabian.
158 Brooke Schedneck, *Thailand's International Meditation Centers: Tourism and the Global Commodification of Religious Practices* (New York: Routledge, 2017), 9–10.
159 Mat McCann, "Tourism, Difference and Authenticity in an Age of Anxiety: Paul Bowles' *The Sheltering Sky*," in *Lit & Tour: Ensaios Sobre Literatura E Turismo*, ed. Sílvia Quintero and Rita Baleiro (Famalicão: Edições Húmus, 2014), 154.

Bibliography

Adler, Judith. "Cultivating Wilderness: Environmentalism and Legacies of Early Christian Asceticism." *Comparative Studies in Society and History* 48, no. 1 (2006): 4–37.
Ahmed, Sara. "A Phenomenology of Whiteness." *Feminist Theory* 8, no. 2 (2007): 149–168.
Anand, Dibyesh. "Western Colonial Representations of the Other: The Case of Exotica Tibet." *New Political Science* 29, no. 1 (2007): 23–42.

Arjana, Sophia. *Pilgrimage in Islam: Traditional and Modern Practices*. London: Oneworld, 2017.

Arjana, Sophia. *Buying Buddha, Selling Rumi: Orientalism and the Mystical Marketplace*. London: Oneworld, 2020.

Bandy, Joe. "Managing the Other of Nature: Sustainability, Spectacle, and Global Regimes of Capital in Ecotourism." *Public Culture* 8 (1996): 539–566.

Bauman, Zygmunt. "From Pilgrim to Tourist: Or a Short History of Identity." In *Questions of Cultural Identity*, edited by Stuart Hall and Paul Du Gay, 18–36. London: Sage, 1996.

Bauman, Zygmunt. *Liquid Modernity*. New York: Polity, 2000.

Bellone, Tamara, Salvatore Engel-Di Mauro, Francesco Fiermonte, Emiliana Armano, and Linda Quiquivix. "Mapping as Tacit Representations of the Colonial Gaze." In *Mapping Crisis: Participation, Datafication and Humanitarianism in the Age of Digital Mapping*, edited by Doug Specht, 17–37. London: University of London Press, 2020.

Bender, Barbara. "Place and Landscape." In *Handbook of Material Culture*, edited by Christopher Tilley, Webb Keane, Susanne Küchler, Michael Rowlands, and Patricia Spyer, 303–314. London: Sage Publications, 2006.

Bennike, Rune. "'A Summer Place': Darjeeling in the Tourist Gaze." In *Darjeeling Reconsidered: Histories, Politics, Environments*, edited by Townsend Middleton and Sara Shneidermann, 54–73. New York: Oxford University Press, 2018.

Brown, Stephen. "No Then There: Of Time, Space, and the Market." In *Time, Space, and the Market: Retroscapes Rising*, edited by Stephen Brown and John F. Sherry, Jr. New York: Routledge, 2015.

Bruner, Edward M. "Transformation of Self in Tourism." *Annals of Tourism Research* 18, no. 2 (1991): 238–250.

Buzard, James. *The Beaten Track: European Tourism, Literature, and the Way to 'Culture,' 1800–1918*. New York: Oxford University Press, 1993.

Choe, Jaeyeon and Luh Putu Mahyuni. "Sustainable and Inclusive Spiritual Tourism Development in Bali as a Long-Term Post-Pandemic Strategy." *International Journal of Religious Tourism and Pilgrimage* 11, no. 2 (2023): 100–111.

Choe, Jaeyeon and Michael O'Regan. "Faith Manifest: Spiritual and Mindfulness Tourism in Chiang Mai, Thailand." *Religions* 11, no. 4 (2020): 177–187.

Cohen, Erik. "A Phenomenology of Tourist Experiences." *Sociology* 13 (1979): 179–201.

Cohen, Erik. "Pilgrimage and Tourism: Convergence or Divergence." In *Sacred Journeys: The Anthropology of Tourism*, edited by Alan Morinis, 47–61. Westport: Greenwood Press, 1992.

Cohen-Hattab, Kobi. "Zionism, Tourism, and the Battle for Palestine: Tourism as a Political-Propaganda Tool." *Israel Studies* 9, no. 1 (2004): 61–85.

Coleman, Simon. "A Tale of Two Centres? Representing Palestine to the British in the Nineteenth Century." *Mobilities* 2, no. 3 (2007): 331–345.

Colley, Ann C. *Victorians in the Mountains: Sinking the Sublime*. Burlington, VT: Ashgate, 2010.

Connell, John. "Island Dreaming: The Contemplation of Polynesian Paradise." *Journal of Historical Geography* 29, no. 4 (2003): 554–581.

Deloria, Philip J. *Playing Indian*. New Haven: Yale University Press, 1998.

Di Giovine, Michael and Jaeyeon Choe. "Geographies of Religion and Spirituality: Pilgrimage beyond the 'Officially' Sacred." *Tourism Geographies: An International Journal of Tourism Space, Place and Environment* 21, no. 3 (2019): 361–383.

Fabian, Johannes. *Time and the Other: How Anthropology Makes Its Object*. New York: Columbia University Press, 2014.

Friedl, Harald A. "'Places of Power': Can Individual 'Sacred Space' Help Regain Orientation in a Confusing World?: A Discussion of Mental Health Tourism to Extraordinary Natural Sites in the Context of Antonovsky's 'Sense of Coherence' and Maslow's 'Hierarchy of Needs." In *The Routledge Handbook of Health Tourism*, edited by Melanie Kay Smith and László Puckzó, 347–364. New York: Routledge, 2017.

Gammon, Sean. "Chapter 2: Secular Pilgrimage and Sport Tourism." In *Sport Tourism: Interrelationships, Impacts and Issues*, edited by Brent W. Richie and Daryl Adair, 30–45. Clevedon: Channel View Publications, 2004.

Graburn, Nelson H. "Tourism: The Sacred Journey." In *Hosts and Guests: The Anthropology of Tourism*, edited by Valene L. Smith, 21–36. Philadelphia: University of Pennsylvania Press, 1989.

Graburn, Nelson H. and Naomi M. Leite. "Always in Process: Edward Bruner, American Anthropology, and the Study of Tourism." In *The Ethnography of Tourism: Edward Bruner and Beyond*, edited by Naomi M. Leite, Quetzil E. Castañeda, and Kathleen M. Adams, 49–64. Lanham: Lexington Books, 2019.

Gregory, Derek. "Emperors of the Gaze: Photographic Practices and Productions of Space in Egypt, 1839–1914." In *Picturing Place: Photography and the Geographical Imagination*, edited by Joan M. Schwartz and James R. Ryan, 196–225. New York: I.B. Tauris, 2003.

Gunn, Clare A. *Vacationscape: Designing Tourist Regions*. New York: Van Nostrand Reinhold, 1988.

Heintzman, Paul. "Nature-Based Recreation and Spirituality: A Complex Relationship." *Leisure Sciences* 32, no. 1 (2009): 72–89.

Hitchcock, Michael. *Tourism, Development, and Terrorism in Bali*. New York: Routledge, 2007.

Hollingshead, Michael. *The Man Who Turned on the World*. London: Blond and Briggs, 1973.

Houston, David L. R. "Five Miles Out: Communion and Commodification Among the Mountaineers." In *Tarzan Was an Eco-Tourist . . . and Other Tales in the Anthropology of Adventure*, edited by Luis Vivanco and Robert Gordon, 147–160. New York: Berghahn Books, 2006.

Howard, Christopher A. "Touring the Consumption of the Other: Imaginaries of Authenticity in the Himalayas and Beyond." *Journal of Consumer Culture* 16, no. 2 (2016): 354–373.

Hughes, George. "Tourism and the Geographical Imagination." *Leisure Studies* 11, no. a (1992): 31–42.

Iancu, Anca-Luminata. "Spaces of Their Own: Emotional and Spiritual Quests in *Under the Tuscan Sun* and *Eat, Pray, Love*." *Journal of Research in Gender Studies* 4, no. 1 (2014): 439–452.

Ivakhiv, Adrian J. *Claiming Sacred Ground: Pilgrims and Politics at Glastonbury and Sedona*. Bloomington: Indiana University Press, 2001.

Kahn, Miriam. "Tahiti Intertwined: Ancestral Land, Tourist Postcard, and Nuclear Test Site." *American Anthropologist* 102, no. 1 (2000): 7–26.

Kahn, Miriam. "Tahiti: The Ripples of a Myth on the Shores of the Imagination." *History and Anthropology* 14, no. 4 (2003): 307–326.

Kim, Hanung. "Another Tibet at the Heart of Qing China: Location of Tibetan Buddhism in the Mentality of the Qing Chinese Mind at Jehol." In *Greater Tibet: An Examination of Borders, Ethnic Boundaries, and Cultural Areas*, edited by P. Christiaan Klieger, 37–56. Lanham: Rowman & Littlefield, 2015.

Klieger, P. Christiaan. "Research Notes: Shangri-La and the Politicization of Tourism in Tibet." *Annals of Tourism Research* 19 (1992): 122–124.

Knipp, Thomas R. "Kenya's Literary Ladies and the Mythologizing of the White Highlands." *South Atlantic Review* 55, no. 1 (1990): 1–16.

Lalvani, Suren. "Consuming the Exotic Other." *Critical Studies in Mass Communication* 12 (1995): 263–286.

Larasati, R. Diyah. "Eat, Pray, Love Mimic: Female Citizenship and Otherness." *South Asian Popular Culture* 8, no. 1 (2010): 29–95.

Leyerle, Blake. "Landscape as Cartography in Early Christian Pilgrimage Narratives." *Journal of the American Academy of Religion* 64, no. 1 (1996): 119–134.

Liechty, Mark. "Building the Road to Kathmandu: Notes on the History of Tourism in Nepal." *Himalaya* 25, nos. 1/2 (2005): 19–28.

Liechty, Mark. "The Key to an Oriental World: Boris Lissanevitch, Kathmandu's Royal Hotel and the 'Golden Age' of Tourism in Nepal." *Studies in Nepali History and Society* 15, no. 2 (2010): 253–295.

Liechty, Mark. *Far Out: Countercultural Seekers and the Tourist Encounter in Nepal.* Chicago: The University of Chicago Press, 2017.

Lorkin, Patricia M. E. "Imperial Nostalgia; Colonial Nostalgia: Differences of Theory, Similarities of Practice?" *Historical Reflections* 39, no. 3 (2013): 97–111.

Lovell, Jane and Howard Griffin. "Unfamiliar Light: The Production of Enchantment." *Annals of Tourism Research* 92 (2022): 1–17.

Lyons, Paul. *American Pacificism: Oceania in the U.S. Imagination.* New York: Routledge, 2006.

MacCannell, Dean. "Staged Authenticity: Arrangements of Social Space in Tourist Settings." *American Journal of Sociology* 79, no. 3 (1973): 589–603.

MacCannell, Dean. *The Tourist: A New Theory of the Leisure Class.* New York: Shocken Books, 1989.

MacCannell, Dean. "The Ego Factor in Tourism." *Journal of Consumer Research* 29, no. 1 (2002): 146–151.

Marston, Kendra. "The World Is Her Oyster: Negotiating Contemporary White Womanhood in Hollywood's Tourist Spaces." *Cinema Journal* 55, no. 4 (2016): 3–27.

McCann, Mat. "Tourism, Difference and Authenticity in an Age of Anxiety: Paul Bowles' *The Sheltering Sky.*" In *Lit & Tour: Ensaios Sobre Literatura E Turismo,* edited by Sílvia Quintero and Rita Baleiro, 149–163. Famalicão: Edições Húmus, 2014.

McDonnell, Siobhan. "Selling 'Sites of Desire': Paradise in Reality Television, Tourism, and Real Estate Promotion in Vanuatu." *The Contemporary Pacific* 30, no. 2 (2018): 413–435.

Mickey, Ethel L. "'Eat, Pray, Love' Bullshit': Women's Empowerment through Wellness at an Elite Professional Conference." *Journal of Contemporary Ethnography* 48, no. 1 (2018): 1–25.

Murphy, Ryan, dir. *Eat, Pray, Love.* Columbia Pictures, 2010.

Narayanan, Yamini and Jim Macbeth. "Deep in the Desert: Merging the Desert and the Spiritual through 4WD Tourism." *Tourism Geographies* 11, no. 3 (2009): 369–389.

Norman, Alex. *Spiritual Tourism: Travel and Religious Practice in Western Society.* London: Continuum, 2011.

Norman, Alex and Jennifer J. Pokorny. "Meditation Retreats: Spiritual Tourism Well-Being Interventions." *Tourism Management Perspectives* 24 (2017): 201–207.

Norum, Roger Edward. "The Unbearable Likeness of Being a Tourist: Expats, Travel and Imaginaries in the Neo-colonial Orient." *International Review of Social Research* 3, no. 1 (2013): 27–47.

O'Carroll, John. "The Island after Plato: A 'Western' Amnesia." *Southern Review* 31 no. 3 (1998): 265–281.

Olsen, Daniel H. "Religious Tourism: A Spiritual or Touristic Experience?" In *Routledge Handbook of Tourist Experience,* edited by Richard Sharpley, 391–407. New York: Routledge, 2022.

Pearson, W. H. "Intimidation and the Myth of Tahiti." *The Journal of Pacific History* 4 (1969): 199–217.

Peleggi, Maurizio. "Consuming Colonial Nostalgia: The Monumentalisation of Historic Hotels in Urban South-East Asia." *Asia Pacific Viewpoint* 46, no. 3 (2005): 255–265.

Picard, Michel. "'Cultural Tourism' in Bali: Cultural Performances as Tourist Attraction." *Indonesia* 49 (1990): 37–74.

Pratt, Marie Louise. "Scratches of the Face of the Country; or, What Mr. Barrow Saw in the Land of the Bushmen." *Critical Inquiry* 12, no. 1 (1985): 119–143.

Robinson, Michael F. *The Lost White Tribe: Explorers, Scientists, and the Theory That Changed a Continent.* New York: Oxford University Press, 2016.

Rubin, Rehav. "Ideology and Landscape in Early Printed Maps of Jerusalem." In *Ideology and Landscape in Historical Perspective: Essays on the Meanings of Some Places in the Past*, edited by Alan R. H. Baker and Gideon Biger, 15–30. New York: Cambridge University Press, 1992.

Saissi, Mohammed. "The Symptoms of Orientalism in Pre-Contemporary Western Travel Writings on Morocco." *International Uni-Scientific Research Journal* 2, no. 36 (2021): 240–161.

Salazar, Noel B. "Tourism Imaginaries: A Conceptual Approach." *Annals of Tourism Research* 39, no. 2 (2012): 863–882.

Salazar, Noel B. "Imagineering Otherness: Anthropological Lenses in Contemporary Tourism." *Anthropological Quarterly* 86, no. 3 (2013): 669–696.

Schedneck, Brooke. *Thailand's International Meditation Centers: Tourism and the Global Commodification of Religious Practices.* New York: Routledge, 2017.

Schedneck, Brooke. "Religious and Spiritual Retreats." In *The Routledge Handbook of Religious and Spiritual Tourism*, edited by Daniel H. Olsen and Dallen J. Timothy, 191–203. New York: Routledge, 2022.

Scriven, Richard, "Geographies of Pilgrimage: Meaningful Movements and Embodied Mobilities." *Geography Compass* 8, no. 4 (2014): 249–261.

Shamma, Tarek. "Horror and Likeness: The Quest for the Self and the Imagining of the Other in *The Sheltering Sky*." *Critical Arts* 25, no. 2 (2011): 242–258.

Sharpley, Richard. "Tourism and Spirituality: Green Places, Blue Spaces, and Beyond." In *The Routledge Handbook of Religious and Spiritual Tourism*, edited by Daniel H. Olsen and Dallen J. Timothy, 152–165. New York: Routledge, 2022.

Sharpley, Richard and Priya Sundaram. "Tourism: A Sacred Journey? The Case of Ashram Tourism, India." *International Journal of Tourism Research* 7 (2005): 161–171.

Shelton, Anthony Alan. "Museum Ethnography: An Imperial Science." In *Cultural Encounters: Representing 'Otherness'*, edited by Elizabeth Hallam and Brian V. Street, 157–193. New York: Routledge, 2000.

Simpson, Colin. *Katmandu.* Sydney: Angus and Robertson, 1967.

Singh, Shalini. "Secular Pilgrimages and Sacred Tourism in the Indian Himalayas." *GeoJournal* 64, no. 3 (2005): 215–223.

Smith, Jonathon Z. "Religion, Religions, Religious." In *Critical Terms for Religious Studies*, edited by Mark C. Taylor, 269–284. Chicago: University of Chicago Press, 1998.

Stausberg, Michael. *Religion and Tourism: Crossroads, Destinations and Encounters.* New York: Routledge, 2011.

Sternberger, Dolf. *Panorama, Oder Ansichten Vom 19. Jahrhundert.* Hamburg, 1955 (English version published as *Panorama of the Nineteenth Century.* New York: Urizen Books, 1977).

Stoler, Ann Laura. *Carnal Knowledge and Imperial Power: Race and the Intimate in Colonial Rule.* Berkeley: University of California Press, 2010.

Tamaira, A Marata. "From Full Dusk to Full Tusk: Reimagining the 'Dusky Maiden' through the Visual Arts." *The Contemporary Pacific* 22, no. 1 (2010): 1–35.

Taylor, Charles. "Modern Social Imaginaries." *Public Culture* 14, no. 1 (2002): 91–124.

Tinker, George E. "Native/First Nation Theology: Response." *Journal of Feminist Studies in Religion* 22, no. 2 (2006): 116–121.

Turner, Victor. "The Center Out There: Pilgrim's Goal." *History of Religions* 12, no. 3 (1973): 191–230.

Urbain, Jean-Didier. "The Tourist Adventure and His Images." *Annals of Tourism Research* 16 (1989): 106–118.

Urry, John. *The Tourist Gaze*. London: SAGE Publications, 2002.

Von Mossner, Alexa Weik. "Encountering the Sahara: Embodiment, Emotion, and Material Agency in Paul Bowles's *The Sheltering Sky*." In *Environmental Awareness and the Design of Literature*, edited by Francois Specq, 116–135. Leiden: Brill, 2016.

Vuconíc, Boris. *Tourism and Religion*. New York: Pergamon, 1996.

Watson, Nick J. "Nature and Transcendence: The Mystical and Sublime in Extreme Sports." In *Sport and Spirituality: An Introduction*, edited by Jim Parry, Simon Robinson, Nick Watson, and Mark Nesti, 95–115. New York: Routledge, 2007.

Williams, Ruth. "Eat, Pray, Love: Producing the Female Neoliberal Spiritual Subject." *The Journal of Popular Culture* 47, no. 3 (2014): 613–633.

Yamashita, Shinji. *Bali and Beyond: Explorations in the Anthropology of Tourism*. New York: Bergahn Books, 2003.

3

IMAGINING AFRICA

> Knowledge of the unknown world was mapped as a metaphysics of gender
> violence—not as the expanded recognition of cultural difference—and was
> validated by the new Enlightenment logic of private property and posses-
> sive individualism. In these fantasies, the world is feminized and spatially
> spread for male exploration.[1]
>
> Anne McClintock

Achille Mbembe famously wrote that for the European and American, Africa
exists as an idea, "an incomparable monster, a silent shadow and mute place
of darkness, existing as no more than a lacuna."[2] Hegel's insistence that
Africa was ahistorical, that it had no history except what belonged to the
Asian or European worlds, is an example of this long-held attitude toward
Africa.[3] Ideas about Africa, as Mbembe reminds us, are often focused on
darkness and horror. H. Rider Haggard's novel *She*, discussed at length in a
later chapter, reflects European anxieties about the continent, its people, and
the dangers it purportedly poses. In that book, an invincible queen monster
rules over an underground kingdom of African cannibals. Africanism—the
European imagination about Africa—is present in this text and many others,
creating a map of Africa full of darkness and horror.[4]

Race lies at the center of European and American beliefs about Africa, seen
in the ways Africans were treated and written about by white colonial settlers and in the way African immigrants from former colonies have been, and
continue to be, treated in Europe. Represented as both monsters and sexual
objects, Africans have been subjected to levels of dehumanization that would
be unbelievable were they not etched in the pages of history. Race also works

DOI: 10.4324/9781003361725-4

in the imagination about Africa through the fantasies about lost white civilizations. These myths place whiteness at the center of the continent—as the *raison d'être* for Africa's greatness. Among these tales are the white Africans of Gambaragara encountered by Henry Morgan Stanley, the character Prester John (who ruled over an East African kingdom), and the ancient Hebrew or Mediterranean people who built Zimbaoë ("Great Zimbabwe").[5] Tales of the Lost Tribes of Israel included Africa, which were popular among Europeans. The Portuguese claimed that tribes in South America were descendants of one these tribes; a rabbi published a book about it, titled *Esperança de Israel* (*Spes Israelis*) (c. 1650).[6]

Today, Africa is linked to tourist imaginaries about adventure, the danger of the safari, and the risks of the African bush. As an adventure experience, Africa ticks off many of the boxes for the tourist, who has a certain level of uncertainty about what they might experience.[7] Tourist imaginaries originate in colonial literature. Semi-autobiographical and fictionalized treatments of Europeans in Africa often include tragedies such as the loss of a lover (in the case of Karen Blixen in *Out of Africa*) or the death of a main character (as in the death of Port in Paul Bowles's *The Sheltering Sky*). In these novels, the landscape becomes a European space through colonialism. As one scholar reminds us, Victorians adopted places through "the masterful narrative converting local landscape into European knowledge."[8] One of these adoptees is Karen, the suburb in Nairobi named after Karen Blixen.

The formation of tourist imaginaries, which include mystical landscapes, relies on Africa's incredible beauty. Landscape and bodies are often co-identified. As Yosefa Loshitzky has explained, "Africa is both convivial and hostile, hospitable and rejecting, unpolluted and fly infested. Africans are both ravishingly winsome and grotesquely repulsive. They have healthy, sculpted bodies or degenerate, demonized ones."[9]

African bodies, simultaneously seen as hostile figures and decorative motifs, are found in places that Europeans mapped as remote, desolate, and empty of civilization. Jarrod Hore calls this the "disembodied vision on nature."[10] In these cases, indigenous inhabitants were either separated (erased) from their lands or represented in problematic depictions, such as the monsters of Africa and the barbaric Indians of North America. As Hore explains,

> The settler obsession with land and territory necessitated its presentation as empty and available, which in turn put pressure on the depiction of certain types of bodies in landscapes. These pressures led to a kind of visual partition between ethnographic and wilderness visions of the same places.[11]

The colonial division of Africa into regions like North Africa, West Africa, and Sub-Saharan Africa reflect histories of European occupation and settlement. Africa is typically understood as two large regions located north and south of the Sahara.[12] Such a vision erases the history of trade, community, family, and lineages across the desert as if they had not existed for hundreds or even thousands of years. True African histories were often irrelevant in the production of a new vision of landscapes.

This chapter focuses on Kenya, Algeria, and Morocco (with minor attention given to Tunisia). Kenya is an important mystical landscape, formulated through British colonialism, literature, and the safari. African landscapes eventually became tourist spaces that include *nature-based tourism*, which relies on ideas like periphery, undeveloped, and remote, the very ideas central to colonial settlers and the denial of African control over the land.[13] Tourists who are not solely interested in leisure (i.e., lying on a beach) are often interested in more meaningful experiences. For these individuals, "their personal identity is formed and informed by the search for spiritual and transcendental experiences that provide meaning."[14] This is the kind of tourism we find in Kenya's safari business.

The Maghreb is the other focus of this chapter. The French colonial history of this region (1830–1962) began with the occupation of Algeria in 1830 and spread to neighboring areas.[15] The French theory of desertification (the destruction of the environment by the Arabs) was a critical part of the colonial project. It relied on Biblical views of an ancient land of Edenic gardens ruined by the Arabs and their land practices. Diana Davis describes this as a "colonial environmental history" that sought to return the Maghreb to its former glory as the most fertile and agriculturally rich place on earth.[16] From France's point of view, Europeans were destined to restore Algeria and other colonies to their former Roman glory.

Algeria, Morocco, and Tunisia were all linked through the French occupation and then became connected through tourism. Thomas Cook & Son first opened an office in Algiers in 1887, and then in 1902 in Tunis.[17] The *Compagnie Générale Transatlantique* (CGT), a colonial fleet that served ports along the coast, made all this possible as a critical part of the tourism industry in the region. The linking of France with Algiers, Oran, and other cities illustrates just how tourism was an appendage of colonialism, of the French *la mission civilisatrice*, something seen throughout this book in many places.[18] When the French had the centennial of 100 years of rule in Algeria in 1930, it was no surprise that these events were also hugely lucrative for tourism.[19] Algeria was also popular with the English, who comprised many of the tourists to Algiers before 1914 and had their own newspaper, church, and Anglican and Scots Presbyterian clerics.[20]

Colonial nostalgia is a powerful part of the mystical landscapes that bring tourists to Africa today. Kenya's safari business is steeped in nostalgia through hotel design, clothing, advertising, and offerings at resorts—such as watching the film *Out of Africa* (1985) in the place it was written.

Morocco, the most popular country for tourists in the Maghreb, also relies on Orientalist tropes that allow tourists to "discover" the country through "ideas about Morocco" or what scholars have called "a series of 'Moroccan dreams.'"[21]

Books about Africa's mystical landscapes are often focused on European and American lives, with the landscape and its indigenous population serving as a kind of "*mise en scène* for the personal drama of white people."[22] In Africa, tourism was formulated by colonial ideas about mystical landscapes linked to personal transformation. The landscapes of Africa, including the Kenyan savannah and the Maghrebi desert, are imagined as dangerous, seductive, and religiously charged spaces where Europeans and Americans love, fight, and die on a continent that is not theirs. We begin with two novels that reflect these ideas, describing different parts of the continent through the desires of foreigners—one a European settler, and the other, tourists seeking a temporary home. *Out of Africa* and *The Sheltering Sky* are very different texts, but they share a longing for meaning in a world that had lost its spiritual compass.

Out of Africa and *The Sheltering Sky*

Out of Africa

Perhaps no book or film is as important in the *imaginaire* about Kenya as *Out of Africa*. As Susan Hardy Aiken writes, "'I had a farm in Africa.' The famous words, alluring microcosm of the book they begin, have repeatedly transported Anglo-American readers to the lost paradise that forms the mythic subtext of Out of Africa."[23] This autobiographical book by Isak Dinesen presents the settler as existing outside of the colonial world that she lived and benefited from. As Simon Lewis explains,

> The occupation of farming by whites in Africa—even if those whites saw themselves as independent and idealist aristocrats—was a significant part of the general colonial occupation of the land; while individual farmers, like Karen Blixen, might present their struggles with drought, disease, etc. as elemental, those struggles are also economic.[24]

Penned by the colonial settler Karen Blixen, the novel tells a story of Karen, her lovers, and the benevolent guardianship of her employees. In Dinesen's life, her employees were disenfranchised from their land by violent colonial policies. In several places, she describes her love for African things; in these instances, African people are listed as possessions. In one place, she describes what she loves: "this lovely country, my dear natives, my horses and dogs" and in another, the things she uses, "my black folk, guns, and dogs."[25] While her affection is expressed throughout the book, it is a colonial affection. As Annie Gagiano explains,

> That she did earn the genuine devotion of many Kenyans seems undeniable. But her fondness for the possessive pronoun in expressions such as "my people" is dubious. These are expressions of (her) commitment and recognition (of Kenyan people), and simultaneously a demotion of those to whom she refers.[26]

The ways in which Blixen thinks of Africa as *naturally hers* are part of a larger set of problematic ways she views Africans. She creates an "emotional relationship between the created self and the land" which is a land that is not really hers.[27] But the way she Otherizes the African is of more concern. Like anthropologists of the past, Blixen places the indigenous people of Kenya in a different time, denying that she and they exist in the same space. Blixen places the African in a world "before culture" and even includes "references to passions that smell 'of the stone age' and to a Kikuyu sense of justice unchanged for two thousand years."[28]

Blixen is strongly maternalistic and at times even goes as far to refer to Africans as "my boys" and "my squatters." The possessives used throughout the book are part of a larger framing of Africa as belonging to Blixen as the "master" and "husbandman" of her colonized land.[29] As Susan Hardy Aiken points out, she also makes claims about being everyone's friend, a brother, a sister, a mother, where the " 'I' here constitutes herself as subject by becoming an Adamic namer in this latter-day Eden."[30]

The extent to which Blixen dehumanizes local Africans is situated in the way the land is viewed, filled with strange creatures, both animal and human. At one point, Blixen writes of "the discovery of the dark races," and in another place, she talks of "[t]he old dark clear-eyed Native of Africa, and the old clear-eyed elephant—they are alike."[31] This kind of sentiment about non-Europeans was common among white settlers, who were horrified by the large numbers of Indians moving into the colony (by 1921, Europeans were outnumbered 2 to 1), and as one English writer and colonist put it, "If the colonisation of Africa is to be a success it must be entrusted to the best among the colonising race, not to the remittance man and the indentured coolie."[32]

Like other colonial writers, Blixen created the landscape that she claims, which was a foreign place—in this case, Africa. The efforts of white settlers to create a European space on African soil were extensive and at times, stunted by the realities of colonial life. As Terence Ranger explains,

> Few whites in Africa, however, maintained domestic establishments of a size which would have allowed the full "traditional" panoply of the British

servant hierarchy. A more elaborate application of European neo-traditions of subordination came with the restructuring of African armies.[33]

The challenges were enormous; despite this, fantasies about an English lifestyle often mediated people's misery. The horseback ride at dawn, polo matches, and the safari were all distractions from the realities of settler life.[34] Like many other settlers, Blixen was eventually defeated—by "dysentery, droughts, locusts, slump" and personal costs, all exposing the "fragility of settler ambition."[35]

The ease with which Blixen writes of her African farm and her Africans ignores a colonial history that included stealing land from local Africans. Blixen writes adoringly of the Africans in her care, and she was not physically abusive toward the Kikuyu. However, when the Mau Mau movement emerges a few decades later, with the slogan "land and freedom," it results in over 20,000 Africans being killed, 1,090 of these in public hangings by the British government.[36]

Blixen is one example of how the erasure of Africans and their experiences, hopes, dreams, and triumphs helped to remap the land as a European space. Often this mapping included outrageous fantasies of adventure. Florence Riddell's *Kenya Mist* includes a scene where "Michaela Dundas pushes a pram with her illegitimate child in it across the African 'veldt' while carrying a rifle to protect against lion attacks."[37] Civilizing the landscape, through a pram and rifle, planting English flowers, or having high tea were all common motifs. Jay Mary Arthur's study of the settler colonists in Australia includes the observation that, "to use the lexicon of the *un*land is to see the country as *potentially* fenced, grazed, drained, cleared, populated, known, explored, discovered, named, and so on—potentially colonised. The place is deficient because it is not colonised."[38]

Blixen's novel is an example of Fabian's denial of coeval time, where the subject (the African) is denied the same temporal space as the producer of knowledge through the colonial gaze. An effective colonial strategy, white settlers "temporalized" the space they inhabited, spatialized time, resulting in landscapes being subjected to "new versions of territoriality."[39] Africa ceased to become a place attached to the space and time of Africans and became something quite different—a landscape modeled upon European visions of space. In modern Kenya, colonial nostalgia is the dominant way tourists think of themselves in Africa, a land imagined as a place full of adventure, danger, and mystical power.

The Sheltering Sky

Paul Bowles lived in Morocco as an expatriate for many years. Although his writings include references to the country, its cities of Marrakesh and

Fez, and its landscape, the novel *The Sheltering Sky* is his most famous. Set in Algeria, it is based on his experiences in both Morocco and Algeria. *The Sheltering Sky* was made into a film directed by Bernardo Bertolucci that explores the disintegrating relationship of a wealthy couple, Port and Kit Moresby, who travel to Algeria to immerse themselves in the Orient, a landscape viewed as a salvation for the ills of Western modernity. As one study notes, "Their cold relationship belies their loveless and arid marriage which is emblematic of psychological and social malaise which is a byproduct of Western post-war civilization."[40]

Maps figure prominently in both the text and film. The desert, as well as the entire region of North Africa, is viewed as a place that exists for the purposes of the European and American traveler. The Sahara is a main character, a place that is both the tableau on which Port and Kit's anxieties, fears, and desires are played out and an active agent. The desert ultimately kills Port, who dies an agonizing death, far away from the civilization of European-occupied cities, and Kit loses her mind at the end of the book in the Sahara.

Port feels he belongs nowhere and everywhere.[41] The world is there for him to experience, reflecting a world in which colonial mapping includes the enjoyment of foreign territories and foreign bodies. Biskra, the Algerian desert city promoted by the French as a tourist destination in the late nineteenth century, boasting naked women, singers, dancers, and prostitutes, was an early example of the sensual desert experience available to foreign men.[42] In the novel, Port experienced what had long been promised to European and American tourists.

The story and film reflect Orientalism's focus on the seductive enticement of the East, which when held at a distance, provides exotic and pleasurable enjoyment, but when engaged with directly, can be deadly. In the film, when Port engages with a prostitute, he is severely beaten; later in the film when he lies dying of typhoid, the sounds of the Qur'an in the call to prayer are heard, signifying the dangers of immersing oneself in a Muslim land. These episodes represent the "tragic consequences of this transition" from West to East.[43] With scenes of the desert, veiled women, Arabic music, and a Muslim villain, Bertloucci uses Orientalist conventions throughout the film. The seduction by the prostitute is one of the most obvious examples linking sensuality with the East: "Marhnia dances to the psychedelic tunes of local music as she takes off her upper garment."[44]

Analyses of the novel and film point to the ways that the characters use the Orient to escape from their unsatisfactory and empty lives, a common trope in narratives of mystical tourism. In *The Sheltering Sky*, the search for enchantment is complicated by the realities of colonial rule. France's brutality in North Africa included several massacres that took place while Bowles was living there as an expatriate. In 1943, the French killed thousands of Tunisians protesting the deposing of Moncef Bey; in 1945, they killed thousands of Algerians in other protests; and in 1947, they killed hundreds in Casablanca.[45]

The characters show an "inability to question the political implications of their actions and the practices of colonial rule," while the text and film function as "a cautionary tale against stereotypical ethnocentric narratives about immersing oneself in exotic cultures to escape one's existential, social, psychological, or even sexual dilemmas."[46] Beyond the means of escape, which provides a model of mystical tourism, the novel and film also present the Orient as a penetrable space. Yosefa Loshitzky describes how this penetration is expressed in violent detail, the "penetration into the Sahara and Africa" mirroring the penetration of a prostitute by Port and the rape of Kit by a Muslim Tuareg.[47]

In the end, the main characters, Port and Kit, face tragic consequences because of their search for enchantment. In Port's case, he loses his life. Kit winds up in a relationship with Belqassim, a local tribesman, after she goes native. In a disturbing scene, he holds her down in a violent sexual encounter (a rape).[48] This is the consequence for an American going native in an Islamic space.[49] Both the novel and film express the "fantasies and fetishness of Oriental/African/Arab/Otherness, most of them concerned with the hypersexualization and hypersensualization of the Other."[50]

The desert is a main character in the book and film. In the film, it serves as a representation of the character's journey inwards—a tactile image of the spiritual quest often attached to places like Algeria. As Kit descends into madness in her quest for meaning, this journey is illustrated through the desert, "a geographic metaphor for the private id of the heroine as well as for the collective id of Western civilization."[51] Apart from the Freudian analyses of Port and Kit's journey into the desert, it is an example of pioneering that requires the erasure of Africans (much like Blixen's). The desert is a transformative space precisely because it is viewed as empty. Brian Edwards explains how Bowles utilizes the frontier thesis in the novel; this is "the translatability of the American frontier."[52]

At the end of the film, Kit has a nervous breakdown, hardly able to speak when her friend Tunner finds her in a hospital, where she is receiving care after being beaten by Belqassim's wives. The sheltering sky has fallen and permanently damaged her, represented by one of the final scenes of the film. Kit wanders into a café, meets Paul Bowles, and when he asks her if she is lost, she replies "Yes." The desert has "the upper hand in the struggle between wilderness and civilization."[53] This struggle communicates the idea of the strange, mysterious, and powerful Orient, which is safer when held at the militarized distance modeled by colonial power. Today, tourists experience the desert in a decolonized Morocco, seeking the mystical landscape created by the Western imagination.

Mapping Africa

All maps "tell us 'where we are'" but more importantly, maps are "descriptions of cultural as well as natural terrain."[54] The European mapping of Africa says more about European ideas of race and gender than about Africa or her people. Europe still has a hold on the continent in various ways. Even intellectually, Africans are linked to Europe unjustly. As Anthony Appiah reminds us, postcolonial African writers are "almost entirely dependent for their support on two institutions: the African university—an institution whose intellectual life is overwhelmingly constituted as Western—and the Euro-American publisher and reader."[55]

Joseph Massad uses the word *ethnopornography* to categorize the lurid, erotic, exaggerated, and salacious ways that Europeans think about foreign bodies and their desires.[56] He argues that the interest in the sex lives of colonized (and any non-European) people included the work of anthropologists studying "Africa, Asia, Australia, and the Americas."[57] When Africa was viewed with this lens, the results included mythologies about African bodies that have persisted for centuries.

The story of Saartjie (Sarah) Baartman (also known as the Venus of Hottentot) is a horror story that emerges from the history of French colonialism in Africa, her genitals dissected after her death to claim she was deformed (which of course she was not), culminating in Napoleon's surgeon general describing her organs as "closer to those of a monkey" in a sick attempt to argue for white supremacy.[58] The anthropologist and historian of Oceania Greg Dening began his 2003 essay on the future of academia with her story and colonialism's links to anthropology, history, and other disciplines: "She had been paraded on the stages in Piccadilly, Bartholemew's Fair, the Haymerket, and in aristocratic salons. She was made to squat and bend and stride by her trainer, the better to expose her protruding buttocks and enlarged genitals," and as Dening reminds us, "the Hottentots were the soft porn of empire."[59]

This crime reflected not only French beliefs about race, beauty, monstrosity, and aesthetics, but also a larger European system of thought that was inspired by Enlightenment evolutionary theory. As Partha Mitter explains, "By the 1850s, black had come to symbolize evil and degraded, the very opposite of chaste white."[60] The myth of the Hottentot tribe from southern Africa included claims that they were the "missing link" in human evolution, and Sarah was displayed alongside animals, "fairground creatures."[61] The comparisons to animals included Geoffrey Saint-Hilaire's claim that her face was like an orangutang and her behind like the mandrill monkey, placing her between the human and monkey families.[62]

France's practice of taking captive Africans back to France included children brought home as house pets. As Robin Mitchell documents in her book on French attitudes toward girls and women from the colonies, "Eighteenth-century French nobility delighted in keeping black children as the equivalent of house pets."[63] The *incomparable monster* Mbembe refers to at the opening of this chapter is France, not Africa. Mbembe's statement about Africa is also reflected in colonial cartography. As LeFebvre remarked,

> However, the essentialization of Africa on the basis on the basis of distinct ethnic groups evacuated all local political realities and erased all historical perspective in favor of a logic that presented human organizations in Africa as based on fundamentally immutable family structures.[64]

While horrors were being inflicted on Africa's people, Europeans were pillaging the continent of its resources. Its cultural treasures ended up in the private collections of wealthy Europeans or in museums. One example is "the British Museum's cataloging of African art seized during the punitive expedition against Benin."[65] These colonial constructions of the continent shaped the way we view Africa today, particularly its natural resources. Because tourism has been shaped by these constructions, we can see how the standard set of expectations revolve around the same ideas established hundreds of years ago—exoticism and adventure. As one study explains,

> These tactics of marketing nature through adventure, surprise, exhilaration, scarcity, and exotic Edenic scenes assist in spectacularizing nature as a commodity, appropriating more generalized interests in exhilarating consumption and nature as a place of ecological reconnection.[66]

Peter Merrington links pageantry to these practices, which become part of early tourism on the continent, where "people and places become types and backdrops."[67]

European constructions of the continent and its people were also seen in museum exhibits, which were organized according to the evolutionary system that had been in vogue since the Enlightenment. The British Museum's collections used the concept of the "primitive" in their classification system and the Bristol Museum had a room that focused on ethnography and the division of its artifacts "according to their racial origins."[68] Predictably, African cultures were explained due to the gloomy, dirty, smelly, and noxious environment they occupied, which highlighted the "ugly" and "barbaric" African people and their "deformed, crude, degenerative, and ugly" art.[69] These same ideas were imposed upon Americans of African descent in the United States, who were described as childlike and violent.[70]

Attempts to overturn this negative view of the African continent and her people came much later through African anthropologists, who challenged colonial anthropology and its racist systems of classification. As Adebayo

Olukoshi and Francis Nyamnjoh explain, the postcolonial turn in African anthropology is linked to Pan-Africanism,

> Mafeje spent the best part of his life contesting the racialized epistemological underpinnings of a system of social knowledge production into which Africans have been co-opted and schooled as passive consumers without voice even on matters pertaining to their very own realities and existence.[71]

Negative depictions of Africans are found in all kinds of literary texts. Pierre Loti (Louis Marie-Julien Viadud) is a writer whose works include *The Marriage of Loti* (1878), discussed in Chapter 6, and *Aziyadé* (1876), discussed in Chapter 7. Both novels place the author in love affairs with foreign women (a Polynesian and a Turkish harem girl, respectively). In *Aziyadé*, he describes an African woman as "hideous" and "like a monkey."[72] This character is contrasted to the beauty of the light-skinned Aziyadé, whose eyes were "that shade of sea green, which was celebrated in the past by the poets."[73]

As discussed earlier, the *beautiful* Africans were light-skinned, like the white tribe that lived on the slopes of Gambaragara who Stanley supposedly encountered. The details about these people were sketchy, but they supposedly retreated to the mountain's "snowy summit, where high walls of rock surrounded a crater lake hundreds of yards in diameter."[74] Later this story was revised, when it was clear that humans did not live at these high altitudes, but the other important point is that the Gambaragara people lived in a secret place, much like other stories about "discovered" and "special" people—an African Shangri-La.

It was these *geographical imaginations* about the continent that created spaces in which mystical landscapes flourished. As one study explains, "Geographical imaginations refers to our mental images or perspectives of peoples and places that are inherently imbued with the politics of representation."[75] In Africa, the geographical imagination includes ideas about African landscapes imbued with mysticism, often through nature mysticism and the perceived differences of African and European cultures and people. Capitalism perceives the natural environment as a product that exists for monetization. As Rosaleen Duffy explains, "One of the main processes through which nature can be reconfigured through tourism is via commodification. This involves the creation of economic value from landscapes, animals and experiences."[76]

In Islamic Studies, Africa occupies a blurry place due to its identification with North Africa and the large numbers of Muslims who live on the continent. In a sense, Africa exists in two spaces—Africa and the Orient. As one study notes,

> Moreover, French colonial Africa, in all its variegated ecological, economic, social and cultural contexts, transcends the usual analytical

distinction between Orientalism and Africanism, as well as escaping from the chronological difficulties of a colonial history too narrowly limited to a specific region.[77]

African Orientalism is a force in the colonial world and the topographies imposed on the continent. As Peter Merrington explains, one of the places this is seen is in the transposition of Egypt and its icons on different spaces, "A particular interlude in this figurative pageant is offered by the role of Freemasonry within British imperial ideology with its 'Egyptian' rituals and genealogy."[78]

One of the effects of this framing of Africa, and especially of North Africa, is seen in European and American consumer practices. The products viewed as exotic are a form of colonial consumption seen in the popularity of Orientalist aesthetics, which for consumers, included many African spaces. One example was the marketing of cigarettes under names like Mecca, Medina, Omar, and Fatima, as well as Camels.[79] The imagery used often featured scenes or people from Africa.

These images and many other cultural forms were part of the Romantic Orientalism that existed alongside the darker themes in colonialism's fixation on the Orient. The emulation of Persian and Arabic styles often existed alongside the more violent themes found among writers, painters, and other agents of the colonial empire in North Africa and elsewhere.[80]

In Africa, the mental images formed in the colonial era become powerful ways in which the continent and its people are seen. Africa was often identified with its rich wildlife and natives that were thought to be dangerous in precolonial times. As a Kenya Government report from 1924 stated, East Africa is a land of the "unknown, a place inhabited by exotic and hostile African tribes such as the Maasai and the Sukuma, and dangerous wild animals."[81] Novels about Africa such as Paul Bowles's novel *The Sheltering Sky* often point to the difference between the West and other spaces stuck in a past time, attaching phrases like "the mechanized age he wanted to forget" to Americans, and juxtaposing this to the primitive and exotic cultures of North Africa.[82]

Africa has a history of incredible violence at the hands of Europeans. As David Ward reminds us, the farms of Kenya were not naturally gifted to Europeans, but more likely "secured by murder and sustained by extortion."[83] Despite these grim historical realities, colonial nostalgia often wins out, resulting in the idea of the continent as a place of noble Europeans and domesticated Africans living in a land imbued with intense mystical promise. In the words of one scholar, Africa often lives in the imagination as a colonial possession full of "Edenic illusions," the same illusions that dominate the business of mystical tourism today.[84] Mystical landscapes are born from these histories of settler colonialism.

IMAGE 3.1 Fatima Cigarette.

Source: photo courtesy of Wikimedia

Africa is often presented as a mystical place that offers the renewal of spirit or other such experience to the American and European. The tourist traveling to Africa seeks a place seen as stuck in time, thus allowing them to experience "life as it once was." The racial overtones of this are rather obvious—they cast Africans as primitive. Tourist materials make claims like "Africa will make you a better person" and "the 'civilized world' is far behind . . . in the land that's been hardly touched since man first walked the earth."[85] As discussed in the previous chapter, this loss of enchantment is believed to be part of the modern condition, and as something that mystical tourism exploits for profit, Africa continues to be one of its prime locations.

Mystical landscapes are built upon the fantasies that Europeans, and later Americans, place on colonized and occupied territories. This process took place through a discourse that included colonial writings and institutions, as well as literature, art, and film. In the case of Africa, the lives of white settlers, who in many cases were extremely wealthy, played a prominent role in mapping Africa. This includes the visits by members of the British royal family to Kenya and other colonies, or by the "lord and ladies, dukes and earls" who made up a disproportionate number of white settlers in the Kenya colony.[86]

A proliferation of novels about Kenya, often with steamy plotlines, included lines such as: "Petronia saw his lips first; sheer chiseled red perfection. The sort of lips that could kiss any woman down the road to Hell!"[87] As could be expected, some of these novels contained anti-Black and anti-Semitic references including "n*****" and "tight fisted Hebrews."[88] While many novels took place in Kenya, the racism held by British settlers was found among other British settler communities. In the eastern Cape, land had been annexed from Xhosa territory, and when settlers were confronted with the antislavery and pro-aboriginal movement in Britain, they resolved to make "common cause" with other settlers, which included characterizing indigenous rights as a dangerous form of "interference" that would result in the savage African taking the upper hand.[89]

Kenya, Morocco, and Algeria are popular places in the mystical tourist marketplace, each representing an assemblage of myths and dreams about the continent and the white tourist's place within it. Kenya is a necessary part of this study of mystical tourism in Africa, for the "images, ideas, and associations," by which it is known are often extended to the entire continent.[90] Kenya is often identified with royal patronage, aristocrats having champagne safaris, and a landscape full of wildlife (but where local Africans were erased, if not through colonial policies, then figuratively).

Thanks in some part to the popularity of the film *Out of Africa*, in the recent modern period the continent has become a place associated with the "Safari Look" and the memorable accent of Meryl Streep as Karen Blixen, which punctuates the film's iconic and sublime landscape.[91] In reality, the history of Kenya is extremely violent. Stories of abuses against Africans at the hands of white settlers populate the historical record. In one instance, three settlers, Ewart Grogan, Russell Bowker, and Captain Thord Gray, thrashed three African men with a hippopotamus hide whip.[92]

The mapping of colonial Africa and its foundation for the mystical tourism that exists today relies on larger patterns of subjugation and fantasy in the continent at the hands of Europeans. Two of the myths used to map

Africa as a space for white settlers, and later white tourists, are the myths of *terra nullius* (the empty land theory) and the extinction model. In southern Africa, claims about the disappearance of the Bushmen and stories of the last "boshie man" were used to argue that as they were "utterly gone," as one official in the Cape government put it, Europeans should naturally step in to manage affairs.[93] As places that exist in the imagination of so many Europeans and others, tourists still refer to a singular Africa. It is as if the distinct cultures, languages, and communities are all one, when in fact there are an almost dizzying number of these different and distinct peoples. Within Kenya alone, there are the Kikuyu, the Ogiek, the Mukogodo, the Maasai, the Endorois, and many others (too many to list here).[94]

These colonial mythologies created a plethora of "cultural commodities."[95] Today, this exists in the form of safaris, the success of clothing like Banana Republic, the Moroccan style that is found everywhere from Paris runways to the aisles of Target's rug section, the popularity of Algerian writers and films, and of course, mystical tourism. These are commodities manufactured out of a history that includes the violent occupation, subjugation, and sometimes extermination of local populations. We begin this exploration of this history in Kenya or, as the early colonists called it, "Kenya colony."

Kenya

Kenya did not become an important colony until late in Britain's great game for European dominance on the continent. The Imperial British East India Company was initially only interested in the Kingdom of Buganda, having established forts between Mombasa and the lake region, and the East African Protectorate was not declared until 1895.[96] European settlement was slow at first, but it eventually picked up after the initial years, including failures like the socialist Freeland Association (1894), which disbanded within a year.[97] Starting in the early 1900s, settlers began to arrive in larger numbers and soon took over wide swaths of land, beginning in 1903 with 117 applications for land and tripling the following year.[98] Many of the settlers spent years trying to create a successful farm or business but were always outnumbered by both Africans (in the millions) and Indians (in the thousands). As John Lonsdale put it, "A 'white man's country' in Kenya was always 'an exotic fantasy.'"[99]

The role British royals played in Kenya and other parts of Africa is an important part of the history of the West's fantasies about the continent. As Robert Aldrich has noted, from the late 1800s onwards the touring of colonies and occupied lands, or even places where the British existed behind the scenes, was popular, from Queen Victoria's son Alfred's tours in the late 1800s to the imperial tours in 1919–1925 by Edward VIII to the recent tours by young royals like William, Catherine, and Harry.[100] Viewed as a part of tradition and as a way to maintain support for the royal household, tours have been a large part of the life of monarchs, with the late Queen Elizabeth (the most traveled royal in history) visiting 128 countries a total of 271 times.[101] The British, as well as other Europeans and later, well-heeled Americans, have emulated royals, which as we shall see, is a behavior that has led to the popularity of safaris today.

The colonial reach of the British royal family is global, seen in the statues of Queen Victoria around the world. As Charles Reed points out,

> There are perhaps more statues of Queen Victoria than of any non-religious figure in history. She sits or stands among whizzing automobiles in Auckland, in front of neo-Gothic façades in Cape Town—in bustling metropolises and provincial towns, near churches, mosques, and temples.[102]

Aristocrats who emulated the royal family were often inspired to emigrate to the colonies, which usually resulted in disastrous consequences for the local population. The places these people inhabited covered much of the world; at the height of their power, the British Empire controlled "a quarter of the world's land surface and nearly a quarter of their inhabitants."[103] Royal trips to Africa play a large role in the colonial mythology on which mystical tourism on the continent is based. In the series *The Crown*, Elizabeth and Philip are portrayed in a romantic lens. Philip defends his new bride against a group of elephants and Elizabeth loves the savannah. Her love for the colony is also shown in her disappointment and sadness when her trip is cut short.

From the beginning, Kenya lived in the imagination of Europeans as a place of magic and danger. Settlers often expressed fears that local Africans would use powerful poison on their spears and witchcraft to kill them.[104] In contrast, the landscape was represented as intoxicating, beautiful, and romantic. The ways in which local Africans were categorized reflected the racial order that Europeans placed upon them. The Somali (whom Europeans believed were more like them because of their physical features, including their "thin lips") were viewed as aristocratic, and the Kikuyu, on whose ancestral lands the settlers lived, were described as "a cunning, craven, dishonest, deceitful, lacy, cruel, and unstable people."[105]

The role of British, Dutch, German, and other settlers is a critical part of the remapping of the land of Kenya and other parts of Africa. As Will Jackson explains,

> While Kenya's aristocratic settlers comprised only a "visible minority" (the phrase is Caroline Shaw's), their lasting legacy was their contribution towards a mythology that has lived on, albeit in transmuted form, to the present day. In fiction, memoir and later, film, Kenya Colony has consistently been depicted as a place of loyal servants and resplendent views, of

sundowners in the evening and journeys down roads that were dusty in the dry season and oceans of mud in the rains.[106]

The remapping of Africa included the taking of land by white settlers and major transportation projects that were used to plunder the continent's resources and to develop tourism. The Kenya-Uganda railway allowed for the building of hotels for tourists including the Hotel Stanley and the Nairobi Club.[107] Authority over the country was expressed in railways, hotels, the large and small European farms that covered the countryside, and in the dress of British settlers and adventurers. As one study puts it, "The uniforms and prescribed clothing brilliantly enhanced the imperial spectacle and the dominant power this represented."[108]

The people of Kenya, like so many other occupied, colonized peoples, bear a history of suffering at the hands of Europeans. Settlers tracked down laborers who left their farms and harmed or killed them (reminiscent of the way runaway slaves were dealt with in the United States), and if laborers killed animals to eat, domestic or wild, they were cruelly punished with "rough justice."[109] These punishments were part of a colonial ideology that viewed the land as important and the native inhabitants as disposable or nonexistent. As Achille Mbembe explains, this is the idea of *territorium nullius*, an "uninhabited and masterless land."[110]

The environmental costs in Kenya have included a devastating depopulation of wild animals. After the establishment of the East African Protectorate on June 15, 1895, hunting by Europeans led to a rapid decline in wildlife as well as the destruction of their habitat.[111] As John Akama has shown, wildlife was protected through a series of native taboos against hunting them, including elephants, lions, and leopards.[112] Colonial and state policies rejected the voices of indigenous Africans, with disastrous results for wildlife and their environment.[113] Unplanned resorts built in marine areas has also resulted in the destruction of entire ecosystems and the exploitation of turtles and other wildlife.[114] Adulphe Delegorgue's account of a colonial hunt boasted of killing 500 buffaloes, four hippopotamuses, 200 wild boar, and 43 elephants, among other animals.[115]

The cultural effects were devastating, with the loss of ways of life and economic stability through a variety of colonial policies. Settler farmers and local African life were intimately linked, with the former causing "conflict, starvation, disease, and a loss of land" through the withholding of medicines during disease outbreaks as well as a myriad of other colonial policies designed to punish locals.[116] The persecution of Africans who hunted for subsistence included targeting the Waliangaru who were imprisoned and sentenced to hard labor, resulting in the culture nearly becoming extinct.[117] The colonial occupation of the land is linked to the poverty of Kenyans through policies that benefited white settlers and had disastrous consequences for

Africans. Kenya's land was intentionally underdeveloped by the British, resulting in cheap land prices and reducing the "viability of indigenous farming" through policies against the Kikuyu and others.[118] Africans then became laborers instead of being owners, while white farmers enjoyed subsidies from colonial authorities.[119] Colonial violence affected every member of the community. Women and children were taken, forced into sexual slavery or labor, and forcibly moved away from their homelands.[120]

The colonial mapping of Kenya includes a rich iconography focused on wildlife, seen in everything from documentary films to children's entertainment. African wildlife is the dominant subject of documentaries, while human stories are often ignored.[121] This is a direct consequence of the policies of colonial authorities over the past 200 years, which includes placing people on reserves, the impoverishment of communities, and the destruction of family and community units. As one study notes, "Settlers generally argue that there was not an 'indigenous presence,' stating instead that there were 'no local people' in the White Highlands of Kenya or the Midlands of Zimbabwe."[122] Of course this was not true, but colonizers claimed it was the reality, what Mbembe calls the colonial logic of "destroying and creating, creating by destroying."[123]

The Safari

The safari is perhaps the most famous tourist practice that emerges out of colonialism in Kenya. The safari was popularized by the royal family and emulated by British settlers, featured in Dinesen's *Out of Africa* and seen in the popularity of African safaris among tourists today. New settlers in Kenya were largely from the "gentlemanly" class and as historians have pointed out, "Kenya's wildlife attracted large numbers of aristocratic sportsmen, who frequently bagged land as well as game."[124]

The British royal family has a long history tied to hunting African wildlife. In 1860, Prince Edward shot upon a massive herd of wildlife described by one scholar as "a rather grotesque 'hunting' trip": in his numerous trips, he hunted an incredible array of animals, including antelope, deer, elephants, and other exotics.[125] Hunting by the royal family and wealthy British and white settlers inspired big game hunting by the wealthy that resulted in the destruction of wildlife populations and their habitats. The safari is important politically, because it "was perceived as a major symbol of European dominance over nature in general and society in particular."[126]

As we have seen, the safari was popularized by the royal family, early British and other European aristocrats, and other wealthy visitors to Kenya. By the 1920s, the first "champagne safaris" became a fixture in travel writing and newspaper features as well as the very important genres of "fiction and memoir."[127] Africa eventually replaced North America as the primary tourist destination for wildlife, while the two—the wild west and Africa—remained linked in the imagination of Europeans. Buffalo Bill's *Wild West* show was one of the ways that the ideas about hunting, wild territories, and white warrior men within it were spread. Played in May 1887 to an audience in London that included the Prince of Wales and Queen Victoria, its European run from 1887 to 1906 included "over five hundred venues" and "millions of spectators."[128] The exploitation of America's wild west and its extension into Africa included President Theodore Roosevelt's champagne safari in 1909–1910.[129] Roosevelt played an important role in popularizing Kenya to wealthy Americans. His trip included 200 support trackers, skinners, and porters; in the end, he returned with "over 3000 specimens of African game."[130]

There was romance to the "dinner in the bush" and the "open spaces" Kenya offered, for by this time it had been cleared of much of its local African population, who had been moved onto reserves or were gone altogether.[131] White settlers included those who kept to the fancy clothing of Europe's upper classes with white waistcoats and formal dresses and others who did safari in "dressing gowns and pajamas."[132] This was part of the appeal of Kenya, for it offered a vision of colonization that allowed Europeans (and some Americans) to act as they wanted, creating imaginary worlds that to some extent, remain to this day. The people of Happy Valley were among the wealthiest and most decadent, part of a crowd of famous expatriates who originated the phrase: "Are you married, or do you live in Kenya?"[133]

White settlers loved the safari, which was a common motif in descriptions of Kenya, books like *Out of Africa*, and today is seen in tourist advertising. The way in which Africans were referred to, as "little apes" and other terrible phrases, exposes the ways that wildlife was valued over humans by settlers, an idea seen today in the tourism industry.[134] The safari, in many ways, is linked to the entire business of mystical tourism, with its focus on a land that is mysterious and dangerous, but ultimately transformative for the individual.

These collective memories are marketed to tourists who want to experience something of the colonial age through a kind of colonial nostalgia for adventure and exotic experience. As detailed in this book, tourism is directly linked to colonialism, a fact I document in each case study, from Kenya to Tahiti. Thomas Cook Travel boasted of the great "vision of colonization" in Kenya and extolled the settlers who made a living from the land, "making homes and raising children to inhabit their glorious tradition."[135] Since then, Kenya has been associated with colonialism, its fashion, and at times, its decadence. The benefit to Kenya's people has been incredibly small. According to a 1991 study, just over 2 percent of the 300 million USD earned by Kenya's parks were returned to the people of the country.[136]

In popular culture, Kenya is often presented as a place for tourists to experience nature in landscapes seemingly empty of the people who live there. *The Lion King* is one example of representations of Africa without people.

As Simon Lewis explains, "Disney's box-office smash *The Lion King* is not only that corporation's sole animated feature film to have been set in Africa, it is also the only one to be completely devoid of human presence."[137] A direct result of Europe's mapping of the land, tourists have typically viewed wildlife as more important than humans.[138]

The erasure of Africans from the landscape is a result of the colonial mapping of Kenya and its efforts to create a white space in East Africa. As recounted throughout this chapter, the imagination about Kenya is rooted in a search for meaning. White settlers were invested in the colonial project. Comparisons of "Kenya's hills to English downs," the popularity of English gardening (especially orchids), and the efforts to make English suppers were all examples of this white mapping.[139] At the same time, they also were on a search for authentic experiences missing in an industrialized Europe that could not offer the adventure of Africa. Kenya provided a space for not only adventure, but also contemplation, in a land where the white settler was king of his or her world.

The Maghreb

The French occupied Algeria in 1830, beginning one of the most brutal European occupations in Africa. French philosopher Pierre Bourdieu was teaching at a university in Bourdeaux when he became compelled to record what he observed, both in written reflections and in photographs. Bourdieu felt that he could be a voice for the voiceless, and in many of his writings one sees how anti-colonial he was. In *Le Déracinement*, he writes, "War and persecution have finished off what had been started by colonial policy and the generalization of monetary exchanges."[140]

Following the occupation of Algeria, the French seized Tunisia (1881–1883), and later, Morocco fell under French control (and a portion under Spanish control) in 1912.[141] Algeria established some of the standards for colonial policies in these other places. Algeria was etched into the European consciousness through brutal French policies against Algerians both in Algeria and in France. Gillo Pontecorvo's film *Battle of Algiers* (1966) remains the most famous film about the French in Africa to this day.

The colonial *imaginaire* in North Africa relied on the fantasy of an ancient landscape of lush forests that had been laid waste by Arabs, transformed into a barren desert—the subject of a 39-volume colonial study named *Exploration scientifique de l'Algerie*.[142] The desert, which became a key fixture of Orientalist writing and painting and a site of the mystical landscape, was also the *raison d'être* of the colonizing project. The mapping of Africa was a major focus of French colonial geographers, who, in addition to universities in Paris and other French cities, had a place at the École des Lettres and its university in Algiers, which from 1880 had a chair in geography.[143] Under

Édouard Cat, courses were "directly linked with contemporary French colonial events," created after events such as the Berlin Conference of 1885, such as the class "Madagascar," and during the Archinard Campaign of 1891, courses included "the French Sahara" and "Morocco."[144]

The French had political interests in classifying the Amazigh people as lost ancestors whose land had been stolen by Arab invasions. In Algeria, the concept that the Amazigh was "the primitive who represents the past of Europeans" was used to argue that they were, in fact, related to Romans, Greeks, and Germans.[145] For the French, the Amazigh were gentle pastoralists and the Arabs were invading wanderers, still unsettled due to their primitive culture.[146] To Orientalists, "North Africa was believed to be inhabited by a predominantly Berber—that is, European population."[147] This view of history was used to divide the Amazigh and Arabs; it also suggested that the French and others belonged in North Africa. Algeria was the place of ancient Roman granaries and agricultural production until the "hordes of Arab nomads and their rapacious herds" destroyed the land.[148]

The French obsession with desertification had its source in other French colonies, especially the "forested tropical island" that represented the Garden of Eden.[149] While the desert became associated with spiritual regeneration in later eras, the early colonial period in North Africa was characterized by a negative view of the desert. It was viewed as a place of evil, or at least immorality, thus fitting for the Arab.[150] The French colonies benefited from these ideas, which resulted in the criminalizing of land tenure by the local population.[151]

Algerian women play a prominent role in the colonial imagination about Algeria. Famously represented in Orientalist art, the Algerian woman is presented as "no more than a source for sexual pleasure" in paintings like Delacroix's *Women of Algiers in Their Apartment* (1834).[152] The foundation of French Orientalist painting was in the exotic fantasies about the East. The founder of the Society of French Orientalist Painters, Léonce Bénédite, was fascinated with Africa and the Orient from a young age, including the "sonorous names" of cities and the visual topography he encountered in Orientalist products of Muslims and Tunisian Jews.[153]

Algerians living under French occupation and those who emigrated to France were subjected to racial policies that, to some extent, exist to this day in the form of the politics surrounding veiling that target North African immigrants. Algeria "formed an integral part of France" and as Stam and Shohat remark, Algerians were subjected to the "Code Indigene" and in France, to "curfews and police brutality and a segregated existence in *bidonvilles*."[154] Malek Alloula's famous work on the colonial harem and other genres of French photography of French girls and women illustrates another form of colonial violence in visual portrayals that were sexual, brutal, and pornographic, with images mass produced for postcards and other commodified products. Colonial photography included naked Algerian women in harems or posing as lesbians, portrayals that fit Orientalist notions of a perverse and sexual culture that included violent men and sensual women who could only be subdued by colonial force.[155]

Algeria stands as a particularly infamous case of colonialism in Africa, in part due to its military force and brutality that included the torture and rape of girls and women and examples of pornography in colonial images. When the FLN agent Djamila Bouppacha was imprisoned by the French, she was raped with a bottle and tortured, facts that came to light when she was released in 1962 as part of a general amnesty at the end of Algeria's war for independence.[156] One million Algerians were killed in that war, which was one-third of the population.

Algeria was subjected to escalating episodes of violence that resulted when it was impossible for 50,000 French troops to subdue over three million Algerians.[157] When the Algerians won their independence, the voices of Islamic reformists were at the center. For all the French propaganda about Algeria being a nation aligned with European history, the history of the Arabs and the importance of Arabic and Islam were critical parts of Algerian anti-colonial writings. Mubarak al-Mili's *Tarikh al Jaza'ir fil Qadim wal Hadith* was published in 1928/1932 (in two volumes), and Ahmad Tawfiq al-Madani's *Kitab al-Jaza'ir*, published in 1932, contained the slogan, "Islam is my religion, Arabic is my language, Algeria is my fatherland"—the official slogan of Algerian independence.[158]

The Protectorate of Morocco was established by the French in 1921 and operated the colony through a careful manipulation of Alaouite notables, whose religious center was the Medieval city of Fez.[159] The French did not lose their grip on power until Sidi Mohamed ben Youssef, chosen to be "a pliable *dahir*-stamping sovereign," became the ant-colonial *Amir al-mu-iminin* (commander of the faithful), eventually becoming Mohammed V, the king of a free Morocco.[160]

French land policies in Morocco followed the established colonial environmental system in Algeria, where the narrative about Arab destruction and French salvation of the land was used to take land from local populations and declare forests state property.[161] Views about the desert eventually transitioned, in part due to the occupation of the territory by French *colons* and differing attitudes toward nature. The desert was seen as a spiritual place by many French artists, for example, who we now call French Orientalists.[162]

During their rule, the French interest in historic preservation, seen in the *medina* (the old city), was linked to a colonial project of classification that included French-run museums, a reflection of the idea that Arabs were stuck in time. Johannes Fabian's critique of the colonial gaze is also seen in the French fixation on the past and refusal to allow Moroccans to modernize under their rule. French colonial administrators looked up to the British, whom they viewed as being the model of how to treat their colonial subjects, "as 'a separate race' which belonged to a different civilization and which the British respected and helped to evolve within the limits of its own traditions."[163] French policies surrounding the preservation of the past involved establishing a colonial museum in Fez (which still exists at the courtyard of Dar Batha) and the construction of a gate, *Bab Bou Jeloud*, that "cut through the reinforced medina wall" so that an optimal view of the Sidi Lezzaz Mosque and the Bou Inania Medersa could be created.[164] An example of what Derek Gregory calls the *scopic regime*—the visual and visualization— were of critical importance in the colonial gaze.

The education system was another place where French and other Moroccans, such as Arabs and the Amazigh, were separated. As Hamid Irbouh documents in his book, French and European children would be educated and trained in the practices of "carrying out various forms of colonial exploitations," and the education of the local population (excluding Franco-Jewish schools, which were a different matter) was focused on trades and other low-paying professions that did not allow for class movement.[165] The colonial regime also marked a strict ethnic division between the Arabs and Amazigh, something that Mohamed V would have to deal with in his rule, which was complicated by his attempts to undo colonial policies like the French education system, which he Arabized.[166]

The city of Fez was also subjected to building codes that aligned with the "Fassi style" that would include colonial buildings like the College Moulay Idris, where Religious Studies was eliminated and replaced with science, and French was the language of instruction.[167] Perhaps most importantly, these policies were directed toward a larger goal—tourism. As Stacey Holden notes, in addition to preserving the medina because it was adjacent to the new homes of wealthy French nationals, there was a larger and more ambitious goal, "Second, the protectorate intended to develop Morocco as a destination for foreign tourists seeking to experience unfamiliar lifestyles."[168] The education system supported both these goals. It focused on the training of locals in the arts and trades so that they could build *villes nouvelles* in cities like Casablanca, Rabat, Marrakesh, Fez, and Meknes.[169] It also trained artists to perpetuate the old styles that would lead to a landscape that was focused on a visual culture that appealed to tourists.[170] The French viewed these *unfamiliar lifestyles* as a central part of a tourist program that reflected Orientalist fantasies about Morocco and more broadly, North Africa and Islamic cultures.

Africa's Mystical Landscapes

As I have suggested, mystical landscapes are best understood as spaces that become places. Once empty spaces on a map, they became places imbued with meaning or value.[171] Spatial locations include "pasts, presents, and futures."[172] However, colonial mapping often erases the past and creates a new present that reflects the colonial imagination about a place. In Africa, these ideas about place were complicated by the mapping of the continent, a process which created fields of meaning based on colonially ordered regions. East Africa is often identified with the wild and open savannah and the animals that occupy a landscape that is both beautiful and promises the regeneration of the human spirit. North Africa is typically aligned with Orientalist ideas about Islam, the desert, and the promise of spiritual renewal. In both schemes, Africans are often erased from the environment or relegated to marginal spaces on the borderlands of the imagination.

The idea of Kenya as a place of colonial romance is a large part of its appeal to tourists. In a sense, visiting Kenya is a way to imagine oneself in the past, as one of the settlers who "believed Kenya was their home."[173] As Brett Shadle explains, "They created spaces which would be permanent and white. They built brick or stone homes and planted flower gardens to mark off their space from the bush."[174] The colonial style is so popular that it is re-created at safari resorts and in the safari style worn by tourists from Prince Charles to the average shopper at Banana Republic or Recreational Equipment Incorporated (REI).

Literature is a place where we see the idea of a mystic Africa expressed, as we have seen in the example of Karen Blixen. In Nadine Gordimer's *The Conservationist*, Africa is a place for renewal and healing, much like the safaris and resorts that the wealthy travel to in Kenya. In the words of Simon Lewis, the character Mehring perceives "the farm as a natural (African) place to escape to when he has had too much (European) capitalist culture."[175] Colonial nostalgia tourism is popular in Kenya, a form of mystical tourism that is predicated on the longing for a past when white Europeans occupied the landscape. The growth of ecotourism is another key part of the mystical tourism industry—tourists seek a transcendent experience while helping to preserve the natural environment. The safari is one of the best examples of this as a genre of travel focused on the preservation of national parks. Scholars of ecotourism have pointed out how ecological movements and the quest for exotic, authentic experience abroad are linked, where "the romanticism and nostalgia for sustainable living and a widespread organicism became linked with the exciting tourist experiences to be had in adventurous journeys, breathtaking scenery, and often, trips to exotic lands."[176]

Nostalgia tourism is a big business in Kenya. Safari camps include luxury accommodations that include places like the Karen Blixen Camp, which promises an experience of the colonial past and includes reproductions of her furniture.[177] The Karen Blixen Camp has an impressive website with Kenya's mystical landscape at its center. It offers "renewal" and "tranquility" and "promises to rejuvenate the spirit."[178] The nostalgia for the colonial days of the past is also part of the marketing: "Karen Blixen Camp offers an authentic 'yesteryear' experience," "a feeling of the 1920s," and the promise that one will "step back in time."[179] In addition to wellness treatments, visitors can watch *Out of Africa* in the bush—an experience that intimates the true colonial gaze. The Camp combines colonial nostalgia and the mystical landscape in one package. The imagery associated with the safari is not limited to big game resorts in Kenya. In Sharm El Sheikh in Egypt, the *Meridien* (now owned by the Savoy hotel chain) "attempts to conjure up an image of a colonial Africa of big game hunting with 'colonial' furniture and paintings of elephants and lions."[180]

Morocco is often conflated with other parts of North Africa, part of the mystique of the Maghreb region that also includes Algeria and Tunisia. The desert remains an important part of the appeal of tourism. Scholars have identified three correlates of the nature experience that results in a spiritual change: being in nature, being away from one's regular environment, and something called "place processes," which include things like contemplation, observation of nature, and time to think about one's existence.[181] When tourists go into nature, especially places considered "wilderness," they may be experiencing latent Christian ideas focused upon God's creation.[182]

The focus of travel in North Africa is often the desert, a space seen as "cleansing," "purifying," and "uplifting."[183] As noted in earlier chapters, a sense of emptiness is often experienced by the mystical tourist in spaces viewed as uninhabited by humans. This view is predicated on colonial fantasies of empty space, which naturally became colonial territories. Tourists venturing into the desert have a Christian experience without acknowledging it, for the desert has been associated with mystical experience since the desert fathers. As Adler writes,

> Enduring motifs of wilderness romance find their first templates in literary treatments and popular cults of "Desert Fathers" as human exemplars, and desert itself as sanctity's distinctive habitat: penitential, sacramental, redemptive, self-creative space of the first order.[184]

Tourists who travel to these mystical landscapes often reflect these themes through their interest in sparse lodging, hopes of redemption, and spiritual rituals.

Mystical landscapes do not always rely on these constructions of empty space, but when they do, they erase the local human populations living around them. In one study of a mystical tourist camp in Tunisia, the authors remark that it is "in the sandy area close to the village of Sabria in the vicinity of the oasis town of Douz."[185] Despite the presence of nearby locals, the participants in the camp experience (which includes other elements of scarcity like fasting and a limited diet) view themselves as being alone, with one commenting, "It was a requirement to go to the source, to go into an empty space, to go to something huge and big, and to go to something where there wasn't anything man can bring along."[186]

Morocco is the most popular destination for tourists wanting to experience the Maghreb. While there are exceptions, like the history and heritage tours offered by companies like Geographic Expeditions, which are geared for the highly educated and wealthy traveler, the country's tourism industry is largely focused on the mystical landscape. The appeal for many tourists is in the exotic experience that Morocco has to offer—the colorful casbah, high mountains, and the magical desert. Studies of tourists visiting Morocco's desert include testimonies about being "released by the 'emptiness' of the space" in a powerful landscape viewed as a site of "wonder and transcendence."[187]

The desert, once portrayed as evidence of the Arab destruction critical to French colonial policies on desertification, is now a place of mystical enchantment. As one of the many tour companies that offer tours to the Sahara boasts, the desert is "a vast reflection of your soul" that offers reconnection "with your true self" through a "deep journey" and experience of "inner and outer liberation," promising "powerful healing modalities, evolutionary growth, and the most life-changing transformation of your life."[188] Once deemed a colonial problem to solve, the Sahara is now the answer to the tourist's existential problems, a mystical landscape one can experience for the right price.

Notes

1 McClintock, 23.
2 Achille Mbembe, *On the Postcolony* (Berkeley: University of California Press, 2001), 9.
3 Merrington, 334.
4 Bruce Mazlish, "A Triptych: Freud's *The Interpretation of Dreams*, Rider Haggard's *She*, and Bulwer-Lytton's *The Coming Race*," *Comparative Studies in Society and History* 35, no. 4 (1993): 727.
5 Robinson 2016, 3, 45, 108, 109, 112. The Hamitic thesis proposed that white Africans (likely just lighter-skinned Africans) were the result of an ancient invasion tied to Biblical lore. See Robinson, 8–10. See Robinson, 128, for Portuguese and other reports of white Africans.
6 Michael Talbot, "Divine Imperialism: The British in Palestine, 1753–1842," in *The British Abroad Since the Eighteenth Century, Volume 2: Experiencing Imperialism*, ed. Martin Farr and Xavier Guégan (New York: Palgrave Macmillan, 2013), 38. See also Merrington, 336–337.
7 Peter Varley, "Confecting Adventure and Playing with Meaning: The Adventure Commodification Continuum," *Journal of Sport & Tourism* 11, no. 2 (2006): 176.
8 Coleman 2007, 337.
9 Loshitzky 2000, 58.
10 Hore, 107.
11 Hore, 107.

12 Bellone et al., 31.
13 Colin Michael Hall and Stephen W. Boyd, "Nature-Based Tourism in Periph-eral Areas: Development or Disaster?," in *Nature-Based Tourism in Peripheral Areas: Development or Disaster*, ed. Colin Michael Hall and Stephen W. Boyd (Buffalo: Clevedon, 2005), 3–6.
14 Olsen, 402.
15 Diana K. Davis, "Desert 'Wastes' of the Maghreb: Desertification Narratives in French Colonial Environmental History of North Africa," *Cultural Geographies* 2004, no. 4 (2004): 360.
16 Davis, 360, 362.
17 Perkins, 37.
18 Perkins, 4, 410.
19 Perkins, 49.
20 Marc Walter, *Voyages around the World* (New York: Friedman, 2002), 128.
21 Claudio Minca and Lauren Wagner, *Moroccan Dreams: Oriental Myth, Colonial Legacy* (New York: I. B. Tauris, 2016), xvii, xix.
22 Jamyang Norbu, "Behind the Lost Horizon: Demystifying Tibet," in *Imagining Tibet: Perceptions, Projections, and Fantasies*, ed. Thierry Dodin and Heinz Räther (Boston: Wisdom Publications, 2001), 374.
23 Susan Hardy Aiken, "Consuming Isak Dinesen," in *Isak Dinesen and Narrativity*, ed. Gurli A. Woods (Montreal: McGill-Queen's University Press, 1994), 7.
24 Lewis, 69.
25 Isak Dinesen (Karen Blixen), *Out of Africa* (Harmondsworth: Penguin, 1984), 327, 314. Quoted in Lewis, 74.
26 Annie Gagiano, "Blixen, Ngugi: Recounting Kenya," in *Ngugi Was Thiong'o: Texts and Contexts*, ed. Charles Cantalupo (Trenton: Africa World Press, 1995), 105.
27 Knipp, 5.
28 Knipp, 7.
29 Aiken 1994, 15.
30 Aiken 1994, 15.
31 Blixen, 6. Quoted in Knipp, 6.
32 Elspeth Huxley, *White Man's Country: Lord Delamere and the Making of Kenya*, Volume 1 (London: MacMillan, 1935), 64. Quoted in Jackson, 348.
33 Terence Ranger, "The Invention of Tradition in Colonial Africa," in *The Invention of Tradition*, ed. Eric Hobsbawn and Terence Ranger (Cambridge: Cambridge University Press, 2014), 453.
34 John Lonsdale, "Kenya: Home County and African Frontier," in *Settlers and Expatriates: Britons Over the Seas*, ed. Robert Bickers (New York: Oxford University Press, 2010), 78.
35 Lonsdale, 79.
36 Rose Miyonga, " 'We Kept Them to Remember': Tin Trunk Archives and the Emotional History of the Mau Mau War," *History Workshop Journal* 96 (2023): 97.
37 C. J. D. Duder, "Love and the Lions: The Image of White Settlement in Kenya in Popular Fiction, 1919–1939," *African Affairs* 90, no. 360 (1991): 431.
38 Jay Mary Arthur, *The Default Country: A Lexical Cartography of Twentieth-Century Australia* (Sydney: University of New South Wales, 2003), 85. Quoted in Lynch, 183.
39 Hore, 109. (emphasis in original)
40 Ahmad Gholi, Masoud Ahmadi Mousaabad, and Maryam Raminnia, "Journey to Loss and Fixation of Western Identity in Bernardo Bertolucci's Movie Adaptation of Sheltering Sky," *Journal of Language, Teaching and Research* 7, no. 5 (2016): 954.

41 Mossner, 123.
42 Perkins, 39.
43 Shamma, 126.
44 Shamma, 128.
45 Brian T. Edwards, "Sheltering Screens: Paul Bowles and Foreign Relations," *American Literary History* 17, no. 2 (2005): 321.
46 Shamma, 137.
47 Loshitzky 2000, 54.
48 Shamma, 134.
49 Shamma, 134.
50 Yosefa Loshitzky, *The Radical Faces of Godard and Bertolucci* (Detroit: Wayne State University Press, 1995), 122.
51 Loshitzky 1995, 130.
52 Brian Edwards, "Sheltering Screens: Paul Bowles and Foreign Relations," *American Literary History* 17, no. 2 (2005): 316.
53 Loshitzky 1995, 132.
54 Leyerle, 138.
55 Anthony Kwame Appiah, *In My Father's House* (New York: Oxford University Press, 1992), 149.
56 Joseph A. Massad, *Desiring Arabs* (Chicago: The University of Chicago Press, 2007).
57 Massad.
58 Mitchell, 38–41.
59 Greg Dening, "The Comaroffs Out of Africa: A Reflection Out of Oceania," *The American Historical Review* 108, no. 2 (2003): 471.
60 Partha Mitter, "The Hottentot Venus and Western Man: Reflections on the Construction of Beauty in the West," in *Cultural Encounters: Representing 'Otherness'*, ed. Elizabeth Hallam and Brian V. Street (New York: Routledge, 2000), 45.
61 Gilles Boëtsch and Pascal Blanchard, "The Hottentot Venus: Birth of a 'Freak'," in *Human Zoos: Science and Spectacle in the Age of Colonial Empires*, ed. Pascal Blanchard, Nicolas Bancel, Gilles Boëtsch, Eric Deroo, Sandrine Lemaire, and Charles Forsdick (Liverpool: Liverpool University Press, 2008), 62, 64.
62 Boëtsch and Blanchard, 65.
63 Mitchell 2020, 23.
64 Lefebvre, 201.
65 Donaldson 1999, 685.
66 Bandy, 553.
67 Merrington, 355.
68 Shelton, 158.
69 Shelton, 182, 183.
70 Melville J. Herskovits, *The Myth of the Negro Past* (Boston: Beacon Press, 1958), 1, 22.
71 Adebayo Olukoshi and Francis Nyamnjoh, "The Postcolonial Turn: An Introduction," in *The Postcolonial Turn: Re-Imagining Anthropology and Africa*, ed. René Devisch and Francis Nyamnjoh (Leiden: African Studies Centre, 2011), 4. Africanism is a broad subject with different methodological concerns. One of the best works on Pan-Africanism is Hakim Adi's *Pan-Africanism: A History* (New York: Bloomsbury Academic, 2018).
72 Loti 1867, 33, 35.
73 Loti 1867, 13.
74 Robinson, 14. Robinson details the stories told to Stanley by the Ganda commander, Colonel Sekajugu, on pages 13–15.
75 Mary Mostafanezhad and Margaret Byrne Swain, "Afterword—Beyond Anthropology: Ethnography in Tourism Studies," in *The Ethnography of Tourism:*

Edward Bruner and Beyond, ed. Naomi M. Leite, Quetzil E. Castañeda, and Kathleen M. Adams (Lanham: Lexington Books, 2019), 247.

76 Rosaleen Duffy, "Interactive Elephants: Nature, Tourism and Neoliberalism," *Annals of Tourism Research* 4 (2014): 92.
77 Blais, Deprest, and Singaravelou, 147.
78 Merrington, 328.
79 Naomi Rosenblatt, "Orientalism in American Popular Culture," *Penn History Review* 16, no. 2 (2009): 60.
80 Zachary Lockman, *Contending Visions of the Middle East: The History and Politics of Orientalism* (New York: Cambridge University Press, 2004), 69.
81 John S. Akama, "The Evolution of Tourism in Kenya," *Journal of Sustainable Tourism* 7, no. 1 (1999): 11.
82 McCann, 152. Quoted from Bowles, *The Sheltering Sky*.
83 David Ward, *The Country and the City* (Oxford: Oxford University Press, 1989), 51.
84 Aiken 1994, 7.
85 Bruner, 239.
86 Will Jackson, "White Man's Country: Kenya Colony and the Making of a Myth," *Journal of East African Studies* 5, no. 2 (2011): 344.
87 Duder, 430.
88 Duder, 432.
89 Alan Lester, "Constructing Colonial Discourse: Britain, South Africa, and the Empire in the Nineteenth Century," in *Postcolonial Geographies*, ed. Alison Blunt and Cheryl McEwan (New York: Continuum, 2002), 34.
90 Jackson, 346.
91 Aiken 1994, 3.
92 Brett Lindsay Shadle, *The Souls of White Folk: White Settlers in Kenya, 1900s–1920s* (Manchester: Manchester University Press, 2015), 1.
93 Hanzimanolis, 45.
94 Robert K. Hitchcock, Maria Sapignoli, and Wayne A. Babchuk, "Settler Colonialism, Conflicts, and Genocide: Interactions between Hunter-Gatherers and Settlers in Kenya, And Zimbabwe and Northern Botswana," *Settler Colonial Studies* 5, no. 1 (2014): 1–2.
95 Jackson, 345.
96 Shadle, 12.
97 Dane Kennedy, *Islands of White: Settler Society and Culture in Kenya and Southern Rhodesia, 1890–1939* (Durham: Duke University Press, 1987), 21.
98 Shadle, 14.
99 Lonsdale, 76.
100 Robert Aldrich, "Visiting the Family and Introducing the Royals: British Royal Tours of the Dominions in the Twentieth Century and Beyond," *Royal Studies Journal* 5, no. 1 (2018): 2.
101 Aldrich, 3.
102 Charles Reed, *Royal Tourists, Colonial Subjects and the Making of a British World* (Manchester: Manchester University Press, 2016), 1.
103 Helen Callaway, "Dressing for Dinner in the Bush: Rituals of Self-Definition and British Imperial Authority," in *Dress and Gender: Making and Meaning in Cultural Contexts*, ed. Ruth Barnes and Joanne B. Eicher (New York: Bloomsbury, 1993), 233.
104 Hitchcock, Sapignoli, and Babchuk, 6.
105 Kennedy, 160, 161.
106 Jackson, 345.
107 Akama 1999, 11.
108 Callaway, 246.

109 Hitchcock, Sapignoli, and Babchuk, 3.
110 Mbembe, 183.
111 John S. Akama, "The Evolution of Wildlife Conservation Policies in Kenya," *Journal of Third World Studies* 15, no. 2 (1998), 104–105.
112 Akama 1998, 104.
113 Akama 1998, 107.
114 Akama 1999, 19.
115 Hanzimanolis, 38.
116 Hitchcock, Sapignoli, and Babchuk, 17.
117 Akama 1998, 108.
118 Lewis, 69.
119 Lewis, 69.
120 Hitchcock, Sapignoli, and Babchuk, 4.
121 Lewis, 73.
122 Hitchcock, Sapignoli, and Babchuk, 18.
123 Mbembe, 189.
124 Kennedy, 92, 44.
125 Reed, 18.
126 Akama 1999, 12.
127 Jackson, 349.
128 David Wrobel, "Prologue: Exceptionalism, Globalism, and Transnationalism—the West, America, and the World across Centuries," in *The Popular Frontier: Buffalo Bill's Wild West and Transnational Mass Culture*, ed. Frank Christianson (Norman: University of Oklahoma Press, 2017), 6, 10.
129 Jackson, 349.
130 Akama 1999, 13.
131 Jackson, 350.
132 Jackson, 351.
133 Duder, 431.
134 Lonsdale, 84.
135 Thomas Cook, *Travels in East Africa* (London: Thomas Cook and Son, 1936), n.p. Quoted in Jackson, 351.
136 Tensie Whelan, "Ecotourism and Its Role in Sustainable Development," in *Nature Tourism: Managing the Environment*, ed. Tensie Whelan (Washington: Island Press, 1991), 11.
137 Lewis, 73.
138 Akama 1999, 13.
139 Lonsdale, 85–86.
140 Pierre Bourdieu, *Le Déracinement: La Crise de L'agriculture Traditionelle en Algérie* (Paris: Editions de Minuit, 1964), 23. Quoted in Pierre Bourdieu, "Habitus and Habitat," in *Picturing Algeria: Pierre Bourdieu*, ed. Franz Schultheis and Christine Frisinghelli (New York: Columbia University Press, 2012), 68.
141 Lockman, 72.
142 Davis, 362.
143 Singaravelou, 152.
144 Singaravelou, 152.
145 Abdelmajid Hannoum, *Violent Modernity: France in Algeria* (Cambridge: Harvard University Press, 2010), 83–84.
146 Davis, 366.
147 Hannoum, 85.
148 Davis, 363.
149 Davis, 368. Tahiti, examined in a later chapter, is an example of the Edenic paradise.

150 Davis, 369.
151 Davis, 374–375.
152 Saissi, n.p.
153 Roger Benjamin, *Orientalist Aesthetics: Art, Colonialism, and French North Africa, 1880–1930* (Berkeley: University of California Press, 2003), 58.
154 Stam and Shohat 2012, 29. (emphasis in original)
155 Malek Alloula, *The Colonial Harem*, trans. Myrna Godzich and Wlad Godzich (Minneapolis: University of Minnesota Press, 1986), 89, 103.
156 Alloula, xii. Simone Beauvoir campaigned for her release. Some intellectuals, like Albert Camus, who was a *pied noir*, were staunchly pro-colonialist, arguing against independence for Algerians. A *pied noir* was a person born in Algeria, but of French ancestry.
157 Hamid Irbouh, *Art in the Service of Colonialism: French Art Education in Morocco 1912–1956* (New York: I. B. Tauris, 2013), 73.
158 Mansoor Moadell, *Islamic Modernism, Nationalism, and Fundamentalism: Episode and Discourse* (Chicago: University of Chicago Press, 2005), 267. Al-Mili's title translates to *A History of Algeria in Antiquity and in Modern Times* and al-Madani's to *The Book of Algeria*. Nearly one-third of Algeria's population died during the war for independence.
159 Stacy E. Holden, "The Legacy of French Colonialism: Preservation in Morocco's Fez Medina," *APT Bulletin: The Journal of Preservation Technology* 39, no. 4 (2008): 6.
160 Jonathon Wyrtzen, *Making Morocco: Colonial Intervention and the Politics of Identity* (Ithaca: Cornell University Press, 2015), 248.
161 Davis, 379.
162 Davis, 377.
163 Irbouh, 75.
164 Holden, 7. The colonial government also changed another gate they deemed was too influenced by European style.
165 Irbouh, 71–72.
166 Wyrtzen, 284–286. The word "Berber" is confused with the word "barbarian," so I use Amazigh instead. See Fazia Äitel, *We Are Imazighen: The Development of Algerian Berber Identity in Twentieth-Century Literature and Culture* (Gainesville: University Press of Florida, 2014).
167 Holden, 8.
168 Holden, 9–10.
169 Irbouh, 2.
170 Irbouh, 2.
171 Yi-Fu Tuan, *Space and Place: The Perspective of Experience* (Minneapolis: University of Minnesota Press, 1977), 6.
172 Thomas S. Bremer, "Sacred Spaces and Tourist Places," In *Tourism, Religion and Spiritual Journeys*, ed. Dallen J. Timothy and Daniel H. Olsen (New York: Routledge, 2006), 27.
173 Shadle, 11.
174 Shadle, 11.
175 Lewis, 73.
176 Bandy, 542.
177 Jackson, 356.
178 Karenblixencamp.com (accessed January 15, 2025).
179 Karenblixencamp.com (accessed January 15, 2025).
180 Jessica Jacobs, *Sex, Tourism and the Postcolonial Encounter: Landscapes of Longing in Egypt* (London: Ashgate, 2010), 49.
181 Heintzman, 77.

182 Heintzman, 77.
183 Moufakkir and Selmi, 111.
184 Adler, 10.
185 Moufakkir and Selmi, 111.
186 Moufakkir and Selmi, 111, 113.
187 Minca and Wagner, 189, 190.
188 Desertmajesty.com (accessed January 16, 2025).

Bibliography

Adi, Hakim. *Pan-Africanism: A History*. New York: Bloomsbury Academic, 2018.
Adler, Judith. "Cultivating Wilderness: Environmentalism and Legacies of Early Christian Asceticism." *Comparative Studies in Society and History* 48, no. 1 (2006): 4–37.
Aiken, Susan Hardy. "Consuming Isak Dinesen." In *Isak Dinesen and Narrativity*, edited by Gurli A. Woods, 3–24. Montreal: McGill-Queen's University Press, 1994.
Äitel, Fazia. *We Are Imazighen: The Development of Algerian Berber Identity in Twentieth-Century Literature and Culture*. Gainesville: University Press of Florida, 2014.
Akama, John S. "The Evolution of Wildlife Conservation Policies in Kenya." *Journal of Third World Studies* 15, no. 2 (1998): 103–116.
Akama, John S. "The Evolution of Tourism in Kenya." *Journal of Sustainable Tourism* 7, no. 1 (1999): 6–25.
Aldrich, Robert. "Visiting the Family and Introducing the Royals: British Royal Tours of the Dominions in the Twentieth Century and Beyond." *Royal Studies Journal* 5, no. 1 (2018): 1–14.
Allers, Roger and Rob Minkoff. *The Lion King*. Walt Disney Features Animation, 1994.
Alloula, Malek. *The Colonial Harem*. Translated by Myrna Godzich and Wlad Godzich. Minneapolis: University of Minnesota Press, 1986.
Appiah, Kwame Anthony. *In My Father's House*. New York: Oxford University Press, 1992.
Arthur, Jay Mary. *The Default Country: A Lexical Cartography of Twentieth-Century Australia*. Sydney: University of New South Wales Press, 2003.
Bandy, Joe. "Managing the Other of Nature: Sustainability, Spectacle, and Global Regimes of Capital in Ecotourism." *Public Culture* 8 (1996): 539–566.
Bellone, Tamara, Salvatore Engel-Di Mauro, Francesco Fiermonte, Emiliana Armano, and Linda Quiquivix. "Mapping as Tacit Representations of the Colonial Gaze." In *Mapping Crisis: Participation, Datafication and Humanitarianism in the Age of Digital Mapping*, edited by Doug Specht, 17–37. London: University of London Press, 2020.
Benjamin, Roger. *Orientalist Aesthetics: Art, Colonialism, and French North Africa, 1880–1930*. Berkeley: University of California Press, 2003.
Bertolucci, Bernardo, dir. *The Sheltering Sky*. Warner Brothers, 1990.
Blais, Hélène, Florence Deprest, and Pierre Singaravelou. "French Geography, Cartography and Colonialism: Introduction." *Journal of Historical Geography* 37 (2011): 146–148.
Boëtsch, Gilles and Pascal Blanchard. "The Hottentot Venus: Birth of a 'Freak'." In *Human Zoos: Science and Spectacle in the Age of Colonial Empires*, edited by Pascal Blanchard, Nicolas Bancel, Gilles Boëtsch, Sandrine Lemaire, and Charles Forsdick, 62–72. Liverpool: Liverpool University Press, 2008.
Bourdieu, Pierre (with Abdelmalek Sayad). *Le Déracinement: La Crise de L'agriculture Traditionalle en Algérie*. Paris: Éditions de Minuit, 1964.

Bourdieu, Pierre. "Habitus and Habitat." In *Picturing Algeria: Pierre Bourdieu*, edited by Franz Schultheis and Christine Frisinghelli, 67–89. New York: Columbia University Press, 2003.

Bowles, Paul. *The Sheltering Sky*, 1949. Reprint. New York: Ecco Press, 1998.

Bremer, Thomas S. "Sacred Spaces and Tourist Places." In *Tourism, Religion and Spiritual Journeys*, edited by Dallen J. Timothy and Daniel H. Olsen, 25–35. New York: Routledge, 2006.

Bruner, Edward M. "Transformation of Self in Tourism." *Annals of Tourism Research* 18, no. 2 (1991): 238–250.

Callaway, Helen. "Dressing for Dinner in the Bush: Rituals of Self-Definition and British Imperial Authority." In *Dress and Gender: Making and Meaning in Cultural Contexts*, edited by Ruth Barnes and Joanne B. Eicher, 232–247. New York: Bloomsbury, 1993.

Coleman, Simon. "A Tale of Two Centres? Representing Palestine to the British in the Nineteenth Century." *Mobilities* 2, no. 3 (2007): 331–345.

Cook, Thomas. *Travels in East Africa: Cook's Handbook for Kenya Colony, Uganda, Tanganyika Territory and Zanzibar*. London: Thomas Cook and Son, 1936.

Davis, Diana K. "Desert 'Wastes' of the Maghreb: Desertification Narratives in French Colonial Environmental History of North Africa." *Cultural Geographies* 11, no. 4 (2004): 359–387.

Dening, Greg. "The Comaroffs Out of Africa: A Reflection Out of Oceania." *The American Historical Review* 108, no. 2 (2003): 471–478.

Dinesen, Isak (Karen Blixen). *Out of Africa*, 1937, Reprint. Harmondsworth: Penguin, 1984.

Donaldson, Laura E. "On Medicine Women and White Shame-ans: New Age Native Americanism and Commodity Fetishism as Pop Culture Feminism." *Signs* 24, no. 3 (1999): 677–696.

Duder, C. J. D. "Love and the Lions: The Image of White Settlement in Kenya in Popular Fiction, 1919–1939." *African Affairs* 90, no. 360 (1991): 427–438.

Duffy, Rosaleen. "Interactive Elephants: Nature, Tourism, and Neoliberalism." *Annals of Tourism Research* 44 (2014): 88–101.

Edwards, Brian. "Sheltering Screens: Paul Bowles and Foreign Relations." *American Literary History* 17, no. 2 (2005): 307–334.

Gagiano, Annie. "Blixen, Ngugi: Recounting Kenya." In *Ngugi wa Thiong'o: Texts and Contexts*, edited by Charles Cantalupo, 95–110. Trenton: Africa World Press, 1995.

Gholi, Ahmad, Masoud Ahmadi Mousaabad, and Maryam Raminnia. "Journey to the Loss and Fixation of Western Identity in Bernardo Bertolucci's Movie Adaptation of Sheltering Sky." *Journal of Language, Teaching and Research* 7, no. 5 (2016): 953–957.

Hall, Colin Michael and Stephen W. Boyd. "Nature-Based Tourism in Peripheral Areas: Development or Disaster?" In *Nature-Based Tourism in Peripheral Areas: Development of Disaster*, edited by Michael C. Hall and Stephen W. Boyd, 3–17. Buffalo: Clevedon, 2005.

Hannoum, Abdelmajid. *Violent Modernity: France in Algeria*. Cambridge, MA: Harvard University Press, 2010.

Hanzimanolis, Margaret. "Eight Hen Per Man Per Day: Shipwreck Survivors and Pastoral Abundance in Southern Africa." In *Navigating African Maritime History*, edited by Carina E. Ray and Jeremy Rich, 33–55. Liverpool: Liverpool University Press, 2009.

Herskovits, Melville J. *The Myth of the Negro Past*. Boston: Beacon Press, 1958.

Hitchcock, Robert K., Maria Sapignoli, and Wayne A. Babchuk. "Settler Colonialism, Conflicts, and Genocide: Interactions between Hunter-Gatherers and Settlers in Kenya, and Zimbabwe and Northern Botswana." *Settler Colonial Studies* 5, no. 1 (2015): 1–26.

Holden, Stacy E. "The Legacy of French Colonialism: Preservation in Morocco's Fez Medina." *APT Bulletin: The Journal of Preservation Technology* 39, no. 4 (2008): 5–11.

Hore, Jarrod. *Visions of Nature: How Landscape Photography Shaped Settler Colonialism*. Berkeley: University of California Press, 2022.

Huxley, Elspeth. *White Man's Country: Lord Delamere and the Making of Kenya, 2 Volumes*. London: MacMillan, 1935.

Irbouh, Hamid. *Art in the Service of Colonialism: French Art Education in Morocco 1912–1956*. New York: I.B. Tauris, 2013.

Jackson, Will. "White Man's Country: Kenya Colony and the Making of a Myth." *Journal of East African Studies* 5, no. 2 (2011): 344–368.

Jacobs, Jessica. *Sex, Tourism and the Postcolonial Encounter: Landscapes of Longing in Egypt*. London: Ashgate, 2010.

Kennedy, Dane. *Islands of White: Settler Society and Culture in Kenya and Southern Rhodesia, 1890–1939*. Durham: Duke University Press, 1987.

Knipp, Thomas R. "Kenya's Literary Ladies and the Mythologizing of the White Highlands." *South Atlantic Review* 55, no. 1 (1990): 1–16.

Lefebvre, Camille. "We Have Tailored Africa: French Colonialism and the 'Artificiality' of Africa's Borders in the Interwar Period." *Journal of Historical Geography* 37 (2011): 191–202.

Lester, Alan. "Constructing Colonial Discourse: Britain, South Africa and the Empire in the Nineteenth Century." In *Postcolonial Geographies*, edited by Cheryl McEwan and Alison Blunt, 29–45. New York: Continuum, 2002.

Lewis, Simon. "Culture, Cultivation, and Colonialism in 'Out of Africa' and Beyond." *Research in African Literatures* 31, no. 1 (2000): 63–79.

Leyerle, Blake. "Landscape as Cartography in Early Christian Pilgrimage Narratives." *Journal of the American Academy of Religion* 64, no. 1 (1996): 119–134.

Lockman, Zackary. *Contending Visions of the Middle East: The History and Politics of Orientalism*. New York: Cambridge University Press, 2004.

Lonsdale, John. "Kenya: Home County and African Frontier." In *Settlers and Expatriates: Britons Over the Seas*, edited by Robert Bickers, 74–111. New York: Oxford University Press, 2010.

Loshitzky, Yosepha (Yosefa). *The Radical Faces of Godard and Bertolucci*. Detroit: Wayne State University Press, 1995.

Loshitzky, Yosefa. "Orientalist Representations: Palestinians and Arabs in Some Postcolonial Film and Literature." In *Cultural Encounters: Representing 'Otherness'*, edited by Elizabeth Hallam and Brian V. Street, 51–71. New York: Routledge, 2000.

Loti, Pierre. *Aziyadé*, 1867. Reprint. Paris: North Star, 2016.

Massad, Joseph A. *Desiring Arabs*. Chicago: The University of Chicago Press, 2007.

Mazlish, Bruce. "A Triptych: Freud's The Interpretation of Dreams, Rider Haggard's *She*, and Bulwer-Lytton's *The Coming Race*." *Comparative Studies in Society and History* 35 no. 4 (1993): 726–745.

Mbembe, Achille. *On the Postcolony*. Berkeley: University of California Press, 2001.

McCann, Mat. "Tourism, Difference and Authenticity in an Age of Anxiety: Paul Bowles' *The Sheltering Sky*." In *Lit & Tour: Ensaois Sobre Literatura E Turismo*, edited by Sílvia Quintero and Rita Baleiro, 149–163. Famalicão: Edições Húmus, 2014.

McClintock, Anne. *Imperial Leather: Race, Gender and Sexuality in the Colonial Contest*. New York: Routledge, 1995.

Merrington, Peter. "A Staggered Orientalism: The Cape-to-Cairo Imaginary." *Poetics Today* 22, no. 2 (2001): 323–364.

Minca, Claudio. "'The Bali Syndrome': The Explosion and Implosion of 'Exotic' Tourist Spaces." *Tourism Geographies* 2, no. 4 (2000): 389–403.

Minca, Claudio and Lauren Wagner. *Moroccan Dreams: Oriental Myths, Colonial Legacy*. New York: I.B. Tauris, 2016.

Mitchell, Robin. *Vénus Noire: Black Women and Colonial Fantasies in Nineteenth-Century France*. Athens: University of Georgia Press, 2020.

Mitter, Partha. "The Hottentot Venus and Western Man: Reflections on the Construction of Beauty in the West." In *Cultural Encounters: Representing 'Otherness'*, edited by Elizabeth Hallam and Brian V. Street, 35–50. New York: Routledge, 2000.

Miyonga, Rose. "'We Keep Them to Remember': Tin Trunk Archives and the Emotional History of the Mau Mau War." *History Workshop Journal* 96 (2023): 96–114.

Moadell, Mansoor. *Islamic Modernism, Nationalism, and Fundamentalism: Episode and Discourse*. Chicago: University of Chicago Press, 2005.

Mostafanezhad, Mary and Margaret Byrne Swain. "Afterword—Beyond Anthropology: Ethnography in Tourism Studies." In *The Ethnography of Tourism: Edward Bruner and Beyond*, edited by Naomi M. Leite, Quetzil E. Castañeda, and Kathleen M. Adams, 239–248. Lanham: Lexington Books, 2019.

Moufakkir, Omar and Noureddine Selmi. "Examining the Spirituality of Spiritual Tourists: A Sahara Desert Experience." *Annals of Tourism Research* 70 (2018): 108–119.

Norbu, Jamyang. "Behind the Lost Horizon." In *Imagining Tibet: Perceptions, Projections, and Fantasies*, edited by Thierry Dodin and Heinz Räther, 373–378. Boston: Wisdom Publications, 2001.

Olsen, Daniel H. "Religious Tourism: A Spiritual or Touristic Experience?" In *Routledge Handbook of Tourist Experience*, edited by Richard Sharpley, 391–407. New York: Routledge, 2022.

Olukushi, Adabayo and Francis Nyamnjoh. "The Postcolonial Turn: An Introduction." In *The Postcolonial Turn: Reimagining Anthropology and Africa*, edited by René Devisch and Francis Nyamnjoh, 1–28. Leiden: African Studies Center, 2011.

Perkins, Kenneth J. "The Compagnie Générale Transatlantique and the Development of Saharan Tourism in North Africa." In *The Business of Tourism: Place, Faith, and History*, edited by Philip Scranton and Janet F. Davidson, 34–55. Philadelphia: University of Pennsylvania Press, 2009.

Pollack, Sydney, dir. *Out of Africa*. Los Angeles: Universal Studios, 1985.

Pontecorvo, Gillo, dir. *Battle of Algiers*. Los Angeles: Allied Artists, 1966.

Ranger, Terence. "The Invention of Tradition in Colonial Africa." In *The Invention of Tradition*, edited by Eric Hobsbawm and Terence Ranger, 450–461. New York: Cambridge University Press, 2015.

Reed, Charles. *Royal Tourists, Colonial Subjects and the Making of a British World, 1860–1911*. Manchester: Manchester University Press, 2016.

Robinson, Michael F. *The Lost White Tribe: Explorers, Scientists, and the Theory that Changed a Continent*. New York: Oxford University Press, 2016.

Rosenblatt, Naomi. "Orientalism in American Popular Culture." *Penn History Review* 16, no. 2 (2009): 51–63.

Saissi, Mohammed. "The Symptoms of Orientalism in Pre-Contemporary Western Travel Writings on Morocco." *International Uni-Scientific Research Journal* 2, no. 36 (2021): 240–261.

Shadle, Brett Lindsay. *The Souls of White Folk: White Settlers in Kenya, 1900s–1920s*. Manchester: Manchester University Press, 2015.

Shamma, Tarek. "Horror and Likeness: The Quest for the Self and the Imagining of the Other in *The Sheltering Sky*." *Critical Arts* 25, no. 2 (2011): 242–258.

Shelton, Anthony Alan. "Museum Ethnography: An Imperial Science." In *Cultural Encounters: Representing 'Otherness'*, edited by Elizabeth Hallam and Brian V. Street, 157–193. New York: Routledge, 2000.

Singaravelou, Pierre. "The Institutionalisation of 'Colonial Geography' in France, 1880–1940." *Journal of Historical Geography* 37 (2011): 149–157.

Stam, Robert and Ella Shohat. *Race in Translation: Culture Wars around the Postcolonial Atlantic*. New York: New York University Press, 2012.

Talbot, Michael. "Divine Imperialism: The British in Palestine, 1753–1842." In *The British Abroad Since the Eighteenth Century, Volume 2: Experiencing Imperialism*, edited by Martin Farr and Xavier Guégan, 36–53. New York: Palgrave Macmillan, 2013.

Tuan, Yi-Fu. *Space and Place: The Perspective of Experience*. Minneapolis: University of Minnesota Press, 1977.

Varley, Peter. "Confecting Adventure and Playing with Meaning: The Adventure Commodification Continuum." *Journal of Sports & Tourism* 11, no. 2 (2006): 173–194.

Von Mossner, Alexa Weik. "Encountering the Sahara: Embodiment, Emotion, and Material Agency in Paul Bowles's *The Sheltering Sky*." In *Environmental Awareness and the Design of Literature*, edited by Francois Specq, 116–135. Leiden: Brill, 2016.

Walter, Marc. *Voyages Around the World*. New York: Friedman, 2002.

Ward, David. *The Country and the City*. Oxford: Oxford University Press, 1979.

Whelan, Tensie. "Ecotourism and Its Role in Sustainable Development." In *Nature Tourism: Managing for the Environment*, edited by Tensie Whelan, 3–16. Washington, DC: Island Press, 1991.

Wrobel, David. "Prologue: Exceptionalism, Globalism, and Transnationalism—The West, America, and the World Across the Centuries." In *The Popular Frontier: Buffalo Bill's Wild West and Transnational Mass Culture*, edited by Frank Christianson, 3–12. Norman: University of Oklahoma Press, 2017.

Wyrtzen, Jonathon. *Making Morocco: Colonial Intervention and the Politics of Identity*. Ithaca: Cornell University Press, 2015.

4

SHANGRI-LA

Indeed, the recognition of any Asian spiritual guide, real or fictional, is predicated on his conformity to general features that are paradigmatically encapsulated in the icon of the Oriental Monk: his spiritual commitment, his clam demeanor, his Asian face, his manner of dress, and—most obviously—his peculiar gendered character.[1]

Jane Naomi Iwamura

Shangri-La

The Orient is a fictional region invented by Europeans. Encompassing lands and islands, mountains and deserts, it stretches from North Africa to maritime Southeast Asia. Within the Western imagination, the East has often functioned as a site of paradise that was simultaneously located in numerous places. As Mohammed Saissi explains,

Consequently, the geographical area was validated as a fictional venue where passionate Westerners, mainly writers and painters, would have access to a realm of illimited fantasies and, parallelly, secure an imaginary space where they could turn away from their monotonous life in their home countries.[2]

Edward Said argued that the East is an imaginary site of mystical experience that is part of the West's fantasies about the Orient. The Himalayas is a region where people have been chasing myths for centuries. The indigenous Bon, the Hindu, and the Buddhist cultures all play key roles in the marketing of Nepal and Tibet as part of the "timeless" East.[3] In George Johnston's book

DOI: 10.4324/9781003361725-5

about his travels in Tibet, he describes the mountains as "a valley musical with the song of roaring rivers and the softer, chuckling gurgle of cascades, a valley of a million flowers glittering in bright warm sunshine."[4]

The mountains of Nepal and Tibet are examples of "power places" that "have long had a mythical spell cast over them" and pull people to them.[5] Tibet has often been likened to Shangri-La and its geographical isolation, Buddhist practices, and its people and land have been linked to mysticism.[6] As Donald Lopez has written, for the West, Tibet was not just any Buddhist society, but the "domain of lost wisdom."[7] Nepal, the site of the highest mountain in the world, also holds an important space in the Western imagination. Nepal was known as "the last home of mystery" once it was believed that Tibet's mystical secrets were known.[8] A sacred space for Hindus and Buddhists, British colonial agents, mountaineers, and travelers have also constructed it as a land imbued with mystical possibility. Nepal was closed to most foreign travelers until the 1950s, when "at least a century's worth of pent up desire could finally be satisfied through tourism."[9] The Rana family rule (1846–1951) kept most tourists out, which did not end until February of 1951, coinciding with the Chinese invasion of Tibet and shifting many of the fantasies about Tibet to its neighbor.[10] The most famous mountain in the world, Everest, exists in a national park that links Nepal with Tibet through the Sagarmatha National Park's northern boundary, which forms the frontier with the Tibet Autonomous Region of China.[11]

The immense beauty of Tibet and Nepal, accompanied by their extreme environments and populated with Eastern religions identified with mystical experience, are all critical parts of the story of the mapping of the Himalayas as a mystical landscape. We begin this exploration in the Himalayas with James Hilton's classic book, *Lost Horizon*. A powerful influence on the European and American *imaginaire* about the highest mountains in the world and the people who live there, this novel is where Shangri-La was born.

Lost Horizon

James Hilton's *Lost Horizon* was published in 1933. Set in a magical valley where people lived to an incredibly old age, Shangri-La's community is presided over by a Catholic priest who is 300 years old. A strongly Orientalist novel, it features Chinese characters, pottery, and other Eastern decorative elements. In addition, a Chinese monk (Chang) and female student (Lo-Tsen) are guided by Father Perrault, who oversees a place hidden from the impending collapse of the outside world. The landscape "cut off" from the rest of the world through an "orthographic barrier" maps a geography that only exists once Europeans discover it.[12]

There are numerous theories about the inspiration for the novel. One was inspired by Tseiben-hegen, a *lama* who looked 40 years younger than his real

age, who Hilton viewed as a proof of the power of the hermit's life.[13] Another
theory is that the American Joseph Rock, an explorer and botanist, inspired
Lost Horizon, for Hilton likely read Rock's writings and based the character
of Rutherford (the narrator of the story) on him.[14] The novel was so popular
that Roosevelt named his retreat Shangri-La (it is now Camp David) and
quoted the novel in his 1937 "quarantine speech."[15]

The location of the mythical Shangri-La is debated by scholars. In Hilton's
text, Shangri-La refers to a specific hidden valley, an idea that was later
applied to the entire Tibetan Plateau.[16] In 1944, the writer and adventurer
George Johnston sought to discover the "real" Shangri-La (one of many
who did so) and believed that the ancient *lamasery* of Konka Gomba was
the inspiration for Hilton's novel.[17] In what was an incredible coincidence,
he met a female Chinese mystic at the *lamasery*, whom he called "The Mystery Woman of Snow Mountain," an uncanny resemblance to Hilton's Lo-
Tsen.[18] Johnston declared after he spent the night at the lamasery that he had
slept at Shangri-La and was even more shocked when he met the "beautiful
Chinese girl."[19]

Scholars have placed *Lost Horizon* in different genres, including the imperial romance or "lost worlds romance," genres that both inspired colonialist fantasies and furnished the "imaginary potential" that led to the science
fiction of the twentieth century.[20] Hilton's novel has several Imperial Gothic
elements, which include the occult, the supernatural, and a queered Asia.[21] Its
focus on the Asian frontier was certainly colonial, but the fact that the characters ended up in Shangri-La when the British were ousted from Afghanistan
causes one to question Hilton's support of the British colonial project. One
might also see the novel, the plane's hijacking, and the result—the arrival in
a magical valley—as a meditation on the "end of colonialism."

Lost Horizon is a critical text in the history of Tibet and the larger Himalayan region because it represents the departure from seeing Buddhism as
"the epitome of a degenerate priest religion" and the establishment of the
Himalayas as the space where "the imaginary spiritual map of mankind"
could be finally realized.[22] The Shangri-La depicted in the novel has similarities to the Tibetan myth of *Śambala* (Shambhala), "a legendary land
hidden behind impassable mountains, where wisdom and harmony prevail
even as darkness and chaos rule the outside world."[23] According to Tibetan
tantric texts,

> Shambhala is shaped like a giant lotus and is filled with sandalwood for-
> ests and lotus lakes, all encircled by a great range of snowy peaks. In the
> center of the kingdom is the capital of Kalāpa, where the luster of the pal-
> aces, made from gold, silver, and jewels, outshines the moon; the walls of
> the palaces are plated with mirrors that reflect a light so bright that night
> is like day.[24]

For Tibetans, the physical reality of Shambhala was a more complicated matter. As scholar Blayne Harcey explains,

> Certainly, Tibetans had imaginations about Shambhala. The collection of 11th century Kalachakratantra texts from which Shambhala emerges describe real socio-political realties and present macrocosmic and microcosmic depictions. Thus, Shambhala is both a real place and, in the non-duality of Madhyamika philosophy, a non-real place.[25]

The book begins with two old friends meeting and one telling a story about a man named Hugh Conway, a British colonial agent who had an incredible experience in a hidden valley in Tibet. The story of his Tibetan adventure in a magical valley focuses on Conway, a high British consul; Mallinson, Vice-Consul in the British government; Miss Brinklow, a missionary; and Barnard, an American. Conway and his fellow travelers end up in the magical valley after their plane is hijacked and purposely crashed in the mountains. This brings them to Shangri-La. Many mystical landscapes are inspired by Christian imagery. As the scholar Ying Tian notes, the location of the magical valley of Shangri-La, and the fascination with it in the West, may be influenced by the Biblical verse Genesis 2:8: "The Lord planted a garden in Eden, in the East."[26]

Before they crash, Conway looks out the window of the plane and witnesses the beautiful scenery of Asia. As Hilton writes,

> Far away, at the very limit of distance, lay range upon range of snow-peaks, festooned with glaciers, and floating, in appearance, upon vast levels of cloud. They compassed the whole of the circle, merging towards the west in a horizon that was fierce, almost garish in coloring, like an impressionist back-drop done by some half-mad genius.[27]

This scene foreshadows the land they will be trapped in—beautiful, remote, and completely outside the norms of British life. When the plane crash lands (the travelers do not find out until later that the crash was purposeful—a hijacking), the mountains that surround them are described as shining "on a far horizon like a row of dog-teeth," introducing a foreboding atmosphere.[28] The land is "mountains on top of mountains" and wherever they looked, there was no way out.[29] The entrapment of the characters suggests the Imperial Gothic.

Derek Gregory's colonial politics of vision ("scopic power") is voiced throughout the novel—Conway's gaze out of the plane, the sighting of mountains when they crash land in the high mountains and survey the land that surrounds them, and the scanning of the territory once they are in the magical valley of Shangri-La. The travelers walk to the place the pilot called

Shangri-La and, on the way, spot edelweiss.[30] The European flower functions as a form of colonial imprinting on Tibet, signaling a safer, European type of space, what Hilton describes as "the first welcome sign of more hospitable levels."[31]

When Shangri-La is finally sighted, the travelers step "out of the mist into clear, sunny air" and then see a "strange and half-incredible sight."[32] Like many occurrences in the novel—the sighting of edelweiss and the head lama being French, not Tibetan—Europe enters the landscape of Tibet, mapping it as a space for lost Europeans in need of spiritual enlightenment, but with some of the comforts of Europe. The pavilions of the *lamasery* (the monastery) have "none of the grim deliberation of a Rhineland castle," yet they are fantastic and beautiful.[33] The meals served at the *lamasery* are a mixture of Asian and European foods, "pomelo, tea, and chupatties."[34] The library at Shangri-La had all the European great books (some of the titles which Hilton names), as well as some Asian texts.[35]

Other items in Hilton's text point to European culture, including symbols of empire. Cigars and coffee represent colonial territories under the control of Portuguese, Dutch, and British military forces. Ying Tian notes that "cigar" and "cigarettes" appear in the novel 19 times, illustrating how important tobacco was in the colonial economy, eventually resulting in a tobacco export number of more than 20 million pounds.[36] Even in Shangri-La, tobacco, a prize product of the British, and coffee, lucrative for several colonial empires, show themselves. The tentacles of empire are present even in Shangri La—the secret, magical valley where time stands still. Once at Shangri-La, as Conway steps out on into the courtyard to view the valley below, he expresses his desire to inspect and survey the valley like any other colonial agent.[37]

Hilton's vision of a European monastery within a hidden valley in inner Asia is part of a large corpus of fantasies that Europeans had about Tibet and the Himalayas. Levi Dowling was one of many Christians who claimed Jesus spent his lost years in Tibet, a story he knew from his special access to secret religious texts.[38] The nineteenth century was full of tales of the discovery of white civilizations around the world—in northern Japan, the Philippines, the interiors of Africa, and the Arctic.[39] Tibet was one of these myths, located in a magical land hidden from the Occident until its discovery by explorers, missionaries, adventurers, and other travelers.

Within this Orientalist milieu is the magical Shangri-La, where time is slowed and people lived to an extremely old age. When the head lama, a priest named Perrault, tells Conway about the mystical space of Shangri-La, he says, "But you, it may be, are destined to be more fortunate, since by the standards of Shangri-La your sunlit years have scarcely yet begun."[40] Shangri-La gets its mysticism from its location in Tibet, but it is continually linked and ratified by Christianity. As the high lama/priest explains to

Conway, "the Christian ethic may at last be fulfilled, and the meek shall inherit the earth."[41]

Tibetan scholar Jamyang Norbu has described Hilton's book as the story of white colonials and their servants in a mystical land. As he describes it, *Lost Horizon* is an expression of white fantasies about Asia.

> The head lama is European, as are most of the top brass of Shangri-La. The Tibetans are essentially superstitious peasants and laborers, hewers of wood and drawers of water—coolies—for the white elite of Shangri-La. The intermediary between the white elite and the native Tibetans is, appropriately enough, a Chinese who acts as the major-domo of the Shangri-La monastery.[42]

Chinese are the main Oriental characters because Tibetans were too "obscure" at the time of Hilton's writing, when the West had already attached certain ideas to China and its people.[43]

The novel was likely influenced by Hilton's anxieties about an impending calamity (world war), which was expressed in the lamasery's library and its collection of great Western literature that needed to be saved in case the world outside the valley collapsed.[44] The ending of the book finds Conway helping Mallinson escape, and Conway then searching endlessly for the valley he has lost. Conway's endless search is for a mystical utopia, a "non-place" that exists only in the wild depths of the imagination.[45]

Both the novel and the resulting film elicit a sense of the mystical landscape of Tibet, with its secret mountains and magical monasteries, places identified with stories of monks who can bend spoons and move objects with their minds. In the film, the musical score was used to create "a mood of mystical power" alongside fantastic sets that created a world that could only exist in the imagination.[46] These fantasies and their inscription on the Himalayas helped to create the mystical landscapes sought in tourism. The history of these landscapes begins nearly a thousand years before, in the thirteenth-century Christian imagination.

The Himalayan Imaginary

Tibetans are not a lost Christian culture, but Hilton's novel is not far from the way Tibet was imagined in the thirteenth through nineteenth centuries. One French Catholic claimed that a Tibetan monastery was in fact an atrophied form of Christianity; in 1620, a Jesuit named Antonio de Andrade described the Tibetan religion as a corrupted and degenerate form of his faith, gone amuck because of Tibet's geographical isolation; and two centuries later, a theory emerged to map Tibet as a Christian space through stories of Jesus spending years in the Himalayas.[47] Later accounts of Tibet also relied on fantasies about Christianity. In the early twentieth century, the Polish traveler Ferdinand Antoni Ossendowski published an account of his journey in Inner Asia that claimed a "King of the World" lived in an underground land, north of Tibet.[48]

Shangri-La presents a vision of paradise that relies on belief in a mystical land with magical lamas, yeti, and other miraculous and supernatural happenings. As a scholar of religion, I do not deny the existence of these beliefs, nor do I make a judgment about whether they are real or fictive. However, there is no denying the popularity of these ideas in the West. In the spiritual autobiography written by a German convert to Tibetan Buddhism, he writes,

> In the uninhabited or sparsely inhabited regions of the world the mind expands unobstructed and undeflected. Its sensitivity is not blunted by the continuous interference of other mind activities or by the meaningless noise and chatter of modern life, and therefore it can enter into communication with those minds that are spiritually attuned to it, either by affection or by sharing certain experiences of the inner life.[49]

He then makes this statement: "This explains the frequency of telepathic phenomena among the inhabitants of Tibet—not only among the highly trained, but even among the simplest people."[50]

Paradise is a fluid category. As scholars have noted, it is a concept that shifts depending on location. In her study of tourism in Hawai'i and the Philippines, Vernadette Vicuña Gonzalez explains how paradise is often linked to the threat of violence:

> In other words, paradise is by no means natural—it is conjured through imaginative labor, sustained by such economic apparatuses as plantation and tourism industries and the hierarchized societies they engender, secured through the threat and reality of violence or the promise of rescue, and continually contested by the people who live there.[51]

To many outsiders, the Himalayas represent paradise.

The history of Nepal and Tibet is characterized by their geographical isolation, British mapping, the study of Hinduism and Buddhism, and tales of a magical landscape. The Himalayas are identified with both danger and immense mystical power. As a place believed to be filled with magical lamas and mystical mountains, it has also been a popular site for mystical experience since the emergence of modern tourism. Tibet has not always had this status, however. Victorian and Edwardian travelers described the Tibetans as dirty, uncivilized, ugly, and childlike, illustrating how the idea of Tibetans as mystical people has been a process embedded in Orientalist and Romantic thought.[52]

British colonial agents and travelers in the nineteenth century referred to Tibetan Buddhism as "the Lama religion" and the Dalai Lama as "a Moloch in human shape," illustrating that the romantic view of Tibet was not without its detractors.[53] Early sentiments about the Tibetan form of Buddhism often reflected a paranoia about its similarities to Catholicism, such as the use of rosaries, as evidence of the devil's work and attempts of "demonic plagiarism" to lead good Christians away from the true religion.[54]

The immense size of this mountain region, which lies between the Indus and Brahmaputra rivers, contributes to its popularity with foreigners. As one author puts it, "The sheer aura of Himalayan physicality sublimates into sacred metaphysical depths, for which it is called the mountain of mountains."[55] Sagarmatha/Chomolungma, or Everest as it is known in the West, is in many respects, the ultimate colonial conquest, and as we shall see, it helped to remap Nepal in profound ways. Everest is the colonial name for the mountain that for centuries has been known as Chomolungma (Goddess Mother of the World) to Tibetans and by Sagarmatha (Head of the Earth Touching Heaven) to Nepalis.[56]

The business of mountain climbing is a critical part of the colonial mapping of the Himalayas, inspired by the sport of mountaineering, invented by the British in the 1800s.[57] In fact, climbing mountains as a form of exploration and achievement goes back much further. Claims about Peter of Aragon climbing Cangou (in the Pyrenees) are unverified, but later ascents, to Mount Aiguille in 1492, and to Mount Pilatus in 1555, point to the long history of mountaineering in Europe.[58] Ascents of mountains were also attributed to Petrarch (1355) and Conrad Gesner, the Swiss naturalist, in 1543.[59] The first recorded ascent of a mountain was not achieved by a European. In 633, the monk En no Shokaku climbed Mt. Fuji.[60]

The establishment of the sport is traced to the founding of the Alpine Club in 1857 in Britain and in 1858, the publication of the book *Peaks, Passes, and Glaciers*.[61] Originally a sport of the middle class, it later became associated with scientific study, athleticism, and romanticism.[62] In McNee's study of late Victorian mountaineering, he explains how, for mountaineers and adventurers, the focus on sublime experience shifted to the "haptic sublime," which involved imminent danger and often physical pain.[63] Concerns about social class and the enthusiasm for imperialism led to European attempts on foreign mountains in places like the Caucasus and the Himalayas. As middle-class adventurers began to populate the European Alps, the Alps were seen as less desirable sites for upper class mountaineers, and the interest in new colonies (not "colonized" by the regular tourist) contributed to interest in Nepal.[64]

Nepal has a complex relationship with its two large neighboring countries, India and China. The geopolitics surrounding Nepal's Buddhist heritage, which includes Lumbini, the birthplace of Gautama Buddha, includes efforts by the Chinese to ensure Nepal does not promote anti-Chinese activities within its borders; for Nepal, India is viewed as meddling in their internal affairs.[65] Nepal's relationship with China is largely economic, but also involves efforts by China to control Buddhist sites and the cultural narrative about Buddhism over the claims about the Buddha made by India. India and Nepal also have tensions surrounding Buddhist heritage sites.[66]

Nepal's popularity with tourists is due to its high mountains, which include eight of the highest elevations on earth, resulting in a mountaineering industry that exists as a form of neocolonialism, where tourists acquire "symbolic capital through gazing upon, trekking through or ascending to the top of the highest mountains in the world."[67] Neocolonialism is also seen in the economic control of Nepal's people, who are often dependent on the mountaineering industry for their livelihood. Within the boundaries of the Sagarmatha National Park, nearly 65 percent of households are dependent on the tourist industry.[68]

Tibet's status is much different, as a colonized and occupied land claimed to be part of China. The way in which Tibet continues to exist as a magical and enduring site of Buddhism is a critical part of its mapping as a site of mystical power and experience, "as a realm in which the other-worldly was manifest in various forms and where spiritual wisdom lost to the West was preserved for the seeker after esoteric 'truths.'"[69] The status of Tibet as a mystical landscape has not only survived its occupation by China, but Nepal has also flourished, a result of the belief that mystic power has remained an indestructible part of the landscape. Before exploring the European history of the Himalayas, it is important to understand how local populations view their environment as a sacred and mystical place.

Himalaya's Religious Landscapes

Mountains are important spaces in Hindu and Buddhist thought. For Hindus, mountains are often closer to the gods and thus "more efficacious" as *tirthas*, the crossing places that function as sites of pilgrimage in India, Nepal, Tibet, and other landscapes that reflect a Hindu cosmology.[70] Muktinath, which is sacred to both Hindus and Buddhists, is one example, located in the Annapurna Himalayas in Nepal, on the Damodar Himal that borders the Autonomous Region of Tibet.[71] For Westerners, the Himalayas have long been a "site of mystical alterity" tied to the purity of nature.[72]

Both Nepal and Tibet are of sacred importance to Hindus and Buddhists as sites of religious pilgrimage and as the home of mystical figures from gods to sages. Mountains are the homes of many gods, spirits, and traditions. In Hinduism and Buddhism, they are often locations of *tirthas*, the "thin spaces" where mystical power and the gods are most accessible. *Tirthas* are located all over Nepal and Tibet in mountains, rivers, streams, and other sites. Shaligrams, smooth, black ammonite fossils, which are worshipped by Hindus as a form (*murti*) of the god Visnu (Vishnu), are also linked to these *tirthas* through their linking of different landscapes and sacred spaces, which scholar Holly Walters describes as "spiritual embodiment involving landscapes and nature that cross multiple boundaries of and link together Hindu, Buddhist, and shamanic traditions."[73]

In addition to being the location of *tirthas*, mountains are also the abodes of local and regional gods. One example of this is Adam's Peak in Sri Lanka, where Hindus believe Lord Shiva left his footprint during the world-creation dance. In Tibetan Buddhism, the mountains are often the home of local deities who have been tamed in service of Buddhism or serve as the location of treasure houses where relics and other objects are kept.[74] As Todd Lewis explains, "Doctrinally, both Indic Buddhism and Hinduism represent powerful ideological formulations of spiritual conquest. Texts recount founders converting local deities, and saints conquering indigenous ritualists and demons."[75]

While Nepal and Tibet are separate places and cultures, the region of Nepal focused on in this chapter, Solu-Khombu, is home to the Sherpas, who are linked to Tibet historically, ethnically, and religiously. As Ortner reminds us, "Their ancestors migrated from eastern Tibet in the sixteenth century, and they remain closely related ethnically to Tibetans."[76] This migration was likely due to conditions created by cooling from the Little Ice Age and resulted in the population of Sherpa being established in what is now Nepal.[77] The oldest Tibetan monasteries were built over a 1,000 years ago, with the oldest being Samye which dates from the eighth century. Sherpas in the modern period began building monasteries in Solu-Khombu in the early twentieth century, the first two founded in 1916 and 1924.[78] The first nunnery was established in 1925 and completed three years later.[79] The presence of Sherpas as early as 1531 and the popularity of Pangboche and Dingboche villages as meditation sites suggest that while Sherpas may have found an empty land to settle in, there were at least wandering mystics who frequented the area.[80] The European belief in the Himalayas as a mystical landscape was intensified by the closing of Tibet to outsiders after 1792, which challenged "the European project of gathering empirical knowledge but left considerable space for imaginal constructions that only enhanced the lure of the 'Forbidden Land.'"[81]

Tibet and Nepal are connected in other ways, including in religious matters that are important to the subject of this book—mystical spaces. One example is Muktinath, part of a sacred pilgrimage that started in Kathmandu and ended in Mt. Kailash (Gang Rinpoche) in Tibet.[82] It is sacred to Hindus, and its main temple, Vishnu Mandir, houses an image of Vishnu and includes temples for other gods and goddesses, as well as a Shaligram (which is worshipped as Vishnu for Hindus and a Tibetan deity for Buddhists).[83]

There is a long history of Vishnu being worshipped through Buddha images.[84] At Muktinath, the image of Vishnu is a Tibetan deity named Lokeswar, a *boddhisatva*.[85] There is also a building shared by Hindus and

Buddhists, the Jwala Mai (Temple of the Miraculous Fire) that sits among the five temples that form the site.[86] Historically, the King of Nepal, who is believed to be a reincarnation of Vishnu, has performed *puja* at Muktinath; and after Pashupatinath, it is the most sacred site for Hindus and Buddhists.[87] Nepal and Tibet have many of these shared cultural traditions including their pilgrimages at Mount Kailash.

Kailash

Kailash is a sacred landscape connected with many religious myths and narratives, religious pilgrimages, religious objects such as the pearl relics, and holding meaning due to their role in spiritual renewal.[88] Mountains are not only important for religious pilgrims. The Himalaya's sacred power has played a critical role in its tourism history as well. The name "Kathmandu" was evocative of exoticism and mystic possibilities. It has always had a "romantic pull" that reflected the belief people had about it being "isolated and mysterious."[89] As one study notes, "[f]requently lying in remote areas and requiring long journeys from the profane life of villages or towns, mountains have been represented in mythologies as the sacred domain of gods and spirits."[90] The Himalayas are no exception, as this region of Asia is believed to be both a "sacred landscape and a spiritual utopia."[91]

Kailash is believed by Hindus to be the manifestation of Meru on earth.[92] It is not summitted, but is visited by Hindus, Buddhists, and followers of the Bon religion. As Simon Piasecki explains, Hindus believe that the god Shiva sits "in eternal meditation with his wife Kali" on its peak; for Buddhists, it is the center of their cosmology; for the Bon, it is the sacred center; and for the Jains, it is where Rishabhana achieved enlightenment.[93] The Bon, whose beliefs predate the Buddhists in Tibet, have a sacred geography that places Kailash (Mount Ti se) as the location of the Silver Castle (the old name for the area, *Khyung lung dngul mkhar*) and the "center of the world."[94]

Tibet's Mount Kailash is an integral part of Asian sacred geography, with hundreds of mountains and temples within India and beyond its borders being named after the semi-mythical place north of India that is believed to be populated with *yakṣas* and *devas*, and at its top, it is the abode of Lord Indra (and Lord Shiva), as well as a place the Gautama Buddha visited.[95] Diana Eck describes Kailash as the most important abode of Shiva (who has many abodes), the "mountain manifestation, so they say, of Shiva's *linga* of light—the one that pierced the earth in the beginning of time."[96] For worshipers of Shiva, it is the most sacred journey. As one pilgrim expresses,

On top is the abode of Lord Shiva. Sprawling below us the sacred Manasarovar, where a ritual bath will deliver a pilgrim to Lord Brahma's Paradise, and a drink of its holy waters relinquishes the sins of a hundred lifetimes.[97]

In Hindu sacred geography, Kailash is often transposed on not only different places such as Tibet, but also far-off locations like the temple complex in
West Java called Prambanan ("the Indonesian Kailash").

Kailash is believed to be the palace of Demchong, a Tibetan god, and as
noted earlier, its summit is believed to be the domain of Shiva.[98] For Hindus,

IMAGE 4.1 Photo of Prambanan, Yogyakarta Region, Indonesia.

Source: photo courtesy of author

IMAGE 4.2 Photo of Prambanan, Yogyakarta Regency, Indonesia.

Source: photo courtesy of author

Kailash is believed to be the real Meru, the center of the universe, and other religions also view it as extremely sacred. As one scholar notes, the identification of Kailash with Meru is because, "in time the mystical Meru and the earthly Kailas merged in people's minds. Early wanderers to the source of the four great Indian rivers . . . found to their wonder that each one rose near a cardinal point of Kailas."[99] Kailash is also a place where Tibetan relics are found, especially the small pearl-like beads (*ring bsrel/ringsel*) located near the stones and rivers on the mountain.[100] These objects also signify the mystic power of mountains, as they are believed to be a sign of a Buddhist saint's sacred power, what Rachel Guidoni describes in one saint as "as sign of his high spiritual power" that included pearls coming out of his bones "weeks after his cremation."[101]

Kailash is visited by Hindus, Buddhists, and other pilgrims, and is one of the most sacred places on earth. It is also an important part of the West's understanding of Tibet as a mystical land. Pilgrims circumambulate the mountain in a ritual known as the *kora* (*parikrama*), which is dangerous (many pilgrims die during their attempts to do this pilgrimage) and includes passing through the *chorten*, which is a liminal space, and through many geographical formations at high altitudes that are believed to be Buddhist, Hindu, and Bon gods.[102] One of the most intense mystical sites of the journey is the Vajra Yogini burial ground, which is a cemetery not of corpses but "of previous lives—it is where pilgrims practice death, often laying among the rocks."[103] The objects that surround pilgrims who lie among the jagged rocks are the "mimesis of a corpse" and include the teeth and hair of other pilgrims.[104]

The spiritual center of this pilgrimage is the field of boulders which is above the burial ground of past lives, which is 3,000 feet higher than the Everest base camp. As Piasecki says, it is a space where "a human being cannot survive."[105] Here, pilgrims face Yama, the King of Death, and may provide drops of their own blood and "drop them on the earth" alongside pieces of clothing and clumps of hair, all preparation for the soul's journey to the next life.[106] As noted above, rocks and boulders, which are a common feature of this journey, are also sites of Tibetan relics in the form of the pearls that signify a saint, found near rocks on Kailash.[107]

Hindu pilgrims who reach this point try to bathe in the pool of Goddess Parvati/Kali, the *Gaurī Kunda* (Gowri Kindam), where she was believed to have seduced Siva, an act that requires the breaking of ice, for this is at an altitude of over 18,500 feet.[108] As one pilgrim describes it, "The unbearable cold provides the pilgrim with the direct experience of the truth that body and soul are indeed separate entities."[109] The path of return is taken once one has experienced the death and rebirth, if they have survived the journey, and by the meditation cave of Milarepa.[110] The final ascent to Drölma-la includes circumambulating the Drölma Stone, where Drölma "disappeared in the form of 21 wolves" after leading Götsangpa to the site.[111]

Kailash is an important part of the history of Tibet in the Western imagination. McKay points out that in the nineteenth century, the mountain's spiritual status was of no interest, but this would change as more travelers visited the region surrounding the Kailash-Mansarovar region.[112] Despite some early travelers' impressions that Kailash was important, as the twentieth century began, "English language works did not subscribe to Kailas as a place of religious significance."[113] Charles Sherring (1868–1940), who worked for the Indian Civil Service, published the book *Western Tibet and the British Borderlands* in 1906, which was focused on a British audience (and an educated Indian one) and the colonial goal of economic improvement to the area.[114] Despite the problems with the book, including inaccuracies as to Kailash's sacred status for Hindus and its success as an argument for opening Tibet and expanding the empire, it was the "first modernist account" of the mountain and survives as the "basis for the predominant understanding of the sacrality if the region."[115] Other works followed Sherring's book, including *Three Years in Tibet*, an account of the travels of a Japanese Buddhist monk, and Sven Hedin's writings, which described Kailash as the site of "ageless sanctity."[116]

Hedin's works were published at a time when Orientalist ideas about the East, including Tibet, were particularly strong. His quest to be the first person to see hidden valleys and mountaintops was part of the hubris of the time, when European explorers failed to consider that Tibetans had already "discovered" these hidden places long before. However, the "white spots" he wanted to find (blank spaces) were part of his larger interest in experiencing the sublime.[117] Landscapes were also a critical part of mapping, as the "gaze from up high" had the potential to form the basis for the mapping, surveillance, and occupation of new territory.[118] McKay has pointed to some of the more questionable aspects of Hedin's methodology, which include a lack of command of Sanskrit and a reliance on Orientalist scholars, resulting in unintentional mistakes that reveal a lack of knowledge of Indian religious texts.[119] These methodological issues may be because Hedin, while being a geographer, was never employed at a university.[120] The understanding of Kailash was, of course, a reflection of colonial interests, and the texts that did this work were accepted not only by the British, but by Indians as well, sidelining other perspectives and studies on Kailash.[121]

Kailash is an example of how Tibet's religious traditions encourage the mapping of Tibet as a mystical land that can cure the problems of the individual coming from the West. Foreign pilgrims have documented their mystical experiences on the pilgrimage, including Winand Callewaert, the eminent scholar. His mystical experience on the pilgrimage in 1996 included these moments:

> I tried my familiar Christian lines. Total darkness. I prayed to Krishna, the Guru of the Sikhs, and to Shiva, Lord of the Devas, with all the lines in my memory, but He kept not only his third eye closed. All eyes of the divine were closed to me. It was an experience I shall and should never forget. Finally I concentrated on the mountain I had not yet seen. A piece of rock covered by a glacier, that much I knew. No words, no priests, no traditions. Pure transcendence.[122]

Bishop describes how places like Nepal and Tibet function in the West's search for enchantment through the "desire to reclaim its 'lost soul' in other times and places."[123] It is not necessary that tourists to these places are religious; in fact, most would never say they are Hindu or Buddhist. However, they identify the region as holding mystical powers that they are seeking. The idea of Tibet was created by colonial knowledge. Following Foucault, Bishop writes, "The 'truth' about a place such as Tibet, therefore, was no discovered, but produced as a result of specific social and imaginative relationships."[124]

Orientalism has always played a dominant role in the imagination about the Himalayas, a region viewed as one in need of documentation and surveillance because of its old age and the inability of Asians to save what was quickly disappearing with the onset of modernity. Donald Lopez explains how Tibet and, by extension, Tibetans were viewed as relics of the past:

> It has been the conviction of European (and later American) Orientalists that the classical age is forever lost, leaving them the task of the preservation and care of its remnants, most often in the form of textual and artistic artifacts; contemporary Asians have allowed this classical age to pass into near oblivion, and thereby have forfeited their proprietary rights over its remains.[125]

China's development of tourism in Tibet has influenced the ways foreigners view Tibet, who fear that it will become less authentic. Robert Sheperd explains how these reflect Orientalist ideas of Tibet:

> These concerns resonate so much because one narrative about Tibet dominates and shapes both academic and popular cultural Euro-American views of Tibet: a pre-Maoist Tibet of holiness and harmony that has been ruined by, first, a Maoist drive to physically destroy Tibet's cultural and spiritual Being and, more recently, a post-Maoist commodification of any authenticity in Tibet that survived Mao.[126]

Tibetans are also viewed as people always engaged in resistance, either covertly or overtly, suggesting that they are a group of people who are relentlessly brave.[127]

The Himalayan mountains are an *extreme* environment. The high altitudes where Chomolungma/Sagarmatha and Kailash are located at are part of a small set of places known as alpine environments, which are fragile. They are both rare and special, as this study points out:

> Soils are young and thin, environments are cold and harsh, plant growth cycles are slow, and even minor forms of disturbance can take decades to heal. They cover 3 percent of the world's surface and are inhabited by

more than 10,000 species of plant, making alpine environments the most
biodiverse habitats in the world.[128]

One way that colonialism has been extended into the twenty-first century
is in tourist businesses like the mountaineering industry in Nepal. The local
guides, known as *Sherpas*, and the foreign adventurers, called *Sahib*, exist in
a binary relationship that reflects the colonial themes of conquest and servi-
tude. Although Sherpas are paid for their services, the relationship revolves
around a hierarchy with the goal of conquest. As Sherry Ortner explains,
white athlete-tourists follow a "western ideology of 'conquest' and the acquisition of symbolic capital through gazing upon, trekking through, or ascending to the top of the highest mountains in the world."[129] At the center of these
neocolonial journeys of symbolic conquest is the extreme environment of the
Himalayas.

Sagarmatha/Chomolungma and Mysticism in Extreme Sports

The focus on extremes found in today's wellness culture also is seen in sports
and travel, where athletes and tourists push themselves to their physical
limits. Scholars have likened these "peak experiences" to mystical experiences, what Nick Watson calls "nature mysticism."[130] The concept of "flow"
is sometimes invoked by scholars to refer to the moments in these experiences when athlete-tourists experience transcendence.[131] Extreme sports, also
known as adventure sports, action sports, and "Whizz sports," have their
roots in the 1960s countercultural movement that also brought tourists to
Nepal and Tibet.[132]

One space where we see this focus on sparsity is in the mountain-climbing
business, which relies on wealthy Americans and Europeans (and, at times,
others, including several famous Japanese climbers) and their desire to summit dangerous and often deadly mountains. In Nepal, even people who have
no interest in going to base camps or to higher altitudes (Kathmandu is at
4,600 feet) typically do a trek. Trekking is a big business in Nepal, usually
to Everest base camp or the Annapurna range; as one non-athlete tourist put
it, this is a "rite of passage"—something that is expected from the tourist.[133]
As is often the case with tourism, a paltry amount of revenues go to the local
communities, with one study placing the benefit to Nepalese communities at
10 percent.[134] While the trekking business did not take off for several decades after Nepal was opened to tourists, foreigners began trekking almost
immediately after the country opened to tourism. A 1955 book documents a
female Swiss adventurer and her travels to places she likely had no permis-
sion to be in, including the Khumbu Valley.[135]

Discourses about science, the body, and aesthetics are seen in the mountaineering industry that dominates the Western imagination about Nepal

today. It should also be noted that in addition to their exploits in the Himalayas, the British had other mountaineering experiences in the Andes and in Aotearoa (New Zealand), which they called the "Southern Alps."[136] As Jarrod Hore explains, this "reinforced settler territoriality in the highlands of the South Island by integrating them with well-known European landscapes like the Alps."[137]

Sparsity is a prominent theme in the promotion of Nepal and Tibet as destinations for mystical tourism. One example of the focus on sparsity is seen in the physical limits that climbers have and the lengths they go to transcend these limits. Perhaps the best example of this are the oxygen tanks that litter Mount Everest, sometimes lying close to climbers whose lives were lost on the mountain. The harsh climate and high altitudes of the Himalayas did not preclude foreign climbers from bringing their favorite things on an attempted ascent, and items were usually carried by Sherpas, along with climbing equipment and necessary provisions. Sherry Ortner tells how during a 1938 attempt, Bill Tilman played chess and read titles like *Seventeenth Century Verse* and Montaigne's *Essays*.[138] Today, as the climbing business has boomed, climbers have changed what they bring—now it's espresso makers and iPads, instead of the classics of European literature.[139]

The achievement of summiting Sagarmatha/Chomolungma (Everest) can be understood to be in direct relationship with the bodily sacrifices made to get there. This is much like the detox and extreme dieting culture, where affluence and leisure are in a relationship with the restrictions placed on one's body. As Dana Logan writes,

> The real miracle, however, happens beyond the laws of physics. Flesh, bodily fluids, and internal "toxins" not only disappear through detoxification, but also transfigure the materiality of the body and the world, creating abundance out of absence.[140]

While climbing the famous mountain is often at the center of people's minds when they think of Nepal, most visitors are trekkers who traverse high altitudes and spiritual seekers who view the Himalayas as a mystical landscape. Tengboche monastery is one popular site visited by trekkers.[141] However, the entire landscape is viewed as special and spiritually potent.

The romanticism attached to Tibet is also seen in the mountaineering industry in Nepal. Mountaineering as a scientific endeavor and pastime of middle-class British men was overtaken by the Romantics in the second half of the nineteenth century, when physicists like J.J. Thompson at Cambridge lost faith in the empirical and utilitarian ideology that had dominated scientific study, which was replaced by a more metaphysical approach.[142] The view of mountains also changed, as noted by scholar David Robbins:

Far from being a backdrop against which a bourgeoisie could demonstrate its powers, mountains were seen as a repository of truths, harmonies, and sensibilities which had been lost with industrialism, and mountaineering was viewed as a way of recovering them.[143]

Tibet provides a different type of experience, where the high altitudes are endured for the privilege of visiting what remains of an important Buddhist tradition, impacted by the occupation of Tibet by China in 1953 and the destruction of much of its religious culture. Nepal's Solu-Khombu region is also important for religious reasons, but most tourists to the Everest region are focused on trekking, sightseeing, and climbing.

Nepal has always been a land of mystique, in part due to its physical location. Popular with tourists in the 1950s and hippies in the 1960s, it has remained a destination for climbers as well as those in search of the mystical powers associated with Nepal's landscape and people. As one study notes, "During the 1950s, media outlets in the West commonly referred to Kathmandu as the 'forbidden kingdom'; one Newsweek article in 1955 even heralded the city as a 'genuine Shangri-La.'"[144] Early climbers talked of climbing the highest mountain in the world in spiritual terms, as a transcendent experience that provided an escape from modernity.[145] Sherpas, on the other hand, were characterized as physically strong (a product of the Himalayan environment), but lacking the "spirit" to want to ascend the mountain on their own.[146] Linked to their Tibetan origins, Sherpas are Buddhists and have often been identified as being connected to Tibetan Buddhism, setting themselves apart from their Nepali Hindu countrymen.[147]

In the century preceding 1951, the year the modern Nepali state was founded, the country was mostly closed to tourists. Even the British were only allowed "3 or 4 visitors a year to the British residency compound in Kathmandu," at a time when Tibet (also isolated from most tourism) saw five times that number.[148] The beginning of Nepal's tourist industry began with Sir Edmund Hillary's ascent of Everest in 1953. A few years later, 24 wealthy Thomas Cook travelers visited Nepal as a side excursion on their cruise, which was docked in Bombay.[149] They stayed at the Royal Hotel, which became a center of expatriate activity, visited by "a steady stream of thirsty mountaineers, diplomats, explorers, spies, missionaries, aid workers, big-game hunters, and yeti enthusiasts—along with the rich and famous tourists."[150] The first tourist visas were issued in 1955, and for several years the majority of tourists were older wealthy Americans, a much different crowd than today's younger backpackers and climbers.[151]

In the 1960s, tourism in Nepal was influenced by the hashish supply (cannabis was outlawed in 1973) as well as other available drugs like opium and heroin, with spiritual seekers also making up many of the travelers to the country.[152] A Harvard connection included Richard Alpert, who, after being fired from the university, met Bhagwan Dass (Ram Dass) at the Tibetan Blue restaurant and became one of his disciples.[153] Even after cannabis was outlawed in Nepal, the idea of Kathmandu as a haven for escapism remained, its status as a mystical land forever enshrined in the Western imagination.

Authenticity is a key component of Nepal's tourist industry, which is focused on trekking and the mystical attributes attached to the nation and its mountains. There are competing ideas about who is an authentic tourist that one gets from expatriates living in places like Kathmandu. What is important here, however, is what is at the center of beliefs about Nepal as a mystical place, and this is situated in the idea that mountain areas are authentic because they are untamed. As Howard explains, for Nepal, this involves "a quality ascribed to remote, mountain landscapes and the traditional people living amid them."[154]

Religious scholars have long argued about whether sport is a religion. Sport has beliefs, rituals, communities, and pilgrimages. As Sean Gammon points out,

> Arguments abound suggesting the similarity of sport and religion; whether comparing the church or temple with the sports stadia and the shrine-like qualities of halls of fame, or in the ritualistic characteristics practiced on both field of play and terraces.[155]

Even if one contends that sport is not a religion, there are several resemblances, including "invoking a sense of belonging, purpose and consolation."[156]

Chomolungma/Sagarmatha has its own colonial history, which is an important part of the story of mystical tourism in Nepal and India. British mountaineers focused their interests on the Royal Geographical Society in London and the Himalayan Club in Darjeeling; the latter sought out Himalayan migrants for guides, including Sherpas.[157] This included the most famous Sherpa of all time, Tenzing Norgay, who grew up "watching adults carry salt and wood loads [from] as far away as Darjeeling."[158] The story of how Norgay became the most famous Sherpa in history in 1953 is linked to the colonial mapping of the region and how British viewed Sherpas and other communities in India and Nepal. Norgay spent years working as a laborer in Darjeeling and made the mistake of cutting his braid, so he would not appear too "rustic," a mistake that caused him to be rejected from the Himalayan Club for the 1933 expedition, as members thought he was a Nepali and not a Sherpa.[159] Two years later, he reapplied for the next expedition and "made sure that he conformed to the British recruiters' image of a genuine Sherpa."[160]

Sagarmatha/Chomolungma (Everest) is the most famous mountain in the world. As such, it holds a privileged place in the Western consciousness. Its role in the tourism industry is one way this is shown, but the extreme sports industry is also tied to the goal of scaling mountaintops that is originally located in Everest history. Mountaineering today is a business, not a mystical journey, and is focused on the acquisition of yet another thing. David Houston writes about mountaineering, "It is not an escape or a departure from civilization, it is an extension of it, an accessory."[161] The expense of climbing Everest suggests that while Nepal has a wide variety of tourists, the climbers who attempt the highest mountain in the world are able to pay close to six figures for getting the privilege of attempting this journey.[162]

The popularity of mountain wear is situated in the long history of Nepal in the Western imagination. The sponsorship of climbers has become common for the most elite athletes, resulting in the success of outdoors clothing in the wider society. As Christopher Driscoll points out,

> Ironically, while not many within western society actually climb big mountains, climbers have long made headlines for various climbing efforts, and in recent years, through company affiliations such as Mammut, The North Face, Berghaus, and Patagonia, big mountain climbers today contribute to contemporary western notions of style.[163]

While female climbers (and some minorities) have become more common in recent years, climbing Everest has largely been the domain of white men. Men make a disproportionate amount of the participants in climbs and are the "popular culture representatives."[164] Bravery and glory are commonly invoked by both groups of climbers and those creating discourse about them such as journalists, suggesting the importance of the norms identified with white masculinity. The Sherpas, whose male members serve as guides for foreign climbers, lie outside this discourse as a group whose economic situation is the reason for their involvement in such a dangerous journey.[165] As Sherry Ortner reminds us,

> For the sahbs, the risk of death is what makes the sport glorious; for the Sherpas there is nothing noble about the risk at all; there is only a kind of threat that must be managed, negotiated."[166]

The threat of death is something that can be experienced by climbers by peering over a cliff or glimpsing "into the abyss."[167] However, for the Sherpas these risks are undertaken because of financial survival.

Tibet and the Spiritual Quest

In Tibet, tourists are attracted to practices of Buddhism that have survived for centuries through the Chinese invasion and the continued occupation of Tibet. Tibet is the ancestral homeland that remains a sacred landscape for

Tibetans who now live in a diaspora brought about by the Chinese invasion of the country in 1959. For Tibetan Buddhists (there are also Tibetan Muslims, discussed in the Introduction to this book, and others, including the Bon, whom I will discuss shortly), Tibet is the home to a lineage of Dalai Lamas who are believed to be "emanations of the Boddhistava Avalokishesh-vara," the Boddhisatva of compassion.[168]

As discussed earlier, the casting of Tibet as a pure Buddhist land ignores the presence of Tibetan Muslims and others in the history of Tibet. As David G. Atwill notes, "Despite the characterization of Khache as perpetual non-natives in many foreign accounts of Lhasa, Tibetan Muslims lived as Tibetans among Tibetans by the early seventeenth century."[169] The presence of Muslims in Tibet went against the vision of the land as a purely Buddhist space. When Robert Crozier and Harold "Mac" McCullum crashed their plane in Tibet in 1942, they were first greeted with "As salaam alaikum"—a detail that was excluded from media—an example of the "larger erasure of Tibetan Muslims, or Khache, from almost all accounts of Tibet."[170]

Exotica Tibet is the name given to the "exoticized Western representations of Tibet" by scholar Dibyesh Anand.[171] It relies on the mystical power attached to the Himalayan mountains, to the Tibetan Buddhist religion, and to Tibetan bodies. The prohibition against tourists to the region added to the mystery and cycle of mythical stories about Tibet's magical lands, including the claims of the *yeti*. The kingdom of Lo (Mustang) was not opened to outsiders until the 1980s, providing a long period in which the lore about Tibet could flourish.[172] The idea of a mystical Tibet is so powerful that today, Han Chinese live as migrant tourists (Zangpiaos), "sojourners" who see Tibet as "a utopian spiritual home," an idea located in the Western vision of Shangri-La.[173]

Tibet, as a locus of mystical Buddhism, is also home to an older religion—the Bon (Bonpo), which remains an important part of Tibetan religious practice in the *Bon dKar* (white Bon) and *Bon gNak* (black Bon).[174] As Holly Walters notes, this religion not only predated Buddhism, but has also long had a close relationship with it,

> According to some accounts, black Bon was indigenous to Mustang before white Bon, which became mixed with eleventh and twelfth-century Tibetan Buddhism of the Skahkya-pa sect arriving from the north and continued mixing with other indigenous practices (such as the *dhami-jhankri* shamanic traditions) throughout the Kali Gandaki River valley up until the nineteenth century.[175]

Nepal and Tibet are not purely Hindu or Buddhist, although at times they have been described that way by foreigners, and as Walters points out in her study of shaligrams, this landscape is characterized by complexity.[176]

The way scholars arrived at these ideas about foreign places was often based on ignorance, fantasy, or both. This is true of India when Hinduism was constructed out of the confusion and wonderment Europeans had when traveling and studying the religions popular in the Indus Valley.[177] The identification of mystical landscapes with India and her religions is a colonial and historical process with numerous effects. As Richard King explains,

> The rise of Hindu- and Buddhist-inspired groups throughout the West, much of contemporary New Age mythology as well as media advertising and popular culture in general, demonstrates the ongoing cultural significance of the idea of the "Mystic East," and the continued involvement of the West in a romantic and exotic fantasy of Indian religions as deeply mystical, introspective and otherworldy in nature.[178]

Hinduism was eventually overtaken by Buddhism as the most popular Eastern mystical religion, something seen in Nepal where Buddhism is monetized as part of the tourism industry, and Hinduism is often ignored or downplayed.[179]

Tibet has been a popular setting for novels like Hilton's *Lost Horizon* and films like *Seven Years in Tibet* (1997). Even Sherlock Holmes has an interlude in Tibet, after he is killed by falling off a cliff in Switzerland and later resurrected by Sir Arthur Conan Doyle, who explains the detective's absence with a story about him traveling for two years in Tibet and studying with a lama.[180] In *The Adventure of the Empty House*, Holmes states, "I traveled for two years in Tibet, therefore, and amused myself by visiting Lhassa, and spending some days with the head lama."[181]

In Tibet, "knowledge" about the territory was often based on nonscientific methods. As Dibyesh Anand has written, "In situations where the culture was relatively unknown—like the Tibetan—hearsay, legends, and fantasies performed an even more important archival function."[182] Among these were stories of magical monks and creatures like the *yeti*. The *yeh-teh* or *meh-teh* (snow-man or bear-man in Tibetan) was a figure that predates European fascination with it, but the claims of sightings by a Swiss expedition, efforts to collect evidence of yeti tracks, and the involvement of cryptozoologists all helped to create a kind of mania about the mythical creature.[183] The *yeti* even made his way into a *Tintin* story, in which Tintin's friend Chang was rescued and cared for by the human-like creature.[184] Stories of magical monks are still common among Tibetan Buddhists, including white converts who follow the tantric forms of Buddhism that characterize this branch of the religion. It is important to note that beliefs in the fantastic also link Nepal and Tibet.

The poverty of Tibetans plays a role in the idea of *Exotica Tibet*. In early twentieth-century traveler accounts, poverty is often mentioned as an innate quality of Tibetans. George Knight wrote about Tibet, "it is a land of mountains, monasteries and monks, land of women, dogs and dirt, country of the great unwashed."[185] The tourism industry in Tibet is focused on the surviving communities of Buddhists who have had a slow resurgence over the past half century. Beginning in 1979 under Hu Yaobang, tourism was slowly opened to foreigners, which initially included only 1,000–2,000 tourist visas per year, a number that by the mid-1980s was 20 times this number.[186]

The Price of Tourism

Nepal has been deeply impacted by its framing as a destination for sublime and mystical experience, which from the early days of mountaineering made it the ultimate site of conquest for adventurers and today for elite athletes. The business of climbing the tallest mountain on earth has resulted in devastating losses for Nepal, from environmental damage to the loss of human life. The trails used by trekkers and climbers in Nepal are often the same ones used for centuries by traders who traveled between Nepal and Tibet. As one study notes, "Prior to tourism, the Thame route was the most intensively used route, as Khumbu traders used it to access the Nangpa La (pass) to cross over into Tibet."[187]

A survey of geographic studies of Sagarmatha clearly illustrates the damage caused by tourism in the region. In my reading of four studies, the academic opinion was unanimous: the climbing industry has caused environmental violence on Nepal's alpine environment. Deforestation, overgrazing by livestock herds, tourist demands for resources, and other forms of land misuse are all part of this process, in addition to more obvious problems like waste, including human waste, that has grown exponentially with the growing numbers of tourists in Nepal.[188] The often unreasonable expectations of foreign mountaineers have effects in other ways, contributing to the death of Sherpas who guide them and resulting in the death of climbers who are in too much of a rush to acclimate ("summit fever").[189]

Curiously, there is no "pack it in/pack it out" policy ethic as practiced by many North American campers and hikers. Instead, human, food, and other waste are left behind. In addition, timber and other resources are exploited. In some cases, mitigation efforts involve locals, which appears to have a positive impact on the rates of destruction. As Alton Byers notes in one of his many studies of the problem, "These better forest conditions were said to be in part related to the presence of *shingo-* and *osho-naua*, or village-appointed forest and field guards with the power to fine villagers found cutting wood or abusing the community-defined land-use regulations."[190] I did not find a reference to fining tourists, however, which suggests the problematic nature of tourist spaces that are also home to local communities.

The Everest climbing region is not the only one in Nepal that has seen environmental effects of tourism. In Alton Byers' study of the Makalu-Barun

National Park, he documents the impact of tourists and the businesses that support them. This area's popularity with trekkers is due to overcrowding of the Everest treks and its access to the highest "trekking Peak," Mera Peak.[191] Lodges in Kothe and other settlements for trekkers have resulted in problems including human waste, timber harvesting, and large amounts of glass beer bottles, all "huge accumulations" in "direct response to tourist demands for a varied diet."[192]

The human costs of the climbing business, an industry that largely benefits foreign entities, from guiding companies to clothing and gear manufacturers, include a huge loss of Sherpa lives. Anthropologist Sherry Ortner has written several excellent books on the Sherpas, their religious communities, culture, and their important role in Himalayan mountaineering. In her 1999 study, which is based on decades of fieldwork in Nepal, she writes,

> Indeed for some climbing Sherpas, nearly every expedition they worked for had had a fatal accident. And it is probably fair to say that there is no Sherpa at all—man, woman, or child, climber or nonclimber—who does not personally know a fellow Sherpa who was killed in mountaineering.[193]

The emergence of Sherpas as climbing guides is tied to the occupation of Tibet by China in 1953, when the frontier with Tibet was closed, ending the long-standing trade of salt and wool from Tibet and iron, wheat, and barley from Nepal.[194] One impact of the climbing business is its effect on the land, which as discussed earlier, is a sacred landscape tied to nature. In villages, forests were often destroyed to build homes and lodges for tourists, thus altering the sacred landscape of Nepal.[195]

The impact on religious and cultural traditions can also be seen in the transition of an economy based on trade and other activities to one focused on tourism. The Sherpa and other communities in Nepal have been forced to change their religious rituals as a response to the environmental effects of tourism. One example is the Khumbu Alpine Conservation Committee's banning of juniper for *puja* (worship) that were performed in the Everest region.[196] The cultural costs of the climbing industry include the transition of the Himalayas from a religious space to a capitalist space. Starting in the 1960s, when the Everest became such a popular destination for climbers, the mountains were seen as "the home of the gods," a designation that has now become "a place of work."[197]

The effects of the Himalayan mountaineering business on religious practices are also seen in the ways that Buddhist authorities have been forced to change their position on religious principles. In the beginning, the lamas were not supportive of Sherpas' involvement in expeditions on Everest due to concerns about angering the gods and the safety of their community members, which included danger from creatures far more terrible than the *yeti* and the presence of demons on the mountain.[198] As Ortner explains, after large donations by the *sahib* were made to monasteries, the lamas seemed to come around to supporting the expeditions, an example of how "the Sherpas are not free agents."[199] This suggests that Sherpas' need to go along with the desires of foreigners is linked to Buddhist practice in problematic ways.

Tibet has a radically different history than Nepal. As a place that has suffered a violent invasion and occupation by the Chinese military, the imagination about Tibet is located both in these events and its status as the site of Shangri-La. The belief that Tibet is special and that it holds a sacred and distinct kind of mystical power is linked to its near destruction; European and American Buddhist converts who follow the Tibetan lineages and teachers have often voiced the idea that these same Tibetan traditions must be saved. The number of tourists entering Tibet (called the Tibetan Administrative Region) has steadily climbed since China opened the territory to foreign visitors. However, the majority of visitors have been Chinese. Between 1995 and 2000, approximately two million tourists visited Tibet and 80 percent of these were from China.[200] Today, these numbers are even larger. Chinese tourists include adventure travelers as well as drifters, called *Zangpiaos* (piao or "drifter") by some scholars, who spend anywhere "between 2 and 20 years or even longer in Tibet without long-term stable employment."[201] They are often on spiritual searches, wishing to be removed from the work culture of the Chinese society.[202]

The development of tourism in Tibet by the Chinese government has radically changed the landscape. One example is the Qinghai-Tibet Highway, an asphalted, 2,000-km highway that connects China to Tibet.[203] Popular with Chinese millennial mountain bikers, it provides excitement, physical challenges, and cultural interactions with Tibetans.[204] As one study noted, overnight homestays with Tibetan families were the highlight of the experience for many of these tourists because "[h]ospitality and offering help is seen as characteristic of Tibetan people; this was experienced and highly valued."[205] This view reflects the larger Orientalist vision of Tibet held by Chinese, whose government has been classified as being premodern and subjects needing to be made "modern."[206] For many Chinese, the Tibetans are viewed as *zang* (dirty) from the Han point of view, the lack of bathing being one in a long list of behaviors viewed as backwards and anti-modern,

> They are known to retain some cultural traits that most Han cannot fathom—bathing seldom, spending time and money on religious activities, eating much meat and dairy products rather than grain and vegetables (which, in any case, do not grow easily at Tibet's elevation).[207]

Efforts to overlay a kind of Chinese visual topography on Tibet have included the People's Square, which was placed in front of the Potala Palace, and the transition of the Dalai Lama's former home (his summer palace, Nor-bulingka) into a park and museum.[208] These attempts to secularize the religious past reflect a kind of religious and cultural violence that has been only somewhat successful. According to Robert Sheperd, the Lama's old bathtub has become a kind of shrine in which "[b]ills are tossed in as offerings, and Tibetan peasants bow and pray when passing."[209]

Mystical Landscapes of the Himalayas

Nepal and Tibet are popular sites of mystical tourism that function in different ways—one as a site of mystical mountains and the other as a place of mystical landscapes and Tibetan bodies. One theoretical frame for understanding the appeal of Nepal and its great mountain is the concept of "power places." These places are often imbued with a religious significance, but they are also often sites that are culturally colonized as international tourism icons.[210] As discussed earlier, Nepal is subject to a colonial gaze that finds its power in the mountaineering industry. Although foreign tourists do not *possess* Nepal's mountains, they possess them through the *scopic regime* of adventure tourism. The mountaineering industry relies on the belief that Nepal is a mystical landscape and that climbing its highest mountain is for many a deeply spiritual experience.

Tibet remains a site of mystical tourism for several different groups of tourists. European and American converts to Tibetan Buddhism are particularly interested in experiencing Buddhism, which for the Chinese, is treated as an "acceptable" religion if it is integrated into the state.[211] What this means for Tibetan Buddhism is that it is under surveillance and control due to its potential to be backwards, in the eyes of government authorities, "Together, these stances have led to greater regulation and surveillance of monks, the deployment of monasteries as tourist attractions, and the transformation of major religious holidays into state-sponsored celebrations."[212]

As discussed earlier, many Chinese tourists visit Tibet in part due to their proximity and because of Tibet's status as a site of spiritual and mystical experience. The Zangpiaos who often spend decades in Tibet, wandering the landscape, going from job to job, are one example. Jinfu Zhang's study of this subset of Chinese travelers explains how important Tibet's mystical reputation is for Zangpiaos, "Meanwhile, Zangpiaos' spiritual quests, lying in concepts like 'scaredness,' 'soul,' and '(spiritual) shock,' coincide with the symbolic Shangri-La or Shambhala image of Tibet and tie them to Tibet."[213] *Zang piao* (drifters in Tibet) and *la piao* (drifters in Lhasa) are temporary settlers.[214] These groups of Chinese tourists are not settler colonists because they do not seek to replace the Tibetan population. Specifically drawn to Tibet as a mystical landscape, they see themselves as transformed by the environment.

Some drifters even adopt Tibetan names, which may be given by Tibetan friends.[215]

The fascination that drifters have with Tibetans as special and mystical is situated in ideas about the landscape. These include the embodied Tibetan practices of pilgrimage to Lhasa and monasteries and rituals like the spinning of prayer wheels (*ma ni 'khor lo*), which is performed around monasteries.[216] Monasteries are sites of mystic power, founded by lamas and other religious figures who often have cycles of narratives about mystical powers and visions surrounding them. The popularity of Tibet as a mystical landscape is also an opportunity for Chinese officials to market locations like Xiahe and Gannan and the entire prefecture of Gansu as "Tibetan spaces." The effort to present these as "exemplary models of consumable Tibetan culture" is problematized by their multiethnic and multireligious populations, which include Muslim Hui.[217] The promotion of these sites is tied to the popularity of the idea of Shangri-La among Chinese and other tourists.[218]

The question of what constitutes an authentic religious experience in Tibet is affected by tourist beliefs about a mystical Tibet, which means that Tibetans either fulfill these fantasies or are cast as nonauthentic, ruined by Sinicization. Mystical tourism, then, doesn't necessarily exist in the capital of Lhasa, but in the isolated parts of the country. Tibetans are expected to be all "that contemporary Westerners have dreamed about—religious, exotically different, devoted to tradition, and above all today, oppressed."[219]

Mystical tourism in Tibet is shaped by these expectations. Western tourists look for the fantasy of Tibet, a land full of monks who were fully supported and focused solely on study and meditation, which itself is a place that never existed.[220] This vision of Tibet is part of larger fantasies of the virtual Orientalism propagated in cinema and other forms of cultural expression in the United States. Jane Naomi Iwamura has argued that the "Oriental monk" is a dominant way that Americans see Buddhism and other Asian religions. The popularity of the Oriental monk as a recognizable symbol of Asian spirituality helps to explain the appeal of the Dalai Lama, whose status as "an American pop cultural figure" is linked to celebrity endorsements of the Free Tibet movement by famous Buddhists like Richard Gere.[221] The "lama fever" attached to Tibet is also a colonial move that allows "psychic resolution and healing" but fails to challenge America's own history of colonialism, the land taken, the children stolen from their parents, and the millions of Native American lives taken.[222]

The introspective monk is a popular figure in the American imagination about the East, so much so that other Tibetan men, such as the "Lhasa Tibetans" who run successful businesses and spend as much as $17,000 on the latest men's fashion, are aberrations of the romanticized Tibet.[223] In addition to the idea of the magical monks are the Tibetan nuns, who are often left out of representations of Tibet that focus more closely on male Buddhist practitioners. American followers of Buddhism may not know that the Tibetan word for woman means *low rebirth*.[224] However, gender and other social inequities in Tibetan culture are often overlooked because the focus is on a mystical landscape that has been a powerful part of the West's imagination and remains so. In Dan Smyer Yü's book on the mindscape of Tibet, he writes, "To enter Tibet is a gift" because "It is a unique bond, an affordance, between the traveler and the Tibetan landscape that deserves sympathetic understanding not moral judgment from social scientists."[225] My hope is that I have been sympathetic in my attempt to understand the ineffable and mystical landscape of the Himalayas.

Notes

1 Jane Naomi Iwamura, *Virtual Orientalism: Asian Religions and American Popular Culture* (New York: Oxford University Press, 2011), 6.
2 Saissi, n.p.
3 Strausberg, 124–125.
4 George Johnston, *Journey Through Tomorrow* (Melbourne: F. W. Cheshire, 1947), 223.
5 Strausberg, 124.
6 Shangri-La has become a generic term ascribed to several other places located in the Orient, including Bali, an island examined in a later chapter. See also Note 15.
7 Donald Lopez, *Prisoners of Shangri-La: Tibetan Buddhism and the West* (Chicago: University of Chicago Press, 2018), 6.
8 See Liechty 2017, 21–23.
9 Liechty 2017, 3.
10 Liechty 2017, 9, 25.
11 Alton Byers, "Contemporary Human Impacts on Alpine Ecosystems in the Sagarmatha (Mt. Everest) National Park, Khumbu, Nepal," *Annals of the Association of American Geographers* 95, no. 1 (2005): 114. Everest is the colonial name for the mountain, but it is known as Sagarmatha to Nepalese and Chomolungma to Tibetans.
12 Paul Beedie, "A History of Mountaineering Tourism," in *Mountaineering Tourism*, ed. Ghazali Musa, James Higham, and Anna Thompson-Carr (New York: Routledge, 2015), 49.
13 Neuhaus, 133.
14 Ying Tian, "Shangri-La and the Imperial Imagination in James Hilton's *Lost Horizon*," *ANQ* 37, no. 3 (2024): 415.
15 Neuhaus, 133. Shangri-La was also the name given to China in U.S. bombing raids on Japan and the name of an aircraft carrier in WWII. See Stausberg, 125.
16 Paul Genoni and Tanya Dalziell, "George Johnston's Tibetan Interlude: Myth and Reality in Shangri-La," *Journeys* 18, no. 2 (2017): 3.
17 Genoni and Dalziell, 8–10.
18 Genoni and Dalziell, 20.
19 Johnston 1947, 316, 346, 349.
20 Mather, 231.
21 Mather, 237, 238.
22 Stausberg, 125.
23 Thierry Dodin and Heinz Räther, "Imagining Tibet: Between Shangri-La and Feudal Oppression," in *Imagining Tibet: Perceptions, Projections, and Fantasies*, ed. Thierry Dodin and Heinz Räther (Boston: Wisdom Publications, 2001), 396.

24 Lopez 2018, 182.
25 Email exchange with Blayne Harcey, February 21, 2025.
26 Tian, 416.
27 James Hilton, *Lost Horizon* (1933: repr., New York: Harper Perennial, 2012), 37.
28 Hilton, 47.
29 Hilton, 47.
30 Hilton, 65.
31 Hilton, 65.
32 Hilton, 67.
33 Hilton, 67.
34 Hilton, 86.
35 Hilton, 98.
36 Tian, 419.
37 Tian, 417. See also Hilton, 105.
38 Liechty 2017, 18.
39 Robinson 2016, 4.
40 Hilton, 160.
41 Hilton, 165.
42 Norbu, 374.
43 Michael Hutt, "Looking for Shangri-La: From Hilton to Lāmichhāne," in *The Tourist Image: Myths and Myth Making in Tourism*, ed. Tom Selwyn (New York: John Wiley & Sons, 1996), 51.
44 Liechty 2017, 17.
45 Hutt, 52.
46 John R. Hammond, *Lost Horizon Companion: A Guide to the James Hilton Novel and Its Characters, Critical Reception, Film Adaptations and Place in Popular Culture* (Jefferson: McFarland & Company, 2008), 139.
47 Lee Feigon, *Demystifying Tibet: Unlocking the Secrets of the Land of Snows* (Chicago: Elephant Paperbacks, 1998), 16–17.
48 Neuhaus, 126. Hedin, who is discussed later in this chapter, criticized these stories as fabrications. See Neuhaus, 126–129.
49 Lama Anagarika Govinda, *The Way of the White Clouds* (New York: Overlook Press, 1966), 113.
50 Govinda, 113.
51 Gonzalez, 8.
52 Neuhaus, 47.
53 Alastair Lamb, *British India and Tibet: 1766–1910* (New York: Routledge & Kegan Paul, 1960), 69, 89. Quote about Dalai Lama is from Karl Friedrich August Gützlaff, *China Opened*, Volume 1 (London: Smith, Elder & Company, 1838), 284.
54 Donald S. Lopez, Jr. "New Age Orientalism: The Case of Tibet," *Tricycle: The Buddhist Review* 3, no. 3 (1994): 37.
55 Singh, 218.
56 Gyan P. Nyaupane, "Mountaineering on Mt. Everest: Evolution, Economy, Ecology and Ethics," in *Mountaineering Tourism*, ed. Ghazali Musa, James Higham, and Anna Thompson-Carr (New York: Routledge, 2015), 265.
57 David Robbins, "Sport, Hegemony and the Middle Class: The Victorian Mountaineers," *Theory, Culture & Society* 4 (1987): 583.
58 Berry, 113.
59 McNee, 5.
60 Beedie, 45.
61 Robbins, 584.
62 Robbins, 585, 588.

63 McNee, 151.
64 McNee, 211.
65 Kalyan Bhandari, "Tourism and the Geopolitics of Buddhist Heritage in Nepal," *Annals of Tourism Research* 75 (2019): 61.
66 Thanks to Blayne Harcey for discussing these conjoined histories and their effect on Lumbini and other sites.
67 Beedie, 48, 44.
68 Colin Michael Hall, "Mountaineering and Climate Change," in *Mountaineering Tourism*, ed. Ghazali Musa, James Higham, and Anna Thompson-Carr (New York: Routledge, 2015), 240. Nepali climbers also climb the mountains within the park. See Sanjay K. Nepal and Yang (Sunny) Mu, "Mountaineering, Commodification and Risk Perceptions in Nepal's Mt. Everest Region," *Mountaineering Tourism*, ed. Ghazali Musa, James Higham, and Anna Thompson-Carr (New York: Routledge, 2015), 251.
69 McKay, 379.
70 Donald A. Messerschmidt, "The Hindu Pilgrimage to Muktinath, Nepal, Part 1: Natural and Supernatural Attributes of a Sacred Field," *Mountain Research and Development* 9, no. 2 (1989): 89.
71 Messerschmidt, Part 1, 92. The Bhotia, as they are known by the Nepalese, are Buddhists who live in this area and are often found alongside the many Hindu pilgrims who visit Muktinath.
72 Liechty 2017, 14.
73 Holly Walters, "Cornerstones: Shaligrams as Kin," *The Journal of Religion* 102, no. 1 (2022): 94, 103.
74 Blayne Harcey, E-mail communication, February 21, 2025.
75 Todd T. Lewis, "Himalayan Religions in Comparative Perspective: Considerations Regarding Buddhism and Hinduism across Their Indic Frontiers," *Himalaya* 14, no. 1 (1994): 29.
76 Ortner 1999, 12.
77 Byers 2005, 115.
78 Ortner 1999, 90.
79 Ortner 1999, 93.
80 Byers 2005, 117.
81 McKay 2016, 379–380. McKay has written elsewhere about the British agents who were stationed in Tibet from 1904 to 1947. As he has noted, "The myth of Tibet as an unknown land of mystery depends on ignoring the presence of these officials." See Alex McKay, "The Establishment of the British Trade Agencies in Tibet: A Survey," *Journal of the Royal Asiatic Society* 2, no. 3 (1992): 399.
82 McKay, 399.
83 Messerschmidt, Part 1, 94, 96.
84 See John Holt, *The Buddhist Visnu: Religious Transformation, Politics, and Culture* (New York: Columbia University Press, 2004).
85 Messerschmidt, Part 1, 94, 96.
86 Donald A. Messerschmidt, "The Hindu Pilgrimage to Muktinath, Part 2: Vaishnava Devotees and Status Reaffirmation," *Mountain Research and Development* 9, no. 2 (1989): 107.
87 Myra Shackley, *Managing Sacred Sites: Service Provision and Visitor Experience* (New York: Continuum 2001), 149.
88 Edwin Bernbaum, "Sacred Mountains: Themes and Teachings," *Mountain Research and Development* 26, no. 4 (2006): 304–305.
89 Liechty 2010, 266.
90 Howard, 357.
91 Howard, 357.

92 Piasecki, 17.
93 Piasecki, 17.
94 Tsering Thar, "Mount Ti se (Kailash) Area: The Center of the Himalayan Civilization," *East and West* 50, nos. 1/4 (2009): 25–26, 28.
95 K. T. S. Sarao, "Kailash," *Encyclopedia of Indian Religions: Buddhism and Jainism*, ed. K. T. S. Sarao and J. D. Long (Dordrecht: Springer Science Business Media, 2017), 607.
96 Diana Eck, *India: A Sacred Geography* (New York: Harmony Books, 2012), 198–199.
97 Pradeep Chamaria, *Kailash Manasarovar: On the Rugged Road to Revelation* (New Delhi: Abhinav Publications, 1996), 17.
98 Bernbaum, 306.
99 Colin Thubron, *To a Mountain in Tibet* (London: Vintage, 2012), 5.
100 Rachel Guidoni, "Conceptions on Tibetan Relics," in *Nature, Culture and Religion at the Crossroads in Asia*, ed. Marie Lecomte-Tilouine (New York: Routledge, 2017), 264, 268.
101 Guidoni, 266.
102 Piasecki, 18–19.
103 Piasecki, 20.
104 Piasecki, 20.
105 Piasecki, 21.
106 Sarao, 615.
107 Guidoni 268.
108 Piasecki, 21.
109 Sri Swami Satchidananda, *Kailash Journal: Pilgrimage into the Himalayas* (Yogaville: Integral Yoga Publications, 1984), 104.
110 Piasecki, 21.
111 Sarao, 615. Drölma is the Tibetan name for Tara. Götsangpa was the founder of the Drukpa Kagyu tradition of Buddhism in Tibet.
112 McKay 2016, 380, 384.
113 McKay 2016, 386.
114 McKay 2016, 388, 390, 393.
115 McKay 2016, 398.
116 McKay 2016, 398, 399, 401.
117 Staffan Bergwik, "Elevation and Emotion: Sven Hedin's Mountain Expedition to Transhimalaya, 1906–1908," *Centaurus* 62 (2020): 653.
118 Bergwick, 657.
119 McKay 2016, 403–404.
120 Bergwick, 651.
121 McKay 2016, 409.
122 Winand M. Callewaert, "On the Way to Kailash," in *Pilgrimage in Tibet*, ed. Alex McKay (Surrey: Curzon Press, 1998), 114.
123 Liechty 2005, 21.
124 Bishop, 12.
125 Donald S. Lopez, Jr., "Foreigner at the Lama's Feet," in *Curators of the Buddha: The Study of Buddhism under Colonialism*, ed. Donald S. Lopez, Jr. (Chicago: University of Chicago Press, 1995), 252.
126 Robert Sheperd, "UNESCO and the Politics of Cultural Heritage in Tibet," *Journal of Contemporary Asia* 36, no. 2 (2006): 244–245.
127 Adams, 515.
128 Byers 2005, 112.
129 Ortner 1999, 44.
130 Watson, 104.

131 Varley, 178.
132 Watson, 97.
133 Norum, 38.
134 Bandy, 559.
135 Liechty 2017, 49.
136 Berry, 118.
137 Hore, 86.
138 Ortner 1999, 34.
139 Ortner 1999, 288.
140 Logan, 608.
141 Byers 2005, 115.
142 Robbins, 595.
143 Robbins, 595.
144 Liechty, 267. Quoted in Norum, 30.
145 Ortner 1999, 36–37.
146 Ortner 1999, 42.
147 Ortner 1999, 94.
148 Liechty 2005, 20.
149 Norum, 32.
150 Liechty 2010, 254. Quoted in Norum, 32.
151 Liechty 2005, 20.
152 Liechty 2005, 22, 25.
153 Liechty 2005, 23.
154 Howard, 355.
155 Gammon, 35.
156 Gammon, 41.
157 Jayeeta Sharma, "Himalayan Darjeeling and Mountain Histories of Labour and Mobility," in *Darjeeling Reconsidered: Histories, Politics, Environments*, ed. Townsend Middleton and Sara Shneiderman (New York: Oxford University Press, 2018), 91, 93.
158 Sharma, 94.
159 Sharma, 94–95.
160 Sharma, 95.
161 Houston, 154.
162 Beedie and Hudson, 628–629. According to Beedie and Hudson, the cost of a permit alone was $70,000 in 2003.
163 Christopher Driscoll, "Sublime Sahib: White Masculinity Formation in Big Mountain Climbing," *Culture and Religion* 21, no. 1 (2020): 44.
164 Driscoll, 49.
165 The Khumbu Icefall is one of the most dangerous parts of the journey and is often affixed with ladders and ropes for the first expedition of the year. The most dangerous work is given to Sherpas, with foreigners avoiding the highest risks of death. See Beedie and Hudson, 633.
166 Ortner 1997, 140.
167 Varley, 179.
168 Klieger, 123.
169 Atwill, 7.
170 Atwill, 13, 15.
171 Anand, 24.
172 Shackley, 150.
173 Honggen Xiao and Jinfu Zhang, "Liquid Identities: Han Sojourners in Tibet," *Annals of Tourism Research* 88 (2021): 2, 8.
174 Walters 2020, 117.

175 Walters 2020, 117–118.
176 Walters 2020, 124.
177 See Richard King, "Orientalism and the Modern Myth of 'Hinduism,'" *Numen* 46, no. 2 (1999): 146–185.
178 Richard King, *Orientalism and Religion: Postcolonial Theory, India and 'the Mystic East'* (New York: Routledge, 1999), 142.
179 Liechty 2017, 325.
180 Feigon, 20.
181 Arthur Conan Doyle, *Sherlock Holmes and Dr. Watson: A Textbook of Friendship*, ed. Christopher Morley (New York: Harcourt, Brace and Company, 1944), 294.
182 Anand, 29.
183 Liechty 2017, 56–57.
184 Liechty 2017, 63. See also Tintin in Tibet (1960).
185 George Knight, *Intimate Glimpses of Mysterious Tibet and Neighbouring Countries* (London: Golden Vista Press, 1930), 25. Quoted in Anand, 33.
186 Klieger, 124.
187 Sanjay K. Nepal and Stella Amor Nepal, "Visitor Impacts on Trails in the Sagarmatha (Mt. Everest) National Park, Nepal," *Ambio* 33, no. 6 (2004): 335.
188 Byers 2005, 116–117.
189 Nepal and Mu, 253, 256–258.
190 Byers 2005, 115.
191 Alton Byers, "Contemporary Human Impacts on Subalpine and Alpine Ecosystems of the Hinku Valley, Makalu-Barun National Park and Buffer Zone, Nepal," *Himalaya* 33, no. 1 (2014): 28.
192 Byers 2014, 31.
193 Ortner 1999, 7.
194 Hans Caspary, "The Cultural Landscape of Sagarmatha National Park," in *Cultural Landscapes of Universal Value: Components of a Global Strategy*, ed. Bernd von Droste, Mechtild Rössler, and Harald Plachter (Jena: Gustav Fischer Verlag, 1995), 155.
195 Caspary, 158.
196 Alton Byers, "A Comparative Study of Tourism Impacts on Alline Ecosystems in the Sagarmatha (Mt. Everest) National Park, Nepal, and the Huascarán National Park, Peru," in *Ecotourism and Environmental Sustainability: Principles and Practice*, ed. Tim Gale and Jennifer Hill (New York: Routledge, 2009), 56.
197 Driscoll, 48.
198 Ortner 1997, 148–149.
199 Ortner 1997, 149.
200 Sheperd 2006, 245.
201 Jinfu Zhang, "Drifting Home: The Quests of Chinese Tourist-Migrants in Tibet," *Journal of Travel Research* 63, no. 6 (2024): 1461.
202 Zhang, 1462.
203 Akke Folmer, Ali (Tanya) Tengxiage, Hanny Kadijk, and Alastair John Wright, "Exploring Chinese Millennials' Experiential and Transformative Travel: A Case Study of Mountain Bikers in Tibet," *Journal of Tourism Futures* 5, no. 2 (2019): 145.
204 Folmer, Tengxiage, Kadijk, and Wright, 148–151.
205 Folmer, Tengxiage, Kadijk, and Wright, 151.
206 Sheperd 2006, 251.
207 Susan D. Blum, *Portraits of 'Primitives': Ordering Human Kinds in the Chinese Nation* (Lanham: Rowman & Littlefield, 2001), 132.
208 Sheperd 2006, 253.

209 Sheperd 2006, 253.
210 Stausberg, 98.
211 Adams, 517.
212 Adams, 517.
213 Zhang, 1462. See also Y. Tuan, *Space and Place* (Minneapolis: University of Minnesota Press, 1977), 150.
214 Hong Zhu and Junxi Qian, "'Drifting' in Lhasa: Cultural Encounter, Contested Modernity, and the Negotiation of Tibetanness," *Annals of the Association of American Geographers* 105, no. 1 (2015): 145.
215 Zhu and Qian, 150.
216 Zhu and Qian, 151.
217 Chris Vasantkumar, "Dreamworld, Shambala, Gannan: The Shangrilazation of China's 'Little Tibet'," in *Mapping Shangrila: Contested Landscapes in the Sino-Tibetan Borderlands*, ed. Emily T. Yeh and Christopher R. Coggins (Seattle: University of Washington Press, 2014), 54.
218 Mather, 233.
219 Adams, 523.
220 Adams, 524.
221 Iwamura, 162.
222 Iwamura, 164–165.
223 Adams, 529.
224 See Victress Hitchcock's film, *Blessings: The Tsoknyi Nuns of Tibet* (2009).
225 Dan Smyer Yü, *Mindscaping the Landscape of Tibet: Place, Memorability, Ecoaesthetics* (Boston: De Gruyter, 2015), 49.

Bibliography

Adams, Vincanne. "Karaoke as Modern Lhasa, Tibet: Western Encounters with Cultural Polities." *Cultural Anthropology* 11, no. 4 (1996): 510–546.
Anand, Dibyesh. "Western Colonial Representations of the Other: The Case of Exotica Tibet." *New Political Science* 29, no. 1 (2007): 23–42.
Annaud, Jean-Jacques. *Seven Years in Tibet.* Sony Pictures, 1997.
Atwill, David G. *Islamic Shangri-La: Inter-Asian Relations and Lhasa's Muslim Communities, 1600 to 1960.* Oakland: University of California Press, 2018.
Bandy, Joe. "Managing the Other of Nature: Sustainability, Spectacle, and Global Regimes of Capital in Ecotourism." *Public Culture* 8 (1996): 539–566.
Beedie, Paul. "A History of Mountaineering Tourism." In *Mountaineering Tourism*, edited by Ghazali Musa, James Higham, and Anna Thompson-Carr, 40–54. New York: Routledge, 2015.
Beedie, Paul and Simon Hudson. "Emergence of Mountain-Based Tourism." *Annals of Tourism Research* 30, no. 3 (2003): 625–643.
Bergwik, Staffan. "Elevation and Emotion: Sven Hedin's Mountain Expedition to Transhimalaya, 1906–1908." *Centaurus* 62 (2020): 647–669.
Berry, Evan. *Devoted to Nature: The Religious Roots of American Environmentalism.* Berkeley: University of California Press, 2015.
Bhandari, Kalyan. "Tourism and the Geopolitics of Buddhist Heritage in Nepal." *Annals of Tourism Research* 75 (2019): 58–69.
Birnbaum, Edwin. "Sacred Mountains: Themes and Teachings." *Mountain Research and Development* 26, no. 4 (2006): 304–309.
Bishop, Peter. *The Myth of Shangri-La: Tibet, Travel Writing and the Western Creation of Sacred Landscape.* Berkeley: University of California Press, 1989.
Blessings: The Tsoknyi Nuns of Tibet. Directed by Victress Hitchcock, 2009.

Blum, Susan D. *Portraits of 'Primitives': Ordering Human Kinds in the Chinese Nation*. Lanham: Rowman & Littlefield Publishers, 2001.

Byers, Alton. "Contemporary Human Impacts on Alpine Ecosystems in the Sagarmatha (Mt. Everest) National Park, Khumbu, Nepal." *Annals of the Association of American Geographers* 95, no. 1 (2005): 112–140.

Byers, Alton. "A Comparative Study of Tourism Impacts on Alpine Ecosystems in the Sagarmatha (Mt. Everest) National Park, Nepal and the Huascarán National Park, Peru." In *Ecotourism and Environmental Sustainability: Principles and Practices*, edited by Tim Gale and Jannifer Hill, 51–71. New York: Routledge, 2009.

Byers, Alton. "Contemporary Human Impacts on Subalpine and Alpine Ecosystems of the Hinku Valley, Makalu-Barun National Park and Buffer Zone, Nepal." *Himalaya* 33, no. 1 (2014): 25–41.

Callewaert, Winand M. "On the Way to Kailash." In *Pilgrimage in Tibet*, edited by Alex McKay, 108–116. Surrey: Curzon Press, 1998.

Capra, Frank, dir. *Lost Horizon*. Columbia Pictures, 1937.

Caspary, Hans. "The Cultural Landscape of Sagarmatha National Park." In *Cultural Components of Universal Value: Components of a Global Strategy*, edited by Bernd von Droste, Mechtild Rössler, and Harald Plachter, 154–160. Jena: Gustav Fischer Verlag, 1995.

Chamaria, Pradeep. *Kailash Manasarovar: On the Rugged Road to Revelation*. New Delhi: Abhinav Publications, 1996.

Dodin, Thierry and Heinz Räther. "Imagining Tibet: Between Shangri-La and Feudal Oppression." In *Imagining Tibet: Perceptions, Projections, and Fantasies*, edited by Thierry Dodin and Heinz Räther, 391–416. Boston: Wisdom Publications, 2001.

Doyle, Arthur Conan. *Sherlock Holmes and Dr. Watson: A Textbook of Friendship*. Edited by Christopher Morley. New York: Harcourt, Brace and Company, 1944.

Driscoll, Christopher. "Sublime Sahib: White Masculinity Formation in Big Mountain Climbing." *Culture and Religion* 21, no. 1 (2020): 43–57.

Eck, Diana L. *India: A Sacred Geography*. New York: Harmony Books, 2012.

Feigon, Lee. *Demystifying Tibet: Unlocking the Secrets of the Land of the Snows*. Chicago: Elephant Paperbacks, 1998.

Folmer, Akke, Ali (Tanya) Tengxiage, Hanny Kadijk, and Alastair John Wright. "Exploring Chinese Millennials' Experiential and Transformative Travel: A Case Study of Mountain Bikers in Tibet." *Journal of Tourist Futures* 5, no. 2 (2019): 142–156.

Gammon, Sean. "Chapter 2: Secular Pilgrimage and Sport Tourism." In *Sport Tourism: Interrelationships, Impacts and Issues*, edited by Brent W. Richie and Daryl Adair, 30–45. Clevedon: Channel View Publications, 2004.

Genoni, Paul and Tanya Dalziell. "George Johnston's Tibetan Interlude: Myth and Reality in Shanri-La." *Journeys* 18, no. 2 (2017): 1–27.

Gonzalez, Vernadette Vicuña. *Securing Paradise: Tourism and Militarism in Hawai'i and the Philippines*. Durham: Duke University Press, 2013.

Govinda, Lama Anagarika. *The Way of the White Clouds*. New York: The Overlook Press, 1966.

Guidoni, Rachel. "Conceptions on Tibetan Relics." In *Nature, Culture and Religion at the Crossroads of Asia*, edited by Marie Lecomte-Tilouine, 260–282. New York: Routledge, 2017.

Gützlaff, Karl Friedrich August. *China Opened, Volume One*. London: Smith, Elder & Company, 1838.

Hall, Colin Michael. "Mountaineering and Climate Change." In *Mountaineering Tourism*, edited by Ghazali Musa, James Higham, and Anna Thompson-Carr, 240–249. New York: Routledge, 2015.

Hammond, John R. *Lost Horizon Companion: A Guide to the James Hilton Novel and Its Characters, Critical Reception, Film Adaptations and Place in Popular Culture*. Jefferson: McFarland & Company, 2008.

Hergé. *Tintin in Tibet*. NYC: Little Brown Books, 1975.

Hilton, James. *Lost Horizon*, 1933. Reprint. New York: Harper, 2012.

Hitchcock, Victress, dir. *Blessings: The Tsoknyi Nuns of Tibet*. Chariot Films, 2009.

Holt, John Clifford. *The Buddhist Visnu: Religious Transformation, Politics, and Culture*. New York: Columbia University Press, 2004.

Hore, Jarrod. *Visions of Nature: How Landscape Photography Shaped Settler Colonialism*. Berkeley: University of California Press, 2022.

Houston, David L. R. "Five Miles Out: Communion and Commodification Among the Mountaineers." In *Tarzan Was an Eco-Tourist . . . and Other Tales in the Anthropology of Adventure*, edited by Luis Vivanco and Robert Gordon, 147–160. New York: Berghahn Books, 2006.

Howard, Christopher A. "Touring the Consumption of the Other: Imaginaries of Authenticity in the Himalayas and Beyond." *Journal of Consumer Culture* 16, no. 2 (2016): 354–373.

Hutt, Michael. "Looking for Shangri-la: From Hilton to Lāmichhāne." In *The Tourist Image: Myths and Myth Making in Tourism*, edited by Tom Selwyn, 49–60. New York: John Wiley & Sons, 1996.

Iwamura, Jane Naomi. *Virtual Orientalism: Asian Religions and American Popular Culture*. New York: Oxford University Press, 2011.

Johnston, George. *Journey Through Tomorrow*. Melbourne: F. W. Cheshire, 1947.

King, Richard. "Orientalism and the Modern Myth of 'Hinduism." *Numen* 46, no. 2 (1999): 146–185.

King, Richard. *Orientalism and Religion: Postcolonial Theory, India and 'The Mystic East'*. New York: Routledge, 1999.

Klieger, P. Christiaan. "Research Notes: Shangri-La and the Politicization of Tourism in Tibet." *Annals of Tourism Research* 19 (1992): 122–124.

Knight, George. *Intimate Glimpses of Mysterious Tibet and Neighbouring Countries*. London: Golden Vista Press, 1930.

Lamb, Alastair. *British India and Tibet: 1766–1910*. New York: Routledge & Kegan Paul, 1960.

Lewis, Todd T. "Himalayan Religions in Comparative Perspective: Considerations Regarding Buddhism and Hinduism across Their Indic Frontiers." *Himalaya* 14, no. 1 (1994): 25–46.

Liechty, Mark. "Building the Road to Kathmandu: Notes on the History of Tourism in Nepal." *Himalaya* 25, nos. 1/2 (2005): 19–28.

Liechty, Mark. "The Key to an Oriental World: Boris Lissanevitch, Kathmandu's Royal Hotel and the 'Golden Age' of Tourism in Nepal." *Studies in Nepali History and Society* 15, no. 2 (2010): 253–295.

Liechty, Mark. *Far Out: Countercultural Seekers and the Tourist Encounter in Nepal*. Chicago: The University of Chicago Press, 2017.

Logan, Dana W. "The Lean Closet: Asceticism in Postindustrial Consumer Culture." *Journal of the American Academy of Religion* 85, no. 3 (2017): 600–628.

Logan, Joshua, dir. *South Pacific*. 20th-Century Fox, 1958.

Lopez, Donald S. Jr. "New Age Orientalism: The Case of Tibet." *Tricycle: The Buddhist Review* 3, no. 3 (1994): 37–43.

Lopez, Donald S. Jr. "Foreigner at the Lama's Feet." In *Curators of the Buddha: The Study of Buddhism Under Colonialism*, edited by Donald Lopez, Jr., 251–295. Chicago: The University of Chicago Press, 1995.

Lopez, Donald S. Jr. *Prisoners of Shangri-La: Tibetan Buddhism and the West*. Chicago: University of Chicago Press, 2018.

Mather, Jeffrey. "Captivating Readers: Middlebrow Aesthetics and James Hilton's *Lost Horizon.*" *CEA Critic* 79, no. 2 (2017): 231–243.

McKay, Alex. "The Establishment of the British Trade Agencies in Tibet: A Survey." *Journal of the Royal Asiatic Society* 2, no. 3 (1992): 399–421.

McKay, Alex. *Kailas Histories: Renunciate Traditions and the Construction of Himalayan Sacred Geography.* Leiden: Brill, 2016.

McNee, Alan. *The New Mountaineer in Late Victorian Britain.* London: Palgrave Macmillan, 2016.

Messerschmidt, Donald A. "The Hindu Pilgrimage to Muktinath, Part 1: Natural and Supernatural Attributes of the Sacred Field." *Mountain Research and Development* 9, no. 2 (1989): 89–104.

Messerschmidt, Donald A. "The Hindu Pilgrimage to Muktinath, Part 2: Vaishnava Devotees and Status Reaffirmation." *Mountain Research and Development* 9, no. 2 (1989): 105–118.

Murphy, Ryan, dir. *Eat, Pray, Love.* Columbia Pictures, 2010.

Nepal, Sanjay K. and Yang (Sunny) Mu. "Mountaineering Commodification and Risk Perceptions in Nepal's Mt. Everest Region." In *Mountaineering Tourism,* edited by Ghazali Musa, James Higham, and Anna Thompson-Carr, 250–264. New York: Routledge, 2015.

Nepal, Sanjay K. and Stella Amor Nepal. "Visitor Impacts on Trails in Sagarmatha (Mt. Everest) National Park." *Ambio* 33, no. 6 (2004): 334–340.

Neuhaus, Tom. *Tibet in the Western Imagination.* New York: Palgrave Macmillan, 2012.

Norbu, Jamyang. "Behind the Lost Horizon." In *Imagining Tibet: Perceptions, Projections, and Fantasies,* edited by Thierry Dodin and Heinz Räther, 373–378. Boston: Wisdom Publications, 2001.

Norum, Roger Edward. "The Unbearable Likeness of Being a Tourist: Expats, Travel and Imaginaries in the Neo-colonial Orient." *International Review of Social Research* 3, no. 1 (2013): 27–47.

Nyaupane, Gyan P. "Mountaineering on Mt. Everest: Evolution, Economy, Ecology and Ethics." In *Mountaineering Tourism,* edited by Ghazali Musa, James Higham, and Anna Thompson-Carr, 265–271. New York: Routledge, 2015.

Ortner, Sherry. "Thick Resistance: Death and the Cultural Construction of Agency in Himalayan Mountaineering." *Representations* 59 (1997): 135–162.

Ortner, Sherry. *Life and Death on Mt. Everest: Sherpas and Himalayan Mountaineering.* Princeton: Princeton University Press, 1999.

Piasecki, Simon. "A Mountain as Multiverse: Circumnavigating the Realities and Meta-Realities of a Kailas Pilgrim." *Performance Research* 24, no. 2 (2019): 16–23.

Robbins, David. "Sport, Hegemony and the Middle Class: The Victorian Mountaineers." *Theory, Culture & Society* 4 (1987): 597–601.

Robinson, Michael F. *The Lost White Tribe: Explorers, Scientists, and the Theory that Changed a Continent.* New York: Oxford University Press, 2016.

Saissi, Mohammed. "The Symptoms of Orientalism in Pre-Contemporary Western Travel Writings on Morocco." *International Uni-Scientific Research Journal* 2, no. 36 (2021): 240–261.

Sarao, K. T. S. "Kailash." In *Encyclopedia of Indian Religions: Buddhism and Jainism,* edited by K. T. S. Sarao and Gang Rinpoche, 607–619. Dordrecht: Springer Science Business Media, 2017.

Satchidananda, Sri Swami. *Kailash Journal: Pilgrimage into the Himalayas.* Yogaville: Integral Yoga Publications, 1984.

Shackley, Myra. *Managing Sacred Sites: Service Provision and Visitor Experience.* New York: Continuum, 2001.

Sharma, Jayeeta. "Himalayan Darjeeling and Mountain Histories of Labour and Mobility." In *Darjeeling Reconsidered: Histories, Politics, Environments*, edited by Townsend Middleton and Sara Shneidermann, 74–96. New York: Oxford University Press, 2018.

Sheperd, Robert. "UNESCO and the Politics of Cultural Heritage in Tibet." *Journal of Contemporary Asia* 36, no. 2 (2006): 243–257.

Singh, Shalini. "Secular Pilgrimages and Sacred Tourism in the Indian Himalayas." *GeoJournal* 64, no. 3 (2005): 215–223.

Stausberg, Michael. *Religion and Tourism: Crossroads, Destinations and Encounters*. New York: Routledge, 2011.

Thar, Tsering. "Mount Ti se (Kailash) Area: The Center of Himalayan Civilization." *East and West* 59, no. 1/4 (2009): 25–30.

Thubron, Colin. *To a Mountain in Tibet*. London: Vintage, 2012.

Tian, Ying. "Shangri-La and the Imperial Imagination in James Hilton's *Lost Horizon*." *ANQ (A Quarterly Journal of Short Articles, Notes and Reviews)* 37, no. 3 (2024): 414–422.

Tuan, Yi-Fu. *Space and Place: The Perspective of Experience*. Minneapolis: University of Minnesota Press, 1977.

Varley, Peter. "Confecting Adventure and Playing with Meaning: The Adventure Commodification Continuum." *Journal of Sports & Tourism* 11, no. 2 (2006): 173–194.

Vasantkumar, Chris. "Dreamworld, Shambala, Gannan: The Shangrilazation of China's 'Little Tibet'." In *Mapping Shangrila: Contested Landscapes in the Sino-Tibetan Borderlands*, edited by Emily T. Yeh and Christopher R. Coggins, 51–73. Seattle: University of Washington Press, 2014.

Walters, Holly. *Shaligram Pilgrimage in the Nepal Himalayas*. Amsterdam: Amsterdam University Press, 2020.

Walters, Holly. "Cornerstones: Shaligrams as Kin." *The Journal of Religion* 102, no. 1 (2022): 93–119.

Watson, Nick J. "Nature and Transcendence: The Mystical and Sublime in Extreme Sports." In *Sport and Spirituality: An Introduction*, edited by Jim Parry, Simon Robinson, Nick Watson, and Mark Nesti, 95–115. New York: Routledge, 2007.

Xiao, Honggen and Jinfu Zhang. "Liquid Identities: Han Sojourners in Tibet." *Annals of Tourism Research* 88 (2021): 1–12.

Yü, Dan Smyer. *Mindscaping the Landscape of Tibet: Place, Memorability, Ecoaesthetics*. Boston: De Gruyter, 2015.

Zhang, Jinfu. "Drifting Home: The Quests of Chinese Tourist-Migrants in Tibet." *Journal of Travel Research* 63, no. 6 (2024): 1459–1472.

Zhu, Hong and Junxi Qian. "Drifting; in Lhasa: Cultural Encounter, Contested Modernity, and the Negotiation of Tibetness." *Annals of the Association of American Geographers* 105, no. 1 (2015): 144–161.

5

BALI HA'I

Up through step-like terrace fields, imprisoning the gleam of water, tinged green with spears of rice. Slender palm trees curved under giant green nuts. The air grew cooler. Now we were among sheer cliffs and tangled jungle growth. The verdure blazed with poinsettia crimson. The air was like a well-honed edge of chilled steel. We burst forth into a place without foliage, a tattered, shaggy village perched upon a ridge. Before us was grey, black emptiness.

Hickman Powell, from *The Last Paradise*[1]

Paradise is an ancient idea linked to Christianity and the search for a new Eden. In the imaginative geography of the "New World," Columbus's search for the mythical El Dorado exists alongside "God's paradise."[2] The search for a perfect place has occupied many explorers and travelers. The Himalayas promise transformations at high altitudes, and tropical islands promise mystical experiences at sea level. As Michael Stausberg explains,

While the mountain paradise of Shangri-La is linked to the imagery of a remote kind of spiritual exaltation with an air of detachment and asceticism, the island paradises are stereotypically ascribed a sensual form of spirituality with a focus on bodies and bodily movements and pleasures.[3]

Perhaps no place on earth is more evocative of Eden than Bali. In the 1920s, it was called "the last paradise," an idea that survives a hundred years later.[4] Popular as a travel destination for wellness and spirituality, it is a key site in the global mystical marketplace. In Shinji Yamashita's study of Bali, he writes,

DOI: 10.4324/9781003361725-6

"Paradise was not simply discovered there: it was created."[5] These visions of Bali are found in tourist materials, novels, and films and include "dancing girls, exotic festivals, romantic landscapes, and wave-kissed beaches."[6] Bali is a *touristed landscape* that reflects a desire for a potentially transformative experience:

> In these landscapes, and the places they constitute and represent, interest in experiencing them reflects aspects of desire as well as multiple positions of sensory engagement, attraction, and legibility—ways in which landscapes can be read, imagined and experienced, from diverse points of views and positions of orientation.[7]

Bali continues to be seen as the "generic icon of paradise in the South Seas" despite the Pacific being a complex geographical and imaginary site.[8] Many texts, paintings, and films have created the mystical presentation of Bali, including some of the earliest films of any South Seas islands, such as *Bali the Unknown* (a short documentary produced in 1922).[9] The magical island of Bali is an idealized space for tourists, an exotic tropical island with the conveniences found in Melbourne or Los Angeles. In movies like *The Road to Bali* (1952) and *South Pacific* (1958), Bali is represented as a "paradise among paradises" and "what the filmmakers imagined a Balinese temple would look like" was achieved with cardboard cutouts of Hindu holy sites.[10] As in the other places examined in this book, the imaginative geographies of Southeast Asia are linked to the history of colonialism:

> The representations of other places, people, landscapes, cultures and natures; the ways in which they project the desires, fantasies and prejudices of their authors; and the intricacies of knowledge and power between the subjects and objects of these representations.[11]

As this chapter shows, these representations become important in the mystical landscapes of Bali, and perhaps to a lesser extent, Thailand. Both are formulated upon the fetishization of the two religions identified with the Orient, Hinduism, and Buddhism.[12]

Bali's nicknames, which include "the last paradise" and "island of the gods," reflect Romanticized ideas about the Balinese resistance to missionaries and a culture that is a "living museum," which include the staging of culture found at hotels, resorts, and restaurants.[13] Bali Ha'i, "the 'one perfect island'" and a place clouded "in mist and mystery," is more an idea than a reality.[14] Among the most important figures in the history of this imaginative vision of Bali is the German-Russian artist Walter Spies. In addition to living in Bali for many years, producing some of the most beautiful and evocative paintings of the island, and supporting Balinese artists, Walter adopted the Balinese culture. We now turn to the story of his life and death in the islands he loved.

The Incredible Life of Walter Spies

Walter Spies, born in 1895, was a German born in Moscow who became one of Bali's most famous residents in the twentieth century. Spies was an important artist of the magical realism style, a photographer, a research guide for anthropologists and writers, and a scholar. The magical realism style includes the transgression of categories and often a "fluid" rendering of human forms.[15] In addition to an art style, it was a philosophy that reflected Walter's life as a gay man who rejected the super-masculinist and nationalist art of Germany.

Walter loved Bali and more generally, Indonesia. He hosted celebrities like Charlie Chaplin and sold his paintings to wealthy Europeans and Americans who visited the islands. His homosexuality was well known to the Balinese and did not seem to be important; he was a friend to many local families and by all accounts, loved by Balinese, Javanese, European and American tourists, celebrities, and many others. From a young age, Walter seemed destined to settle somewhere outside Europe. After the Great War, Spies was detained as a young man to an enemy camp due to his ancestry, where he encountered nomadic groups like the Tartars, who sparked his interest in Asia.[16] Spies moved to Ubud, Bali, in August 1927, two years after his first visit to the island, where he lived in a small cottage and wrote to his mother about how happy he was to be away from Europe. 1927 was also the year the Nazis had their first major rally.[17] As it turns out, as much as he tried to avoid the unraveling of Europe, the activities of the Nazis would indirectly lead to his death in 1942 at the young age of 46.[18]

Spies painted bucolic scenes of Bali with Balinese people, wildlife, and domesticated animals like the water buffalo. Influenced by German Romanticism, his paintings include *Die Landschaft und ihre Kinder*, one of the many pieces that idealize the Balinese life.[19] These portrayals express a simple, beautiful existence, free of the problems that plagued Europe. This painting and others by Spies portray the Balinese as gentle pastoralists. Spies portrayed the Balinese people in a magico-realist style that was more concerned with "a cultivated sense of Asian male harmony and proportion" than homoerotic or sexual themes.[20] The style in which he drew and painted Balinese men was also ideological. In *Banyan with Two Young Balinese*, we have one example:

> Once again, he avoided plating the two with any Winckelmann-style muscles. The representation was what could be called an Orientalist stereotype of "delicate, lotus-eyed boys." But, viewed as a response to the

Nazi-driven images of manhood sweeping his homeland, Walter's drawings offered a queering dissent.[21]

As he settled into life in Bali, his paintings were widely recognized for their
beauty, exhibited in the Bali Museum, and sold to tourists and collectors
from abroad. Spies was involved in the *Pita Maha*, an Ubud-based arts association that was integral to the development of the arts on the island and is
still important today.[22] He also helped to revive the museum, which had been
destroyed by an earthquake in 1917.[23] He was protective of the Balinese and
feared for their future. He was relieved to be settled in a small island as far
away from Germany as one could get.

Spies was a Renaissance man. He was a musician, dancer and choreogra-
pher, photographer, and muse for the most famous novel about Bali, Vicki
Baum's *Love and Death in Bali* (1937), for which he provided much of the
ethnography.[24] Spies took photographs that utilized special effects to create a
magical feeling. As Balinese scholar I Made Bayu Pramana has suggested, his
use of smoke created a "mystical nuance."[25] Spies was part of a larger group
of artists, writers, and musicians who lived in Bali in the twentieth century,
including artist Miguel Covarrubias, writer Vicki Baum (whose friendship
with Spies inspired her book), and composer Colin McPhee.[26] Spies and his
group of friends led a Bohemian lifestyle and viewed Bali as a culture worth
objectifying and protecting. Spies and others in his circle deeply loved Bali
and her people, inadvertently contributing to the idea of Bali as a mystical
landscape.

Spies's sexuality was an open secret and when he was arrested for acts with
a minor, the young man's relatives defended Walter. Ultimately, it was his
German ancestry, not his queerness, that ended his time in Bali and proved
fatal. The Dutch arrested Walter and interred him in numerous jails, moving
him around repeatedly, but he continued to draw and paint with whatever
supplies he could get.[27] He stayed at one jail in Ngawi and at another in
Sumatra. Finally, the Dutch planned to send him to Sri Lanka, where *en
route* his ship was bombed by the Japanese, and he died.[28] Walter's body was
never found and lies in the graveyard of the largest ocean on earth.

There were two prophetic episodes in Walter's life that deserve mentioning.
The first is the death of his cousin Conrad. As mentioned in other chapters,
mystical landscapes are often tied to unexplained events. In the weeks preceding Conrad's death in a shark attack in the waters the Balinese avoided,
Conrad made comments about his death, even pointing to a place in the
European cemetery in Denpasar where he would be buried, an event that followed his consultation with a Balinese astrological calendar that predicted a
death of someone young on Conrad's birthday.[29] On March 5, 1932, Spies,
Conrad, and Elly Beinhorn, the famous German aviator, drove to the beach
at Lebih; in the car, Conrad had joked about how he would be eaten by

Kala Rahu, a Balinese monster with only a head.[30] Walter and Conrad often enjoyed swimming in the ocean, a place the Balinese avoided due to ashes being deposited and the presence of demons.[31] Shortly after he entered the water, he was attacked by a shark, who tore all the flesh off one leg and most of his fingers.[32] He was buried in the same cemetery where he had predicted he would lie.

The second prophetic incident in Walter's life involves his last artwork, a painting of Ezekiel, a curious subject as he had never been explicitly interested in Biblical themes.[33] The artwork has been lost, but contemporaries (in jail) of Walter described it, so we have some idea of its content (e.g., it was composed of three panels). It is the subject of the painting that is most interesting—a prophet who was warned by God, "Son of man, with one blow I am about to take away from you the delight of your eyes. Yet do not lament or weep or shed any tears. Groan quietly; do not mourn the dead."[34] This was his last known painting before the light in his eyes went dark. He drowned in the same ocean that he had swam in so many times when the Japanese bombed the ship he was on.

A Dutch Eden

The mapping of territories in the minds of Europeans and Americans has often focused on escapism. Bali has long been identified as an example of anti-modernity and understood as "the homeland of a traditional culture insulated from the modern world and its vicissitudes."[35] Bali is still viewed as an escape from the modern world despite the island's fast-food restaurants, nightclubs, and luxurious resorts. Its many temples (older studies place the number of Hindu temples at 4,661) and public festivals make it a destination for tourists wishing to experience a mystical landscape.[36]

Bali, situated east of Java and west of the Sunda Islands and surrounded by the Bali Strait (to the west), the Java Sea (to the north), the Lombok Strait (to the east), and the Indian Ocean (to the south), covers 5,632 km and is divided into seven regencies.[37] Mount Agung and Mount Batur are the two most sacred mountains on an island full of tropical forests, beaches, and rice terraces. The social imagination about Bali as a paradise originated with the Dutch period of colonization, when all aspects of Balinese culture and style were legislated to reconstitute "what the Dutch thought Balinese culture must have been."[38] Like other colonial outposts, Bali was documented in photos, first through Wijnand Otto Van Nieuwenkamp, who was sent to the island by Governor General Van Heutz, and a few years later by Gregor Krause, whose book of images remains famous today, in part for its many nude photos of the Balinese people.[39]

The beliefs about Bali's mystical qualities are attached to its Hindu religion, which is viewed as a timeless tradition that survived modernity. Bali's

IMAGE 5.1 Photo of Bali Rice Field, Bali, Indonesia.

Source: photo courtesy of author

Buddhist history is less well known, but scholars have documented early contacts between Southeast Asia and the Himalayas. As one study notes, clay votive amulets (Tib. *T'sat'sas*) have been found in Bali, and "Traveling Buddhist monks such as I-Tsing (690 CE) and Atis'a (1040 CE) also record that there were pilgrims and scholars moving routinely between Southeast Asia, the Gangetic plains, and the Himalayan highlands."[40]

Bali has also been viewed through the lens of the U.S. military. The idea of "Bali-Hai" is attached to the experience of American servicemen in the film *South Pacific*.[41] Tahiti and Hawai'i are mystical landscapes underpinned by occupation and settler colonialism by France and America, while Bali is part of the Dutch colonial project. However, Bali has often been included in the geographical region known as the "South Seas" and travelers often associated other sites in the Pacific with Bali. In Hickman Powell's travelogue of Bali in the 1920s, he encounters a European traveler who had come from Tahiti, a place renowned for its beautiful and amorous females:

> A man from Tahiti came to Bali. The man from Tahiti was stroking a brown girl's silken hair. "The girls of the South Seas are gentle, friendly things," he said. "Their little tendernesses are very pleasant."[42]

When the Balinese girl showed no interest in the man, he remarked that he liked Tahiti better.[43]

Bali's status as an island is a critical part of its construction as a mystical landscape. Islands and especially tropical ones are understood as spaces of difference, which can be understood as separate from the mainland. Indonesia has no mainland—it is a country with over 10,000 islands—but Java is in many ways its political center.[44] Bali fulfills many fantasies of the island paradise—it is beautiful, the locals are friendly, and it is on "island time."[45] Unlike Thailand, whose Buddhist identity is well established in tourist literature, Bali's status as an island with a Hindu majority within the largest Muslim nation on earth is often obscured or denied. When telling people that I have spent a lot of time in Java, for example, I have often heard the comment made by tourists that they have "been to Bali, but not Indonesia." The fact that tourists can fly directly to Denpasar and bypass Jakarta helps to explain the cognitive disassociation people make when separating Bali from the rest of the archipelago.

The erasure of Indonesia as a nation reveals both the power of mystical landscapes and a soft form of Islamophobia. While Bali was framed as a highly developed special culture, it was considered a paradise because of its Hindu majority. Bali was an island "not yet 'corrupted' by Islam."[46] Even today, the Balinese people are often described as special, different, and having a superior culture to the Javanese. These claims deny facts about Balinese history, the social problems in Bali today, and the Muslim minority in Bali, who typically have close and loving relationships with their Hindu compatriots.[47] The story of Bali follows an outline similar to other colonized territories that are imagined as mystical places. Out of the colonial milieu of administrators, writers, artists, and travelers in Bali, an idyllic Hindu culture emerged. Most writings give no consideration of the links between Hindus, Buddhists, Muslims, and other religionists, or the fact that Hindus and Muslims live together quite peacefully on the small island.

From the beginning, Bali's Dutch colonial record demonstrated a belief that Balinese culture was superior to the Javanese form of Islam that eventually dominated the island next door. Cornelius de Houtman, the Dutch captain who first encountered Bali, had a documented hostility toward Muslims (and Catholics).[48] Early accounts of Bali (*Baly*) called it *Hollandiola* and described its Hindu inhabitants as heathens, which meant "non-Muslim" or simple (polytheistic).[49] It would not be long before the Dutch had cast the island as the new Eden.

The Dutch expedition to the Malay world in 1597 led to the colonial empire of the Dutch East Indies, whose capital Jakarta was called Batavia and whose fascination with Bali focused on its Hindu religion.[50] An island known for its warfare, practice of widow burning (*sutee*), its slave trade, and the massacres of the Balinese by the Dutch was replaced by the geographic vision of an island paradise with happy and cheerful natives. In a sense, both these ideas about Bali are exaggerated stereotypes. The practice of widow burning was based on Portuguese Goa, what Gombrich calls an "adapted stereotype," and the image of the Balinese king with a parasol riding in a wagon was based on the Dutch *bolderwagon*.[51] Slavery existed but was exaggerated to make the argument that Bali's leaders were cruel and must be replaced by the Dutch, who would preserve the rights of the friendly commoners.[52] The beginnings of the Dutch occupation of Bali were focused on slavery, the primary interest of the Dutch East Indies Company (known as the VOC or the *Vereenigde Oost-Indische Compagnie*).[53] The *puputans* (mass suicides) of Balinese royalty and their followers in 1904 and 1908 signaled the beginning of colonial rule (by both the Dutch and the British).[54] The mass suicides also had a profoundly negative impact on the Dutch colonial state, for the events of 1904 and 1908 were looked at with horror by foreigners.[55]

The Dutch were keenly interested in preserving certain aspects of the culture of Bali, what is known as *Baliseering* ("The Balinization of Bali").[56] In some ways, Bali never recovered from the Dutch casting the island as both a "site of erotic pleasures" and an exotic landscape with mystical powers.[57] The Dutch ruled until the Japanese occupation in 1942, which was followed by independence, a number of political crises, and eventual stability as the third largest democracy in the world.[58] Even the Japanese had tourist plans for Bali during their brief occupation of Indonesia, which included making the island a part of Japan's "Beautiful South," an imperial fantasy that ended with their defeat.[59] The anthropologists who characterized Bali in terms of its "harmony" also fixed the island in the past.[60]

Early reports from Dutch explorers who visited the island are problematic, often relying on stereotypical ideas about Hinduism from India and extrapolating these onto the island. As anthropologist James Boon has stated, "The first images of Balinese culture were happily inscribed on western consciousness following a stop there in 1597 by Cornelius de Houtman's renowned *eertse schipvaart* to the East Indies."[61] Boon, who spent his career studying Bali and more broadly, Indonesia, notes that the early Dutch impressions of Bali were based on observations that were, at best, "inadequate stereotypes" that resulted in an idea of Bali as an exotic land with an "absolute monarchy" and "happy irrigationalists."[62] In truth, of course, Bali had the same social conditions as other islands, but these were swept away in the ocean of romantic and mystical ideas about the Hindu island within an archipelago dominated by Muslims.[63]

Bali's Hindu culture was viewed as an heir to the Majapahit in Java (1293–1517). This empire was linked to "a form of imagining as it arose out of an encounter with another formidable Asian entity, the Yuan Dynasty of China that had tried to invade Java without success."[64] The view of the Dutch and other colonial Europeans like Raffles was that the *Wong Majapahit* (the elite Hindus) were foreign Javanese who subjected the population to a caste system, a belief that was based more on mythology and stereotypes about Hinduism from India than evidence.[65] Bali had beautiful beaches but no natural harbors, which made it difficult to be developed as part of the Dutch East Indies trade empire. In 1914, six years after the fall of the last Balinese kingdom to the Dutch, tourist brochures extolling the "Garden of Eden" were produced.[66]

The Dutch mapped the island as a tropical version of their homeland. The Balinese aristocracy, which the Dutch identified with their Javanese ancestors, was viewed as tyrannical, ruling the peaceful local Balinese who had to be liberated by the Dutch.[67] As Howe states, "They were really not very different from their colonial masters. With its dams, dykes, and canals, Bali reminded the Dutch of their homeland, and could be seen as 'little Holland.'"[68] The influence of the Romantic movement on ideas about foreign places had a dark side, which influenced the Dutch. Romanticism was far from the philosophical movement that influenced some of the greatest art of the nineteenth and twentieth centuries. It also functioned as a "territorial ideology" that included settler colonies and their European inhabitants.[69] The Romantic focus on time and the promise of possibilities was made real by the end of old systems (Balinese independence) and the new order (colonialism).

Late Colonialism and Independence

Photography played a key role in creating the mystical landscape of Bali. W.O.J. Niewenkamp and Gregor Krause both published large books of photographs that included beautiful images of the Balinese, many of the women topless, and of Hindu rituals, which were viewed as evidence of the survival of an old and idyllic culture. The photos of Niewenkamp were also used for Dutch military operations in the conquest of the Kingdoms of Bandung, Tabanan, and Klungkung.[70] Gregor Krause's book *Bali* (1912) created a photographic essay that included images of Bali's people and her famous rice fields.[71] As Hitchcock writes, ignoring the bloody history of colonialism, Krause presented Bali as a place marked by the "timelessness of tourist exotica."[72] Among the most evocative early impressions of the island were the many works by artists who traveled to the island or settled there. For the Dutch, the island existed as a time capsule of Hinduism that represented a kind of "colonial mapping" of the island.[73] However, Bali was not an ideal island for typical colonial ventures. It was too mountainous to have plantations and had no valuable natural resources (unlike the Spice Islands), but it did provide a place for colonial agents to create a tourist industry.[74]

Hickman Powell and Andrew Roosevelt also traveled to Bali and produced the popular book of photographs and reflections on Bali titled *Bali the Last Paradise* (1930).[75] Spies and his friends settled in Bali for extended periods of time, several of them writing about Bali's mystical landscape and people, and anthropologists followed, including Margaret Mead and Clifford Geertz.[76] One of Mead's remarks about the Balinese shows how entranced some anthropologists were with the island and her people: "The Balinese are unusually photogenic and tend to compose in groups so that half the work of photography is done for the photographer."[77]

Several friends of Walter Spies wrote books about Bali. Miguel Covarrubias's *Island of Bali* (1937) is a lengthy and detailed study that includes Bali's history, rituals, customs, and a fair amount of opinion on the Hindus and other religious groups. Covarrubias described the Muslims in negative ways as "the Arabs with their forbidding black beards" and the Javanese as "Muslim fanatics."[78] Like his contemporaries, Covarrubias viewed the Bali and the Balinese as special.

> The slender Balinese bodies are as much a part of the landscape as the palms and breadfruit trees, and their smooth skins have the same tone as the earth and as the brown rivers where they bathe; a general color scheme of greens, greys, and ochres, relieved here and there by brightly colored sashes and tropical flowers.[79]

Colin McPhee, another friend of Spies, wrote a book about Bali called *A House in Bali* (1944). He describes the landscape even more poetically:

> I preferred to drive at random through the island, getting lost in the network of back roads that ran up into the hills where, as you looked down towards the seas, the flooded rice-fields lay shining in the sunlight like a broken mirror. The sound of music seemed forever in the air. People sang

in the fields or in the streams as they bathed. From behind village walls rose the sound of flutes and cymbals as invisible musicians rehearsed at all hours of the day and night.[80]

These books make it apparent how Bali became the icon of the South Seas paradise.

Bali has gone by several eponyms, including Shangri-La, the Garden of Eden, and the last paradise.[81] The idea that one could "experience" the culture of others became linked to social class through the differentiation between offerings for working class tourists and the wealthy.[82] This can be seen in Bali, where the masses of tourists frequent Kuta and Seminyak, but the wealthy, including celebrities, choose the exclusive resorts found outside Ubud. Today, Bali is seen as an amalgamation of all the Orient's most wonderful qualities. As Adrian Vickers explains, "Tahiti called to Gauguin with the beauty, beaches and tropical climate of the South Seas; India lured travelers with its Eastern mystery and Hinduism; but Bali's image combines all the attractions."[83] However, when a traveler came to Bali seeking amorous and free love, as Charlie Chaplin did, he was disappointed; and Margaret Mead's husband found the Balinese as strict as "his own England."[84]

The fascination with Bali as a place that exemplifies a perfect example of Hinduism began early. As one scholar put it,

> Since the days of Raffles, Bali had been seen as a "living museum" of Majapahit Java, and the enlightened colonial policy designed for the island aimed to preserve Balinese culture, and even return it to its former state.[85]

In fact, in 1908, the island was promoted as "the Gem of the Lesser Sunda Isles."[86]

Bali differs from Java, whose Hindu and Buddhist temples are largely in ruins yet hold a special place in the hearts of many Javanese Muslims. A visit to the Dieng Plateau, where the oldest Hindu temples are found, or to Borobudur, the largest Buddhist temple in the world, will show that the largest community of tourists are Muslims from Java and other islands in the archipelago. As one study notes, these visitors believe these spaces to be associated with their ancestors, thus spiritually powerful and worthy of visiting.[87] Bali's temples are an example of a living religion, and as such, they are not like Java's ruins, but rather places where mystical power is real. As Sarah Tiffin has argued, the theme of Java's "ruined *candis*" reflects the "passing of a high point in the island's artistic and creative history but also hinted at the momentous implications of a wider social and cultural deterioration" and its replacement with a "sadly degenerative" Muslim culture.[88]

The role of Bali in Indonesia's nationalist programs is an important part of its tourist history. In the late 1930s, the nationalists urged the banning of media that showed Balinese women with bare breasts, a widespread practice among Balinese.[89] Bali's status as a tourist site often came in conflict with the efforts to create an "undivided nation state," something that in later decades was sacrificed for a booming tourism industry that helped buffer poor economic conditions.[90] Bali's status as an idyllic destination is tied both to its history of colonial occupation and later to Indonesian politics under Sukarno and Suharto.

The newly independent Indonesia (August 17, 1945) was focused on creating an "undivided nation state," which was expressed in Bali in the commemorations of the *puputans* in the Badung "fight to the death" slogan in the monument in Denpasar.[91] In the 1960s, Sukarno used Japanese war reparations to fund the Bali Beach Hotel in Sanur, and when Suharto became president, he chose Bali as the focus of tourism development in the country.[92] The development of Bali as a tourist haven is steeped in violence, existing as a kind of symbol of the nation rising out of the ashes. As Robert Sheperd describes it,

> After coming to power in the aftermath of a 1965 military coup that left hundreds of thousands of citizens dead, Indonesian President Suharto's New Order government officially proclaimed tourism to be a key tool of nation-building.[93]

In 1971, "Cultural Tourism" (*Pariwisata Budaya*) was adopted as the guiding concept for the island.[94] During the New Order era (1965–1998), Bali also was impacted by a simplistic way of viewing society that focused on a "single cultural type" and downplayed ethnic diversity.[95] The impact on the Balinese of these efforts includes the development of tourism at the cost of cultural survival. The belief that Bali represented both an economic resource and a "cultural peak" was used to foster national pride, initiated by Ki Hajar Dewantara (Raden Mas Soewardi Soerjaningrat), the First Minister of Education of the Republic of Indonesia, whose commitment to cultivating a national culture would be influential for years after his death.[96]

The development of Bali as an island tourist site, which continued during this era, has its origins in the colonial geography of Bali, as noted earlier. If it had been amenable to plantations or mining, the Dutch would not have turned to tourism.[97] It is important to understand that Bali's tourism industry is situated in the kind of *scopic power* of the colonial regime discussed by Derek Gregory and other scholars, where the siting of the island was used to create a place out of space.

The impact on Bali's traditional agrarian life is evident in the development of Denpasar, Kuta, Sanur, and Nusa Dua. Once fishing villages with "dry crop farming, cattle raising, and some sawah farming," these are now some of the most popular resort areas on the island.[98] In the case of Kuta, which saw a rapid growth of the tourism sector in 1970–1980, the character of the village changed architecturally, representing the takeover of the industry and the disappearance of the traditional village. As one study notes, "Many of the compound walls which once fronted the street have been torn down to facilitate construction of restaurants and shops, while vacant land adjacent to residences has also been utilized for development."[99]

Brand Bali

The first time I flew to Bali, I remember walking on the tarmac at the Denpasar International Airport and encountering an enormous Hindu god. The airport is small, surprisingly so for such a popular site of tourism. Driving through Denpasar, I am always reminded that Bali is a tourist capital, full of coffee shops, T-shirt stands, fancy restaurants, and countless spa businesses. It is almost as if the carving reminds one of where they are—an island largely populated with Hindus. But the population is in service to tourists, who visit the temples and drive through villages on their rented mopeds.[100] Long gone is the Bali where agriculture was the main economy. In 1971, agriculture accounted for nearly 60 percent of the island's economy, and as of 2020 it was less than 20 percent.[101] Bali is almost solely focused on tourism and its commodification of Hinduism includes resorts, spas, and restaurants named after gods and goddesses.

Bali's first major colonial encounter is understood through a story of two Dutch seamen who abandoned their ship due to the "irresistible charms" of the local women.[102] *Bali Ha'i* is a recognizable phrase attached to the island, found on numerous products that sell exotic and mystical curatives. Bali Ha'i has its origins in the 1958 film *South Pacific*, a musical with U.S. military men stuck on their base, with the "mysterious island" of Bali Ha'i —the place of beautiful women (hence the song "There Is Nothing Like a Dame").[103] Today, Balinese Hinduism exists as both a culture and the center of the island's tourism, which was no easy feat. The designers of the modern tourist industry in Indonesia had to strike a careful balance between exploiting the exotic aspects of the islands and keeping everyone united. Indonesia is the most ethnically and linguistically diverse nation in the world, with over 300 languages and more than 200 ethnic groups. As Robert Sheperd explains,

> A tourism policy aimed at domestic stability sought, in effect, to limit ethnicity as an identity marker to artistic and vague cultural displays, while simultaneously subordinating ethnicity to religious identity, the goal being both to create and manage a pan-Indonesian identity.[104]

This balance doesn't work perfectly. Bali remains a beautiful island with beaches, coffee farms, health retreats, and five-star resorts. At the same time, parts of the island are overrun with development, including Denpasar, Kuta, and even the artist center of Ubud. Sheperd describes these places:

> In Ubud, art galleries, craft shops and espresso bars compete for business with French and Italian restaurants and bookshops stocking the *New York Times*, while in Kuta, surf shops and all-you-can-drink night clubs compete with pizzerias and the Hard Rock Café for the cash of drunken Australians and rebel Japanese (They get tanned).[105]

Places identified with mystical tourism have special brands. Bali's branding may not have anything remotely to do with the island. As one study notes, "The leitmotif of 'Bali' has come to stand for almost anything vaguely equatorial and exotic, and the proliferation of the 'Bali' brand name continues apace."[106] Elizabeth Gilbert's book *Eat, Pray, Love* and the film it inspired helped to promote Bali as a mystical landscape. *Eat, Pray, Love* is a cultural phenomenon that includes the book, film, and a line of products launched to coincide with the movie's release that focused on mystical and transformational qualities identified with Bali. Gilbert's book expresses her desire to experience the poverty of the mystical Balinese. As noted in Chapter 1, Gilbert's fascination with the Balinese is built upon the fantasy of poverty as a natural conduit to mysticism. Gilbert did not invent the mystical Hinduism that is identified with Bali—the Dutch did—but she did popularize it for an American audience.

The way this fantasy is expressed is not limited to *Eat, Pray, Love*; poverty is a popular theme in the wellness industry. In the case of *Goop*, Gwyneth Paltrow's wildly successful company that sells products focused on exotic potions, fasting, and detoxification, we see how poverty can be framed as a fun, experimental, and temporary state for the wealthy. In Paltrow's case, she did a "food stamp challenge" that she failed, giving herself a C-grade due to her inability to be poor: "As I suspected, we only made it through four days, when I personally broke and had some chicken and fresh vegetables (and in full transparency, half a bag of black licorice)."[107]

The theme of island poverty is one aspect of the Bali brand, but other businesses market their products through the exotic and mystical qualities attached to the island, showcased in resorts that cost thousands of dollars per night. Thailand and Bali are both sites of the "imaginative consumption of both metaphysical 'pilgrimage' within the global wellness industry."[108]

Bali's Mystical Landscapes

Bali, like other large islands in the Indonesian archipelago, includes mountains, which are sacred to Hindus. The largest of these, Gunung Agung, is home to the largest Hindu temple, Pura Besakih. Many religions believe mountains are sacred and that they are the home of the gods. Kailash in Tibet, Emei Shan in China, Uluru in Australia, and Sagarmatha/Chomolungma in Nepal are examples.[109] The Balinese believe the environment has a cosmic order that must be respected and maintained. Tourists visit Bali to experience this mystical landscape, reflecting the *ecospirituality* that marks many of the sites in this book.[110]

Balinese beliefs in the landscape, mountains, oceans, sacred spaces, and sacred directions are all part of a larger Hindu understanding of the cosmos. The *Tri Hita Karana* doctrine is characterized by three "harmonious relationships" that can be understood as the three causes of happiness.[111] This philosophy is rooted in *Tri* (three), *Hita* (prosperous), and *Karana* (cause), which can be understood through *Parahyangan* (harmony between humans and *Brahman*), *Pawongan* (harmony between humans), and *Palemahan* (harmony between humans and nature).[112] These principles are used to regulate non-tourist areas and include agricultural organizations (*Subak*) and rules surrounding the preservation of nature, which must be observed for balance in the environment.[113] This system is a different kind of mapping than we find in tourist areas, which violate these Balinese Hindu norms of purity and balance.[114] Tourists who seek experiences outside the beach resorts of Kuta and other more commercialized tourist districts are often seeking "power places" that are linked to specific sacred geographical sites.[115]

The Hindu design of landscapes and gardens is shaped by *Tri Angga*, which views mountains as the most sacred geography and oceans as the lowest.[116] Villages are organized by this principle, where gardens are used to grow plants used for making daily offerings to the gods.[117] The placement of everything in the Hindu universe is important, so much so that when the enormous statue of Wisnu (which is 121 meters tall and has a wingspan of 64 meters) was placed in southern Bali, Hindus protested because it was not in a Northeast position.[118]

Bali's mystical tourism industry is focused not only on hotels and resorts that offer transformative therapies and products, but also on an enormous array of businesses, images, and themes that one encounters the moment they arrive in Denpasar. Tourists view Hinduism as an exotic curiosity and often conflate it with Buddhism. While the form of Hinduism practiced in Bali can contain Buddhist imagery, there is not a sizeable Buddhist population on the island. Meditation retreats are popular in Bali, evidence of the ways that Buddhism has become identified with meditation, which carries "its own set of imaginaries."[119] American and European yoga instructors often do trainings and retreats for their clients in Bali. These are very different than traditional rituals involving *panditas* (Hindu priests) and the *sad kerthi* (local wisdom) of the Balinese.[120]

Indonesia receives approximately 20 million visitors every year, and half of them go to Bali.[121] Australians compose a large sector of these tourists, and some scholars have suggested that a trip to Bali is a "crucial rite of passage."[122] Some Australians may even view Bali as an imaginary extension of their geography, which might explain some of the more problematic behavior noted by media and in academic studies of the excessive use of alcohol, moped accidents, and issues. Casting Bali as a tourist territory for Australians means that for some, Bali is not a mystical landscape, but rather an island on which to party. Much like tourists in the Gili Islands to the east of Bali, the focus of some tourists is on partying, nightclubs, and drinking.[123] Fantasies about living the island life are seen not only in seasonal tourists, but also in foreigners who have longer stays in Bali or are there year-round, often living out a neocolonial life with a maid (*pembantu*) and benefiting from the inequalities in wealth between Indonesia and other nations.[124]

The mystical landscape of Bali, which includes its mountains, beaches, and rice fields, has suffered the effects of a large tourist industry. The busy city of Denpasar, with its fast-food restaurants, traffic, and shopping malls, the busy beaches of Kuta, and the growing popularity of Ubud in the island's interior have all threatened the idea of Bali as a Shangri-La. No longer "the last paradise," tourists have started to look elsewhere for the Balinese experience, turning to the nearby island of Lombok, touted as "The Bali of Ten Years Ago!"[125]

In addition to less-crowded islands like Lombok, Bali is the site of what Claudio Minca calls "The Bali Syndrome," the reterritorialization of well-established exotic tourist spaces that are separated into popular and more exclusive and private sites.[126] This preserves the exotic space from complete destruction by the tourist industry that has taken over. As Minca explains, "'Mature' tourism, therefore, seeks to protect and separate itself from the creature of its own making which now threatens to destroy it."[127] Minca uses the word "re-territorialization" to describe this phenomenon, which may include tourist spaces with microcosms of the host culture.[128] This ensures that tourists do not have to venture out into the "real" social spaces, which may destroy their idyllic illusions of a mystical paradise.

Kuta is a highly trafficked tourist area with several levels of accommodation catering to tourists with differing levels of income and taste. Minca describes it as a "chaos of lights, bars, discotheques" and "hard drugs and prostitution," while Sanur is a kind of midway location, and Nusa Dua the site of elite "high class tourism."[129] The economic situation for many Balinese includes foreign ownership of most hotels, a prostitution business that involves foreign expats in leadership roles, and statements from expats about how they feel like a "queen" or a "king" in Bali, a lifestyle that often includes servants.[130] These dynamics illustrate how for some, Bali is not only a mystical landscape, but also one imbued with colonial nostalgia.

Nusa Dua became a development project in the late 1970s when it was apparent that a tourist boom was on its way.[131] As part of the Bali master plan for tourism, hotels in Kuta, Sanur, and Nusa Dua were built, creating options for tourists with different budgets. One of the most impressive hotels is the Renaissance at Nusa Dua, owned by Marriott, a resort with everything a tourist needs—three pools, an elaborate play center for children, conference and event facilities, a hair salon, and views of the ocean from many of the rooms (there is no access to the beach). The Renaissance is an enormous and luxurious hotel, but at 146 U.S. dollars for high season, it is 10 percent of the price of comparable resorts in Hawai'i.

The Renaissance resort offers a beautiful and affordable vacation for families and other tourists who don't want the crowds, bars, and other bothersome issues of Kuta and other highly developed areas with beaches. For those who want an exclusive hotel that focuses on Bali's mystical landscape, there are many choices, including the Oberoi (their property in Lombok is even more stunning) and the Mandapa Preserve, owned by Ritz-Carlon. The Mandapa, located in Ubud, promises guests "a 'temple' of their own." Ubud is a small city in inland Bali that is popular with tourists for its mystical power. Known to tourists for its "restorative powers," its name originates from *ubad* (medicine), which refers to the local medicinal plants that grow in the area's jungles.[132] Numerous therapeutic services in Ubud are connected to the surrounding mystical landscape, including yoga, Ayurvedic "detoxes," Native American healing, energy cleansing, and aquasoma, often led by American women who charge exorbitant fees.[133]

The Mandapa markets itself as a "sanctuary for the body and soul in a mystical landscape," "an indigenous Balinese village" that offers a respite for "mind, body, and soul" and comes with a butler (*patih*), adding a little colonial nostalgia to one's experience.[134] Packages include a "Voyage of Discovery" and the "Enchanted Moments," options that offer the exotic character of Bali and the enchantment of an authentic culture. The importance of enchantment is critical in the marketing of high-end Balinese properties, which promise an experience different than home and also from Bali's crowded cities, beaches, and nightclubs.

The ways that tourists experience Bali's mystical landscape are not limited to hotels and resorts. Cultural tourism includes Mandapa's immersion in a Balinese village and the many temples and other cultural sites on the island popular with foreign tourists.[135] Wellness tourism includes offerings at luxury hotels like Mandapa. However, it is also a business that can involve local healers and practitioners. Ubud is believed to have a "natural potency" that is tied to the landscape and local communities that offer home spa services and homemade products like aromatherapy oils.[136] Hydrotherapy, massage, and other treatments are believed to alleviate headaches, create a feeling of calmness, and have other benefits tied to local wisdom and the Balinese environment with its plants and trees such as coconut and other tropical fauna.[137]

Wellness tourism can also involve Bali's environment, which is believed to have sacred qualities that are important not only for local Hindus and Muslims, but also for non-native tourists and long-term residents. Activities focused on wellness include "yoga, meditation, self-purification, and other spiritual activities."[138] Because Bali is viewed as a special environment imbued with unexplainable (i.e., mystical) powers, these activities practiced in Bali are viewed as being more efficacious than when practiced in one's home country. Participants in yoga have indicated that practicing yoga and meditation in Bali brings "joy and harmony with my surroundings" and that they "feel more in balance spiritually," and one participant stated, "I learned yoga and meditation for a while already, but learning yoga in Bali is a different experience."[139]

Yoga is offered at hotels, resorts, and yoga studios. Foreign teachers regularly offer yoga retreats in Bali, appealing to customers who believe the practice is more meaningful in a foreign and exotic location. The kind of yoga most practiced in Bali uses *asana* movements, which are not found in Balinese texts like Vrespatitatva and Jnanatatva.[140] Hindu yoga practices like "*ahimsa* (non-violence, *satya* (truth), *asteya* (not wanting other people's property), *brahmacarya* (abstinence from sexual pleasure), and *aparigraha* (abstinence from luxury)" are not part of these tourist yoga practices, which are focused more on food discipline and physical health.[141] Yoga promises that tourists will "gain enlightenment and meaning."[142] Balinese scholar Gede Sutarya describes how the COVID pandemic created a space for "on-off tourism"— yoga offerings that are offline (in Bali) and online (featuring Balinese scenery).[143] The Balinese environment is an important part of these businesses and includes places like the Munivara Ashram in Ubud.

Foreign yoga instructors far outnumber local teachers in Bali. At one Ubud studio, there were 22 foreign and 3 local yoga teachers.[144] Yoga pilgrimage has grown in popularity, in part because of the novel *Eat, Pray, Love* (2006), in which Elizabeth Gilbert seeks a religious teacher (*balian*) in her spiritual quest.[145] This pilgrimage is a tourist practice for some foreigners and follows the traditions of Sumantra, who utilizes "the mythology of Rsi Markendya" (an ancient sage who visited Bali according to tradition) in *tirtayatra* (the practice of visiting sacred waters).[146] Ubud is an important site both for yoga practitioners (with many yoga and wellness businesses) and for the yoga pilgrimage, which includes a tradition about Rsi Markendya visiting the Pucak Payogan Temple and other sites.[147]

The *melukat* ritual is a ritual of self-purification that also involves sacred waters sourced from one of the many sources on the island—temples, rivers, the ocean, or holy water sanctified by a Hindu priest at his home.[148] Popular with tourists, Indonesian scholars have noted that it is an "instagramable" event that attracts people through social media posts, serves as a "background view," and creates interest for tourists seeking a special experience.[149] *Melukat* is intended to clear one's body and mind from sickness, anxiety, nightmares, and other afflictions.[150] Foreigners who have done the ceremony remarked that they feel "cleansed and blessed," "a special spiritual feeling," and that it gave them "a feeling of calmness and [a] harmonious feeling."[151]

Water's importance in *melukat* reflects the importance of *tirthas* (crossing places) in Hinduism. Bali's water is often featured at temples, gardens, in rituals, and other spaces; and in the *melukat* ritual, it is viewed as a cure for mental illnesses and disorders.[152] Popular places for this ceremony include Pura Dalem Pingit, Pakraman Village, and Sebatu Gianyar.[153] Water is also linked to fertility and the importance of water as a principle of Tri Hita Karana is seen in the location of temples on lakes and coasts and is important in other areas of Balinese life such as the support of crops by the gods.[154]

Melukat is also connected to yoga and the sacred landscape of Ubud. The spiritual teacher Sumantra, who leads the yoga pilgrimage discussed earlier, often includes a visit to Campuhan, Ubud, for a sacred midnight bath.[155] As noted earlier, Ubud is believed by both local Balinese and some tourists to be a sacred place. The understanding of Ubud as "medicine" (*ubad* means medicine) is specifically tied to yoga practices and its holy waters, including the Campuhan River, places sanctified by spiritual teachers in the Hindu tradition who performed specific ceremonies like Eka Dasa Rudra.[156]

Bali continues to attract tourists of all kinds from around the world, including religious tourists from India, domestic tourists from Indonesia, Singaporeans on short holidays, Australians, yoga enthusiasts, long-term residents from Europe and elsewhere (expats), and spiritual seekers. Scholars have pointed to Bali's status as both a site of "spiritual magnetism" and a popular "tourist imaginary."[157] Bali means something quite different to its Indonesian residents. The participation in yoga classes at hotels and resorts with swimming pools, spas, and other services is contrasted with locals who visit sacred springs and the homes of Hindu guides.[158] Bali has two mystical landscapes—one for tourists and the other for Hindus and other religious Indonesians, including many Javanese Muslims, who view Bali with love and adoration as a place that survived the ravages of colonialism.

The White Lotus

The third season of *The White Lotus* (2025) takes place in Thailand at an idyllic resort punctuated by walkways, tropical forest, and Buddhist iconography. Unlike previous seasons, which take place in Hawai'i and Italy, Season 3 includes a strong emphasis on religion. The opening sequence of *The White Lotus* features a montage of Thai paintings of humans, monkeys, and foliage. It ends with sea monsters devouring humans, an example of the

East's exotic allure and inherent danger. Throughout history, the Orient has often been seen through "depictions of landscapes inhabited with all manner of terrible things."[159]

Buddhism plays a central role in the show, serving as the center of several plotlines. Gaitok, a security guard at the resort, struggles with Buddhism when he is forced to learn how to shoot a gun and, ultimately, when he must violate the Buddhist teaching of non-harm/nonviolence (*ahimsa*). Piper is the daughter of the Ratliff family, who has dragged her family to Thailand, telling them that she is interviewing a Buddhist monk for her senior thesis, but later revealing there is no thesis, just a plan to spend a year meditating at a nearby Buddhist monastery. After spending a night at the monastery, Piper decides it is not for her, complaining the next day to her parents about the dirty sheets and nonorganic food. Piper's father Timothy, who is contemplating his own mortality, also engages with the monastery, meeting with the head monk who imparts some Buddhist wisdom about the meaning of life. Rick, who is in Thailand to confront and perhaps murder someone from his parent's past, seeks help from a meditation teacher at the resort to help him deal with his own suffering, which has made him an unhappy and toxic partner to his much younger girlfriend Chelsea.

Piper Ratliff, who convinces her family to travel to Thailand instead of Bali (a place evoked by one of the characters when she wonders what they are doing in Thailand instead of their usual Asian spot, Bali), is perhaps the best example of the mystique of Buddhism in the tropics. As Brooke Schedneck has written, Thailand's Buddhist identity has been used to construct an example of tourism's *imaginaries of meditation*.[160] As she explains,

> These imaginaries are transmitted in promotional materials and through any visual or textual medium about a place, including novels, art, movies, postcards, memoirs, and blogs. Imaginaries of meditation have also become known through popular film and TV references, museum collections of meditating Buddha statues, and numerous popular manuals of meditation.[161]

The White Lotus creates a powerful mystical landscape that centers meditation as a key feature of its narrative.

The White Lotus's wealthy American and European clientele, who seek a luxury experience in Thailand, a nation known for its Buddhist culture, are an example of the West's vision of the East as a place of mystical healing. Both Bali and Thailand are centers of the colonial Oriental imagination, "part of an expansive list of exotic places associated with the East that are imbued with magical, mystical powers."[162] In particular, Thailand has been fetishized as a Buddhist landscape, much like Nepal and Tibet, whose other religious communities are ignored or conflated with Buddhism.

In *The White Lotus*, Buddhism is incorporated in the resort's spa therapies, environment, and decor. The show opens with the murder(s) that take place in the final episode, then begins several days earlier and tells the viewer the backstory to the tragic end of several of the show's favorite characters. Natasha is an employee of *The White Lotus* resort in Hawai'i (and featured in Season 2) whose story continues in Season 3. In the opening scenes of the first episode, Natasha's son Zion attempts to escape the gunfire that has erupted by jumping into the waters surrounding an enormous statue of the Buddha. A body (or bodies) float by him, but the viewer does not know their identity until the end of the series.

The opening and penultimate scenes of *The White Lotus* are not the only ones to feature images of Buddhism. Hanuman is featured throughout the series, a symbol of devotion amidst a decadent and wealthy tourist culture. A large statue of the Buddha is shown in both scenes at the hotel (filmed at the Four Seasons Resort Koh Samui) and in Bangkok, suggesting a tension between Thailand's culture of kindness and religion that is polluted by its tourist industry. In a violent scene that unfolds in the last episode, one of the doomed characters begs to meet with his meditation coach, but while waiting for his turn, he is unable to fight off his demons and tragedy unfolds. One cannot help but think of the Buddha's teachings on the war within the self and the suffering it can cause in the world.

Thailand's Mystical Landscapes

Thailand's popularity as a tourist destination is not only due to its Buddhist culture, but is also a result of a beautiful environment that is rich with wildlife. As one example, elephants are a large part of the tourist industry, with elephant rides, elephant shows, and even elephant paintings available for foreign visitors to purchase. The importance of elephants as a source of labor is an old practice, and today, the country has over 3,000 elephants of which 2,000 are privately owned and 1,000 live in national parks.[163] Bali also has elephants, including those who live at a resort with a hotel and preserve where tourists can ride the elephants, see them paint colorful pictures, feed them fruit, and learn about the fragile population of the animal in Indonesia and Malaysia.

Like Bali, Thailand has been subjected to fantasies about mystical power. Although Thailand was never officially colonized and occupied, it was influenced by Britain in the modern period, greatly impacting the culture of the country and the practice of Buddhism. Britain considered the Kingdom of Siam a part of its colonial territories, despite the country being officially free from colonial overlords. One place this influence of the West is seen is in the marketing of Buddhism as a commodity. I include Thailand in this chapter to show how Buddhism functions as a popular desire for tourists traveling to Southeast Asia.

Thailand is a popular tourist destination due to its lucrative and well-known Buddhist meditation, yoga, and wellness offerings, all of which reflect the importance of the mystical landscape. Brooke Schedneck has written how "Thailand's exotic allure" and meditation's status as "a universal symbol of peace, relaxation, and anti-modernity" have contributed to its lucrative tourism industry.[164] Thailand is a popular site for tourists who believe that the country is "an exotic center and its meditation practice" that exists as "a marker of difference."[165] Thailand's appeal lies in its mystical landscape and also relies on the role of Buddhist monks as icons of Western popular culture, what Iwamura calls "the Oriental monk."[166]

Siam, as Thailand was formerly known, was never officially colonized, but its leaders had to constantly strategize to make sure it would not be Britain's next colony. In 1887, King Rama V ordered a survey for what would become the state railway of Thailand, which would help to develop the country economically while showing it did not need a paternalistic caretaker in the form of a colonial government.[167] The railway was a continuation of policies by his predecessor, King Rama IV (1851–1868), who initiated government-sponsored media to help "Siam maintain its sovereignty and stave off threat from Western superpowers."[168] These policies were designed to counter the threats of imperialism that could have resulted in the occupation of the country.[169]

Despite Thailand's successes in staying independent, the influence of British and other European powers on the society is seen in its mapping. Between 1850 and 1910, Siam became "bordered," representing the ways in which even independent lands were impacted by the concept of "bounded territorial space."[170] Colonial ideology is also apparent in numerous other spaces, from the organization of government to attitudes toward *farang* (Westerners), who are often seen as smarter and more capable than Asians. One example is found in the marketing of Buddhism through "Monk Chats" in Chiang Mai, where Buddhism is marketed as a product, and farang are viewed as "smart enough to understand complex Buddhist teachings."[171]

One of the effects of foreign influence in Thailand is its long-term impact on the practice of Buddhism. Buddhism, once a religion that was practiced within independent communities, became centralized under a government ministry in Thailand. The creation of administrative units to control various parts of the territory, a common practice of European governments, was adopted by Thailand. One of the effects on Buddhism was the imposition of a centralized form of Thai religion on local festivals and celebrations, which was coupled with the commoditization of religion for tourism.[172]

In Thailand, the practice of Buddhism was changed as part of the modern governance of the country, creating a situation that affected the ways in which people interacted with their beliefs and sacred spaces. As Ploysri Porananond explains,

> The centralization of Buddhism in Thailand, the consequence of which was that all temples which used to be owned by local communities were then placed under the Department of Religion in Bangkok and the monks who used to be titled or appointed by local people as temple members were placed under the Department under Central Government, can be considered as one of the major factors in the decline of Buddhism in Thailand.[173]

One effect of this change is on how people practice Buddhism in Thailand. In 2003, the Jed Lin Temple began making a large sand pagoda, which was ostensibly designed to "present Lanna culture to the tourists."[174] However, this is an example of the importance of consumerism in Thai society more than authentic Buddhism. The sand pagoda is simply "not a meaningful part" of the "lives or beliefs" of the Lanna people.[175]

Chiang Mai is one of the most popular tourist destinations in Thailand. It was the capital of the people of the Lanna kingdom 700 years ago, and as a major Buddhist center, it is populated with many Buddhist temples.[176] Meditation centers in Thailand run by Buddhist monks are very popular with Westerners seeking the enchantment and authenticity missing from their lives at home. As Brooke Schedneck has argued, religious leaders in Thailand have "molded their religious practices to fit with Romantic Orientalist ideas of a 'mystical' and 'ancient' Eastern spirituality."[177]

The mystical landscapes of Thailand reflect the importance of Buddhism in the nation's culture and the preoccupation of foreign tourists with the religion and the practices linked to it, including yoga and meditation. The tourist materials used to market Thailand as a mystical landscape often include the image of a lone white tourist meditating in nature. One example is a young woman meditating on a lotus flower, an example of the "magic" associated with meditation in Thailand and an example of the many scenes of the "tourist meditating in an exotic, almost fantastic, scene."[178]

The insertion of white bodies in the Thai landscape illustrates the mapping of space by white bodies. The achievement of mystical states suggests that a Thai Buddhist teacher is unnecessary. Brooke Schedneck notes in her ethnography of tourist pamphlets that there were no Thai or other Asian teachers shown leading meditation for a group of foreigners.[179] Yoga is another practice associated with Buddhism featured at many tourist locations in Thailand. It has been described as a form of "transformational tourism" that when offered abroad, in exotic locations, gains a kind of authenticity that comes from a "source" of the tradition.[180] Advertisements for yoga also suggest the importance of white bodies and their independence from Asian expertise.

Bali Ha'i **181**

In yoga retreats in Thailand, geographical exploration is a part of these transformative experiences that include both "internal and external pilgrimage" that are "consumed in reconstituted ways by global yogis."[181] McCartney uses the term *Yogaland* to describe these experiences, which is used by yoga tourists who seek the "utopian-inspired meta-space where life is celebrated," which includes places in both Bali and Thailand.[182] The mystical landscape of the global yogi is the "antithesis" to the enchantment experienced outside of these special places.[183] As we learn in the next chapter, Bali and Thailand are just two of the island nations in the South Pacific that have a powerful place in the Western imagination.

Notes

1 Hickman Powell, *The Last Paradise: An American's 'Discovery' of Bali in the 1920s* (Singapore: Oxford University Press, 1982), 4–5.
2 Margaret Jolly, "Contested Paradise: Dispossession and Repossession in Hawai'i," *The Contemporary Pacific* 30, no. 2 (2018): 356.
3 Stausberg, 128.
4 Yamashita, 7.
5 Yamashita, 25.
6 I. Nyoman Darma Putra and Michael Hitchcock, "Bali Imagined in the Context of Tourism," *E-Journal of Tourism* 8, no. 2 (2021): 202.
7 Carolyn Cartier, "Introduction: Touristed Landscapes/Seductions of Place," in *Seductions of Place: Geographical Perspectives on Globalization and Touristed Landscapes*, ed. Carolyn Cartier and Alan A. Lew (New York: Routledge, 2005), 4.
8 Allon, 25. The South Seas has had shifting geographical identities, sometimes including Indonesia and other places in the Asian Pacific and other times restricting itself to Polynesia and its islands, which are the focus of the next chapter.
9 Robert C. Schmitt, "South Sea Movies, 1913–1943," *Hawaii Historical Review* 2, no. 11 (1968): 433.
10 Hitchcock 2007, 15.
11 Carolina Sánchez Palencia, "'The Tropics Make It Difficult to Mope': The Imaginative Geography of Alexander Payne's *The Descendants* (2011)," *International Journal of English Studies* 15, no. 2 (2015): 86.
12 I. Gede Sutarya, "The Potentials and Prospects of Yoga Pilgrimage Exploration in Bali Tourism," *International Journal of Religious Tourism and Pilgrimage* 8, no. 8 (2021): 129.
13 Yamashita, 27, 33, 75.
14 Judith Schlachter, "Reclaiming Paradise: Cinema and Hawaiian Nationhood," *Pacific Studies* 38, nos. 1/2 (2015): 232.
15 Gary L. Atkins, *Imagining Gay Paradise: Bali, Bangkok, and Cyber-Singapore* (Hong Kong: Hong Kong University Press, 2012), 71.
16 Yamashita, 29.
17 Atkins, 74.
18 Atkins, 142.
19 Yamashita, 31.
20 Atkins, 75.
21 Atkins, 76.
22 Putra and Hitchcock, 203.

23 Atkins, 88.

24 Written by German author Vicki Baum, the novel was first translated into English in 1937.

25 I. Made Pramana, "Photography as a Bridge: To Intercultural Interaction in Bali during the Netherlands Indies Colonial Period of the 1920s–1930s," *Lekesen: Interdisciplinary Journal of Asia Pasific Arts* 2, no. 2 (2019): 57.

26 Leo Howe, *The Changing World of Bali: Religion, Society and Tourism* (New York: Routledge, 2005), 27.

27 Atkins, 135.

28 Michael Hitchcock, "Bali: A Paradise Globalized," *Pacific Tourism Review* 4 (2000): 67.

29 Atkins, 90.

30 Atkins, 90.

31 Atkins, 89.

32 Atkins, 90.

33 Atkins, 139.

34 Biblical verse quoted by Atkins, 140.

35 Michel Picard, "Cultural Heritage and the Tourist Capital," in *International Tourism: Identity and Change*, ed. Marie-Françoise Lanfant, John B. Allcock, and Edward M. Bruner (London: Sage, 1995), 45.

36 Hitchcock 2000, 65.

37 Luchman Hakim, Jae-Eun Kim, and Sun-Kee Hong, "Cultural Landscape and Ecotourism in Bali Island, Indonesia," *Journal of Ecology and Field Biology* 32, no. 1 (2009): 2.

38 Howe 2005, 18.

39 Pramana, 55–56. See Gregor Krause, *Bali 1912* (1920; repr., Singapore: Pepper Publications, 1998).

40 Lewis 1994, 38. Scholars debate questions about the cohabitation of Hinduism and Buddhism in Java and Bali, even today.

41 Allon, 25.

42 Powell, 152.

43 Powell, 152. The next chapter focuses on the romanticized views that Europeans had of Tahiti.

44 The capital of Indonesia is being relocated to Kalimantan, a process that will take many years and might shift the political focus away from Java.

45 Godfrey Baldacchino, "Island Tourist Experiences," in *Routledge Handbook of Tourist Experience* (New York: Routledge, 2022), 501.

46 Henk Schulte Nordholt, "Some Visits to Bali," *Itinerario* 4, no. 2 (1980): 84.

47 For a study of the Balinese Muslims, see Sophia Arjana's forthcoming book on Indonesian Islam, provisionally titled *The Mosque with the Thatched Roof: Magical Forests, Ocean Spirits, and Other Stories from Indonesia* (Oxford, 2026).

48 Atkins, 72.

49 James A. Boon, *The Anthropological Romance of Bali, 1597–1972: Dynamic Perspectives on Marriage & Caste, Politics & Religion* (New York: Cambridge University Press, 1977), 11–12.

50 Allon 28–29.

51 Hitchcock 2000, 65.

52 Hitchcock 2000, 66.

53 Ana Dragojlovic, *Beyond Bali: Subaltern Citizens and Post-Colonial Intimacy* (Amsterdam: Amsterdam University Press, 2016), 27.

54 Allon, 29.

55 Dragojlovic, 28.

56 Dragojlovic, 29.
57 Allon, 30.
58 India and the United States are the two largest by population number, followed by Indonesia.
59 Putra and Hitchcock, 203.
60 Nordholt, 85.
61 James A. Boon, "The Birth of the Idea of Bali," *Indonesia* 22 (1976): 72.
62 Boon 1976, 81.
63 The history of Islam in Indonesia is complex, and the archipelago was still populated by many Hindus at the time of Dutch contact.
64 Putra and Hitchcock, 198. *Pahit* means "bitter" and may be a reference to this period of invasion by the Chinese.
65 Putra and Hitchcock, 198–199.
66 Atkins, 73.
67 Howe 2005, 20.
68 Howe 2005, 21. Here, Howe quotes James A. Boon, *The Anthropological Romance of Bali, 1597–1972: Dynamic Perspectives in Marriage & Caste, Politics & Religion* (New York: Cambridge University Press, 1977), 15.
69 Hore, 142.
70 Pramana, 55.
71 Hitchcock, 30.
72 Hitchcock, 30.
73 Salazar 2013, 680.
74 Pramana, 55.
75 Pramana, 56.
76 While famous and widely read, Geertz viewed Bali in ways that were somewhat problematic, but his work inspired later generations of scholars.
77 Margaret Mead, "The Art and Technology of Fieldwork," in *A Handbook of Method in Cultural Anthropology*, ed. Raoul Naroll and Ronald Cohen (Garden City: Natural History Press, 1970), 259. Quoted in Boon 1977, 67.
78 Miguel Covarrubias, *Island of Bali* (New Clarendon: Tuttle Publishing, 1973), xxvi, 23.
79 Covarrubias, 9.
80 Colin McPhee, *A House in Bali* (North Clarendon: Tuttle Publishing, 1944), 17.
81 Allon, 25.
82 Norum, 37.
83 Adrian Vickers, *Bali: A Paradise Created* (Singapore: Tuttle Publishing, 2012), 16.
84 Vickers, 168–169.
85 Picard 1990, 39.
86 Picard 1990, 40.
87 William Chapman, *A Heritage of Ruins: The Ancient Sites of Southeast Asia and Their Conservation* (Honolulu: University of Hawai'i Press, 2013), 6.
88 Sarah Tiffin, "Raffles and the Barometer of Civilisation: Images and Descriptions of Ruined Candis in 'the History of Jav'," *Journal of the Royal Asiatic Society* 18, no. 3 (2008): 360, 359.
89 Hitchcock 2007, 33.
90 Hitchcock 2007, 34–35.
91 Hitchcock 2000, 68.
92 Picard 1990, 41. Construction on the Bali Beach Hotel began in 1963. See Vickers, 252–252 for a discussion of the early tourist boom in Bali, which the anti-Communist purges in 1955 and 1956 affected.
93 Robert Sheperd, "'A Green and Sumptuous Garden': Authenticity, Hybridity, and the Bali Tourism Project," *South East Asia Research* 10, no. 1 (2002): 63.

94 Picard 1995, 49.
95 Picard 1995, 49.
96 Hitchcock 2000, 68.
97 Putra and Hitchcock, 201.
98 Antonia Hussey, "Tourist Destination Areas in Bali," *Contemporary Southeast Asia* 3, no. 4 (1980): 376.
99 Hussey, 379.
100 *Candi* is the old Javanese word for temple or sanctuary. They are also known by the word *pura*.
101 Williams 2014, 630.
102 Hitchcock 2000, 65.
103 Hitchcock 2000, 63.
104 Sheperd 2002, 65.
105 Sheperd 2002, 94.
106 Hitchcock 2007, 37.
107 Logan, 613.
108 Patrick McCartney, "Yoga-Scapes, Embodiment and Imagined Spiritual Tourism," in *Tourism and Embodiment*, ed. Catherine Palmer and Hazel Andrews (New York: Routledge, 2019), 86.
109 Alan A. Lew and Guosheng Han, "A World Geography of Mountain Trekking," in *Mountaineering Tourism*, ed. Ghazali Musa, James Higham, and Anna Thompson-Carr (New York: Routledge, 2015), 21.
110 McCartney, 91.
111 Hakim, Kim, and Hong, 2.
112 Anak Agung Sagung Laksmi Dewi, Mella Ismelina Farma Rahayu, and Anak Agung Ngurah Adhi Wibisama, "Green Tourism in Sustainable Tourism Development in Bali Based on Local Wisdom," *Jurnal Dinamika Hukum* 23, no. 2 (2023): 118.
113 Dewi, Rahayu, and Wibisama, 120–122.
114 Dewi, Rahayu, and Wibisama, 124.
115 McCartney, 95.
116 Hakim, Kim, and Hong, 4.
117 Hakim, Kim, and Hong, 5–6.
118 Bart Verheijen and I. Nyoman Darma Putra, "Balinese Cultural Identity and Global Tourism: The Garuda Wisnu Kencana Cultural Park," *Asian Ethnicity* 21, no. 3 (2020): 425.
119 Schedneck 2017, 9.
120 Anak Agung Ayu Ngurah Sri Rahayu Gorda, Kadek Januarsa Adi Sudharma, and Ketut Elly Sutrisni, "*Melukat* Ritual for Commercialization and Protection toward Cultural Tourism in Bali," in *Advances in Social Science, Education and Humanities Research* (Proceedings of the 3rd International Conference on Business Lawa and Local Wisdom in Tourism, Atlantis Press, Dordrecht, 2023), 621, 628.
121 Verheijen and Putra, 428. This is a 2019 statistic.
122 Allon, 26.
123 The one time I stayed near Kuta beach, the hotel was overrun with drunk tourists. This included Australians walking around topless at our hotel, to the horror of the Balinese and Javanese staff.
124 Claudia Bell, " 'We Feel Like the King and Queen': Western Retirees in Bali, Indonesia," *Asian Journal of Social Science* 45 (2017): 274, 277. Foreigners who stay for extended periods of time are required to hire a maid or other local staff, an arrangement that generates income for local families while placing them in labor situations with foreigners where they may be verbally abused or worse.

125 Minca, 397.
126 Minca, 389.
127 Minca, 393.
128 Minca, 395.
129 Minca, 395–396.
130 Claudia Bell, "Eat, Pray, Love, Ethics: Researching Expats and Tourists in Bali," in *Qualitative Ethics in Practice*, ed. Martin Tolich (Walnut Creek: Left Coast Press, 2016), 162, 163, 164, 167.
131 Raymond Noronha, "Paradise Reviewed: Tourism in Bali," in *Tourism: Passport to Development? Perspectives on the Social and Cultural Effects of Tourism in Developing Countries*, ed. Emanuel de Kadt (New York: Oxford University Press, 1979), 196, 200.
132 Claudia Bell, "The New Age Tourist Brand-Wagon in Ubud, Bali: Eat Pay Love!," *South Asian Research Journal of Arts, Language and Literature* 1, no. 3 (2019): 76.
133 Bell 2019, 78.
134 Mandapa website (accessed January 19, 2025).
135 Ida Bagus Nyoman Mantra, I. Nyoman Suparsa, and Nengah Dwi Handayani, "Cultural and Wellness Tourism: The Potential of Yoga, Meditation and Self-Purification Ceremony," *SOSHUM (Jurnal Sosial dan Humaniora)* 13, no. 2 (2023): 112.
136 Pradana Gede Yoga Kharisma and Parwati Komang Shanty Muni, "Local-Wisdom-Based Spa Tourism in Ubud Village of Bali, Indonesia," *RJOAS* 68, no. 8 (2017): 190–191.
137 Kharisma and Muni, 193.
138 Mantra, Suparsa, and Handayani, 111.
139 Mantra, Suparsa, and Handayani, 113–114.
140 I. Gede Sutarya and I. Dewa Ayu Hendrawathy, "Theological Critics to Yoga Tourism in Bali" (Conference Paper, International Conference on Theology, Philosophy and Religious, Nua Dusa, Bali, November 29, 2018), n.p.
141 Sutarya and Hendrawathy, n.p.
142 I. Gede Sutarya, "On-Off Hybrid Spiritual Tourism in the New Normal Era," *Southeast Asia: A Multidisciplinary Journal* 24, no. 2 (2024): 97.
143 Sutarya 2024, 95. The tourist numbers in Bali declined due to the COVID pandemic, with over six million visitors to Bali in 2019 and only 371,000 in 2022. The numbers have since bounced back. See Sutarya 2024, 99.
144 Sutarya 2021, 128.
145 Sutarya 2021, 127.
146 Sutarya 2021, 128, 129.
147 Sutarya 2021, 130.
148 Mantra, Suparsa, and Handayani, 115, *Melukat* is also known as *malukat*.
149 Putu Ratna Juwita Sari, Ni Nyoman Sri Wisudawati, and Ni Made Dhlan Rani Yullanthi, "The 'Melukat' Tradition as Millennial Religious Tourism in Bali," *Jurnal Antropologi: Isu-Isu Social Buudaya* 24, no. 2 (2022): 245.
150 Mantra, Suparsa, and Handayani, 116.
151 Mantra, Suparsa, and Handayani, 116.
152 Mantra, Suparsa, and Handayani, 117.
153 Sari, Wisudawati, and Yullanthi, 242.
154 Hakim, Kim, and Hong, 6.
155 Sutarya 2021, 130.
156 Sutarya 2021, 130.
157 Choe and Mahyuni, 101–102.
158 Choe and Mahyuni, 105.

159 Sophia Rose Arjana, *Muslims in the Western Imagination* (New York: Oxford University Press, 2015), 87.
160 Schedneck 2017, 9.
161 Schedneck 2017, 9–10.
162 Arjana 2020, 76.
163 Rosaleen Duffy and Lorraine Moore, "Neoliberalizing Nature? Elephant-Back Tourism in Thailand and Botswana." *Antipode* 42, no. 3 (2010): 754.
164 Schedneck 2017, 111.
165 Schedneck 2017, 11.
166 Iwamura, 13.
167 Napawan Tantivejakul, "The State Railway of Siam and the Origin of Tourism Public Relations in Thailand (1917–1941)," *Corporate Communications: An International Journal* 29, no. 2 (2024): 9.
168 Tantivejakul, 11.
169 Tantivejakul, 17.
170 Anderson, 173. As Anderson explains, the spaces marked by stones and other objects became replaced by national "borders."
171 Brooke Schedneck, "Religious Others, Tourism, and Missionization: Buddhist 'Monk Chats' in Northern Thailand," *Modern Asian Studies* 52, no. 6 (2018): 1890, 1913.
172 Sudarat Auttarat and Nivej Poonsukcharoen, "A Spiritual Journey? Using Religious Storytelling to Enhance Tourism in Northern Thailand," *The International Journal of Religion and Spirituality in Society* 12, no. 2 (2022): 84.
173 Ploysri Porananond, "Tourism and the Transformation of Ritual Practices with Sand Pagodas in Chiang Mai, Northern Thailand," *Tourism Review* 70, no. 3 (2015): 176.
174 Porananond, 173.
175 Porananond, 173.
176 Porananond, 168.
177 Schedneck 2017 10.
178 Schedneck 2017, 119.
179 Schedneck 2017, 119.
180 Melanie Kay Smith and Ivett Sziva, "Yoga, Transformation and Tourism," in *The Routledge Handbook on Health Tourism*, ed. Melanie Kay Smith and László Puczkó (New York: Routledge, 2017), 168, 172.
181 McCartney, 89.
182 McCartney, 89.
183 McCartney, 89.

Bibliography

Allon, Fiona. "Bali as Icon: Tourism, Death, and the Pleasure Periphery." *Humanities Research* 11, no. 1 (2004): 24–41.
Anderson, Benedict. *Imagined Communities: Reflections on the Origin and Spread of Nationalism.* New York: Verso, 2006.
Arjana, Sophia. *Muslims in the Western Imagination.* New York: Oxford University Press, 2015.
Arjana, Sophia. *Buying Buddha, Selling Rumi: Orientalism and the Mystical Marketplace.* London: Oneworld, 2020.
Arjana, Sophia. *The Mosque with the Thatched Roof: Magical Forests, Ocean Spirits, and Other Stories from Indonesia.* New York: Oxford University Press, 2026.
Atkins, Gary L. *Imagining Gay Paradise: Bali, Bangkok, and Cyber-Singapore.* Hong Kong: Hong Kong University Press, 2012.

Auttarat, Sudarat and Nivej Poonsukcharoen. "A Spiritual Journey? Using Religious Storytelling to Enhance Tourism in Northern Thailand." *The International Journal of Religion and Spirituality in Society* 12, no. 2 (2022): 83–97.

Baldacchino, Godfrey. "Island Tourist Experiences." In *Routledge Handbook of the Tourist Experience*, edited by Richard Sharpley, 498–507. New York: Routledge, 2022.

Baum, Vicki. *Love and Death in Bali*, 1937. Reprint. North Clarendon: Tuttle, 2011.

Bay, Michael, dir. *Pearl Harbor*. Touchstone Pictures, 2001.

Bell, Claudia. "Eat, Pray, Love, Ethics: Researching Expats and Tourists in Bali." In *Qualitative Ethics in Practice*, edited by Martin Tolich, 159–170. Walnut Creek: Left Coast Press, 2016.

Bell, Claudia. "'We Feel Like the King and Queen': Western Retirees in Bali, Indonesia." *Asian Journal of Social Science* 45 (2017): 271–293.

Bell, Claudia. "The New Age Tourist Band-Wagon in Ubud, Bali: Eat Pay Love!" *South Asian Research Journal of Arts, Language and Literature* 1, no. 3 (2019): 74–82.

Boon, James A. "The Birth of the Idea of Bali." *Indonesia* 22 (1976): 70–83.

Boon, James A. *The Anthropological Romance of Bali, 1597–1972: Dynamic Perspectives in Marriage & Caste, Politics & Religion*. New York: Cambridge University Press, 1977.

Cartier, Carolyn. "Introduction: Touristed Landscapes/Seductions of Place." In *Seductions of Place: Geographical Perspectives on Globalization and Touristed Landscapes*, edited by Carolyn Carter and Alan A. Lew, 1–19. London: Routledge, 2005.

Chapman, William. *A Heritage of Ruins: The Ancient Sites of Southeast Asia and Their Conservation*. Honolulu: University of Hawai'i Press, 2013.

Choe, Jaeyeon and Luh Putu Mahyuni. "Sustainable and Inclusive Spiritual Tourism Development in Bali as a Long-Term Post-Pandemic Strategy." *International Journal of Religious Tourism and Pilgrimage* 11, no. 2 (2023): 100–111.

Covarrubias, Miguel. *Island of Bali*, 1937. Reprint. North Clarendon: Tuttle Publishing, 1973.

Crowe, Cameron, dir. *Aloha*. Columbia Pictures, 2015.

Dewi, Anak Agung Sagung Laksmi, Mella Ismelina Farma Rahayu, and Anak Agung. "Green Tourism in Sustainable Tourism Development in Bali Based on Local Wisdom." *Jurnal Dinamika Hukum* 23, no. 1 (2023): 111–130.

Donaldson, Roger, dir. *The Bounty*. Los Angeles: Orion Pictures, 1984.

Dragojlovic, Ana. *Beyond Bali: Subaltern Citizens and Post-Colonial Intimacy*. Amsterdam: Amsterdam University Press, 2016.

Duffy, Rosaleen and Lorraine Moore. "Neoliberalizing Nature? Elephant-Back Tourism in Thailand and Botswana." *Antipode* 42, no. 3 (2010): 742–766.

Flaherty, Robert, dir. *Moana (Moana: A Romance of the Golden Age)*. Paramount Pictures, 1926.

Forby, Marc, dir. *Princess Kaiulani*. Roadside Attractions, 2009.

Gilbert, Elizabeth. *Eat, Pray, Love: One Woman's Search for Everything Across Italy, India and Indonesia*. New York: Penguin Books, 2006.

Gorda, Anak Agung Ayu Ngurah Sri Rahayu, Kadek Januarsa Adi Sudharma, and Ketut Elly Sutrisni. "Melukat Ritual for Commercialization and Protection Toward Cultural Tourism in Bali." In *Advances in Science, Education and Humanities Research* (Proceedings of the 3rd International Conference on Business Law and Local Wisdom Traditions), 618–629. Dordrecht: Atlantis Press, 2023.

Hakim, Luchman, Jae-Eun Kim, and Sun-Kee Hong. "Cultural Landscape and Ecotourism in Bali Island, Indonesia." *Journal of Ecology and Field Biology* 32, no. 1 (2009): 1–8.

Hemmings, Kaui Hart. *The Descendants*. New York: Random House, 2007.
Hitchcock, Michael. "Bali: A Paradise Globalized." *Pacific Tourism Review* 4 (2000): 63–73.
Hitchcock, Michael. *Tourism, Development, and Terrorism in Bali*. New York: Routledge, 2007.
Hore, Jarrod. *Visions of Nature: How Landscape Photography Shaped Settler Colonialism*. Berkeley: University of California Press, 2022.
Howe, Leo. *The Changing World of Bali: Religion, Society and Tourism*. New York: Routledge, 2005.
Hussey, Antonia. "Tourist Destination Areas in Bali." *Contemporary Southeast Asia* 3, no. 4 (1980): 374–385.
Iwamura, Jane Naomi. *Virtual Orientalism: Asian Religions and American Popular Culture*. New York: Oxford University Press, 2011.
Jolly, Margaret. "Contested Paradise: Dispossession and Repossession in Hawai'i." *The Contemporary Pacific* 30, no. 2 (2018): 355–377.
Kharisma, Pradana Gede Yoga and Parwati Komang Shanty Muni. "Local-Wisdom-Based Spa Tourism in Ubud Village of Bali, Indonesia." *RJOAS* 68, no. 8 (2017): 188–196.
Krause, Gregor. *Bali 1912*, 1920. Reprint. Singapore: Pepper Publications, 1998.
Lew, Alan A. and Guosheng Han. "A World Geography of Mountain Trekking." In *Mountaineering Tourism*, edited by Ghazali Musa, James Higham, and Anna Thompson-Carr, 19–39. New York: Routledge, 2015.
Lewis, Todd T. "Himalayan Religions in Comparative Perspective: Considerations Regarding Buddhism and Hinduism Across Their Indic Frontiers." *Himalaya* 14, no. 1 (1994): 25–46.
Lloyd, Frank, dir. *Mutiny on the Bounty*. Los Angeles: MGM, 1935.
Logan, Dana W. "The Lean Closet: Asceticism in Postindustrial Consumer Culture." *Journal of the American Academy of Religion* 85, no. 3 (2017): 600–628.
Mantra, Ida Bagus, I Nyoman Suparsa, and Negah Dwi Handayani. "Cultural and Wellness Tourism: The Potential of Yoga, Meditation, and Self-Purification Ceremony." *SOSHUM (Jurnal Sosial dan Humaniora)* 13, no. 2 (2013): 109–119.
McCartney, Patrick. "Yoga-scapes, Embodiment, and Imagined Spiritual Tourism." In *Tourism and Embodiment*, edited by Catherine Palmer and Hazel Andrews, 86–106. New York: Routledge, 2019.
McPhee, Colin. *A House in Bali*. New Clarendon: Tuttle Publishing, 1944.
Mead, Margaret. "The Art and Technology of Fieldwork." In *A Handbook of Method in Cultural Anthropology*, edited by Raoul Naroll and Ronald Cohen, 246–265. Garden City: Natural History Press, 1970.
Minca, Claudio. "'The Bali Syndrome': The Explosion and Implosion of 'Exotic' Tourist Spaces." *Tourism Geographies* 2, no. 4 (2000): 389–403.
Murnau, F.W., dir. *Tabu: A Story of the South Seas*. Paramount Pictures, 1931.
Nordholt, Henk Schulte. "Some Visits to Bali." *Itinerario* 4, no. 2 (1980): 83–89.
Noronha, Raymond. "Paradise Reviewed: Tourism in Bali." In *Tourism: Passport to Development? Perspectives on the Social and Cultural Effects of Tourism in Developing Countries*, edited by Emanuel de Kadt, 177–204. New York: Oxford University Press, 1979.
Norum, Roger Edward. "The Unbearable Likeness of Being a Tourist: Expats, Travel and Imaginaries in the Neo-colonial Orient." *International Review of Social Research* 3, no. 1 (2013): 27–47.
Palencia, Carolina Sánchez. "'The Tropics Make It Difficult to Mope' The Imaginative Geography of Alexander Payne's *The Descendants* (2001)." *International Journal of English Studies* 15, no. 2 (2015): 81–95.
Payne, Alexander, dir. *The Descendants*. Fox Searchlight Pictures, 2011. DVD.

Picard, Michel. "'Cultural Tourism' in Bali: Cultural Performances as Tourist Attraction." *Indonesia* 49 (1990): 37–74.

Picard, Michel. "Cultural Heritage and Tourist Capital: Cultural Tourism in Bali." In *International Tourism: Identity and Change*, edited by Marie-Françoise Lanfant, John B. Allcock, and Edward M. Bruner, 44–66. London: Sage, 1995.

Pommer, Erich, dir. *The Beachcomber*. Paramount Pictures, 1938.

Porananond, Ploysri. "Tourism and the Transformation of Ritual Practice with Sand Pagodas in Chiang Mai, Northern Thailand." *Tourism Review* 70, no. 3 (2015): 165–178.

Powell, Hickman. *The Last Paradise: An American's 'Discovery' of Bali in the 1920s.* Singapore: Oxford University Press, 1982.

Pramana, I. Made Bayu. "Photography as a Bridge: To Intercultural Interaction in Bali During the Netherlands Indies Colonial Period of the 1920s–1930s." *Lekesen: Interdisciplinary Journal of Asia Pacific Arts* 2, no. 2 (2019): 54–58.

Putra, I. Nyoman Darma and Michael Hitchcock. "Bali Imagined in the Context of Tourism." *E-Journal of Tourism* 8, no. 2 (2021): 197–206.

Salazar, Noel B. "Imagineering Otherness: Anthropological Lenses in Contemporary Tourism." *Anthropological Quarterly* 86, no. 3 (2013): 669–696.

Sari, Putu Ratna Juwita, Ni Nyoman Sri Wisudawati, and Ni Made Dhlan Rani Yulianthi. "The 'Melukat' Tradition as Millennial Religious Tourism in Badung, Bali." *Jurnal Antropologi: Isu-Isu Social Budya* 24, no. 2 (2022): 241–248.

Schedneck, Brooke. *Thailand's International Meditation Centers: Tourism and the Global Commodification of Religious Practices*. New York: Routledge, 2017.

Schedneck, Brooke. "Religious Others, Tourism, and Missionization: Buddhist 'Monk Chats' in Northern Thailand." *Modern Asia Studies* 52, no. 6 (2018): 1888–1916.

Schlachter, Judith. "Reclaiming Paradise: Cinema and Hawaiian Nationhood." *Pacific Studies* 38, no. 1/2 (2015): 229–252.

Schmitt, Robert C. "South Sea Movies, 1913–1943." *Hawaii Historical Review* 2, no. 11 (1968): 433–452.

Sheperd, Robert. "'A Green and Sumptuous Garden': Authenticity, Hybridity, and the Bali Tourism Project." *South East Asia Research* 10, no. 1 (2002): 63–97.

Smith, Melanie Kay and Ivett Sziva. "Yoga, Transformation and Tourism." In *The Routledge Handbook on Health Tourism*, edited by Melanie Kay Smith and László Puczkó, 168–180. New York: Routledge, 2017.

Stausberg, Michael. *Religion and Tourism: Crossroads, Destinations and Encounters.* New York: Routledge, 2011.

Sutarya, I. Gede. "The Potential and Prospects of Yoga Pilgrimage Exploration in Bali Tourism." *International Journal of Religious Tourism and Pilgrimage* 8, no. 8 (2021): 127–135.

Sutarya, I. Gede. "On-Off Hybrid Spiritual Tourism in the New Normal Era." *Southeast Asia: A Multidisciplinary Journal* 24, no. 2 (2024): 95–106.

Sutarya, I. Gede and I. Dewa Ayu Hendrawathy Putri. "Theological Critics to Yoga Tourism in Bali." *Conference Paper, International Conference on Theology, Philosophy and Religious 2018*, November 29, 2018.

Tantivejakul, Napawan. "The State Railway of Siam and the Origin of Tourism Public Relations in Thailand (1917–1941)." *Corporate Communications: An International Journal* 29, no. 1 (2024): 9–23.

Tiffin, Sarah. "Raffles and the Barometer of Civilisation: Images and Descriptions of Ruined Candis in 'The History of Java'." *Journal of the Royal Asiatic Society* 18, no. 3 (2008): 341–360.

Toland, Gregg and John Ford, dir. *December 7th*. Office of War Information, 1943.

Van Dyke, W.S., dir. *White Shadows in the South Seas*. Metro-Goldwyn-Meyer (MGM), 1928.

Verheijen, Bart and I. Nyoman Darma Putra. "Balinese Cultural Identity and Global Tourism." *Asian Ethnicity* 21, no. 3 (2020): 425–442.

Vickers, Adrian. *Bali: A Paradise Created*. Singapore: Tuttle Publishing, 2012.

Walker, Hal, dir. *Road to Bali*. Paramount Pictures, 1952.

White, Mike, dir. *The White Lotus* (Season 3). Los Angeles: HBO, 2025.

Williams, Ruth. "Eat, Pray, Love: Producing the Female Neoliberal Spiritual Subject." *The Journal of Popular Culture* 47, no. 3 (2014): 613–633.

Yamashita, Shinji. *Bali and Beyond: Explorations in the Anthropology of Tourism*. New York: Bergahn Books, 2003.

6

DREAMS OF THE SOUTH PACIFIC

> Paradise is not a generic or static term—it specifically refers to an idea
> of passivity and penetrability engendered by imperialism as an alibi for
> domination.[1]
>
> Vernadette Vicuña Gonzalez

Islands are vulnerable to radical re-imaginings, and as one scholar notes,
"Few islands have excited imaginations more than those of the Pacific."[2]
Geographically and figuratively, islands are little universes that exist apart
from the rest of the world:

> Islands offer the allure of seemingly complete worlds, introspective eco-
> systems, secured by boundaries: empathy and control are simultaneously
> possible. Sea and island can be taken in panoptically as a singular insular
> whole.[3]

The islands of the South Pacific include high islands, majestic volcanic peaks,
and coral atolls, all tropical paradises in the eyes of colonial explorers, artists, and tourists. Isolated, small, and different than European landscapes, the
islands of the South Pacific have been tied to physical and spiritual rebirth in
literature, painting, and cinema.

The colonial mapping of the Pacific Ocean included the academic construction of three cultural and linguistic groupings: Polynesia (many islands);
Melanesia (black islands or, more accurately, the islands of black-skinned
peoples); and Micronesia (small islands).[4] Polynesia was a word first used
by Charles de Brosses in 1756, describing the many islands discovered in the

DOI: 10.4324/9781003361725-7

Pacific, which was further elaborated upon in 1832 by J. Dumont d'Urville for the triangle (the Polynesian triangle) of islands between Rapa Nui (Easter Island), the Hawaiian Islands, and Aotearoa (New Zealand).[5] The different names for the islands in the Pacific Ocean also reflect romantic (South Seas) and military (Oceania, due to Hawaii's growing importance) sensibilities.[6] Romantic fantasies about the islands are reflected in the status of Polynesians as popular characters in literature and films, including films about the mutiny on *the Bounty*, an event that took place in 1789.

The racial classification of the people of the Pacific is part of the colonial history of the islands. The racial overtones of these classifications are seen in the focus on cannibalism in Melanesia, a practice that also existed among the lighter-skinned Polynesians.[7] The contrast between European representations of Polynesia and Melanesia illustrates how race was tied to the mapping of colonized islands. John Connell has explained how the people of Vanuatu and New Caledonia were seen as "repugnant" and how Melanesians were viewed as "Negroes," part of a "racialized geography" that replaced earlier views about the region.[8] In contrast, the lighter-skinned Polynesians were viewed as a lost Aryan race. As anthropologist Bengt Danielsson writes,

> In the Pacific, as the ocean is called (with as little justification for half of it lies north of the Equator and it is far from the Pacific), there are three large island groups: Micronesia and Melanesia in the western and Polynesia in the eastern half. This division is based on decisive cultural and racial differences between the three island groups.[9]

Cannibalism was an object of fascination for Europeans and later Americans. One study notes how 111 *kanaks* from New Caledonia were put on display at an exhibition in Paris at the *Palais des Colonies* where they reenacted cannibalism "with wooden tibias while letting out screams" (the exhibition was located close to the zoo, which was no accident).[10] The people who lived on islands were variously described as beautiful, erotic, lazy, friendly, dangerous, and cannibalistic. Images of islanders included a broad field of popular literature, fine art, and performance art—paintings, poetry, novels, circus attractions—all focused on salacious tales of cannibals. Songs like "King and Queen of Cannibal Islands" and "The Banquet Song of the Tonga Islands" were wildly popular; the latter was Emerson's favorite song as a child.[11]

As noted in the previous chapter, the terminology used for the islands in the South Pacific can be confusing. *South Seas* is used both for Polynesia and for islands farther away, including Bali. Early films about the Pacific Ocean and its cultures include 1938's *The Beachcomber*, which "was set in the Dutch East Indies, but in theme and treatment might just as well been given a Samoan or Tuamotuan locale."[12] The two archipelagos examined in this chapter are Tahiti and Hawai'i. *Tahiti* refers to the two main islands and

Moorea, all the Society Islands, and at times, the entirety of French colonies in the Pacific.[13] The islands of Hawai'i include the best-known one, Oahu, with its famous beach Waikiki, and other islands including the island *of* Hawaii, also known as "the big island."

The mapping of islands in the South Seas often relied on fantasies about bodily renewal through an idyllic landscape and its people. Descriptions of the islands often resembled Greek myths and promised renewal through the sexual consumption of female bodies. This was especially true in Tahiti, which is identified with the most powerful sexual imagery in the Pacific. The Hawaiian Islands were quickly incorporated into an American settler imagination that includes Jack London's identification as a *kama'aina* (local) [as opposed to a newcomer (*makihini*)].[14]

Mapping the geographical imagination about Polynesia reflected an interest in primitivism. The South Pacific stood as a place untouched by time where Europeans could "return" to the simpler days of human existence, living off fish, bananas, breadfruit, and other exotic fruits while discovering their true selves. As Michael Sturma explains, "For many Europeans, Tahiti represented an encounter with a more 'primitive' version of themselves."[15] However, there was also the need to civilize the natives, what Paul Lyons has coined "American Pacificism," the "double logic that the islands are imagined at once as places to be civilized and as escapes from civilization."[16]

Tahiti is famous for "the powerful place it occupies in the imagination (the place of blue lagoons, sunny skies, white sandy beaches, coconut palms, virile men and seductive women)" which "overshadows and crowds out the reality."[17] Tahiti, like the Hawaiian Islands, is also intimately connected to foreign militaries. As Teresia Teaiwa has written, the Pacific is "a strategic and commercial space where European, American, and Asian desires are played out."[18]

The South Pacific is one of the most romanticized, exotified, and eroticized parts of the earth.[19] As Michael Sturma has written, it is "often referred to not so much to a geographical spot as to a dreamlike state of mind."[20] The experiences of transcendence recorded by early travelers and artists like Gauguin and sought out by modern tourists are partially due to the island environment. Scholars have suggested that nature-based spiritual experiences are often due to an individual's immersion in a different physical environment. Isolation is a factor found in these experiences that has been found to be "conducive to renewal and restoration."[21] This chapter explores the ways that these islands were formulated by Westerners into mystical landscapes that offer special and transformative experiences for the tourist.

French naval officer and writer Pierre Loti's *The Marriage of Loti* is one of the most famous tales of the South Seas that contributed to the vision of Tahiti as a mystical landscape. The novel was one of several fictionalized tales of Loti's consummation of sexual affairs with non-European girls and women. Like many texts and paintings, it presents the South Pacific as a place where men could be physically and spiritually born anew. These rebirths were often focused on the bodies of island maidens. In *The Marriage of Loti*, Rarahu is the focus of Loti's experience in the beautiful and mystical landscape of Otaheite.

The Marriage of Loti

Pierre Loti is one of the most important creators of the *imaginaire* about Tahiti. Born Louis-Marie-Julien Viaud, he was, to use Ali Behdad's term, a "cultural transvestite."[22] He was racist, describing Indian men as "women, monkeys, and wild beasts" and the Chinese as revolting, while supporting movements like Egyptian nationalism.[23] In a later chapter, we will learn how he identified as an "Oriental," dressing up in Turkish clothes and claiming to be a Muslim.[24] In the context of the South Pacific, his book *The Marriage of Loti* was critical to the formation of the islands as mystical landscapes. *The Marriage of Loti* was an especially popular text among the French public. Described by one scholar as an exercise in narcissism, it tells a story of Polynesia dying "slowly and beautifully to satisfy the decadent nostalgia of a European romantic."[25] Loti was not only popular with the French public, but he also influenced Gauguin, who fetishized Loti's island girl (Rarahu) as living an "utterly idle existence, free of responsibilities and concerns save to dream, bathe, sing, and wander through the woods."[26]

Bodily difference is a popular colonial theme that was often used to suggest an evolutionary difference between Europeans and others. The descriptions of Rarahu and other Tahitians in *The Marriage of Loti* often include comparisons to animals and children. They were like "lively gold-fish," had "monkey-like high spirits," they were a "race of giants," and were "grown-up children;" they were "addicted to day-dreams, music, fine fruit, flowers, and running water;" one queen was "a thorough old savage with pointed teeth;" and Rarahu was "a little savage."[27] The descriptions of Tahitians as animals were part of a larger discourse that imagined the peoples of the South Pacific as examples of the premodern "natural man," who in *Gulliver's Travels* are described not as humans, but as horses.[28]

Loti's description of Rarahu in the opening pages of the novel has been cited as an example of the ways that European romantics viewed girls and women from the islands. The text describes Rarahu's features in exquisite detail. Rarahu's "eyes were of tawny black, full of exotic languor and coaxing softness, like those of a kitten when it is stroked; her eyelashes so long and black that you might have taken them for painted feathers."[29] Later in the same paragraph, Loti writes, "Rarahu was small, beautiful in proportion and mould; her bosom was purely formed and polished; her arms as perfect as an antique."[30]

Loti's idealization of young girls (Rarahu was 14 when she met Loti) and women contrasts starkly to how he describes older Tahitians and the Chinese merchants who lived in Papeete. The Chinese are presented as "an object of disgust and horror," and one Chinese man described in the text had "bony limbs" and wore his hair "like a woman's."[31] Worst of all, "his sensual old eyes glittered with an odious leer."[32]

In the end, Loti abandons Rarahu and returns to Europe, and afterwards, she dies of consumption (tuberculosis). Loti's dream of Rarahu describes a horrible scene where she is taken by the undead monsters of Polynesia, the *tupapa'u*.[33] Scholars have suggested that this ending is linked to feelings of desire and horror that were often attached to foreign bodies. The identification of foreign sexualities with horror is common in colonial writing and was likely inspired by fears of miscegenation (racial mixing), reflecting ideas about monstrous births and impure bloodlines that had long circulated among Europeans. The novel ends with a frightening scene of Rarahu's death, imagined by Loti in a dream, where her corpse "laughed aloud" after being taken by the monsters who had surrounded her, with their long hairs covering their faces, their "motionless" bodies watching Loti through "closed eyes."[34] The island maiden died once the colonial actor was finished with her—because she only existed for his pleasure.

Encountering the Islands

The people of the South Pacific had a sophisticated sense of their place in the world. This knowledge included maps of the Pacific Ocean that placed their island within a history of voyaging across the largest areas of ocean on earth. Rod Edmond tells one story of the precision of these island cartographies:

> In 1768 Tupaia, a priest from the Tahitian group of islands, drew Cook a map of his world. Taking its centre at Tahiti, the map showed seventy-four islands scattered across a large oceanic area measuring about three thousand miles from east to west and a thousand miles from north to south. The islands were arranged in concentric circles based on sailing times from the maps centre rather than on linear distance.[35]

The long-held theory of *Terra Australis Incognito* was the (mythical) huge continent that would be found in the Southern Hemisphere and which, as one Oceanic historian explained to me years ago, was believed to "balance the earth so it would not tip over."[36] Europeans believed that this huge land mass was Solomon's Ophir or a Pythagorean "antipodean continent."[37] The myth of the land mass was not dispelled until Cook's second voyage, when he severed it "from Australia and shrinking it to the size of Antarctica."[38] In place of the continent that balanced the earth, the many islands in the South

Pacific emerged as a new imaginary space for Europeans. As it turned out, Pacific Islanders had a more accurate and realistic view of the world than Europeans. The Pacific Ocean is the largest ocean in the world and home to an incredible diversity of cultures and languages. These facts were unknown to the early explorers, who were focused on finding the mythical continent.

Wallis made the first European landfall in Tahiti in 1767, a moment that forever changed the way Europeans thought about the region. A violent encounter for Tahitians, with many killed by Wallis, for Europeans it established the beginning of a field of representations that remains in force to this day.

> From this moment western representations of the Pacific were to form important chapters in the history of the Enlightenment and Romanticism, of nineteenth-century Christianity, science and social theory, of modern painting, anthropology and popular culture.[39]

Bougainville reached Otaheite (Tahiti) one year later in 1768 and named it *La Nouvelle Cythère* after the Greek island, a reflection of the Tahitian's public affections and a reference to the Greek goddess of love, Aphrodite.[40]

The invention of the South Pacific as a premodern Eden was also influenced by the popularity of travel literature, which conflated "travel and romance" and was more akin to the modern fiction novel than scientific observations about an actual place observed and studied.[41] Islands were objects of adventure, and at times, of romance in these stories. A strict separation between fiction and nonfiction did not exist; even by the eighteenth century, when Defoe's *Robinson Crusoe* was released, nonfiction was a form of historical fiction. Defoe, much like other writers of the era, was interested in creating believable worlds: "Defoe's realism is not the conventional realism of the novel. He did not aim to suspend disbelief, but to do away with it completely."[42]

John Hawkesworth's 1773 book, *An Account of the Voyages*, combined impressions from several voyages to Tahiti, including those of Wallis, Cook, and Carteret, which were exaggerated and retold with creative flair. This book included accounts of the Tahitian religion and their amorous public physical expressions of affection, which tantalized the public. One only needs to read an excerpt to see how Tahiti became a place identified with sexual freedom:

> A young man, near six feet high, performed the rites of Venus with a little girl about eleven or twelve years of age, before several of our people, and a great number of the natives, without the sense of its being indecent or improper, but, as appeared, in perfect conformity to the custom of the place.[43]

Today, Tahiti remains identified with romance and beauty that are believed to be redemptive for the tourist.

Islands are extremely seductive environments, due to their inaccessibility and isolation, what Carolyn Cartier calls the "essence reduced" into "mythic form" of the beachscape.[44] As we will learn, these islands are often left out of colonial histories, a result of what Paul Lyons calls *Pacificism*, which ignores the environmental and human devastation wrought upon the people of Oceania. Like other spaces in this book, the European colonial mind is involved in the mapping of this region, as is the American. In the Pacific, the colonial state was not simply white but multiracial and one dominated by shifting powers and the tensions between Japan and the United States.[45] Today, the islands are often subjected to the effects of these larger political forces, including nuclear contamination (from the French and Americans) and the fear of nuclear war (from North Korea and its rival states).

By 1900, virtually every island in the South Pacific had come under foreign occupation by the French, British, Spanish, and Americans.[46] The human and environmental cost of colonialism included population decimation (e.g., over 90 percent of the Chamorro in Guam died from disease) and the elimination of traditions (the end of the *kapu* legal system in the Hawaiian Islands due to foreign trade).[47] Fervent missionary activity in the islands resulted in the erasure of religious traditions that were lost, although in a few lucky cases they have seen a resurgence in recent years.

The way that Europeans viewed the South Pacific was often contradictory—both a pathway to the wealthy resources of Asia and an isolated colonial outpost.[48] While the Pacific Ocean, the largest in the world, is nowhere near Europe, and the Hawaiian Islands are nowhere near the West Coast, the islands were mapped as a part of Europe and the United States for centuries. James Michener, whose writings helped to create the image of the Hawaiian Islands so popular today, wrote in 1951, "There is only one sensible way to think of the Pacific Ocean today. It is the highway between Asia and America."[49] Of Tahiti, Michener wrote, "Tahiti insists upon relaxation" and "Tahiti has unique sex freedom," mirroring the words of explorers like Wallis and Bougainville over 200 years earlier.[50]

Oftentimes stories about the South Pacific were exaggerated, based on fantasies of romantic and sensual islanders. When I was an undergraduate in college, where I majored in Pacific Island studies, I heard a story of the boat that nearly disintegrated in a South Pacific harbor, the result of European travelers removing its nails to trade for sexual favors with the lascivious natives. I thought I had imagined (or misremembered) this story, but while reading the work of anthropologist Miriam Kahn I discovered that the tale was, in fact, popular in London. As Kahn writes,

> For example, when Samuel Wallis arrived in Tahiti on the *HMS Dolphin*, he and his men bartered beads, mirrors and iron for food and sex (Tahitians especially coveted nails, which they used to make fishhooks). When

Wallis returned to England, the story widely circulated that the *HMS Dolphin* nearly fell apart as sailors ripped nails one by one from the ship.[51]

Another scholar describes how the sailors "began pulling the nails for their hammocks" and then "pulled nails out of the ship," a crime for which Wallis flogged the worst offenders.[52]

Polynesia continues to exist as an idyllic region because of the romantic projections on the islands that are perpetuated in tourism and popular culture. Defoe's *Robinson Crusoe*, Stevenson's *Treasure Island*, and Wyss's *Swiss Family Robinson* are three examples of such projections, all focused on the fantasy of white folks going native on beautiful islands. Stevenson described the Marquesas Islands in these words: "The scent of the land, of a hundred fruits and flowers, flows forth on the caressing air."[53]

As noted earlier, the islands are also associated with sexuality, situated in a reliance upon "pleasurable anticipation."[54] O'Dwyer has remarked, "Subsequently it has acquired a definitely sexual cast and become laden with the baggage of erotic expectation."[55] In the case of Tahiti, a place that is perhaps best known for Europe's sexual fantasies of the native islands, this process was due to the musings of explorers like Wallis, Bougainville, and Cook, whose description of the islands as a "veritable garden of Eden" became memorialized.[56] The impressions of these men and their crew were, in part, a reflection of the Romantic literary tradition: "They referred to a golden age, to noble savages, paradise, beautiful nature and so on, and in these respects they were followers of Rousseau and the Deists."[57]

This history created a set of expectations for visitors that tourism would exploit. Anthropologists like Bronislaw Malinowski (*The Sexual Life of Savages*, 1929) and Margaret Mead (*Coming of Age in Samoa*, 1928) characterized islanders as sexually uninhibited and wildly sensual. Their studies had a lasting impact; Paul Theroux's travel book published in the 1990s refers to Malinowski's work, seven decades earlier.[58] Today, tourism relies on the stereotype of the South Seas maiden in its advertising, illustrating the lasting impact of the mapping of the Pacific as a site of sensual mystic pleasures.

Pacificism is one way that foreign interventions in the region can be understood and that describes the ways that colonialism defines the peoples of the South Pacific.[59] Heather Waldroup suggests the term *Polynesianism* to define the ways the West has imagined the Pacific. As she explains, "Pleasure is a defining aspect of Polynesianism: the exoticism, mystery and intimacy afforded by such images accounts for their primacy in popular spaces."[60] As we learn in this chapter, pleasure, through the islands of Polynesia and the bodies of their inhabitants, is identified with their mystical landscapes.

Islands, Military, and Tourism

The mapmakers of imaginative geographies often mark the inhabitants of territories in troubling ways. The influence of evolutionary theory was often seen in the mapping of newly encountered places; in the Pacific, for instance, in the theory of two different races—Polynesians and Melanesians.[61] At the time, the noble savage was a fantasy that loomed large in the minds of Europeans, who were influenced by Jean-Jacques Rousseau and the journals of explorer Louis Antoine de Bougainville, who called Tahiti "la Nouvelle Cythère" and in whose journals "everything about the noble savage could be found."[62]

Islands are sites of a specific kind of difference—exoticism. In Tahiti, once called New Cythera or Otaheite, the idea of unrestrained sensuality was always identified with women.[63] French navigator Louis Antoine de Bougainville was influenced by Rousseau's vision of the primitive noble savage, which helped to inform the explorer's impressions of Tahiti as an "Edenic wonderland" filled with naked, sexually ravenous females.[64] Bougainville's observations included many comments about girls: "The girl carelessly dropt a cloth, which covered her, and appeared to the eyes of all beholders, such as Venus shewed herself to the Phrygian shepherd, having, indeed, the celestial form of that goddess."[65] One study describes the colonial view of Tahitians as a list of fantasies,

> They dedicated much of their time to love, which they pursued without shame or jealousy, even in the witness of a circle of friends and to the accompaniment of hymeneal tunes played on a nose-flute. Their women were the most obliging in the world, and their only fault, if indeed it was one, was that they had no concept of private property. In one extreme version of this picture, they drank nothing but water or coconut milk, had no wars and their language had no indigenous word for *kill*.[66]

Tahiti and Hawai'i are important parts of a larger history of colonialism and empire in the Pacific. Today, they exist as colonies (or "neo-colonies"). As Ron Edmond has pointed out, colonialism was not a uniform practice in the Pacific; it included annexation, pressures from settlers, and the actions of a rogue naval officer.[67] There were incredible distances between colonial powers and their possessions. France, located thousands of miles away from the islands known as "French Polynesia," and Hawai'i, which lies in the middle of the Pacific Ocean, are nowhere near their occupiers' borders. The Hawaiian Islands function within a larger mapping of American power and control that is tied to American ideas about identity.

The profound notion that the continent, from the Atlantic to the Pacific, had been a divinely ordained American space all along, and never really a globally contested one, also undergirded this envisioning of western settlement as the ultimate expression of the unfolding story of American democracy and liberty.[68]

The militaries of France and the United States and their nuclear weapons are intimately connected to the histories of these places. *Solar ecology* views the island as "the contained space of a laboratory."[69] Postwar scientists even went as far as stating, "Thus, ecologists need not feel bashful about attacking ecosystems so long as they observe the rules of good science."[70] While these two ideas may seem incongruent—the contained laboratory and the poisoned ecosystem—they both reflect that the environments and lives of indigenous people were believed to be expendable.

Tourism is linked to military projects in several ways. Colonial-era travel writings, fiction, and art often helped to create fictive worlds where the indigenous people, the Ma'ohi (Tahitian) and Kānaka Maoli (Hawaiian) people, were presented as premodern, childlike, and in need of a paternal caretaker—the French and American governments. As Vernadette Vicuña Gonzalez explains,

> While these travel narratives ranged from outright racist portrayals to the more nostalgic romanticization of untouched and undiscovered premodern life, as a whole their production of the world as backwards and in need of uplift served to justify the military project that would soon secure these territories as colonial outposts.[71]

One of the goals of this book is to produce an act of remembrance that works to reinstate precolonial senses of space. The island groups examined in this chapter are the ancestral homes of the Ma'ohi (Tahitian) and Kānaka Maoli (Native Hawaiian) people. The use of Kānaka Maoli reflects the goal of achieving a new Hawaiian nation, the Kānaka Maoli lāhui, that is "sovereign" but rejects the notion of a "geopolitically bound nation," and Te Ao A'ohi is "an indigenous replacement for the colonially possessive term 'La Polynésia Française' (French Polynesia)."[72] Tahiti was shortened from the indigenous *Tahiti-nui mare'are'a*—the Great Tahiti of the Golden Haze.[73] The inclusion of these names in this book is an effort to remind the reader who the people originally tied to these islands, their lands, mountains, and oceans are.

Mapping Otaheite

Tahiti is a prime example of the ways Polynesia has been envisioned as a paradise, and more specifically, as a place of spiritual power and mysticism. Samuel Wallis and the crew of his ship, *the Dolphin*, first sighted what they thought was the "southern continent" (Terra Australis) on June 18, 1767, and the myth of Tahiti as a new Eden was born.[74] The "cold lands under grey skies a harsh repressive urban and industrial landscape" in Europe were compared to the idyllic "hot islands in warm blue seas" of Tahiti.[75]

The "discovery" of these islands by Europeans took place at a time when, as noted earlier, the Romantic movement was popular, evident in the ways that the islands were written about in Classical terms. Tahiti as the "new Cythera" and the importance of islands in antiquity, including Plato's writings, are two examples.[76] The use of Cythera by Bougainville, who called it the "new utopia," was used to honor Aphrodite, who supposedly arose out of the sea at Cythere.[77] From the beginning, Tahiti was mapped as a place attached to Classical and European notions of place. Samuel Wallis, the British captain who arrived in 1767, and Louis Antoine de Bougainville, the French explorer who arrived in 1768, were instrumental in mapping the islands of Tahiti, Bora Bora, and surrounding smaller atolls as a natural and sensual paradise.[78]

The notion of recapturing what had been lost is a powerful part of the Enlightenment. Turning away from wonderment and the mystical qualities of nature was at the center of Europe's projections on the islands and her people. The sexual objectification of females began with the openness to sexual relations that some islanders exhibited, according to the accounts of explorers. Beginning with Wallis, reports of naked or partially naked girls and women were a feature of explorers' accounts.[79] The stark contrast of the islands' so-called lack of morality vis-à-vis European rules around romantic relationships was enticing to sailors and other travelers to the islands, resulting in the idea that Tahitian (and other) girls and women were sexually available, amorous, and patently "uninhibited."[80]

Artists also encouraged this view of island women—above all, Paul Gauguin. Gauguin was always a colonial fellow. During the colonial exhibit at Paris's *Exposition Universelle* of 1889, he picked up a piece of a frieze that had fallen off a Javanese building, taking it home with him.[81] Later, he turned from collecting artifacts of exotic cultures to fixating on women from these same lands. Gauguin long had fantasies of traveling far from France and living with a bevy of native women; about Madagascar he said, the women were "so to speak, obligatory."[82] This kind of sentiment was common among French men, for "Black women helped France's white men and women fantasize about their black colonies and often served as substitutes for making sense of white bodies 'behaving badly.'"[83]

Eventually, Gauguin settled in Tahiti, and his paintings became famous, especially his series of *Eves* that represented the themes of sex, sin, and paradise on the tableau of Tahitian female bodies. While these paintings are focused on the Tahitian woman, his first model was a Tongan, preferred over the Tahitian women, for he found them either "tainted" by French blood or "too evocative of cannibal pasts."[84] Gauguin is well known to Pacific Islanders for his fantasies about their girls and women. He is also linked to the legacy of colonialism and the havoc it wrought on societies in the region. In the novel by Sia Figiel, *Where We Once Belonged* (1996), the character Siniva is an object of lust who walks around Apia, the capital, bare breasted, yelling at tourists, "Go back to where you came from, you fucking ghosts! Gaugin is dead! There is no paradise!"[85] The way Polynesian childhood and sexuality were portrayed for Western audiences created a space where fantasies about rejuvenation through the land and bodies of islanders could be enjoyed by tourists, seen today in many tourist locations around the Pacific.

This vision of the South Pacific as a paradise remains popular today in a variety of forms, most of all tourism, which relies on promises of bodily and spiritual fulfillment, much like the promises made in the past by explorers. In the interwar period, the French public was still engaging with Gauguin's vision of Polynesian women. At the *Exposition Coloniale Paris* held in 1931, visitors could observe women from New Caledonia, about which one Frenchman enthusiastically exclaimed, "Gaugin's women exist; I have seen them in the New Caledonia pavilion."[86]

Polynesia exists in a liminal space that is neither East nor West, a region of "betwixt and between" like the pilgrimage journey. There is no "paradise," of course, but only a fabrication of Eden by tourists who could enjoy the islands without concern for the devastation wrought by its visitors. Magazines like *National Geographic* and *Geographical Magazine* helped to form these ideas in the American imagination, where as late as 2020 places like Samoa are described as a "tropical paradise."[87]

Otaheite was the most popular group of islands for Romantic writers and artists to fantasize about the Pacific. As noted earlier, Pierre Loti penned several books about himself traveling to a foreign land and consummating an affair with a local woman (called a *vahine* in Tahiti). The plotline was simple: "boy meets exotic girl; boy possesses exotic girl; boy leaves exotic girl."[88] His book about Loti is the most famous. This plotline was patterned along the idea of colonial consumption, where the occupier could easily obtain an object he wanted, consume it, and discard it when finished. Tahiti is perhaps the best example of the "fetishized object of the male gaze" in the Pacific, a place that seduces because it is an object of the colonial male gaze.[89]

The flipside of these fantasies was the sinfulness identified with Polynesia that, in the words of one scholar, "necessitated redemption by trader, administrator and above all missionary."[90] The devastation of the islands has been extensive, including their use as penal colonies, nuclear testing sites, and military bases.[91] As in Africa, the Americas, and other colonial territories, taking indigenous people from their lands to do "tours" of Europe and serve as specimens of exotic places and people are part of the colonial history of the South Pacific.

Omai was one of several people from the islands who were taken to Europe as a curiosity for the wealthy.[92] James Cook took Omai from Ra'iatea to England, setting off a Polynesian style popular in London that included Tahitian porches, wallpaper evocative of the South Seas, and artificial lakes meant to resemble the lagoons of coral atolls.[93] He was incredibly popular, an example of the ways Europeans viewed foreign bodies as tableaus for their fantasies about the noble savage. As Miriam Khan writes,

> Omai, always seen as friendly and charming, became the darling of English society. His benefactors dressed him in silk shirts and velvet jackets. He met the king, learned [to] ice skate and shoot, dined in London's best homes and was popular with the ladies.[94]

One account stated that he met with no fewer than 12 ladies a day and was a charmer.[95] His representations in paintings show him to be handsome and typically wearing flowing robes made from *tapa*, the painted bark cloth worn by many Polynesians.[96] Omai was luckier than most, for after his tour of England he eventually returned home alive. Ahutoru, brought to Paris by Bougainville, died on his way home.[97] Other "exotic people" brought to Europe seldom survived their captivity and tours of Europe. When the artist George Catlin brought Indians from North America to London's Egyptian Hall in 1840, the same place that housed artifacts from Cook's voyages, they died—first two Iowas and then two Ojibwas.[98] As David Wrobel writes,

> Caitlin had effectively placed the story of American empire and its devastating impact on indigenous peoples into a larger global context of the terrible human consequences of imperialism and colonialism.[99]

One of the most famous paintings of Tahiti is John Webber's 1777 portrait of the daughter of a chief in Ra'iatea, whose name was Poedua, but what many do not know is that this painting was based on the period she was kidnapped and held hostage by Captain Cook between November 25 and 29, 1877.[100] Webber's *A Portrait of Poedua* hangs in the Royal Museum of Greenwich, showing a woman with her breasts exposed, her lower half draped by a cloth, with a faint smile on her face. The reality is that when Poedua was kidnapped, according to witnesses, she was weeping, inconsolable, and terrified: "The Indians finding themselves thus caught in a Snare fell a crying, especially the beautiful Poiedooa [Poedua] who was not to be pacified."[101]

Colonial regimes are well known for their policies of attacking the societies they occupy. In the case of the Ma'ohi people, this was achieved through several strategies. The indigenous language (*reo maohi*) was outlawed in 1963, making way for "French linguistic and cultural dominance."[102] As Miriam

Khan points out, this is an overwhelming and undeniable effect of the cultural violence inflicted upon the islands.

> This colonial grip manifests itself daily in numerous ways. Tahitian children devote the majority of their school day to learning French language, history, and geography. Postsecondary education, other than at the Centre Universitaire de Polynésie Française on the island of Tahiti, is usually limited to universities in France since French is the only language officially taught to Tahitians.[103]

The erasure of indigenous language and in its place, the requirement of the colonial language, are a common tactic of colonial regimes.

During the Second World War (WWII), U.S. soldiers were stationed in Bora Bora (one of Tahiti's islands) and the once tranquil island, which had no paved roads or cars, became a place of roads, prefab buildings, planes, and foreigners.[104] The French occupation of the islands also had an impact on their quest to become a nuclear power. The CEP (*Centre d'expérimentation du Pacifique*) used the islands of Moruroa and Fangataufa to test nuclear weapons.[105] This was a cultural disaster, bringing benefits to the wealthy class of French and demi (mixed) families, migration from the outer islands, urbanization, and the loss of traditional economies based on fishing and farming.[106] The nuclear testing on Moruroa was cast in the language of male, colonial penetration. The naming of the campaigns as "Brigitte" and "Hortensia" reflected the French view of the atolls "as a series of barren, female striking zones" and the efforts to "induce the paralyzing colonial amnesia" that would pave the way for the mystical tourism industry that thrives in the islands today.[107]

The cultural violence this transformation caused included the effects of tourism on the local population, the loss of indigenous farming, and the resulting economic disenfranchisement. In a 1975 study by Claude Robineau, the results of French occupation are documented and include Tahitians holding "the lowest employment positions" and vanilla and copra production falling from 150.6 tons in 1960 to 5.9 tons in 1967.[108] The nuclear testing on Moruroa resulted in bans on fish and coconut from the island and the death of inhabitants after ingesting these foods, with rates of numerous types of cancers skyrocketing in the years following the atmospheric tests of weapons.[109] The modern human costs of colonialism in French Polynesia include poverty, alcoholism, and domestic violence, as well as the effect on the environment. In the words of one scholar, "And the Tahitians? They continued to receive the many foreigners with hospitality. In return they got venereal disease, small pox, fire arms, and Christianity."[110]

The colonial mindset of the French is unrepentant, so much so that President Flosse reacted to the protests against testing with a denunciation of

Tahitians, "those who want to fade the colors of Gaugin, extinguish the voice of Jacques Brel, and obliterate the memory of Paul-Émile Victor."[111] Tahiti is projected as French, which is evident through the production of postcards that feature naked women adorned by tropical flowers. As one well-known photographer remarked, the models used are French because the customers "don't want her skin to be too dark, her nose too broad, or her thighs too strong."[112] Images of white bodies in these spaces are about erasure. As McDonnell describes it,

> These are not simply images of sex, sand, and sea; they are images that flatten the landscape by obscuring other histories and people and place. By centering on white, female, and scantily clad bodies, the visual images enable foreign claims to possession, whether through tourism and real estate.[113]

Hawai'ian Landscapes

Hawai'i was considered a "natural" part of the United States despite its location over 2,500 miles from the coast of California. The colonization of the Hawaiian Islands by missionaries, American businessmen, and the U.S. military took place against the protests of the monarchy and its people, as well as those white settlers who were loyal to the monarchy. In 1820, Calvinist missionaries arrived in the islands, and soon Hawaiian cultural traditions were outlawed, while white settlers facilitated the purchase of land by foreigners, factors which eroded Native Hawaiian agency over their own land and affairs.[114] Hawaiians were often described as fun loving and lazy, even simple, stereotypes exploited by the Americans in their annexation plans.[115] Queen Lili'uokalani was vilified for her "low morality" and described as a tyrant.[116] In cartoons, she was presented as an African American, a way to vilify her for her skin color and attach the Queen's body to the vile hatred of Americans of African descent.[117] Supporters of the settler state often referred to Hawaii's land system as "feudal" to imply that the American control of the islands was akin to the Revolutionary War and its liberation from European medievalism.

The colonization of Hawai'i is linked to U.S. militarism. After the deposition of the queen, King Kalākaua became the Americans' next target. In 1873, a reconnaissance mission confirmed the islands as an ideal place for a military port, and in 1887, the king was forced to sign the Bayonet Constitution, which was followed by Pearl Harbor being gifted to the U.S. military and the voting rights of Hawaiian men restricted.[118] The Bayonet Constitution got its name from the threats by Sanford Dole and Lorrin Thurston, both from missionary families, who "assembled a white militia in order to 'inspire' the king to sign the document."[119]

Hawaii's annexation was a long game that had been in the works for many years. The Reciprocity Treaty of 1875 had a clause that set up the annexation and the Bayonet Constitution was signed by the king at gunpoint, allowing for a revised treaty and making way for the incorporation of the islands into the United States.[120] The protests from Native Hawaiians, scholars, and activists led to the incorporation of antiannexationist documents in over 75 Hawaiian language newspapers.[121] In 1893, the Hawaiian government was overthrown, backed by an American warship, and 45 percent of the land was handed over to the United States.[122] Restitution of the monarchy was popular not only among Native Hawaiians but also among some white (*haole*) families.[123] On July 4, 1894, the Republic of Hawaii was established, and in colonial settler fashion, Sanford Dole, the offspring of missionaries and the family attached to the Dole pineapple found in most supermarkets, became its president.[124]

Like Tahiti, Hawai'i illustrates the way the South Pacific exists as an imaginary region of fantasies for the tourist. In addition to the impact on indigenous Hawaiians, the impact of the military on their lands is another form of violence, one that has remapped the islands as a paradise with an enormous military presence. Hawai'i has been identified with the U.S. military since the late nineteenth century, and as scholars have pointed out, it is one of many places that represent the "linked genesis of tourist and military practices."[125]

Indigenous scholar Teresia Teaiwa describes this as *militourism*, "a phenomenon by which military or paramilitary forces ensure the smooth running of a tourist industry, and that same tourist industry masks the military force behind it."[126] The military activities of the United States in the Pacific go far beyond the region where the Hawaiian Islands are located. While France is the nuclear power that usually comes to mind first, it is not alone in testing nuclear weapons on islands in this part of the world. The history of this relationship includes the testing of nuclear weapons on Bikini and Enewetak and the production of postcards from these events for soldiers.[127]

The popularity of the Hawaiian Islands as a tourist site is intimately connected to the U.S. military. Hawai'i is identified not only with the U.S. Naval base of Pearl Harbor, of course, but also with beautiful beaches, Hawaiian music featuring the steel string guitar and ukulele, the *luau*, and the *hula*.

The *hula* is a critical part of the history of Hawai'i as a site of tourism, which illustrates how foreign bodies are imagined and constructed as products for tourists. As Adria Imada has written, "A significant but understudied cultural performance imported from a besieged nation to imperial sites, *hula* became a novel part of urban and regional entertainments in the US and Europe which rendered Hawaiian bodies into hypervisible commodities."[128]

Hula was revitalized as a cultural form by King Kalākaua, making it a recognizable part of the island culture for audiences worldwide.[129] Imada's study of *hula* in the waning days of the monarchy and the first years of Hawai'i after annexation (1892–1896) documents how audiences formed an idea about the islands from these performances that rendered Hawaiian women as both savage and desirable: "Hawaiian women could be read as menacing or gentle, but their eroticism and racial subordination remained constant."[130] Hula was also a way that the islands were mapped as a *haole* (white) space through utilizing an ancient art form and transferring it to white, American bodies. The performers of hula (the "Aloha Maids") who came to the United States in the 1930s and 1940s were *hapa-haole* with light skin and slender figures, the "preferred phenotype."[131] This phenotype became the hula girl found in tourist brochures, on posters, and in other paraphernalia that enticed tourists to travel to Hawai'i and experience the magic of the islands for themselves.

The human costs of U.S. colonialism in Hawai'i were catastrophic. According to the late scholar and activist Haunani-Kay Trask,

Ravaged by introduced diseases (syphilis, measles, influenza, whooping cough, cholera), the indigenous population fell from an estimated half million in 1778 to less than 48,000 in 1878—a decline by a ratio of more than ten to one.[132]

IMAGE 6.1   Photo of Hula Girls.

Source: photo courtesy of National Parks Gallery, Public Domain

In addition to the depopulation of Hawaiians by disease, white settlers moved in, making the Kānaka Maoli "partial subjects of an empire that was happy to take their lands but not exactly sure what to do with its nonwhite peoples."[133]

The history of violence against the Hawaiian people includes the forceful end of the Hawaiian monarchy, radical changes in the society brought about by American statehood and its institutions, and a long list of environmental crimes, many of which involve the U.S. military and their numerous installations on the islands, notably Oahu. Among the most radical changes in Hawaiian society was land ownership. Hawaiians did not have communal land ownership in the sense that everyone shared the islands equally. Traditionally, the land was not "owned," although it did "belong to the highest-ranking chief."[134] This system included the inheritance of land, which was dependent on the chief's agents (the *konohiki*), but ultimately the land was associated with the commoners, as Jocelyn Linnekin explains: "The land was intrinsically identified with the *maka'aina*, the long-time residents on the land."[135]

The Hawaiian system of caring for the land did not resemble the American model of private property. The people cared for the land, and if they did this to the satisfaction of the lesser chiefs, the land remained in the family. It was a way of life that ensured continuity for most families, and as one scholar pointed out, "[n]o one's property rights were capable of being sold, however, neither the commoners' nor the chiefs'."[136] However, with the annexation, this changed, and many *maka'aina* lost claims to the land their families had lived on, sometimes for generations, due to a filing deadline that many missed, when white settlers claimed Hawaiian land.[137] This is known as the Great Mahele.

Another shift in land tenure was that Native Hawaiians had challenges accepting private ownership (*kuleanas*), as the land had traditionally been cared for within extended family groups.[138] Another factor was that many Hawaiians were "land-rich but cash-poor," resulting in the loss of land for income and sustenance.[139] Scholars disagree on the history of the Great Mehele, with some believing that it was a way to distribute lands that would be easily taken if held solely by the monarchy. The late Native Hawaiian scholar Haunani-Kay Trask believed that it resulted from pressures by American business interests.[140] The colonial-military mapping of the land and waters of Hawai'i can be seen in the environmental assaults on sacred lands. The establishment of a coaling station at Pearl Harbor River was the first step in the annexation of the islands, ending the use of the harbor, called *Ke Awa Lau o Pu'uloa*, for fishing and taro farming.[141] It is now a Superfund site, with massive amounts of pollutants from the military waste getting deposited in the waters.[142]

The military has a history of symbolic violence against local people, including during the prewar and WWII periods. One example is found in the photographs of "Rip" Henry Yeager, who was a navy man and amateur photographer.[143] He took several thousand photographs of women in various states of undress who were in prisoner camps in Micronesia.[144] These photos included both white and Asian women baring breasts or completely naked, communicating "sexual availability."[145] These provocative images also appeared on the sides of military planes in Honolulu, illustrating how the reach of the United States resulted in a kind of panopticon that portrayed women as available to men—what O' Dwyer calls an "ethnographic envisioning."[146]

Kaho'olawe is another place where violence against the land of the Kānaka Maoli people has been perpetrated. While the U.S. government has characterized the island as a bare strip of sand ideal for bombing practice, the Kānaka Maoli have identified Kanaloa (its traditional name) as a sacred place (*wahi pana*).[147] The framing of Kaho'olawe as empty was used to "void female space to be filled by male, human subjects on behalf of the United States," much like the myths of an empty Kenyan landscape and the vanishing American Indian.[148] The bombing of the island of Kaho'olawe by the U.S. military continued to destroy the island even after it was recognized to contain hundreds of historic sites important to the Hawaiian people.[149] The Hawaiian *'ohana* (people) were responsible for stopping the bombing through the PKO (Protect Kaho'olawe 'Ohana) movement, which resulted in the 1997 cessation of military practice on the island.[150] Jonathan Kamakawiwo'ole Osorio, who is dean of Hawai'inuiākea, the School of Hawaiian Knowledge, explains how the Navy continued to bomb ancestral sites even after the island was recognized as a site of ancestral places important to the Hawaiian people,

> Since March 1981, the entire island of Kaho'olawe has been recognized as an archaeological district after it was placed on the U.S. National Register of Historic Places. One of the ways in which the 'Ohana continued to challenge the Navy's activities was in its capacity as stewards of the archaeological sites that were not only threatened but occasionally struck by shells and bombs.[151]

The PKO was successful in limiting the Navy's activities and ultimately stopping them completely, illustrating how tenuous U.S. control of the land is against the power of the *'aina* (people).

More recently, indigenous land rights advocates and non-Hawaiians concerned with protecting the land converged during the construction of the H-3 interstate on Oahu. First conceived as part of the Eisenhower Interstate and Defense Highway System in 1960, it took nearly 40 years to complete at a price tag of 1.3 billion U.S. dollars.[152] In 1993, five Native Hawaiian women occupied the Hālawa Valley, after concerns about the bulldozing of sacred sites in the valley were dismissed by the Bishop Museum, eventually resulting in the rerouting of the highway and protection of some of the sites.[153]

The effect on the Hawaiian people has been one of loss and trauma. The South Pacific was a popular region for missionaries who wished to convert the populations of islands in the South Pacific to Christianity. In the early 1990s, when I spent time in Fiji, I recall meeting missionaries from the United States at the hotel where I stayed. In the late nineteenth century, the attitude of early Americans toward the loss of Hawaiian culture was reflected in comments about idolatry and ancient superstition. As American businessman Charles Morris boasted, "The Hawaiians left themselves by their own act without a religion, and celebrated with a jubilee their deliverance from an oppressive superstition."[154] The language of the Kānaka Maoli ('Ōlelo Hawai'i) was outlawed in 1896, another way to "civilize" the indigenous population and remake the islands into a new, American space.[155] According to Kānaka Maoli scholar Lisa Kahaleole Hall, the usage of the blood quantum system to determine Hawaiian identity today is another way the U.S. government has been able to determine who is Kānaka Maoli.[156]

The marketing of Hawai'i is situated in a form of colonial nostalgia focused on the post-WWII era, its music, costuming, and clothing, all ways to communicate that Hawai'i is a part of America and its most idealized era. Absent from these representations is the acknowledgement of the lands stolen from indigenous Hawaiians; instead, the "retro paradigm" reigns supreme.[157] As Janet Borgerson and Jonathan Schroeder explain, "The present image for consumption remains steeped in fifties kitsch: hula girls, luaus, easy-listening island music, aloha shirts, Trader Vic's style pupu platters and rum drinks."[158] Mystical tourism is steeped in this nostalgia.

One interesting intersection of colonialism, tourism, and mysticism is seen in the genre of stories about ghosts and spirits of Hawaiians who intercede against the wheels of progress. Perhaps nowhere was this more present than during the construction of H-3, where sightings and witness accounts of the strange and unexplained powers of the island abounded. These included freak accidents, ghost sightings, and noises, all reported by a wide number of people, from activists to construction workers.[159] Indeed, it appears that the mystical power of Hawai'i is alive and well, even on a superhighway.

Today, Native Hawaiians continue to be connected to their ancestral lands. Hawai'i is rich with petroglyph sites, including those found on the Big Island. The distribution of these petroglyphs suggests that place was important, for they are distributed in a purposeful and intentional manner at "certain sites with spiritual associations."[160] In archaeologist Georgia Lee's study of these motifs on the island of Hawai'i, she notes that at Kaeo (southern Kohala), a Hawaiian family came to the site where she was working and left an offering (pū'olo), signifying that the memory of these places has survived colonialism.[161]

It is important to understand that there have been efforts to recognize native rights in Hawai'i, which have to date been largely unsuccessful.[162] The issue of protections for Kānaka Maoli is complicated by their legal treatment under the U.S. law. Unlike Native Americans, who are "recognized" through tribes, Native Hawaiians do not have this form of relationship. As a result, the Hawaiian people "are deprived of options outside of categorization by racial or ethnic lines, which results in an equal protection issue" but also makes it challenging to take legal action against Hawaiian names, products, and words.[163] Unlike Native Americans and Native Alaskans, Kānaka Maoli do not have federal recognition and are severely restricted in their recourse through legal channels.

The identification of the islands as an exotic playground for white Americans mapped the islands as a new space for settlers from the mainland. Painting and advertisements for tourism were two spaces in which white women assumed Native Hawaiian bodies. In the image *Ukelele Lady* (1925), a white woman is shown with Hawaiian clothes holding a ukelele, sitting underneath a palm tree.[164] The ways in which white and Native Hawaiian cultures are in tension is seen in cinema. We turn now to the popularity of the islands in movies, including the 2011 film, *The Descendants*.[165]

From *The Bounty* to *The Descendants*

The portrayal of the South Seas in cinema includes early black-and-white films that featured a combination of ethnographic and fictionalized elements. Between 1913 and 1943, over 165 films about the Pacific Islands were produced, including the earliest footage from 1898 by Burton Holmes.[166] One famous early film is *Tabu* (1931), written by Robert Flaherty and directed by F.W. Murnau. It tells the story of a young Tahitian pearl fisherman and his one true love.[167] *Tabu* is both a travelogue and feature film and as such, both documents the life of Tahitians in the 1930s while projecting fantasies about it for a Western audience. *Tabu* was surrounded by mystery and rumors of ancient curses, apropos for a film about moral taboos in a place often imbued with magical powers. According to reports of the filming, the director and his crew occupied ancient burial grounds, and as a result, various people died during the shooting, ending with the death of Murnau a week before the film's opening. Murnau is an important historical character in the history of the South Pacific. Initially, the shooting of *Tabu* was to take place in Bali, where he had visited his friend Walter Spies.[168] Murnau bought several of Walter's paintings before his death.[169]

Robert Flaherty was also the director of *Moana: A Romance of the Golden Age*, a film made a few years earlier than *Tabu* in 1926. This film also combined ethnographic footage with a romantic story, which in this case was focused on Moana and Faangase.[170] Set in Samoa, another idyllic island, the film was a culmination of Flaherty's two years on the island studying and documenting local traditions. These films, which exist as bridges between ethnography and dramatic cinema, illustrate how Polynesia was constructed as a paradise, in both academic works and the arts. In cinema, the South Seas have continued to be popular locations for films about paradise, such as in the films about *the Bounty*'s mutiny. Hawai'i has also been identified with American military prowess.

In the modern era, perhaps no other film encapsulates the imagination about Tahiti better than *The Bounty*. The mutiny on the ship is a famous historical event, which sets it apart from some of the more creative narratives about Tahiti. Today, Captain Bligh and Fletcher Christian are names that many people recognize, in part due to knowledge about the events surrounding the mutiny of 1789 and the popularity of depictions of these events, including the 1935 film, which became a classic. After the mutiny took place, Christian and the other mutineers settled in Pitcairn Island with their island love interests (often represented as the reason for the mutiny), but what happened after this was less of a romance than a horror story. Filmic versions of the mutiny include 1935, 1962, and 1984 movies that tell fictionalized versions of the events on the ship and exploit romantic ideas about the women of Otaheite.[171]

The mutiny took place on April 28, 1789, when Captain Bligh was forced into the ship's launch with supplies and two of the more unpopular members of the crew, while the majority of crew stayed on the boat with Fletcher Christian.[172] Two months later, *the Bounty* arrived at Pitcairn Island, with nine British men, six Polynesian men, and 12 Polynesian women, after which they set *the Bounty* on fire on January 23, 1790.[173] Over the next three years, the small society fell apart, with murders of both British and Polynesian men and the abandonment of Pitcairn by others.[174] The 1984 film *The Bounty* starred Anthony Hopkins as a villainous Captain Bligh and Mel Gibson as a sympathetic, perhaps even heroic, sailor Fletcher Christian. According to some scholars, it was the only one of the films to make the beauty of Tahitian women central to the presentation of the story.[175]

Like Tahiti, Hawai'i has also been a popular setting for films.[176] More than 50 films were made on or about the islands from 1920 to 1939.[177] WWII is a major focus of films about the South Pacific. The Japanese bombing of Pearl Harbor was depicted in Ford's *December 7th* (1943), a documentary that focuses on the "unique 'Aloha culture' of Hawaii" which is portrayed as serene, peace-loving, and full of "warm, friendly people."[178] Like many other films about the South Pacific, it exploits the romanticized view of the islands, with no reference to the Kānaka Maoli. The film won the Oscar for best short documentary in 1943 and was followed by other films about the attacks, including *Tora! Tora! Tora!*, a film that was a Japanese and American coproduction.[179]

In these films, the American military is at the center. *Pearl Harbor* (2001) presents Hawai'i as an idyllic playground for well-intentioned white soldiers and nurses with virtually no sign of Pacific Islanders or Asians except for the nefarious Japanese who bombed Oahu on December 7, 1941. Like *December 7th*'s "land of sugar cane and pineapple fields," this film exploits the beautiful landscape while making it clear that it is American territory, what one study describes as Hollywood's fixation on "distinctly US adventures, obstacles, and contributions."[180] American settlers and military men and women are at the center of the film, while most of the Japanese are on the periphery as arch-villains. The film also includes vague scenes of Japanese Americans acting suspiciously, suggesting they were helping in the bombing.[181] The mapping of Hawai'i in these films presents the islands as a site of American power and redemption. The island of Oahu is presented as an idealistic American space (one local complained that Hawai'i was "not Minnesota"), achieved through its "erasure of Hawai'i's Asian and Polynesian communities."[182]

A few big studio films have given attention to Kānaka Maoli land issues. One is Cameron Crowe's *Aloha* (2015). Criticisms regarding Emma Stone's casting as a part-Asian character diverted attention away from the movie's focus on Hawaiian sovereignty issues. As one critic noted, the casting of white actors in Asian roles is part of a larger problem that Hollywood has with Asian American representation and inclusion, which includes a system that is "already deeply troubled and racist."[183] However, *Aloha* includes a lengthy series of scenes with Dennis "Bumpy" Pu'ohunua Kanahele, the current leader of the Nation of Hawaii movement, where he negotiates for more land for his community of Native Hawaiians who live at the *Pu'uhonua o Waimanalo*.[184]

Aloha is the best-known nondocumentary film that includes the sovereignty movement in its storyline. *Princess Kaiulani* (also known by the title Barbarian Princess, 2009) is another film that attempts to provide a sense of Hawaiian history, in this case from the view of a member of the royal family. Several documentaries have been produced about Hawaiian land, language, and legal struggles over the past few decades, including *Act of War: The Overthrow of the Hawaiian Nation* (1993), *Hawaii: A Voice for Sovereignty* (2009), *Noho Hewa: The Wrongful Occupation of Hawai'i* (2008), and *Pidgin: The Voice of Hawaii* (2009).[185]

The Descendants (2011) presents a complex view of the state of contemporary Hawai'i. Despite its criticisms, including the role of a Native Hawaiian played by George Clooney instead of a Hawaiian or other Polynesian actor, it gave "massive publicity to Native Hawaiian political issues," perhaps more than any film made to date.[186] Clooney plays a *kama'āina haole*, a white person who is a descendant of American missionaries.[187] In the film's story, Clooney's ancestors include a white American who had married a Hawaiian princess, leaving a huge piece of land for their future family members.

The Descendants is based on a book by Hawaiian writer Kaui Hart Hemmings. The film revolves around the struggles of Clooney's character, a lawyer named Matt King. King is a soon-to-be single dad whose struggles include reconciling his feelings about his wife, who is on life support after a jet ski accident, whom he recently learned had cheated on him, and dealing with his family's huge land holdings of 25,000 acres. The land Matt King controls (as the executor of a large family estate) is a part of a former missionary family's holdings. Matt is part Hawaiian, although he states in the film that he is "haole as shit." The complications of Matt's identity reveal the imperialism of Hawai'i, located in sugar and pineapple plantations, and more recently, real estate. Adra Imada explains the early white families, known as the "Big Five."

> Blending paternalism and brutal strikebreaking, the Big Five ruled the plantations with a tight fist, befitting the Calvinist backgrounds of their dictators. The Hawaiian colony, with its racialized workforce of Native Hawaiians and Asians, produced agricultural commodities for the metropole and absorbed the inflated exports of the mother country.[188]

The Hawaiian landscape plays a central character in the film, which opens with scenes of Honolulu's traffic and Matt's comment, "Paradise? Paradise can go fuck itself."[189] The scenes of Hawai'i include "a woman in a wheelchair, an old Asian man, a homeless person with her dog on a beach" and the film "shuns the stereotypical trope further by showing rain in Hawai'i, mist on the beaches, and crowded residential neighborhoods."[190] *The Descendants* disrupts the tourist vision of the islands and instead presents an ecosystem on the verge of collapse.

The film has two intersecting plots. The first involves King's wife, who will soon be taken off life support. The second focuses on the land that Matt is responsible for, whose sale will result in a huge commission for his wife's lover, the realtor King tracks down with the help of his eldest daughter, who had revealed the affair to her dad. There are few Native Hawaiians in the film (like the passenger on an inter-island flight). As other scholars have noted, Payne connects emotional and ideological themes through the Hawaiian landscape.[191] A sense of the island before U.S. imperialism is communicated in a scene when Matt takes his girls to view the land that they inherited on the southeast coast of Kauai. In the end, despite pressures from his cousins and threats of lawsuits, Matt decides that, as executor of the King fortune, he will not sell the land to developers. When Matt says that he didn't do anything to get the land, this is a statement about the injustice that characterizes the history and the status of Hawaiians.

As stated earlier, the land in *The Descendants* plays a role in the film. Matt King's wealth comes from the land his ancestors inherited through marriage to a member of the royal family, and his family benefits from the exploitation this union created. A critique of the film is the absence of Kānaka Maoli people, which suggests the conscious erasure of a past that is unsettled. Hawaiian sovereignty and land protection issues today are seen in the fights over the construction of the H-3 super highway and the massive telescope on Mauna Kea. The voices of Hawaiians are critical in understanding how the colonial mapping of the islands by white settlers is being eroded.

Mauna Kea, or *Mauna a Wākea*, is the tallest mountain in the island chain and an important site in the cosmology of the Kānaka Maoli, as the *piko* (navel) of earth and the most sacred place in the Hawaiian universe.[192] Protests over the TMT (thirty-meter telescope) reflect concerns about the struggle to maintain a Hawaiian landscape and honor the ancestors. No'eau Peralto is a descendant of *kupuna* from Koholālele, Hāmākua, Hawai'i, who is the executive director of hui Mau (Hui Mālama I ke Ala 'Ūlili), an *'ohana* (Native Hawaiian) organization focused on sustainable, ecological, and ancestral systems that benefit the people and reconnect them to the land.[193]

Peralto, who holds a doctorate in Indigenous Politics, explains how Mauna a Wākea is a part of the history of the Kānaka Maoli and an important part of Hawaiian cosmology. In his words, "It has been said that we are branches of the genealogical trees established long ago by our kupuna who birthed us into existence. I ulu nō ka lālā I ke kumu."[194] Hawaiians are connected to the land in a reciprocal and "familial relationship" due to the interconnectedness of people and land ('āina), which makes it necessary to protect and care for the land.[195] For Kānaka Maoli, the mountain is also "the pink that connects us to the heavens," and it is the place where "life-giving waters" from the clouds are shared with the land below.[196] The first images that come to mind when thinking of Hawai'i and its landscapes may be its volcanoes, pristine beaches, and dramatic cliffs at places like the Na Pali coast. As discussed earlier, Kānaka Maoli have been struggling to take some of these lands back. Against the work of Hawaiians is the enormous tourist industry, whose use of land and water and production of trash threaten the very paradise people come to experience. More importantly, it threatens the physical and cultural survival of the Kānaka Maoli.

Mystical Landscapes in the South Pacific

Tourist materials in Tahiti include a recycling of the old fantasies of island maidens available to white foreign men as well as images of the ownership of territory by white women. One way this is communicated is through the inclusion of white females on tropical beaches. As Siobhan McDonnell points out, "White, bikini-clad women are a regular motif in real estate and tourism images across the Pacific, serving as a reminder of who is defining this 'paradise.'"[197] Tahiti inspires a large host of products that range from postcards to chocolate wrappers on the Bounty Bar, whose ads feature consumers "opening" the bars and being transported to a Tahitian beach and experiencing sensual pleasures identified with the local population.[198]

The image of Tahiti as a destination for seekers of a paradise on earth stands in direct contrast to what Tahitians find valuable about their home. For Tahitians, the land and sea have a complementary relationship, with each realm providing sustenance (yams and breadfruit, fish and seafood), but what is even more important is that the sea, which is such a focus of tourism, is not seen as desirable by the indigenous population.[199] As one Tahitian put it, "Tahitians don't care to live next to the sea or to have a view of water. They see the water all the time. It's nothing special. Tourists are the only ones who crave the water."[200]

Tahiti does not see huge numbers of tourists due to its distance from major airports and the high travel expense. As a comparison, Hawai'i receives about 35 times as many tourists as Tahiti.[201] As an overseas territory, *erritoire d'outre-mer*, holidays like Bastille Day remain important occasions, and as a sign of the ways that French culture had been transposed on the islands, Polynesian festivals (*heivas*) accompany these holidays.[202] Tourists who come to Tahiti and other nearby islands find a place defined by its beauty and promise as a special, timeless landscape or seascape.

The Tahitian product most associated with its mystical landscape is *mono'i*, or "monoi de Tahiti," which is coconut oil scented with *tiare* (gardenia).[203] *Mono'i* is a "sacred oil" that traditionally was prepared in different ways, using a special coconut oil with the addition of fat (usually from a crab) and flowers or sandalwood.[204] Similar oils are found across French Polynesia and in other parts of the South Pacific (in Polynesian cultures like Samoa).[205] Perhaps most importantly, it is used in "religious, magical, and medicinal practices" and is connected to the ancestors and traditions within the Maohi community.[206]

The tourist industry in Hawai'i is linked to the presence of the U.S. military in the islands, as noted earlier. It is focused on nostalgia, seen in tourist spaces and souvenir products, as well as on other areas of pop culture. As Camilla Fojas writes,

> Pop culture locates Hawai'i as the origin of tiki culture, volcano sacrifices, friendly and happy natives, grass skirts, hula girls, and surfer boys, thereby helping install the symbolic coordinates of one of the largest U.S. tourist industries. These ideas and icons are supported by the mainland interpretation of aloha culture, embodied by the welcoming native offering up the bounties of Hawai'i to the weary traveler.[207]

Calendars with Hawaiian images that advertise the islands often featured white hula girls, usually sitting on a beach under the moonlight, with the

Pacific Ocean beside them. These images place white bodies in Hawaiian space, thus rendering the islands a colonially occupied mystical landscape, promising bodily and spiritual rejuvenation through the beauty of an American paradise. The "aloha culture" is at the center of the imagination about the islands, a problematic use of the indigenous language. Kānaka Maoli scholars have criticized the way that *huna* and *kahuna* have been extended to non-Hawaiians, calling them the "plastic shamans of Hawaiian spirituality."[208]

Hawai'i is also viewed as a romantic destination, seen in many films about weddings, including *Waikiki Wedding* (1937) and *Blue Hawaii* (1961), the tune "The Hawaiian Wedding Song," and the huge wedding business that caters to Japanese tourists.[209] These weddings often feature new chapels that are only used for weddings; in some cases, they represent a remapping of Hawaiian royal lands for the tourism industry. One case is the Aloha ke Akua chapel, which sits on the former property of King Kamehameha IV and was built by the large wedding company World of Aloha.[210]

Aloha culture is everywhere, with Hawaiian-style music piped into airports and hotel lobbies, tropical drinks served at every bar and restaurant, and island flowers placed on pillows and towels in hotel rooms. The Aulani Disney resort uses large amounts of water for its gardens, pools, and water features, which is only possible because of the colonial history of the island, when sugar plantations diverted water from the windward side to the dry side of the island.[211] Kānaka Maoli groups have been concerned about water (*wai*) issues, which involve sustaining native foods like kalo (*taro*) and religious beliefs.[212] As the Kānaka Maoli attorney and scholar Kapua Sproat explains,

> As island people who rely on fresh water to survive, Kanaka Maoli developed an intimate and complex relationship with our resources. In addition to providing a foundation for Indigenous society, fresh water was also deified as a kinolau or physical embodiment of Kāne, one of the four principal *akua* (ancestors or gods) of the Maoli pantheon.[213]

The Aulani resort features indigenizing through native artists, at least one of whom has said their motifs contain critiques of the Aulani property.[214] Hotels and resorts like Aulani feature therapeutical products that exploit the island's tropical environment, including creams, perfumes, soaps, massages, and body wraps using coconut, lilikoi, mango, pineapple, and sea salt. In *White Shadows in the South Seas* (1928), a popular early film about the South Seas, the massage is presented as a mystically powerful body treatment. This is no ordinary massage. It is "the secret and sacred massage of Polynesia."[215]

Spa treatments and portable products that tourists take home are one side of Hawaii's tourist experience tied to the mystical landscape, with a long history in the geographical imagination about the islands. Aulani re-creates a landscape that reflects the idea of Hawai'i as a mystical landscape, claiming that it is a space that "immerses" the guest in "local magic" through features like the "ancient therapy" of hydrotherapy, which promises to "boost the immune system and regulate circulation."[216] A homeless population of *Kānaka Maoli* live near the resort, evidence of the human price of mystical tourism in the Aloha state.[217]

Notes

1 Gonzalez, 7.
2 Connell, 555.
3 Connell, 555.
4 For an excellent history of Oceania and the intersection of European and Pacific Islander histories, see Marshall Sahlins, *Islands of History* (Chicago: University of Chicago Press, 1987). The death of Captain Cook is an especially well-known historical episode that is analyzed in this book; see Chapter 4: Captain James Cook; or, The Dying God."
5 Anne-Marie d'Hauteserre, "Maintaining the Myth: Tahiti and Its Islands," in *Seductions of Place: Geographical Perspectives on Globalization and Touristed Landscapes*, ed. Carolyn Cartier and Alan A. Lew (New York: Routledge, 2005), 195.
6 Edmond, 16.
7 Sturma, 10.
8 Connell, 559.
9 Bengt Danielsson, *Love in the South Seas: Sex and Family Life of the Polynesians, Based on Early Accounts as Well as Observations by the Noted Swedish Anthropologist* (Honolulu: Mutual Publishing, 1986), 13. Quoted in Teaiwa, 253.
10 Kahn, 324.
11 Lyons, 35.
12 Schmitt, 433.
13 D'Hauteserre, 194.
14 John P. Eperjesi, *The Imperialist Imaginary: Visions of Asia and the Pacific in American Culture* (Hanover: Dartmouth College Press, 2005), 106.
15 Sturma, 29.
16 Lyons, 27.
17 Kahn 2003, 308.
18 Teresia Teaiwa, "Reading Paul Gaugin's *Noa Noa* with Epeli Hau'ofa's *Kisses in the Nederends*: Militourism, Feminism, and the 'Polynesian' Body," in *Inside Out: Literature, Cultural Politics, and Identity in the New Pacific*, ed. Vilson Hereniko (Lanham: Rowman & Littlefield, 1999), 251. The late Dr. Teaiwa was a Kiribati and an African American scholar.
19 Also called the "South Seas" in earlier days.
20 Sturma, 9. See also Gavin Daws, *A Dream of Islands: Voyages of Self-Discovery in the South Seas* (Brisbane: W. W. Norton & Company, 1980), xi.
21 Heintzman, 78.
22 Sharif Gemie, "Loti, Orientalism and the French Colonial Experience," *Journal of European Area Studies* 8, no. 2 (2000): 150, 152.
23 Gemie, 157, 160.
24 Gemie, 162. The Victorian artist William Holman Hunt also dressed up as an Arab, a way of "physically translating the Holy Land" for his fellow Christians in London. See Coleman 2007, 332.

25 Edmond, 20.
26 Nancy Perloff, "Gauguin's French Baggage: Decadence and Colonialism in Tahiti," in *Prehistories of the Future: The Primitivist Project and the Culture of Modernism*, ed. Elazar Barkan and Ronald Bush (Stanford: Stanford University Press, 1995), 238.
27 Pierre Loti, *The Marriage of Loti* (1878; repr., London: Forgotten Books, 2012), 20, 21, 28, 40, 59, 117, 126.
28 Rennie, 76.
29 Loti 1878, 16.
30 Loti 1878, 16.
31 Loti 1878, 43, 44.
32 Loti 1878, 45.
33 Jolly 2004, 32.
34 Loti 1878, 216.
35 Edmond, 1.
36 See Edmond, 6, for a history of *Terra Australis Incognito*, which first emerged in Western thought in the first two centuries with Pomponius Mela and Ptolemy.
37 Rennie, 39.
38 Rennie, 90.
39 Edmond, 7.
40 Sturma, 16.
41 Rennie, 58–59.
42 Rennie, 65.
43 Joseph Banks, *The 'Endeavour' Journal of Joseph Banks*, ed. J. C. Beaglehole (Sydney: Angus and Robertson Ltd., 1962), 128.
44 Cartier 2005, 15.
45 Seri Luangphinith, "Tropical Fevers: 'Madness' and Colonialism in Pacific Literature," *The Contemporary Pacific* 16, no. 1 (2004): 60.
46 David A. Chappell, "The Postcontact Period," in *The Pacific Islands: Environment and Society (Revised Edition)*, ed. Moshe Rappaport (Honolulu: University of Hawai'i Press, 2103), 141.
47 Chappell, 139.
48 Jack London's characterization of Asians as threatening and menacing in comparison to the "soft primitivism" reserved for Hawaiians is one example. See Eperjesi, 110, 112.
49 James Michener, *Return to Paradise* (New York: Random House, 1951), 436.
50 Michener, 45–46.
51 Kahn 2003, 310.
52 Henri J. M. Claessen, "Tahiti and the Early European Visitors," in *European Imagery and Colonial History in the Pacific*, ed. Toon van Meijl and Paul van der Grijp (Saarbrüken: Verlag für Entwicklungspolitik Breitenbach GmbH, 1994), 16.
53 Daws, xii.
54 O' Dwyer, 35.
55 O' Dwyer, 35.
56 Claaesen, 19.
57 Claaesen, 25.
58 Sturma, 136.
59 Tamaira, 15.
60 Heather Leigh Waldroup, "Traveling Images: Representations of the South Pacific from Colonial and Postcolonial Worlds" (PhD dissertation, University of California, Santa Cruz, 2004), 33. Quoted in Tamaira, 15.
61 Edmond, 8.
62 Claaesen, 14.

63 Loti 1878, 125.
64 Tamaira, 7.
65 Louis Antoine de Bougainville, *A Voyage Round the World*, trans. John Reinhold Forster (New York: De Capo Press, 1967), 1967, 219. Quoted in Tamaira, 7.
66 Pearson, 200. (emphasis in original)
67 Edmond, 12.
68 Wrobel, 4.
69 Elizabeth DeLoughrey, "Heliotropes: Solar Ecologies and Pacific Radiations," in *Postcolonial Ecologies: Literatures of the Environment*, ed. Elizabeth DeLoughrey and George B. Handley (New York: Oxford University Press, 2011), 238.
70 Eugene Odum, "Ecology and the Atomic Age," *ASB Bulletin* 4, no. 2 (1957): 28. Quoted in DeLoughrey, 239.
71 Gonzalez, 12.
72 Dina El Dessouky, "Activating Voice, Body, and Place: Kanaka Maoli and Ma'ohi Writings for Kaho'olawe and Moruroa," in *Postcolonial Ecologies: Literatures of the Environment*, ed. Elizabeth DeLoughrey and George B. Handley (New York: Oxford University Press, 2011), 255.
73 Rennie, 84.
74 Rennie, 84.
75 Connell, 556.
76 Connell, 556.
77 D'Hauteresse, 198.
78 Kahn 2003, 309.
79 Rennie, 85.
80 Connell, 556.
81 Perloff, 233.
82 Perloff, 236.
83 Mitchell 2020, 3.
84 Teaiwa, 254,
85 Sia Figiel, *Where We Once Belonged* (New York: Kaya, 1999), 192. Quoted in Luangphinith, 75.
86 André Maurois, *Sur le vif, L'exposition coloniale* (Paris: Degorce, 1931), 13. Quoted in Herman Lebovics, "The Zoos of the Exposition Coloniale Internationale, Paris 1931," in *Human Zoos: Science and Spectacle in the Age of Colonial Empires*, ed. Pascal Blanchard, Nicolas Bancel, Gilles Boëtsch, Eric Deroo, Sandrine Lemaire, and Charles Forsdick (Liverpool: Liverpool University Press, 2008), 372.
87 Douglas Chadwick, "The Samoan Way," *National Geographic* 98, no. 1 (2000), 72. See also Connell, 567.
88 Gemie, 153.
89 D'Hauteserre, 199.
90 Connell, 558.
91 Connell, 561.
92 His name was more likely Mai, with the O added by Europeans by mistake. According to scholars, O means "it is" and sometimes prefaced a proper name; thus, it is likely his real name was Mai. See Rennie, 126.
93 Daws, 11.
94 Khan 2003, 310.
95 Rennie, 126.
96 Rennie, 126.
97 Kahn 2003, 324.
98 Wrobel, 8.

 99 Wrobel, 8–9.
100 Tamaira, 11.
101 J. C. Beaglehole, ed., *The Journals of Captain James Cook on His Voyages of Discovery: The Voyage of the Resolution and Discovery 1776–1780. Part I* (Cambridge: Cambridge University Press, 1967), 248. Quoted in Tamaira, 13.
102 El Dessouky, 260.
103 Kahn, 10.
104 Kahn 2003, 316.
105 Kahn 2003, 317.
106 Kahn 2003, 317.
107 El Dessouky, 261.
108 Claude Robineau, "The Tahitian Economy and Tourism," in *A New Kind of Sugar: Tourism in the Pacific*, ed. Ben R. Finney and Karen Ann Watson (Honolulu: The East-West Center, 1975), 67, 69.
109 Kahn 2000, 14.
110 Claaesen, 28.
111 Chanel Didier, "Por relancer le tourisme en Polynésie: Promotion de 545 millions CFP!," *La Dépêche de Tahiti*, November 30, 1995. Quoted in Kahn 2000, 21.
112 Kahn 2000, 16.
113 McDonnell, 427.
114 Gonzalez, 10.
115 Fojas, 22.
116 Fojas, 22.
117 Lyons, 36.
118 Gonzalez, 10.
119 Eperjesi, 120.
120 Fojas, 96.
121 Fojas, 23.
122 Eperjesi, 122. The Committee of Annexation was renamed the Committee on Safety, signifying the need to take over the islands for the safety of its white settlers. See Eperjesi, 120–122.
123 Lyons, 156.
124 Lyons, 155.
125 O' Dwyer, 34.
126 Teaiwa, 251.
127 DeLoughrey, 240.
128 Adria Imada, "Transnational Hula as Colonial Culture," *The Journal of Pacific History* 46, no. 2 (2011): 152. (emphasis in original)
129 Imada 2011, 152.
130 Imada 2011, 168.
131 Adria Imada, "Hawaiians on Tour: Hula Circuits through the American Empire," *American Quarterly* 56, no. 1 (2004): 130.
132 Haunani-Kay Trask, "Fighting the Battle of Double Colonization: The View of an Hawaiian Feminist," *Ethnies: Human Rights and Tribal Peoples (Renaissance in the Pacific)* 4, nos. 8,9,10 (1989): 62. The late Dr. Trask was a Native Hawaiian scholar and activist.
133 Gonzalez, 46.
134 Joceyln Linnekin, "The *Hui* Lands of Keanae: Hawaiian Land Tenure and the Great Mahele," *The Journal of the Polynesian Society* 92, no. 2 (1983): 171.
135 Linnekin, 171.
136 Stuart Banner, "Preparing to Be Colonized: Land Tenure and Legal Strategy in Nineteenth-Century Hawaii," *Law & Society Review* 39, no. 2 (2005): 281.
137 Linnekin, 173–174.

138 Linnekin, 174.
139 Banner, 304.
140 Trask, 62.
141 Fojas, 97.
142 Fojas, 97–98.
143 O' Dwyer, 38.
144 O' Dwyer, 38, 42.
145 O' Dwyer, 42.
146 O' Dwyer, 42–43.
147 El Dessouky, 255.
148 El Dessouky, 261.
149 Trask, 64.
150 Jonathan Kamakawiwo'ole Osorio, "Hawaiian Souls: The Movement to Stop the U.S. Military Bombing of Kaho'olawe," in *A Nation Rising: Hawaiian Movements for Life, Land, and Sovereignty*, ed. Erin Kahunawaika'ala, Ikaika Hussey, and Noelani Goodyear-Kaōpua (Durham: Duke University Press, 2014), 137, 141, 157.
151 Osorio, 138.
152 Gonzalez, 69.
153 Gonzalez, 71, 75,
154 Charles Morris, *Our Island Empire: A Hand-Book of Cuba, Porto Rico, Hawaii, and the Philippine Islands* (Philadelphia: J. B. Lippincott Company, 1899), 231.
155 El Dessouky, 260.
156 Lisa Kahaleole Hall, " 'Hawaiian at Heart' and Other Fictions," *The Contemporary Pacific* 17, no. 2 (2005): 405.
157 Janet Borgerson and Jonathan Schroder, "The Lure of Paradise: Marketing the Retro-Escape of Hawaii," in *Time, Space, and the Market: Retroscapes Rising* (New York: Routledge, 2015), 220.
158 Borgerson and Schroder, 220.
159 Gonzalez, 74.
160 Georgia Lee, "Wahi Pana: Legendary Places on Hawai'i Island," in *Inscribed Landscapes: Marking and Making Place*, ed. Bruno David and Meredith Wilson (Honolulu: University of Hawai'i Press, 2002), 80.
161 Lee, 87.
162 President Cleveland sought the restoration of the monarchy in 1893. See Angela Louise R. Tiangco, "Selling Aloha: The Fight for Legal Protections over Native Hawaiian Culture," *William & Mary Journal of Race, Gender, and Social Justice* 29, no. 2 (2022/2023): 493.
163 Angela Louise R. Tiangco, "Selling Aloha: The Fight for Legal Protections Over Native Hawaiian Culture," *William & Mary Journal of Race, Gender, and Social Justice* 29, no. 2 (2022/2023): 493.
164 DeSoto Brown, *Hawaii Recalls: Nostalgic Images of the Hawaiian Islands: 1910–1950* (New York: Routledge and Kegan Paul International, 1982), 60.
165 As a disclaimer, I am distantly related to the film's star George Clooney. I have never met him, and my familial ties to the Clooneys exist through the marriage of Rosemary Clooney to one of the Boones, who are my relatives.
166 Schmitt, 433.
167 *Moving Images of the Pacific Islands: A Catalogue of Films and Videos (Occasional Paper 34)*, ed. Melissa C. Miller (Honolulu: University of Hawaii Press, 1989), 155.
168 See Atkins on the relationship between Walter Spies and Murnau.
169 Atkins, 87.
170 *Moving Images of the Pacific Islands: A Catalogue of Films and Videos (Occasional Paper 34)*, 106.
171 Sturma, 43.

172 Rennie, 143.
173 Rennie, 166.
174 Sturma, 43.
175 Sturma, 49.
176 Hawai'i has also been a popular site for television, with shows like *Magnum P.I.* and *Hawai'i Five-O*.
177 Schlachter, 231.
178 Carl Boggs, "Pearl Harbor: How Film Conquers History," *New Political Science* 28, no. 4 (2006): 455–456.
179 Geoffrey M. White, "Disney's Pearl Harbor: National Memory at the Movies," *The Public Historian* 24, no. 4 (2002): 101.
180 Boggs, 455, 453.
181 White 2002, 111.
182 White 2002, 112.
183 Sylvia Shin Huey Chong, "What Was Asian American Cinema?," *Cinema Journal* 56, no. 3 (2017): 131. Crowe apologized for the casting.
184 This piece of land was given to the Hawaiian sovereignty movement in exchange for leaving a beach they were occupying. This movement is known as the Nation of Hawaii, which is different than the Kingdom of Hawai'i movement, which seeks the restoration of the monarchy.
185 Schlachter, 233, 236, 237, 240.
186 Fojas, 199.
187 Imada 2004, 115.
188 Imada 2004, 115.
189 *The Descendants* (2011), dir. Alexander Payne. 01:24.
190 Schlachter, 244.
191 Palencia, 83.
192 Jolly 2018, 358.
193 https://www.alaulili.com/about-us.html (accessed January 26, 2025).
194 Leon No'eau Peralto, "Portrait. Mauna a Wākea, Hānau Ka Mauna, the Piko of Our Ea," in *A Nation Rising: Hawaiian Movements for Life, Land, and Sovereignty*, ed. Erin Kahunawaika'ala, Ikaika Hussey, and Noelani Goodyear-Kaōpua (Durham: Duke University Press, 2014), 233. This phrase translates to "[t]he branches grow because of the trunk."
195 Peralto, 234, 235.
196 Peralto, 236.
197 McDonnell, 426.
198 Kahn 2003, 313, 319.
199 Kahn 2000, 11.
200 Kahn 2000, 11.
201 d'Hauteserre, 206.
202 d'Hauteserre, 208, 204.
203 Kate Stevens, "Repackaging Tradition in Tahiti? Mono'i and Labels of Origin in French Polynesia," *The Contemporary Pacific* 30, no. 1 (2018): 70.
204 Stevens, 77.
205 Stevens, 77.
206 Stevens, 78.
207 Fojas, 94.
208 Kahaleole Hall, 411. *Kuna* refers to "secret" or traditional knowledge held by Hawaiian people.
209 Mary G. McDonald, "Tourist Weddings in Hawai'i: Consuming the Destination," in *Seductions of Place: Geographical Perspectives on Globalization and Touristed Landscapes*, ed. Carolyn Cartier and Alan A. Lew (New York: Routledge, 2005), 176–177.
210 McDonald, 190.

211 Jolly 2018, 363.
212 D. Kapua'ala Sproat, "A Question of Wai: Seeking Justice through Law for Hawai'i's Streams and Communities," in *A Nation Rising: Hawaiian Movements for Life, Land, and Sovereignty*, ed. Erin Kahunawaika'ala, Ikaika Hussey, and Noelani Goodyear-Kaōpua (Durham: Duke University Press, 2014), 201, 202. Kapua Sproat is a Native Hawaiian who works as an attorney and is also a scholar.
213 Sproat, 202.
214 Jolly 2018, 364.
215 Jeffrey Geiger, "Imagined Islands: 'White Shadows in the South Seas' and Cultural Ambivalence," *Cinema Journal* 41, no. 3 (2002): 112.
216 https://www.disneyaulani.com/spa-fitness/kula-wai-hydrotherapy-garden/ (accessed January 26, 2025).
217 Jolly 2018, 364.

Bibliography

Atkins, Gary L. *Imagining Gay Paradise: Bali, Bangkok, and Cyber-Singapore*. Hong Kong: Hong Kong University Press, 2012.
Banks, Joseph. *The 'Endeavour' Journal of Joseph Banks*. Edited by John Cawte Beaglehole. Sydney: Angus and Robertson, Ltd., 1962.
Banner, Stuart. "Preparing to Be Colonized: Land Tenure and Legal Strategy in Nineteenth-Century Hawaii." *Law & Society Review* 39, no. 2 (2005): 272–314.
Beaglehole, J. C., ed. *The Journals of Captain James Cook on His Voyages of Discovery. The Voyage of the Resolution and Discovery 1776–1780. Part I*. Cambridge: Cambridge University Press, 1967.
Boggs, Carl. "Pearl Harbor: How Film Conquers History." *New Political Science* 28, no. 4 (2006): 451–466.
Borgerson, Janet and Jonathan Schroeder. "The Lure of Paradise: Marketing the Retro-Escape of Hawaii." In *Time, Space and the Market: Retroscapes Rising*, edited by Stephen Brown and John F. Sherry, Jr., 219–237. New York: Routledge, 2015.
Brown, DeSoto. *Hawaii Recalls: Nostalgic Images of the Hawaiian Islands: 1910–1950*. New York: Routledge and Kegan Paul International, 1982.
Cartier, Carolyn. "Introduction: Touristed Landscapes/Seductions of Place." In *Seductions of Place: Geographical Perspectives on Globalization and Touristed Landscapes*, edited by Carolyn Carter and Alan A. Lew, 1–19. London: Routledge, 2005.
Chadwick, Douglas. "The Samoan Way." *National Geographic* 98, no. 1 (2000).
Chappell, David A. "The Postcontact Period." In *The Pacific Islands: Environment and Society (Revised Edition)*, edited by Moshe Rappaport, 138–146. Honolulu: University of Hawaii Press, 2013.
Chong, Sylvia Shin Huey. "What Was Asian Cinema?" *Cinema Journal* 56, no. 3 (2017): 130–135.
Claaesen, Henri J. M. "Tahiti and the Early European Visitors." In *European Imagery and Colonial History in the Pacific*, edited by Toon van Meijl and Paul van der Grijp, 14–31. Saarbrüken: Verlag für Entwicklungspolitik Breitenbach GmbH, 1994.
Coleman, Simon. "A Tale of Two Centres? Representing Palestine to the British in the Nineteenth Century." *Mobilities* 2, no. 3 (2007): 331–345.
Connell, John. "Island Dreaming: The Contemplation of Polynesian Paradise." *Journal of Historical Geography* 29, no. 4 (2003): 554–581.

Danielsson, Bengt. *Love in the South Seas: Sex and Family Life of the Polynesians, Based on Early Accounts as Well as Observations by the Noted Swedish Anthropologist.* Honolulu: Mutual Publishing, 1986.

Daws, Gavan. *A Dream of Islands.* Brisbane: W.W. Norton and Company, 1980.

De Bougainville, Louis Antoine. *A Voyage Round the World.* Translated by John Reinhold Forster. New York: Da Capo Press, 1967.

DeLoughrey, Elizabeth. "Heliotropes: Solar Ecologies and Pacific Radiations." In *Postcolonial Ecologies: Literatures of the Environment*, edited by Elizabeth DeLoughrey and George B. Handley, 235–253. New York: Oxford University Press, 2011.

D'Hauterserre, Anne-Marie. "Maintaining the Myth: Tahiti and Its Islands." In *Seductions of Place: Geographical Perspectives on Globalization and Touristed Landscapes*, edited by Carolyn Carter and Alan A. Lew, 193–208. London: Routledge, 2005.

Didier, Chanel. "Por relancer le tourisme en Polynésie: Promotion de 545 millions CFP!" *La Dépêche de Tahiti*, November 30, 1995.

Edmond, Rod. *Representing the South Pacific: From Cook to Gaugin.* Cambridge: Cambridge University Press, 2009.

El Dessouky, Dina. "Activating Voice, Body, and Place: Kanaka Maoli and Ma'ohi Writings for Kaho'olawe and Moruroa." In *Postcolonial Ecologies: Literatures of the Environment*, edited by Elizabeth DeLoughrey and George B. Handley, 254–272. New York: Oxford University Press, 2011.

Eperjesi, John R. *The Imperialist Imaginary: Visions of Asia and the Pacific in American Culture.* Hanover: Dartmouth University Press, 2005.

Figiel, Sia. *Where We Once Belonged.* New York: Kaya, 1999.

Fojas, Camilla. *Islands of Empire: Pop Culture & U.S. Power.* Austin: University of Texas Press, 2014.

Geiger, Jeffrey. "Imagined Islands: 'White Shadows in the South Seas' and Cultural Ambivalence." *Cinema Journal* 41, no. 3 (2002): 98–121.

Gemie, Sharif. "Loti, Orientalism and the French Colonial Experience." *Journal of European Area Studies* 8, no. 2 (2000): 149–165.

Gonzalez, Vernadette Vicuña. *Securing Paradise: Tourism and Militarism in Hawai'i and the Philippines.* Durham: Duke University Press, 2013.

Hall, Lisa Kahaleole. "'Hawaiian at Heart' and Other Fictions." *The Contemporary Pacific* 17, no. 2 (2005): 404–413.

Heintzman, Paul. "Nature-Based Recreation and Spirituality: A Complex Relationship." *Leisure Sciences* 32, no. 1 (2009): 72–89.

Imada, Adria L. "Hawaiians on Tour: Hula Circuits Through the American Empire." *American Quarterly* 56, no. 1 (2004): 111–149.

Imada, Adria L. "Transnational Hula as Colonial Culture." *The Journal of Pacific History* 46, no. 2 (2011): 149–176.

Jolly, Margaret. "Contested Paradise: Dispossession and Repossession in Hawai'i." *The Contemporary Pacific* 30, no. 2 (2018): 355–377.

Jolly, Roslyn. "South Sea Gothic: Pierre Loti and Robert Louis Stevenson." *English Literature in Translation, 1880–1920* 47, no. 1 (2004): 28–49.

Kahn, Miriam. "Tahiti Intertwined: Ancestral Land, Tourist Postcard, and Nuclear Test Site." *American Anthropologist* 102, no. 1 (2000): 7–26.

Kahn, Miriam. "Tahiti: The Ripples of a Myth on the Shores of the Imagination." *History and Anthropology* 14, no. 4 (2003): 307–326.

Lebovics, Herman. "The Zoos of the Exposition Coloniale Internationale, Paris 1931." In *Human Zoos: Science and Spectacle in the Age of Colonial Empires*, edited by Pascal Blanchard, Nicolas Bancel, Gilles Boëtsch, Sandrine Lemaire, and Charles Forsdick, 369–376. Liverpool: Liverpool University Press, 2008.

Lee, Georgia. "Wahi Pana: Legendary Places on Hawai'i Island." In *Inscribed Landscapes: Marking and Making Place*, edited by Bruno David and Meredith Wilson, 79–92. Honolulu: University of Hawai'i Press, 2002.

Linnekin, Joycelyn. "The *Hui* Lands of Keanae: Hawaiian Land Tenure and the Great Mahele." *The Journal of the Polynesian Society* 92, no. 2 (1983): 169–188.

Loti, Pierre. *The Marriage of Loti (Rarahu)*, 1878. Reprint. London: Forgotten Books, 2012.

Luangphinith, Seri. "Tropical Fevers: 'Madness' and Colonialism in Pacific Literature." *The Contemporary Pacific* 16, no. 1 (2004): 59–85.

Lyons, Paul. *American Pacificism: Oceania in the U.S. Imagination*. New York: Routledge, 2006.

Maurois, André. *Sur le vif, L'exposition coloniale*. Paris: Degorce, 1931.

McDonald, Mary G. "Tourist Weddings in Hawai'i: Consuming the Destination." In *Seductions of Place: Geographical Perspectives on Globalization and Touristed Landscapes*, edited by Carolyn Carter and Alan A. Lew, 171–192. London: Routledge, 2005.

McDonnell, Siobhan. "Selling 'Sites of Desire': Paradise in Reality Television, Tourism, and Real Estate Promotion in Vanuatu." *The Contemporary Pacific* 30, no. 2 (2018): 413–435.

Michener, James. *Return to Paradise*. New York: Random House, 1951.

Mitchell, Robin. *Vénus Noire: Black Women and Colonial Fantasies in Nineteenth-Century France*. Athens: University of Georgia Press, 2020.

Morris, Charles. *Our Island Empire: A Hand-book of Cuba, Porto Rico, Hawaii, and the Philippine Islands*. Philadelphia: J.B. Lippincott Company, 1899.

Moving Images of the Pacific Islands: A Catalogue of Films and Videos (Occasional Paper 34). Edited by Melissa C. Miller. Honolulu: University of Hawaii Press, 1989.

Odum, Eugene. "Ecology and the Atomic Age." *ASB Bulletin* 4, no. 2 (1957): 27–29.

O'Dwyer, Carolyn. "Tropic Knights and Hula Belles: War and Tourism in the South Pacific." *Journal for Cultural Research* 8, no. 1 (2004): 33–50.

Osorio, Jonathan Kamakawiwo'ole. "Hawaiian Souls: The Movement to Stop the U.S. Bombing of Kaho'olawe." In *A Nation Rising: Hawaiian Movements for Life, Land, and Sovereignty*, edited by Noelani Goodyear-Ka'ōpua, Ikaika Hussey, and Erin Kahunawaika'ala Wright, 137–160. Durham: Duke University Press, 2014.

Palencia, Carolina Sánchez. "'The Tropics Make It Difficult to Mope' The Imaginative Geography of Alexander Payne's *The Descendants* (2001)." *International Journal of English Studies* 15, no. 2 (2015): 81–95.

Payne, Alexander, dir. *The Descendants*. Fox Searchlight Pictures, 2011. DVD.

Pearson, W. H. "Intimidation and the Myth of Tahiti." *The Journal of Pacific History* 4 (1969): 199–217.

Peralto, Leon No'eau. "Portrait. Auna a Wākea: Hanau Ka Mauna, The Piko of Our Ea." In *A Nation Rising: Hawaiian Movements for Life, Land, and Sovereignty*, edited by Noelani Goodyear-Ka'ōpua, Ikaika Hussey, and Erin Kahunawaika'ala Wright, 234–243. Durham: Duke University Press, 2014.

Perloff, Nancy. "Gaugin's French Baggage: Decadence and Colonialism in Tahiti." In *Prehistories of the Future: The Primitivist Project and the Culture of Modernism*, edited by Elazar Barkan and Ronald Bush, 226–269. Stanford: Stanford University Press, 1995.

Rennie, Neil. *Far-Fetched Facts: The Literature of Travel and the Idea of the South Seas*. Oxford: Clarendon Press, 1995.

Robineau, Claude. "The Tahitian Economy and Tourism." In *A New Kind of Sugar: Tourism in the Pacific*, edited by Ben R. Finney and Karen Ann Watson, 61–76. Honolulu: The East-West Center, 1975.

3

Sahlins, Marshall. *Islands of History*. Chicago: University of Chicago Press, 1985.

Schlachter, Judith. "Reclaiming Paradise: Cinema and Hawaiian Nationhood." *Pacific Studies* 38, no. 1/2 (2015): 229–252.

Schmitt, Robert C. "South Sea Movies, 1913–1943." *Hawaii Historical Review* 2, no. 11 (1968): 433–452.

Sproat, D. Kapua'ala. "A Question of Wai: Seeking Justice Through Law for Hawaii's Streams and Communities." In *A Nation Rising: Hawaiian Movements for Life, Land, and Sovereignty*, edited by Noelani Goodyear-Ka'ōpua, Ikaika Hussey, and Erin Kahunawaika'ala Wright, 199–219. Durham: Duke University Press, 2014.

Stevens, Kate. "Repackaging Tradition in Tahiti? Mono'i and Labels of Origin in French Polynesia." *The Contemporary Pacific* 20, no. 1 (2018): 70–106.

Sturma, Michael. *South Sea Maidens: Western Fantasy and Sexual Politics in the South Pacific*. Westport: Greenwood Press, 2002.

Tamaira, A. Marata. "From Full Dusk to Full Tusk: Reimagining the 'Dusky Maiden' through the Visual Arts." *The Contemporary Pacific* 22, no. 1 (2010): 1–35.

Teaiwa, Teresia. "Reading Paul Gaugin's *Noa Noa* with Epeli Hau'ofa's *Kisses in the Nederends*: Militourism, Feminism, and the 'Polynesian' Body." In *Inside Out: Literature, Cultural Politics, and Identity in the New Pacific*, edited by Vilson Hereniko, 249–263. Lanham: Rowman & Littlefield, 1999.

Tiangco, Angela Louise R. "Selling Aloha: The Fight for Legal Protections Over Native Hawaiian Culture." *William & Mary Journal of Race, Gender, and Social Justice* 29, no. 2 (2022/2023): 489–518.

Trask, Haunani-Kay. "Fighting the Battle of Double Colonization.: The View of an Hawaiian Feminist." *Ethnies: Human Rights and Tribal Peoples (Special Issue: Renaissance in the Pacific)* 4, no. 8, 9, 10 (1989): 61–67.

Waldroup, Heather Leigh. "Traveling Images: Representations of the South Pacific from Colonial and Postcolonial Worlds." PhD diss., University of California, Santa Cruz, 2004.

White, Geoffrey M. "Disney's Pearl Harbor: National Memory at the Movies." *The Public Historian* 24, no. 4 (2002): 97–115.

Wrobel, David. "Prologue: Exceptionalism, Globalism, and Transnationalism—The West, America, and the World across the Centuries." In *The Popular Frontier: Buffalo Bill's Wild West and Transnational Mass Culture*, edited by Frank Christianson, 3–12. Norman: University of Oklahoma Press, 2017.

7

HOLY LANDSCAPES

In the colonial postcard, time is reorganized as spectacle; through the choreographing of fetish icons, history is organized into a single, linear narrative of progress. Photography became the servant of imperial progress.[1]

Anne McClintock

The genocide in Gaza made Palestine a necessary part of this study.[2] As I watched the violence unfold, first with the Hamas attacks on Israelis, then with massacres by the IOF (Israeli Occupation Forces) of children, pregnant women, infants, boys and men, journalists, and aid workers, I felt what many were experiencing—a sense of helplessness and disbelief. I remembered these words from Charles Taylor about how the post-WWII world had enshrined human rights for all people:

The whole development reaches its culmination in our time, in the period after the Second World War, in which the notion of rights that are prior to and untouchable by political structures becomes widespread—although they are now called "human" rather than "natural" rights.[3]

Somehow, these rights do not apply to Palestinians.

Mapping is often linked to tourism through the fulfillment of desires and myths about the past. This chapter examines Egypt and Palestine through racial ideologies, historical mythologies, and colonial nostalgia. Linked to French, British, and American colonial powers, Palestine and Egypt have landscapes that are ancient, spiritually powerful, and mystical. My aim is to suggest how these social imaginaries construct the

DOI: 10.4324/9781003361725-8

mystical landscapes that are familiar to us today in Egypt's ancient ruins and Palestine's religious sites.

For centuries, European history was identified with ancient Egypt, myths that became realized in the tourist experience. The focus of early tourism in Egypt on the ancient attractions, while bypassing everything Islamic, illustrates how Europeans viewed themselves in the long arc of history:

> For the tourist, the trajectory of civilization begins in Pharaonic Egypt, advances to Greco-Roman times, progresses to the European Renaissance, and culminates in modern Western culture, entirely bypassing the achievements of Islamic civilization.[4]

For colonial Europeans, Palestine was linked to a Christian nostalgia for the Holy Land. Simon Coleman suggests that Palestine was a land "that could be 'read' like a text," seen in the observations of Christians who traveled there and identified each place with the Bible.[5] Palestine also functioned as a nationalist project for many Christians in England; the transposition of Britain on Palestine included Biblical scholars like Isaac Watts (1674–1748), who "replaced the names of Israel and Judah with that of Britain" and "Jewish kings with those of Great Britain" in a Christianizing and Anglicizing of the Jewish texts.[6] Christian Zionism, known as Restorationism, the "belief in a literal return of the Jews to the Holy Land as fulfilment of Biblical prophecy and precondition of Christ's 1,000-year rule (Millenarianism)" was a popular idea reflected in travel accounts, art, and government policy during the Mandate period.[7] British Israelites included Restorationist ideologues like Rev. Thomas Reader, Charles Thompson, and Robert Tyron, who called Palestine "cursed" as long as it was occupied by Arabs.[8] Americans were also preoccupied with Biblical geography, which reflected American ideologies about the promised land and new Americans as the chosen people.[9]

The experiences of British and other tourists in Egypt and the Holy Land were often inspired by the Bible. Earlier forms of tourism also impacted these colonial-era journeys, including the Grand Tour of the eighteenth and nineteenth centuries and the emergence of companies like Thomas Cook & Son.[10] Part of a long history of overlaying a Christian topography of the Holy Land and its neighbors, seventeenth- and eighteenth-century maps included sites like the Garden of Eden, offering a vision of landscape that was both Christian and imaginary.[11] In Egypt, missionaries largely focused on the Copts through such organizations as the Church Missionary Society of Great Britain, which arrived in 1819, and the United Presbyterian Church of North America, which arrived several decades later (1854).[12] In Palestine, missionary efforts were often inseparable from colonial activities and the emergence of tourism.

The links between colonialism and tourism are apparent in both Egypt and Palestine. Timothy Mitchell explains how tourists to Egypt attempted to copy the experience they had at world's fairs and exhibitions, where elaborate dioramas were built of the Orient and "tours" of a fake "Cairo" were taken on donkeys.[13] These were imaginary colonial expeditions where Africans and islanders from the South Pacific were also displayed. Early modern tourists needed a viewing point. Egypt was the panopticon that was a critical part of the colonial experience. The minaret in general was used as a viewing tower, and the pyramids were scaled to survey the territory. Tourists even climbed on top of the Sphinx to have their photo taken and survey the landscape.[14] In Mitchell's words, "The point of view was not just a place set apart, outside the world or earlier. It was ideally a position from where, like the authorities in the panopticon, one could see and yet not be seen."[15]

Christian theology lies at the foundation of the tourist industry in Egypt and Palestine. This is an important difference from other places examined in this book. In the Himalayas, for example, the British imagination was more situated in Christian ideas about the sublime, related to the Bible but not directly to *Biblical places*. Thomas Cook viewed tourism in the Middle East as a missionary opportunity, offering tours designed for ministers.[16] One of many illustrations of the ways that Christian evangelism was embedded in tourism in Egypt and Palestine from the beginning is seen in missionary activities. Efforts to convert Jews predate the booming tourist industry of the 1880s. In 1795, the London Society for Promoting Christianity Amongst the Jews, known as the LJS, was founded, and after initially focusing on Britain and Africa, they set their sights on Palestine.[17] The LJS (London Jews' Society) established the Palestine Fund in 1825 and the "restoration" of the Jews to the Holy Land became a primary focus of its work.[18] In 1869, Thomas Cook offered a tour to witness the opening of the Suez Canal and visit Egypt and Palestine.[19] Like Cook's tours, which focused on the ancient world of the Egyptians and the Bible, there remains a fascination with the exotic and old cultures of Egypt and the Holy Land. As recently as the 1990s, tourists were visiting "living museums" set up near the pyramids where locals dressed up as ancient Egyptians, something visitors could do as well in a form of touristic cross-dressing.[20] The fixation on the past also led to tourist views of Palestinians, whose architecture, eating utensils, pottery, and technology were all described as primitive.[21]

The creation of *mystical landscapes* in Egypt and Palestine often linked the regions to other distant parts of "the East." One example is found in the writings of Madame Blavatsky, whose Theosophist ideas were a powerful part of early modern mysticism. For Blavatsky, the "Adepts" led both the "Brotherhood of Luxor" and the "Tibetan Brotherhood."[22] Egypt was a prime site for creating a new landscape, with its dangerous Nile full of crocodiles; the mysterious desert; and its ancient pyramids and temples filled with mystery, danger, and curses. Palestine's mystical landscapes had a religious power that came from its identification with Christianity, which was later used to establish a tourism industry that relied on the reenactment of ancient religious narratives like the Sermon on the Mount. The interest in Palestine from the colonial period to the present is seen in the huge corpus of documents, photos, and material objects that emerge from the Holy Land.

> Examples of such would include John Banvard's theatrical Holy Land panoramas, Frederick Church's Holy Land paintings, Robert Morris's sales of "Holy Land Cabinets" of bits of stone, wood, flowers, seeds, and other items, and even the large-scale Holy Land garden erected along the shores of the lake at the Chautauqua Assembly, the institution launched in 1874, according to the son of its founder John Heyl Vincent, as "a gigantic Palestine class."[23]

These productions helped to create the mystical landscape of the Holy Land.

The mystical landscapes of Egypt were born out of colonial map-making. Napoleon's invasion (1799), Muhammad Ali's rule in the 1830s, Turkish rule in the early 1840s, the Ottoman and British Mandate periods, and the establishment of Israel have all influenced the mapping of Palestine (and, to some extent, Egypt).[24] Egypt was considered part of the "Bible Lands," which were locations adjacent to Palestine or mentioned in the Bible.[25] The explosion of interest in the Holy Land and Bible Lands was directly tied to the growth of colonial powers in the nineteenth century. The number of works published in the 40 years following Edward Robinson's work was nearly equal to the number of studies published over the previous 1,500 years.[26] The scramble to control the land of the Bible was on and there was no way to stop it.

The Snake Charmer and the Imperial Gothic

Images of the mystical Orient are not only found in photographs of landscapes, paintings, literature, and cinema. Gérôme's painting *The Snake Charmer* (1879) and H. Rider Haggard's novel *She: A History of Adventure* (1887) also are examples of popular cultural forms that express common Orientalist themes—exotic lands, sexual danger, and the grotesque. The Orientalist painter Jean-Leon Gérôme is known for his portrayals of the more lascivious elements of Orientalist subjectivities. As noted in Chapter 3, the Society of French Orientalist Painters was inspired by encounters with the "fairyland" of the Orient and Africa experienced by its founder, Léonce Bénédite, whose views of the Orient, while being fantastic and full of wonder, were not necessarily focused on the violence and wild sensuality seen in the works of some French Orientalist painters.[27] Bénédite was not one of Gérôme's biggest fans, perhaps due to the painter's status as a self-made millionaire or differences in aesthetics or style.[28]

Naomi Rosenblatt has illustrated how the Orientalist aesthetic was a popular fixture among European, then American, consumers, creating a "material Orientalism" that reflected the "use of deep, warm colors, exotic patterns, and depictions of oases, harems, mosques, and bazaars."[29] Gérôme's painting is recognized today as the cover image for Said's classic 1978 book on Orientalism. The painting represents the fantasies of Europeans like Flaubert's characters Emma Bovary and Frédéric Moreau, whose daydreams include "harems, princesses, princes, slaves, veils, dancing girls and boys, sherberts, ointments, and so on."[30] *The Snake Charmer* was painted around 1879 and portrays an assortment of Orientalist images, but not in a way that makes sense. A work of muddled Orientalism, Gérôme's painting is focused on evoking a feeling of the exotic, as opposed to the documentation more common to the colonial scholar.[31] As Hossam Mahdy explains,

> The painting is an art-historical pastiche of the following: figures with Ottoman faces, dressed in Balkan costumes, watching a naked boy as a snake charmer (a scene unknown in Ottoman culture; the boy is standing on a prayer mat (a most unlikely behavior at the time); the wall is decorated with Iznik tile panels, with Qajar Persian or Indian armor hung on the wall.[32]

Orientalist literature also identified the dangers of Egypt and the larger North African region. Among these is Henry Rider Haggard's novel *She: A History of Adventure* (1887). Haggard is best known for his stories about lost worlds and peoples, perhaps most famously for *King Solomon's Mines* (1885). His novels were focused on the colonial scramble for Africa and were an inspiration for later works of adventure, including the character of Indiana Jones. *She* and its sequel, *Ayesha*, were focused on Egypt, a landscape viewed as both mystical and dangerous in the late nineteenth and early twentieth centuries.

She is one of several novels by Haggard that are part of the "lost race literature" genre.[33] Haggard, like other Brits of his generation, had a fascination with Africa and the Middle East that was complicated, expressing both racism and admiration for different cultures. He wrote not only of "splendidly barbaric" and "most strange" people and rituals, but also of the importance of civilizing the natives.[34] The villain in this novel is a monstrous woman, a queen who has lived over 2,000 years and who lords over a lost African civilization, using her special powers. The novel's African setting, its Arab characters, and its foreign monsters make it an example of the muddled Orientalism that often characterizes cultural forms of the East over the past couple of centuries.

She is a long novel at nearly 300 pages. Haggard was a popular "middle-brow" author who was not known for literary prose. As Daniel Dougherty writes, "Despite his limitations as a writer, he was and remains popular, and many of his novels have never been out of print."[35] The story follows the adventures of Horace Holly and the young man he has been asked to raise from the age of five, Leo Vincey. Leo's ancestors are connected to the evil monster queen, a connection that begins to be uncovered on his twenty-fifth birthday through the opening of an Eastern box of treasures that includes a chest with sphynxes and a collection of mysterious artifacts. Amenartas is the key to Leo's past, a princess who is linked to the passing of a pot sherd from father to son and the reason for the adventure undertaken in the novel.[36]

Haggard's novels often emphasize the occult and the belief in previous lives. Haggard was known to participate in séances in which he had visions of his life as an ancient man in Britain, a Black man, and an Egyptian (a vision he had twice).[37] In the novel, we see his fascination with previous lives through Leo, whom the queen, Ayesha, believes to be a reincarnation of her lover Kallikrates, who she killed in a jealous rage. Kallikrates and his wife's son are Leo's ancestors from 2,000 years ago. *She* is focused on avenging this murder and killing the queen of the secret kingdom, which is populated by African cannibals. Haggard includes visuals of foreign scripts and other visual details in the book, including drawings of mysterious letters, images of the sherd of Amenartas, a partial glyph, and various instructions.[38] The novel is a mishmash of exotic and fantastic events and details, including "destructive storms, lost civilizations, supernatural murders, and caverns full of beautifully preserved corpses."[39]

The two adventurers take two colonial servants (an Arab and their servant from England, who was Leo's au pair from the age of five) and encounter a variety of wonders that include a lost race of people, the Amahaggers, who guide them to the kingdom of the monster queen, a place called Kôr, an underground land, where the queen immolates herself and dies (temporarily; she is brought back in the sequel, *Ayesha*). The death of Ayesha, described over a few pages, transforms her beauty into a monstrous spectacle, for she ages 2,000 years in a matter of minutes. She is described as a monkey, a tortoise, and parchment. The monster she turns into is the opposite of her appearance in the preceding nearly 300 pages—a beautiful and veiled woman who becomes a horrendous creature.[40]

The book contains numerous Orientalist details such as the language that appears in the evil kingdom on its columns, which appeared more like "Chinese" than any other language.[41] The inclusion of ancient languages in a visual form within Imperial Gothic, adventure, and other colonial-era genres was not uncommon. Stoker's mummy tale, *The Jewel of Seven Stars* (1903), includes reproductions of hieroglyphs.[42] This is one of many texts that present Egypt as a mystical landscape. The figure of the mummy, who becomes an object of terror in both literature and film, is tied to Egypt's desert, a place full of mystery, curses, and ancient religious power.

Scholars have suggested that these references, the monster queen's wish to rule in Europe, and the frequent use of "yellow," may reflect the anxieties about Chinese bodies, foreign threats, and the "yellow peril" extant when Haggard was writing the novel.[43] In *She*, Haggard provides a fictionalized treatment of the colonial male's fantasies, which include a fascination with Africa, the women of the Orient, and their dangerous sexual energy. The importance of philology in the novel also suggests colonial anxieties about the language of the foreign Other. Ayesha is a master of languages and is more adept at them than Holly. She is also identified as being racially superior to Arabs because she is more closely related to the "mother Syriac" that is now extinct.[44]

The monster's end is also significant within the colonial geography of the Orient. Ayesha's status as "parchment" relegates her to a distant past, far from the modernity identified with the British and their colonial adventures. She has been found, she has been destroyed, and she is known, much like the rest of the world that has been "discovered" by the British, French, Germans, and others. Ayesha represents the siting and control of the world, so often attached to colonial geography. She wears a veil but is revealed through her destruction. In the end, colonial power is victorious against the African/Oriental Other.

Pyramids and Jesus

Egypt is a mystical landscape, thanks in part to its popularity with Orientalists, whose travels to Cairo, the desert, and Egypt's ancient wonders helped to establish it as a site of power and magic. Gérard Nerval (the pen name of Gérard Labrunie) was an important French Orientalist who traveled to Egypt in 1842. His writings helped to establish the idea of Egypt as a place of intense spiritual renewal. As one of his biographer's notes, "The mystic East would provide him the magic cure for his physical and mental ills. He would . . . find there perchance the inner harmony he had lost in the morass of modern life."[45] Said describes how Nerval's presentation of Egypt and the entire Orient is "like the veils he sees in Cairo," a concealment of "a deep rich fund of female sexuality."[46]

Viewed as a place of decay and backwardness, Egypt is the focus of numerous studies on how colonial discourse attempted to validate its French and British occupation. In 1892, Milner's *England in Egypt* explained that British interference in the country's affairs was "not exercised to impose an uncongenial foreign system upon a reluctant people" but rather was "a force making for the triumph of the simplest ideas of honesty, humanity, and justice."[47] This attitude was strongly held among the British, with few detractors.

Among the few anti-colonial voices was E.M. Forster, who wrote that the Europeans were

> aliens in Egypt and have come to exploit it; they despise Oriental ways, they are agnostics or Christians who have no sympathy for Islam, and they feel for the natives a fear that too often proceeds from a bad conscience.[48]

Egypt was linked to other places in the European imagination, including other parts of Africa.[49] The myth of Great Zimbabwe insisted a white people built the great African city, including claims that the massive bird carvings at the site were of Assyrian, Phoenician, or Egyptian origin.[50] Europeans also claimed that Hamitic people, descendants of Noah, built the great pyramids, as Africans could not possibly have had such an advanced culture.[51] The excavation of mummies was used to try and prove these theories; it included measuring over 100 Egyptian skulls, resulting in the decapitated bodies being used as benches to sit on.[52] All of these efforts were directed at finding evidence of white, or European, Africans. They represent the failed attempts to map Africa as a white space, attempts invented so that white settlers could be seen as resettling their land.[53]

The imaginative geography of Egypt also included gendered maps. Travel writings are also well known among historians and scholars of religion for their sensual content. For many, the landscape of the Orient was likened to a woman to be conquered; some accounts even describe geographical features as breasts and likened journeys into deserts and waterways as sexual experiences. Homoeroticism included the desires of European men like Gustave Flaubert, whose *Voyage en Egypte* included descriptions of his night with a prostitute, the "feeling of her stomach against my buttocks . . . her mound warmer than her stomach, heated me like a hot iron," and his plans for sex with a young boy, "You reserve the bath for yourself . . . and skewer the lad in one of the rooms."[54] These kinds of desires, jarring and at times, revolting, are common themes in travel writing and when juxtaposed with the theological mapping of the region, illustrate how the landscapes of Egypt and Palestine were subjected to all kinds of imaginative techniques.

As discussed earlier, in addition to colonial desire, the explosion of tourism in the region reflects European and American beliefs in the origins of Christianity and the desire to travel abroad. In the past, the Holy Land was the goal of Christian pilgrims, who viewed everything through a religious lens. In the nineteenth century,

> Various rituals, such as kissing the ground or washing the feet upon setting foot in the Holy Land often marked the passage from the secular to the holy. During their stay, the pilgrims focused solely on Palestine's sacred, religious treasures.[55]

Egypt was linked to these desires in part due to its proximity to Palestine, but also because of its status as an important site in Biblical narratives, what was called a "Bible land."

Modern tourism can be more complex than the religious pilgrimages of the past, which were focused solely on religious sites. What was once a purely religious journey became one that involved a wish to experience different cultures and a desire to educate oneself.[56] Historians of tourism have shown how the Grand Tour of the sixteenth century led to the creation of an industry that did cater to include not only the wealthy, but also the middle class, resulting in the establishment of companies like Thomas Cook and American Express, both of which included organized tours of the Middle East.[57] Tourism may be a form of pilgrimage, but it is also an activity with strong colonial overtones. As Joe Bandy writes,

> This is accompanied by a dramatic expansion of (neo/post) colonialism, in which the ambassador or invader from the overdeveloped world is no longer only a merchant or a multinational seeking resources and labor, but also a tourist seeking to gaze at the differences of the natural and primitive Other.[58]

Modern tourists of Egypt and Palestine, while they may have had religious interests, often visited Cairo, Jerusalem, and other famous sites as part of a large Mediterranean tour.[59]

The ways in which locals (Arabs, Turks, Persians, and others) and Europeans viewed their environment were vastly different. In Michelle Woodward's study of Orientalist and modernist photography, she examines two family photography studios—the Sébah family in Istanbul and the Bonfil family in Beirut, illustrating the differences between subjects who were unposed and posed and environments that were ordered and disordered.[60] The Sébah's portraits "emphasize order and modernity within indigenous historical structures," while the Bonfil's, as Europeans who adopted Beirut as their home, communicated a "vision of a static, romantically traditional world whose people could be described through familiar character-types from the Bible or tales from *1001 Nights*."[61]

Mystical landscapes were a tableau on which colonial powers imposed a Christian map that sought to replace the indigenous or local ways of understanding place. Europeans had a particular view of Egypt and Palestine that insisted Arabs, Bedouins, and others, including Arab Jews, were incapable of ruling themselves. In his book on Egypt, the First Earl of Cromer, Evelyn Baring, describes Arabs as "wanting in the logical faculty," "too apathetic" and "too ignorant," "emotional, ignorant, and credulous," and easily led away by "agitators."[62] Egyptians and all Arabs needed to be ruled over. In Egypt, one result was a new landscape that reflected the colonial gaze of the desert, pyramids, and other ancient wonders. In Palestine, these ideas were extended to Arabs and others, including Arab Jews, who were subjected to European hygiene programs to make them good Israeli citizens.

Egypt and Palestine are mystical landscapes created out of an imaginative geography that is unapologetically European, Christian, and colonial. The links between colonial possession and tourism are more than apparent in the history of Egypt. As Fekri Hassan explains, "Ancient Egypt was essential for the new colonial paradigm because by possessing the antiquities of Egypt, the colonial powers inherited the claim to cultural hegemony."[63] Tourism in Egypt is linked to this project through transportation, Orientalism, and the early tour companies. Hassan also wants us to see how the fact that "ancient Egypt was romanticized as a land of mystery" is part of a larger European project of identifying with the Roman Empire.[64] This was an especially popular attitude among the French, as demonstrated by their colony in Algeria, and the British, who saw themselves as linked to Palestine.

Orientalism's Scopic Regime

Orientalism has a strong presence in this book, and as I have argued in other chapters, it is useful in studying the lands that comprise Europe's fictive "East." The Arabian desert became transposed onto different geographies, seen in the use of *simoom* and *haboob* to describe dust storms in the American Southwest.[65] The colonial imagination does, at times, cross boundaries; as numerous scholars have argued, the Orient is an idea that finds itself in all kinds of strange places.

Consumption is a critical piece of the history of mapping. The ways that Europeans thought about the East were informed by not only the Bible, of course, but also a rich mythology about exotic lands far away that held mystical power. While Orientalism was certainly a critical part of this vision, it also involved an ancient past that was observable and surveyable. The belief that European men had ownership over the world was reiterated in numerous Orientalist texts.

For example, in Loti's *Aziyadé*, he surveys the land like a good colonial agent: "My house in Pera was situated in a secluded spot overlooking the Golden Horn and the distant panorama of the Turkish city."[66] Later in the novel, Loti writes, "I'm free to go wherever I choose," suggesting that for the foreigner living in Ottoman Turkey, the territory is his to explore.[67] The role of consumptive Orientalism, where the colonial agent or tourist figuratively consumed girls and women, is another part of the historical record. Among the examples is the genre of romantic literature that includes the work of Pierre Loti (Louis-Marie-Julien Viaud) and his novel, *Aziyadé* (1879), detailing the author's affair with a harem girl. *Aziyadé* follows the plot of his other novels, detailing sexual escapades with exotic girls and women and reflects Loti's fixation in his private life on the Orient. As Sharif Gemie has written, Loti took on the appearance and identity of a Turkish or other Muslim from the Orient, wearing their clothing, speaking Arabic and Persian, and decorating his home in Rochefort in an Arab style.[68]

Perhaps there is no better example of the intersection of Orientalism with academics within the cataloging and classification of Egypt than the Orientalist scholar Edward Lane. Born in Hereford in 1801, he became one of the most important voices in the mapping of Egypt as a subject for other scholars to study and for tourists to visit.[69] Most famous for his *Description of Egypt* (also known as *Notes and Views in Egypt and Syria*) and *Manners and Customs of the Modern Egyptians*, Lane went on to become an Arabic linguist whose lexicon *Madd al-Qamus* illustrated his excellent command of the language.[70]

Travelogues and first-hand accounts by colonial scholars were an important part of the Orientalist project. It was also seen in the works by artists and writers, even people who never left London or Paris. As Ali Behdad has argued, photography was an instrumental part of this project, offering an experience that helped to formulate a particular idea about the East and its wonders.

> The Orientalist photograph has a supplementary function, providing the viewer with a visually objective experience of "the Orient," otherwise unavailable to most people. Orientalist photography, therefore, neither displaced its painterly counterpart nor did it outdate its textual precursor, but rather joined them to further the project of Orientalism as a dominant mode of representation.[71]

In Egypt, photography played an important role in staging the country for the public. Derek Gregory describes this as the "importance of a visual thematic in colonial appropriation," which included practices such as uncovering monuments to create the best sketch.[72] Photography and artwork, including etchings and drawings, were eventually used to create a vision of Egypt being the origins of a "distinctively European history."[73] Thus, Egypt was remapped as an ancient European space—an empty landscape with no local inhabitants. The "empty spaces" on these maps, much like what took place in Kenya and later in the American West, allowed Europeans to create a landscape that held mystical promise. As Derek Gregory explains, "Early photographers tacitly represented Egypt as a vacant space awaiting its (re) possession and reclamation by Europe."[74]

This gaze, which scholars often refer to as the *Oriental gaze,* or the *consuming gaze,* is found in an almost endless number of practices and products related to Egypt and Palestine. There were exhibitions, the founding of museums focused on the Orient (or another part of the world that had been surveyed and was now controlled by a European power), and the Orientalist texts that could be found on the streets of London and Paris; there were also products that included the "Turkish shawl" and the "turban"-like headdresses; Oriental costumes worn by men; and the use of Oriental motifs, people, and places in advertising.[75]

In Palestine, Orientalism was deployed against the Oriental Jew, with claims that they were filthy and unhealthy. Palestine's Jews were viewed as "objects of hygienic transformation," for, as one British Mandate physician remarked, "We are here to bring the West . . . *not only to ourselves*, but to the entire backward Orient, which must rise to a clean hygienic life."[76] Zionist programs of hygiene and cleanliness reflected the ways that British travelers viewed local Arabs, for "travelers were warned to keep a civil and aesthetic distance from Middle Easterners and their reportedly-barbaric habits" and to even "look away" from them.[77]

Orientalism sees everything through the lens of European (and eventually, American) cultural narcissism. The Orient only exists as a self-referential tool that sees the region that exists *for the West*. As Aiken explains, "Orientalism is a discourse, in Foucauldian terms, and here that discourse can be seen in the process of self-construction; a circular, self-referential discursive regime is constituting itself around the scholarship of self and others."[78]

Edward Said was not particularly interested in the role of scriptural geography, apart from the focus on redemption of the land from the Arabs.[79] As he writes in *Culture and Imperialism* (1993),

> On the one hand, one can with any other than a political or ideological justification speak of the modern "Arab mind," with its alleged propensity to violence, its culture of shame, the historical overdetermination of Islam, its political semantics, its degeneration *vis-à-vis* Judaism and Christianity?[80]

However, he was interested in geographical imaginaries and their location in systems of power, and above all, in the colonial apparatus of agents, writers, artists, and scholars serving the interests of empire.

Orientalism includes numerous fantasies, some of which have been explored in earlier chapters. The mystical power of Tibet and Nepal is one example of the imagination's role in constructing the geography of the Orient as a site of difference and exoticism. In Egypt and Palestine, these fantasies are also part of a vast literary corpus. One example is found in the writings of Christian ministers and lay people who visited the East. In his visit to Damascus, Josias Leslie Porter, an Irish Presbyterian priest, remarked, "It resembles, in fact, some scene in fairyland; and one feels, on beholding it, that that glowing descriptions in the 'Arabian Nights' were not mere pictures of fantasy."[81]

The claims of Arabs living in the past, another example of the denial of coeval time in the colonial record, were used to argue that the disintegration of the Orient was due to the Muslim inability to think, write, or study history. Jay Mary Arthur describes this practice as a kind of statement of knowledge coming into being, what she calls the "declaration of a *terra nullius* of knowledge."[82] In the case of Egypt and Palestine, Orientalism describes the attitudes of Europeans as the creators of knowledge. The ways that travelers approached the Holy Land were complex. Protestant Christians had several competing concerns when they visited the Holy Land. They had to balance the need for distance with the proximity they had to the sacred, which was worsened by anxieties about other Christians (Catholics and Orthodox Christians) whose practices included more direct access to the Divine.[83] These anxieties drove Protestants to do uncivilized things. In Trollope's novel *The Bertrams*, travelers have a picnic on the Tomb of St. James and at one point, Miss Todd exclaims, "I declare, these tombs are very nice tables, are they not?"[84]

The Orientalist imagination about Egypt is expressed in the images created by travelers and artists who visited Cairo, the pyramids, and the Nile. Photographers like Douglas Sladen prepared tourists for what they would see in cities like Cairo, which was viewed as being an example of the pre-modern humans who lived on streets that were "low" and "native" and "unspoiled."[85] Fabian's denial of coevalness was expressed as a matter of fact, for these encounters between the modern European or American and the medieval Arab denied that Muslims lived in the same time, or world, as those from the Occident. Mitchell's analysis of the impact of the exhibition and the world's fair on early tourists to Egypt reflects this denial of time. When tourists sought a view of the landscape below, from a minaret or the top of a pyramid, they were attempting to re-create pictures they had seen back home.

The way travelers described Arabs was often as monsters—nonhuman or subhuman characters who occupied lands under colonial control. In Florence Nightingale's travel writings on Egypt, she described the local Arabs in Alexandria as "an intermediate race between the monkey and the man," and her impressions of the Nile included describing people as "choosing to upon the ground like reptiles" and "like beasts," a tree as "the only thing human," humans living in "nests" and "baying like jackals," and other Arabs moving "like lizards."[86] The Nile was not only a site of wonder, horror, and danger, but it was also a self-contained waterway of mini-nations, created by tourists who flew their nation's flag, created a racialized order of servants, and transformed the *dahabeah* into a little colonial universe.[87] Derek Gregory describes it as "stage directions and scriptings" that transformed the boats into viewing platforms and Egypt into a "transparent space."[88] For the tourist, the Nile was a moving panopticon.

Egypt was described as a place in disarray due to its control by the Arabs, with only glimpses of its former magnificence available for the traveler to observe or experience. For Florence Nightingale, Cairo was a city situated in the mystique of the *Arabian Nights*. As Derek Gregory puts it, "She is indeed dissolving history into the space of mythology—into the space of Arabian nights—and she later underlines this distinction: 'Cairo is not Egyptian,' she announced, 'it is Arabian.'"[89]

The tourist industry was largely developed by J.M. Cook, who conducted tours of Egypt, cruises of the Nile, and in Europe and the United States utilized the practice of blocking out hotel rooms to save their clients' money (an idea that their competitor, Henry Glaze, invented), developed the "circular note" (a precursor to the coupon), and set up a ticket agency system.[90] Egypt offered an extremely lucrative opportunity as "a large territory that could be developed as a closed-enclave tourism economy."[91] Within 30 years (1872–1900), the numbers of tourists visiting Egypt grew from 400 to over 50,000 per year, and as the interest in Egypt boomed, so did tomb robbing and the plundering of resources.[92] Tourists were mostly interested in Egypt's ancient ruins and sights, not its Islamic culture. Like other places in the Orient, the locals were seen as either disturbances to the colonial vision of the landscape or evidence of a culture stuck in the distant past.

Egypt's status as a popular tourist site is linked to Egyptology, Orientalism, and the production of consumable goods in Europe and America. As Derek Gregory has shown, due to the pyramids and other archaeological wonders, the importance of "sights and views" and of the landscapes viewed atop pyramids and other high points (a desert version of the Himalayas in terms of its scopic quality) was "made visible as a panoramic totality."[93] These practices show how the scopic regime of colonialism was linked to tourism.

Holy Land Imaginations

Scriptural geography helped to form ideas of the Holy Land in the Christian imagination, creating a vision of Palestine that remains powerful today. As Edwin James Aiken has argued, "These texts are both created from geographical imagination and subsequently serve to help create geographical imaginaries in others: they are both products of and productive of geographic imaginaries."[94] This process relied on the use of secondary texts, which were often highly imaginative. A strongly modern project, the authors of scriptural geography viewed the Orient as a place fallen from grace, in disarray, a wasteland of crumbling monuments that were disappointing to the tourist.[95] This is why Arab and other indigenous voices were excluded from the literature of Orientalism. It was part of the colonial logic—to exclude these voices because they were incapable of speaking for themselves was part of the "Western progress that must be imposed on a chronologically static society."[96]

One of the key myths in the construction of Israel as a modern state is that Arabs are not worthy of the land. This claim emerged in the Orientalist era, and as we shall see, it is a critical part of Zionist propaganda even though it originated much earlier. When Christian Orientalists were writing about the Holy Land, they were using the imagination. Many of these writers never left Europe, yet we find words like decay, forgotten, and ruins. As Aiken writes, this was part of a system of discourse that helped to rationalize later periods of colonial occupations: "In just a way the holy landscape of the present is subservient to holy landscape's biblical past. The contemporary, largely Muslim, inhabitants of the Holy Land are viewed as inferior to the population as imagined in the past."[97]

In George Adam Smith's writings, he uses phrases like "crumbling precipices and corries choked with debris" and "Except for the blue water . . . it is a dreary world" to suggest a land that has not fulfilled its glorious promise.[98] These "negative stereotypes," to borrow Alan Dowty's phrase, illustrated the ways that Christian travelers in the Holy Land resented Muslim control of a land that they viewed as mapped by Christian experience and history. Chateaubriand characterized the Muslims as despotic and Islam as "a religion hostile to civilization," foreshadowing the ways Palestinians and Arab Muslims are characterized today.[99]

Sacred geography also used photography to confirm the Biblical record through a cataloging of places and incidents. This project involved a recovery of a "sacred terrain" that identified Christianity with the topography of Palestine.[100] However, this was not only a project focused on mapping Biblical land. The British viewed themselves as linked to the Holy Land. The surveys conducted in the 1860s "mapped British presence on a land over which the British believed they had dominion by right of a spiritual connection intimately tied to their national identity."[101] At the time of these geographical studies tied to the Bible, Palestinians had a sense of their national boundaries, which under the Ottomans not only comprised the southern part of *bilad al-Sham* (Greater Syria) but also represented the ancestral home of Arabs who had lived in the region for many centuries and already had a growing intelligentsia.[102]

One mapping strategy used in Palestine by the British was to copy the movements of the Hebrews, a practice seen in the *Ordnance Survey of the Peninsula of Sinai*, where the British party followed "in the footsteps of the ancient Israelites."[103] The photographs from this expedition not only told this story, but also documented the occupation of the land by the British and the indigenous loss of the territory to them.[104] As Ben-Arieh points out, in most nineteenth-century studies, the Arab populations were minimized or simply erased.[105]

Tourism in Palestine was largely undeveloped in the nineteenth century, falling short of European expectations for traveling abroad. In the late 1860s, there were only a handful of acceptable hotels for tourists, including the Mediterranean Hotel (about which there is conflicting information and at least three locations), the Melita, and the Rosenthal.[106] Travelers often characterized the older sites as disintegrating, ugly, or somehow lacking in aesthetics, suggesting that the Orient was in decay, a strong theme at the time. One visitor to the Rosenthal Hotel described the Church of the Holy Sepulcher as having a "clumsy dome" and the homes that surrounded the hotel as having a "monotonous flatness."[107]

Other travel accounts of Jerusalem reflected the Romantic Orientalism popular with many Europeans and Americans of the nineteenth and twentieth centuries. Critical to these views was the idea of a land located in the past (Christianity) that could simply not be controlled by the present (a Muslim-majority Palestine). Travelers, scholars, and religious pilgrims ruminated about the landscape as if it were their own, insisting on a Christian mapping of a Muslim land and ignoring the very real ways these religions were linked. Within the writings about the Holy Land as a Christian space, interrupted by Muslim bodies, there was also a strong tradition of ridiculing the sites and traditions of Eastern Christians, people who, from the Protestant point of view, were bizarre. James Silk Buckingham expressed what others felt when visiting the Church of the Holy Sepulcher, which he called "a temple combining the most surprising mixture of credulity and imposition, devotion and wickedness, that has ever issued from any one source since the world began."[108]

Mapping Palestine

Palestine has been subjected to a rich set of fantasies, many of which are linked to Israeli occupation and settlements. However, the mapping of Palestine as part of Europe is older and more complex. Its colonial forms are found not only within Israeli policies, but also in the British and American understandings of a place linked to Biblical and territorial imaginings. These ideas are a critical part of understanding Palestine today. It is important to understand how Palestine came to be—as both a place and an idea.

While the modern state of Israel is linked to Jewish Zionists, the role of evangelical Christians in its founding was critical. Above all, the modern mapping of Palestine is a Christian and colonial project, with Zionism jumping in at the endgame once the territory had been colonized by the British. Simon Coleman describes how the colonial gaze is really the gaze of a Christian god: "The Holy Land is not only a land whose history is deeply implicated with that of the West; it also provides a landscape wherein the gaze of the believer is subordinated to that of the 'sacred eyes' of Christ."[109] Such an optic leaves no room for anything or anyone else, including the Palestinian people.

Christian Zionism is an extremely important part of the history of Palestine and Israel. In May 1865, at Westminster Abbey, in the room named after Jerusalem, the Palestine Exploration Fund was established.[110] As Mohammad Sakhnini writes,

> The establishment of the Palestine Exploration Fund, which surveyed the land and its population, and also the rise of evangelical fervor in Britain calling for restoring the Jews to the land of their ancestors, as Bar-Yosef has shown, reflected the influential role of Britain in the region, especially in the period after the British government approved of the creation of the office of British Consul in Jerusalem, one fronted in 1838 by William Tanner Young, a fervent Christian Zionist.[111]

Here, we see how mapping the territory of Palestine was linked directly to the projects of British colonialism, Christian evangelism, anti-Semitism, and Zionism.

IMAGE 7.1   Photo of Group of Explorers, Judea District, Palestine, 1867.

Source: photo courtesy of Palestine Exploration Fund/Bridgeman Images

The opening of the Suez Canal in 1869 increased interest in Palestine due to its strategic importance.[112] British and other colonial tourists viewed Arabs as relics of the past and aliens in a Jewish and Christian land. In the book *Earthly Footsteps of the Man of Galilee* (1894), the Muslim presence in the Holy Land is attributed to the failure of Jews and Christians to observe the covenants in the Bible.[113]

The Ottomans viewed Palestine as part of the *Shami* territories, but *Filastin* referred to the Holy Land and, according to scholars, it went beyond the borders controlled by the empire.[114] The *Filastin Risalesi* included the administrative units of Galilee (Akka), Nablus, and Jerusalem, and reflected both religious ideas of the Holy Land and concerns over the colonial ambitions of the British, French, and others who had aims to take over their lands.[115]

The end of WWI brought the dissolution of the Ottoman Empire, which introduced new ways of understanding Palestine as a distinct entity. During the Great War, Palestine's geographical position was "between Ottoman Bilad al-Sham and British-controlled Egypt," but, with British colonial rule, came a new set of concerns about how Palestine would be defined and controlled.[116] Nadi Abusaada documents the transition of Palestinians from looking to the model of a Greater Syria to their realization that Palestine needed to be a distinct national space (a result, in part, of the British endorsement of Zionism).[117] Palestinians had complex views of a national geography and their place within it, but they consistently identified as Palestinians and with the land on which they and their ancestors lived. The Arabic word for patriotism, *wataniyya*, is linked to the Arabic word for home, *watan*. Despite the shifts in Palestinians' own geographical imaginary, Palestinians viewed the land as something they were connected to through their ancestral ties to the land, their homes, and their farms. In 1923, the British civil administration was established in Palestine, and the Palestinian Revolts took place in 1936–1939.[118] These events made it even more clear to Palestinians that they would need to defend their land against occupation, British interests, and European settlers.

At the same time that British, American, and Zionist efforts to remake Palestine into a European space were afoot, Arab Palestinians and their allies launched projects like the Arab Exhibition, which featured women artists like Nicola Saig and was held in the Palace Hotel, which had an Arab style.[119] These exhibitions, the first in 1933 and the second in 1934, featured Arab products from across the region, but perhaps more importantly, they offered a venue where the concepts of unity (*wihda*), independence (*istiqlal*), and economic rebirth (*nahda iqtisadiya*) were used to advocate for the public display of Arab culture.[120] While the tide of colonialism and European immigration under the British was strong, Palestinians made public efforts to argue for their voice. While this was taking place, tourism to Palestine was expanding beyond the religious class, artists, and the wealthy. In 1934, the

Worker's Travel Association (WTA) began offering tours of Palestine, which also included trips to Egypt and opened the region to more travelers, including those who wanted a "holiday."[121]

Mapping is not limited to the drawings of cartographers. In Palestine, the efforts by the British to project a Christian identity upon a land that was inhabited by numerous religious groups is apparent at numerous sites. The museum of antiquities in Jerusalem is one example of how Ottoman and Islamic cultures were erased and replaced with a European one that was deemed superior and modern. The museum changed from being the *Ottoman Museum* (1901–1917) to the *British Palestine Museum of Antiquities* (1921–1930) and then to the *Palestine Archaeological Museum* (1930–1935); today, it is known as the Rockefeller Museum.[122]

When Colonel Ronald Storrs was appointed the Military Governor of Jerusalem in April 1918, he "viewed his role in Jerusalem as part of the grander civilizing mission of returning the holy land to the rule of Christians," a project that included naming places after crusaders, such as Coeur de Lion street.[123] The theme of rescuing Jerusalem, and all of Palestine, from the Turks and recovering the damage done by their mishandling of everything from government systems to antiquities' collections was expressed in Storrs's writings, in which he made remarks like "The Psalms of David and a cloud of unseen witnesses seemed to inspire our work."[124] He also had moments of doubt (and humor) about the Zionist cause. At one point he remarked, "Two hours of Arab grievances drive me into the synagogue, while after an intensive course of Zionist propaganda, I am prepared to embrace Islam."[125]

Storrs appointed the British architect Charles Ashbee as the Civic Advisor and Secretary of the Pro-Jerusalem Society, whose photographs (often panoramas) included views of the Old City, with plans including the destruction of the Ottoman clock tower and which either erased Arabs or rendered them as "ghostly silhouettes" in the Biblical landscape.[126] The handling of the museum's artifacts also illustrates the ways in which the British made assumptions about the competencies of the Ottomans. The first Keeper of the Museum, W.J.T. Phythian-Adams (1888–1967), wrongly assumed there was no catalog and proceeded to re-catalog each item, a laborious task that was unnecessary.[127] When the museum opened in 1921, the address by High Commissioner Lord Herbert Samuel referred to the superiority of British academic methods and the reminder that the museum was "a mission of the salvation of the past."[128]

The efforts to reimagine Palestine as a European space include Zionist visions that predate the founding of Israel. One place this is seen is in hotel architecture, design, and décor from the British Mandate period, which include a sense of "utopian national aspirations" that was often adapted from the Jewish homes that had been lost, what Daniella Ohad Smith describes where she writes, "the homes of Jewish immigrants in Palestine were closely tied to what they had left behind."[129] Linked to the Zionist efforts to create a national tourism industry that would reshape the concept of Palestine, the hotel and the home were spaces in which style reflected the tensions between colonial, Orientalist, and nationalist visions. In the 1930s, Zionist architects created a version of modernism that showed a preference for European minimalism and rejected local design and decorative conventions.[130]

Tourism was a Zionist project that often involved the renaming of places and the creation of new maps that sought to establish the vision of a Jewish topography on a multireligious land. Zionist maps of Jerusalem often depicted Jewish neighborhoods and sites in greater detail and relegated places like the Old City to a smaller part of a map, seen in Steimansky's 1941/1942 map.[131] The 1935 film *To a New Life*, a project that Israeli scholar Kobi Cohen-Hattab called "a model of celluloid propaganda," and similar work, featured images of Jewish immigrants, the Strauss Medical Center, and Hebrew University, all symbols of the Zionist imagination of what Palestine would become.[132] Tourist materials created by the Yishuv, often with the aid of Americans and Europeans, reinterpreted the landscape of Palestine as Jewish and often erased or substantially mitigated the Palestinians. In one brochure published in 1935, 8 out of 63 photographs focused on Arab Palestine and over a third of its illustrations focused on new building programs associated with Yishuv/Zionist settlers.[133]

Hotels expressed a variety of imaginative geographies ranging from the Biblical to Zionist nationalism. The King David Hotel, which opened in 1931, was designed by Swiss architects and managed by Swiss hoteliers who created an environment that projected numerous Biblical themes, an evocation of "the Jerusalem of the Bible."[134] The lobby included motifs of the shield of Solomon, a relief of the seven fruits and grains of ancient Israel, and a menorah, and the reading room of the hotel reflected the Temple, complete with cedar overlaid with gold, referencing I Kings 6:22.[135] The *Arab Salon*, which was the smoking room, was the one (non-Jewish) Orientalist exception, a hodgepodge of Islamic, Moorish, and other designs.[136]

There were also hotels modeled upon a Zionist modernist style, including the short-lived *Eretz Yisre'eli* style (a blend of indigenous and European motifs) and the Modernist style, which was reflected in the Eden Hotel, opened in the 1920s.[137] The Eden Hotel reflected the aesthetic of the European Jewish home, which was identified with Josef Frank and the aesthetic of the ordinary.[138] Eden made no references to Jerusalem, either historical or contemporary, and offered the Jewish tourist "an Occidental haven from Oriental Jerusalem in its clean surfaces, open spaces" and other qualities.[139] Jerusalem's Jewish hotels often reflected the European culture of Zionist immigrants, with names like Café Europa and the San Remo Hotel.[140]

Cleanliness was a central feature of the Zionist project, which viewed Muslim Palestine as backward and Zionism as a force of modernity and progress. Ironically, Jews and Muslims, who many Christians have viewed as being coconspirators for centuries and as Orientals for several centuries, were distinguished within the Zionist project—one medieval, dirty, and inept (the Arab Oriental) and the other, modern, clean, and progressive (the Jew). As Sarah Irving explains, "The distancing of the 'oriental' from Jewishness—itself seen by many non-Jewish Westerners as intimately bound up with the Orient—was necessary for the articulation of the modern Zionist project."[141] Jerusalem was the focus of Arab Palestinian tourism and was linked to nationalist aspirations and the defense of their lands. Zionist tourist activity had a larger scope, developing hotels at the Sea of Galilee and the Jezreel Valley, where the Jewish focus on development and modernism was coupled with the Christian interest in the Biblical past.[142] Jasmin Daam describes how these projects "brought the Bible to life."[143]

The Israeli Imagination

It is important to understand the character of Palestine before the state of Israel changed its demographics and landscape into a dominantly European and American space. The population was dominated by Arab Muslims, Sunni in orientation, but there were also substantial Christian and Jewish minorities, including Jewish communities in cities like Jerusalem, Hebron, and Safed.[144] These were Arab Jews, who became new members of the Israeli state and were viewed as uncivilized because they were not European. Ella Shohat writes about her experience as an Arab Jew:

> Stripped of our history, we have been forced by our no-exit situation to repress our collective nostalgia, at least within the public sphere. The pervasive notion of "one people" reunited in their ancient homeland actively deauthorizes any affectionate memory of life before Israel.[145]

Nur Masalha has shown how Palestine was Hebraicized through Israelis adopting Hebrew names and changing place names from Arabic to Hebrew, such as Jabal Ideid becoming Har Karkom.[146] When the former Deputy Mayor of Jerusalem (also a historian, a reminder that colonial agents and academics are often indistinguishable) Meron Benvenisti Herbraicized the Arab names on the map, he effectively did a cut-and-paste of Arab superimposed by Jewish ones.[147] Benvenisti wrote in his memoir: "Like all immigrant societies, we attempted to erase all alien names. . . . The Hebrew map of Israel constitutes one stratum in my consciousness, underlaid by the stratum of the previous Arab map."[148] Israeli identity is also predicated on a difficult relationship with the Arab Jew. As Ella Shohat has argued, these Jews are "a diasporic stain to be 'cleansed' through assimilation" and rejected due to their "savage" and "primitive" character.[149]

The colonial mapping of Palestine is directly linked to violence against Palestinians, for it is the *raison d'être* for Israel's existence. Zionism is a project that relies on settler colonialism, a system that requires the elimination or expulsion of an indigenous population (Palestinians) and its replacement with settlers (Jews, largely of European descent).[150] Because it is focused on elimination, it is in a state of constant conflict, war, and violence.[151] Strategies used to eliminate Palestinians include massacres and extrajudicial executions by Israeli soldiers, but they also include policies like the stripping of residency papers from Palestinians living in East Jerusalem.[152]

Israel's colonial imagination includes several myths about Palestine. One claim is that Palestine is a word originating post-1948 or slightly earlier in the twentieth century, when, in fact, it has been in usage for about 1,000 years, as *Filastin*, or *Filastin,* and *al-Ard al-Muqaddasa*, identifying Palestine as the Holy Land.[153] This claim has been discredited by many historians including Israeli scholars like Haim Gerber; as he points out, this is part of the need for "self-critical research" that all scholars of Israel/Palestine should be engaged in.[154] The denial of Palestinian existence, easily disproved by historical sources including property deeds and Palestinian currency, is seen today in the construction of tourist sites on Palestinian land. One example that stands out is the Museum of Tolerance, a kind of "shrine to Zionism" that was built upon a Muslim cemetery in Jerusalem.[155]

Much like the empty-land imaginary the British deployed against Kenyans, in Palestine, we find the "clichés of deficiency" what Jay Mary Arthur cites as part of the settler colonial imaginary.[156] Another myth deployed against Palestinians is that they were "primitive and retrograde."[157] Agriculture is often given as an example of this deficit in Palestinian society—a way to legitimize the colonization of the land by Israelis who supposedly transformed the area from desert to farmland. The problems with this claim are numerous but include Palestinian exports like Jaffa oranges (a huge business before 1948) and barley (which included exporting 40,000 tons a year to Europe).[158]

The primitive and retrograde Orient was also identified with its dirty and sick inhabitants, an idea seen, among other places, in the Jewish health programs focused on British Mandate Jews, who, being non-European, were considered uncivilized. American graduates of the Hadassah Medical Organization were part of a civilizing mission in which many Jews were seen as part of the East and in need of help, including Eastern Europeans, who were viewed as being from a different, underdeveloped world.[159] The American colonial enterprise is evident in such programs, which viewed Israel as a space in which "other" Jews were made into modern subjects who could help to grow a future nation. As for Palestinians, they were often avoided, for nurses "seemed reluctant" to work with them.[160] Palestinians were simply referred to as one of the "non-Jewish communities of Palestine," a way of denying them their identity.[161] The replacement of local/Arab culture with a European one was also seen in architecture, where the local home became a site of "both existing and evolving identities" that stated an Israeli identity through a balance of the Orient and Occident.[162] By the 1960s, Danish-style interiors became popular, and styles like "Identified" and "Non-Conscious" highlighted modern forms, European middle-class elements, and Eurocentric design.[163]

The influence of Zionism on American academia is another way that these mythologies were imposed on U.S. education. This includes not only Jewish American organizations like Hillel and Israel Campus Coalition but also individual scholars committed to Zionist principles and silencing Palestinian voices. One example is S.D. Goitein, who moved to the United States from Israel and whose activities included criticizing postcolonial and Arab thinkers. His claims included that there was an "anti-Israeli obsession" and that there was "a mass psychosis" that existed among Israel's Arab neighbors.[164]

American academics with no Israeli affiliation also have a history of erasing Palestinian history and ignoring Palestinians, including ethnographic studies of refugees and studies within Israel; problems only remedied in the 1980s when scholars began to shift toward postcolonial sources and self-reflection on the problems in past studies.[165] Israeli anthropologists entered the discourse and further created problems by Orientalizing and dehumanizing the Arab population, portraying Palestinians as anti-modern, "a trope diametrically opposed to the self-image of a rational, forward-looking, modernizing Israeli."[166] As Khaled Furani and Dan Rabinowitz point out, this "silence over refugees and peasants was embedded in the larger epistemic political configurations of the question of Palestine."[167]

All these myths and practices are linked to Israel's geographical imagination, which includes a particular vision of what the new state would look like, from its architecture to agricultural settlements that include the modern *kibbutz*. The hotels, malls, government buildings, and homes of Israelis all represent an effort to remake the space of Palestine, which was multiethnic and multireligious, into a place that is Israel. Theodore Herzl had a vision of Israel characterized by "international eclecticism" that would result in "a cosmopolitan society using all the available and accessible opportunities of the modern world—and include its styles."[168] However, instead of Herzl's palazzos and palaces, what resulted was a modernism that has been described by scholars as aesthetically wanting and "cubic."[169] The *kibbutz* is a settler project that, along with *moshavim*, signified new, modern ways that were parts of Zionist nationalism in the 1920s and 1930s.[170] As mentioned earlier, the use of language and the renaming of places in Palestine are other ways the landscape has been remade into a Jewish one. The Arab neighborhood of Silwan, near the Old City in Jerusalem, is called the "City of David" by Israeli settlers who have taken Palestinian homes.[171]

Settler colonialism is a feature of several places in this book, including Kenya, Otaheite, the Hawaiian Islands, Palestine, and the American

Southwest—the focus of the next chapter. Scholars have suggested a set of recurring themes in this type of colonialism, which include "recurring values, images, icons, archetypes, monuments, stories, discourses, lexicons, politics, forgettings, and expectations."[172] However, the category of settler colonialism can also be oversimplified. While Israel certainly represents an effort to achieve a settler colonial state, scholars have argued that they have failed to achieve this as the Palestinians have refused to leave their ancestral lands. As Lorenzo Veracini explains, Palestine/Israel represents a case of both colonial occupation and settler colonialism,

> While the occupation is the absolute precondition for the settlements' establishment and ongoing existence, its success (like that of colonial rule) depends on its ability to maintain the sharp division between colonizer and colonized—the very division that prevents the realization of a successful settler colonial society.[173]

The map created by sectors of occupation and sectors of apartheid results in a map that is, for lack of a better word, confused. In a sense, Palestine is a case where both colonial and settler colonial forms are in tension. Veracini describes this as a kind of segregation in which erasure is not achieved.[174]

The most contested city in the Christian world (with Istanbul a close second), Jerusalem, has always existed in the imagination of Christians, Europeans, and Americans as a place of "sacrality and power."[175] Initially, people's idea of Jerusalem existed through the relics carried back to Europe, a point made by Annabel Jane Wharton in her study of its status as a contested place of religious, political, and territorial control.[176] As she explains, "Jerusalem first circulated in the West in the form of its physical fragments—pieces of stone, drops of oil, bits of bone, particles of wood."[177]

Today, Jerusalem has sacred importance to Jews, Christians, and Muslims, and as a city conquered and reconquered over the past 2,000 years, its religious places have been torn down, been the site of massacres, and survived the ravages of wars and social upheaval. The Temple Mount, abandoned by Christians for half a millennium, was taken by Muslims in 638.[178] It is still sacred to Muslims as the place where Abraham nearly sacrificed Ishmael (in the Islamic version of the story) and where Prophet Muhammad ascended to heaven in the *miraj*. It joins Mecca and Medina in the triad of holy cities that believers should visit in their lifetime. For Muslims, it is a city that has been mapped as an ancient Muslim center of power, a city filled with holy graves, and today, as the symbol of Western colonialism through its proxy, the modern state of Israel. The difficulties Muslims face in accessing the al-Haram al-Sharif, the Dome on the Rock, are viewed as an affront to Muslims, for the Islamic mapping of Jerusalem has this place as its sacred and political center.

Jerusalem has often existed in the form of problematic images and representations, evident in the drawings of the city that include buildings in the wrong places, such as the sketch by one German artist that included a town from his own country, landed the Palestine, "In his depiction of al-Haram al-Sharif, the influential German artist Luigi Mayers imported a stilted baroque onion dome and a well-ordered town square to Palestine," and in another rendering, by William Finden, Jerusalem is set in the Scottish highlands and includes a "western woman being ravaged by Arab bandits in the foreground."[179]

The violent and sexually insatiable Arab man is prominent in many of these depictions of Jerusalem. In a sense, Jerusalem is at the center of an old map that begins with the death of Christ and continues to this day. Christianity has been at the center this entire time: "For modern travelers as for premodern pilgrims, the Bible mapped the holy land. Jerusalem was indecipherable without the Hebrew Bible and the New Testament."[180] Jews were largely silenced through most of this through expulsion, pogroms, and genocide, until the Zionist movement and the state of Israel gave them a voice.

The possession of Jerusalem has been a preoccupation of Europeans for centuries. Accessibility for tourists was always part of the colonial project, what one nineteenth-century writer described when he wrote that Europeans should invade Ottoman territory and force them to give up the holy land to its rightful owners.[181] These kinds of polemical travelogues also contain sermons about non-European Christians, viewed as sullying the Holy Land with their superstitions. As one excerpt from Lamartine's book on the Holy Land states,

> Alas! If they had only spoiled the stones and ruins of these visible scenes! But what have they not done to the dogmas, the doctrines, the examples of that religion of reason, simplicity, love, and humility, that the Son of Man had taught them at the price of his blood?[182]

Through panoramas that were both textual and pictorial, the colonization of the Orient was found in these material objects, which Wharton describes as the "provocation for possession."[183] Israel is a European, and now, an American project, and one can see these touristic desires in numerous spaces and forms. In Shaul Kelner's study of Jewish tours to Israel, he discusses how the land is "inscribed" using signifiers that work within a "themed environment whose overarching motif is Jewish culture," which he likens to Disneyland.[184] Kelner's book illustrates how Israel is constructed by the government as a "Jewish space," but it is an illusion that is always on the edge of being revealed.

Israel was never solely a Jewish project—it was a Christian and colonial project that was enthusiastically championed by some, but not all, Jews. Jerusalem today is a political project rooted in Christian missionary activity. Evangelical Protestants see the establishment of Israel and the Jewish occupation of Palestine as a necessary part of the End of Days, a belief linked to the popularity of religious tours of the "Holy Land" and the reconstruction of the temple. These reconstructions exist in different forms, at times as models (such is the case of the Jerusalem Holy Land's outdoor model, over 2,000 square meters large) and Orlando's Holy Land Experience temple.[185]

The Mystical Landscapes of Egypt and Palestine

Egypt remains one of the most evocative landscapes in the world, seen in the numerous films that are set in its deserts and on the Nile. Many of these films, which include horror adventures like *The Mummy* (1999) and *The Mummy Returns* (2001) and *Death on the Nile* (2022), focus on the colonial period.[186] Nostalgia for the era of British colonialism includes "images of white linen, potted palms, and ancient tombs in the minds of Westerners."[187] Egypt's ancient civilization is a critical part of its mystical landscape. Sites like the pyramids, the sphinxes, and the many tombs in the desert are "symbolic elements of seduction" that hold secrets, mystery, and magic for tourists.[188] In addition to visiting them, tourists and consumers around the world purchase items related to *Egyptomemes*, "ideas and constellations of ideas related to or affiliated with ancient Egypt."[189]

Egyptomemes often relate to the belief in Egypt as a mystical landscape, found in everything from new religious movements to beauty and wellness products. Both the Nation of Islam and the Five Percenters are new religious movements that contain elements of ancient Egyptian "science." Products that promise miraculous anti-aging results are often linked to Egypt and its long history of mummies and eternal life. One example is Goop's crystal products, including those made of malachite whose magical properties include "a crystal with the power to transform," which Goop sells as a "mystical cleansing product."[190]

The tourist industry in Egypt includes tours of the desert and the Nile as well as resorts focused on these landscapes, which are marketed as being restorative, spiritual, and mystical. The Egyptian Tourism Authority has noted how the "heat, sight, and the light of the desert" are a source of rejuvenation for tourists.[191] Sharm El Sheikh is a resort area in Egypt that features colonial nostalgia identified with big game like elephants and lions to create an exotic ambience that is more East African than Egyptian.[192]

Like other mystical landscapes, the Egyptian desert has been viewed as a source of spiritual power by Europeans, a place where the "complexities of human existence" are explored and a site of introspection, meaning, and spiritual growth.[193] In one example, a study by Iraqi scholars explores the ways that deserts function in both English and Arabic modern literature as the site of spiritual journeys that are focused on reflection and communion with the Divine.[194] As discussed elsewhere in this book, the desert is an important place in the Western consciousness due to its embeddedness in Christian esoteric experiences, which have often been overlaid on foreign topographies from Algeria to Sedona. Tourism in Egypt includes trips to Sinai, where the desert is featured, at times, as an example of the tourists' desire for a place "that remains untouched by modernity."[195] Bedouin-run camps located in the desert offer a respite for tourists seeking solace, reflection, and spiritual experience.[196]

Israeli tourism benefits distinct groups of residents and tourists: Jewish Israelis, Jewish tourists, and Christian tourists. The land of Palestine is mapped to order space through immobility, carceral policies, and separation of Jews and Arabs.[197] The tourist experience must erase Palestinians from "Israeli" land to create certain experiences or at least to try to create them. The belief held among many Israelis that their migration is a kind of spiritual homecoming is tied to the idea of Aliyah or "ascension."[198] This ascension is not only a Zionist ideal, but it is also a goal of mystical practice, suggesting that one's spirituality is higher in the land of Israel. Erik Cohen gives the example of an American Jewish writer who claims "the light of Jerusalem has purifying powers and filters the blood."[199]

The experience of young Jews on birthright trips that are sponsored by the Israeli government is tied to the land and identified with Jewish bodies and experiences, a themed environment that is constructed around Jewish narratives and symbols. The popularity of Safed among Jewish tourists relies on the creation of a mystical landscape that reminds one of Kelner's use of Disneyland as a metaphor for Israel, although it is more focused on "flowy dresses" and "1960s counterculture" than Biblical narratives.[200] As Kelner writes, "The state is a symbol and a container for symbols of which the diasporans are the consumers."[201]

Christian tourists have been seeking transformative mystical experiences in Palestine for centuries. In the twentieth century, Protestants used maps to create these possibilities. As Jasmin Daam notes, "The physical presence of travelers at Biblical sites allegedly allowed them to access the biblical revelation and to spiritually access the site."[202] The role of Jewish guides in these experiences includes promoting a "Hebrew map" on the Palestinian landscape that is sponsored by the Israeli government.[203] The staging of lectures on Protestant tours in the Holy Land often utilizes the Biblical sites featured by tour companies, which include mountaintops with panoramic views where the Sermon on the Mount is read to true believers.[204] These tourist offerings promise transformative religious experiences through incorporating tourist views that circumscribe colonized and occupied land, made possible through the support of (mostly) European and American Christians, often through Jewish immigrant bodies, and by silencing and effectively erasing Palestinians—both Arab Muslims and Arab Christians.

Israel is often re-created as a simulacrum at various places in the United States. Orlando's *Holy Land Experience Theme Park*, which boasts several attractions including a reconstruction of the Jewish Temple in Jerusalem, capitalizes on the mystique of Palestine for profit while erasing the Palestinian people. Foods offered include the Jaffa Hot Dog, Arabian Chicken Wrap, and Bedouin Beef Pita Pockets, but beyond this, there is no mention of the Arab or Muslim population.[205] Arabic "musak" is "piped through the speakers," one of the ways that Orientalism is at play at the theme park, in addition to costuming and architecture.[206] As Joan Branham suggests, far from being accidental, these choices are likely a way to identify the "two groups of chosen people in God's eyes, Jews and Christians."[207] As we shall see in the next chapter, belief in a group of chosen people is a fundamental part of manifest destiny, the occupation of North America, and the expulsion of American Indians from their lands—all of which helped to create the mystical landscapes of the American West.

Notes

1 McClintock, 125.
2 Palestine refers to the land recognized by Arab speakers, whether Muslim or Christian, as their ancestral home. Palestinian is used in this chapter to refer to Arab speakers who may be Muslim or Christian. Yishuv refers to "the Jewish immigrant community of the Mandate." See Jasmin Daam, *Tourism and the Emergence of Nation-States in the Arab Eastern Mediterranean* (Amsterdam: Amsterdam University Press, 2022), 126.
3 Taylor 2002, 124.
4 Suan Slyomovics, "Cross-Cultural Dress and Tourist Performance in Egypt," *Performing Arts Journal* 11, nos. 3/4 (1989): 139.
5 Coleman 2007, 334.
6 Willie James Jennings, *The Christian Imagination: Theology and the Origins of Race* (New Haven: Yale University Press, 2010), 210, 211.
7 Talbot, 37.
8 Talbot, 37, 39, 43.
9 Hilton Obenzinger, *American Palestine: Melville, Twain, and the Holy Land Mania* (Princeton: Princeton University Press, 1999), 5.
10 Kobi Cohen-Hattab and Yosi Katz, "The Attraction of Palestine: Tourism in the Years 1850–1948," *Journal of Historical Geography* 27, no. 2 (2001): 168.
11 Butlin 1992, 38. See Butlin's discussion of *An Historical Geography of the Old Testament* (1701), 37–39.
12 Moadell, 82.
13 Mitchell 1988, xiv, 10.
14 Walter, 147.
15 Mitchell 1988, 24.
16 Stausberg, 3.
17 Yaron Perry and Elizabeth Yodim, *British Mission to the Jews in Nineteenth-Century Palestine* (New York: Routledge, 2003), 13–16.

18 Talbot, 44–45.
19 Waleed Hazbun, "The East as an Exhibit: Thomas Cook & Son and the Origins of the International Tourist Industry in Egypt," in *The Business of Tourism: Place, Faith, and History* (Philadelphia: University of Pennsylvania Press, 2009), 16.
20 Slyomovics, 146.
21 Lodwijk van Oord, "The Making of Primitive Palestine: Intellectual Origins of the Palestine-Israel Conflict," *History and Anthropology* 19, no. 3 (2008): 213–214.
22 Liechty 2017, 6.
23 Obenzinger, 3. See also Leon Vincent, *John Heyl Vincent: A Biographical Sketch* (New York: MacMillan Co., 1925), 91.
24 Yehoshua Ben-Arieh, "The Geographical Exploration of the Holy Land," *Palestine Exploration Quarterly* 104, no. 2 (1972): 81–82.
25 Yehoshua Ben-Arieh, "Nineteenth-Century Historical Geographies of the Holy Land," *Journal of Historical Geography* 15, no. 1 (1989): 71. According to Ben-Arieh, the Bible Lands included Egypt, Mesopotamia, northern Syria, Anatolia, Greece, Crete, and Cyprus.
26 Ben-Arieh 1972, 86.
27 Benjamin, 58.
28 Benjamin, 69.
29 Rosenblatt, 53, 58.
30 Said 1978, 190.
31 For a discussion of the difference between the Orientalist style and Orientalist colonial scholarship, see Chapter 3.
32 Mahdy, 161.
33 Robinson 2016, 175.
34 Robinson 2016, 177.
35 Daniel Dougherty, "Reading Eternity: Haggard's *She* and the Immortality in the Fin-de-siècle Novel," *Journal of Comparative Literature and Aesthetics* 47, no. 4 (2024): 107.
36 Katy Brundan, "Translation and Philological Fantasy in H. Rider Haggard's *She*," *Studies in English Literature (SEL) 1500–1900* 58, no. 4 (2018): 964.
37 Matthew A. Fike, "Time Is Not an Arrow: Anima and History in H. Rider Haggard's *She*," *ANQ (A Quarterly Journal of Short Articles, Notes and Reviews)* 28, no. 2 (2015): 107.
38 These items and their letters comprise nearly 19 pages of Haggard's novel. H. Ryder Haggard, *She: A History of Adventure* (Cleveland: Black and Gold House of Books, 2023), 25–44.
39 Dougherty, 107.
40 Mazlish, 734.
41 Haggard, 134.
42 Aintzane Legarreta Mentxaka, "Egypt in Western Popular Culture," *Otherness: Essays and Studies* 6, no. 2 (2018): 165.
43 Fike, 105. The word "yellow" appears in the novel *She* 24 times.
44 Brundan, 968.
45 S. A. Rhodes, *Gerard de Nerval 1808–1855, Poet, Traveler, Dreamer* (New York: Philosophical Library, 1951), 192.
46 Said 1978, 182.
47 Alfred Milner, *England in Egypt* (London: Edward Arnold, 1920), 331. Quoted in Buzard, 318.
48 E. M. Forster, "Egypt," in *Recommendations on the Government of Egypt, by a Committee of the International Section of the Labor Research Department* (London: Labour Research Department, 1920), 3. Quoted in Buzard, 325–326.

49 See Chapter 3 for a further discussion of the myths of white tribes in Africa.
50 Robinson 2016, 115.
51 Robinson 2016, 137.
52 Robinson 2016, 141.
53 Robinson 2016, 8. For the French myths of this idea in Algeria, see Chapter 3.
54 Gregory 1995, 44, 46.
55 Doron Barr and Kobi Cohen-Hattab, "A New Kind of Pilgrimage: The Modern Tourist Pilgrim of Nineteenth-Century and Early Twentieth-Century Palestine," *Middle Eastern Studies* 39, no. 2 (2003): 132.
56 Barr and Cohen-Hattab, 133.
57 Barr and Cohen-Hattab, 133.
58 Bandy, 555.
59 Bar and Cohen-Hattab, 135.
60 Michelle L. Woodward, "Between Orientalist Clichés and Images of Modernization: Photographic Practice in the Late Ottoman Era," *History of Photography* 27, no. 4 (2003): 363, 366, 368.
61 Woodward, 372, 373.
62 Evelyn Baring Cromer, *Modern Egypt* (New York: Macmillan, 1908), 194, 195.
63 Fekri A. Hassan, "Egypt in the Memory of the World," in *Egyptian Archaeology*, ed. Willeke Wendrich (Malden: Wiley-Blackwell, 2010), 265.
64 Hassan, 265.
65 Lynch, 108.
66 Loti 1867, 47.
67 Loti 1867, 59.
68 Gemie, 152, 162.
69 Geoffrey Roper, "Texts from Nineteenth-Century Egypt: The Role of E. W. Lane," in *Travelers in Egypt*, ed. Paul and Janet Starkey (London: Tauris Parke Paperbacks, 2001), 25.
70 Roper, 244, 245, 248.
71 Ali Behdad, "The Orientalist Photograph: An Object of Comparison," *Canadian Review of Comparative Literature* 43, no. 2 (2016): 275.
72 Gregory 2003, 204.
73 Gregory 2003, 206.
74 Gregory 2003, 207.
75 Lalvani, 276.
76 Dafna Hirsch, " 'Interpreters of Occident to the Awakening Orient': The Jewish Public Health Nurse in Mandate Palestine," *Comparative Studies in Society and History* 50, no. 1 (2008): 228. (emphasis in original)
77 Kelly 2015, 629.
78 Aiken 2010, 74.
79 Aiken 2010, 195.
80 Said 1993, 260. (emphasis in original)
81 Josias Leslie Porter, *Five Years in Damascus: Including an Account of the History, Topography, and Antiquities of That City, with Travels and Researches in Palmyra, Lebanon and the Hauran* (London: 1855), 37. Quoted in Aiken 2010, 99.
82 Arthur, 57. Quoted in Lynch, 63.
83 Coleman 2007, 334.
84 Anthony Trollope, *The Bertrams* (1859: repr., Oxford: Oxford University Press, 1947), Chapter XI: 116.
85 Gregory 2003, 220–221.
86 Gregory 1995, 35–36. Excerpts taken from Florence Nightingale's *Letters from Egypt: Journey on the Nile, 1849–50.*
87 The Arab river boat, common on the Nile.

88 Gregory 2001, 117.
89 Gregory 1995, 37.
90 Hazbun, 14–16.
91 Hazbun, 16.
92 Hazbun, 20, 28.
93 Gregory 2001, 115.
94 Aiken 2010, 188.
95 Aiken 2010, 69.
96 Aiken 2010, 75.
97 Aiken 2010, 100.
98 George Adam Smith, *The Book of the Twelve Prophets: Commonly Called Minor*, 2 Volumes (London: 1896–98), 73. Quoted in Aiken 2010, 166.
99 F. A. Chateaubriand, *Travels in Greece, Palestine, Egypt and Barbary*, 2 Volumes (London: Printed for Henry Colburn, 1812), 62. Quoted in Sakhniny, 258.
100 Kathleen Stewart Howe, "Mapping a Sacred Geography: Photographic Surveys by the Royal Engineers in the Holy Land, 1864–68," in *Picturing Place: Photography and the Geographical Imagination*, ed. Joan M. Schwartz and James R. Ryan (New York: I.B. Tauris, 2003), 228–229.
101 Howe, 230.
102 Doumani, 9–10.
103 Howe, 237. The survey was done in 1868–1869.
104 Howe, 237.
105 Ben-Arieh 1989, 76.
106 Shimon Gibson and Rupert L. Chapman, "The Mediterranean Hotel in Nineteenth-Century Jerusalem," *Palestine Exploration Quarterly* 127, no. 2 (1995): 103.
107 Gibson and Chapman, 103.
108 James Silk Buckingham, *Travels in Palestine* (London: Longman, 1821), 252. Quoted in Sakhnini, 257.
109 Coleman 2007, 338.
110 Ben-Arieh 1972, 89.
111 Sakhnini, 251. P.E.F. mapping included many Arabic names, as opposed to earlier maps that only included Biblical names of places. See I. W. J. Hopkins, "Nineteenth-Century Maps of Palestine: Dual-Purpose Historical Evidence," *Imago Mundi* 22 (1968): 34.
112 Cohen-Hattab and Katz, 169.
113 Van Oord, 217. See also *Earthly Footsteps of the Man from Galilee, being Three Hundred and Eighty-Four Original Photographic Views and Descriptions of the Places Connected with the Earthly Life of Our Lord and His Apostles Traced with Note Book and Camera* (1894).
114 Salim Tamari, "Shifting Ottoman Conceptions of Palestine. Part 2: Ethnography and Cartography," *Jerusalem Quarterly* 48 (2011): 10. Shami refers to the area that is now Syria.
115 Tamari, 6.
116 Nadi Abusaada, "'The Reconstruction of Palestine': Geographical Imaginaries after World War I," in *The Social and Cultural History of Palestine: Essays in Honour of Salim Tamari*, ed. Sarah Irving (Edinburgh: Edinburgh University Press, 2023), 102.
117 Abusaada 2023, 108.
118 Abusaada 2023, 108.
119 Nadi Abusaada, "Self-Portrait of a Nation: The Arab Exhibition in Mandate Jerusalem, 1931–34," *Jerusalem Quarterly* 77 (2019): 130, 131.
120 Abusaada 2019, 129.

121 Daam, 123–125.
122 Beatrice St. Laurent and Himmet Taskömür, "The Imperial Museum of Antiquities in Jerusalem, 1890–1930: An Alternative Narrative," *Jerusalem Quarterly* 55 (2013): 37–38.
123 St. Laurent and Taskömür, 26.
124 Ronald Storrs, *Orientations* (London: Ivor Nicholson & Watson, 1937), 464. Quoted in Sr. Laurent and Taskömür, 28.
125 Storrs, 340.
126 Abusaada 2021, 371–374.
127 St. Laurent and Taskömür, 32.
128 St. Laurent and Taskömür, 33.
129 Daniella Ohad Smith, "Hotel Design in British Mandate Palestine: Modernism and the Zionist Vision," *The Journal of Israeli History* 29, no. 1 (2010): 99, 112.
130 Daniella Ohad Smith, "The 'Designed' Israeli Interior, 1960–1977: Shaping Identity," *Journal of Interior Design* 38, no. 3 (2013): 23.
131 Cohen-Hattab 2004, 69.
132 Cohen-Hattab 2004, 71.
133 Daam, 149.
134 Ohad Smith 2010, 104.
135 Ohad Smith 2010, 104–105.
136 Ohad Smith 2010, 105.
137 Ohad Smith 2010, 107–110.
138 Ohad Smith 2010, 114–115.
139 Ohad Smith 2010, 115.
140 Cohen-Hattab and Katz, 174.
141 Sarah Irving, 'This Is Palestine': History and Modernity in Guidebooks to Mandate Palestine," *Contemporary Levant* 4, no. 1 (2019): 68.
142 Daam, 158–163.
143 Daam, 163.
144 Talbot, 40.
145 Ella Shohat, "Dislocated Identities," in *On the Arab-Jew, Palestine, and Other Displacements: Selected Writings* (London: Pluto Press, 2017), 80.
146 Nur Masalha, *The Bible and Zionism: Invented Traditions, Archaeology and Post-Colonialism in Palestine-Israel* (New York: Zed Books, 2007), 68.
147 Harley 2001, 179.
148 Meron Benvenisti, *Conflicts and Contradictions* (New York: Villard Books, 1986), 191–202. Quoted in Harley 2001, 179.
149 Ella Shohat, "The Invention of the Mizrahim," in *On the Arab-Jew, Palestine, and Other Displacements: Selected Writings* (London: Pluto Press, 2017), 102, 109. See Shohat's other essays for further discussion of this issue in this volume, especially in Part I of the book.
150 The author wishes to make an explicit distinction between Jews as an ethnic and religious group and Zionists. The Zionist settlers known as the *Yishuv* are a small section of a Jewish international that includes some of the most vocal challenges to Zionism. According to my reading of Judaism as a religious scholar, this is a critical distinction because the Zionist violence seen in the 75 years of Israel's existence is in direct violation of Jewish principles of justice.
151 John Collins, "A Dream Deferred: Palestine from Total War to Total Peace," in *Studies of Settler Colonialism: Politics, Identity and Culture*, ed. Fiona Bateman and Lionel Pilkington (New York: Palgrave MacMillan, 2011), 173.
152 Saree Makdisi, "Zionism Then and Now," in *Studies of Settler Colonialism: Politics, Identity and Culture*, ed. Fiona Bateman and Lionel Pilkington (New York: Palgrave MacMillan, 2011), 237.

153 Gerber, 26. See also Talbot, 40.

154 Gerber, 26.

155 Makdisi, 238.

156 See Arthur, 85.

157 Gerber, 30.

158 Gerber, 34.

159 Hirsch, 243.

160 Hirsch, 251.

161 Khalidi 1999, 23.

162 Ohad Smith 2013, 24.

163 Ohad Smith 2013, 29–32.

164 Hanan Harif, "A Bridge of Fortress? S.D. Goitein and the Role of Jewish Arabists in the American Academy," *Jewish Social Studies* 26, no. 2 (2021): 80.

165 Khaled Furani and Dan Rabinowitz, "The Ethnographic Arriving of Palestine," *Annual Review of Anthropology* 40 (2011): 480–482.

166 Furani and Rabinowitz, 480.

167 Furani and Rabinowitz, 480.

168 Ita Heinze-Greenberg, "Immigration and Culture Shock," in *Tel Aviv Modern Architecture, 1930–1939*, ed. Irmel Kamp-Bandau, Winfried Nerdinger, and Pe'era Goldman (Munich: Institut für Auslandsbeziehungen, 1994), 36.

169 Heinze-Greenberg, 37.

170 Cohen-Hattab and Katz, 170.

171 Khalidi 1997, 15.

172 Lynch, 25.

173 Veracini, 29.

174 Veracini, 31.

175 Wharton, 45.

176 See Wharton, 45.

177 Wharton, 45.

178 Wharton, 54.

179 Wharton, 157.

180 Wharton, 146.

181 Wharton, 185.

182 Alphonse De Lamartine, *A Pilgrimage to the Holy Land: Comprising Recollections, Sketches, and Reflections, Made During a Tour in the East* (New York: D. Appleton & Company, 1848), 303.

183 Wharton, 183.

184 Shaul Kelner, *Tours That Bind: Diaspora, Pilgrimage, and Israeli Birthright Tourism* (New York: New York University Press, 2010), 203, 103.

185 Joan R. Branham, "The Temple That Won't Quit: Constructing Sacred Space in Orlando's Holy Land Experience Theme Park," *CrossCurrents* 59, no. 3 (2009): 358, 359, 363.

186 *Death on the Nile* (2022) is a remake of the 1978 film.

187 Julia Ashton, "Camels, Sand, and Pyramids: Struggles with Tourism in the Land of the Pharaohs" (Proceedings of the National Conference on Undergraduate Research, April 11–13, 2015), 523.

188 Cartier 2005, 7.

189 Hassan, 267.

190 https://goop.com/beauty/skin/malachite-skin-care/ (accessed January 25, 2025).

191 Egyptian Tourism Authority, quoted in Ashton, 523.

192 Jacobs, 49.

193 Ahmed Khashea Naji and Mohamad Fleih Hassan, "Mapping Desert Narratives: A Systematic Review of Desert Representations on Postmodern English

and Arabic Fiction," *Multidisciplinary Reviews* (2025): n.p., https://doi.org/10.
31893/multiv.2025048.
194 Naji and Hassan, n.p.
195 Jacobs, 53.
196 Jacobs, 53.
197 Julie Peteet, *Space and Mobility in Palestine* (Bloomington: Indiana University
Press, 2017), 31.
198 Cohen 1979, 191.
199 Cohen 1979, 192. Here Cohen is quoting a *Time* magazine review of Bellow's
book *To Jerusalem and Back* (1976).
200 Kelner, 85–86.
201 Kelner, 87.
202 Daam, 128.
203 Jackie Feldman, "Constructing a Shared Bible Land: Jewish Israeli Guiding Performances for Protestant Pilgrims," *American Ethnologist* 34, no. 2 (2007): 355.
204 Feldman, 361.
205 Branham, 366, 374.
206 Branham, 374–375.
207 Branham, 375.

Bibliography

Abusaada, Nadi. "Self-Portrait of a Nation: The Arab Exhibition in Mandate Jerusa-
lem, 1931–34." *Jerusalem Quarterly* 77 (2019): 122–135.
Abusaada, Nadi. "Urban Encounters: Imaging the City in Mandate Palestine." In
*Imaging and Imagining Palestine: Photography, Modernity and the Biblical Lens,
1918–1948*, edited by Karène Sanchez Summerer and Sary Zananiri, 360–389.
Boston: Brill, 2021.
Abusaada, Nadi. "'The Reconstruction of Palestine': Geographical Imaginaries after
World War I." In *The Social and Cultural History of Palestine: Essays in Honour
of Salim Tamari*, edited by Sarah Irving, 102–119. Edinburgh: Edinburgh Univer-
sity Press, 2023.
Aiken, Edwin James. *Scriptural Geography: Portraying the Holy Land*. New York:
Bloomsbury Publishing, 2010.
Arthur, Jay Mary. *The Default Country: A Lexical Cartography of Twentieth-Century
Australia*. Sydney: University of New South Wales Press, 2003.
Ashton, Julia. "Camels, Sands, and Pyramids: Struggles with Tourism in the Golden
Land of the Pharaohs." *Proceedings of the National Conference on Undergradu-
ate Research (NCUR)*, April 11–13, 2013.
Bandy, Joe. "Managing the Other of Nature: Sustainability, Spectacle, and Global
Regimes of Capital in Ecotourism." *Public Culture* 8 (1996): 539–566.
Barr, Doron and Kobi Cohen-Hattab. "A New Kind of Pilgrimage: The Modern Tour-
ist Pilgrim of Nineteenth-Century and Early Twentieth-Century Palestine." *Middle
Eastern Studies* 39, no. 2 (2003): 131–148.
Behdad, Ali. "The Orientalist Photograph: An Object of Comparison." *Canadian
Review of Comparative Literature* 43, no. 2 (2016): 265–281.
Ben-Arieh, Yehoshua. "The Geographical Exploration of the Holy Land." *Palestine
Exploration Quarterly* 104, no. 2 (1972): 81–92.
Ben-Arieh, Yehoshua. "Nineteenth-century Historical Geographies of the Holy
Land." *Journal of Historical Geography* 15, no. 1 (1989): 69–79.
Benjamin, Roger. *Orientalist Aesthetics: Art, Colonialism, and French North Africa,
1880–1930*. Berkeley: University of California Press, 2003.

Benvenisti, Meron. *Conflicts and Contradictions*. New York: Villard Books, 1986.

Branagh, Kenneth, dir. *Death on the Nile*. 20th Century Studios. 2022.

Branham, Joan R. "The Temple That Won't Quit: Constructing Sacred Space in Orlando's Holy Land Experience Theme Park." *CrossCurrents* 59, no. 3 (2009): 358–382.

Brundan, Katy. "Translation and Philological Fantasy in H. Rider Haggard's *She*." *Studies in English Literature 1500–1900* 58, no. 4 (2018): 959–980.

Buckingham, James Silk. *Travels in Palestine*. London: Longman, 1825.

Butlin, Robin A. "Ideological Contexts and the Reconstruction of Biblical Landscapes in the Seventeenth and Early Eighteenth Centuries: Dr. Edward Wells and the Historical Geography of the Holy Land." In *Ideology and Landscape in Historical Perspective: Essays on the Meanings of Some Places in the Past*, edited by Alan R. H. Baker and Gideon Biger, 31–62. Cambridge: Cambridge University Press, 1992.

Cartier, Carolyn. "Introduction: Touristed Landscapes/Seductions of Place." In *Seductions of Place: Geographical Perspectives on Globalization and Touristed Landscapes*, edited by Carolyn Carter and Alan A. Lew, 1–19. London: Routledge, 2005.

Chateaubriand, F. A. *Travels in Greece, Palestine, Egypt and Barbary*. 2 Volumes. London: Printed for Henry Colburn, 1812.

Cohen, Erik. "A Phenomenology of Tourist Experiences." *Sociology* 13 (1979): 179–201.

Cohen-Hattab, Kobi. "Zionism, Tourism, and the Battle for Palestine: Tourism as a Political-Propaganda Tool." *Israel Studies* 9, no. 1 (2004): 61–85.

Cohen-Hattab, Kobi and Yossi Katz. "The Attraction of Palestine: Tourism in the Years 1850–1948." *Journal of Historical Geography* 27, no. 2 (2001): 166–177.

Coleman, Simon. "A Tale of Two Centres? Representing Palestine to the British in the Nineteenth Century." *Mobilities* 2, no. 3 (2007): 331–345.

Collins, John. "A Dream Deterred: Palestine from Total War to Total Peace." In *Studies in Settler Colonialism: Politics, Identity and Culture*, edited by Fiona Bateman and Lionel Pilkington, 169–185. New York: Palgrave MacMillan, 2011.

Cromer, Evelyn Baring (1st Earl of Cromer). *Modern Egypt*. New York: MacMillan Company, 1916.

Daam, Jasmin. *Tourism and the Emergence of Nation-States in the Arab Eastern Mediterranean, 1920s–1930s*. Amsterdam: Amsterdam University Press, 2022.

De Lamartine, Alphonse. *A Pilgrimage to the Holy Land: Comprising Recollections, Sketches, and Reflections, Made During a Tour in the East*. New York: D. Appleton & Company, 1848.

Dougherty, Daniel. "Reading Eternity: Haggard's *She* and the Immortality in the Fin-de-siècle Novel." *Journal of Comparative Literature and Aesthetics* 47, no. 4 (2024): 104–114.

Doumani, Beshara B. "Rediscovering Ottoman Palestine: Writing Palestinians into History." *Journal of Palestine Studies* 21, no. 2 (1992): 5–28.

Feldman, Jackie. "Constructing a Shared Bible Land: Jewish Israeli Guiding Performances for Protestant Pilgrims." *American Ethnologist* 34, no. 2 (2007): 351–374.

Fike, Matthew A. "Time Is Not an Arrow: Anima and History in H. Rider Haggard's *She*." *ANQ (A Quarterly Journal of Short Articles, Notes and Reviews)* 28, no. 2 (2015): 105–109.

Forster, E. M. "Egypt." In *Recommendations on the Government of Egypt, by a Committee of the International Section of the Labour Research Department*. London: Labour Research Department, 1920.

Furani, Khaled and Dan Rabinowitz. "The Ethnographic Arriving of Palestine." *Annual Review of Anthropology* 40 (2011): 475–491.

Gemie, Sharif. "Loti, Orientalism and the French Colonial Experience." *Journal of European Area Studies* 8, no. 2 (2000): 149–165.

Gerber, Haim. "Zionism, Orientalism, and the Palestinians." *Journal of Palestine Studies* 33, no. 1 (2003): 23–41.

Gibson, Shimon and Rupert L. Chapman. "The Mediterranean Hotel in Nineteenth-Century Jerusalem." *Palestine Exploration Quarterly* 127, no. 2 (1995): 93–105.

Gregory, Derek. "Between the Book and the Lamp: Imaginative Geographies of Egypt, 1849–50." *Transactions of the Institute of British Geographers* 20, no. 1 (1995): 29–57.

Gregory, Derek. "Colonial Nostalgia and Cultures of Travel: Spaces of Constructed Visibility in Egypt." In *Consuming Tradition, Manufacturing Heritage: Global Norms and Urban Forms in the Age of Tourism*, edited by Nezar Al Sayyad, 111–151. New York: Routledge, 2001.

Gregory, Derek. "Emperors of the Gaze: Photographic Practices and Productions of Space in Egypt, 1839–1914." In *Picturing Place: Photography and the Geographical Imagination*, edited by Joan M. Schwartz and James R. Ryan, 196–225. New York: I.B. Tauris, 2003.

Guillerman, John, dir. *Death on the Nile*. EMI Distributers, 1978.

Haggard, H. Rider. *She: A History of Adventure*, 1887. Reprint. Black & Gold House of Books, 2023.

Harif, Hanan. "A Bridge or a Fortress? S.D. Goiten and the Role of Jewish Arabists in the American Academy." *Jewish Social Studies* 26, no. 2 (2021): 68–92.

Harley, John B. "New England Cartography and the Native Americans." In *The New Nature of Maps: Essays in the History of Cartography*, edited by Paul Laxton, 169–196. Baltimore: John Hopkins University Press, 2001.

Hassan, Fekri A. "Egypt in the Memory of the World." In *Egyptian Archaeology*, edited by Willeke Wendrich, 259–273. Malden: Wiley-Blackwell, 2010.

Hazbun, Waleed. "The East as an Exhibit: Thomas Cook & Son and the Origins of the International Tourism Industry in Egypt." In *The Business of Tourism: Place, Faith, and History*, edited by Philip Scranton and Janet F. Davidson, 3–33. Philadelphia: University of Pennsylvania Press, 2009.

Heinze-Greenberg, Ita. "Immigration and Culture Shock." In *Tel Aviv Modern Architecture, 1930–1939*, edited by Irmel Kamp-Bandau, Winfried Nerdinger, and Pe'era Goldman, 36–39. Munich: Institut für Auslandsbeziehungen, 1994.

Hirsch, Dafna. "'Interpreters of Occident to the Awakening Orient': The Jewish Public Health Nurse in Mandate Palestine." *Comparative Studies in Society and History* 50, no. 1 (2008): 227–255.

Hopkins, I. W. J. "Nineteenth-Century Maps of Palestine: Dual-Purpose Historical Evidence." *Imago Mundi* 22 (1968): 30–36.

Howe, Kathleen Stewart. "Mapping a Sacred Geography: Photographic Surveys by the Royal Engineers in the Holy Land, 1864–68." In *Picturing Place: Photography and the Geographical Imagination*, edited by Joan M. Schwartz and James R. Ryan, 226–242. New York: I.B. Tauris, 2003.

Irving, Sarah. "'This Is Palestine': History and Modernity in Guidebooks to Mandate Palestine." *Contemporary Levant* 4, no. 1 (2019): 64–74.

Jacobs, Jessica. *Sex, Tourism and the Postcolonial Encounter: Landscapes of Longing in Egypt*. London: Ashgate, 2010.

Jennings, Willie James. *The Christian Imagination: Theology and the Origins of Race*. New Haven: Yale University Press, 2010.

Kelly, Kristine. "Aesthetic Desire and Imperialist Disappointment in Trollope's *The Bertrams* and the Murray *Handbook for Travellers in Syria and Palestine*." *Victorian Literature and Culture* 43 (2015): 621–639.

Kelner, Shaul. *Tours that Bind: Diaspora, Pilgrimage, and Israeli Birthright Tourism*. New York: NYU Press, 2010.

Khalidi, Rashid. *Palestinian Identity: The Construction of Modern National Consciousness*. New York: Columbia University Press, 1997.

Lalvani, Suren. "Consuming the Exotic Other." *Critical Studies in Mass Communication* 12 (1995): 263–286.

Liechty, Mark. *Far Out: Countercultural Seekers and the Tourist Encounter in Nepal.* Chicago: The University of Chicago Press, 2017.

Loti, Pierre. *Aziyadé*, 1867. Reprint. Paris: North Star, 2016.

Lynch, Tom. *Outback & Out West: The Settler-Colonial Environmental Imaginary.* Lincoln: University of Nebraska Press, 2022.

Mahdy, Hossam. "Travellers, Colonisers, and Conservationists." In *Travellers in Egypt*, edited by Paul and Janet Starkey, 157–167. London: Tauris Parke Paperbacks, 2001.

Makdidi, Saree. "Zionism Then and Now." In *Studies of Settler Colonialism: Politics, Identity, and Culture*, edited by Fiona Bateman and Lionel Pilkington, 237–256. New York: Palgrave MacMillin, 2011.

Masalha, Nur. *The Bible and Zionism: Invented Traditions, Archaeology and Post-Colonialism in Palestine-Israel.* New York: Zeb Books, 2007.

Mazlish, Bruce. "A Triptych: Freud's The Interpretation of Dreams, Rider Haggard's *She*, and Bulwer-Lytton's *The Coming Race.*" *Comparative Studies in Society and History* 35, no. 4 (1993): 726–745.

McClintock, Anne. *Imperial Leather: Race, Gender and Sexuality in the Colonial Contest.* New York: Routledge, 1995.

Mentxaka, Aintzane Legarreta. "Egypt in Western Popular Culture: From Bram Stoker to *The Jewel of the Nile.*" *Otherness: Essays and Studies* 6, no. 2 (2018): 162–193.

Milner, Alfred. *England in Egypt.* London: Edward Arnold, 1920.

Mitchell, Timothy. *Colonising Egypt.* Berkeley: University of California Press, 1988.

Moadell, Mansoor. *Islamic Modernism, Nationalism, and Fundamentalism: Episode and Discourse.* Chicago: University of Chicago Press, 2005.

Naji, Ahmed Khashea and Mohamad Fleih Hassan. "Mapping Desert Narratives: A Systematic Review of Desert Representations in Postmodern English and Arabic Fiction." *Multidisciplinary Reviews* (2025): n.p. http://doi.org/10.31893/multiv.2025048

Obenzinger, Hilton. *American Palestine: Melville, Twain, and the Holy Land Mania.* Princeton: Princeton University Press, 1999.

Perry, Yaron and Elizabeth Yodim. *The British Mission to the Jews in Nineteenth-Century Palestine.* New York: Routledge, 2003.

Peteet, Julie. *Space and Mobility in Palestine.* Bloomington: Indiana University Press, 2017.

Porter, Josias Leslie. *Five Years in Damascus: Including an Account of the History, Topography, and Antiquities of that City, with Researches in Palmyra, Lebanon and the Hauran, 2 Volumes.* London, 1855.

Rhodes, S. A. *Gerard de Nerval 1808–1855, Poet, Traveler, Dreamer.* New York: Philosophical Library, 1951.

Robinson, Michael F. *The Lost White Tribe: Explorers, Scientists, and the Theory that Changed a Continent.* New York: Oxford University Press, 2016.

Roper, Geoffrey. "Texts from Nineteenth-Century Egypt: The Role of E. W. Lane." In *Travellers in Egypt*, edited by Paul and Janey Starkey, 244–254. London: Tauris Parke Paperbacks, 2001.

Rosenblatt, Naomi. "Orientalism in American Popular Culture." *Penn History Review* 16, no. 2 (2009): 51–63.

Said, Edward. *Orientalism.* New York: Vintage, 1978.

Said, Edward. *Culture and Imperialism.* New York: Vintage, 1993.

Sakhnini, Mohammad. "James Silk Buckingham (1786–1855) and the Politics of Travel in the Holy Land." *Studies in Romanticism* 62, no. 2 (2023): 249–267.

Shohat, Ella. "Dislocated Identities." In *On the Arab-Jew, Palestine, and Other Displacements: Selected Writings*, 77–86. London: Pluto Press, 2017.

Shohat, Ella. "The Invasion of the Mizrahim." In *On the Arab-Jew, Palestine, and Other Displacements: Selected Writings*, 102–121. London: Pluto Press, 2017.

Slyomovics, Susan. "Cross-Cultural Dress and Tourist Performance in Egypt." *Performing Arts Journal* 11, no. 3/4 (1989): 139–148.

Smith, Daniela Ohad. "The 'Designed' Israeli Interior, 1960–1977: Shaping Identity." *Journal of Interior Design* 38, no. 3 (2013): 21–36.

Smith, Daniella Ohad. "Hotel Design in British Mandate Palestine: Modernism and the Zionist Vision." *The Journal of Israeli History* 29, no. 1 (2020): 99–123.

Smith, George Adam. *The Book of the Twelve Prophets: Commonly Called Minor. 2 Volumes*. London, 1896–98.

Sommers, Stephen, dir. *The Mummy*. Universal Pictures, 1999.

Sommers, Stephen, dir. *The Mummy Returns*. Universal Pictures, 2001.

Stausberg, Michael. *Religion and Tourism: Crossroads, Destinations and Encounters*. New York: Routledge, 2011.

St. Laurent, Beatrice and Himmet Taskömür. "The Imperial Museum of Antiquities in Jerusalem, 1890–1930: An Alternative Narrative." *Jerusalem Quarterly* 55 (2013): 6–45.

Storrs, Ronald. *Orientations*. London: Ivor Nicholson & Watson, 1937.

Talbot, Michael. "Divine Imperialism: The British in Palestine, 1753–1842." In *The British Abroad Since the Eighteenth Century, Volume 2: Experiencing Imperialism*, edited by Martin Farr and Xavier Guégan, 36–53. New York: Palgrave Macmillan, 2013.

Tamari, Salim. "Shifting Ottoman Conceptions of Palestine. Part 2: Ethnography and Cartography." *Jerusalem Quarterly* 48 (2011): 6–16.

Taylor, Charles. "Modern Social Imaginaries." *Public Culture* 14, no. 1 (2002): 91–124.

Trollope, Anthony. *The Bertrams*, 1859. Oxford: Oxford University Press, 1947.

Van Oord, Lodwijk. "The Making of Primitive Palestine: Intellectual Origins of the Palestine-Israel Conflict." *History and Anthropology* 19, no. 3 (2008): 209–228.

Veracini, Lorenzo. "The Other Shift: Settler Colonialism, Israel and the Occupation." *Journal of Palestine Studies* 42, no. 2 (2013): 26–42.

Vincent, John H., J. W. Lee, and R. E. M. Bain, eds. *Earthly Footsteps of the Man of Galilee, Being Three Hundred and Eighty-Four Original Photographic Views and Descriptions of the Places Connected with the Earthly Life of Our Lord and His Apostles Traced with Note Book and Camera*. London, 1864.

Vincent, Leon. *John Heyl Vincent: A Biographical Sketch*. New York: MacMillan Co., 1925.

Walter, Marc. *Voyages Around the World*. New York: Friedman, 2002.

Wharton, Annabel Jane. *Selling Jerusalem: Relics, Replicas, Theme Parks*. Chicago: University of Chicago Press, 2006.

Woodward, Michelle L. "Between Orientalist Clichés and Images of Modernization: Photographic Practice in the Late Ottoman Era." *History of Photography* 27, no. 4 (2003): 363–374.

8

THE MYSTIC WEST

In the European fashioning of American space, cosmographic measure pre-dated and prefigured the encounter with actual nature. Colonists took the view that the Native American population was so much a part of nature (literally savages: "of the woods") that its members were incapable of intellect.[1]

Denis Cosgrove

Black Elk, the Oglala spiritual leader, spent his childhood on the lands that became the Wind Cave National Park, a time about which he remembered his people being happy, when "the two-leggeds and the four-leggeds lived together like relatives, and there was plenty for them and for us."[2] His world radically changed as a result of the establishment of the national park system that eventually pushed American Indians out of lands they used for hunting and fishing. As the park system expanded and his people were excluded from these lands, Black Elk noticed the separation between humans and animals, for the U.S. government had "made little islands for us and other little islands for the four-leggeds."[3] The Grand Canyon National Park has a similar story, a place whose Indian populations were moved as part of the creation of a pocket of "wilderness" to provide a refuge from the industrial landscape of the United States of America.[4] These refuges made out of Indian lands are now mystical landscapes.

American Indians were removed from their lands to make space for the new white settler vision of the landscape.[5] As J.Z. Smith reminded us in an earlier chapter, maps are a device used to erase people from memory. Evan

DOI: 10.4324/9781003361725-9

Berry explains how, in the United States, this was achieved through both
military and legal means,

> With an eye to economic interests the National Forest Service and National
> Park Service eagerly prosecuted traditional Native American land-tenure
> practices. Hunting became poaching, gathering fruits and herbs became
> trespassing, and many tribal efforts toward economic development were
> stymied in the name of conservation.[6]

The idea of the American frontier as the site of a new Europe was situated in ideals of settler colonialism that were communicated in maps, political speeches, laws, and cultural texts. Thomas Jefferson often referred to
Manifest Destiny in his letters and speeches. Examples include his letter to
Archibald Judge Stewart in 1786 ("Our confederacy must be viewed as the
nest from which all America, North and South is to be peopled"); in 1801,
at his inaugural address ("possessing a chosen country, with room enough or
our descendants to the thousandth and thousandth generation"); in an 1803
letter to Virginian John Breckenridge ("When we shall be full on this side,
we may lay off a range of states on the Western bank from the head to the
mouth, & so range after range, advancing compactly as we multiply"); and
in his 1812 letter to John Jacob Astor

> I considered a great public acquisition the commencement of a settlement
> on that point of the Western coast of America, & looked forward with
> gratification to the time when it's descendants should have spread them-
> selves thro' the whole length of that coast.[7]

Settlers of the Western territories of the United States are often described
as "early colonial Americans" and included Englishmen, Germans, Scots,
and Irish. One inspiration for the move westward and the taking of Indian
land was the Biblical verse Genesis 1:28: "God blessed them and God said
to them: Be fertile and increase, fill the earth and master it; rule the fish of
the sea, the birds of the sky, and all the living things that creep on earth."
A Biblical idea that validated notions of Anglo-Saxon culture, Manifest
Destiny promised an empire to the children of Adam.[8] Manifest Destiny
was linked to Christianity in other powerful ways. The motif of nature
as a place of redemption originated in the early days of Christianity. The
"rhetorical self-representations of Protestant settlers" used the desert and
wilderness as descriptions for the entire continent, ideas which eventually
found themselves in the writings of Emerson, and later, into the environmental movement.[9]

The doctrine of Manifest Destiny was so important to early Americans that John Quincy Adams had it entered into the congressional record in 1864.[10] In literature, Manifest Destiny is found in Willa Cather's (1873–1947) prairie novels, where pioneers, "unlike the Pawnees," were white Christians and, thus, "enabled the land to fulfill its true destiny."[11] Cather paints a picture of a land saved from desolation through the labor of white Americans. In *O Pioneers!*, Alexandra's father struggles in the early days of pioneering, but his progeny transforms the land from a "shaggy coat of the prairie" to "a vast checker-board, marked off in squares of wheat and corn; light and dark, dark and light."[12] Cather ends the novel with a declaration of Manifest Destiny: "Fortunate country, that is one day to receive hearts like Alexandra's into its bosom, to give them out again in the yellow wheat, in the rusting corn, in the shining eyes of youth!"[13]

American Progress on Canvas

Manifest Destiny also became a significant theme in painting, a popular subject for both American and European artists. Indians were painted as savage killers in works like Charles Wimar's *The Attack on a Wagon Train* and Frederic Remington's *The Emigrants*, and captive white Americans were featured in paintings like John Mix Stanley's *Osage Scalp Dance*, which placed women and infants at the center of a bloodthirsty group of monstrous Native Americans.[14] These paintings portrayed Indians as "red-skinned assassins" and the "creature of impulse that can only be controlled through fear."[15] In truth, Native Americans were advanced in language, architecture, the arts, and cartography. Like the people of Tahiti, who drew maps of their islands and their position in the vast Pacific Ocean for Europeans, Native Americans had a cartographical sense of their world. In fact, the English and other settlers would not have had maps without their Indian guides helping to create them. As Harley suggests, "Clearly, some if not all American Indians could draw maps at the time of their first contact with the British."[16]

One of the most powerful paintings in this genre is John Gast's 1872 painting *American Progress* (1872), famous for its angel flying over the American West, sanctifying the landscape as a Christian space. As Albert Boime describes, it is a view of the nation that includes an almost impossibly large number of motifs and themes,

> The personification of American Progress, bearing on her forehead the Star of Empire, floats high overhead and leads the parade westward, stringing telegraph wire across the Great Plains and bringing the lights of civilization to the dark wastes of the far West, symbolized by the fleeing Indians and buffalo who are dispelled by the "presence of a wondrous vision."[17]

Paintings by Wimar, Remington, Stanley, and Gast created a visual map of the West where white settlers belonged to the divinely ordained land that Indians were expelled from. Mapping of territory that was Indian land told the story of the U.S. government's military campaigns, laws, and the history of the forced expulsions of Native peoples. As Matthew Baigell explains, in Albert Bierstadt's *The Oregon Trail* (1869), the imminent destruction of Indians is part of the painting's vision of landscape,

> Bierstadt included in his painting all of the western landscapes—forest, plains, mountains, wet and dry areas. On the left, the settlers find water for their cattle, insuring sustenance of life in the West. In the center, the caravan moves over the dry plains toward the distant Indian dwellings, which will soon be obliterated. The sun, symbolizing the Destiny's presence, indicates that all will proceed with minimum discord.[18]

Other paintings more closely resemble maps through their clear lines of territory and space. One example is Fanny Palmer's *Across the Continent: "Westward the Course of Empire Takes Its Way"* (1868), a lithograph that

IMAGE 8.1 Across the Continent: "Westward the Course of Empire Takes Its Way," Frances Flora Bond Palmer, 1868.

Source: Yale University Library, Public Domain

includes a bisection of the canvas.[19] On the left is civilization; in the middle, a railroad and train cut through the land; and on the right, two Indians are stopped by the train—the savage landscape and people are effectively cut off by white progress.

The white settler imagination is reflected in narrative elements found in paintings, popular literature, and films, commonly expressed in scenes of conflicts with Indians, male bonding, and cattle drives.[20] The role of animals, especially cattle and sheep, is identified with race and territory. Anglo-Saxon men were linked to cattle and the Basque and other non-Anglos to sheep.[21] These visions of America, however, came later. New England was a place of magic that hosted Europe's ghosts within it. As David Hall writes, "The people of seventeenth-century New England lived in an enchanted universe. Theirs was a world of wonders."[22] Disenchantment was perhaps even more troubled in the early United States than in Europe. In a sense, early white Americans occupied an old world, living in a universe of voices, the devil, and witches. The fear of Indians and women was prominent, and the two, alongside people of African descent, represented the battle between "Satan and God."[23] Indians were allied with Satan and had to disappear so that God, through the victories of the new Americans over dark forces, could be victorious. This led to the mapping of the American West as a landscape of promise, restoration of the human spirit, and mystic experience.

Hauntings

The desert and mountains of the West are incredibly beautiful. People who live there today frequently refer to the regenerative power of the Rocky Mountains, which is memorialized in John Denver's songs and countless movies. The Southwest exists as a mecca for America's wealthy who have migrated there from both coasts. Boulder, my hometown, once a center of hippie culture and radical activism, is now a city of Lululemon shops, yoga studios, vegan restaurants, life coaches, and intuitive healers who claim they can heal any illness by looking at a person and *feeling* the affliction they might have. Once the home of Arapaho Chief Niwot, the Boulder Valley is now identified with wealthy seekers of mystical experience.

A short drive away, Denver also offers the cool vibe of trendy coffee shops, breweries, and marijuana pharmacies. Underneath this facade is a darker history. Denver International Airport has a famous statue of a blue horse with blazing red eyes that fell on its creator and killed him. Stapleton, the former airport, is now a trendy housing development, one of the many areas of Denver that offers cookie-cutter "affordable" houses, at half a million dollars or more. It is named after Benjamin Franklin Stapleton, who was twice mayor of Denver and a prominent member of the Klu Klux Klan. Denver's other famous white men include John Evans, whose connections to the University of Denver, the Iliff School of Theology, and Northwestern University (located in Evanston, named after him) exist alongside his involvement in one of the worst massacres in the American West, at Sand Creek. As American Indian scholar Tink Tinker (wazhwazhe/Osage Nation) explains,

> Evans and Chivington were the two key Methodist figures involved politically and militarily in the events around the U.S. Army's terrorist murders known as the Sand Creek Massacre, Chivington as the military leader and perpetrator of the crimes, and Evans as the territorial governor complicit by generating a war-making hysteria in the months that led to the army's attack.[24]

Evans, after whom Evanston, Illinois, is named and who founded Northwestern University and the University of Denver (where I earned my doctorate), stoked anti-Indian sentiment for several years, helping to create the conditions for the massacre.[25] Chivington was proud of the attack, which killed over 230 American Indians, many of them children. On the day of the massacre, November 29, 1964, Chivington wrote that his men had killed "between 400 and 500 other Indians" in addition to several chiefs and they had whipped the "savages" in the massacre (which he initially claimed was a "fight," a claim that was later discredited).[26] Chivington's rationale for the massacre was to avenge the murder of a white man whose scalp had been found days earlier, a story that was later changed to claim there were actually 19 scalps.[27]

Stories surrounding Indian atrocities against white settlers often change numerous times, telling historians that they are likely fictitious. Atrocities committed against Indians, however, are well documented in the historical record. As one study notes, "At the same time, many Cheyennes and Arapahos signaled their peaceful intentions by 'holding their hands up.' Chivington's men ignored their pleas, firing on women and children and later mutilating their bodies."[28] In one account, at the end of the massacre, a surviving woman and her child were being herded with a group of ponies, when Colonel Shoup ordered his men to "Take no prisoners."[29] "The woman understood what had just transpired. She sheltered her child, then turned to face away from her murderers, who then did exactly as their commander had ordered."[30] The histories of Stapleton, the KKK, John Evans, and Sand Creek are not well known outside academic and activist circles. Later in this chapter, I will tell the largely forgotten story of a book. It was held in the library of Iliff School of Theology for nearly 100 years and wrapped in the skin of a flayed Indian.

The American West stretches from the plains of Colorado (or Kansas, according to some) to the coastlines of California, Oregon, and Washington. This chapter focuses mainly on the Southwest, a smaller area that includes

272 Colonial Geographies, Tourist Imaginaries, Mystical Landscapes

the states of Arizona, New Mexico, Colorado, and Utah, in part because I have spent a good portion of my life there, but also because of the mysticism attached to it, for it is characterized by "images of forbidding nature, vastness, and mystical grandeur."[31] I made an editorial decision to ignore the borders of these states and focus on specific sites in the lands that make up the region.

Today, the West retains much of the mystique it has had for two centuries as a place of wilderness and exploration. Even Lawrence of Arabia, so instrumental in the British colonial project, after attacking a train with his Arab allies, remarked, "It's the most amateurish, Buffalo Bill sort of performance, and the only people who do it well are the Bedouin."[32] Thus, even across the ocean, in the deserts of the Hijaz, the frontier myth was found in the narrative of British colonialism.[33] This myth was dependent upon the disappearance of the American Indian, which involved the reservation system, Indian schools, and the national park system. Once completed, the landscape could be remade as new American (white) territory that would serve the interests of oil, mining, agriculture, and other businesses, including mystical tourism.

One idea that is iterated in these mystical spaces is that "Everything Happens for a Reason," which is a popular slogan among the self-help, spiritual, New Age, and mystical seekers who often populate places like Boulder, Denver, and Sedona. As scholars have explained, the sentiment that "even bad things are not truly bad" is a convenient way to avoid criticism of the westward expansion of white settlers, the genocide of Native Americans, and the entire project of conquest.[34] The spaces of mystical tourism in the American West are an example of Manifest Destiny and the fulfillment of the idea of God leading the Puritans to the Promised Land: the Promised Land was, and is, Indian land.

The destruction of Indian ways of living includes the care of the land. The Muscogee Creek, whose relationship with the land I discussed in the opening chapter of this book, predicted the effects of the white man and his policies:

> The general prophecy of the Muscogee Creek is that the world will come to an end when the people no longer celebrate the harvest of the green corn in their "busk" ceremony, and tribal prophets warn that the sky will rain blood; when the trees are cut, their sap will be blood, announcing that when the last of the Indians disappear from the land, the land will fall beneath the waters of the ocean.[35]

The resonance of these words today in global warming and disappearing lands is both prophetic and undeniable.

New American Imaginaries

Maps suggest how new landscapes of America were imagined as European spaces. John Harley describes the cartography of the centuries leading up to the American Revolution as "simultaneously a practical instrument for colonial policy, a visual rhetoric for fashioning European attitudes towards the Americas and its people, and an analogue for the acquisition, management and reinforcement of colonial power."[36] John Smith's *Lord Baltimore's Map* and William Wood's *The South Part of New England* show "an already-tamed wilderness," which was, in the words of John Brian Harley, "more acceptable to English eyes."[37] The early writings of American settlers contain similar themes. An excerpt from *Letters from an American Farmer* provides one example: "This formerly rude soil has been converted by my father into a pleasant farm, and in return, it has established all our rights; on it is founded our rank, our freedom, our power as citizens."[38]

The theological framing of American citizenship was based on what the African American theologian Willie James Jennings describes as "the Christian imagination," seen in the intersection between Christianity, whiteness, and land ownership: "With the emergence of whiteness, identity was calibrated through possession of, not possession by, specific land."[39] Private ownership required the erasure of Indians, in part because most tribes did not recognize or agree with a concept of the earth that included ownership of private land. The mapping of the New World provides a blueprint of the ways that Europeans thought about the land and the problem of Indians within it.

The mapping of lands that became the United States began before the Revolutionary War, when the competition for Indian territory formed zones of Native and European control. In Daniel Richter's book of Native American history, he includes several of these maps. One shows the remapping of the region that encompasses Florida to the South, the East Coast up to Maine, the southern border of what is now Canada, and to the West, the Missouri River (Illinois and Missouri).[40]

As Richter explains, foreign powers wasted no time in renaming places and erasing their Indian roots. In the North, there was the Gallic "New France," St. Lawrence Valley, and "le pays des Illinois," and to the South, the Spanish San Marcos and St. Augustine.[41] Long gone were the Indian names for these places. As the Revolutionary War approached, and as a result of wars between the new Americans and British, the map shifted again. Richter calls this phase of mapping (1763–1768) the "racial frontier," and in his book, he includes a map of these Anglo-Indian boundaries.[42]

The use of a European engraving style and the depiction of Indians with Europeanized features in maps were two ways in which the landscapes of North America were envisioned as a natural extension of Europe.[43] European settlers looked at the environment as something to be tamed because it was threatening and dangerous; the forests were the domain of "wood sprites, trolls, and goat men—who defiled women and stole children," mythic creatures superimposed on the woods and mountains of America.[44] Pioneers envisaged the move West as a fight with Indians and the unseen enemy that lurked in the wilderness.[45] In later years, maps delineated good and bad Indians—the ones who were subdued and the ones with whom the United States had no treaties. This was expressed in a civilizational topography that included not only "wild Indians" but also "emigrant tribes" who had been removed from their ancestral lands.[46]

The belief in a frightening environment had its roots in premodern epistemologies that impacted the ways white settlers thought about America. Forests and mountains, "once the monstrosities of the medieval Christian imagination," helped to create the idea of the wilderness as frightful.[47] It was some time before the woods, mountains, and hollers of America were viewed as beautiful and serene. As Evan Berry explains, America's theology of immanence took some time to develop: "Far from being spaces of bewitchment, mountains and forests became key symbols of beauty, healthfulness, and power in American environmental thought."[48] The sublime became a key idea in American consciousness, and by the 1880s, nature was a religious space identified with Christian belief, where "natural wonders, such as Yosemite, the Grand Canyon, Niagara Falls, and Yellowstone, became emblems of divinity."[49]

The U.S. military was critical to this transformation of the landscape. Soldiers relocated, expelled, or massacred Indians in the quest for territory and the making of empty, safe, and serene landscapes for settlers whose views would be uninterrupted by the expelled indigenous populations. The story of the national parks is an important part of this history. A product of Emersonian thought, the photographs and paintings of nature, and the powerful idea of the American frontier, the park system is embedded in the popularity of transcendentalism and the theology of Reformed Protestantism.[50] As Mark Stoll explains in his majestic study of religion and the environmental movement, Emerson released this tradition "from its theological cage and clothed it in glittering, seductive colors."[51]

Photography is an important colonial technology, as documented in the previous chapter's example of the British occupation of Palestine. In the Grand Canyon, photography had its challenges, including the poor quality of early roll film and supply problems on expeditions.[52] George Eastman's developments in photography in the late nineteenth century and the development of the early Kodak camera revolutionized photography, making it easier to capture images without heavy equipment and chemicals that could be damaged *en route* (this also had a huge impact on tourism).[53] John Wesley Powell used stereographs and understood the importance of images in promoting his achievements, which were viewed by the public as accurate proof of the West's natural wonders.[54] Photographers, writers, and artists helped to create an idea of the West that was both mythical and mystical. Photographers Carleton Watkins (1829–1916) and William Henry Jackson (1843–1942) took images that helped to create the idea of America's "wilderness," and painters like Sanford Griffith (1823–1880) created representations of the Grand Canyon, which are some of the earliest in American art.[55]

Albert Bierstadt traveled to the Rocky Mountains in 1859, making sketches that would later help him to create masterpieces like *Indian Encampment, Shoshone Village* (1860), and his many portraits of Indians.[56] Bierstadt was a realistic painter, meticulous in detail; like other painters, he transposed his subject in a manner that would create a particular vision of landscape, even removing a mountain range when painting a river.[57] Other artists took much greater licenses, leaving out geographical features or rearranging them completely, thus helping to create a view of the West that was at once beautiful, fantastic, and fictive. Ethnographic portraiture, including Bierstadt's, often placed the subject—the American Indian—in the past. Another example of Fabian's critique of the West's denial of coeval time, portraits became a genre of the disappearing or already vanished Indian.

Stereoviews, photographs, and wood engravings were used to instill "a romanticized subjectivity, a wistful mythologizing of the views."[58] The use of photography in the settler colonial project of the American West is the story of mapping. As the landscape became reimagined as white space, photographers "used the beauty of the landscape as a metaphor for its potential," an idea used by investors, agriculturists, and other profiteers who viewed the West as an untapped economic opportunity.[59] Evan Berry explains how in this construction of nature, "[t]he role of romantic soteriology as a driving force of these recreational conquests can hardly be overstated."[60] The mountains became sites identified with truth and the kind of secularized religious experience that Protestants, living in an era of disenchantment, sought.

The role of artists in creating the national vision of the American West and its early tourism industry is a critical part of the history of America's mystical landscapes. Thomas Moran was interested in representing the "character of that region," which at times included a manipulation of the reality of the landscape, such as an exaggerated foreground, a photographic manipulation of the scene achieved by moving objects like large branches to the lower part of a photograph.[61] As art historians have noted, the work of artists like Thomas Moran, Frederick Church, and Winslow Homer "reinforced the intellectual concept of a heritage shared by all Americans."[62] It was a shared history that focused on the landscapes of America, emptied of Indian people.[63]

While the foundations of a new American landscape were being overlaid on Indian homelands, survivors who had been expelled from these same lands were fighting for survival. Robert Yellowtail, a tribal leader of the Crow, fought for his tribe his entire life. As a child, he witnessed the deaths of those around him—in a short time, the Crows on his reservation lost 20 percent of their people to disease and other health issues caused by U.S. government policies.[64] The experience of the Crow was shared by many tribal communities. Indian boarding schools also resulted in high death rates, especially from tuberculosis.[65] The harsh realities of the reservation and the boarding school were a world away from the lives of white artists and photographers, who were romanticizing the West for future tourists seeking its spiritual benefits.

Artists were not the only ones who contributed to a new vision of the American West. Christianity also had a major role. There was a profound shift in the status of geological features, which became objects of theological reflection and the churches of the outdoors. In Marjorie Nicolson's foundational book on the genre of mountain studies, she writes, "A century and a half ago, mountains became 'temples of Nature built by the Almighty' and 'natural cathedrals, or natural altars . . . with their clouds resting on them as the smoke of a continual sacrifice.'"[66] In many ways, her book *Mountain Gloom and Mountain Glory: The Development of the Aesthetics of the Infinite* (1959) is a theology of nature, reflexive of Christian ideas about the divine, sacred space, and the blessings of God's creation. Landscape has always been a religious project, and in the United States, the ways it has been constructed are often strongly situated in Protestant Christian ideas about the world. In Terry Tempest Williams' book on the national parks, which she calls a "personal topography," the sacred lands of Indians are places where "we meet the miraculous" and "read Genesis out loud in the Garden of Eden in Arches."[67]

Renamings

The first national park, Yellowstone, was established on lands that were home to the Piegans (Blackfoot), the Crows, the Bannocks, and the Shoshoni (including the Sheepeaters).[68] Interest in Yellowstone began in the early 1850s, a result of U.S. military mapping projects in the area that included expeditions with scientists and artists, which were followed by more expeditions over the following decades.[69] It took about 20 years for the legal acts that established Yellowstone to be put through Congress and signed into law, and on March 1, 1872, the ancestral lands of numerous Indian tribes became the first national park.[70] This marked the beginning of a system that would tear people from their lands and erase Indians from memory or memorialize them into the past through their "ruins" and "ancient cities." After battles between the U.S. military and Indians in 1877, when the last of the Bannocks and Nez Perce were captured or left the area, in Yellowstone, all that remained of Indians were piles of bones and scraps of blankets and clothing.[71]

The creation of the national park system, like other policies that were part of the settler colonial project, was often orchestrated, designed, and operated by the U.S. military. The early days of Yellowstone National Park provide one example where the U.S. military was present in guarding the park, protecting it from pioneers who were illegally hunting on it, and scaring off vandalizers of ancient rocks and other places.[72] Of course, the story of the American West starts in the pre-Revolutionary days of the new America, long before Frederick Jackson Turner's frontier, "an imaginary westward-moving line" that marked the division between "civilization" (white folks) and "savagery" (Indians).[73]

The national parks exist today as a major feature of summer travel, the family road trip, and a destination for foreign tourists. Turner's frontier is divided between cities, towns, and suburbs; miles of urban growth; and sites like the national park. Envisioned as a place for "the people" by transcendentalists and early naturalists, the parks' attractions became popular with the general American public after WWI.[74] Likely due to the popularity of the automobile, the national park is now an indelible feature of the U.S. landscape—once retreats for the rich, now open to everyone at the cost of admission.

Like the East Coast, the American West is a landscape defined by settler colonialism, a system that requires the erasure of old identities and their replacement with a mythology about who these settlers are. Settlers become the original inhabitants, a process seen in America and more recently in Israel. This is the difference between the classic colonies of Europe and settler colonies like the United States. As Lorenzo Veracini explains,

> The difference is absolutely critical: while a colonial society is successful only if the separation between colonizer and colonized is retained, a settler colonial project is ultimately successful only when it *extinguishes* itself—that is, when the settlers cease to be defined as such and become "Natives," and their position becomes normalized.[75]

The renaming of Indian places is another visible way in which places underwent a radical reconceptualization. In Arizona, the mountains known as the San Francisco Peaks (named by the Franciscans) have a host of older Native American names.[76] For the Navajo, the name is *Dook'o'oosliid*; for the Hopi, *Nuva'tukya'ovi*; for the Zuni, *Sunha K'hbchu*; for the Western Apache, *Dzil Tso*; and for the Southern Paiute, *Nuvaxatuh*. Many names of people and mountains are unfamiliar to us. In Sedona, Cathedral Rock, a location of one of the so-called spiritual vortexes, was first named Court Rock by settlers, then Cathedral Rock, to distinguish it from another place called Church Rock—all English names for Indian places.[77]

The remapping of the American West includes a history of Indians in other regions of North America, who were pushed westward. The story told in this chapter is incomplete, but I attempt to provide a sense of how the lands of Native peoples were remapped and how this impacted those who were forced into a different kind of life. Native American ways of being are not focused on ownership; instead, the caretaking of the land and its creations is important. Native American concepts of the sacred are focused on the land, not alienation from it, and the white American commodification, private ownership, and exploitation of the land are an anathema to Indian peoples.[78]

Christianity had a profound role in the removal of Indians, which included acts like arbitrarily taking Indian lands. One record is found in the words of Seneca Indian Annie Young Bumberry, who recalled a time when the Quakers set up a meeting house on her tribe's land, "Somehow the Quakers have been given a deed to the property and now we are told that it is theirs and now they are building a new parsonage there. Our Council House and property was sold to a white man and destroyed."[79] This took place after Collier's Indian New Deal, which tried to stop further land allotment to white settlers, a policy that was ignored.

The forced relocation of American Indians to the West was achieved not only through violent events like the massacres at Wounded Knee and Sand Creek, but also through legislation. The Indian Removal Act of 1870 allowed for the relocation of Indians who lived east of the Mississippi to the west of that river.[80] Other laws like the Timber and Stone Act, the Preemption Act, and the Homestead Act viewed land as available for the taking—in one case, limiting a claim to 160 acres.[81] In Cherokee Nation v. Georgia, the Supreme Court ruled that Indians "did not have legal standing due to their status as a 'domestic, dependent nation.'"[82] This ruling used the act of conquest as the *reason d'être* for further acts of conquest. These are part of a history of laws, policies, and events that destroyed Indian ways of living and remapped the American landscape into regions that were viewed as civilized (cities, agriculture, or natural resource allocation) or areas of wilderness set aside for tourist's enjoyment (national parks).

One place we can see this view is in the Wilderness Act of 1964, which defines wilderness as "an area where the earth and its community of life are untrammeled by man where man himself is a visitor who does not remain."[83] This Act, much like other legislation, denies both Indian connections to these lands and their forced removal from them. Wilderness is a space that is often identified with spiritual and mystical experience, as we shall learn later in this chapter. In particular, the Southwest is described this way. In the words of one fellow scholar, "The words enchanted, magical, and spiritual frequently are used to describe the Southwest. It *is* truly different from other regions of the West."[84]

Myths of the Indian

The mystical landscapes of the West are made possible through the process of historical settler colonization, which includes the removal of Indians from their ancestral lands, the reservation system, and the establishment of the national park system. American Indians have been variously portrayed as savage, violent, noble, and beautiful. When Indians attempted to assimilate to evade removal from their lands, as was the case of Miami Indians like Maconqua, they had limited success.[85] In this case, Indians were accepted after adopting European farming practices or building log houses like their neighbors.[86] More often, different tribes were categorized according to their acquiescence to the U.S. government, military, and white settlers, until these differences disappeared. As a matter of history and guilt, in time all Indians became romanticized as part of the West from long ago. J.Z. Smith wrote that these two visions represent a problematic reasoning:

> What troubles me is that these two portraits of the primitive—the nineteenth century negative evaluation and the twentieth century positive (even nostalgic) appreciation—are but the two sides of the same coin. They are but variations on the even older ambivalence: the Wild Man and the Noble Savage. Both see the primitive as not-like-us.[87]

The idea of the savage Indian was instrumental in the making of the modern West; without this imputed savagery, it would have been impossible to map it as an *American* space. In the mythologies of the Indians, the white man is ever present, often as a hero and at other times as a victim of the savage heathens whom white settlers encountered. It is important to understand that these are mythologies with fabrications and exaggerations, with names and places changed one, two, or endless times. The story of Pocahontas is one example. John Smith told of her rescuing him from certain death at the hands of her father, the chief (whom he calls the "king") of the Powhatan. As one version tells it, Pocahontas "dashed from the crowd, cradled Smith's head in her arms, and 'laid her downe' on top of his 'to save him from death.'"[88] In reality, Pocahontas was kidnapped and forced to convert to Christianity. There was no great love story, only a frightened kidnap victim who became part of the mythology of America.

The identification of the United States as an anti-colonial nation is complicated by the narrative of the American Revolution, an anti-colonial war for independence that, while freeing the United States of British control, was the path forward for imperial actions in the Hawaiian Islands, the Philippines, and Puerto Rico.[89] The mythologizing of an America ignores the centuries of "internal colonialism"—the focus of this chapter—and its exploration of the imaginary about the American West.[90] The American traditions of the summer camp and the establishment of the national park system are contingent on the internal colonization of Indian lands. The "American West" is an area that was Indian land, although it is presented as an empty, vast, and mystical space for the tourist.

As discussed earlier, the creation of the American West is dependent upon the erasure of Indians. This disappearance was achieved not only via genocide and forced removal, but also through literary conventions of the vanishing Indian and the popularity of Indian ghosts in the white American consciousness. Buffalo Bill's *Wild West* show was one of the most popular forms of traveling entertainment in the late nineteenth century and sold tickets based on the idea of the vanishing Indian. As Sam Maddra writes,

> The American Indians were commonly perceived to be a race in decline, and the Wild West show played on this idea by promoting the exhibition as being one of the last chances for the public to see a way of life that was vanishing.[91]

The disappearance of Native Americans from the American landscape was a necessary part of creating the American frontier (and the settlements east of the Mississippi). The vanishing Indian was also a rhetorical and artistic device. As R. David Edmunds explains,

> Images of the "vanishing redmen" permeated newspapers, magazines, and dime novels, while James Earle Frazer's popular sculpture "The End of the Trail," which featured a defeated Plains warrior slumped forward over a downcast horse, seemed to epitomize what was believed to be the Native Americans' fate.[92]

Ghosts were another way that Indians disappeared from the landscape. They were the new specters that replaced the old ones. "In Europe, people were haunted by their own ancestors. In America, we are haunted by the ghosts of Indians."[93] The specter of the Indian, while being a critical part of the formation of the American West, is part of a larger fascination with Indians that goes far beyond the domestic borders of the modern United States. Indians are popular in Europe and Asia as part of New Age Native Americanism (NANA). The numerous "Indian" products sold in Bali, for instance, include dreamcatchers and small clay models of an Indian chief, all for sale on an island across the ocean from American Indian homelands. Laura Donaldson has described the international appeal of NANA in "German Indian clubs" and the "Japanese tourists experiencing Hopi sacred dances, Lakota vision quests, and Ojibway sweat lodges," all part of late capitalism and its practice of making money off other cultures.[94]

While white men were the perpetrators of most of the violence against Indians, white women also played a role. Even in progressive circles of women who fought for the right to vote and championed other communities, including Irish and Chinese immigrants, there was often a disdain or even disgust for the Indians. One example is found in the activism of female journalists Sara Lippincott and Miriam Leslie, who were unsympathetic to Indians while focusing on the struggles of Chinese, Cornish, and Irish immigrants.[95] This fit into the prevailing white feminism of the day, which worked to uphold the power of white society and characterized even the most obvious colonizers and thieves of Indian lands and resources as "gallant."[96]

In addition to all these ways that Indians were abused, tortured, and killed, there exists the figurative erasure found in literature and other forms of popular culture. The Indian was often presented as "disappearing" into the wilderness, then vanishing altogether. Perhaps nowhere is this as emphatic as in James Fenimore Cooper's *The Last of the Mohicans* (1826). The novel is strongly focused on the theme of the vanishing Indian. In one place, an Indian falls "into that deep and yawning abyss" and in another, "down the irrecoverable precipice."[97] The character Magua is sinister in both the book and film, a "savage demon."[98]

Americans may be more familiar with the film starring Daniel Day Lewis and Madelaine Stowe than the book, which provides a compelling and romantic version of the story. In the film, Lewis plays an adopted white man named Hawkeye who has Indian sympathies, and Stowe plays Cora, a kidnapped American. They are madly in love and fight the "bad" Indians. Stowe's sister Alice, played by the angelic Jodhi May, is in love with Uncas, an Indian. In the end, Uncas is murdered by the nefarious Indian Magua and thrown off a cliff. Heartbroken, Alice follows him to her death. The final scene has Cora and Hawkeye escaping while Uncas is remembered as the "last of the Mohicans."

The creation of the sparse wastelands in the American West is part of a colonial history that has brutalized both the environment and its indigenous inhabitants. The creation of this region is linked to violence against Indians through a variety of policies, among them forced expulsion from the Eastern part of the United States westward.[99] Philip Deloria explains this forced migration (which also included massacres and other approaches) here,

> From 1813, when the final defeat of Tecumseh at the Battle of the Thames marked the end of Indian attempts to offer a unified, interregional resistance, until the 1830s, when President Andrew Jackson defied his own Supreme Court and forced the Cherokees to take to what became known as the Trail of Tears, Americans waged war, signed treaties, and used guile and force to relocate hundreds of thousands of Indian people. By the middle of the nineteenth century, most Native people had indeed been made to disappear from the eastern landscape.[100]

What resulted was an East almost completely emptied of Indians and a West in which they were present but often hidden, pushed into the most unproductive lands west of the Mississippi. As soon as I moved to Kentucky from my home state of Colorado, I noticed this absence. Mammoth Cave National Park mentions Indians, but the memorials to Native peoples are largely out West, at places like Sand Creek Massacre National Historic Site in Colorado.[101] National parks are often contested spaces—an example is Devils Tower in Wyoming, which is known as *Mato Tipila* (Bear's Lodge) by several Native communities.[102]

By the nineteenth century, whites claimed that Indians were extinct or that they lived in the past, a strategy that allowed for their status to be dependent on the United States but having "no American civil identity."[103] Priscilla Wald explains how Indians were viewed as "domestic dependent nations" who were "under the guardianship of the state."[104] In other words, Indians were not considered full persons under the law. These ideas created conditions under which land was stolen and children were taken by white parents.

The creation of reservations on which some Indians live today is another chapter in the story of the American West. Once Indians had been largely subdued with violence and forced to move to the West, they were cast as dangerous savages who should be kept separate (Jackson believed they could only evolve if kept apart from whites), and "if they refused to disappear, deserved extermination."[105] After Custer's defeat at Little Big Horn in 1876, the policy shifted and Indians were forced onto reservations, where assimilation could take place through the sale of surplus Indian land to white farmers who could teach Indians the correct way to live.[106] This was a way to keep Indians away from most whites, but allow them "to exist within American national boundaries"—the reservation.[107] As Indian scholars have pointed out, taking land and establishing reservations were just the beginning. The termination of the federal recognition of Native Americans like the Klamath and Menominee was another way, alongside encouraging Indians to relocate to urban centers, of opening their lands to use by the federal government and corporations.[108]

The colonial (internal colonial) strategy of reforming land tenure was disastrous for many indigenous peoples. As discussed in an earlier chapter, the Great Mahele, which may have been intended by the King to help preserve the land for the Hawaiian people (if it was distributed, it would be more difficult to steal than if it was all held by the King), was used to disenfranchise Native Hawaiians from zones of land they had been on for years (or generations). In the case of Indians, the encouragement of so-called "Indian farming" that followed the European style ended up "reducing the amount of Indian land under cultivation" and the loss of "tens of millions of acres."[109]

The national park system, which worked in tandem with the reservations established for some of the remaining tribal communities, was also used to eradicate Indians from the landscape. Mark David Spence's history of Yellowstone, Glacier, and Yosemite shows the ways that the preservation of nature was viewed as incongruous with Indian culture. From the beginning, the clearing of Indians from beautiful natural spaces was viewed as the first step in creating sites of leisure tourism for Americans. In Colorado, the

Mountain Ute were involuntarily removed from areas deemed ideal for the future "pleasure ground and health home of the nation."[110] This idea of nature was firmly grounded in the theology of a reformed Christianity.

It was the spirit of the solitary seeker alone in nature in the twentieth century. It is also the spirit of this Reformed relationship of individual, spirit, and nature, which this generation adapted to parks for the uplift of a democratic people.[111]

National parks became identified with good citizenship and were believed to offer a way to improve a person's character.[112] Men like Theodore Winthrop, author of *Canoe and Saddle* (1862), and Frederick Law Olmstead viewed nature as something that "cultivated the mind and improved the soul," and climbing Mount Rainier was viewed as a transformational act that made men and women "better human beings."[113] Washington, like many states out West, also had a burgeoning naturalist and environmental community, which included organizations like the *Sierra Club* (1892) and the *Mazamas* (1894), which developed into The Mountaineers, a club that exists to this day.[114]

The myth of the vanishing Indian played a major role in the establishment of parks like Yellowstone, where it was claimed that no human had set foot. In reality, humans had been present in the area since the last Ice Age; more recently, it was a major source of food for indigenous peoples including fish, berries, deer, elk, and antelope, as well as a spiritual area due to its hot mineral waters.[115] The Crow were told that because they hunted buffalo, they had no interest in the area, despite their frequent hunting in the mountains for game, and were eventually pushed out entirely and moved to a reservation 200 miles away.[116] Yosemite had an Indian Village, which was first a tourist attraction designed to showcase authentic Indian culture and later was called an eyesore and moved to a secluded part of the park before it was dismantled altogether.[117] Policies used to exclude Indians from lands important to their sustenance and community were often centered on making a park pristine and empty, as if it had never been the land of Indians, but rather an empty wilderness for new Americans to explore.

Children's camps are one place where we find a rich imagination about Indians. Ernest Thomas Seton began Indian cosplay for children in camps in 1901, called the Woodcraft Indians, which was popularized after being documented in the *Ladies' Home Journal* a year later.[118] Summer camps became associated with Indians through the naming of camps, in costuming, and through a healthy body and mind. Camps were intimately linked to American anthropology through an identification with Indian culture. As Philip Deloria explains, white Americans "played Indian" as a child-rearing model: "As ethnography gained greater popular legitimacy in the last decades of the nineteenth century, its primitivist impulses infiltrated American culture, making Seton's Indians seem a more authentic means of raising children than Beard's pioneers."[119] The gendering of children was even cast within Indian cosplay, a program that was linked to the establishment of the Boy Scouts and Girl Scouts. The Camp Fire Girls (who became the Girl Scouts) were focused on learning to cook, care for babies, and learn home economics.[120]

Bioregionalism is another form of "playing Indian," which includes three elements: the recognition that Native Americans lived in harmony with the environment, an acknowledgement that white settlers eliminated or displaced Indians and disrupted this harmonious relationship, and a commitment to be more like Native Americans.[121] One problem with bioregionalism, despite its positive attributes, is that it often refers to Indians as relics of the past, with little or no reference to contemporary Indians, or to the reparations they deserve.[122] Today, the fascination with the "primitive" through playing Indian is seen in numerous spaces.

Burning Man is a festival held in the Black Rock Desert of Nevada every summer. My most recent book discusses the event as a "tribe event," one of the many festivals held around the country that celebrate the primitive and often use cosplay to imitate the "primitive Indian." In the case of Burning Man, participants "comingle many strains of late twentieth-century affinity tribes into a single seething meta-tribe."[123] It is, in the words of Robert Kozinets, a "neotribe" that calls itself Burners.[124] It is important to remember that these imaginings about Indians are situated in an idea of "the West" as a place that is different, wondrous, and strange—a "mythic" place that has the "alluring horizons of possibility."[125] As a place, the West is also a space where difference is at its foundation, for it is "west" of Europe and "west" of the settlements of the early United States, which usually expelled or killed Indians. Much like the frontier of the past, festivals like Burning Man and Wanderlust (which moves to different locations) promise the possibility of personal transformation in a landscape that offers beauty, introspection, and the possibility of mystical experience.

Creating the American West

As discussed earlier, the United States has a colonial and imperialist history. The internal colonialism directed at Indians includes settler violence, military attacks, massacres, disease, enslavement, the kidnapping and murder of children, environmental damage, and cultural colonialism. Narratives about the American West often focus on solitude, reflecting ideas about the search for one's true self in the vast outdoors—a space made empty through the violence inflicted upon Native Americans and, for survivors, expulsion to barren lands known as "reservations." Environmental violence was one way in which the American West was created, both in its current physical form and in the idea of the West as an expansive and barren space. Consider Sedona, examined at the end of this chapter. Before the middle of the nineteenth century, the valley in which Sedona is located had a semitropical climate with high humidity, a perfect place for farming and hunting, qualities that were destroyed by white settlers.[126] Cattle farming and then agriculture in the form of orchards were followed by a drought, then rains, wood harvesting, and mining, all of which created gullies and ravines, resulting in all the topsoil and its vegetation being washed away.[127] Sedona was named after an early white settler.

Tourism in the American Southwest relies on the exploitation of its indigenous populations and the visual optics of their disappearance. John Muir, who helped to make the West famous through his writings about nature and the great outdoors, is one example. In most of his writings, Indians are either absent, erased from the beautiful locations he writes about, or they exist as negative characters stealing or otherwise acting as the villain. In his writings about Alaska, Muir respects Native practices, but as for Indians, they are described as "dirty," "deadly," and "lazy," and as for their place in America, they were viewed as having "no right place in the landscape."[128] It is not until the end of his life, in his book *The Story of My Boyhood and Youth,* that he writes about the Indians as part of the world he loves.[129] Yet, they are still described as undesirables, apart from their hunting skills: "hungry beggars, thieves, and a frightful lurking presence."[130] For Muir and many others, Native Americans were interruptions to the modern gaze. Indians "disturbed the wilderness" that was their ancestral home because they were completely disassociated from it.[131]

The sacred in the American West is both connected to and disconnected from American Indians. In some cases, the cultures of indigenous peoples are used to legitimize the land and its features, something seen in claims about the mystic vortexes that characterize the Sedona landscape, according to some white residents.[132] Conversely, the sacred is constructed upon Christian ideas like "God's presence" and Gnostic spirituality.[133] As Susannah Crockford explains, "Sedona is an example of the social production of the sacred in recent historical memory, a recorded and visible process of sacralization."[134] The question of what these changes mean in terms of sacrality is one issue, but there is also the problem of how tourism functions as a kind of performance. As one study notes,

> Tourists want performances to be lively and accessible to photography, to be safe, to be of short duration, since they have other sites to see and time is limited, and the objects they purchase must be small enough to be taken back on an airplane.[135]

In mystical landscapes, white people often take on Indian identities for a business in healing or other mystical practices. Assuming an Indian identity is also a practice white people have used for cultural cachet, career advancement, and in some cases, to gain scholarships and other benefits. These forms of aggression against Indians are not examined here but are part of the ongoing violence against Indian/Native communities.

The Hollywood Western is a genre famous around the world that has its own subgenres and that has inspired many other genres, including films focused on the spiritual quest. Movies featuring the American West are problematic and none more than the Hollywood Western, a genre that is morally reprehensible for its violence and lack of guilt. Susan Courtney asks this question:

> [H]ow did a popular film genre that routinely pairs democracy with individualism, justice with vigilantism, property rights with conquest, and the right to life (along with "liberty and the pursuit of happiness") with mass murder for so long maintain a reputation as *the* genre of American ideals?[136]

Because these *are* American values.

The Hollywood Western includes the films of John Wayne, who is typically shown as killing Indians with abandon. One of these films, *True Grit* (1969), included scenes shot on my grandmother's ranch in Colorado, and I remember being told about my grandmother briefly meeting Mr. Wayne on the steps of a building (a courthouse, I believe, in Ouray). John Wayne's politics were not very different from how he behaved in films, with a strong dislike for American Indians. In contrast, one film inspired by the Hollywood Western that features a spiritual quest, *Nomadland* (2020), portrays the West as a space emptied of the Indians who once lived there, now a region frequented by itinerant laborers moving between jobs in camper vans and other vehicles, made homeless by the failure of capitalism.

Nomadland, for which Frances McDormand won an Oscar for Best Actress, is based on the nonfiction book *Nomadland: Surviving America in the Twenty-First Century*, by Jessica Bruder (2017), that documents older white North Americans who have lost their homes due to financial pressures brought about by layoffs and other crises. David Brown Morris describes how the book documents its subject, the "workamper," living in vehicles that "serve as cramped escape pods for elderly individuals ejected from a booming economy that has failed them."[137]

The film is directed by Chloe Zhao, whose attention to Native voices is well known from her earlier movie, *The Rider* (2017), which featured the nonprofessional Brady Jandreau, a Lower Brule Sioux, in the main role.[138] *Nomadland* is focused on white nomads, the *workamper* documented in Bruder's book, who go from job to job, most often at Amazon fulfillment centers, which employ more "nomadic van-dwellers" than any other business in the nation.[139]

The Hollywood Western relies on antinomies—"cowboy vs. Indian; garden vs. wilderness; domesticity vs. the company of men."[140] In *Nomadland*, the focus is on white (masculinized) women within a vast landscape, which is presented without any comment regarding how it was emptied of Indians. Patricia White describes how contemporary films about the West function as feminist telling of the story of national territory: "These stories thrum with attention to detail even as they render the landscape in glorious magic-hour images, focusing the genre's intertwined problems of masculine and territorial legitimacy through a feminist lens."[141]

The landscape is ever present in *Nomadland*, noted by critics who have compared the film to the American West (a film "as vast as the American landscape it travels").[142] The focus on individualism reflects the frontier myth that formulated the West in public consciousness. As Tim Lindemann writes, *Nomadland* "reaffirms the myth of the 'wide open spaces' of US landscape which has historically been instrumental in the displacement of people excluded from US national identity on the basis of class, race and gender."[143] The idea of the American West, which serves as the space where the main character escapes to in her journey, is situated in the fantasy that its "wild" nature offers a path to healing and transcendence despite the fact that "the supposed wilderness was not 'wild' at all but had been inhabited for centuries by Indigenous people."[144] When Fern is shown in a mountain stream, contemplating her life and losses, it is a "mythical ritual."[145] This moment and others in the film signify how the West exists for many white North Americans—as a mystical space that offers healing, solace, and even transcendence for the individual in need of respite.

The portrayal of the American West is a mystic space that white Americans have access to, like Fern's mythic ritual. However, for American Indians, land is sacred, and access to its power is cultural. The sacred center of Indian lands is not tied to a historical event, but to creation, and is not available to those outside the community.[146] The Navajo have four mountains that mark the boundaries of their land, and sacred sites are not revealed publicly because they are for the community members—those who have always been in a relationship with it.[147] Assuming that the American West's sacrality is available to people outside these communities is evidence of the remapping done by settler colonialism and its rejection of the beliefs on which this sacrality is supposedly based. One place where this is especially true is in Sedona, Arizona.

Sedona, Arizona

Individuality is a common feature of mystical narratives and suggests that the answers to modernity's miseries can be remedied by nature. Scholars have written about the ways in which consumerism has marginalized religion; when combined with the "cultural influence of individualism," fantasies about visiting the American West are proposed as mystical journeys.[148] The following section examines Sedona. The therapeutic practices and products attached to Sedona are variably marketed as holistic, spiritual, or mystical ways of crafting tourist spaces that try to "engage with the whole self and the balance of body, mind, and spirit" as pathways to improve the "spiritual self."[149]

Sedona began seeing white settlers in larger numbers in the 1820s, a trend that continued with the "gradual confiscation of Indian lands and removal of Indians by the 'right of discovery,'" which was followed by attacks on Indians and, in 1875, the forced removal of the Yavapai-Apache to the San Carlos Reservation.[150] Today, Sedona, Arizona, with its many shades of sandstone and shale geologic features, has a landscape that is recognizable to anyone who has visited the town. It is "nestled at the mouth of the scenic box canyon Oak Creek has carved out of the Mogollon Rim as it plunges down a 3,000-foot gorge to the sloping mesa of the Verde Valley."[151] The area, once populated by Hopi, Navajo, Apache, and Pueblo, is now a popular New Age destination that celebrities, including Oprah Winfrey, have visited. Housing developments reflect the idea of mysticism, which is believed to be attached to the "vortexes" in the area, with names like Harmony Hills, Shadow Estates, and Mystic Hills.[152] These places are part of a cognitive map of Sedona that involves the replacement of a geographical marker with a new understanding of its "siting."[153]

Anyone who has visited, read about, or studied Sedona knows that the idea of *vortexes* is a strong part of the town's identity. Locals (white folks) claim that there are not only vortexes but also "mysterious underground reservoirs of energy," "interdimensional portals," and all sorts of other "spiritual presences."[154] Native American beliefs in the sacredness of Sedona's land are often cited by local spiritualists and mystics as proof of the existence of vortexes—a problematic claim based on the assumption that Native American sacred spaces are for everyone.

Susannah Crockford explains how the remapping of Sedona as a space for white spiritual and mystical experience violates Native beliefs in place. As she writes,

> Most tribes have a sacred center of their ancestral lands, which is permanent in that it came into being with creation and not with a historical event. It is identified with that tribe, who accept responsibility for it and relate all historical events within its confines; for example, Navajo land has four sacred mountains that mark its extent.[155]

Like other New Age and contemporary mystical places, there is a big mish-mash of religions, traditions, beliefs, and practices found in Sedona. As I wrote in my most recent book, this is the kind of cultural colonialism modern mysticism is known for—muddled, confused, and, at the same time, exotic and enticing.[156]

At Sedona, people refer to Christ, a Father God, Love, and Light and use smudge with sage, medicine wheels, and Indian-style drumming as parts of a mystical continuum of experience.[157] References to "Native" and "indigenous" power, spirituality, and traditions are common in Sedona. Many of its Indian critics refer to practitioners of neo-Native spirituality as "whiteshamans" and colonizers.[158] Native languages are also used to present Sedona as a place that is authentic due to its native past, but decidedly under the umbrella of modern mysticism. As Susannah Crockford explains,

> Cross-cultural concepts are seen as equivalent; energy is equated with the Holy Spirit, *prana*, *chi*, and *mana*. We return here to the resemblance between energy and the impersonal forces of early sociological theory, which equated *prana* and *mana* with *orenda* in Iroquois, *manitou* in Algonquin, *wakan* in Dakota, Brahman from Hinduism, *naual* from Mexico and Central America, and many other terms cross-culturally.[159]

The construction of Sedona as a place of vortexes, mysterious powers in the land, energy lines congruent with the Egyptian pyramids, and the former location of the Lemuria temple (related to the lost city of Atlantis) isn't simply New Age silliness, but a way for white settlers to imagine the space as non-Indian.[160] As Adrian Ivakhiv points out, this "allows New Agers to upstage any existing Native land claims by invoking for themselves a higher and more ancient authority presumed by them to be equally or more deeply rooted in the land."[161] Like the white settlers of the past—the frontiersmen and mountain men, miners and cattle barons—the current inhabitants of Sedona also see the area as their own.

An Infamous Book

This chapter concludes with the story of a book in Iliff School of Theology's library. In a way, this book represents what is at stake in this project—the erasure of people through the theft of their lands. Mystical landscapes are dependent on the disappearance of the past, which is a necessary and critical part of the remapping of territory for white bodies. I didn't spend much time in the library where that book was interred from 1893 to 1974. I was a graduate student in the joint doctoral program at the University of Denver and Iliff School of Theology, and later a faculty member at Iliff in a visiting position I held for five years. Iliff's library collections were largely focused on Christianity, including some old and rare books that were encased in glass. Most of my time at Iliff was spent in classes, either taking courses or, years later, teaching a new generation of graduate students. However, a short walk across campus is the University of Denver library, where I spent endless hours and days doing research, finding books, and returning books, until one day I returned the last pile of books, said goodbye to my many years at the two institutions, and set off for a new life in Kentucky.

I heard about the book late in my time at Iliff and somehow it made sense, for I never felt welcomed as a Muslim faculty member, and for me, it was not an easy place to be. As a former administrator told me before resigning, "This is a difficult place to be a woman." When I moved out of my office and we drove away, a car ran into the left side of my husband's Toyota truck, pushing us a few more inches away from the campus. He said, "I wonder if that is a sign from Allah." The book in the library at Iliff was called *The History of Christianity*, "bound in the flayed tanned skin of a murdered American Indian."[162] When my former colleague Tink Tinker learned about the book in 1985, when he was a new faculty member at the School of Theology, he smudged the building with cedar smoke.[163] Even though it was gone, given to members of American Indian Movement (AIM) in 1974 to bury, he wondered why it had been there so long on display for people to see, admire, look at as a curiosity, and fetishize.[164] As I read Tinker's scholarship on the book, one of the facts of the story haunted me—the title. Of course, I thought, the book was called *The History of Christianity*—this is the history of white colonial religion, isn't it? Beyond this, there were less subjective and academic questions related to the book you have been reading. Above all is the current space of Colorado, so much of it occupied by wealthy white yuppies with their Subarus, drinking matcha lattes, and doing yoga and pilates, all made possible by the erasure of Indians.

The book was made from the skin of an Indian murdered in 1774, 1776, or 1779, most likely in Virginia but perhaps Kentucky.[165] There are different versions of the story, one of which claims that the murderer was General Daniel Morgan, a Revolutionary War figure who made trinkets from the skin of an Indian, who perhaps killed his wife and daughter (these details were probably made up, for white people often killed Indians with impunity).[166] The book even has a dedication: "This Latin church history book, written by Johann Lorenz von Moshiem in 1752, is bound in American Indian skin. The Indian was killed in hand-to-hand combat by General David Morgan of Morgantown, West Virginia, on April 1, 1779."[167]

The role of the imagination is a critical part of this story, for no one really knows if the Indian was killed in Virginia or Kentucky (Kentucky has a Morgantown, close to where I live in Bowling Green). The detail about hand-to-hand combat is likely an elaboration, made to valorize the killer who may have murdered the Indian for any host of reasons, from wanting his land to not liking Indians. The part of the story about the Indian being killed because he killed Morgan's wife and daughter is also not linked to any evidence, and another inscription in the book that tells its genealogy (it was handed off to this person, then this person gave it to this reverend) describes Morgan as an "Indian fighter," which suggests the Indian in question was killed as part of a larger campaign, part of what Tinker calls a "Christian invasion" on Indian lands.[168]

As Tinker notes in his research on the book, the elaborate story of the Indian and Morgan includes a claim that his "beautiful young wife and infant daughter" were killed by an "Algonquin warrior" and that after the unarmed Morgan wrestled the tomahawk from the Indian, he killed the Indian.[169] Here is the story of white vengeance against the Indian, a standard narrative in the mythology of the savage Indian that is well known to scholars. In 1955, yet another version of the Morgan story emerged, with Morgan being attacked by two Indians while he was asleep in a field.[170] These endless versions of the story, of David Morgan or Daniel Morgan in Virginia, Kentucky, in 1774, 1776, or 1779, as revenge or as a matter of self-defense, are why we know none of this is true. The only fact that remains is that an Indian was murdered, his skin flayed, tanned, and used as a cover for a book.

How was this incident remembered? In a gruesome and disturbing news article reporting about the donation of the book to Iliff in 1934, the reporter for the *Rocky Mountain News* describes the book's beautiful condition: it was "well preserved," with unbroken skin, "its smoothness and texture equal to those of the finest parchment," and finally, its color "mellowed to deep ivory mottling into saffron, and by an ironic quirk of fate, it endures as a priceless vestment for the teachings of brotherly love."[171]

This grotesque misremembering of the murder of an unnamed Indian is significant for several reasons that lie at the center of this book—above all, for the way the past is misremembered and erased as part of the creation of modern landscapes. The imaginary landscapes of modernity are often built upon the bodies of past peoples, then reformulated in ways that allow for capitalist, neoliberal businesses that include mystical tourism. In 2013, when the graduating class of Iliff raised money for a memorial related to the book, the offer was turned down.[172] If the memorial had been constructed, the work it would have done would have been significant, for it would remind generations what Iliff, the University of Denver, Denver, and Colorado are all founded upon—the murder of Indians.

As this book draws to a close, I quote the words of Grey Eyes, a Wyandot Indian whose people were removed from their lands along the Sandusky River, and Annie Bumberry, the Seneca Indian whose land was taken by the Quakers. After he gave his last sermon in his ancestral lands, for he had converted to Methodism, along with many of his people, Grey Eyes said, "Soon they shall be forgotten, for the onward march of the strong White Man will not turn aside for the Indians graves."[173] In 1937, Annie Bumberry, who was born near Elk River in Oklahoma, when speaking about the home she had inherited from her grandmother, said, "I do not know how long I can stay here as I am told that the water from the Grand River dam will come up to the top of the doors."[174] John Bowes describes this as the removal of Indians that occurred even after they had drawn "their final breath."[175] Bowes stood looking at the waters of Grand Lake, where under the waters were the homes of Bumberry and other Seneca Indians, their ceremonial grounds drowned by America's mapmakers.[176]

Notes

1 Cosgrove 2008, 91.
2 Mark David Spence, *Dispossessing the Wilderness: Indian Removal and the Making of the National Parks* (New York: Oxford University Press, 1999), 3.
3 Spence, 3.
4 Crockford, 59.
5 American Indian and Native American are both used in this chapter to describe the original inhabitants of the United States of America.
6 Berry, 125.
7 Joel Kovarsky, *The True Geography of Our Country: Jefferson's Cartographic Vision* (Charlottesville: University of Virginia Press, 2014), 112–113. Jefferson's fondness for maps in the context of his plans for expansion is discussed in Kovarsky's book on page 128. Excerpts from letters quoted are part of the public domain and located in the National Archives website ("Founders Online").
8 Reginald Horsman, *Race and Manifest Destiny: The Origins of American Racial Anglo-Saxonism* (Cambridge: Harvard University Press, 1981), 86, 90.
9 Adler, 13.
10 Matthew Baigell, "Territory, Race, Religion: Images of Manifest Destiny," *Smithsonian Studies in American Art* 4, no. 3/4 (1990): 8.
11 Lynch, 189.
12 Willa Cather, *O Pioneers!* (public domain), 28.
13 Cather, 114.
14 Baigell, 4–6.
15 Albert Boime, *The Magisterial Gaze: Manifest Destiny and American Landscape Painting c. 1830–1865* (Washington: Smithsonian Institution Press, 1991), 140–141.
16 Harley 2001, 171.
17 Boime, 133.
18 Baigell, 11–12.
19 Boime, 131. See also Boime's discussion of Mount Rushmore, 158–163.
20 Lynch, 7.
21 Lynch, 152.
22 David D. Hall, *Worlds of Wonder, Days of Judgment: Popular Religious Belief in Early New England* (Cambridge: Harvard University Press, 1990), 71.
23 Bergland, 27.
24 George E. "Tink" Tinker, "Redskin, Tanned Hide: A Book of Christian History Bound in the Flayed Skin of an American Indian: The Colonial Romance, Christian Denial and the Cleansing of a Christian School of Theology," *Journal of Race, Ethnicity, and Religion* 5, no. 9 (2014): 11–12. Dr. Tinker is a member of the Osage Nation.
25 Tinker 2014, 12–13.
26 Ari Kellman, *A Misplaced Massacre: Struggling Over the Memory of Sand Creek* (Cambridge: Harvard University Press, 2013), 9.
27 Kellman, 10, 15.

28 Kellman, 28.
29 Joy Masoff, "The Mystery Man of Sand Creek: George Laird Shoup," *Great Plains Quarterly* 39, no. 2 (2019): 194.
30 Masoff, 194.
31 Ivakhiv, 145.
32 T.E. Lawrence, *Lawrence of Arabia: The Selected Letters*, ed. Malcolm Brown (London: Little Books, 2005), 132–133. Quoted in Johnston 2017.
33 Stetler, 161.
34 Crockford, 22.
35 Fixico, 22.
36 John B. Harley, "Rereading the Maps of the Columbian Encounter," *Annals of the Association of American Geographers* 82 (1992): 528.
37 Harley 1988, 70.
38 Baigell, 15.
39 Jennings, 59.
40 Richter, 164.
41 Richter, 166.
42 Richter, 212.
43 Harley 1988, 71.
44 Kim Heacox, *An American Idea: The Making of the National Parks* (Washington: National Geographic Society, 2001), 24.
45 Heacox, 27.
46 D. W. Meinig, "Territorial Strategies Applied to Captive Peoples," in *Ideology and Landscape in Historical Perspective: Essays on the Meanings of Some Places in the Past*, ed. Alan R. H. Baker and Gideon Biger (Cambridge: Cambridge University Press, 1992), 132.
47 Berry, 102.
48 Berry, 102.
49 David E. Nye, *American Technological Sublime* (Stanford: Stanford University Press, 1994), 23.
50 Mark R. Stoll, *Inherit the Mountain: Religion and the Rise of American Environmentalism* (New York: Oxford University Press, 2015), 115.
51 Stoll, 115.
52 David E. Nye, "Visualizing Eternity: Photographic Constructions of the Grand Canyon," in *Picturing Place: Photography and the Geographical Imagination*, ed. Joan M. Schwartz and James R. Ryan (New York: I.B. Tauris, 2003), 81.
53 Douglas Collins, *The Story of Kodak* (New York: Harry Abrams Publishers, 1990), 46–55.
54 Nye 2003, 81–82.
55 Floramae McCarron-Cates, "The Best Possible View: Pictorial Representation in the American West," in *Frederick Church, Winslow Homer, and Thomas Moran: Tourism and the American Landscape*, ed. Gail S. Davidson and Floramae McCarron-Cates (New York: Bulfinch Press, 2006), 75.
56 Lynda S. Ferber, *The Hudson River School: Nature and American Vision* (New York: Rizzoli, 2009), 151.
57 Ferber, 151.
58 McCarron-Cates, 78.
59 Hore, 23, 36.
60 Berry, 119.
61 McCarron-Cates, 90.
62 McCarron-Cates, 107.
63 Artists also created paintings of Indians, but, like much of the representations of Native peoples in America, they were often viewed as evidence of the disappearing Indian.

64 Frederick E. Hoxie and Tim Bernardis, "Robert Yellowtail (Crow)," in *The New Warriors: Native American Leaders Since 1900*, ed. R. David Edmunds (Lincoln: University of Nebraska Press, 2001), 55, 56, 61. The sale of so-called "surplus lands" was one of the issues that Yellowtail battled.

65 Brenda J. Child, *Boarding School Seasons: American Indian Families, 1900–1940* (Lincoln: University of Nebraska Press, 1998), 66–67. Dr. Child is an Ojibwe scholar.

66 Marjorie Hope Nicolson, *Mountain Gloom and Mountain Glory: The Development of the Aesthetics of the Infinite* (New York: W. W. Norton & Company, 1959), 2.

67 Terry Tempest Williams, *The Hour of Land: A Personal Topography of America's National Parks* (New York: Farrar, Straus and Giroux, 2016), 14, 285, Here, Williams refers to Arches National Park, mapping it as a church—a Christian space.

68 Haines, *Volume One*, 21.

69 Haines, *Volume One*, 85, 87, 103.

70 Haines, *Volume One*, 167, 172.

71 Haines, *Volume One*, 238–239.

72 Aubrey L. Haines, *The Yellowstone Story: A History of Our First National Park*, Volume 2 (Niwot: University Press of Colorado, 1996), 3, 21, 27.

73 Ferber, 151.

74 Thomas R. Cox, "Americans and Their Forests: Romanticism, Progress, and Science in the Late Nineteenth Century," *Journal of Forest History* 29, no. 4 (1985): 159.

75 Veracini, 28.

76 Crockford, 34.

77 Crockford, 39.

78 Crockford, 50.

79 Bowes, 211.

80 Bowes, 7.

81 Cox, 161.

82 Bowes, 65.

83 McCloskey, 315.

84 Suzan Campbell, *The American West: People, Places, and Ideas* (Santa Fe: Western Edge Press, 2001), 111.

85 Bowes, 72–73.

86 Bowes, 73.

87 Smith 1993, 297.

88 Timothy J. Shannon and David N. Gellman, *American Odysseys: A History of Colonial America* (New York: Oxford University Press, 2014), 58.

89 Karen M. Morin, "Mining Empire: Journalists in the American West, ca. 1870," in *Postcolonial Geographies*, ed. Alison Blunt and Cheryl McEwan (New York: Continuum, 2002), 154.

90 Morin, 154.

91 Maddra, 135.

92 R. David Edmunds, "Introduction: Twentieth-Century Warriors," in *The New Warriors: Native American Leaders Since 1900*, ed. R. David Edmunds (Lincoln: University of Nebraska Press, 2001), 1.

93 Bergland, 19.

94 Donaldson, 678.

95 Morin, 161, 165.

96 Morin, 165.

97 Quoted in Bergland, 86.

98 See Bergland.

99 My use of the word Indian here is due to conversations I've had with an elder from one of these communities who preferred it to Native American.

100 Deloria, 64–65.

101 Bremer 2022, 169.

102 Bremer 2022, 169.

103 Bergland, 15.

104 Priscilla Wald, *Constituting Americans: Cultural Anxiety and Narrative Form* (Durham: Duke University Press, 1995), 18.

105 Deloria, 104.

106 Deloria, 104.

107 Deloria, 104.

108 M. Annette Jaimes and Theresa Halsey, "American Indian Women: At the Center of Indigenous Resistance in Contemporary North America," in *Dangerous Liaisons: Gender, Nation and Postcolonial Perspectives*, ed. Anne McClintock, Aamir Mufti, and Ella Shohat (Minneapolis: University of Minnesota Press, 1997), 309.

109 Banner, 274.

110 Samuel Bowles, *The Parks and Mountains of Colorado: A Summer Vacation in the Switzerland of America, 1868*, ed. James H. Pickering (Norman: University of Oklahoma Press, 1991), 182. Quoted in Spence, 26.

111 Stoll, 116.

112 Berry, 119.

113 Theodore Catton, *National Park, City Playground: Mount Rainier in the Twentieth Century* (Seattle: University of Washington Press, 2006), 19–20.

114 Jim Kjeldsen, *The Mountaineers: A History* (Seattle: The Mountaineers, 1998), 12, 13. As noted by Kjeldsen, Chinese and Native Americans were excluded from the club for many years. See Kjeldsen, 19.

115 Spence, 43.

116 Spence, 52.

117 Spence, 122–124.

118 Deloria, 96.

119 Deloria, 106.

120 Deloria, 113.

121 Lynch, 225.

122 Lynch, 225.

123 Kevin Kelly, "The Next Burning Ban," in *Burning Man*, ed. John Plunkett and Brad Weiners (San Francisco: HardWired, 1997), 127.

124 Kozinets, 203.

125 Lynch, 9.

126 Ivakhiv, 152.

127 Ivakhiv, 152–153.

128 Spence, 23.

129 Paul Robbins and Sarah A. Moore, "Return of the Repressed: Native Presence and American Memory in John Muir's *Boyhood and Youth*," *Annals of the American Association of Geographers* 109, no. 6 (2019): 1751.

130 Robbins and Moore, 1752.

131 Hore, 130.

132 Crockford, 35.

133 Crockford, 35.

134 Crockford, 35.

135 Bruner, 244.

136 Courtney, 86. Italics in original.

137 David Brown Morris, *Wanderers: Literature, Culture and the Open Road* (New York: Routledge, 2021), 23.

138 Patricia White, "Women Auteurs, Western Promises," *Film Quarterly* 75, no. 4 (2022): 26.
139 Morris, 24.
140 White, 23.
141 White, 26.
142 Jessica Kiang, "Chloe Zhao's Nomadland as Vast as the American Landscape It Travels." *The Playlist*, September 11, 2020, https://theplaylist.net/nomadland-venice-review-20200911/, n.p. Quoted in Lindemann, 39.
143 Tim Lindemann, "Travelling the Scenic Landscape: Community, Nationalism and Precarity in *Nomadland* (2020)," *Empedocles: European Journal for the Philosophy of Communication* 13, no. 1 (2022): 26.
144 Lindemann, 32.
145 Lindemann, 33.
146 Crockford, 50–51.
147 Crockford, 51.
148 Jacqueline Hodder, "Spirituality and Well-Being: 'New Age' and 'Evangelical' Spiritual Expressions among Young People and Their Implications for Well-Being," *International Journal of Children's Spirituality* 14, no. 3 (2009): 199.
149 Catherine Kelly and Melanie Kay Smith, "Journeys of the Self: The Need to Retreat," in *The Routledge Handbook of Health Tourism*, ed. Melanie Kay Smith and László Puczkó (New York: Routledge, 2017), 138, 142.
150 Ivakhiv, 151–152.
151 Ivakhiv, 147.
152 Ivakhiv, 162.
153 Leyerle, 128.
154 Ivakhiv, 167.
155 Crockford, 50–51.
156 See Arjana 2020.
157 Ivakhiv, 176.
158 Ivakhiv, 196.
159 Crockford, 19.
160 Ivakhiv, 187–188.
161 Ivakhiv, 188.
162 Tinker 2014, 6.
163 Tinker 2016, 10.
164 Tinker 2016, 10.
165 Tinker 2014, 23.
166 Tinker 2014, 23–24.
167 Tinker 2014, 25.
168 Tinker 2014, 45, 43.
169 Tinker 2014, 27.
170 Tinker 2014, 29.
171 Tinker 2014, 28.
172 Tinker 2014, 41.
173 Bowes, 148.
174 Bowes, 231.
175 Bowes, 230.
176 Bowes, 233.

Bibliography

Adler, Judith. "Cultivating Wilderness: Environmentalism and Legacies of Early Christian Asceticism." *Comparative Studies in Society and History* 48, no. 1 (2006): 4–37.

Arjana, Sophia. *Buying Buddha, Selling Rumi: Orientalism and the Mystical Marketplace.* London: Oneworld, 2020.

Baigell, Matthew. "Territory, Race, Religion: Images of Manifest Destiny." *Smithsonian Studies in American Art* 4, no. 3/4 (1990): 2–21.

Banner, Stuart. "Preparing to Be Colonized: Land Tenure and Legal Strategy in Nineteenth-Century Hawaii." *Law & Society Review* 39, no. 2 (2005): 272–314.

Bergland, Renée L. *The National Uncanny: Indian Ghosts and American Subjects.* Hanover: University Press of New England, 2000.

Berry, Evan. *Devoted to Nature: The Religious Roots of American Environmentalism.* Berkeley: University of California Press, 2015.

Boime, Albert. *The Magisterial Gaze: Manifest Destiny and American Landscape Painting c. 1830–1865.* Washington: Smithsonian Institution Press, 1991.

Bowes, John P. *Land Too Good for Indians: Northern Indian Removal.* Norman: University of Oklahoma Press, 2016.

Bowles, Samuel. *The Parks and Monuments of Colorado: A Summer Vacation in the Switzerland of America, 1868.* Edited by James H. Pickering. Norman: University of Oklahoma Press, 1991.

Bremer, Thomas S. "The Religious and Spiritual Appeal of National Parks." In *The Routledge Handbook of Religious and Spiritual Tourism,* edited by Daniel H. Olsen and Dallen J. Timothy, 166–178. New York: Routledge, 2022.

Bruner, Edward M. "Transformation of Self in Tourism." *Annals of Tourism Research* 18, no. 2 (1991): 238–250.

Campbell, Suzan. *The American West: People, Places, and Ideas.* Santa Fe: Western Edge Press, 2001.

Cather, Willa. *O Pioneers!* Public Domain. Originally published in 1913.

Catton, Theodore. *National Park, City Playground: Mount Rainier in the Twentieth Century.* Seattle: University of Washington Press, 2006.

Child, Brenda J. *Boarding School Seasons: American Indian Families, 1900–1940.* Lincoln: University of Nebraska Press, 1998.

Collins, Douglas. *The Story of Kodak.* New York: Harry Abrams Publishers, 1990.

Cooper, James Fenimore. *The Last of the Mohicans,* 1826. Reprint. New York: Signet Classics, 2005.

Cosgrove, Denis. *Geography and Vision: Seeing, Imagining and Representing the World.* New York: I.B. Tauris, 2008.

Courtney, Susan. *Split Screen Nation: Moving Images of the American West and South.* New York: Oxford University Press, 2017.

Cox, Thomas R. "Americans and Their Forests: Romanticism, Progress, and Science in the Late Nineteenth Century." *Journal of Forest History* 29, no. 4 (1985): 156–168.

Crockford, Susannah. *Ripples of the Universe: Spirituality in Sedona, Arizona.* Chicago: University of Chicago Press, 2021.

Deloria, Philip J. *Playing Indian.* New Haven: Yale University Press, 1998.

Donaldson, Laura E. "On Medicine Women and White Shame-ans: New Age Native Americanism and Commodity Fetishism as Pop Culture Feminism." *Signs* 24, no. 3 (1999): 677–696.

Edmunds, David. "Introduction: Twentieth-Century Warriors." In *The New Warriors: Native American Leaders Since 1900,* edited by David Edmunds, 1–15. Lincoln: University of Nebraska Press, 2001.

Ferber, Linda S. *The Hudson River School: Nature and the American Vision.* New York: Rizzoli, 2009.

Fixico, Donald L. *The Invasion of Indian Country in the Twentieth Century: American Capitalism and Tribal Natural Resources.* Niwot: University Press of Colorado, 1998.

Haines, Aubrey L. *The Yellowstone Story: A History of Our First National Park, Volume One.* Niwot: University Press of Colorado, 1996.

Haines, Aubrey L. *The Yellowstone Story: A History of Our First National Park, Volume Two*. Niwot: University Press of Colorado, 1996.

Hall, David D. *Worlds of Wonder, Days of Judgment: Popular Religious Belief in Early New England*. Cambridge, MA: Harvard University Press, 1990.

Harley, John Brian. "Silences and Secrecy: The Hidden Agenda of Cartography in Early Modern Europe." *Imago Mundi* 40 (1988): 57–76.

Harley, John Brian. "Rereading the Maps of Columbian Encounter." *Annals of the Association of American Geographers* 82 (1992): 522–542.

Harley, John Brian. "New England Cartography and the Native Americans." In *The New Nature of Maps: Essays in the History of Cartography*, edited by Paul Laxton, 169–196. Baltimore: John Hopkins University Press, 2001.

Hathaway, Henry, dir. *True Grit*. Paramount Pictures, 1969.

Heacox, Kim. *An American Idea: The Making of National Parks*. Washington, DC: National Geographic Society, 2001.

Hodder, Jacqueline. "Spirituality and Well-Being: 'New Age' and 'Evangelical' Spiritual Expressions Among Young People and Their Implications for Well-Being." *International Journal of Children's Spirituality* 14, no. 3 (2009): 197–212.

Hore, Jarrod. *Visions of Nature: How Landscape Photography Shaped Settler Colonialism*. Berkeley: University of California Press, 2022.

Horsman, Reginald. *Race and Manifest Destiny: The Origins of American Racial Anglo-Saxonism*. Cambridge, MA: Harvard University Press, 1981.

Hoxie, Frederick E. and Tim Bernardis. "Robert Yellowtail (Crow)." In *The New Warriors: Native American Leaders Since 1900*, edited by David Edmunds, 55–77. Lincoln: University of Nebraska Press, 2001.

Ivakhiv, Adrian J. *Claiming Sacred Ground: Pilgrims and Politics at Glastonbury and Sedona*. Bloomington: Indiana University Press, 2001.

Jaimes, M. Annette and Theresa Halsey. "American Indian Women: At the Center of Indigenous Resistance in Contemporary North America." In *Dangerous Liaisons: Gender, Nation, and Postcolonial Perspectives*, edited by Anne McClintock, Aamir Mufti, and Ella Shohat, 298–329. Minneapolis: University of Minnesota Press, 1997.

Jennings, Willie James. *The Christian Imagination: Theology and the Origins of Race*. New Haven: Yale University Press, 2010.

Kellman, Ari. *A Misplaced Massacre: Struggling Over the Memory of Sand Creek*. Cambridge, MA: Harvard University Press, 2013.

Kelly, Catherine and Melanie Kay Smith. "Journeys of the Self: The Need to Retreat." In *The Routledge Handbook of Health Tourism*, edited by Melanie Kay Smith and László Puckzó, 138–151. New York: Routledge, 2017.

Kelly, Kevin. "The Next Burning Man." In *Burning Man*, edited by John Plunkett and Brad Wieners, 126–128. San Francisco: HardWired, 1997.

Kiang, Jessica. "Chloe Zhao's Nomadland as Vast as the American Landscape It Travels." *The Playlist*, September 11, 2020, n.p. https://theplaylist.net/nomadland-venice-review-20200911/

Kjeldsen, Jim. *The Mountaineers: A History*. Seattle: The Mountaineers, 1998.

Kovarsky, Joel. *The True Geography of Our Country: Jefferson's Cartographic Vision*. Charlottesville: University of Virginia Press, 2014.

Kozinets, Robert V. "The Moment of Infinite Fire." In *Time, Space and the Market: Retroscapes Rising*, edited by Stephen Brown and John F. Sherry, Jr., 199–216. New York: Routledge, 2015.

Lawrence, T. E. *Lawrence of Arabia: The Selected Letters*. Edited by Malcom Brown. London: Little Books, 2005.

Leyerle, Blake. "Landscape as Cartography in Early Christian Pilgrimage Narratives." *Journal of the American Academy of Religion* 64, no. 1 (1996): 119–134.

Lindemann, Tim. "Travelling the Scenic Landscape: Community, Nationalism and Precarity in *Nomadland* (2020)." *Empedocles: European Journal for the Philosophy of Communication* 13, no. 1 (2022): 25–40.

Lynch, Tom. *Outback & Out West: The Settler-Colonial Environmental Imaginary.* Lincoln: University of Nebraska Press, 2022.

Maddra, Sam. "American Indians in Buffalo Bill's Wild West." In *Human Zoos: Science and Spectacle in the Age of Colonial Empires,* edited by Pascal Blanchard, Nicolas Bancel, Gilles Boëtsch, Sandrine Lemaire, and Charles Forsdick, 134–141. Liverpool: Liverpool University Press, 2008.

Mann, Michael, dir. *The Last of the Mohicans.* 20th Century Fox, 1992.

Masoff, Joy. "The Mystery Man of Sand Creek: George Laird Shoup." *Great Plains Quarterly* 39, no. 2 (2019): 179–210.

McCarron-Cates, Floramae. "The Best Possible View: Pictorial Representation in the American West." In *Frederick Church, Winslow Homer, and Thomas Moran: Tourism and the American Landscape,* edited by Gail S. Davidson and Floramae McCarron-Cates, 75–118. New York: Bulfinch Press, 2006.

McCloskey, Michael. "The Wilderness Act of 1964: Its Background and Meaning." *The Oregon Law Review* 45, no. 4 (1966): 288–321.

Meinig, D. W. "Territorial Strategies Applied to Captive Peoples." In *Ideology and Landscape in Historical Perspective: Essays on the Meanings of Some Places in the Past,* edited by Alan R. H. Baker and Gideon Biger, 125–136. New York: Cambridge University Press, 1992.

Morin, Karen M. "Mining Empire: Journalists in the American West, ca. 1970." In *Postcolonial Geographies,* edited by Cheryl McEwan and Alison Blunt, 152–167. New York: Continuum, 2002.

Morris, David Brown. *Wanderers: Literature, Culture and the Open Road.* New York: Routledge, 2021.

Nicolson, Marjorie Hope. *Mountain Gloom and Mountain Glory: The Development of the Aesthetics of the Infinite.* New York: W. W. Norton & Company, 1959.

Nye, David E. *American Technological Sublime.* Cambridge, MA: MIT Press, 1994.

Nye, David E. "Visualizing Eternity: Photographic Constructions of the Grand Canyon." In *Picturing Place: Photography and the Geographical Imagination,* edited by Joan M. Schwartz and James R. Ryan, 74–95. New York: I.B. Tauris, 2003.

Richter, Daniel. *Facing East from Indian Country: A Native History of Early America.* Cambridge, MA: Harvard University Press, 2001.

Robbins, Paul and Sarah A. Moore. "Return of the Repressed: Native Presence and American Memory in John Muir's *Boyhood and Youth.*" *Annals of the American Association of Geographers* 109, no. 1 (2019): 1748–1757.

Shannon, Timothy J. and David N. Gellman. *American Odysseys: A History of Colonial North America.* New York: Oxford University Press, 2014.

Smith, Jonathon Z. *Map Is Not Territory.* Chicago: University of Chicago Press, 1993.

Spence, Mark David. *Dispossessing the Wilderness: Indian Removal and the Making of the National Parks.* New York: Oxford University Press, 1999.

Stetler, Julia S. "'Painting the Town Read': Buffalo Bill's Indians in the German Media." In *The Popular Frontier: Buffalo Bill's Wild West and Transnational Mass Culture,* edited by Frank Christianson, 155–174. Norman: University of Oklahoma Press, 2017.

Stoll, Mark R. *Inherit the Holy Mountain: Religion and the Rise of American Environmentalism.* New York: Oxford University Press, 2015.

Tinker, George E. "Native/First Nation Theology: Response." *Journal of Feminist Studies in Religion* 22, no. 2 (2006): 116–121.

Tinker, George E. "Redskin, Tanned Hide: A Book of Christian History Bound in the Flayed Skin of an American Indian: The Colonial Romance, Christian Denial, and the Cleansing of a Christian School of Theology." *Journal of Race, Ethnicity, and Religion* 5, no. 9 (2014): 1–43.

Veracini, Lorenzo. "The Other Shift: Settler Colonialism, Israel and the Occupation." *Journal of Palestine Studies* 42, no. 2 (2013): 26–42.

Wald, Priscilla. *Constituting Americans: Cultural Anxiety and Narrative Form.* Durham: Duke University Press, 1995.

White, Patricia. "Women Auteurs, Western Promises." *Film Quarterly* 75, no. 4 (2022): 23–33.

Williams, Terry Tempest. *The Hour of Land: A Personal Topography of America's National Parks.* New York: Farrar, Straus and Giroux, 2016.

Zhao, Chloé, dir. *The Rider.* Sony Pictures Classics, 2017.

Zhao, Chloé, dir. *Nomadland.* Searchlight Pictures, 2021.

POSTSCRIPT

The West in which I grew up was filled with beautiful places—majestic mountains of pine forests and aspen trees, pristine lakes the color of turquoise, and deserts with sunsets of every imaginable color from peach to violet. As I explored these lands as a child and adolescent, I encountered elk, deer, moose, and one time, just missed a bear who had just departed the yard of a cabin once owned by my grandmother. The vast mountains and plains of Colorado that once were the home of this wildlife are now barren wastelands, the water taken for golf courses and flower-filled yards in Arizona and California. From the time I was a young child, the names I was familiar with—Ute, Chipeta, and Ouray—were all part of a world that had long ago been disappeared by white settlers, replaced with condos and national parks, coffee shops and hiking trails, music festivals and celebrities' mansions. It is a land of white people with Indians living as a minority in their homeland. I am one of those white settlers and often think about what the small part of my Indian lineage would think of me, hiking, fishing, and camping on their land, with no connection to my ancestors. I do know that if my Apache ancestor had not killed the cougar who tried to take her baby, by strangling it with her bare hands, while she hung her laundry on the clothesline, I would not be here, writing this book.

Centering Local and Indigenous People: A Path Forward

What, if anything, would be a path forward, to recognize what lies beneath the waters of Grand River Dam? Land acknowledgements are problematic, for they are only words that don't do anything meaningful. The example given by indigenous people includes taking away someone's water, then acknowledging it, but keeping the water. Reparations seem an

DOI: 10.4324/9781003361725-10

impossible dream, given the lack of political support for acknowledging the past. The United States is behind many other countries on these issues.

Aotearoa (New Zealand) offers a model for recognizing the past and involving indigenous peoples in their ancestral lands. At Aoraki (Mount Cook), the Department of Conservation has employed *iwi* interpreters for the past 30 years, providing historical and cultural materials to the public, involving *marae* (a community center of the Māori people), and including art of the Māori in the central reception area.[1] The forms of cultural interpretation offered to the public include brochures, lectures, art, and other materials, all centering the Māori people at Aoraki.[2] Māori approaches to the environment emphasize preexistence, potentiality, historicality, and ecological humanism.[3] This is radically different than the tourism for profit model of European and American societies. Aotearoa also has the Toi Iho Program, which focuses on standards in Māori art and seeks to protect traditional art forms while allowing Māori artists to make a living.[4]

In American national parks, references to American Indians are included, but the practices adopted at Aoraki signify something quite different, where the landscape is situated in a Māori discourse that provides the perspective of the Ngāi Tahu—the *iwi* (people) whose ancestral land is now a tourist site.[5] Australia offers another path to acknowledging and repairing relations between white settlers and indigenous people. Emily Gap is a well-known site in Australia known to the Eastern Arrernte people as Anthwerrke, who in 2009 were given native-title ownership of the site, now managed jointly with the Northern Territory Parks and Wildlife Commission.[6]

Counter-mapping provides another avenue through which colonial mapping can be challenged or even undone. Barbara Bender refers to this as a kind of *subversion* of the gaze.[7] Indigenous beliefs about the environment and people's relationship to ancestral lands, trees, and resources may come in conflict with the goals of government and industry. The Dayak people of Kalimantan, Indonesia, used counter-maps to illustrate their customary claims, which involved specific items, including trees, as opposed to boundaries of territory.[8] *Adat*, or custom, is an important part of Indonesian culture and plays a role in the way space, and maps, are reconciled when resource management is an issue. By using mapping technologies, local people like the Dayak can stake claims to resources they need and challenge the wholesale taking of resources.[9]

The preceding chapter, the end of this book, strives to honor my Apache ancestors, who I have no real sense of, for they are on my father's side, and he is not in my life. The only thing I know about them is that they existed. I was once told a story about an ancestor, who was full-blooded Apache. She was hanging out the wash on the clothesline and had her baby with her. A mountain lion approached and tried to snatch the infant, and my great-great-grandmother (to be honest, she may have been a great-grand-mother, the details are fuzzy) strangled the cat with her bare hands.

I also feel that ending with America represents the historical arc that determines my life. I am a white American and live with the knowledge (and guilt) of slavery and genocide, which is why I began this book with Africa and end with America. My privilege relies upon the history of a world I was not part of but benefit from.

I have often questioned how to fit into the world. A white convert to Islam, married to a Muslim from a distant island, with our four children, only one (from my first marriage) of whom who passes as white. One time, I shared a post on social media about how we were homesick for my husband's village, for our relatives who miss us, for a home I have decorated and sewn quilts for and cried for when we depart for the airport to fly back across the Pacific Ocean. When an academic colleague attacked me for me for saying I missed this place, I realized that home is a fluid concept for some, and for others, it is dependent on the status of me as a colonizer. How much a colonizer am I? I do not own land in the village (foreigners are not allowed to own land in Indonesia, a policy I fully support), but I am my husband's wife, and these are our children. Postcolonialism is complicated, indeed.

As I wrote in my most recent book, the pull of some places—the mountains of the Himalayas, the rice terraces of Bali, the deserts of the Southwest—is undeniable. The Academy dislikes these types of claims about experience and emotion with an immense passion that will surely result in some negative reviews of this book. However, how do we explain the strange and unexplainable happenings told in this book? The explorer who found a real Lo-Tsen when searching for the mythical Shangri-La, the Balinese calendar that predicted the terrible death of the cousin of Walter Spies, the prophecies of Native Americans that if they lost their homelands, environmental disasters would wreck the earth. Mystical landscapes may be more real than we think.

Notes

1 Carr, 441–442.
2 Carr, 442–443.
3 Makere Stewart-Harawira, *The New Imperial Order: Indigenous Responses to Globalization* (New York: Zed Books, 2005), 34–35. Dr. Harawira is a Māori scholar with a Waitaha tribal affiliation.
4 Tiangco, 515.
5 Carr, 443.
6 Lynch, 2.
7 Bender 2006, 307.
8 Nancy Lee Peluso, "Whose Woods Are These? Counter-Mapping Forest Territories in Kalimantan, Indonesia," *Antipode* 27, no. 4 (1995): 384, 392.
9 Peluso, 400.

Bibliography

Bender, Barbara. "Place and Landscape." In *Handbook of Material Culture*, edited by Christopher Tilley, Webb Keane, Susanne Küchler, Michael Rowlands, and Patricia Spyer, 303–314. London: Sage Publications, 2006.

Carr, Anna. "Mountain Places, Cultural Spaces: The Interpretation of Culturally Significant Landscapes." *Journal of Sustainable Tourism* 12, no. 5 (2004): 432–459.

Lynch, Tom. *Outback & Out West: The Settler-Colonial Environmental Imaginary.* Lincoln: University of Nebraska Press, 2022.

Peluso, Nancy Lee. "Whose Woods Are These? Counter-Mapping Forest Territories in Kalimantan, Indonesia." *Antipode* 27, no. 4 (1995): 383–406.

Stewart-Harawira, Makere. *The New Imperial Order: Indigenous Responses to Globalization.* New York: Zed Books, 2005.

Tiangco, Angela Louise R. "Selling Aloha: The Fight for Legal Protections over Native Hawaiian Culture." *William & Mary Journal of Race, Gender, and Social Justice* 29, no. 2 (2022/2023): 489–518.

BIBLIOGRAPHY

Abusaada, Nadi. "Self-Portrait of a Nation: The Arab Exhibition in Mandate Jerusalem, 1931–34." *Jerusalem Quarterly* 77 (2019): 122–135.

Abusaada, Nadi. "Combined Action: Aerial Imagery and the Urban Landscape in Interwar Palestine, 1918–40." *Jerusalem Quarterly* 81 (2020): 20–36.

Abusaada, Nadi. "Urban Encounters: Imaging the City in Mandate Palestine." In *Imaging and Imagining Palestine: Photography, Modernity and the Biblical Lens, 1918–1948*, edited by Karène Sanchez Summerer and Sary Zananiri, 360–389. Boston: Brill, 2021.

Abusaada, Nadi. "'The Reconstruction of Palestine': Geographical Imaginaries after World War I." In *The Social and Cultural History of Palestine: Essays in Honour of Salim Tamari*, edited by Sarah Irving, 102–119. Edinburgh: Edinburgh University Press, 2023.

Adams, Vincanne. "Karaoke as Modern Lhasa, Tibet: Western Encounters with Cultural Politics." *Cultural Anthropology* 11, no. 4 (1996): 510–546.

Adi, Hakim. *Pan-Africanism: A History*. New York: Bloomsbury Academic, 2018.

Adler, Judith. "Cultivating Wilderness: Environmentalism and Legacies of Early Christian Asceticism." *Comparative Studies in Society and History* 48, no. 1 (2006): 4–37.

Ahmed, Sara. "A Phenomenology of Whiteness." *Feminist Theory* 8, no. 2 (2007): 149–168.

Aiken, Edwin James. *Scriptural Geography: Portraying the Holy Land*. New York: Bloomsbury Publishing, 2010.

Aiken, Susan Hardy. "Consuming Isak Dinesen." In *Isak Dinesen and Narrativity*, edited by Gurli A. Woods, 3–24. Montreal: McGill-Queen's University Press, 1994.

Äitel, Fazia. *We Are Imazighen: The Development of Algerian Berber Identity in Twentieth-Century Literature and Culture*. Gainesville: University Press of Florida, 2014.

Akama, John S. "The Evolution of Wildlife Conservation Policies in Kenya." *Journal of Third World Studies* 15, no. 2 (1998): 103–116.

Akama, John S. "The Evolution of Tourism in Kenya." *Journal of Sustainable Tourism* 7, no. 1 (1999): 6–25.

Aldrich, Robert. "Visiting the Family and Introducing the Royals: British Royal Tours of the Dominions in the Twentieth Century and Beyond." *Royal Studies Journal* 5, no. 1 (2018): 1–14.

Allers, Roger and Rob Minkoff, dir. *The Lion King.* Walt Disney Features Animation, 1994.

Allon, Fiona. "Bali as Icon: Tourism, Death, and the Pleasure Periphery." *Humanities Research* 11, no. 1 (2004): 24–41.

Alloula, Malek. *The Colonial Harem.* Translated by Myrna Godzich and Wlad Godzich. Minneapolis: University of Minnesota Press, 1986.

Anand, Dibyesh. "Western Colonial Representations of the Other: The Case of Exotica Tibet." *New Political Science* 29, no. 1 (2007): 23–42.

Anderson, Benedict. *Imagined Communities: Reflections on the Origin and Spread of Nationalism.* New York: Verso, 2006.

Annaud, Jean-Jacques. *Seven Years in Tibet.* Sony Pictures, 1997.

Appiah, Kwame Anthony. *In My Father's House.* New York: Oxford University Press, 1992.

Arjana, Sophia. *Muslims in the Western Imagination.* New York: Oxford University Press, 2015.

Arjana, Sophia. *Pilgrimage in Islam: Traditional and Modern Practices.* London: Oneworld, 2017.

Arjana, Sophia. *Buying Buddha, Selling Rumi: Orientalism and the Mystical Marketplace.* London: Oneworld, 2020.

Arthur, Jay Mary. *The Default Country: A Lexical Cartography of Twentieth-Century Australia.* Sydney: University of New South Wales Press, 2003.

Ashton, Julia. "Camels, Sands, and Pyramids: Struggles with Tourism in the Golden Land of the Pharaohs." *Proceedings of the National Conference on Undergraduate Research (NCUR),* April 11–13, 2013.

Atkins, Gary L. *Imagining Gay Paradise: Bali, Bangkok, and Cyber-Singapore.* Hong Kong: Hong Kong University Press, 2012.

Atwill, David G. *Islamic Shangri-La: Inter-Asian Relations and Lhasa's Muslim Communities, 1600 to 1960.* Oakland: University of California Press, 2018.

Auttarat, Sudarat and Nivej Poonsukcharoen. "A Spiritual Journey? Using Religious Storytelling to Enhance Tourism in Northern Thailand." *The International Journal of Religion and Spirituality in Society* 12, no. 2 (2022): 83–97.

Baigell, Matthew. "Territory, Race, Religion: Images of Manifest Destiny." *Smithsonian Studies in American Art* 4, no. 3/4 (1990): 2–21.

Baldacchino, Godfrey. "Island Tourist Experiences." In *Routledge Handbook of the Tourist Experience,* edited by Richard Sharpley, 498–507. New York: Routledge, 2022.

Bandy, Joe. "Managing the Other of Nature: Sustainability, Spectacle, and Global Regimes of Capital in Ecotourism." *Public Culture* 8 (1996): 539–566.

Banks, Joseph. *The 'Endeavour' Journal of Joseph Banks.* Edited by John Cawte Beaglehole. Sydney: Public Library of New South Wales and Angus & Robertson, 1962.

Banner, Stuart. "Preparing to Be Colonized: Land Tenure and Legal Strategy in Nineteenth-Century Hawaii." *Law & Society Review* 39, no. 2 (2005): 272–314.

Barr, Doron and Kobi Cohen-Hattab. "A New Kind of Pilgrimage: The Modern Tourist Pilgrim of Nineteenth-Century and Early Twentieth-Century Palestine." *Middle Eastern Studies* 39, no. 2 (2003): 131–148.

Baum, Vicki. *Love and Death in Bali,* 1937. Reprint. North Clarendon: Tuttle, 2011.

Bauman, Zygmunt. "From Pilgrim to Tourist: Or a Short History of Identity." In *Questions of Cultural Identity,* edited by Stuart Hall and Paul Du Gay, 18–36. London: Sage, 1996.

Bauman, Zygmunt. *Liquid Modernity.* New York: Polity, 2000.

Bay, Michael, dir. *Pearl Harbor*. Touchstone Pictures, 2001.

Beaglehole, J. C., ed. *The Journals of Captain James Cook on His Voyages of Discovery. The Voyage of the Resolution and Discovery 1776–1780. Part I*. Cambridge: Cambridge University Press, 1967.

Beedie, Paul. "A History of Mountaineering Tourism." In *Mountaineering Tourism*, edited by Ghazali Musa, James Higham, and Anna Thompson-Carr, 40–54. New York: Routledge, 2015.

Beedie, Paul and Simon Hudson. "Emergence of Mountain-Based Tourism." *Annals of Tourism Research* 30, no. 3 (2003): 625–643.

Behdad, Ali. "The Orientalist Photograph: An Object of Comparison." *Canadian Review of Comparative Literature* 43, no. 2 (2016): 265–281.

Bell, Claudia. "Eat, Pray, Love, Ethics: Researching Expats and Tourists in Bali." In *Qualitative Ethics in Practice*, edited by Martin Tolich, 159–170. Walnut Creek: Left Coast Press, 2016.

Bell, Claudia. "'We Feel Like the King and Queen': Western Retirees in Bali, Indonesia." *Asian Journal of Social Science* 45 (2017): 271–293.

Bell, Claudia. "The New Age Tourist Band-Wagon in Ubud, Bali: Eat Pay Love!" *South Asian Research Journal of Arts, Language and Literature* 1, no. 3 (2019): 74–82.

Bellone, Tamara, Salvatore Engel-Di Mauro, Francesco Fiermonte, Emiliana Armano, and Linda Quiquivix. "Mapping as Tacit Representations of the Colonial Gaze." In *Mapping Crisis: Participation, Datafication and Humanitarianism in the Age of Digital Mapping*, edited by Doug Specht, 17–37. London: University of London Press, 2020.

Ben-Arieh, Yehoshua. "The Geographical Exploration of the Holy Land." *Palestine Exploration Quarterly* 104, no. 2 (1972): 81–92.

Ben-Arieh, Yehoshua. "Nineteenth-century Historical Geographies of the Holy Land." *Journal of Historical Geography* 15, no. 1 (1989): 69–79.

Ben-Bassat, Yuval and Yossi Ben-Artzi. "Ottoman Maps of the Empire's Arab Provinces, 1850s to the First World War." *Imago Mundi* 70, no. 2 (2018): 199–211.

Bender, Barbara. "Time and Landscape." *Current Anthropology* 43, no. 4 (2002): S103–S112.

Bender, Barbara. "Place and Landscape." In *Handbook of Material Culture*, edited by Christopher Tilley, Webb Keane, Susanne Küchler, Michael Rowlands, and Patricia Spyer, 303–314. London: Sage Publications, 2006.

Benjamin, Roger. *Orientalist Aesthetics: Art, Colonialism, and French North Africa, 1880–1930*. Berkeley: University of California Press, 2003.

Bennike, Rune. "'A Summer Place': Darjeeling in the Tourist Gaze." In *Darjeeling Reconsidered: Histories, Politics, Environments*, edited by Townsend Middleton and Sara Shneidermann, 54–73. New York: Oxford University Press, 2018.

Benvenisti, Meron. *Conflicts and Contradictions*. New York: Villard Books, 1986.

Bergland, Renée L. *The National Uncanny: Indian Ghosts and American Subjects*. Hanover: University Press of New England, 2000.

Bergwik, Staffan. "Elevation and Emotion: Sven Hedin's Mountain Expedition to Transhimalaya, 1906–1908." *Centaurus* 62 (2020): 647–669.

Bernbaum, Edwin. "Sacred Mountains: Themes and Teachings." *Mountain Research and Development* 26, no. 4 (2006): 304–309.

Berry, Evan. *Devoted to Nature: The Religious Roots of American Environmentalism*. Berkeley: University of California Press, 2015.

Bertolucci, Bernardo, dir. *The Sheltering Sky*. Warner Brothers, 1990.

Bhandari, Kalyan. "Tourism and the Geopolitics of Buddhist Heritage in Nepal." *Annals of Tourism Research* 75 (2019): 58–69.

Birnbaum, Edwin. "Sacred Mountains: Themes and Teachings." *Mountain Research and Development* 26, no. 4 (2006): 304–309.

Bishop, Peter. *The Myth of Shangri-La: Tibet, Travel Writing and the Western Creation of Sacred Landscape*. Berkeley: University of California Press, 1989.

Blais, Hélène, Florence Deprest, and Pierre Singaravelou. "French Geography, Cartography and Colonialism: Introduction." *Journal of Historical Geography* 37 (2011): 146–148.

Blum, Susan D. *Portraits of 'Primitives': Ordering Human Kinds in the Chinese Nation*. Lanham: Rowman & Littlefield Publishers, 2001.

Boëtsch, Gilles and Pascal Blanchard. "The Hottentot Venus: Birth of a 'Freak'." In *Human Zoos: Science and Spectacle in the Age of Colonial Empires*, edited by Pascal Blanchard, Nicolas Bancel, Gilles Boëtsch, Sandrine Lemaire, and Charles Forsdick, 62–72. Liverpool: Liverpool University Press, 2008.

Boggs, Carl. "Pearl Harbor: How Film Conquers History." *New Political Science* 28, no. 4 (2006): 451–466.

Boime, Albert. *The Magisterial Gaze: Manifest Destiny and American Landscape Painting c. 1830–1865*. Washington, DC: Smithsonian Institution Press, 1991.

Boon, James A. "The Birth of the Idea of Bali." *Indonesia* 22 (1976): 70–83.

Boon, James A. *The Anthropological Romance of Bali, 1597–1972: Dynamic Perspectives in Marriage & Caste, Politics & Religion*. New York: Cambridge University Press, 1977.

Borgerson, Janet and Jonathan Schroeder. "The Lure of Paradise: Marketing the Retro-Escape of Hawaii." In *Time, Space and the Market: Retroscapes Rising*, edited by Stephen Brown and John F. Sherry, Jr., 219–237. New York: Routledge, 2015.

Bourdieu, Pierre (with Abdelmalek Sayad). *Le Déracinement: La Crise de L'agriculture Traditionalle en Algérie*. Paris: Éditions de Minuit, 1964.

Bourdieu, Pierre. "Habitus and Habitat." In *Picturing Algeria: Pierre Bourdieu*, edited by Franz Schultheis and Christine Frisinghelli, 67–89. New York: Columbia University Press, 2003.

Bowes, John P. *Land Too Good for Indians: Northern Indian Removal*. Norman: University of Oklahoma Press, 2016.

Bowles, Paul. *The Sheltering Sky*, 1949. Reprint. New York: Ecco Press, 1998.

Bowles, Samuel. *The Parks and Monuments of Colorado: A Summer Vacation in the Switzerland of America, 1868*. Edited by James H. Pickering. Norman: University of Oklahoma Press, 1991.

Branagh, Kenneth, dir. *Death on the Nile*. 20th Century Studios, 2022.

Branham, Joan R. "The Temple That Won't Quit: Constructing Sacred Space in Orlando's Holy Land Experience Theme Park." *CrossCurrents* 59, no. 3 (2009): 358–382.

Bremer, Thomas S. *Blessed with Tourists: The Borderlands of Religion and Tourism in San Antonio*. Chapel Hill: University of North Carolina Press, 2004.

Bremer, Thomas S. "Sacred Spaces and Tourist Places." In *Tourism, Religion and Spiritual Journeys*, edited by Dallen J. Timothy and Daniel H. Olsen, 25–35. New York: Routledge, 2006.

Bremer, Thomas S. "The Religious and Spiritual Appeal of National Parks." In *The Routledge Handbook of Religious and Spiritual Tourism*, edited by Daniel H. Olsen and Dallen J. Timothy, 166–178. New York: Routledge, 2022.

Britton, Stephen. "Tourism, Capital, and Place: Towards a Critical Geography of Tourism." *Society and Space* 9, no. 4 (1991): 451–478.

Brown, DeSoto. *Hawaii Recalls: Nostalgic Images of the Hawaiian Islands: 1910–1950*. New York: Routledge and Kegan Paul International, 1982.

Brown, Stephen. "No Then There: Of Time, Space, and the Market." In *Time, Space, and the Market: Retroscapes Rising*, edited by Stephen Brown and John F. Sherry, Jr. New York: Routledge, 2015.

Brundan, Katy. "Translation and Philological Fantasy in H. Rider Haggard's *She.*" *Studies in English Literature 1500–1900* 58, no. 4 (2018): 959–980.

Bruner, Edward M. "Transformation of Self in Tourism." *Annals of Tourism Research* 18, no. 2 (1991): 238–250.

Buckingham, James Silk. *Travels in Palestine.* London: Longman, 1825.

Butlin, Robin A. "Ideological Contexts and the Reconstruction of Biblical Landscapes in the Seventeenth and Early Eighteenth Centuries: Dr. Edward Wells and the Historical Geography of the Holy Land." In *Ideology and Landscape in Historical Perspective: Essays on the Meanings of Some Places in the Past,* edited by Alan R. H. Baker and Gideon Biger, 31–62. Cambridge: Cambridge University Press, 1992.

Buzard, James. *The Beaten Track: European Tourism, Literature, and the Way to 'Culture,' 1800–1918.* New York: Oxford University Press, 1993.

Byers, Alton. "Contemporary Human Impacts on Alpine Ecosystems in the Sagarmatha (Mt. Everest) National Park, Khumbu, Nepal." *Annals of the Association of American Geographers* 95, no. 1 (2005): 112–140.

Byers, Alton. "A Comparative Study of Tourism Impacts on Alpine Ecosystems in the Sagarmatha (Mt. Everest) National Park, Nepal and the Huascarán National Park, Peru." In *Ecotourism and Environmental Sustainability: Principles and Practices,* edited by Tim Gale and Jannifer Hill, 51–71. New York: Routledge, 2009.

Byers, Alton. "Contemporary Human Impacts on Subalpine and Alpine Ecosystems of the Hinku Valley, Makalu-Barun National Park and Buffer Zone, Nepal." *Himalaya* 33, no. 1 (2014): 25–41.

Callaway, Helen. "Dressing for Dinner in the Bush: Rituals of Self-Definition and British Imperial Authority." In *Dress and Gender: Making and Meaning in Cultural Contexts,* edited by Ruth Barnes and Joanne B. Eicher, 232–247. New York: Bloomsbury, 1993.

Callewaert, Winand M. "On the Way to Kailash." In *Pilgrimage in Tibet,* edited by Alex McKay, 108–116. Surrey: Curzon Press, 1998.

Campbell, Suzan. *The American West: People, Places, and Ideas.* Santa Fe: Western Edge Press, 2001.

Capra, Frank, dir. *Lost Horizon.* Columbia Pictures, 1937.

Carr, Anna. "Mountain Places, Cultural Spaces: The Interpretation of Culturally Significant Landscapes." *Journal of Sustainable Tourism* 12, no. 5 (2004): 432–459.

Cartier, Carolyn. "Introduction: Touristed Landscapes/Seductions of Place." In *Seductions of Place: Geographical Perspectives on Globalization and Touristed Landscapes,* edited by Carolyn Carter and Alan A. Lew, 1–19. London: Routledge, 2005.

Caspary, Hans. "The Cultural Landscape of Sagarmatha National Park." In *Cultural Components of Universal Value: Components of a Global Strategy,* edited by Bernd von Droste, Mechtild Rössler, and Harald Plachter, 154–160. Jena: Gustav Fischer Verlag, 1995.

Cather, Willa. *O Pioneers!* Public Domain (1913).

Catton, Theodore. *National Park, City Playground: Mount Rainier in the Twentieth Century.* Seattle: University of Washington Press, 2006.

Chadwick, Douglas. "The Samoan Way." *National Geographic* 98, no. 1 (2000).

Chamaria, Pradeep. *Kailash Manasarovar: On the Rugged Road to Revelation.* New Delhi: Abhinav Publications, 1996.

Chapman, William. *A Heritage of Ruins: The Ancient Sites of Southeast Asia and Their Conservation.* Honolulu: University of Hawai'i Press, 2013.

Chappell, David A. "The Postcontact Period." In *The Pacific Islands: Environment and Society (Revised Edition),* edited by Moshe Rappaport, 138–146. Honolulu: University of Hawaii Press, 2013.

Chateaubriand, F. A. *Travels in Greece, Palestine, Egypt and Barbary. 2 Volumes.* London: Printed for Henry Colburn, 1812.

Chi, Robert. "Toward a New Tourism: Albert Wendt and Becoming Attractions." *Cultural Critique* 37 (1997): 61–105.

Child, Brenda J. *Boarding School Seasons: American Indian Families, 1900–1940.* Lincoln: University of Nebraska Press, 1998.

Choe, Jaeyeon and Luh Putu Mahyuni. "Sustainable and Inclusive Spiritual Tourism Development in Bali as a Long-Term Post-Pandemic Strategy." *International Journal of Religious Tourism and Pilgrimage* 11, no. 2 (2023): 100–111.

Choe, Jaeyeon and Michael O'Regan. "Faith Manifest: Spiritual and Mindfulness Tourism in Chiang Mai, Thailand." *Religions* 11, no. 4 (2020): 177–187.

Chong, Sylvia Shin Huey. "What Was Asian Cinema?" *Cinema Journal* 56, no. 3 (2017): 130–135.

Claaesen, Henri J. M. "Tahiti and the Early European Visitors." In *European Imagery and Colonial History in the Pacific*, edited by Toon van Meijl and Paul van der Grijp, 14–31. Saarbrüken: Verlag für Entwicklungspolitik Breitenbach GmbH, 1994.

Cohen, Erik. "A Phenomenology of Tourist Experiences." *Sociology* 13 (1979): 179–201.

Cohen, Erik. "Pilgrimage and Tourism: Convergence or Divergence." In *Sacred Journeys: The Anthropology of Tourism*, edited by Alan Morinis, 47–61. Westport: Greenwood Press, 1992.

Cohen-Hattab, Kobi. "Zionism, Tourism, and the Battle for Palestine: Tourism as a Political-Propaganda Tool." *Israel Studies* 9, no. 1 (2004): 61–85.

Cohen-Hattab, Kobi and Yossi Katz. "The Attraction of Palestine: Tourism in the Years 1850–1948." *Journal of Historical Geography* 27, no. 2 (2001): 166–177.

Coleman, Simon. "From the Sublime to the Meticulous: Art, Anthropology and Victorian Pilgrimage to Palestine." *History and Anthropology* 13, no. 4 (2002): 275–290.

Coleman, Simon. "A Tale of Two Centres? Representing Palestine to the British in the Nineteenth Century." *Mobilities* 2, no. 3 (2007): 331–345.

Colley, Ann C. *Victorians in the Mountains: Sinking the Sublime.* Burlington, VT: Ashgate, 2010.

Collins, Douglas. *The Story of Kodak.* New York: Harry Abrams Publishers, 1990.

Collins, John. "A Dream Deterred: Palestine from Total War to Total Peace." In *Studies in Settler Colonialism: Politics, Identity and Culture*, edited by Fiona Bateman and Lionel Pilkington, 169–185. New York: Palgrave MacMillan, 2011.

Connell, John. "Island Dreaming: The Contemplation of Polynesian Paradise." *Journal of Historical Geography* 29, no. 4 (2003): 554–581.

Cook, Terry. "A Reconstruction of the World: George R. Parkin's British Empire Map of 1893." *Cartographica* 21, no. 4 (1984): 53–65.

Cook, Thomas. *Travels in East Africa: Cook's Handbook for Kenya Colony, Uganda, Tanganyika Territory and Zanzibar.* London: Thomas Cook and Son, 1936.

Cooper, James Fenimore. *The Last of the Mohicans*, 1826. Reprint. New York: Signet Classics, 2005.

Corbey, Raymond. "Ethnographic Showcases: Account and Vision." In *Human Zoos: Science and Spectacle in the Age of Colonial Empires*, edited by Pascal Blanchard, Nicolas Bancel, Gilles Boëtsch, Sandrine Lemaire, and Charles Forsdick, 95–113. Liverpool: Liverpool University Press, 2008.

Cosgrove, Denis. *Social Formation and Symbolic Landscape.* Madison: University of Wisconsin Press, 1984.

Cosgrove, Denis. *Geography and Vision: Seeing, Imagining and Representing the World.* New York: I.B. Tauris, 2008.

Courtney, Susan. *Split Screen Nation: Moving Images of the American West and South*. New York: Oxford University Press, 2017.

Covarrubias, Miguel. *Island of Bali*, 1937. Reprint. North Clarendon: Tuttle Publishing, 1973.

Cox, Thomas R. "Americans and Their Forests: Romanticism, Progress, and Science in the Late Nineteenth Century." *Journal of Forest History* 29, no. 4 (1985): 156–168.

Crockford, Susannah. *Ripples of the Universe: Spirituality in Sedona, Arizona*. Chicago: University of Chicago Press, 2021.

Cromer, Evelyn Baring (1st Earl of Cromer). *Modern Egypt*. New York: MacMillan Company, 1916.

Crouch, David, Lars Aronsson, and Lage Wahlström. "Tourist Encounters." *Tourist Studies* 1, no. 3 (2001): 253–270.

Crowe, Cameron, dir. *Aloha*. Columbia Pictures, 2015.

Daam, Jasmin. *Tourism and the Emergence of Nation-States in the Arab Eastern Mediterranean, 1920s–1930s*. Amsterdam: Amsterdam University Press, 2022.

Danielsson, Bengt. *Love in the South Seas: Sex and Family Life of the Polynesians, Based on Early Accounts as Well as Observations by the Noted Swedish Anthropologist*. Honolulu: Mutual Publishing, 1986.

Davis, Diana K. "Desert 'Wastes' of the Maghreb: Desertification Narratives in French Colonial Environmental History of North Africa." *Cultural Geographies* 11, no. 4 (2004): 359–387.

Daws, Gavan. *A Dream of Islands*. Brisbane: W.W. Norton and Company, 1980.

De Bougainville, Louis Antoine. *A Voyage Round the World*. Translated by John Reinhold Forster. New York: Da Capo Press, 1967.

De Lamartine, Alphonse. *A Pilgrimage to the Holy Land: Comprising Recollections, Sketches, and Reflections, Made During a Tour in the East*. New York: D. Appleton & Company, 1848.

Deloria, Philip J. *Playing Indian*. New Haven: Yale University Press, 1998.

DeLoughrey, Elizabeth. "Heliotropes: Solar Ecologies and Pacific Radiations." In *Postcolonial Ecologies: Literatures of the Environment*, edited by Elizabeth DeLoughrey and George B. Handley, 235–253. New York: Oxford University Press, 2011.

Dening, Greg. "The Comaroffs Out of Africa: A Reflection Out of Oceania." *The American Historical Review* 108, no. 2 (2003): 471–478.

De Vorsey, Louis. "Maps in Colonial Promotion: James Edward Oglethorpe's Use of Maps in 'Selling' the Georgia Scheme." *Imago Mundi* 38 (1986): 35–45.

Dewi, Anak Agung Sagung Laksmi, Mella Ismelina Farma Rahayu, and Anak Agung. "Green Tourism in Sustainable Tourism Development in Bali Based on Local Wisdom." *Jurnal Dinamika Hukum* 23, no. 1 (2023): 111–130.

D'Hauterserre, Anne-Marie. "Maintaining the Myth: Tahiti and Its Islands." In *Seductions of Place: Geographical Perspectives on Globalization and Touristed Landscapes*, edited by Carolyn Carter and Alan A. Lew, 193–208. London: Routledge, 2005.

Didier, Chanel. "Por relancer le tourisme en Polynésie: Promotion de 545 millions CFP!" *La Dépêche de Tahiti*, November 30, 1995.

Di Giovine, Michael and Jaeyeon Choe. "Geographies of Religion and Spirituality: Pilgrimage beyond the 'Officially' Sacred." *Tourism Geographies: An International Journal of Tourism Space, Place and Environment* 21, no. 3 (2019): 361–383.

Dinesen, Isak. *Out of Africa*, 1937, Reprint. Harmondsworth: Penguin, 1984.

Dodin, Thierry and Heinz Räther. "Imagining Tibet: Between Shangri-La and Feudal Oppression." In *Imagining Tibet: Perceptions, Projections, and Fantasies*, edited by Thierry Dodin and Heinz Räther, 391–416.

Donaldson, Laura E. "On Medicine Women and White Shame-ans: New Age Native Americanism and Commodity Fetishism as Pop Culture Feminism." *Signs* 24, no. 3 (1999): 677–696.

Donaldson, Roger, dir. *The Bounty*. Los Angeles: Orion Pictures, 1984.

Dougherty, Daniel. "Reading Eternity: Haggard's *She* and the Immortality in the Fin-de-siècle Novel." *Journal of Comparative Literature and Aesthetics* 47, no. 4 (2024): 104–114.

Doumani, Beshara B. "Rediscovering Ottoman Palestine: Writing Palestinians into History." *Journal of Palestine Studies* 21, no. 2 (1992): 5–28.

Doyle, Arthur Conan. *Sherlock Holmes and Dr. Watson: A Textbook of Friendship*. Edited by Christopher Morley. New York: Harcourt, Brace and Company, 1944.

Dragojlovic, Ana. *Beyond Bali: Subaltern Citizens and Post-Colonial Intimacy*. Amsterdam: Amsterdam University Press, 2016.

Driscoll, Christopher. "Sublime Sahib: White Masculinity Formation in Big Mountain Climbing." *Culture and Religion* 21, no. 1 (2020): 43–57.

Duder, C. J. D. "Love and the Lions: The Image of White Settlement in Kenya in Popular Fiction, 1919–1939." *African Affairs* 90, no. 360 (1991): 427–438.

Duffy, Rosaleen. "Interactive Elephants: Nature, Tourism, and Neoliberalism." *Annals of Tourism Research* 44 (2014): 88–101.

Duffy, Rosaleen and Lorraine Moore. "Neoliberalizing Nature? Elephant-Back Tourism in Thailand and Botswana." *Antipode* 42, no. 3 (2010): 742–766.

Eck, Diana L. *India: A Sacred Geography*. New York: Harmony Books, 2012.

Edmond, Rod. *Representing the South Pacific: From Cook to Gaugin*. Cambridge: Cambridge University Press, 2009.

Edmunds, David. "Introduction: Twentieth-Century Warriors." In *The New Warriors: Native American Leaders Since 1900*, edited by David Edmunds, 1–15. Lincoln: University of Nebraska Press, 2001.

Edwards, Brian. "Sheltering Screens: Paul Bowles and Foreign Relations." *American Literary History* 17, no. 2 (2005): 307–334.

El Dessouky, Dina. "Activating Voice, Body, and Place: Kanaka Maoli and Ma'ohi Writings for Kaho'olawe and Moruroa." In *Postcolonial Ecologies: Literatures of the Environment*, edited by Elizabeth DeLoughrey and George B. Handley, 254–272. New York: Oxford University Press, 2011.

Eperjesi, John R. *The Imperialist Imaginary: Visions of Asia and the Pacific in American Culture*. Hanover: Dartmouth University Press, 2005.

Fabian, Johannes. *Time and the Other: How Anthropology Makes Its Object*. New York: Columbia University Press, 2014.

Feigon, Lee. *Demystifying Tibet: Unlocking the Secrets of the Land of the Snows*. Chicago: Elephant Paperbacks, 1998.

Feldman, Jackie. "Constructing a Shared Bible Land: Jewish Israeli Guiding Performances for Protestant Pilgrims." *American Ethnologist* 34, no. 2 (2007): 351–374.

Ferber, Linda S. *The Hudson River School: Nature and the American Vision*. New York: Rizzoli, 2009.

Figiel, Sia. *Where We Once Belonged*. New York: Kaya, 1999.

Fike, Matthew A. "Time Is Not an Arrow: Anima and History in H. Rider Haggard's *She*." *ANQ (A Quarterly Journal of Short Articles, Notes and Reviews)* 28, no. 2 (2015): 105–109.

Fixico, Donald L. *The Invasion of Indian Country in the Twentieth Century: American Capitalism and Tribal Natural Resources*. Niwot: University Press of Colorado, 1998.

Flaherty, Robert, dir. *Moana (Moana: A Romance of the Golden Age)*. Paramount Pictures, 1926.

Fojas, Camilla. *Islands of Empire: Pop Culture & U.S. Power*. Austin: University of Texas Press, 2014.

Folmer, Akke, Ali (Tanya) Tengxiage, Hanny Kadijk, and Alastair John Wright. "Exploring Chinese Millennials' Experiential and Transformative Travel: A Case Study of Mountain Bikers in Tibet." *Journal of Tourist Futures* 5, no. 2 (2019): 142–156.

Forby, Marc, dir. *Princess Kaiulani*. Roadside Attractions, 2009.

Forster, E. M. "Egypt." In *Recommendations on the Government of Egypt, by a Committee of the International Section of the Labour Research Department*. London: Labour Research Department, 1920.

Forster, George. *A Voyage Around the World: Volume 1*. London, 1777.

Foucault, Michel. "Fantasia of the Library." In *Language, Counter-Memory, Practice: Selected Essays and Interviews*, edited by Donald Bouchard, 87–109. Ithaca: Cornell University Press, 1977.

Foucault, Michel and Jay Miskowiec. "Of Other Spaces." *Diacritics* 16, no. 1 (1986): 22–27.

Friedl, Harald A. "'Places of Power': Can Individual 'Sacred Space' Help Regain Orientation in a Confusing World?: A Discussion of Mental Health Tourism to Extraordinary Natural Sites in the Context of Antonovsky's 'Sense of Coherence' and Maslow's 'Hierarchy of Needs.'" In *The Routledge Handbook of Health Tourism*, edited by Melanie Kay Smith and László Puckzó, 347–364. New York: Routledge, 2017.

Furani, Khaled and Dan Rabinowitz. "The Ethnographic Arriving of Palestine." *Annual Review of Anthropology* 40 (2011): 475–491.

Gagiano, Annie. "Blixen, Ngugi: Recounting Kenya." In *Ngugi wa Thiong'o: Texts and Contexts*, edited by Charles Cantalupo, 95–110. Trenton: Africa World Press, 1995.

Gammon, Sean. "Chapter 2: Secular Pilgrimage and Sport Tourism." In *Sport Tourism: Interrelationships, Impacts and Issues*, edited by Brent W. Richie and Daryl Adair, 30–45. Clevedon: Channel View Publications, 2004.

Geiger, Jeffrey. "Imagined Islands: 'White Shadows in the South Seas' and Cultural Ambivalence." *Cinema Journal* 41, no. 3 (2002): 98–121.

Gemie, Sharif. "Loti, Orientalism and the French Colonial Experience." *Journal of European Area Studies* 8, no. 2 (2000): 149–165.

Genoni, Paul and Tanya Dalziell. "George Johnston's Tibetan Interlude: Myth and Reality in Shangri-La." *Journeys* 18, no. 2 (2017): 1–27.

Gerber, Haim. "Zionism, Orientalism, and the Palestinians." *Journal of Palestine Studies* 33, no. 1 (2003): 23–41.

Gholi, Ahmad, Masoud Ahmadi Mousaabad, and Maryam Raminnia. "Journey to the Loss and Fixation of Western Identity in Bernardo Bertolucci's Movie Adaptation of *Sheltering Sky*." *Journal of Language, Teaching and Research* 7, no. 5 (2016): 953–957.

Gibson, Shimon and Rupert L. Chapman. "The Mediterranean Hotel in Nineteenth-Century Jerusalem." *Palestine Exploration Quarterly* 127, no. 2 (1995): 93–105.

Gilbert, Elizabeth. *Eat, Pray, Love: One Woman's Search for Everything Across Italy, India and Indonesia*. New York: Penguin Books, 2006.

Glouberman, Dina and Josée-Ann Cloutier. "Community as Holistic Healer on Health Holiday Retreats: The Case of Skyros." In *The Routledge Handbook of Health Tourism*, edited by Melanie Kay Smith and László Puckzó, 152–167. New York: Routledge, 2017.

Gonzalez, Vernadette Vicuña. *Securing Paradise: Tourism and Militarism in Hawai'i and the Philippines*. Durham: Duke University Press, 2013.

Gorda, Anak Agung Ayu Ngurah Sri Rahayu, Kadek Januarsa Adi Sudharma, and Ketut Elly Sutrisni. "Melukat Ritual for Commercialization and Protection Toward Cultural Tourism in Bali." In *Advances in Science, Education and Humanities*

Research (Proceedings of the 3rd International Conference on Business Law and Local Wisdom Traditions), 618–629. Dordrecht: Atlantis Press, 2023.

Govinda, Lama Anagarika. *The Way of the White Clouds*. New York: The Overlook Press, 1966.

Graburn, Nelson H. "Tourism: The Sacred Journey." In *Hosts and Guests: The Anthropology of Tourism*, edited by Valene L. Smith, 21–36. Philadelphia: University of Pennsylvania Press, 1989.

Graburn, Nelson H. and Naomi M. Leite. "Always in Process: Edward Bruner, American Anthropology, and the Study of Tourism." In *The Ethnography of Tourism: Edward Bruner and Beyond*, edited by Naomi M. Leite, Quetzil E. Castañeda, and Kathleen M. Adams, 49–64. Lanham: Lexington Books, 2019.

Gregory, Derek. *Geographical Imaginations*. Cambridge: Blackwell, 1994.

Gregory, Derek. "Between the Book and the Lamp: Imaginative Geographies of Egypt, 1849–50." *Transactions of the Institute of British Geographers* 20, no. 1 (1995): 29–57.

Gregory, Derek. "Colonial Nostalgia and Cultures of Travel: Spaces of Constructed Visibility in Egypt." In *Consuming Tradition, Manufacturing Heritage: Global Norms and Urban Forms in the Age of Tourism*, edited by Nezar Al Sayyad, 111–151. New York: Routledge, 2001.

Gregory, Derek. "Emperors of the Gaze: Photographic Practices and Productions of Space in Egypt, 1839–1914." In *Picturing Place: Photography and the Geographical Imagination*, edited by Joan M. Schwartz and James R. Ryan, 196–225. New York: I.B. Tauris, 2003.

Guidoni, Rachel. "Conceptions on Tibetan Relics." In *Nature, Culture and Religion at the Crossroads of Asia*, edited by Marie Lecomte-Tilouine, 260–282. New York: Routledge, 2017.

Guillerman, John, dir. *Death on the Nile*. EMI Distributers, 1978.

Gunn, Clare A. *Vacationscape: Designing Tourist Regions*. New York: Van Nostrand Reinhold, 1988.

Gützlaff, Karl Friedrich August. *China Opened, Volume One*. London: Smith, Elder & Company, 1838.

Haggard, H. Rider. *She: A History of Adventure*, 1887. Reprint, Black & Gold House of Books, 2023.

Haines, Aubrey L. *The Yellowstone Story: A History of Our First National Park, Volume One*. Niwot: University Press of Colorado, 1996.

Haines, Aubrey L. *The Yellowstone Story: A History of Our First National Park, Volume Two*. Niwot: University Press of Colorado, 1996.

Hakim, Luchman, Jae-Eun Kim, and Sun-Kee Hong. "Cultural Landscape and Ecotourism in Bali Island, Indonesia." *Journal of Ecology and Field Biology* 32, no. 1 (2009): 1–8.

Hall, Colin Michael. "Mountaineering and Climate Change." In *Mountaineering Tourism*, edited by Ghazali Musa, James Higham, and Anna Thompson-Carr, 240–249. New York: Routledge, 2015.

Hall, Colin Michael and Stephen W. Boyd. "Nature-Based Tourism in Peripheral Areas: Development or Disaster?" In *Nature-Based Tourism in Peripheral Areas: Development of Disaster*, edited by Michael C. Hall and Stephen W. Boyd, 3–17. Buffalo: Clevedon, 2005.

Hall, David D. *Worlds of Wonder, Days of Judgment: Popular Religious Belief in Early New England*. Cambridge, MA: Harvard University Press, 1990.

Hall, Lisa Kahaleole. "'Hawaiian at Heart' and Other Fictions." *The Contemporary Pacific* 17, no. 2 (2005): 404–413.

Hammond, John R. *Lost Horizon Companion: A Guide to the James Hilton Novel and Its Characters, Critical Reception, Film Adaptations and Place in Popular Culture*. Jefferson: McFarland & Company, 2008.

Hannoum, Abdelmajid. *Violent Modernity: France in Algeria*. Cambridge, MA: Harvard University Press, 2010.

Hanzimanolis, Margaret. "Eight Hen Per Man Per Day: Shipwreck Survivors and Pastoral Abundance in Southern Africa." In *Navigating African Maritime History*, edited by Carina E. Ray and Jeremy Rich, 33–55. Liverpool: Liverpool University Press, 2009.

Harif, Hanan. "A Bridge or a Fortress? S.D. Goiten and the Role of Jewish Arabists in the American Academy." *Jewish Social Studies* 26, no. 2 (2021): 68–92.

Harley, John Brian. "Maps, Knowledge, and Power." In *The Iconography of Landscape: Essays on the Symbolic Representation, Design and Use of Past Environments*, edited by Denis Cosgrove and Stephen Daniels, 277–312. Cambridge: Cambridge University Press, 1988.

Harley, John Brian. "Silences and Secrecy: The Hidden Agenda of Cartography in Early Modern Europe." *Imago Mundi* 40 (1988): 57–76.

Harley, John Brian. "Rereading the Maps of Columbian Encounter." *Annals of the Association of American Geographers* 82 (1992): 522–42.

Harley, John Brian. "New England Cartography and the Native Americans." In *The New Nature of Maps: Essays in the History of Cartography*, edited by Paul Laxton, 169–196. Baltimore: John Hopkins University Press, 2001.

Hassan, Fekri A. "Egypt in the Memory of the World." In *Egyptian Archaeology*, edited by Willeke Wendrich, 259–273. Malden: Wiley-Blackwell, 2010.

Hathaway, Henry, dir. *True Grit*. Paramount Pictures, 1969.

Hazbun, Waleed. "The East as an Exhibit: Thomas Cook & Son and the Origins of the International Tourism Industry in Egypt." In *The Business of Tourism: Place, Faith, and History*, edited by Philip Scranton and Janet F. Davidson, 3–33. Philadelphia: University of Pennsylvania Press, 2009.

Heacox, Kim. *An American Idea: The Making of National Parks*. Washington, D.C.: National Geographic Society, 2001.

Heintzman, Paul. "Nature-Based Recreation and Spirituality: A Complex Relationship." *Leisure Sciences* 32, no. 1 (2009): 72–89.

Heinze-Greenberg, Ita. "Immigration and Culture Shock." In *Tel Aviv Modern Architecture, 1930–1939*, edited by Irmel Kamp-Bandau, Winfried Nerdinger, and Pe'era Goldman, 36–39. Munich: Institut für Auslandsbeziehungen, 1994.

Hemmings, Kaui Hart. *The Descendants*. New York: Random House, 2007.

Hergé. *Tintin in Tibet*. NYC: Little Brown Books, 1975.

Herskovits, Melville J. *The Myth of the Negro Past*. Boston: Beacon Press, 1958.

Higham, James, Anna Thomason-Carr, and Ghazali Musa. "Mountaineering Tourism: Activity, People and Place." In *Mountaineering Tourism*, edited by Ghazali Musa, James Higham, and Anna Thompson-Carr, 1–15. New York: Routledge, 2015.

Hilton, James. *Lost Horizon*, 1933. Reprint. New York: Harper, 2012.

Hirsch, Dafna. "'Interpreters of Occident to the Awakening Orient': The Jewish Public Health Nurse in Mandate Palestine." *Comparative Studies in Society and History* 50, no. 1 (2008): 227–255.

Hitchcock, Michael. "Bali: A Paradise Globalized." *Pacific Tourism Review* 4 (2000): 63–73.

Hitchcock, Michael. *Tourism, Development, and Terrorism in Bali*. New York: Routledge, 2007.

Hitchcock, Robert K., Maria Sapignoli, and Wayne A. Babchuk. "Settler Colonialism, Conflicts, and Genocide: Interactions between Hunter-Gatherers and Settlers in Kenya, and Zimbabwe and Northern Botswana." *Settler Colonial Studies* 5, no. 1 (2015): 1–26.

Hitchcock, Victress, dir. *Blessings: The Tsoknyi Nuns of Tibet*. Chariot Films, 2009.

Hodder, Jacqueline. "Spirituality and Well-Being: 'New Age' and 'Evangelical' Spiritual Expressions Among Young People and Their Implications for Well-Being." *International Journal of Children's Spirituality* 14, no. 3 (2009): 197–212.

Holden, Stacy E. "The Legacy of French Colonialism: Preservation in Morocco's Fez Medina." *APT Bulletin: The Journal of Preservation Technology* 39, no. 4 (2008): 5–11.

Hollingshead, Michael. *The Man Who Turned on the World.* London: Blond and Briggs, 1973.

Holt, John Clifford. *The Buddhist Visnu: Religious Transformation, Politics, and Culture.* New York: Columbia University Press, 2004.

Hopkins, I. W. J. "Nineteenth-Century Maps of Palestine: Dual-Purpose Historical Evidence." *Imago Mundi* 22 (1968): 30–36.

Hore, Jarrod. *Visions of Nature: How Landscape Photography Shaped Settler Colonialism.* Berkeley: University of California Press, 2022.

Horsman, Reginald. *Race and Manifest Destiny: The Origins of American Racial Anglo-Saxonism.* Cambridge, MA: Harvard University Press, 1981.

Houston, David L. R. "Five Miles Out: Communion and Commodification Among the Mountaineers." In *Tarzan Was an Eco-Tourist . . . and Other Tales in the Anthropology of Adventure,* edited by Luis Vivanco and Robert Gordon, 147–160. New York: Berghahn Books, 2006.

Howard, Christopher A. "Touring the Consumption of the Other: Imaginaries of Authenticity in the Himalayas and Beyond." *Journal of Consumer Culture* 16, no. 2 (2016): 354–373.

Howe, Kathleen Stewart. "Mapping a Sacred Geography: Photographic Surveys by the Royal Engineers in the Holy Land, 1864–68." In *Picturing Place: Photography and the Geographical Imagination,* edited by Joan M. Schwartz and James R. Ryan, 226–242. New York: I.B. Tauris, 2003.

Howe, Leo. *The Changing World of Bali: Religion, Society and Tourism.* New York: Routledge, 2005.

Hoxie, Frederick E. and Tim Bernardis. "Robert Yellowtail (Crow)." In *The New Warriors: Native American Leaders Since 1900,* edited by David Edmunds, 55–77. Lincoln: University of Nebraska Press, 2001.

Hughes, George. "Tourism and the Geographical Imagination." *Leisure Studies* 11, no. 1 (1992): 31–42.

Hussey, Antonia. "Tourist Destination Areas in Bali." *Contemporary Southeast Asia* 3, no. 4 (1980): 374–385.

Hutt, Michael. "Looking for Shangri-la: From Hilton to Lāmichhāne." In *The Tourist Image: Myths and Myth Making in Tourism,* edited by Tom Selwyn, 49–60. New York: John Wiley & Sons, 1996.

Huxley, Elspeth. *White Man's Country: Lord Delamere and the Making of Kenya, 2 Volumes.* London: MacMillan, 1935.

Iancu, Anca-Luminata. "Spaces of Their Own: Emotional and Spiritual Quests in *Under the Tuscan Sun* and *Eat, Pray, Love.*" *Journal of Research in Gender Studies* 4, no. 1 (2014): 439–452.

Imada, Adria L. "Hawaiians on Tour: Hula Circuits Through the American Empire." *American Quarterly* 56, no. 1 (2004): 111–149.

Imada, Adria L. "Transnational Hula as Colonial Culture." *The Journal of Pacific History* 46, no. 2 (2011): 149–176.

Irbouh, Hamid. *Art in the Service of Colonialism: French Art Education in Morocco 1912–1956.* New York: I.B. Tauris, 2013.

Irving, Sarah. "'This Is Palestine': History and Modernity in Guidebooks to Mandate Palestine." *Contemporary Levant* 4, no. 1 (2019): 64–74.

Ivakhiv, Adrian J. *Claiming Sacred Ground: Pilgrims and Politics at Glastonbury and Sedona.* Bloomington: Indiana University Press, 2001.

Iwamura, Jane Naomi. *Virtual Orientalism: Asian Religions and American Popular Culture.* New York: Oxford University Press, 2011.

Jackson, Will. "White Man's Country: Kenya Colony and the Making of a Myth." *Journal of East African Studies* 5, no. 2 (2011): 344–368.

Jacobs, Jessica. *Sex, Tourism and the Postcolonial Encounter: Landscapes of Longing in Egypt*. London: Ashgate, 2010.

Jaimes, M. Annette and Theresa Halsey. "American Indian Women: At the Center of Indigenous Resistance in Contemporary North America." In *Dangerous Liaisons: Gender, Nation, and Postcolonial Perspectives*, edited by Anne McClintock, Aamir Mufti, and Ella Shohat, 298–329. Minneapolis: University of Minnesota Press, 1997.

Jazeel, Tariq. "Orientalism and the Geographical Imagination." *Geography* 97, no. 1 (2012): 4–11.

Jennings, Willie James. *The Christian Imagination: Theology and the Origins of Race*. New Haven: Yale University Press, 2010.

Johnston, George. *Journey Through Tomorrow*. Melbourne: F. W. Cheshire, 1947.

Johnston, Jeremy M. "'The Wild West Side of American Existence': Theodore Roosevelt, Buffalo Bill Cody, and American Military Exceptionalism." In *The Popular Frontier: Buffalo Bill's Wild West and Transnational Mass Culture*, edited by Frank Christianson, 73–95. Norman: University of Oklahoma Press, 2017.

Jolly, Margaret. "Contested Paradise: Dispossession and Repossession in Hawai'i." *The Contemporary Pacific* 30, no. 2 (2018): 355–377.

Jolly, Roslyn. "South Sea Gothic: Pierre Loti and Robert Louis Stevenson." *English Literature in Translation, 1880–1920* 47, no. 1 (2004): 28–49.

Kabbani, Rana. *Europe's Myths of Orient*. Bloomington: Indiana University Press, 1986.

Kahn, Miriam. "Tahiti Intertwined: Ancestral Land, Tourist Postcard, and Nuclear Test Site." *American Anthropologist* 102, no. 1 (2000): 7–26.

Kahn, Miriam. "Tahiti: The Ripples of a Myth on the Shores of the Imagination." *History and Anthropology* 14, no. 4 (2003): 307–326.

Kellman, Ari. *A Misplaced Massacre: Struggling over the Memory of Sand Creek*. Cambridge, MA: Harvard University Press, 2013.

Kelly, Catherine and Melanie Kay Smith. "Journeys of the Self: The Need to Retreat." In *The Routledge Handbook of Health Tourism*, edited by Melanie Kay Smith and László Puckzó, 138–151. New York: Routledge, 2017.

Kelly, Kevin. "The Next Burning Man." In *Burning Man*, edited by John Plunkett and Brad Wieners, 126–128. San Francisco: HardWired, 1997.

Kelly, Kristine. "Aesthetic Desire and Imperialist Disappointment in Trollope's *The Bertrams* and the Murray *Handbook for Travellers in Syria and Palestine*." *Victorian Literature and Culture* 43 (2015): 621–639.

Kelner, Shaul. *Tours that Bind: Diaspora, Pilgrimage, and Israeli Birthright Tourism*. New York: NYU Press, 2010.

Kennedy, Dane. *Islands of White: Settler Society and Culture in Kenya and Southern Rhodesia, 1890–1939*. Durham: Duke University Press, 1987.

Kernahan, Mel. *White Savages in the South Seas*. London: Verso, 1995.

Khalidi, Rashid. *Palestinian Identity: The Construction of Modern National Consciousness*. New York: Columbia University Press, 1997.

Kharisma, Pradana Gede Yoga and Parwati Komang Shanty Muni. "Local-Wisdom-Based Spa Tourism in Ubud Village of Bali, Indonesia." *RJOAS* 68, no. 8 (2017): 188–196.

Kiang, Jessica. "Chloe Zhao's Nomadland as Vast as the American Landscape It Travels." *The Playlist*, September 11, 2020, n.p. https://theplaylist.net/nomadland-venice-review-20200911/

Kim, Hanung. "Another Tibet at the Heart of Qing China: Location of Tibetan Buddhism in the Mentality of the Qing Chinese Mind at Jehol." In *Greater Tibet:*

An Examination of Borders, Ethnic Boundaries, and Cultural Areas, edited by P. Christiaan Klieger, 37–56. Lanham: Rowman & Littlefield, 2015.

King, Richard. "Orientalism and the Modern Myth of 'Hinduism'." *Numen* 46, no. 2 (1999): 146–185.

King, Richard. *Orientalism and Religion: Postcolonial Theory, India and 'The Mystic East'*. New York: Routledge, 1999.

Kjeldsen, Jim. *The Mountaineers: A History*. Seattle: The Mountaineers, 1998.

Klein, Milton M. "Everyman His Own Historian: Carl Becker as Historiographer." *The History Teacher* 19, no. 1 (1985): 101–109.

Klieger, P. Christiaan. "Research Notes: Shangri-La and the Politicization of Tourism in Tibet." *Annals of Tourism Research* 19 (1992): 122–124.

Knight, George. *Intimate Glimpses of Mysterious Tibet and Neighbouring Countries*. London: Golden Vista Press, 1930.

Knipp, Thomas R. "Kenya's Literary Ladies and the Mythologizing of the White Highlands." *South Atlantic Review* 55, no. 1 (1990): 1–16.

Kosasa, Karen. "Searching for the 'C' Word: Museums, Art Galleries, and Settler Colonialism in Hawai'i." In *Studies in Settler Colonialism: Politics, Identity and Culture*, edited by Fiona Bateman and Lionel Pilkington, 153–168. New York: Palgrave MacMillan, 2011.

Kovarsky, Joel. *The True Geography of Our Country: Jefferson's Cartographic Vision*. Charlottesville: University of Virginia Press, 2014.

Kozinets, Robert V. "The Moment of Infinite Fire." In *Time, Space and the Market: Retroscapes Rising*, edited by Stephen Brown and John F. Sherry, Jr., 199–216. New York: Routledge, 2015.

Krause, Gregor. *Bali 1912, 1920*. Reprint. Singapore: Pepper Publications, 1998.

Lalvani, Suren. "Consuming the Exotic Other." *Critical Studies in Mass Communication* 12 (1995): 263–286.

Lamb, Alastair. *British India and Tibet: 1766–1910*. New York: Routledge & Kegan Paul, 1960.

Larasati, R. Diyah. "Eat, Pray, Love Mimic: Female Citizenship and Otherness." *South Asian Popular Culture* 8, no. 1 (2010): 29–95.

Lawrence, T. E. *Lawrence of Arabia: The Selected Letters*. Edited by Malcom Brown. London: Little Books, 2005.

Lebovics, Herman. "The Zoos of the Exposition Coloniale Internationale, Paris 1931." In *Human Zoos: Science and Spectacle in the Age of Colonial Empires*, edited by Pascal Blanchard, Nicolas Bancel, Gilles Boëtsch, Sandrine Lemaire, and Charles Forsdick, 369–376. Liverpool: Liverpool University Press, 2008.

Lee, Georgia. "Wahi Pana: Legendary Places on Hawai'i Island." In *Inscribed Landscapes: Marking and Making Place*, edited by Bruno David and Meredith Wilson, 79–92. Honolulu: University of Hawai'i Press, 2002.

Lefebvre, Camille. "We Have Tailored Africa: French Colonialism and the 'Artificiality' of Africa's Borders in the Interwar Period." *Journal of Historical Geography* 37 (2011): 191–202.

Lester, Alan. "Constructing Colonial Discourse: Britain, South Africa and the Empire in the Nineteenth Century." In *Postcolonial Geographies*, edited by Cheryl McEwan and Alison Blunt, 29–45. New York: Continuum, 2002.

Lew, Alan A. and Guosheng Han. "A World Geography of Mountain Trekking." In *Mountaineering Tourism*, edited by Ghazali Musa, James Higham, and Anna Thompson-Carr, 19–39. New York: Routledge, 2015.

Lewis, Simon. "Culture, Cultivation, and Colonialism in 'Out of Africa' and Beyond." *Research in African Literatures* 31, no. 1 (2000): 63–79.

Lewis, Todd T. "Himalayan Religions in Comparative Perspective: Considerations Regarding Buddhism and Hinduism across their Indic Frontiers." *Himalaya* 14, no. 1 (1994): 25–46.

Leyerle, Blake. "Landscape as Cartography in Early Christian Pilgrimage Narratives." *Journal of the American Academy of Religion* 64, no. 1 (1996): 119–134.

Liechty, Mark. "Building the Road to Kathmandu: Notes on the History of Tourism in Nepal." *Himalaya* 25, nos. 1/2 (2005): 19–28.

Liechty, Mark. "The Key to an Oriental World: Boris Lissanevitch, Kathmandu's Royal Hotel and the 'Golden Age' of Tourism in Nepal." *Studies in Nepali History and Society* 15, no. 2 (2010): 253–295.

Liechty, Mark. *Far Out: Countercultural Seekers and the Tourist Encounter in Nepal.* Chicago: The University of Chicago Press, 2017.

Lindemann, Tim. "Travelling the Scenic Landscape: Community, Nationalism and Precarity in *Nomadland* (2020)." *Empedocles: European Journal for the Philosophy of Communication* 13, no. 1 (2022): 25–40.

Linnekin, Joycelyn. "The Hui Lands of Keanae: Hawaiian Land Tenure and the Great Mahele." *The Journal of the Polynesian Society* 92, no. 2 (1983): 169–188.

Lloyd, Frank, dir. *Mutiny on the Bounty.* Los Angeles: MGM, 1935.

Lockman, Zackary. *Contending Visions of the Middle East: The History and Politics of Orientalism.* New York: Cambridge University Press, 2004.

Logan, Dana W. "The Lean Closet: Asceticism in Postindustrial Consumer Culture." *Journal of the American Academy of Religion* 85, no. 3 (2017): 600–628.

Logan, Joshua, dir. *South Pacific.* 20th-Century Fox, 1958.

Lonsdale, John. "Kenya: Home County and African Frontier." In *Settlers and Expatriates: Britons Over the Seas*, edited by Robert Bickers, 74–111. New York: Oxford University Press, 2010.

Lopez, Donald S. Jr. "New Age Orientalism: The Case of Tibet." *Tricycle: The Buddhist Review* 3, no. 3 (1994): 37–43.

Lopez, Donald S. Jr. "Foreigner at the Lama's Feet." In *Curators of the Buddha: The Study of Buddhism Under Colonialism*, edited by Donald Lopez, Jr., 251–295. Chicago: The University of Chicago Press, 1995.

Lopez, Donald S. Jr. *Prisoners of Shangri-La: Tibetan Buddhism and the West.* Chicago: University of Chicago Press, 2018.

Lorkin, Patricia M. E. "Imperial Nostalgia; Colonial Nostalgia: Differences of Theory, Similarities of Practice?" *Historical Reflections* 39, no. 3 (2013): 97–111.

Loshitzky, Yosepha (Yosefa). *The Radical Faces of Godard and Bertolucci.* Detroit: Wayne State University Press, 1995.

Loshitzky, Yosefa. "Orientalist Representations: Palestinians and Arabs in Some Postcolonial Film and Literature." In *Cultural Encounters: Representing 'Otherness'*, edited by Elizabeth Hallam and Brian V. Street, 51–71. New York: Routledge, 2000.

Loti, Pierre. *The Marriage of Loti (Rarahu)*, 1878. Reprint. London: Forgotten Books, 2012.

Loti, Pierre. *Aziyadé*, 1867. Reprint. Paris: North Star, 2016.

Lovell, Jane and Howard Griffin. "Unfamiliar Light: The Production of Enchantment." *Annals of Tourism Research* 92 (2022): 1–17.

Luangphinith, Seri. "Tropical Fevers: 'Madness' and Colonialism in Pacific Literature." *The Contemporary Pacific* 16, no. 1 (2004): 59–85.

Lüthy, Barbara, Francesca Falk, and Patricia Purtschert. "Colonialism without Colonies: Examining Blank Spaces in Colonial Studies." *National Identities* 18, no. 1 (2016): 1–9.

Lynch, Tom. *Outback & Out West: The Settler-Colonial Environmental Imaginary.* Lincoln: University of Nebraska Press, 2022.

Lyons, Paul. *American Pacificism: Oceania in the U.S. Imagination.* New York: Routledge, 2006.

MacCannell, Dean. "Staged Authenticity: Arrangements of Social Space in Tourist Settings." *American Journal of Sociology* 79, no. 3 (1973): 589–603.

MacCannell, Dean. *The Tourist: A New Theory of the Leisure Class*. New York: Shocken Books, 1989.

MacCannell, Dean. "The Ego Factor in Tourism." *Journal of Consumer Research* 29, no. 1 (2002): 146–151.

Maddra, Sam. "American Indians in Buffalo Bill's Wild West." In *Human Zoos: Science and Spectacle in the Age of Colonial Empires*, edited by Pascal Blanchard, Nicolas Bancel, Gilles Boëtsch, Sandrine Lemaire, and Charles Forsdick, 134–141. Liverpool: Liverpool University Press, 2008.

Mahdy, Hossam. "Travellers, Colonisers, and Conservationists." In *Travellers in Egypt*, edited by Paul and Janet Starkey, 157–167. London: Tauris Parke Paperbacks, 2001.

Makdidi, Saree. "Zionism Then and Now." In *Studies of Settler Colonialism: Politics, Identity, and Culture*, edited by Fiona Bateman and Lionel Pilkington, 237–256. New York: Palgrave MacMillin, 2011.

Mann, Michael, dir. *The Last of the Mohicans*. 20th Century Fox, 1992.

Mantra, Ida Bagus, I. Nyoman Suparsa, and Negah Dwi Handayani. "Cultural and Wellness Tourism: The Potential of Yoga, Meditation, and Self-Purification Ceremony." *SOSHUM (Jurnal Sosial dan Humaniora)* 13, no. 2 (2013): 109–119.

Marston, Kendra. "The World Is Her Oyster: Negotiating Contemporary White Womanhood in Hollywood's Tourist Spaces." *Cinema Journal* 55, no. 4 (2016): 3–27.

Masalha, Nur. *The Bible and Zionism: Invented Traditions, Archaeology and Post-Colonialism in Palestine-Israel*. New York: Zeb Books, 2007.

Masoff, Joy. "The Mystery Man of Sand Creek: George Laird Shoup." *Great Plains Quarterly* 39, no. 2 (2019): 179–210.

Massad, Joseph A. *Desiring Arabs*. Chicago: The University of Chicago Press, 2007.

Mather, Jeffrey. "Captivating Readers: Middlebrow Aesthetics and James Hilton's *Lost Horizon*." *CEA Critic* 79, no. 2 (2017): 231–243.

Maurois, André. *Sur le vif, L'exposition Coloniale*. Paris: Degorce, 1931.

Mazlish, Bruce. "A Triptych: Freud's *The Interpretation of Dreams*, Rider Haggard's *She*, and Bulwer-Lytton's *The Coming Race*." *Comparative Studies in Society and History* 35, no. 4 (1993): 726–745.

Mbembe, Achille. *On the Postcolony*. Berkeley: University of California Press, 2001.

McCann, Mat. "Tourism, Difference and Authenticity in an Age of Anxiety: Paul Bowles' *The Sheltering Sky*." In *Lit & Tour: Ensaois Sobre Literatura E Turismo*, edited by Sílvia Quintero and Rita Baleiro, 149–163. Famalicão: Edições Húmus, 2014.

McCarron-Cates, Floramae. "The Best Possible View: Pictorial Representation in the American West." In *Frederick Church, Winslow Homer, and Thomas Moran: Tourism and the American Landscape*, edited by Gail S. Davidson and Floramae McCarron-Cates, 75–118. New York: Bulfinch Press, 2006.

McCartney, Patrick. "Yoga-scapes, Embodiment, and Imagined Spiritual Tourism." In *Tourism and Embodiment*, edited by Catherine Palmer and Hazel Andrews, 86–106. New York: Routledge, 2019.

McClintock, Anne. *Imperial Leather: Race, Gender and Sexuality in the Colonial Contest*. New York: Routledge, 1995.

McCloskey, Michael. "The Wilderness Act of 1964: Its Background and Meaning." *The Oregon Law Review* 45, no. 4 (1966): 288–321.

McDonald, Mary G. "Tourist Weddings in Hawai'i: Consuming the Destination." In *Seductions of Place: Geographical Perspectives on Globalization and Touristed Landscapes*, edited by Carolyn Carter and Alan A. Lew, 171–192. London: Routledge, 2005.

McDonnell, Siobhan. "Selling 'Sites of Desire': Paradise in Reality Television, Tourism, and Real Estate Promotion in Vanuatu." *The Contemporary Pacific* 30, no. 2 (2018): 413–435.

McKay, Alex. "The Establishment of the British Trade Agencies in Tibet: A Survey." *Journal of the Royal Asiatic Society* 2, no. 3 (1992): 399–421.

McKay, Alex. *Kailas Histories: Renunciate Traditions and the Construction of Himalayan Sacred Geography.* Leiden: Brill, 2016.

McNee, Alan. *The New Mountaineer in Late Victorian Britain.* London: Palgrave Macmillan, 2016.

McPhee, Colin. *A House in Bali.* New Clarendon: Tuttle Publishing, 1944.

Mead, Margaret. "The Art and Technology of Fieldwork." In *A Handbook of Method in Cultural Anthropology*, edited by Raoul Naroll and Ronald Cohen, 246–265. Garden City: Natural History Press, 1970.

Meinig, D. W. "Territorial Strategies Applied to Captive Peoples." In *Ideology and Landscape in Historical Perspective: Essays on the Meanings of Some Places in the Past*, edited by Alan R. H. Baker and Gideon Biger, 125–136. New York: Cambridge University Press, 1992.

Mentxaka, Aintzane Legarreta. "Egypt in Western Popular Culture: From Bram Stoker to *The Jewel of the Nile.*" *Otherness: Essays and Studies* 6, no. 2 (2018): 162–193.

Merrington, Peter. "A Staggered Orientalism: The Cape-to-Cairo Imaginary." *Poetics Today* 22, no. 2 (2001): 323–364.

Messerschmidt, Donald A. "The Hindu Pilgrimage to Muktinath, Part 1: Natural and Supernatural Attributes of the Sacred Field." *Mountain Research and Development* 9, no. 2 (1989): 89–104.

Messerschmidt, Donald A. "The Hindu Pilgrimage to Muktinath, Part 2: Vaishnava Devotees and Status Reaffirmation." *Mountain Research and Development* 9, no. 2 (1989): 105–118.

Michener, James. *Return to Paradise.* New York: Random House, 1951.

Mickey, Ethel L. "'Eat, Pray, Love' Bullshit': Women's Empowerment through Wellness at an Elite Professional Conference." *Journal of Contemporary Ethnography* 48, no. 1 (2018): 1–25.

Milner, Alfred. *England in Egypt.* London: Edward Arnold, 1920.

Minca, Claudio. "'The Bali Syndrome': The Explosion and Implosion of 'Exotic' Tourist Spaces." *Tourism Geographies* 2, no. 4 (2000): 389–403.

Minca, Claudio and Lauren Wagner. *Moroccan Dreams: Oriental Myths, Colonial Legacy.* New York: I.B. Tauris, 2016.

Mitchell, Robin. *Vénus Noire: Black Women and Colonial Fantasies in Nineteenth-Century France.* Athens: University of Georgia Press, 2020.

Mitchell, Timothy. *Colonising Egypt.* Berkeley: University of California Press, 1988.

Mitter, Partha. "The Hottentot Venus and Western Man: Reflections on the Construction of Beauty in the West." In *Cultural Encounters: Representing 'Otherness'*, edited by Elizabeth Hallam and Brian V. Street, 35–50. New York: Routledge, 2000.

Miyonga, Rose. "'We Keep Them to Remember': Tin Trunk Archives and the Emotional History of the Mau Mau War." *History Workshop Journal* 96 (2023): 96–114.

Moadell, Mansoor. *Islamic Modernism, Nationalism, and Fundamentalism: Episode and Discourse.* Chicago: University of Chicago Press, 2005.

Morin, Karen M. "Mining Empire: Journalists in the American West, ca. 1970." In *Postcolonial Geographies*, edited by Cheryl McEwan and Alison Blunt, 152–167. New York: Continuum, 2002.

Morris, Charles. *Our Island Empire: A Hand-book of Cuba, Porto Rico, Hawaii, and the Philippine Islands*. Philadelphia: J.B. Lippincott Company, 1899.

Morris, David Brown. *Wanderers: Literature, Culture and the Open Road*. New York: Routledge, 2021.

Mostafanezhad, Mary and Tanya Promburom. "'Lost in Thailand': The Popular Geopolitics of Film-Induced Tourism in Northern Thailand." *Social & Cultural Geography* 19, no. 1 (2018): 81–101.

Mostafanezhad, Mary and Margaret Byrne Swain. "Afterword—Beyond Anthropology: Ethnography in Tourism Studies." In *The Ethnography of Tourism: Edward Bruner and Beyond*, edited by Naomi M. Leite, Quetzil E. Castañeda, and Kathleen M. Adams, 239–248. Lanham: Lexington Books, 2019.

Moufakkir, Omar and Noureddine Selmi. "Examining the Spirituality of Spiritual Tourists: A Sahara Desert Experience." *Annals of Tourism Research* 70 (2018): 108–119.

Moving Images of the Pacific Islands: A Catalogue of Films and Videos (Occasional Paper 34). Edited by Melissa C. Miller. Honolulu: University of Hawaii Press, 1989.

Murnau, F. W., dir. *Tabu: A Story of the South Seas*. Paramount Pictures, 1931.

Murphy, Ryan, dir. *Eat, Pray, Love*. Columbia Pictures, 2010.

Naji, Ahmed Khashea and Mohamad Fleih Hassan. "Mapping Desert Narratives: A Systematic Review of Desert Representations in Postmodern English and Arabic Fiction." *Multidisciplinary Reviews* (2025): n.p. http://doi.org/10.31893/multiv.2025048

Narayanan, Yamini and Jim Macbeth. "Deep in the Desert: Merging the Desert and the Spiritual through 4WD Tourism." *Tourism Geographies* 11, no. 3 (2009): 369–389.

Nepal, Sanjay K. and Stella Amor Nepal. "Visitor Impacts on Trails in Sagarmatha (Mt. Everest) National Park." *Ambio* 33, no. 6 (2004): 334–340.

Nepal, Sanjay K. and Yang (Sunny) Mu. "Mountaineering Commodification and Risk Perceptions in Nepal's Mt. Everest Region." In *Mountaineering Tourism*, edited by Ghazali Musa, James Higham, and Anna Thompson-Carr, 250–264. New York: Routledge, 2015.

Neuhaus, Tom. *Tibet in the Western Imagination*. New York: Palgrave Macmillan, 2012.

Nicolson, Marjorie Hope. *Mountain Gloom and Mountain Glory: The Development of the Aesthetics of the Infinite*. New York: W. W. Norton & Company, 1959.

Nir, Yeshayahu. *The Bible and the Image: The History of Photography in the Holy Land 1839–1899*. Philadelphia: University of Pennsylvania Press, 1985.

Nolan, Christopher, dir. *Oppenheimer*. Universal Pictures, 2023.

Noor, Farish A. *The Long Shadow of the 19th Century: Critical Essays on Colonial Orientalism in Southeast Asia*. Petaling Jaya: Matahari Books, 2021.

Norbu, Jamyang. "Behind the Lost Horizon." In *Imagining Tibet: Perceptions, Projections, and Fantasies*, edited by Thierry Dodin and Heinz Räther, 373–378. Boston: Wisdom Publications, 2001.

Nordholt, Henk Schulte. "Some Visits to Bali." *Itinerario* 4, no. 2 (1980): 83–89.

Norman, Alex. *Spiritual Tourism: Travel and Religious Practice in Western Society*. London: Continuum, 2011.

Norman, Alex and Jennifer J. Pokorny. "Meditation Retreats: Spiritual Tourism Well-Being Interventions." *Tourism Management Perspectives* 24 (2017): 201–207.

Noronha, Raymond. "Paradise Reviewed: Tourism in Bali." In *Tourism: Passport to Development? Perspectives on the Social and Cultural Effects of Tourism in Developing Countries*, edited by Emanuel de Kadt, 177–204. New York: Oxford University Press, 1979.

Norum, Roger Edward. "The Unbearable Likeness of Being a Tourist: Expats, Travel and Imaginaries in the Neo-colonial Orient." *International Review of Social Research* 3, no. 1 (2013): 27–47.

Nyaupane, Gyan P. "Mountaineering on Mt. Everest: Evolution, Economy, Ecology and Ethics." In *Mountaineering Tourism*, edited by Ghazali Musa, James Higham, and Anna Thompson-Carr, 265–271. New York: Routledge, 2015.

Nye, David E. *American Technological Sublime*. Cambridge, MA: MIT Press, 1994.

Nye, David E. "Visualizing Eternity: Photographic Constructions of the Grand Canyon." In *Picturing Place: Photography and the Geographical Imagination*, edited by Joan M. Schwartz and James R. Ryan, 74–95. New York: I.B. Tauris, 2003.

Obenzinger, Hilton. *American Palestine: Melville, Twain, and the Holy Land Mania*. Princeton: Princeton University Press, 1999.

O'Carroll, John. "The Island after Plato: A 'Western' Amnesia." *Southern Review* 31, no. 3 (1998): 265–281.

Odum, Eugene. "Ecology and the Atomic Age." *ASB Bulletin* 4, no. 2 (1957): 27–29.

O'Dwyer, Carolyn. "Tropic Knights and Hula Belles: War and Tourism in the South Pacific." *Journal for Cultural Research* 8, no. 1 (2004): 33–50.

Olsen, Daniel H. "Religious Tourism: A Spiritual or Touristic Experience?" In *Routledge Handbook of Tourist Experience*, edited by Richard Sharpley, 391–407. New York: Routledge, 2022.

Olukushi, Adabayo and Francis Nyamnjoh. "The Postcolonial Turn: An Introduction." In *The Postcolonial Turn: Reimagining Anthropology and Africa*, edited by René Devisch and Francis Nyamnjoh, 1–28. Leiden: African Studies Center, 2011.

Olwig, Kenneth. *Landscape, Nature, and Body Politic*. Madison: University of Wisconsin Press, 2002.

Ortner, Sherry. "Thick Resistance: Death and the Cultural Construction of Agency in Himalayan Mountaineering." *Representations* 59 (1997): 135–162.

Ortner, Sherry. *Life and Death on Mt. Everest: Sherpas and Himalayan Mountaineering*. Princeton: Princeton University Press, 1999.

Osorio, Jonathan Kamakawiwo'ole. "Hawaiian Souls: The Movement to Stop the U.S. Bombing of Kaho'olawe." In *A Nation Rising: Hawaiian Movements for Life, Land, and Sovereignty*, edited by Noelani Goodyear-Ka'ōpua, Ikaika Hussey, and Erin Kahunawaika'ala Wright, 137–160. Durham: Duke University Press, 2014.

Palencia, Carolina Sánchez. "'The Tropics Make It Difficult to Mope' The Imaginative Geography of Alexander Payne's *The Descendants* (2001)." *International Journal of English Studies* 15, no. 2 (2015): 81–95.

Pallander, Edwin. *The Log of an Island Wanderer: Notes of Travel in the Eastern Pacific*. London: C. Arthur Pearson, 1901.

Payne, Alexander, dir. *The Descendants*. Fox Searchlight Pictures, 2011. DVD.

Pearson, W. H. "Intimidation and the Myth of Tahiti." *The Journal of Pacific History* 4 (1969): 199–217.

Peleggi, Maurizio. "Consuming Colonial Nostalgia: The Monumentalisation of Historic Hotels in Urban South-East Asia." *Asia Pacific Viewpoint* 46, no. 3 (2005): 255–265.

Peluso, Nancy Lee. "Whose Woods Are These? Counter-Mapping Forest Territories in Kalimantan, Indonesia." *Antipode* 27, no. 4 (1995): 383–406.

Peralto, Leon No'eau. "Portrait. Auna a Wākea: Hanau Ka Mauna, The Piko of Our Ea." In *A Nation Rising: Hawaiian Movements for Life, Land, and Sovereignty*, edited by Noelani Goodyear-Ka'ōpua, Ikaika Hussey, and Erin Kahunawaika'ala Wright, 234–243. Durham: Duke University Press, 2014.

Perkins, Kenneth J. "The Compagnie Générale Transatlantique and the Development of Saharan Tourism in North Africa." In *The Business of Tourism: Place, Faith, and History*, edited by Philip Scranton and Janet F. Davidson, 34–55. Philadelphia: University of Pennsylvania Press, 2009.

Perloff, Nancy. "Gaugin's French Baggage: Decadence and Colonialism in Tahiti." In *Prehistories of the Future: The Primitivist Project and the Culture of Modernism*, edited by Elazar Barkan and Ronald Bush, 226–269. Stanford: Stanford University Press, 1995.

Perry, Yaron and Elizabeth Yodim. *The British Mission to the Jews in Nineteenth-Century Palestine*. New York: Routledge, 2003.

Peteet, Julie. *Space and Mobility in Palestine*. Bloomington: Indiana University Press, 2017.

Piasecki, Simon. "A Mountain as Multiverse: Circumnavigating the Realities and Meta-Realities of a Kailas Pilgrim." *Performance Research* 24, no. 2 (2019): 16–23.

Picard, Michel. "'Cultural Tourism' in Bali: Cultural Performances as Tourist Attraction." *Indonesia* 49 (1990): 37–74.

Picard, Michel. "Cultural Heritage and Tourist Capital: Cultural Tourism in Bali." In *International Tourism: Identity and Change*, edited by Marie-Françoise Lanfant, John B. Allcock, and Edward M. Bruner, 44–66. London: Sage, 1995.

Pollack, Sydney, dir. *Out of Africa*. Los Angeles: Universal Studios, 1985.

Pommer, Erich, dir. *The Beachcomber*. Paramount Pictures, 1938.

Pontecorvo, Gillo, dir. *Battle of Algiers*. Los Angeles: Allied Artists, 1966.

Porananond, Ploysri. "Tourism and the Transformation of Ritual Practice with Sand Pagodas in Chiang Mai, Northern Thailand." *Tourism Review* 70, no. 3 (2015): 165–178.

Porter, Josias Leslie. *Five Years in Damascus: Including an Account of the History, Topography, and Antiquities of that City, with Researches in Palmyra, Lebanon and the Hauran, 2 Volumes*. London, 1855.

Powell, Hickman. *The Last Paradise: An American's 'Discovery' of Bali in the 1920s*. Singapore: Oxford University Press, 1982.

Pramana, I. Made Bayu. "Photography as a Bridge: To Intercultural Interaction in Bali During the Netherlands Indies Colonial Period of the 1920s–1930s." *Lekesen: Interdisciplinary Journal of Asia Pasific Arts* 2, no. 2 (2019): 54–58.

Pratt, Marie Louise. "Scratches of the Face of the Country; or, What Mr. Barrow Saw in the Land of the Bushmen." *Critical Inquiry* 12, no. 1 (1985): 119–143.

Putra, I. Nyoman Darma and Michael Hitchcock. "Bali Imagined in the Context of Tourism." *E-Journal of Tourism* 8, no. 2 (2021): 197–206.

Queirós, Margarida. "Edward Soja: Geographical Imaginations from the Margins to the Core." *Planning Theory and Practice* 17, no. 1 (2016): 154–160.

Ranger, Terence. "The Invention of Tradition in Colonial Africa." In *The Invention of Tradition*, edited by Eric Hobsbawm and Terence Ranger, 450–461. New York: Cambridge University Press, 2015.

Rasch, William. "Enlightenment as Religion." *New German Critique* 108 (2009): 109–131.

Reed, Charles. *Royal Tourists, Colonial Subjects and the Making of a British World, 1860–1911*. Manchester: Manchester University Press, 2016.

Rennie, Neil. *Far-Fetched Facts: The Literature of Travel and the Idea of the South Seas*. Oxford: Clarendon Press, 1995.

Rhodes, S. A. *Gerard de Nerval 1808–1855, Poet, Traveler, Dreamer*. New York: Philosophical Library, 1951.

Richter, Daniel. *Facing East from Indian Country: A Native History of Early America*. Cambridge, MA: Harvard University Press, 2001.

Robbins, David. "Sport, Hegemony and the Middle Class: The Victorian Mountaineers." *Theory, Culture & Society* 4 (1987): 597–601.

Robbins, Paul and Sarah A. Moore. "Return of the Repressed: Native Presence and American Memory in John Muir's *Boyhood and Youth*." *Annals of the American Association of Geographers* 109, no. 1 (2019): 1748–1757.

Robineau, Claude. "The Tahitian Economy and Tourism." In *A New Kind of Sugar: Tourism in the Pacific*, edited by Ben R. Finney and Karen Ann Watson, 61–76. Honolulu: The East-West Center, 1975.

Robinson, Michael F. *The Lost White Tribe: Explorers, Scientists, and the Theory That Changed a Continent*. New York: Oxford University Press, 2016.

Robinson, Zac. "Early Alpine Club Culture and Mountaineering Literature." In *Mountaineering Tourism*, edited by Ghazali Musa, James Higham, and Anna Thompson-Carr, 105–117. New York: Routledge, 2015.

Roper, Geoffrey. "Texts from Nineteenth-Century Egypt: The Role of E. W. Lane." In *Travellers in Egypt*, edited by Paul and Janey Starkey, 244–254. London: Tauris Parke Paperbacks, 2001.

Rosenblatt, Naomi. "Orientalism in American Popular Culture." *Penn History Review* 16, no. 2 (2009): 51–63.

Rubin, Rehav. "Ideology and Landscape in Early Printed Maps of Jerusalem." In *Ideology and Landscape in Historical Perspective: Essays on the Meanings of Some Places in the Past*, edited by Alan R. H. Baker and Gideon Biger, 15–30. New York: Cambridge University Press, 1992.

Sahlins, Marshall. *Islands of History*. Chicago: University of Chicago Press, 1985.

Said, Edward. *Orientalism*. New York: Vintage, 1978.

Said, Edward. "Yeats and Decolonization." In *Nationalism, Colonialism, and Literature: Terry Eagleton, Fredric Jameson, and Edward Said*, 69–95. Minneapolis: University of Minnesota Press, 1990.

Said, Edward. *Culture and Imperialism*. New York: Vintage, 1993.

Saissi, Mohammed. "The Symptoms of Orientalism in Pre-Contemporary Western Travel Writings on Morocco." *International Uni-Scientific Research Journal* 2, no. 36 (2021): 240–261.

Sakhnini, Mohammad. "James Silk Buckingham (1786–1855) and the Politics of Travel in the Holy Land." *Studies in Romanticism* 62, no. 2 (2023): 249–267.

Salazar, Noel B. "Tourism Imaginaries: A Conceptual Approach." *Annals of Tourism Research* 39, no. 2 (2012): 863–882.

Salazar, Noel B. "Imagineering Otherness: Anthropological Lenses in Contemporary Tourism." *Anthropological Quarterly* 86, no. 3 (2013): 669–696.

Sandon, Emma. "Projecting Africa: Two British Travel Films of the 1920s." In *Cultural Encounters: Representing 'Otherness'*, edited by Elizabeth Hallam and Brian V. Street, 109–147. New York: Routledge, 2000.

Sarao, K. T. S. "Kailash." In *Encyclopedia of Indian Religions: Buddhism and Jainism*, edited by K. T. S. Sarao and Gang Rinpoche, 607–619. Dordrecht: Springer Science Business Media, 2017.

Sari, Putu Ratna Juwita, Ni Nyoman Sri Wisudawati, and Ni Made Dhlan Rani Yulianthi. "The 'Melukat' Tradition as Millennial Religious Tourism in Badung, Bali." *Jurnal Antropologi: Isu-Isu Social Budya* 24, no. 2 (2022): 241–248.

Satchidananda, Sri Swami. *Kailash Journal: Pilgrimage into the Himalayas*. Yogaville: Integral Yoga Publications, 1984.

Schedneck, Brooke. *Thailand's International Meditation Centers: Tourism and the Global Commodification of Religious Practices*. New York: Routledge, 2017.

Schedneck, Brooke. "Religious Others, Tourism, and Missionization: Buddhist 'Monk Chats' in Northern Thailand." *Modern Asia Studies* 52, no. 6 (2018): 1888–1916.

Schedneck, Brooke. "Religious and Spiritual Retreats." In *The Routledge Handbook of Religious and Spiritual Tourism*, edited by Daniel H. Olsen and Dallen J. Timothy, 191–203. New York: Routledge, 2022.

Schlachter, Judith. "Reclaiming Paradise: Cinema and Hawaiian Nationhood." *Pacific Studies* 38, no. 1/2 (2015): 229–252.

Schmitt, Robert C. "South Sea Movies, 1913–1943." *Hawaii Historical Review* 2, no. 11 (1968): 433–452.

Scriven, Richard. "Geographies of Pilgrimage: Meaningful Movements and Embodied Mobilities." *Geography Compass* 8, no. 4 (2014): 249–261.

Setler, Julia S. "'Painting the Town Red': Buffalo Bill's Indians in German Media." In *The Popular Frontier: Buffalo Bill's Wild West and Transnational Mass Culture*, edited by Frank Christianson. Norman: University of Oklahoma Press, 2017.

Shackley, Myra. *Managing Sacred Sites: Service Provision and Visitor Experience.* New York: Continuum, 2001.

Shadle, Brett Lindsay. *The Souls of White Folk: White Settlers in Kenya, 1900s–1920s.* Manchester: Manchester University Press, 2015.

Shamma, Tarek. "Horror and Likeness: The Quest for the Self and the Imagining of the Other in *The Sheltering Sky*." *Critical Arts* 25, no. 2 (2011): 242–258.

Shannon, Timothy J. and David N. Gellman. *American Odysseys: A History of Colonial North America.* New York: Oxford University Press, 2014.

Sharma, Jayeeta. "Himalayan Darjeeling and Mountain Histories of Labour and Mobility." In *Darjeeling Reconsidered: Histories, Politics, Environments*, edited by Townsend Middleton and Sara Shneidermann, 74–96. New York: Oxford University Press, 2018.

Sharpley, Richard. "Tourism and Spirituality: Green Places, Blue Spaces, and Beyond." In *The Routledge Handbook of Religious and Spiritual Tourism*, edited by Daniel H. Olsen and Dallen J. Timothy, 152–165. New York: Routledge, 2022.

Sharpley, Richard and Priya Sundaram. "Tourism: A Sacred Journey? The Case of Ashram Tourism, India." *International Journal of Tourism Research* 7 (2005): 161–171.

Shelton, Anthony Alan. "Museum Ethnography: An Imperial Science." In *Cultural Encounters: Representing 'Otherness'*, edited by Elizabeth Hallam and Brian V. Street, 157–193. New York: Routledge, 2000.

Sheperd, Robert. "'A Green and Sumptuous Garden': Authenticity, Hybridity, and the Bali Tourism Project." *South East Asia Research* 10, no. 1 (2002): 63–97.

Sheperd, Robert. "UNESCO and the Politics of Cultural Heritage in Tibet." *Journal of Contemporary Asia* 36, no. 2 (2006): 243–257.

Shohat, Ella. "Dislocated Identities." In *On the Arab-Jew, Palestine, and Other Displacements: Selected Writings*, 77–86. London: Pluto Press, 2017.

Shohat, Ella. "The Invasion of the Mizrahim." In *On the Arab-Jew, Palestine, and Other Displacements: Selected Writings*, 102–121. London: Pluto Press, 2017.

Simpson, Colin. *Katmandu.* Sydney: Angus and Robertson, 1967.

Singaravelou, Pierre. "The Institutionalisation of 'Colonial Geography' in France, 1880–1940." *Journal of Historical Geography* 37 (2011): 149–157.

Singh, Shalini. "Secular Pilgrimages and Sacred Tourism in the Indian Himalayas." *GeoJournal* 64, no. 3 (2005); 215–223.

Slyomovics, Susan. "Cross-Cultural Dress and Tourist Performance in Egypt." *Performing Arts Journal* 11, no. 3/4 (1989): 139–148.

Smith, Bernard. *Imagining the Pacific: In the Wake of the Cook Voyages.* New Haven: Yale University Press, 1992.

Smith, Daniela Ohad. "The 'Designed' Israeli Interior, 1960–1977: Shaping Identity." *Journal of Interior Design* 38, no. 3 (2013): 21–36.

Smith, Daniella Ohad. "Hotel Design in British Mandate Palestine: Modernism and the Zionist Vision." *The Journal of Israeli History* 29, no. 1 (2020): 99–123.

Smith, George Adam. *The Book of the Twelve Prophets: Commonly Called Minor.* 2 Volumes. London, 1896–98.

Smith, Jonathon Z. *Map Is Not Territory.* Chicago: University of Chicago Press, 1993.

Smith, Jonathon Z. "Religion, Religions, Religious." In *Critical Terms for Religious Studies*, edited by Mark C. Taylor, 269–284. Chicago: University of Chicago Press, 1998.

Smith, Melanie Kay and Ivett Sziva. "Yoga, Transformation and Tourism." In *The Routledge Handbook on Health Tourism*, edited by Melanie Kay Smith and László Puczkó, 168–180. New York: Routledge, 2017.

Soja, Edward. *Postmodern Geographies: The Reassertion of Space in Critical Social Theory*. New York: Verso, 1989.

Soja, Edward. *Thirdspace: Journeys to Los Angeles and Other Real and Imagined Places*. Oxford: Blackwell, 1996.

Sommers, Stephen, dir. *The Mummy*. Universal Pictures, 1999.

Sommers, Stephen, dir. *The Mummy Returns*. Universal Pictures, 2001.

Spence, Mark David. *Dispossessing the Wilderness: Indian Removal and the Making of the National Parks*. New York: Oxford University Press, 1999.

Sproat, D. Kapua'ala. "A Question of Wai: Seeking Justice Through Law for Hawaii's Streams and Communities." In *A Nation Rising: Hawaiian Movements for Life, Land, and Sovereignty*, edited by Noelani Goodyear-Ka'ōpua, Ikaika Hussey, and Erin Kahunawaika'ala Wright, 199–219. Durham: Duke University Press, 2014.

Stam, Robert and Ella Shohat. *Race in Translation: Culture Wars Around the Postcolonial Atlantic*. New York: New York University Press, 2012.

Stausberg, Michael. *Religion and Tourism: Crossroads, Destinations and Encounters*. New York: Routledge, 2011.

Sternberger, Dolf. *Panorama, Oder Ansichten Vom 19. Jahrhundert*. Hamburg, 1955 (English version published as *Panorama of the Nineteenth Century*. New York: Urizen Books, 1977).

Stetler, Julia S. "'Painting the Town Read': Buffalo Bill's Indians in the German Media." In *The Popular Frontier: Buffalo Bill's Wild West and Transnational Mass Culture*, edited by Frank Christianson, 155–174. Norman: University of Oklahoma Press, 2017.

Stevens, Kate. "Repackaging Tradition in Tahiti? Mono'i and Labels of Origin in French Polynesia." *The Contemporary Pacific* 20, no. 1 (2018): 70–106.

Stevenson, Robert Louis. *In the South Seas*. London: Chatto and Windus, 1912.

Stewart-Harawira, Makere. *The New Imperial Order: Indigenous Responses to Globalization*. New York: Zed Books, 2005.

St. Laurent, Beatrice and Himmet Taskömür. "The Imperial Museum of Antiquities in Jerusalem, 1890–1930: An Alternative Narrative." *Jerusalem Quarterly* 55 (2013): 6–45.

Stoler, Ann Laura. *Carnal Knowledge and Imperial Power: Race and the Intimate in Colonial Rule*. Berkeley: University of California Press, 2010.

Stoll, Mark R. *Inherit the Holy Mountain: Religion and the Rise of American Environmentalism*. New York: Oxford University Press, 2015.

Storrs, Ronald. *Orientations*. London: Ivor Nicholson & Watson, 1937.

Strauss, Claudia. "The Imaginary." *Anthropological Theory* 6, no. 3 (2006): 322–344.

Sturma, Michael. *South Sea Maidens: Western Fantasy and Sexual Politics in the South Pacific*. Westport: Greenwood Press, 2002.

Sutarya, I. Gede. "The Potential and Prospects of Yoga Pilgrimage Exploration in Bali Tourism." *International Journal of Religious Tourism and Pilgrimage* 8, no. 8 (2021): 127–135.

Sutarya, I. Gede. "On-Off Hybrid Spiritual Tourism in the New Normal Era." *Southeast Asia: A Multidisciplinary Journal* 24, no. 2 (2024): 95–106.

Sutarya, I. Gede and I. Dewa Ayu Hendrawathy Putri. "Theological Critics to Yoga Tourism in Bali." *Conference Paper, International Conference on Theology, Philosophy and Religious 2018*, November 29, 2018.

Talbot, Michael. "Divine Imperialism: The British in Palestine, 1753–1842." In *The British Abroad Since the Eighteenth Century, Volume 2: Experiencing Imperialism*, edited by Martin Farr and Xavier Guégan, 36–53. New York: Palgrave Macmillan, 2013.

Tamaira, A. Marata. "From Full Dusk to Full Tusk: Reimagining the 'Dusky Maiden' through the Visual Arts." *The Contemporary Pacific* 22, no. 1 (2010): 1–35.

Tamari, Salim. "Shifting Ottoman Conceptions of Palestine. Part 2: Ethnography and Cartography." *Jerusalem Quarterly* 48 (2011): 6–16.

Tantivejakul, Napawan. "The State Railway of Siam and the Origin of Tourism Public Relations in Thailand (1917–1941)." *Corporate Communications: An International Journal* 29, no. 1 (2024): 9–23.

Taylor, Charles. "Modern Social Imaginaries." *Public Culture* 14, no. 1 (2002): 91–124.

Taylor, Charles. *A Secular Age*. Cambridge, MA: Harvard University Press, 2007.

Teaiwa, Teresia. "Reading Paul Gaugin's *Noa Noa* with Epeli Hau'ofa's *Kisses in the Nederends*: Militourism, Feminism, and the 'Polynesian' Body." In *Inside Out: Literature, Cultural Politics, and Identity in the New Pacific*, edited by Vilson Hereniko, 249–263. Lanham: Rowman & Littlefield, 1999.

Thar, Tsering. "Mount Ti se (Kailash) Area: The Center of Himalayan Civilization." *East and West* 59, no. 1/4 (2009): 25–30.

Thubron, Colin. *To a Mountain in Tibet*. London: Vintage, 2012.

Tian, Ying. "Shangri-La and the Imperial Imagination in James Hilton's *Lost Horizon*." *ANQ (A Quarterly Journal of Short Articles, Notes and Reviews)* 37, no. 3 (2024): 414–422.

Tiangco, Angela Louise R. "Selling Aloha: The Fight for Legal Protections Over Native Hawaiian Culture." *William & Mary Journal of Race, Gender, and Social Justice* 29, no. 2 (2022/2023): 489–518.

Tiffin, Sarah. "*Raffles and the Barometer of Civilisation: Images and Descriptions of Ruined Candis in* 'The History of Java'." *Journal of the Royal Asiatic Society* 18, no. 3 (2008): 341–360.

Tilley, Christopher. "Introduction: Identity, Place, Landscape and Heritage." *Journal of Material Culture* 11, no. 1/2 (2006): 7–32.

Tinker, George E. "Native/First Nation Theology: Response." *Journal of Feminist Studies in Religion* 22, no. 2 (2006): 116–121.

Tinker, George E. "Redskin, Tanned Hide: A Book of Christian History Bound in the Flayed Skin of an American Indian: The Colonial Romance, Christian Denial, and the Cleansing of a Christian School of Theology." *Journal of Race, Ethnicity, and Religion* 5, no. 9 (2014): 1–43.

Toland, Gregg and John Ford, dir. *December 7th*. Office of War Information, 1943.

Trask, Haunani-Kay. "Fighting the Battle of Double Colonization.: The View of an Hawaiian Feminist." *Ethnies: Human Rights and Tribal Peoples (Special Issue: Renaissance in the Pacific)* 4, no. 8, 9, 10 (1989): 61–67.

Trollope, Anthony. *The Bertrams*, 1859. Oxford: Oxford University Press, 1947.

Tuan, Yi-Fu. *Space and Place: The Perspective of Experience*. Minneapolis: University of Minnesota Press, 1977.

Tuchman, Barbara W. *Bible and Sword: England and Palestine from the Bronze Age to Balfour*. New York: Ballantine Books, 1984.

Turner, Victor. "The Center out There: Pilgrim's Goal." *History of Religions* 12, no. 3 (1973): 191–230.

Urbain, Jean-Didier. "The Tourist Adventure and His Images." *Annals of Tourism Research* 16 (1989): 106–118.

Urry, John. *The Tourist Gaze*. London: SAGE Publications, 2002.

Urry, John. "The Place of Emotions Within Place." In *Emotional Geographies*, edited by Liz Bondi, Joyce Davidson, and Mick Smith, 77–83. London: Routledge, 2016.

Usick, Patricia. "William John Bankes' Collection of Drawings of Egypt and Nubia." In *Travellers in Egypt*, edited by Paul and Janet Starkey, 51–60. London: Tauris Parke Paperbacks, 2001.

Van Dyke, W.S., dir. *White Shadows in the South Seas*. Metro-Goldwyn-Meyer (MGM), 1928.

Van Oord, Lodwijk. "The Making of Primitive Palestine: Intellectual Origins of the Palestine-Israel Conflict." *History and Anthropology* 19, no. 3 (2008): 209–228.

Varley, Peter. "Confecting Adventure and Playing with Meaning: The Adventure Commodification Continuum." *Journal of Sports & Tourism* 11, no. 2 (2006): 173–194.

Vasantkumar, Chris. "Dreamworld, Shambala, Gannan: The Shangrilazation of China's 'Little Tibet'." In *Mapping Shangrila: Contested Landscapes in the Sino-Tibetan Borderlands*, edited by Emily T. Yeh and Christopher R. Coggins, 51–73. Seattle: University of Washington Press, 2014.

Veracini, Lorenzo. "The Other Shift: Settler Colonialism, Israel and the Occupation." *Journal of Palestine Studies* 42, no. 2 (2013): 26–42.

Verheijen, Bart and I. Nyoman Darma Putra. "Balinese Cultural Identity and Global Tourism." *Asian Ethnicity* 21, no. 3 (2020): 425–442.

Vickers, Adrian. *Bali: A Paradise Created*. Singapore: Tuttle Publishing, 2012.

Vincent, John H., J. W. Lee, and R. E. M. Bain, eds. *Earthly Footsteps of the Man of Galilee, Being Three Hundred and Eighty-Four Original Photographic Views and Descriptions of the Places Connected with the Earthly Life of Our Lord and His Apostles Traced with Note Book and Camera*. London, 1864.

Vincent, Leon. *John Heyl Vincent: A Biographical Sketch*. New York: MacMillan Co., 1925.

Von Mossner, Alexa Weik. "Encountering the Sahara: Embodiment, Emotion, and Material Agency in Paul Bowles's *The Sheltering Sky*." In *Environmental Awareness and the Design of Literature*, edited by Francois Specq, 116–135. Leiden: Brill, 2016.

Vuconíc, Boris. *Tourism and Religion*. New York: Pergamon, 1996.

Wald, Priscilla. *Constituting Americans: Cultural Anxiety and Narrative Form*. Durham: Duke University Press, 1995.

Waldroup, Heather Leigh. "Traveling Images: Representations of the South Pacific from Colonial and Postcolonial Worlds." PhD diss., University of California, Santa Cruz, 2004.

Walker, Hal, dir. *Road to Bali*. Paramount Pictures, 1952.

Walter, Marc. *Voyages Around the World*. New York: Friedman, 2002.

Walters, Holly. *Shaligram Pilgrimage in the Nepal Himalayas*. Amsterdam: Amsterdam University Press, 2020.

Walters, Holly. "Cornerstones: Shaligrams as Kin." *The Journal of Religion* 102, no. 1 (2022): 93–119.

Ward, David. *The Country and the City*. Oxford: Oxford University Press, 1979.

Watson, Nick J. "Nature and Transcendence: The Mystical and Sublime in Extreme Sports." In *Sport and Spirituality: An Introduction*, edited by Jim Parry, Simon Robinson, Nick Watson, and Mark Nesti, 95–115. New York: Routledge, 2007.

Wharton, Annabel Jane. *Selling Jerusalem: Relics, Replicas, Theme Parks*. Chicago: University of Chicago Press, 2006.

Whelan, Tensie. "Ecotourism and Its Role in Sustainable Development." In *Nature Tourism: Managing for the Environment*, edited by Tensie Whelan, 3–16. Washington, DC: Island Press, 1991.

White, Geoffrey M. "Disney's *Pearl Harbor*: National Memory at the Movies." *The Public Historian* 24, no. 4 (2002): 97–115.

White, Mike, dir. *The White Lotus* (Season 3). Los Angeles: HBO, 2025.

White, Patricia. "Women Auteurs, Western Promises." *Film Quarterly* 75, no. 4 (2022): 23–33.

Williams, Ruth. "Eat, Pray, Love: Producing the Female Neoliberal Spiritual Subject." *The Journal of Popular Culture* 47, no. 3 (2014): 613–633.

Williams, Terry Tempest. *The Hour of Land: A Personal Topography of America's National Parks*. New York: Farrar, Straus and Giroux, 2016.

Willson, Gregory B., Alison J. McIntosh, and Anne L. Zahra. "Tourism and Spirituality: A Phenomenological Analysis." *Annals of Tourism Research* 42 (2013): 150–168.

Woodward, Michelle L. "Between Orientalist Clichés and Images of Modernization: Photographic Practice in the Late Ottoman Era." *History of Photography* 27, no. 4 (2003): 363–374.

Wrobel, David. "Prologue: Exceptionalism, Globalism, and Transnationalism—The West, America, and the World Across the Centuries." In *The Popular Frontier: Buffalo Bill's Wild West and Transnational Mass Culture*, edited by Frank Christianson, 3–12. Norman: University of Oklahoma Press, 2017.

Wyrtzen, Jonathon. *Making Morocco: Colonial Intervention and the Politics of Identity*. Ithaca: Cornell University Press, 2015.

Xiao, Honggen and Jinfu Zhang. "Liquid Identities: Han Sojourners in Tibet." *Annals of Tourism Research* 88 (2021): 1–12.

Yamashita, Shinji. *Bali and Beyond: Explorations in the Anthropology of Tourism*. New York: Bergahn Books, 2003.

Yü, Dan Smyer. *Mindscaping the Landscape of Tibet: Place, Memorability, Ecoaesthetics*. Boston: De Gruyter, 2015.

Zhang, Jinfu. "Drifting Home: The Quests of Chinese Tourist-Migrants in Tibet." *Journal of Travel Research* 63, no. 6 (2024): 1459–1472.

Zhao, Chloé, dir. *The Rider*. Sony Pictures Classics, 2017.

Zhao, Chloé, dir. *Nomadland*. Searchlight Pictures, 2021.

Zhu, Hong and Junxi Qian. "'Drifting in Lhasa': Cultural Encounter, Contested Modernity, and the Negotiation of Tibetness." *Annals of the Association of American Geographers* 105, no. 1 (2015): 144–161.

GLOSSARY OF INDIGENOUS AND LOCAL PLACES

Al Jazá'ir (Arabic)	l'Algérie (Algeria)	(French)
Anfa (Aureba)	Casablanca	(Portuguese)
Anthwerrke (Arrernte)	Emily Gap	(English)
Aoraki (Māori)	Mt. Cook	(English)
Aotearoa (Māori)	New Zealand	(English)
Bandung (Indonesian)	Bandsoeng	(Dutch)
Bogor (Indonesian)	Buitenzorg	(Dutch)
Chomolungma (Tibetan/Sherpa)	Everest	(English)
Jakarta (Indonesian)	Batavia	(Dutch)
Kānaka Maoli lāhui (Kānaka Maoli)	Hawai'i	(English)
Ke Tiritiri o te Moana (Māori)	Southern Alps	(English)
Maghreb (Arabic)	North Africa	(English)
Mauna a Wākea (Hawaiian)	Mauna Kea	(English)
Mi tse a-da-zi (Minnetaree)	Yellowstone	(English)
Oghá P'o'oge (Tewa)	Santa Fe	(Spanish)
Sagarmatha (Nepali)	Everest	(English)
Tageldit n Lmeyrib (Tamazight)	Morocco	(Spanish)
Tahiti-nui mare'are'a (Ma'ohi)	Tahiti	(French)
Yanaguana (Payaya)	San Antonio	(Spanish)
Yootó (Navajo)	Santa Fe	(Spanish)
Zimbaoë (Shona)	Great Zimbabwe	(English)

INDEX

Adat 302

Africa 6, 14, 24, 25, 29–31, 35–36, 39, 54, 58, 63, 72, 83–87, 91–100; Algeria 24, 26, 28, 70, 85, 88–90, 102–104, 237; Great Zimbabwe (*Zimbaoë*) 84, 235; Happy Valley (Kenya) 101; Kenya 6, 54, 94, 97–102, 106–107; Maghrib (North Africa) 24, 41, 85, 102–105; Morocco 89, 104–105, 107–108; South Africa 36, 39

Africans 28, 29, 84, 87–88, 90–100, 101–102, 106; Amazigh 103, 105; Endorois 97; Kikuyu 87, 88, 97, 98; Maasai 94; Mukugodo 97; Ogiek 97; Sukuma 94

Ahmed, Sara 12, 63–64

'*Aina* 209

American West 7–8, 27, 33, 34, 40, 54, 62, 267–276, 271–272

anthropology/anthropologists 3–4, 13–14, 27–29, 36, 91, 283–284

Aotearoa (New Zealand) 15–16, 136, 191–192, 302

Arabic 28, 89, 94, 104, 238, 245, 248, 253–255

Arabs 90, 103–104, 108, 232–233, 236–242, 245–255, 272

Australia 10, 36, 62, 88, 91, 172, 195, 302

authenticity 8, 12–13, 15, 53–64, 69, 102, 106–107, 134, 138, 146, 174, 180, 283–284, 289

Bali Ha'i 170

Bali Syndrome 173

Bali 14, 26–27, 53, 55–57, 63, 65, 158–176; Balinese Hinduism 68, 162–168, 170–176

Bauman, Zygmunt 12–13, 60, 69: Liquid Modernity (theory) 57

Bible 60, 229, 230, 231–232, 237, 245, 247–248, 252, 267; Biblical mapping 5, 30, 36, 38, 67–68, 85, 122, 162, 229, 230, 242, 243, 246–248, 254, 267

Black Elk 266

blank spaces (*terra nullius*) 9, 10, 13, 14, 33, 39–41, 69–70, 84, 90, 96–97, 101–102, 105–108, 133

Bon (Bonpo) 119, 129, 132, 140

Bougainville, Louis Antoine de 198, 199, 201

Bourdieu 102

Britain 36, 42, 96, 126, 178, 229, 230, 233, 244; British Royal Family 96–98, 100; British Mandate 231

Buddhism 64, 121–128, 137, 139–142, 145–147, 159, 163–164, 172, 177–181

Buffalo Bill (traveling show) 42, 101, 272, 280

Bumberry, Annie 278, 291, 292

Cairo 230, 234–236, 240–241

Candi 169

Cannibalism 16, 83, 192, 201–202, 233
Centre d' experimentation du Pacifique 204
China 11, 120, 124, 126–127, 137, 143, 144, 166, 172
Christianity 38, 40, 59, 67–70, 107, 122–125, 133, 229–230, 235–237, 239–246, 248, 251–254, 267–268, 273–276, 285, 291
Cinema 33, 38, 72, 96, 98–99, 234, 287–288; *Aloha* 213; *Battle of Algiers* 102; *Bali the Unknown* 159; *The Beachcomber* 192; *Blue Hawaii* 217; *The Bounty* 212; *Death on the Nile* 253; *December 7th* 213; The *Descendants* 213–215; *Lion King (The)* 101–102; *Last of the Mohicans* 281; *Lost Horizon* 124; *Moana: A Romance of the Golden Age* 211–212; *The Mummy* 253; *The Mummy Returns* 253; *Nomadland* 287–288; *Oppenheimer* 40; *Out of Africa* 85, 86–88, 96; *Pearl Harbor* 213; *Seven Years in Tibet* 141; *The Sheltering Sky* 40, 89–90; *South Pacific* 159, 164, 170; *Tabu* 211; *The Road to Bali* 159; *Waikiki Wedding* 217; *White Shadows in the South Seas* 217
colonialism 3, 6–9, 24–28, 31–42; colonial geography 35–36; colonial maps/mapping 2, 4, 13, 25, 26, 36, 37, 41, 89, 91–97, 102–103, 105–108, 123, 136, 162–166, 242–248; colonial nostalgia 54–56, 58, 85–88, 94101, 106–107, 173, 174, 210, 216, 253; colonial surveys 3, 8, 242
Communitas 13
Cook, James 16, 195, 198, 203
Cook, Thomas 53, 85, 101, 137, 231, 236
counter-maps 24, 302

Description de l' Egypte 52
deserts 15, 33, 38, 40–41, 56, 69–70, 72, 85–86, 89–90, 102–108, 233–237, 249, 253–254, 272, 284; American Southwest 267, 270, 272, 284; Sahara 41, 84–85, 89–90, 102–103, 108
Dinesen, Isak (Karen Blixen) 25, 63, 86–88

Disenchantment/Enchantment 3, 6, 13, 15, 54, 85, 89–90, 108, 134, 174, 180–181, 270, 275
Dutch 1–3, 26, 33, 63, 65, 71, 98–99, 123, 161–167, 169, 170; Dutch East Indies 1–3, 71, 165, 166, 193

Eat, Pray, Love (book and film) 56, 66, 171, 175
Ebstorf Map 68
Eden 71, 85, 87, 92, 94, 103, 122, 158, 162–166, 196, 198–202, 229, 276
Egeria 67–68
Egypt 28–31, 37, 52–53, 107, 228–237, 253–254
Ethnopornography 91
Everest (Chomolungma/Sagarmatha) 8–9, 14, 29, 71, 120, 126, 136–140, 142–144
Exotica Tibet 140
Exposition Universalle 201

Fabian, Johannes 72, 88, 104, 240, 275
Farang 179
Flaubert, Gustave 57, 235
Foucault 5, 14–15, 41
France 24, 35, 42, 57, 85, 164, 199–201, 206; French Africa 35–36, 91–92, 102–105

Gauguin 58, 168, 194, 201–202
Gaza 28, 32, 228
gendered orientalism 32, 37, 42, 103, 235
genocide 228, 252, 272, 279–280, 303
geographical imagination 27–28, 30, 31–35, 93, 193, 217–218, 241, 250–251
Goop 40, 171, 253
Graceland 62
grey eyes 291

Haole 207
Harley, John Brian 4, 7, 13, 14, 268, 272–273
Hawai'i 5, 53, 125, 205–215; Bayonet Constitution 27, 205–106; Kaho'olawe 209; legal status of Hawaiians 211; Mauna Kea 215
Heiva 216
Heterotopia 14–15
Hollandiola 165

Holy Land 5, 10, 30, 32, 53, 60, 67–68,
229–231, 235, 240, 241–246,
249–253
Hula 206–207, 210, 216–217
human zoos 26–27

Imaginaire 13–14, 28, 86, 102,
120, 194
imaginative geographies 6–9, 32–35,
199, 247
Imperial Gothic 121–122, 233
India 28, 31, 32, 36, 56, 62, 126–127,
129, 141, 165–166, 168; Darjeeling
5, 138
Indian Removal Act of 1870, 278
Indian removal 8, 27, 278–283, 288,
292; and *ghosting* 6–8, 27
Indonesia 33, 164, 168–170;
development of tourism 169–170;
Kalimantan 302; Sumatra 161;
see also Bali and Java
Islands 1–3, 37, 38, 41–42, 53, 64, 71,
159, 164, 191–192, 197, 199, 201
Israeli tourism 246–248, 254–255

Japan 3, 31, 123, 133, 135, 161–162,
166, 169, 171, 197, 212–213,
217, 280
Java 1–3, 41, 130–131, 162–164, 166,
168; Bandung 1–3; Jakarta 3, 33–34,
164, 165; Semarang 3
Jerusalem 28–29, 236, 243–253

Kailash (*Kailās*) 10, 41, 129–135
Kama'aina 193
Kānaka Maoli 200, 208, 211, 212, 213,
215, 217–218
Kanaks 192
Kant 71
Kapu 197
Konohiki 205

La mission civilisatrice 85
La Nouvelle Cythère 196, 199, 201
Lamasery 121, 123
landscapes 1–12, 27, 34, 37–42, 57–59,
67–69, 86
Lane, Edward 30–31, 238
LeFebvre, Henri 12, 13, 92
literature 3, 37, 38, 70, 72, 84, 85, 96,
106, 191–192, 196, 231–232, 237,
241, 253–254, 270, 281; *Aziyadé*
32, 93, 237–238; *The Bertrams* 240;

The Conservationist 106; *The Jewel
of the Seven Stars* 233–234; *Kenya
Mist* 88; *King Solomon's Mines*
232; *The Last of the Mohicans* 281;
Lost Horizon 120–124, 141; *Love
and Death in Bali* 161; *Marriage of
Loti* 32, 37, 42, 193–195, 202; *O
Pioneers!* 268–270; *Out of Africa*
63, 86–88; *Robinson Crusoe* 196,
198; *She: A History of Adventure*
231–234; *Sheltering Sky (The)* 40,
72, 88–90; *Swiss Family Robinson*
198; *Treasure Island* 198; *Where
Once We Belonged* 202
London 32, 38, 53, 101, 138, 203, 230,
238–239
Lumbini 8, 126–127

Ma'ohi 200, 203, 216
magical realism 160
Makihini 193
manifest destiny 26, 255, 267–272
Māori 15, 16, 38, 302
map-making 4, 13, 26, 28, 35–39, 231
Mato Tipila 282
Mbembe, Achille 83, 92, 99, 100
Melukat (Balinese tradition) 175–176
Militourism 206
mountaineering 8–9, 10, 26, 28, 29, 71,
126–127, 135–139, 142–145
mountains 5, 6, 28, 38, 40, 41, 59,
71, 108, 119–120, 122, 124–132,
134–135, 136–138, 140, 144–145,
171–172, 273–276, 283, 287;
Aoraki 25, 302; Kailash 41,
129–135; Mount Agung 162; Mount
Batur 162; Mount Denali 38; Mauna
Kea 215; Mount Rainier 283
Muddled Orientalism 31, 232
Muir, John 285
Museums 2, 13–14, 26, 31, 35–37, 92,
104–105, 145, 159, 161, 168, 203,
209–210, 230, 238–239, 246, 249
Muslims 31, 39, 59, 93–94, 103, 140,
165, 167–168, 175–176, 240, 242,
248, 251–255
Mystical landscapes 53, 55, 62–63,
67–72, 86, 96, 105–108, 145–147,
171–176, 180–181, 214–218,
253–255
mystical tourism 15, 41–42, 56–59,
63–67, 90, 94–98, 106–107, 136,
145–146, 171–172, 272

Napoleon 52, 91, 231
National Parks (U.S.) 54, 266–267,
    282–283, 302; Devil's Tower 282;
    Grand Canyon 266; Wind Cave
    266; Yellowstone 5, 274, 276–277,
    282–283
Native Americans 6–7, 27, 35, 56,
    60; Apache 10, 301, 302, 277,
    288; Arapaho 271; Bannocks 276;
    Cherokee 8, 278; Cheyenne 271;
    Crow 275–276; Minnetaree 5;
    Navajo 277, 287, 288; Oglala 266;
    Osage 60, 268, 271; Pawnee 268;
    Pequot 9; Piegans/Blackfoot 276;
    Seneca 278, 291–292; Shoshoni 276;
    Ute 283, 301; Wyandot 291
neocolonialism 15, 26, 127
Nepal 8, 9–10, 29, 55–57, 64, 70–71,
    120, 142–144
New England 7, 37, 270, 273
Nile River 25, 53, 230–231, 240,
    241, 253

'Ohana 209, 215
Omai (Mai) 10, 27, 203
Orientalism (book) 69
orientalism 2, 28–31, 33–37, 52–53,
    70, 93–95, 134, 146, 194, 232,
    237–241, 243, 255
Orientalizing 30

Pacificism 197, 198
painting 3, 27, 38, 52, 102, 103, 160,
    162, 191, 196, 203, 211, 231–232,
    268–270, 275–276; Across the
    Continent; "Westward the Course
    of Empire Takes Its Way," 269;
    American Progress 268; A Portrait
    of Poedua 203; The Attack on a
    Wagon Train 268; Banyan with Two
    Young Balinese 160; Die Landschaft
    und ihre Kinder 160; Indian
    Encampment, Shoshone Village 275;
    Osage Scalp Dance 168; The Snake
    Charmer 231–232: Ukelele Lady
    211; Women of Algiers in Their
    Apartment 106
Palais des Colonies 192
Palestine Exploration Fund 244
Palestine 32, 33–34, 38, 39–40, 52–53,
    60, 228–231, 239
Pan-Africanism 92–93
Panditas 172

Paradise 14, 27, 41–42, 63–64, 70–71,
    126, 129, 158–159, 164–165,
    168, 196
Pariwisata Budaya 169
Patih 174
Pembantu 173
Philippines 5, 123, 125, 279
photography 30–32, 52, 103–104,
    161, 166–167, 228, 236, 238, 242,
    274–275
Pilgrimage 10–15, 16, 58–62, 68–69,
    127–133, 146, 171, 175, 181
Pita Maha 161
Pocahontas 279
Polynesianism 198
Power Places 120, 145, 172
Prambanan 130, 131
Puja 129, 143
Puputans 165, 169
pyramids 52, 230–231, 235–237,
    240–241, 253, 289

race 12, 30, 83–84, 192, 195, 240
Raffles, Stamford 2, 166, 168
religion (concept) 59–60
remapping 7, 33, 39, 57, 98–99, 217,
    273, 277–279, 287–288; through
    renaming 8–9, 37–38, 273, 276–278

sacred geography 129–130, 172, 242
Safari 6, 54–55, 58, 84–85, 88, 96,
    99–102, 106–107
Sahib 135, 139, 144
Said, Edward 24, 25, 69, 119, 239
Sand Creek Massacre 270–271, 278,
    281–282
Scopic regime 12, 35, 104, 122–123,
    145, 169, 237–241
Scotland 58
Sedona 8, 40, 54, 277, 285–289;
    vortexes 285, 288–289
Shambhala 121–122, 145
Shangri-La 10, 11, 119–124, 125
Sherpas 8–9, 128–135, 139, 142–144
Smith, JZ 4, 59, 266, 279
Soja, Edward 11–12; Thirdspace 12
Solar ecology 209
South Pacific (region) 5, 14, 37,
    41, 197
Spies, Walter 159–162, 167, 211
Spiritual tourism 58–59, 64
Stevenson, Robert Louis 37, 198
Sutee 165

Tahiti (*Otaheite*) 42, 64, 193, 200–205
Tangata whenua 15
Taylor, Charles 13, 31, 57, 65, 228
Terra Australis Incognito 195, 201
Territorium nullius 99
Thailand 41, 55, 159, 164, 171, 176–181
Thebaid 69–70
Tibet 10, 29, 38, 39, 70, 120–124, 139–142, 144–145; Lhasa 8, 140, 145–146; Mustang 9, 140; Yeti
Tirtayatra 175
Tirthas 127–128, 176
Tourism 12–13, 52–58, 60–63, 173–176; Tours 24, 53, 55, 97–98, 202, 203, 229, 230, 236, 241, 245–246, 252–255
Tourist imaginaries 57, 62–64, 84
Tri Hita Karana 172
Tupapa'u 195
Turkey 31, 93, 194, 231, 237–239; Ottoman(s) 231, 232, 237, 245, 246, 252

United States of America 5–6, 25, 26, 42, 62, 92, 99, 146, 197, 200, 205–211, 241, 250, 255, 266–276, 279–281

Villes nouvelles 105

Wallis, Samuel 196, 198, 200–201
Wataniyya 245
wellness 40, 53, 55, 58, 59–60, 66, 69, 107, 135, 158, 171, 174–176, 179, 253
White Lotus (*The*) (tv series) 176–178
whiteness 12, 63–64, 83–84, 87; and theology 274; white Africans 84
wilderness 6–7, 27, 70, 90, 107, 266–267, 272–287
Wounded Knee Massacre 278

yoga 58, 172, 174–176, 180–181

Zangpiaos 140, 144–146
Zionism 39–40, 52, 239, 242, 244–254; Christian Zionism 229, 244; Zionism and architecture 246–248

For Product Safety Concerns and Information please contact our EU
representative GPSR@taylorandfrancis.com
Taylor & Francis Verlag GmbH, Kaufingerstraße 24, 80331 München, Germany

www.ingramcontent.com/pod-product-compliance
Lightning Source LLC
Chambersburg PA
CBHW050333270326
41926CB00016B/3429

9 7 8 1 0 3 2 4 2 2 1 1 4